P9-DTB-588

Complete Solutions Guide

Introductory Chemistry: A Foundation
Introductory Chemistry
Basic Chemistry

Fourth Edition

Complete Solutions Guide

Introductory Chemistry: A Foundation
Introductory Chemistry
Basic Chemistry

Fourth Edition

Zumdahl

James F. Hall
University of Massachusetts Lowell

Houghton Mifflin Company
Boston   New York

Editor-in-Chief: Kathi Prancan
Associate Editor: Marianne Stepanian
Editorial Assistants: Sarah Gessner and Joy Park
Senior Manufacturing Coordinator: Marie Barnes
Executive Marketing Manager: Andy Fisher

Printed in the U.S.A.

ISBN: 0-395-95544-0

2 3 4 5 6 7 8 9-BB-03 02 01

Table of Contents

Preface

This guide contains complete solutions for the end-of-chapter problems in the fourth editions of *Introductory Chemistry*, *Introductory Chemistry: A Foundation*, and *Basic Chemistry* by Steven S. Zumdahl. Several hundred new problems and questions have been prepared for the new editions of the text, which we hope will be of even greater help to your students in gaining an understanding of the fundamental principles of chemistry.

We have tried to give the most detailed solutions possible to all the problems, even though some problems give repeat, drill practice on the same subject. Our chief attempt at brevity is to give molar masses for compounds without showing the calculation (after the subject of molar mass itself has been discussed). We have also made a conscious effort in this guide to solve each problem in the manner discussed in the textbook. The instructor, of course, may wish to discuss alternative methods of solution with his or her students.

One topic that causes many students concern is the matter of significant figures, and the determination of the number of digits to which a solution to a problem should be reported. To avoid truncation errors in the solutions contained in this guide, the solutions typically report intermediate answers to one more digit that appropriate for the final answer. The final answer to each problem is then given to the correct number of significant figures based on the data provided in the problem.

Many very dedicated people have worked long hours to prepare this guide. Particular thanks go to Leslie di Verdi of Colorado State University for carefully checking the manuscript for accuracy, and to Sarah Gessner, Editorial Assistant at Houghton Mifflin, for her patience, competence, and good cheer.

James F. Hall
University of Massachusetts Lowell
James_Hall@uml.edu

Chapter 1   Chemistry: An Introduction

1.   Obviously, the answer to this question depends on your own experience. You might consider such things as how oven and drain cleaners work, why antifreeze keeps your car's radiator from freezing, why cuts and scrapes are often cleaned with hydrogen peroxide, how a "permanent wave" curls hair, etc.

2.   Examples: physician (understanding cellular processes, understanding how drugs and bloodtests work); lawyer (understanding scientific/forensic laboratory tests for use in court); pharmacist (understanding how drugs work, and interactions between drugs); artist (understanding the various media used in art work); photographer (understanding how the film exposure and developing chemical processes occur and how they can be controlled and modified); farmer (understanding which pesticide or fertilizer is needed and how these chemicals work); nurse (understanding how various tests and drugs may affect the patient's wellbeing).

3.   There are obviously many such examples. Many new drugs and treatments have recently become available thanks to research in biochemistry and cell biology. New long-wearing, more comfortable contact lenses have been produced by research in polymer and plastics chemistry. Special plastics and metals were prepared for the production of compact discs to replace vinyl phonograph records.

4.   There are, unfortunately, many examples. Chemical and biological weapons are still being produced in some countries. Although the development of new plastics has been a boon in many endeavors, this also increases our depletion of fossil fuels and our solid waste problems. Although many exciting new drugs and treatments have become available, the same biotechnology may lead to testing procedures for determining whether a person has a genetic likelihood of developing a particular disease, which may make it impossible or difficult for that person to obtain health or life insurance.

5.   This answer depends on your own experience.

6.   This answer depends on your own experience, but consider the following examples: oven cleaner (the label says it contains sodium hydroxide; it converts the burned on grease in the oven to a soapy material that washes away); drain cleaner (the label says it contains sodium hydroxide; it dissolves the clog of hair in the drain); stomach antacid (the label says it contains calcium carbonate; it makes me belch and makes my stomach feel better); hydrogen peroxide (the label says it is a 3% solution of hydrogen peroxide; when applied to a wound, it bubbles); depilatory cream (the label says it contains sodium hydroxide; it removes unwanted hair from skin).

7.   David and Susan first recognized the problem (unexplained medical problems). A possible explanation was then proposed (the glaze on their china might be causing lead poisoning). The explanation was tested by experiment (it was determined that the china did contain lead). A full discussion of this scenario is given in the text.

8.   Answer will depend on student experience.

9.   The steps are: (1) recognizing the problem and stating it clearly; (2) proposing possible solutions to or explanations of the problem; and (3) performing experiments to test the solutions or explanations.

10.   a.   quantitative - a number (measurement) is indicated explicitly
       b.   qualitative - only a qualitative description is given
       c.   quantitative - a numerical measurement is indicated
       d.   qualitative - only a qualitative description is given
       e.   quantitative - a number (measurement) is implied
       f.   qualitative - a qualitative judgment is given
       g.   quantitative - a numerical quantity is indicated

11.   A hypothesis is a *possible* explanation of a single observed phenomenon. A theory or model consists of a set of tested hypotheses which give an overall explanation of some part of nature.

12.   A natural law is a *summary of observed, measurable behavior* that occurs repeatedly and consistently. A theory is our attempt to *explain* such behavior. The conservation of mass observed during chemical reactions is an example of a natural law. The idea that the universe began with a "big bang" is an example of a theory.

13.   Scientists are human, too. When a scientist formulates a hypothesis, he or she wants it to be proven correct. In academic research, for example, scientists want to be able to publish papers on their work to gain renown and acceptance from their colleagues. In industrial situations, the financial success of the individual and of the company as a whole may be at stake. Politically, scientists may be under pressure from the government to "beat the other guy."

14.   Most applications of chemistry are oriented toward the interpretation of observations and the solving of problems. Although memorization of some facts may *aid* in these endeavors, it is the ability to combine, relate, and synthesize information that is most important in the study of chemistry.

15.   Chemistry is not merely a list of observations, definitions, and properties. Chemistry is the study of very real interactions among different samples of matter, whether within a living cell, or in a chemical factory. When we study chemistry, at least in the beginning, we try to be as general and as nonspecific as possible, so that the *basic principles* learned can be applied to many situations. In a beginning chemistry course, we learn to interpret and solve a basic set of very simple problems, in the hopes that the method of solving these simple problems can be extended to more complex real life situations later on. The actual solution to a problem, at this point, is not as important as learning how to recognize and interpret the problem, and how to propose reasonable, experimentally testable hypotheses.

16.   In real life situations, the problems and applications likely to be encountered are not simple textbook examples. One must be able to observe an event, hypothesize a cause, and then test this hypothesis. One must be able to carry what has been learned in class forward to new, different situations.

Chapter 2   Measurements and Calculations

1.   4

2. 10^4

3.   4,512

4.   Because 0.0021 is less than one, the exponent will be *negative*. Because 4540 is greater than one, the exponent will be *positive*.

5.   a.   0.06235

       b.   7229

       c.   0.000005001

       d.   86,210

6.   a. -5; 6.7×10^{-5}

       b.   6; 9.331442×10^6

       c. -4; 1×10^{-4}

       d.   4; 1.631×10^4

7.   a.   The decimal point must be moved four places to the left, so the exponent is positive 4; $12,500 = 1.25 \times 10^4$

       b.   The decimal point must be moved seven places to the left, so the exponent is positive 7; $37,400,000 = 3.74 \times 10^7$

       c.   The decimal point must be moved 23 places to the left, so the exponent is positive 23; $602,300,000,000,000,000,000,000 = 6.023 \times 10^{23}$

       d.   The decimal point must be moved two places to the left, so the exponent is positive 2; $375 = 3.75 \times 10^2$

       e.   The decimal point must be moved two places to the right, so the exponent is negative 2; $0.0202 = 2.02 \times 10^{-2}$

       f.   The decimal point must be moved one place to the right, so the exponent is negative 1; $0.1550 = 1.550 \times 10^{-1}$

       g.   The decimal point must be moved five places to the right, so the exponent is negative 5; $0.0000104 = 1.04 \times 10^{-5}$

       h.   The decimal point must be moved nineteen places to the right, so the exponent is -19; $0.0000000000000000000129 = 1.29 \times 10^{-19}$

8.   a.   The decimal point must be moved six places to the left, so the exponent is positive 6; $9,367,421 = 9.367421 \times 10^6$

      b.   The decimal point must be moved three places to the left, so the exponent is positive 3; $7241 = 7.241 \times 10^3$

      c.   The decimal point must be moved four places to the right, so the exponent is negative 4; $0.0005519 = 5.519 \times 10^{-4}$

      d.   The decimal point does not have to be moved, so the exponent is zero; $5.408 = 5.408 \times 10^0$

      e. 6.24×10^2 is already written in standard scientific notation.

      f.   The decimal point must be moved three places to the left, and the resulting exponent of positive three must be combined with the exponent of negative two in the multiplier; $6,319 \times 10^{-2} = 6.319 \times 10^1$

      g.   The decimal point must be moved nine places to the right, so the exponent is negative nine; $0.000000007215 = 7.215 \times 10^{-9}$

      h.   The decimal point must be moved one place to the right, so the exponent is negative 1; $0.721 = 7.21 \times 10^{-1}$

9.   a.   The decimal point must be moved three places to the right; $6.441 \times 10^3 = 6,442$

      b.   The decimal point must be moved five places to the left; $5.991 \times 10^{-5} = 0.00005991$

      c.   The decimal point must be moved four places to the right; $2.001 \times 10^4 = 20,010$

      d.   The decimal point must be moved three places to the left; $1.997 \times 10^{-3} = 0.001997$

      e.   The decimal point must be moved one place to the left; $7.871 \times 10^{-1} = 0.7871$

      f.   The decimal point must be moved one place to the right; $1.001 \times 10^1 = 10.01$

      g.   The decimal point must be moved four places to the left; $9.721 \times 10^{-4} = 0.0009721$

      h.   The decimal point must be moved six places to the right; $2.015 \times 10^6 = 2,015,000$

      i.   The decimal point must be moved two places to the left; $5.583 \times 10^{-2} = 0.05583$

      j.   The decimal point must be moved six places to the left; $4.227 \times 10^{-6} = 0.000004227$

k.   The decimal point must be moved three places to the right;
$9.734 \times 10^3 = 9,734$

l.   The decimal point must be moved one places to the right;
$1.000 \times 10^1 = 10.00$

10. a.   The decimal point must be moved two places to the right;
$4.83 \times 10^2 = 483$

b.   The decimal point must be moved four places to the left;
$7.221 \times 10^{-4} = 0.0007221$

c.   The decimal point does not have to be moved; $6.1 \times 10^0 = 6.1$

d.   The decimal point must be moved eight places to the left;
$9.11 \times 10^{-8} = 0.0000000911$

e.   The decimal point must be moved six places to the right;
$4.221 \times 10^6 = 4,221,000$

f.   The decimal point must be moved three places to the left;
$1.22 \times 10^{-3} = 0.00122$

g.   The decimal point must be moved three places to the right;
$9.999 \times 10^3 = 9,999$

h.   The decimal point must be moved five places to the left;
$1.016 \times 10^{-5} = 0.00001016$

i.   The decimal point must be moved five places to the right;
$1.016 \times 10^5 = 101,600$

j.   The decimal point must be moved one place to the left;
$4.11 \times 10^{-1} = 0.411$

k.   The decimal point must be moved four places to the right;
$9.71 \times 10^4 = 97,100$

l.   The decimal point must be moved four places to the left;
$9.71 \times 10^{-4} = 0.000971$

11. To say that scientific notation is in *standard* form means that you have a number between 1 and 10, followed by an exponential term. The numbers given in this problem are *not* between 1 and 10 as written.

a. $4381 \times 10^{-4} = (4.381 \times 10^3) \times 10^{-4} = 4.381 \times 10^{-1}$

b. $98,784 \times 10^4 = (9.8784 \times 10^4) \times 10^4 = 9.8784 \times 10^8$

c. $78.21 \times 10^2 = (7.821 \times 10^1) \times 10^2 = 7.821 \times 10^3$

d. 9.871×10^{-4} is already written in standard scientific notation.

e. $0.009871 \times 10^7 = (9.871 \times 10^{-3}) \times 10^7 = 9.871 \times 10^4$

f. $42,221 \times 10^4 = (4.2221 \times 10^4) \times 10^4 = 4.2221 \times 10^8$

g. $0.00008951 \times 10^6 = (8.951 \times 10^{-5}) \times 10^6 = 8.951 \times 10^1$

h. $0.00008951 \times 10^{-6} = (8.951 \times 10^{-5}) \times 10^{-6} = 8.951 \times 10^{-11}$

12.   To say that scientific notation is in *standard* form means that you have a number between 1 and 10, followed by an exponential term. The numbers given in this problem are *not* between 1 and 10 as written.

a. $142.3 \times 10^3 = (1.423 \times 10^2) \times 10^3 = 1.423 \times 10^5$

b. $0.0007741 \times 10^{-9} = (7.741 \times 10^{-4}) \times 10^{-9} = 7.741 \times 10^{-13}$

c. $22.7 \times 10^3 = (2.27 \times 10^1) \times 10^3 = 2.27 \times 10^4$

d. 6.272×10^{-5} is already written in standard scientific notation.

e. $0.0251 \times 10^4 = (2.51 \times 10^{-2}) \times 10^4 = 2.51 \times 10^2$

f. $97,522 \times 10^{-3} = (9.7522 \times 10^4) \times 10^{-3} = 9.7522 \times 10^1$

g. $0.0000097752 \times 10^6 = (9.7752 \times 10^{-6}) \times 10^6 = 9.7752 \times 10^0$ (9.97752)

h. $44,252 \times 10^4 = (4.4252 \times 10^4) \times 10^4 = 4.4252 \times 10^8$

13.   a. $1/1033 = 9.681 \times 10^{-4}$

b. $1/10^5 = 1 \times 10^{-5}$

c. $1/10^{-7} = 1 \times 10^7$

d. $1/0.0002 = 5 \times 10^3$

e. $1/3,093,000 = 3.233 \times 10^{-7}$

f. $1/10^{-4} = 1 \times 10^4$

g. $1/10^9 = 1 \times 10^{-9}$

h. $1/0.000015 = 6.7 \times 10^4$

14.   a. $1/0.00032 = 3.1 \times 10^3$

b. $10^3/10^{-3} = 1 \times 10^6$

c. $10^3/10^3 = 1 (1 \times 10^0)$; any number divided by itself is unity.

d. $1/55,000 = 1.8 \times 10^{-5}$

e. $(10^5)(10^4)(10^{-4})/10^{-2} = 1 \times 10^7$

f. $43.2/(4.32 \times 10^{-5}) = \dfrac{4.32 \times 10^1}{4.32 \times 10^{-5}} = 1.00 \times 10^6$

g. $(4.32 \times 10^{-5})/432 = \dfrac{4.32 \times 10^{-5}}{4.32 \times 10^{2}} = 1.00 \times 10^{-7}$

h. $1/(10^{5})(10^{-6}) = 1/(10^{-1}) = 1 \times 10^{1}$

15.   International System (*SI*)

16.   grams

17.   a. 10^{3}

b. 10^{-2}

c. 10^{-3}

d. 10^{-1}

e. 10^{-9}

f. 10^{-6}

18.   a.   mega-

b.   milli-

c.   nano-

d.   mega-

e.   centi-

f.   micro-

19.   meter

20.   A mile represents, by definition, a greater distance than a kilometer. Therefore 100 mi represents a greater distance than 100 km.

21.   centimeter

22.   quart

23.   100 km (approximately 62 mi)

24.   kilogram

25.   5.22 cm

26.   1.62 m is approximately 5 ft, 4". The woman is slightly taller.

27.   c

28.   d

29.   c

30.   d (the other units would give very large numbers for the distance)

31.   Table 2.6 indicates that a dime is 1 mm thick.

$$10 \text{ cm} \times \frac{10 \text{ mm}}{1 \text{ cm}} \times \frac{1 \text{ dime}}{1 \text{ mm}} \times \frac{\$1}{10 \text{ dimes}} = \$10$$

32.   Table 2.6 indicates that the diameter of a quarter is 2.5 cm.

$$1 \text{ m} \times \frac{100 \text{ cm}}{1 \text{ m}} \times \frac{1 \text{ quarter}}{2.5 \text{ cm}} = 40 \text{ quarters}$$

33.   When we use a measuring scale to the *limit* of precision, we *estimate* between the smallest divisions on the scale: since this is our best estimate, the last significant digit recorded is uncertain.

34.   uncertainty

35.   The third figure in the length of the pin is uncertain because the measuring scale of the ruler has *tenths* as the smallest marked scale division. The length of the pin is given as 2.8*5* cm (rather than any other number) to indicate that the point of the pin appears to the observer to be *half way* between the smallest marked scale divisions.

36.   The scale of the ruler shown is only marked to the nearest *tenth* of a centimeter; writing 2.850 would imply that the scale was marked to the nearest *hundredth* of a centimeter (and that the zero in the thousandths place had been estimated).

37.   a.   four

       b.   five

       c.   four

       d.   one

       e.   three (the decimal point makes the zeroes significant)

       f.   three (because the number is written in scientific notation)

       g.   six

       h.   five

38.   a.   probably only two

       b.   infinite (a definition)

       c.   infinite (a definition)

       d.   probably only 1

       e.   three (the race is defined to be exactly 500. miles)

39.   remain unchanged

40.   final

41. a.   1,570,000 (or better, 1.57×10^6)

     b. 2.77×10^{-3}

     c.   84,600 (or better, 8.46×10^4)

     d.   0.00117

     e.   0.0776

42. a. 4.23×10^{-1}

     b. 7.12×10^6

     c. 4.45×10^{-4}

     d. 2.30×10^{-4}

     e. 9.72×10^5

43. a.   102.40 (1.0240×10^2)

     b.   16.0

     c.   1.639

     d.   7.36

44. a. 3.42×10^{-4}

     b. 1.034×10^4

     c. 1.7992×10^1

     d. 3.37×10^5

45. smallest

46. decimal

47. two significant figures (based on 0.0043 having two significant figures)

48. three

49. only one (based on 121.2 being known only to the first decimal place)

50. none

51. a.   102.623 (the answer can only be given to the third decimal place
           since 97.381 is only known to the third decimal place)

     b.   236.2 (the answer can only be given to the first decimal place
           since 171.5 is only known to the first decimal place)

     c.   3.0814 (the answer can only be given to the fourth decimal place
           since 1.2012 is only known to the fourth decimal place)

d.   4.67 (the answer can only be given to the second decimal place since 13.21 is only known to the second decimal place)

52.   a.   641.0 (the answer can only be given to one decimal place, since 212.7 and 26.7 are only given to one decimal place)

b.   1.327 (the answer can only be given to three decimal places, since 0.221 is only given to three decimal places)

c.   77.34 (the answer can only be given to two decimal places, since 26.01 is only given to two decimal places)

d.   Before performing the calculation, the numbers have to be converted so that they contain the same power of ten.
$2.01 \times 10^2 + 3.014 \times 10^3 = 2.01 \times 10^2 + 30.14 \times 10^2 = 32.15 \times 10^2$
This answer should then be converted to *standard* scientific notation, $32.15 \times 10^2 = 3.215 \times 10^3 = 3{,}215$.

53.   a.   2.26 (the answer can only be given to three significant figures because each number in the problem is known only to three significant figures)

b. 8.4×10^{22} (the answer can only be given to two significant figures because 0.14 is only given to two significant figures)

c. 1.5×10^5 (the answer can only be given to two significant figures because 4.0×10^4 is only given to two significant figures)

d. 6.67×10^{12} (the answer can only be given to three significant figures because each of the numbers in the problem is only given to three significant figures)

54.   a.   124 (the answer can only be given to three significant figures because 0.995 is only given to three significant figures)

b. 1.995×10^{-23} (the answer can only be given to four significant figures because 6.022×10^{23} is only given to four significant figures)

c. 1.14×10^{-2} (the answer can only be given to three significant figures because 0.500 is only given to three significant figures.)

d. 5.3×10^{-4} (the answer can only be given to two significant figures because 0.15 is only given to two significant figures)

55.   a. $[2.3232 + 0.2034 - 0.16] \times (4.0 \times 10^3) =$
$[2.3666] \times (4.0 \times 10^3) = 9.4664 \times 10^3 = 9.5 \times 10^3$

b. $[1.34 \times 10^2 + 3.2 \times 10^1]/(3.32 \times 10^{-6}) =$
$[13.4 \times 10^1 + 3.2 \times 10^1]/(3.32 \times 10^{-6}) =$
$[16.6 \times 10^1]/(3.32 \times 10^{-6}) = 5.00 \times 10^7$

c. $(4.3 \times 10^6)/[4.334 + 44.0002 - 0.9820] =$
     $(4.3 \times 10^6)/[47.3522] = 9.1 \times 10^4$

d. $(2.043 \times 10^{-2})^3 = 8.527 \times 10^{-6}$

56.   a. $(2.0944 + 0.0003233 + 12.22)/7.001 =$
           $(14.3147233)/7.001 = 2.045$

b. $(1.42 \times 10^2 + 1.021 \times 10^3)/(3.1 \times 10^{-1}) =$
     $(142 + 1021)/(3.1 \times 10^{-1}) = (1163)/(3.1 \times 10^{-1}) = 3751 = 3.8 \times 10^3$

c. $(9.762 \times 10^{-3})/(1.43 \times 10^2 + 4.51 \times 10^1) =$
     $(9.762 \times 10^{-3})/(143 + 45.1) = (9.762 \times 10^{-3})/(188.1) = 5.19 \times 10^{-5}$

d. $(6.1982 \times 10^{-4})^2 = (6.1982 \times 10^{-4})(6.1982 \times 10^{-4}) = 3.8418 \times 10^{-7}$

57.   conversion factor

58.   an infinite number (a definition)

59. $\dfrac{1 \text{ mi}}{1760 \text{ yd}} \blacktriangleleft \quad \dfrac{1760 \text{ yd}}{1 \text{ mi}}$

60. $\dfrac{1000 \text{ mL}}{1 \text{ L}} \blacktriangleleft \quad \dfrac{1 \text{ L}}{1000 \text{ mL}}$

61. $\dfrac{\$0.79}{1 \text{ lb}}$

62. $\dfrac{1 \text{ lb}}{\$0.79}$

63.   a. $36 \text{ ft} \times \dfrac{12 \text{ in.}}{1 \text{ ft}} = 432 \text{ in.} = 4.3 \times 10^2 \text{ in (2 significant figures)}$

b. $36 \text{ in.} \times \dfrac{1 \text{ ft}}{12 \text{ in.}} = 3.0 \text{ ft}$

c. $6.25 \text{ mi} \times \dfrac{1.6093 \text{ km}}{1 \text{ mi}} = 10.1 \text{ km}$

d. $6.25 \text{ km} \times \dfrac{1 \text{ mi}}{1.6093 \text{ km}} = 3.88 \text{ mi}$

e. $552 \text{ kg} \times \dfrac{1000 \text{ g}}{1 \text{ kg}} = 552,000 \text{ g} = 5.52 \times 10^5 \text{ g}$

f. $552 \text{ g} \times \dfrac{1 \text{ kg}}{1000 \text{ g}} = 0.552 \text{ kg}$

g. $552 \text{ lb} \times \dfrac{1 \text{ kg}}{2.2046 \text{ lb}} = 250. \text{ kg}$

h. $55 \text{ min} \times \dfrac{1 \text{ hr}}{60 \text{ min}} = 0.92 \text{ hr}$

64.   a. $2.23 \text{ m} \times \dfrac{1.094 \text{ yd}}{1 \text{ m}} = 2.44 \text{ yd}$

b. $46.2 \text{ yd} \times \dfrac{1 \text{ m}}{1.094 \text{ yd}} = 42.2 \text{ m}$

c. $292 \text{ cm} \times \dfrac{1 \text{ in.}}{2.54 \text{ cm}} = 115 \text{ in.}$

d. $881.2 \text{ in.} \times \dfrac{2.54 \text{ cm}}{1 \text{ in.}} = 2238 \text{ cm}$

e. $1043 \text{ km} \times \dfrac{1 \text{ mi}}{1.6093 \text{ km}} = 648.1 \text{ mi}$

f. $445.5 \text{ mi} \times \dfrac{1.6093 \text{ km}}{1 \text{ mi}} = 716.9 \text{ km}$

g. $36.2 \text{ m} \times \dfrac{1 \text{ km}}{1000 \text{ m}} = 0.0362 \text{ km}$

h. $0.501 \text{ km} \times \dfrac{1000 \text{ m}}{1 \text{ km}} \times \dfrac{100 \text{ cm}}{1 \text{ m}} = 5.01 \times 10^{4} \text{ cm}$

65.   a. $62.5 \text{ cm} \times \dfrac{1 \text{ in.}}{2.54 \text{ cm}} = 24.6 \text{ in.}$

b. $2.68 \text{ in.} \times \dfrac{2.54 \text{ cm}}{1 \text{ in.}} = 6.81 \text{ cm}$

c. $3.25 \text{ yd} \times \dfrac{1 \text{ m}}{1.0936 \text{ yd}} = 2.97 \text{ m}$

d. $4.95 \text{ m} \times \dfrac{1.0936 \text{ yd}}{1 \text{ m}} = 5.41 \text{ yd}$

e. $62.5 \text{ cm} \times \dfrac{1 \text{ in.}}{2.54 \text{ cm}} \times \dfrac{1 \text{ yd}}{36 \text{ in.}} = 0.684 \text{ yd}$

f. $2.45 \text{ mi} \times \dfrac{1 \text{ km}}{0.62137 \text{ mi}} = 3.94 \text{ km}$

g. $4.42 \text{ m} \times \dfrac{1.0936 \text{ yd}}{1 \text{ m}} \times \dfrac{36 \text{ in.}}{1 \text{ yd}} = 174 \text{ in}$

h. $5.01 \text{ kg} \times \dfrac{1 \text{ lb}}{0.45359 \text{ kg}} \times \dfrac{16 \text{ oz}}{1 \text{ lb}} = 177 \text{ oz}$

66. a. $254.3 \text{ g} \times \dfrac{1 \text{ kg}}{1000 \text{ g}} = 0.2543 \text{ kg}$

b. $2.75 \text{ kg} \times \dfrac{1000 \text{ g}}{1 \text{ kg}} = 2.75 \times 10^3 \text{ g}$

c. $2.75 \text{ kg} \times \dfrac{1 \text{ lb}}{0.45359 \text{ kg}} = 6.06 \text{ lb}$

d. $2.75 \text{ kg} \times \dfrac{1 \text{ lb}}{0.45359 \text{ kg}} \times \dfrac{16 \text{ oz}}{1 \text{ lb}} = 97.0 \text{ oz}$

e. $534.1 \text{ g} \times \dfrac{1 \text{ lb}}{453.59 \text{ g}} = 1.177 \text{ lb}$

f. $1.75 \text{ lb} \times \dfrac{453.59 \text{ g}}{1 \text{ lb}} = 794 \text{ g}$

g. $8.7 \text{ oz} \times \dfrac{1 \text{ lb}}{16 \text{ oz}} \times \dfrac{453.59 \text{ g}}{1 \text{ lb}} = 2.5 \times 10^2 \text{ g}$

h. $45.9 \text{ g} \times \dfrac{1 \text{ lb}}{453.59 \text{ g}} \times \dfrac{16 \text{ oz}}{1 \text{ lb}} = 1.62 \text{ oz}$

67. $\$20.00 \times \dfrac{\text{DM } 1.74}{\$1.00} = \text{DM } 34.80$ (assuming the exchange rate is exact)

$\text{DM } 100.0 \times \dfrac{\$1.00}{\text{DM } 1.74} = \$57.47$ (assuming the exchange rate is exact)

68. $190 \text{ mi} = 1.9 \times 10^2 \text{ mi}$ to two significant figures

$1.9 \times 10^2 \text{ mi} \times \dfrac{1 \text{ km}}{0.62137 \text{ mi}} = 3.1 \times 10^2 \text{ km}$

$3.1 \times 10^2 \text{ km} \times \dfrac{1000 \text{ m}}{1 \text{ km}} = 3.1 \times 10^5 \text{ m}$

$1.9 \times 10^2 \text{ mi} \times \dfrac{5{,}280 \text{ ft}}{1 \text{ mi}} = 1.0 \times 10^6 \text{ ft}$

69. To decide which train is faster, both speeds must be expressed in the *same unit* of distance (either miles or kilometers)

$\dfrac{225 \text{ km}}{1 \text{ hr}} \times \dfrac{1 \text{ mi}}{1.6093 \text{ km}} = 140. \text{ mi/hr}$

So the Boston-New York trains will be faster.

70. $1 \times 10^{-10} \text{ m} \times \dfrac{100 \text{ cm}}{1 \text{ m}} = 1 \times 10^{-8} \text{ cm}$

$$1 \times 10^{-8} \text{ cm} \times \frac{1 \text{ in.}}{2.54 \text{ cm}} = 4 \times 10^{-9} \text{ in.}$$

$$1 \times 10^{-8} \text{ cm} \times \frac{1 \text{ m}}{100 \text{ cm}} \times \frac{10^9 \text{ nm}}{1 \text{ m}} = 0.1 \text{ nm}$$

71.   Fahrenheit

72.   Celsius

73.   212°F; 100°C

74.   273

75.   100

76.   Fahrenheit (F)

77. $t_K = t_C + 273$ $t_C = (t_F - 32)/1.80$

    a.   −155 + 273 = 118 K

    b.   200 + 273 = 473 K

    c.   −52 + 273 = 221 K

    d.   101 °F = 38.3 °C; 38.3 + 273 = 311 K

    e.   −52 °F = −46.6 °C; −46.6 + 273 = 226 K

    f.   −196 + 273 = 77 K

78. $t_C = t_K - 273$

    a.   275 − 273 = 2°C

    b.   445 − 273 = 172°C

    c.   0 − 273 = −273°C

    d.   77 − 273 = −196°C

    e.   10,000. − 273 = 9727°C

    f.   2 − 273 = −271°C

79. $t_C = (t_F - 32)/1.80$

    a.   (45 − 32)/1.80 = 13/1.80 = 7.2 °C

    b.   (115 − 32)/1.80 = 83/1.80 = 46 °C

    c.   (−10 − 32)/1.80 = −42/1.80 = −23 °C

d.   Assuming 10,000°F to be known to two significant figures:
(10,000 − 32)/1.80 = 5500 °C

80. $t_F = 1.80(t_C) + 32$

a.   1.80(78.1) + 32 = 173 °F

b.   1.80(40.) + 32 = 104 °F

c.   1.80(−273) + 32 = −459 °F

d.   1.80(32) + 32 = 90. °F

81.   a.   1.80(−40) + 32 = −40°F

b.   (−40 −32)/180 = −40 °C

c.   232 - 273 = −41 °C

d.   232 K = −41 °C; 1.80(−41) + 32 = −42 °F

82.   a. $t_C = (t_F − 32)/1.80 = (−201 °F −32)/1.80 = (−233)/1.80 = −129.4$ °C

−129.4 °C + 273 = 143.6 = 144 K

b.   −201 °C + 273 = 72 K

c. $t_F = 1.80(t_C) + 32 = 1.80(351$ °C$) + 32 = 664$ °F

d. $t_C = (t_F − 32)/1.80 = (−150$ °F $− 32)/1.80 = −101$ °C

83.   volume

84. g/cm^3 (g/mL)

85.   lead

86.   100 in^3

87.   low

88.   Density is a *characteristic* property of a pure substance; all samples of
the same pure substance have the *same* density.

89.   aluminum (2.70 g/cm^3)

90.   copper

91.
$$density = \frac{mass}{volume}$$

a. m = 4.53 kg = 4530 g

$$d = \frac{4530 \text{ g}}{225 \text{ cm}^3} = 20.1 \text{ g/cm}^3$$

b. v = 25.0 mL = 25.0 cm^3

$$d = \frac{26.3 \text{ g}}{25.0 \text{ cm}^3} = 1.05 \text{ g/cm}^3$$

c. m = 1.00 lb = 453.59 g

$$d = \frac{453.59 \text{ g}}{500. \text{ cm}^3} = 0.907 \text{ g/cm}^3$$

d. m = 352 mg = 0.352 g

$$d = \frac{0.352 \text{ g}}{0.271 \text{ cm}^3} = 1.30 \text{ g/cm}^3$$

92.   density = $\dfrac{\text{mass}}{\text{volume}}$

a. $d = \dfrac{122.4 \text{ g}}{5.5 \text{ cm}^3} = 22 \text{ g/cm}^3$

b. $v = 0.57 \text{ m}^3 \times (\dfrac{100 \text{ cm}}{1 \text{ m}})^3 = 5.7 \times 10^5 \text{ cm}^3$

$$d = \frac{1.9302 \times 10^4 \text{ g}}{5.7 \times 10^5 \text{ cm}^3} = 0.034 \text{ g/cm}^3$$

c. $m = 0.0175 \text{ kg} \times \dfrac{1000 \text{ g}}{1 \text{ kg}} = 17.5 \text{ g}$

$$d = \frac{17.5 \text{ g}}{18.2 \text{ mL}} = 0.962 \text{ g/mL} = 0.962 \text{ g/cm}^3$$

d. $v = 0.12 \text{ m}^3 \times (\dfrac{100 \text{ cm}}{1 \text{ m}})^3 = 1.2 \times 10^5 \text{ cm}^3$

$$d = \frac{2.49 \text{ g}}{1.2 \times 10^5 \text{ cm}^3} = 2.1 \times 10^{-5} \text{ g/cm}^3$$

93. $d = \dfrac{75.0 \text{ g}}{62.4 \text{ mL}} = 1.20 \text{ g/mL}$

94. $d = \dfrac{75.2 \text{ g}}{89.2 \text{ mL}} = 0.843 \text{ g/mL}$

95. $m = 1.45 \text{ kg} \times \dfrac{10^3 \text{ g}}{1 \text{ kg}} = 1.45 \times 10^3 \text{ g}$

$$d = \frac{1.45 \times 10^3 \text{ g}}{542 \text{ mL}} = 2.68 \text{ g/mL}$$

96. $m = 3.5 \text{ lb} \times \dfrac{453.59 \text{ g}}{1 \text{ lb}} = 1.59 \times 10^3 \text{ g}$

$v = 1.2 \times 10^4 \text{ in}^3 \times (\dfrac{2.54 \text{ cm}}{1 \text{ in}})^3 = 1.97 \times 10^5 \text{ cm}^3$

$d = \dfrac{1.59 \times 10^3 \text{ g}}{1.97 \times 10^5 \text{ cm}^3} = 8.1 \times 10^{-3} \text{ g/cm}^3$

The material will float.

97.   The volume of the iron can be calculated from its mass and density:

$v = 52.4 \text{ g} \times \dfrac{1 \text{ cm}^3}{7.87 \text{ g}} = 6.66 \text{ cm}^3 = 6.66 \text{ mL}$

The liquid level in the graduated cylinder will rise by 6.66 mL when the cube of metal is added, giving a final volume of $(75.0 + 6.66) = 81.7$ mL

98. $5.25 \text{ g} \times \dfrac{1 \text{ cm}^3}{10.5 \text{ g}} = 0.500 \text{ cm}^3 = 0.500 \text{ mL}$

11.2 mL + 0.500 mL = 11.7 mL

99.
a. $50.0 \text{ g} \times \dfrac{1 \text{ cm}^3}{2.16 \text{ g}} = 23.1 \text{ cm}^3$

b. $50.0 \text{ g} \times \dfrac{1 \text{ cm}^3}{13.6 \text{ g}} = 3.68 \text{ cm}^3$

c. $50.0 \text{ g} \times \dfrac{1 \text{ cm}^3}{0.880 \text{ g}} = 56.8 \text{ cm}^3$

d. $50.0 \text{ g} \times \dfrac{1 \text{ cm}^3}{10.5 \text{ g}} = 4.76 \text{ cm}^3$

100.   a. $50.0 \text{ cm}^3 \times \dfrac{19.32 \text{ g}}{1 \text{ cm}^3} = 966 \text{ g}$

b. $50.0 \text{ cm}^3 \times \dfrac{7.87 \text{ g}}{1 \text{ cm}^3} = 394 \text{ g}$

c. $50.0 \text{ cm}^3 \times \dfrac{11.34 \text{ g}}{1 \text{ cm}^3} = 567 \text{ g}$

d. $50.0 \text{ cm}^3 \times \dfrac{2.70 \text{ g}}{1 \text{ cm}^3} = 135 \text{ g}$

101. a.   three

      b.   three

      c.   three

102. a. 3.011×10^{23} = 301,100,000,000,000,000,000,000

      b. 5.091×10^{9} = 5,091,000,000

      c. 7.2×10^{2} = 720

      d. 1.234×10^{5} = 123,400

      e. 4.32002×10^{-4} = 0.000432002

      f. 3.001×10^{-2} = 0.03001

      g. 2.9901×10^{-7} = 0.00000029901

      h. 4.2×10^{-1} = 0.42

103. a. 4.25×10^{2}

      b. 7.81×10^{-4}

      c. 2.68×10^{4}

      d. 6.54×10^{-4}

      e. 7.26×10^{1}

104. a.   centimeters

      b.   meters

      c.   kilometers

      d.   centimeters

      e.   millimeters

105. a. $1.25 \text{ in.} \times \dfrac{1 \text{ ft}}{12 \text{ in.}} = 0.104 \text{ ft}$

           $1.25 \text{ in.} \times \dfrac{2.54 \text{ cm}}{1 \text{ in.}} = 3.18 \text{ cm}$

      b. $2.12 \text{ qt} \times \dfrac{1 \text{ gal}}{4 \text{ qt}} = 0.530 \text{ gal}$

           $2.12 \text{ qt} \times \dfrac{1 \text{ L}}{1.0567 \text{ qt}} = 2.01 \text{ L}$

      c. $2640 \text{ ft} \times \dfrac{1 \text{ mi}}{5280. \text{ ft}} = 0.500 \text{ mi}$

           $2640 \text{ ft} \times \dfrac{1.6093 \text{ km}}{5280. \text{ ft}} = 0.805 \text{ km}$

      d. $1.254 \text{ kg} \times \dfrac{10^{3} \text{ g}}{1 \text{ kg}} \times \dfrac{1 \text{ cm}^{3}}{11.34 \text{ g}} = 110.6 \text{ cm}^{3}$

      e. $250. \text{ mL} \times 0.785 \text{ g/mL} = 196 \text{ g}$

f. $3.5 \text{ in}^3 \times (\dfrac{2.54 \text{ cm}}{1 \text{ in.}})^3 = 57 \text{ cm}^3 = 57 \text{ mL}$

$57 \text{ cm}^3 \times 13.6 \text{ g/cm}^3 = 7.8 \times 10^2 \text{ g} = 0.78 \text{ kg}$

106.   a. $36.2 \text{ blim} \times \dfrac{1400 \text{ kryll}}{1 \text{ blim}} = 5.07 \times 10^4 \text{ kryll}$

b. $170 \text{ kryll} \times \dfrac{1 \text{ blim}}{1400 \text{ kryll}} = 0.12 \text{ blim}$

c. $72.5 \text{ kryll}^2 \times (\dfrac{1 \text{ blim}}{1400 \text{ kryll}})^2 = 3.70 \times 10^{-5} \text{ blim}^2$

107. $110 \text{ km} \times \dfrac{1 \text{ hr}}{100 \text{ km}} = 1.1 \text{ hr}$

108. $52 \text{ cm} \times \dfrac{1 \text{ in.}}{2.54 \text{ cm}} = 20. \text{ in.}$

109. $45 \text{ mi} \times \dfrac{1.6093 \text{ km}}{1 \text{ mi}} = 72.4 \text{ km}$

$38 \text{ mi} \times \dfrac{1.6093 \text{ km}}{1 \text{ mi}} = 61.2 \text{ km}$

1 gal = 3.7854 L

highway: 72.4 km/3.7854 L = 19 km/L

city: 61.2 km/3.7854 L = 16 km/L

110. $1 \text{ lb} \times \dfrac{1 \text{ kg}}{2.2 \text{ lb}} \times \dfrac{\$1}{F5} \times \dfrac{11.5F}{1 \text{ kg}} = \$1$

111. $15.6 \text{ g} \times \dfrac{1 \text{ capsule}}{0.65 \text{ g}} = 24 \text{ capsules}$

112. $°X = 1.26°C + 14$

113. $v = 4/3(\pi r^3) = 4/3(3.1416)(0.5 \text{ cm})^3 = 0.52 \text{ cm}^3$

$d = \dfrac{2.0 \text{ g}}{0.52 \text{ cm}^3} = 3.8 \text{ g/cm}^3 \text{ (the ball will sink)}$

114. $d = \dfrac{36.8 \text{ g}}{10.5 \text{ L}} = 3.50 \text{ g/L}$ $(3.50 \times 10^{-3} \text{ g/cm}^3)$

115.   a. $25.0 \text{ g} \times \dfrac{1 \text{ cm}^3}{0.000084 \text{ g}} = 2.98 \times 10^5 \text{ cm}^3$

b. $25.0 \text{ g} \times \dfrac{1 \text{ cm}^3}{13.6 \text{ g}} = 1.84 \text{ cm}^3$

c. $25.0 \text{ g} \times \dfrac{1 \text{ cm}^3}{11.34 \text{ g}} = 2.20 \text{ cm}^3$

d. $25.0 \text{ g} \times \dfrac{1 \text{ cm}^3}{1.00 \text{ g}} = 25.0 \text{ cm}^3$

116.   for ethanol, $100. \text{ mL} \times \dfrac{0.785 \text{ g}}{1 \text{ mL}} = 78.5 \text{ g}$

for benzene, $1000 \text{ mL} \times \dfrac{0.880 \text{ g}}{1 \text{ mL}} = 880. \text{ g}$

total mass, 78.5 + 880. = 959 g

117.   three

118.   a.   negative

b.   negative

c.   positive

d.   zero

e.   negative

119.   a.   positive

b.   negative

c.   negative

d.   zero

120.   a.   2; positive

b.   11; negative

c.   3; positive

d.   5; negative

e.   5; positive

f.   0; zero

g.   1; negative

h.   7; negative

121.   a.   4; positive

b.   6; negative

c.   0; zero

d.   5; positive

e.   2; negative

122. a.   1; positive

      b.   3; negative

      c.   0; zero

      d.   3; positive

      e.   9; negative

123. a.   The decimal point must be moved two places to the left, so the exponent is positive 2; $529 = 5.29 \times 10^2$

      b.   The decimal point must be moved eight places to the left, so the exponent is positive 8; $240,000,000 = 2.4 \times 10^8$

      c.   The decimal point must be moved seventeen places to the left, so the exponent is positive 17; $301,000,000,000,000,000 = 3.01 \times 10^{17}$

      d.   The decimal point must be moved four places to the left, so the exponent is positive 4; $78,444 = 7.8444 \times 10^4$

      e.   The decimal point must be moved four places to the right, so the exponent is negative 4; $0.0003442 = 3.442 \times 10^{-4}$

      f.   The decimal point must be moved ten places to the right, so the exponent is negative 10; $0.000000000902 = 9.02 \times 10^{-10}$

      g.   The decimal point must be moved two places to the right, so the exponent is negative 2; $0.043 = 4.3 \times 10^{-2}$

      h.   The decimal point must be moved two places to the right, so the exponent is negative 2; $0.0821 = 8.21 \times 10^{-2}$

124. a.   The decimal point must be moved five places to the left; $2.98 \times 10^{-5} = 0.0000298$

      b.   The decimal point must be moved nine places to the right; $4.358 \times 10^9 = 4,358,000,000$

      c.   The decimal point must be moved six places to the left; $1.9928 \times 10^{-6} = 0.0000019928$

      d.   The decimal point must be moved 23 places to the right; $6.02 \times 10^{23} = 602,000,000,000,000,000,000,000$

      e.   The decimal point must be moved one place to the left; $1.01 \times 10^{-1} = 0.101$

      f.   The decimal point must be moved three places to the left; $7.87 \times 10^{-3} = 0.00787$

g.   The decimal point must be moved seven places to the right;
$9.87 \times 10^7 = 98,700,000$

h.   The decimal point must be moved two places to the right;
$3.7899 \times 10^2 = 378.99$

i.   The decimal point must be moved one place to the left;
$1.093 \times 10^{-1} = 0.1093$

j.   The decimal point must be moved zero places;
$2.9004 \times 10^0 = 2.9004$

k.   The decimal point must be moved four places to the left;
$3.9 \times 10^{-4} = 0.00039$

l.   The decimal point must be moved eight places to the left;
$1.904 \times 10^{-8} = 0.00000001904$

125.   To say that scientific notation is in *standard* form means that you have a number between 1 and 10, followed by an exponential term. The numbers given in this problem are *not* between 1 and 10 as written.

a. $102.3 \times 10^{-5} = (1.023 \times 10^2) \times 10^{-5} = 1.023 \times 10^{-3}$

b. $32.03 \times 10^{-3} = (3.203 \times 10^1) \times 10^{-3} = 3.203 \times 10^{-2}$

c. $59933 \times 10^2 = (5.9933 \times 10^4) \times 10^2 = 5.9933 \times 10^6$

d. $599.33 \times 10^4 = (5.9933 \times 10^2) \times 10^4 = 5.9933 \times 10^6$

e. $5993.3 \times 10^3 = (5.9933 \times 10^3) \times 10^3 = 5.9933 \times 10^6$

f. $2054 \times 10^{-1} = (2.054 \times 10^3) \times 10^{-1} = 2.054 \times 10^2$

g. $32,000,000 \times 10^{-6} = (3.2 \times 10^7) \times 10^{-6} = 3.2 \times 10^1$

h. $59.933 \times 10^5 = (5.9933 \times 10^1) \times 10^5 = 5.9933 \times 10^6$

126.   a. $1/10^2 = 1 \times 10^{-2}$

b. $1/10^{-2} = 1 \times 10^2$

c. $55/10^3 = \dfrac{5.5 \times 10^1}{1 \times 10^3} = 5.5 \times 10^{-2}$

d. $(3.1 \times 10^6)/10^{-3} = \dfrac{3.1 \times 10^6}{1 \times 10^{-3}} = 3.1 \times 10^9$

e. $(10^6)^{1/2} = 1 \times 10^3$

f. $(10^6)(10^4)/(10^2) = \dfrac{(1 \times 10^6)(1 \times 10^4)}{(1 \times 10^2)} = 1 \times 10^8$

g. $1/0.0034 = \dfrac{1}{3.4 \times 10^{-3}} = 2.9 \times 10^2$

h. $3.453/10^{-4} = \dfrac{3.453}{1 \times 10^{-4}} = 3.453 \times 10^4$

127. meter

128. kelvin, K

129. 100 km (see inside back cover of textbook)

130. centimeter

131. 250. mL

132. 0.105 m

133. 100 km/hr = 62.1 mi/hr; you would not violate the speed limit.

134. 1 kg (100 g = 0.1 kg)

135. 4.25 g (425 mg = 0.425 g)

136. 10 cm (1 cm = 10 mm)

137. significant figures (digits)

138. 2.8 (the hundredths place is estimated)

139. a.   one

b.   one

c.   four

d.   two

e.   infinite (definition)

f.   one

140. a.   0.000426

b. 4.02×10^{-5}

c. 5.99×10^6

d.   400.

e.   0.00600

141. a.   0.7556

      b.   293

      c.   17.01

      d.   432.97

142. a.   2149.6 (the answer can only be given to the first decimal place, since 149.2 is only known to the first decimal place)

      b. 5.37×10^3 (the answer can only be given to two decimal places since 4.34 is only known to two decimal places; since the power of ten is the same for each number, the calculation can be performed directly)

      c.   Before performing the calculation, the numbers have to be converted so that they contain the same power of ten.

            $4.03 \times 10^{-2} - 2.044 \times 10^{-3} =$

            $4.03 \times 10^{-2} - 0.2044 \times 10^{-2} =$

            3.83×10^{-2} (the answer can only be given the second decimal place since 4.03×10^{-2} is only known to the second decimal place)

      d.   Before performing the calculation, the numbers have to be converted so that they contain the same power of ten.

            $2.094 \times 10^5 - 1.073 \times 10^6 =$

            $2.094 \times 10^5 - 10.73 \times 10^5 =$

            -8.64×10^5

143. a. 5.57×10^7 (the answer can only be given to three significant figures because 0.0432 and 4.43×10^8 are only known to three significant figures)

      b. 2.38×10^{-1} (the answer can only be given to three significant figures because 0.00932 and 4.03×10^2 are only known to three significant figures)

      c.   4.72 (the answer can only be given to three significant figures because 2.94 is only known to three significant figures)

      d. 8.08×10^8 (the answer can only be given to three significant figures because 0.000934 is only known to three significant figures)

144. a. $(2.9932 \times 10^4)(2.4443 \times 10^2 + 1.0032 \times 10^1) =$

            $(2.9932 \times 10^4)(24.443 \times 10^1 + 1.0032 \times 10^1) =$

            $(2.9932 \times 10^4)(25.446 \times 10^1) = 7.6166 \times 10^6$

b. $(2.34 \times 10^2 + 2.443 \times 10^{-1})/(0.0323) =$

$(2.34 \times 10^2 + 0.002443 \times 10^2)/(0.0323) =$

$(2.34 \times 10^2)/(0.0323) = 7.24 \times 10^3$

c. $(4.38 \times 10^{-3})^2 = 1.92 \times 10^{-5}$

d. $(5.9938 \times 10^{-6})^{1/2} = 2.4482 \times 10^{-3}$

145. $\dfrac{1 \text{ L}}{1000 \text{ cm}^3}$ $\dfrac{1000 \text{ cm}^3}{1 \text{ L}}$

146.   1 year/12 months; 12 months/1 year

147.   a. $8.43 \text{ cm} \times \dfrac{10 \text{ mm}}{1 \text{ cm}} = 84.3 \text{ mm}$

b. $2.41 \times 10^2 \text{ cm} \times \dfrac{1 \text{ m}}{100 \text{ cm}} = 2.41 \text{ m}$

c. $294.5 \text{ nm} \times \dfrac{1 \text{m}}{10^9 \text{ nm}} \times \dfrac{100 \text{ cm}}{1 \text{ m}} = 2.945 \times 10^{-5} \text{ cm}$

d. $404.5 \text{ m} \times \dfrac{1 \text{ km}}{1000 \text{ m}} = 0.4045 \text{ km}$

e. $1.445 \times 10^4 \text{ m} \times \dfrac{1 \text{ km}}{1000 \text{ m}} = 14.45 \text{ km}$

f. $42.2 \text{ mm} \times \dfrac{1 \text{ cm}}{10 \text{ mm}} = 4.22 \text{ cm}$

g. $235.3 \text{ m} \times \dfrac{1000 \text{ mm}}{1 \text{ m}} = 2.353 \times 10^5 \text{ mm}$

h. $903.3 \text{ nm} \times \dfrac{1 \text{ m}}{10^9 \text{ nm}} \times \dfrac{10^6 \text{ } \mu\text{m}}{1 \text{ m}} = 0.9033 \text{ } \mu\text{m}$

148.   a. $908 \text{ oz} \times \dfrac{1 \text{ lb}}{16 \text{ oz}} \times \dfrac{1 \text{ kg}}{2.2046 \text{ lb}} = 25.7 \text{ kg}$

b. $12.8 \text{ L} \times \dfrac{1 \text{ qt}}{0.94633 \text{ L}} \times \dfrac{1 \text{ gal}}{4 \text{ qt}} = 3.38 \text{ gal}$

c. $125 \text{ mL} \times \dfrac{1 \text{ L}}{1000 \text{ mL}} \times \dfrac{1 \text{ qt}}{0.94633 \text{ L}} = 0.132 \text{ qt}$

d. $2.89 \text{ gal} \times \dfrac{4 \text{ qt}}{1 \text{ gal}} \times \dfrac{1 \text{ L}}{1.0567 \text{ qt}} \times \dfrac{1000 \text{ mL}}{1 \text{ L}} = 1.09 \times 10^4 \text{ mL}$

e. $4.48 \text{ lb} \times \dfrac{453.59 \text{ g}}{1 \text{ lb}} = 2.03 \times 10^3 \text{ g}$

f. $550 \text{ mL} \times \dfrac{1 \text{ L}}{1000 \text{ mL}} \times \dfrac{1.0567 \text{ qt}}{1 \text{ L}} = 0.58 \text{ qt}$

149. $9.3 \times 10^7 \text{ mi} \times \dfrac{1 \text{ km}}{0.62137 \text{ mi}} = 1.5 \times 10^8 \text{ km}$

$1.5 \times 10^8 \text{ km} \times \dfrac{1000 \text{ m}}{1 \text{ km}} \times \dfrac{100 \text{ cm}}{1 \text{ m}} = 1.5 \times 10^{13} \text{ cm}$

150.   Assuming exactly 6 gross, 864 pencils

151. $t_K = t_c + 273$

a. $0 + 273 = 273 \text{ K}$

b. $25 + 273 = 298 \text{ K}$

c. $37 + 273 = 310. \text{ K}$

d. $100 + 273 = 373 \text{ K}$

e. $-175 + 273 = 98 \text{ K}$

f. $212 + 273 = 485 \text{ K}$

152.   a.   Celsius temperature $= (175 - 32)/1.80 = 79.4 \text{ °C}$

kelvin temperature $= 79.4 + 273 = 352 \text{ K}$

b. $255 - 273 = -18 \text{ °C}$

c. $(-45 - 32)/1.80 = -43 \text{ °C}$

d. $1.80(125) + 32 = 257 \text{ °F}$

153. $\text{density} = \dfrac{\text{mass}}{\text{volume}}$

a. $d = \dfrac{234 \text{ g}}{2.2 \text{ cm}^3} = 110 \text{ g/cm}^3$

b. $m = 2.34 \text{ kg} \times \dfrac{1000 \text{ g}}{1 \text{ kg}} = 2340 \text{ g}$

$v = 2.2 \text{ m}^3 \times \left(\dfrac{100 \text{ cm}}{1 \text{ m}}\right)^3 = 2.2 \times 10^6 \text{ cm}^3$

$d = \dfrac{2340 \text{ g}}{2.2 \times 10^6 \text{ cm}^3} = 1.1 \times 10^{-3} \text{ g/cm}^3$

c. $m = 1.2 \text{ lb} \times \dfrac{453.59 \text{ g}}{1 \text{ lb}} = 544 \text{ g}$

$$v = 2.1 \text{ ft}^3 \times (\frac{12 \text{ in}}{1 \text{ ft}})^3 \times (\frac{2.54 \text{ cm}}{1 \text{ in}})^3 = 5.95 \times 10^4 \text{ cm}^3$$

$$d = \frac{544 \text{ g}}{5.95 \times 10^4 \text{ cm}^3} = 9.1 \times 10^{-3} \text{ g/cm}^3$$

d. $$m = 4.3 \text{ ton} \times \frac{2000 \text{ lb}}{1 \text{ ton}} \times \frac{453.59 \text{ g}}{1 \text{ lb}} = 3.90 \times 10^6 \text{ g}$$

$$v = 54.2 \text{ yd}^3 \times (\frac{1 \text{ m}}{1.0936 \text{ yd}})^3 \times (\frac{100 \text{ cm}}{1 \text{ m}})^3 = 4.14 \times 10^7 \text{ cm}^3$$

$$d = \frac{3.90 \times 10^6 \text{ g}}{4.14 \times 10^7 \text{ cm}^3} = 9.4 \times 10^{-2} \text{ g/cm}^3$$

154. $$85.5 \text{ mL} \times \frac{0.915 \text{ g}}{1 \text{ mL}} = 78.2 \text{ g}$$

155. $$50.0 \text{ g} \times \frac{1 \text{ mL}}{1.31 \text{ g}} = 38.2 \text{ g}$$

156. $$m = 155 \text{ lb} \times \frac{453.59 \text{ g}}{1 \text{ lb}} = 7.031 \times 10^4 \text{ g}$$

$$v = 4.2 \text{ ft}^3 \times (\frac{12 \text{ in}}{1 \text{ ft}})^3 \times (\frac{2.54 \text{ cm}}{1 \text{ in}})^3 = 1.189 \times 10^5 \text{ cm}^3$$

$$d = \frac{7.031 \times 10^4 \text{ g}}{1.189 \times 10^5 \text{ cm}^3} = 0.59 \text{ g/cm}^3$$

157. Volume = 21.6 mL – 12.7 mL = 8.9 mL

$$d = \frac{33.42 \text{ g}}{8.9 \text{ mL}} = 3.8 \text{ g/mL}$$

158. a. 23 °F
      b. 32 °F
      c. –321 °F
      d. –459 °F
      e. 187 °F
      f. –459 °F

Chapter 3   Matter and Energy

1.   matter

2.   solid, liquid, gas (vapor)

3.   incompressible: solids, liquids; compressible: gases

4.   Liquids

5.   fixed in position: solids; move freely: liquids and gases

6.   gaseous

7.   Liquids and gases both have no rigid shape and take on the shape of their containers (because the molecules in them are free to move relative to each other). Liquids are essentially incompressible, whereas gases are readily compressible.

8.   stronger

9.   The gaseous 10-g sample of water has a much *larger* volume than either the solid or liquid samples. While the 10-g sample of water vapor contains the same amount of water as the solid and liquid sample (the same number of water molecules), there is a great deal of empty space in the gaseous sample.

10.   Gases are easily compressed into smaller volumes, whereas solids and liquids are not. Since a gaseous sample consists mostly of empty space, it is this empty space which is compressed when pressure is applied to a gas.

11.   physical

12.   chemical

13.   the orange color

14.   the substance reacts with iron(II) sulfate

15.   An ice cube consists of water in its solid state. This solid state is characterized by a closely packed, regular array of water molecules in a crystal lattice. Because of the close-packing of the molecules, intermolecular forces between water molecules are very strong, and the molecules are more or less fixed in position. As heat is applied to an ice cube, the molecules of water absorb the energy being applied and begin to vibrate and move more and more strongly, until finally the molecules are able to separate physically from one another to form the liquid state. As more heat is applied to the liquid state, the energy being applied is again converted to the energy of motion (kinetic energy) of the molecules. The water molecules move quickly and more violently, and the tendency increases for molecules at the surface of the liquid to be moving in such a direction as to escape from the bulk of liquid. As heat continues to be applied, more and more molecules will have sufficient energy to escape from the surface of the liquid until

the liquid is vaporizing rapidly (boiling). None of the changes described above involves the breaking of chemical bonds or the production of a new substance, so the changes are physical in nature, rather than chemical.

16. Electrolysis is the passage of an electrical current through a substance or solution to force a chemical reaction to occur. Electrolysis causes chemical changes to take place that would ordinarily not take place on their own. When an electrical current is passed through water, the current causes the water molecules to break down into their constituent elements (hydrogen gas and oxygen gas).

17. a. physical;   this represents only a change in state

    b. chemical;   when the alcohol in the brandy burns, it is converted into other substances (carbon dioxide and water)

    c. chemical;   the acid reacts with the glass and converts it into other substances

    d. physical;   this represents only a change in freezing point

    e. chemical;   since the antacid produces a new substance (carbon dioxide), this can only be a chemical change

    f. chemical;   the metal case of the battery is converted into other substances, which allows the battery to leak

    g. chemical;   the cellulose which make up the cotton fibers is converted into other substances, leaving a hole

    h. physical;   milk contains protein, and when the vinegar is added, the acidity of the vinegar causes a change in the protein's shape, making it insoluble in water.

    i. physical;   when you stop pulling on the rubber, it goes back to its original shape

    j. physical;   this represents just a change in state

    k. physical;   the acetone dissolves the lacquers in the nail polish, forming a solution (which is not a chemical process)

18. a. chemical;   the scorch represents the oxidation of the material

    b. physical;   the gas in the tires decreases in volume with temperature

    c. chemical;   tarnish on silver is caused by reaction of the silver with sulfur or oxygen

d.   chemical;   the ethyl alcohol in the wine is oxidized to acetic acid

e.   chemical;   the oven cleaner contains sodium hydroxide which converts greases in the oven into soaps

f.   chemical;   an ordinary flashlight battery is constructed with a zinc casing which serves as one of the electrodes. As the battery discharges, the zinc is oxidized.

g.   chemical;   the acids attack the calcium phosphate matrix of the teeth

h.   chemical;   the charring represents the breakdown of the sugar

i.   chemical;   iron in the blood catalyzes the decomposition of the hydrogen peroxide into oxygen gas (and water)

j.   physical;   this is just a change in state; carbon dioxide, only in the gaseous state, is still present after the sublimation

k.   chemical;   chlorine is an oxidizing agent and can change the chemical nature of the dyes in the fabrics

19.   chemical

20.   element

21.   compounds

22.   Compounds

23.   When we say that a compound always has the same composition, we mean that the molecules of that compound always contain the same type and number of atoms of its constituent elements.

24.   Typically, the properties of a compound and the elements that constitute it are very different.   Consider the properties of liquid *water* and the hydrogen and oxygen gases from which the water was prepared. Consider the properties of *sodium chloride* (table salt) and the sodium metal and chlorine gas from which it might have been prepared.

25.   the same

26.   a variable

27.   A solution is a homogeneous mixture in which the solute is uniformly dispersed on a molecular level in the solvent. Simple mixtures are typically nonhomogeneous and the dispersion of the components may not be on the molecular level.

28.   solutions: window cleaner, shampoo, rubbing alcohol
       mixtures: salad dressing, jelly beans, the change in my pocket

29.   a.   mixture (fat, water, sugar, protein, etc.)

       b.   mixture (wood pulp, cotton, coloring agents, etc.)

       c.   pure substance

       d.   mixture

       e.   mixture (iron, and perhaps nickel, carbon, chromium, etc.)

30.   a.   mixture

       b.   mixture

       c.   mixture

       d.   pure substance

31.   a.   homogeneous (if nothing has been mixed in with the ice cream)

       b.   heterogeneous

       c.   homogeneous

       d.   heterogeneous

       e.   heterogeneous

32.   a.   homogeneous

       b.   heterogeneous

       c.   heterogeneous

       d.   homogeneous

       e.   the paper itself is basically homogeneous in appearance

33.   Consider a salt solution (sodium chloride in water). Since water boils
       at a much lower temperature than sodium chloride, the water can be
       boiled off from the solution, collected, and subsequently condensed back
       into the liquid state. This separates the two chemical substances.

34.   Consider a mixture of salt (sodium chloride) and sand. Salt is soluble
       in water, sand is not. The mixture is added to water and stirred to
       dissolve the salt, and is then filtered. The salt solution passes
       through the filter, the sand remains on the filter. The water can then
       be evaporated from the salt.

35. If water is added to the sample, and the sample is then heated to boiling, this should dissolve the benzoic acid but not the charcoal. The hot sample could then be *filtered*, which would remove the charcoal. The solution which passed through the filter could then be cooled, which should cause some of the benzoic acid to crystallize, or the solution could be heated carefully to boil off the water leaving benzoic acid behind.

36. The solution is heated to vaporize (boil) the water. The water vapor is then cooled so that it condenses back to the liquid state, and the liquid is collected. After all the water is vaporized from the original sample, pure sodium chloride will remain. The process consists of physical changes.

37. energy

38. the calorie

39. In a sample of ice, the water molecules are held relatively rigidly in fixed positions in the crystal. As heat is applied, the water molecules begin to vibrate back and forth, but still basically remain in their original positions until the melting point is reached. When the melting point is reached, the forces which held the molecules in position in the crystal are overcome, and the molecules begin to move around much more freely, although they are still held within the bulk volume of the liquid. As the liquid continues to be heated, the molecules move more quickly and more freely until the boiling point is reached. At the boiling point, the forces holding the molecules in the liquid are overcome, and the individual molecules are moving so quickly and freely that they are able to escape from the volume of the liquid. As the molecules of the vapor continue to be heated, they move more and more quickly.

40. As the steam is cooled from 150 °C to 100 °C, the molecules of vapor gradually slow down as they lose kinetic energy. At 100 °C, the steam condenses into liquid water, and the temperature remains at 100 °C until all the steam has condensed. As the liquid water cools, the molecules in the liquid move more and more slowly as they lose kinetic energy. At 0 °C, the liquid water freezes.

41. lower

42. temperature

43. $526 \text{ J} \times \dfrac{25.0 \text{ g}}{7.40 \text{ g}} = 1.78 \times 10^3 \text{ J}$

44. $526 \text{ J} \times \dfrac{55 \text{ °C}}{17 \text{ °C}} = 1.7 \times 10^3 \text{ J}$

45. a. $7845 \text{ cal} \times \dfrac{4.184 \text{ J}}{1 \text{ cal}} = 3.282 \times 10^4 \text{ J} = 32.82 \text{ kJ}$

  b. $4.55 \times 10^4 \text{ cal} \times \dfrac{4.184 \text{ J}}{1 \text{ cal}} = 1.90 \times 10^5 \text{ J} = 190. \text{ kJ}$

  c. $62.142 \text{ kcal} \times \dfrac{4.184 \text{ kJ}}{1 \text{ kcal}} = 2.600 \times 10^2 \text{ kJ} = 2.600 \times 10^5 \text{ J}$

  d. $43{,}024 \text{ cal} \times \dfrac{4.184 \text{ J}}{1 \text{ cal}} = 1.800 \times 10^5 \text{ J} = 180.0 \text{ kJ}$

46. Since 1.000 cal = 4.184 J, then 1.000 kcal = 4.184 kJ

  a. $462.4 \text{ kJ} \times \dfrac{1 \text{ kcal}}{4.184 \text{ kJ}} = 110.5 \text{ kcal}$

  b. $18.28 \text{ kJ} \times \dfrac{1 \text{ kcal}}{4.184 \text{ kJ}} = 4.369 \text{ kcal}$

  c. $1.014 \text{ kJ} \times \dfrac{1 \text{ kcal}}{4.184 \text{ kJ}} = 0.2424 \text{ kcal}$

  d. $190.5 \text{ kJ} \times \dfrac{1 \text{ kcal}}{4.184 \text{ kJ}} = 45.53 \text{ kcal}$

47. a. $55{,}322 \text{ cal} \times \dfrac{1 \text{ kcal}}{1000 \text{ cal}} = 55.322 \text{ kcal}$

  b. $972 \text{ cal} \times \dfrac{1 \text{ kcal}}{1000 \text{ cal}} = 0.972 \text{ kcal}$

  c. $442{,}800 \text{ cal} \times \dfrac{1 \text{ kcal}}{1000 \text{ cal}} = 442.8 \text{ kcal}$

  d. $5.26 \times 10^4 \text{ cal} \times \dfrac{1 \text{ kcal}}{1000 \text{ cal}} = 52.6 \text{ kcal}$

48. a. $12.30 \text{ kcal} \times \dfrac{1000 \text{ cal}}{1 \text{ kcal}} = 12{,}300 \text{ cal} \ (1.230 \times 10^4 \text{ cal})$

  b. $290.4 \text{ kcal} \times \dfrac{1000 \text{ cal}}{1 \text{ kcal}} = 290{,}400 \text{ cal} \ (2.904 \times 10^5 \text{ cal})$

  c. $940{,}000 \text{ kcal} \times \dfrac{1000 \text{ cal}}{1 \text{ kcal}} = 940{,}000{,}000 \text{ cal} \ (9.4 \times 10^8 \text{ cal})$

  d. $4201 \text{ kcal} \times \dfrac{1000 \text{ cal}}{1 \text{ kcal}} = 4{,}201{,}000 \text{ cal} \ (4.201 \times 10^6 \text{ cal})$

49. a. $243,000 \text{ J} \times \dfrac{1 \text{ kJ}}{1000 \text{ J}} = 243 \text{ kJ}$

b. $4.184 \text{ J} \times \dfrac{1 \text{ kJ}}{1000 \text{ J}} = 4.184 \times 10^{-3} \text{ kJ}$

c. $0.251 \text{ J} \times \dfrac{1 \text{ kJ}}{1000 \text{ J}} = 2.51 \times 10^{-4} \text{ kJ}$

d. $450.3 \text{ J} \times \dfrac{1 \text{ kJ}}{1000 \text{ J}} = 0.4503 \text{ kJ}$

50. a. $45.62 \text{ kcal} \times \dfrac{4.184 \text{ kJ}}{1 \text{ kcal}} = 190.9 \text{ kJ}$

b. $72.94 \text{ kJ} \times \dfrac{1 \text{ kcal}}{4.184 \text{ kJ}} = 17.43 \text{ kcal}$

c. $2.751 \text{ kJ} \times \dfrac{1 \text{ kcal}}{4.184 \text{ kJ}} \times \dfrac{1000 \text{ cal}}{1 \text{ kcal}} = 657.5 \text{ cal}$

d. $5.721 \text{ kcal} \times \dfrac{4.184 \text{ kJ}}{1 \text{ kcal}} \times \dfrac{1000 \text{ J}}{1 \text{ kJ}} = 2.394 \times 10^{4} \text{ J}$

51. Temperature increase = 75.0 – 22.3 = 52.7°C

$145 \text{ g} \times 4.184 \text{ J/g °C} \times 52.7°C \times \dfrac{1 \text{ cal}}{4.184 \text{ J}} = 7641.5 \text{ cal} = 7.64 \times 10^{3} \text{ cal}$

52. Heat = mass × specific heat capacity × temperature change

specific heat capacity = Heat/(mass × temperature change)

72.4 kJ = 72,400 J

specific heat capacity = $\dfrac{72,400 \text{ J}}{(952 \text{ g})(10.7 \text{ °C})} = 7.11 \text{ J/g °C}$

53. Table 3.2 gives the specific heat capacity of gold as 0.13 J/g °C
Temperature increase = 155 – 120. = 35°C
25.0 g × 0.13 J/g °C × 35°C = 113.75 J = 1.1×10^{2} J

54. Table 3.2 gives the specific heat of silver as 0.24 J/g °C
Temperature increase = 15.2 –12.0 = 3.2 °C
1.25 kJ = 1250 J
1250 J = (mass of silver) × 0.24 J/g °C × 3.2 °C
mass of silver = 1627 g = 1.6×10^{3} g silver

55.   Table 3.2 gives the specific heat capacity of iron as 0.45 J/g °C.

50. joules is the heat that is applied to the sample of iron, and must equal the product of the mass of iron, the specific heat capacity of the iron, and the temperature change undergone by the iron (which is what we want).

Heat = mass × specific heat capacity × temperature change

50. J = 10. g × 0.45 J/g °C × ΔT

$$\Delta T = \frac{50.\ J}{10.\ g \times 0.45\ J/g\ °C} = 11\ °C$$

56.   Table 3.2 gives the specific heat capacity of iron as 0.45 J/g °C.

Heat = mass × specific heat capacity × temperature change

Temperature change = 75.5 - 40.1 = 35.4 °C

Heat = 852.2 g × 0.45 J/g °C × 35.4 °C = 1.4×10^4 J

57. $0.24\ \dfrac{J}{g\ °C} \times \dfrac{1\ cal}{4.184\ J} = 0.057\ \dfrac{cal}{g\ °C}$

58. $0.13\ \dfrac{J}{g\ °C} \times \dfrac{1\ cal}{4.184\ J} = 0.031\ \dfrac{cal}{g\ °C}$

59.   It is not really necessary to calculate the temperature changes experienced by the metals. For metal samples of equal mass, the metal with the smallest specific heat capacity will experience the largest temperature change when a given amount of heat is applied. Remember that the specific heat capacity represents the ability of the substance to absorb heat energy.

60.   Specific heat capacities are given in Table 3.2

for gold,   25.0 g × 0.13 J/g °C × 20. °C = 65 J

for mercury,   25.0 g × 0.14 J/g °C × 20. °C = 70. J

for carbon,   25.0 g × 0.71 J/g °C × 20. °C = 360 J

61.   Heat = mass × specific heat capacity × temperature change

The temperature change is 92 – 10. = 82 °C

540. J = 22.5 g × s × 82 °C

$$s = \frac{540.\ J}{22.5\ g \times 82\ °C} = 0.29\ J/g\ °C$$

62. 1251 J = 35.2 g × (specific heat capacity) × 25.0 °C

    specific heat capacity = 1.42 J/g °C

63. mixture, compound

64. Since *X* is a pure substance, the fact that two different solids form when electrical current is passed indicates that *X* must be a compound.

65. Chalk must be a compound, since it loses mass when heated, and appears to change into a substance with different physical properties (the hard chalk turns into a crumbly substance).

66. Since vaporized water is still the *same substance* as solid water, no chemical reaction has occurred. Sublimation is a physical change.

67. a. $4.52 \text{ cal} \times \dfrac{1 \text{ kcal}}{1000 \text{ cal}} = 4.52 \times 10^{-3} \text{ kcal}$

    b. $5.27 \text{ kcal} \times \dfrac{4.184 \text{ kJ}}{1 \text{ kcal}} \times \dfrac{1000 \text{ J}}{1 \text{ kJ}} = 2.20 \times 10^{4} \text{ J}$

    c. $852{,}000 \text{ cal} \times \dfrac{4.184 \text{ J}}{1 \text{ cal}} \times \dfrac{1 \text{ kJ}}{1000 \text{ J}} = 3.56 \times 10^{3} \text{ kJ}$

    d. $352.4 \text{ kcal} \times \dfrac{4.184 \text{ kJ}}{1 \text{ kcal}} = 1474 \text{ kJ}$

    e. $5.72 \text{ kJ} \times \dfrac{1 \text{ kcal}}{4.184 \text{ kJ}} \times \dfrac{1000 \text{ cal}}{1 \text{ kcal}} = 1.37 \times 10^{3} \text{ cal}$

    f. $4.52 \times 10^{3} \text{ J} \times \dfrac{1 \text{ kJ}}{1000 \text{ J}} = 4.52 \text{ kJ}$

68. 2.5 kg of water = 2,500 g

    Temperature change = 55.0 − 18.5 = 36.5 °C

    2500 g × 4.184 J/g °C × 36.5 °C = 3.8 × 10⁵ J

69. For a given mass of substance, the substance with the *smallest* specific heat capacity (gold, 0.13 J/g °C) will undergo the *largest* increase in temperature. Conversely, the substance with the largest specific heat capacity (water, 4.184 J/g °C) will undergo the smallest increase in temperature.

70. No calculation is necessary: aluminum will lose more heat because it has the higher specific heat capacity.

71.   Heat evolved by hydrogen: 5.0 g × 120. J/g = 600 J (6.0 × 10^2 J)

Heat evolved by methane: 10. g × 50. J/g = 500 J (5.0 × 10^2 J)

Total heat evolved by burning: 600 + 500 = 1100 J (1.1 × 10^3 K)

For any substance, $Q = m \times s \times \Delta T$. Let T_f represent the final temperature reached by the water. Then $\Delta T = (T_f - 25\ °C)$

1.1×10^3 J = 500. g × 4.184 J/g °C × $(T_f - 25\ °C)$

$(T_f - 25\ °C) = 0.53\ °C$

$T_f = 25 + 0.53 = 25.5\ °C = 26\ °C$

To the limits of measurement indicated in the problem, the temperature would not effectively increase. A relatively large amount of water was used to absorb the heat evolved by the combustion, and water has a very large heat capacity (this is why water is so often used as a coolant).

72.   For any substance, $Q = m \times s \times \Delta T$. The quantity of heat gained by the water in this experiment must equal the total heat lost by the metals (i.e., the *sum* of the amount of heat lost by the iron and the amount of heat lost by the aluminum).

$(m \times s \times \Delta T)_{water} = (m \times s \times \Delta T)_{iron} + (m \times s \times \Delta T)_{aluminum}$

If T_f represents the final temperature reached by this system, then

$[m \times s \times (T_f - 22.5\ °C)]_{water}$

$\quad = [m \times s \times (100\ °C - T_f)]_{iron} + [m \times s \times (100\ °C - T_f)]_{aluminum}$

$[97.3\ g \times 4.184\ J/g\ °C \times (T_f - 22.5\ °C)]$

$\quad = [10.00\ g \times 0.45\ J/g\ °C \times (100\ °C - T_f)]$

$\qquad + [5.00\ g \times 0.89\ J/g\ °C \times (100\ °C - T_f)]$

$407.1(T_f - 22.5) = 4.50(100 - T_f) + 4.45(100 - T_f) = 8.95(100 - T_f)$

$407.1 T_f - 9160. = 895 - 8.95 T_f$

$416.1 T_f = 10,055$ which gives $T_f = 24.2\ °C$

73.   Let T_f represent the final temperature reached.

For the hot water, heat lost = 50.0 g × 4.184 J/g °C × $(100. - T_f)$

For the cold water, heat gained = 50.0 g × 4.184 J/g °C × $(T_f - 25)$
Heat lost by the hot water must *equal* heat gained by the cold water.

$$50.0 \text{ g} \times 4.184 \text{ J/g °C} \times (100. - T_f) = 50.0 \text{ g} \times 4.184 \text{ J/g °C} \times (T_f - 25)$$

$$209.2(100 - T_f) = 209.2(T_f - 25)$$

$$(100 - T_f) = (T_f - 25)$$

$$2T_f = 125 \text{ °C}$$

$$T_f = 62.5 \text{ °C} = 63 \text{ °C}$$

74. $(m \times s \times \Delta T)_{water} = (m \times s \times \Delta T)_{iron}$

Let T_f represent the final temperature reached by the system

$$[75 \text{ g} \times 4.184 \text{ J/g °C} \times (T_f - 20.)] = [25.0 \text{ g} \times 0.45 \text{ J/g °C} \times (85 - T_f)]$$

$$314(T_f - 20.) = 11.4(85 - T_f)$$

$$314T_f - 6280 = 961 - 11.3T_f$$

$$325T_f = 7241$$

$$T_f = 22.3 \text{ °C} = 22 \text{ °C}$$

75. Liquids and gases both flow freely and take on the shape of their container. The molecules in liquids are relatively close together and interact with each other, whereas the molecules in gases are far apart from each other and do not interact with each other.

76. far apart

77. physical

78. chemical

79. physical

80. chemical

81. state

82. electrolysis

83. a.   physical;   milk contains protein, and when the vinegar is added, the acidity of the vinegar causes a change in the protein's shape, making it insoluble in water (see Chapter 21)

    b.   chemical;   exposure to the oxygen of the air allows bacteria to grow which cause the chemical breakdown of components of the butter.

c.   physical;   salad dressing is a physical mixture of water soluble and insoluble components, which only combine temporarily when the dressing is shaken.

d.   chemical;   milk of magnesia is a *base*, which chemically reacts with and neutralizes the acid of the stomach.

e.   chemical;   steel consists mostly of iron, which chemically reacts with the oxygen of the atmosphere.

f.   chemical;   carbon monoxide combines chemically with the hemoglobin fraction of the blood, making it impossible for the hemoglobin to combine with oxygen.

g.   chemical;   cotton consists of the carbohydrate cellulose, which is broken down chemically by acids.

h.   physical;   sweat consists mostly of water, which consumes heat from the body in evaporating.

i.   chemical;   although the biochemical action of aspirin is not fully understood, the process is chemical in nature.

j.   physical;   oil molecules are not water soluble, and are repelled by the moisture in skin.

k.   chemical;   the fact that one substance is converted into two other substances demonstrates that this is a chemical process.

84.   a.   heterogeneous

b.   heterogeneous

c.   heterogeneous (unless you work hard to get all the lumps out!)

d.   although strictly heterogenous, it may appear homogeneous

e.   heterogeneous

85.   a.   heterogeneous

b.   homogeneous

c.   heterogeneous

d.   homogeneous (assuming there are no imperfections in the glass)

e.   heterogeneous

86.   9.0 J (It requires twice as much heat to warm twice as large a sample over the same temperature interval.)

87.   Since it requires 103 J to heat the iron over a temperature change of 25° (from 25° to 50°C), it will require 206 J (twice as much heat) to heat the same sample of iron over a temperature change of 50° (from 25° to 75°).

88.   a. $44.21 \text{ cal} \times \dfrac{4.184 \text{ J}}{1 \text{ cal}} = 185.0 \text{ J}$

     b. $162.4 \text{ cal} \times \dfrac{4.184 \text{ J}}{1 \text{ cal}} = 679.5 \text{ J}$

     c. $3.721 \times 10^3 \text{ cal} \times \dfrac{4.184 \text{ J}}{1 \text{ cal}} = 1.557 \times 10^4 \text{ J}$

     d. $146.2 \text{ kcal} \times \dfrac{1000 \text{ cal}}{1 \text{ kcal}} \times \dfrac{4.184 \text{ J}}{1 \text{ cal}} = 6.117 \times 10^5 \text{ J}$

89.   a. $52.18 \text{ kJ} \times \dfrac{1 \text{ kcal}}{4.184 \text{ kJ}} = 12.47 \text{ kcal}$

     b. $4.298 \text{ J} \times \dfrac{1 \text{ cal}}{4.184 \text{ J}} \times \dfrac{1 \text{ kcal}}{1000 \text{ cal}} = 1.027 \times 10^{-3} \text{ kcal}$

     c. $5.433 \times 10^3 \text{ J} \times \dfrac{1 \text{ cal}}{4.184 \text{ J}} \times \dfrac{1 \text{ kcal}}{1000 \text{ cal}} = 1.299 \text{ kcal}$

     d. $455.9 \text{ kJ} \times \dfrac{1 \text{ kcal}}{4.184 \text{ kJ}} = 109.0 \text{ kcal}$

90.   a. $5.442 \times 10^4 \text{ J} \times \dfrac{1 \text{ kJ}}{1000 \text{ J}} = 54.42 \text{ kJ}$

     b. $5.442 \times 10^4 \text{ J} \times \dfrac{1 \text{ cal}}{4.184 \text{ J}} = 1.301 \times 10^4 \text{ cal}$

     c. $352.6 \text{ kcal} \times \dfrac{4.184 \text{ kJ}}{1 \text{ kcal}} = 1475 \text{ kJ}$

     d. $17.24 \text{ kJ} \times \dfrac{1 \text{ kcal}}{4.184 \text{ kJ}} = 4.120 \text{ kcal}$

91.   Table 3.2 gives the specific heat capacity of gold as 0.13 J/g °C.

     Temperature increase = 75.0 − 20.0 = 55.0 °C

     Heat required = 25.0 g × 0.13 J/g ° × 55.0 °C = 178.8 J = 1.8×10^2 J

     (which is equivalent to 0.18 kJ, 0.043 kcal, 43 cal)

92.   The specific heat capacity of water is 4.184 J/g °C.

Temperature increase = 39 − 25 = 14 °C.

75 g × 4.184 J/g °C × 14 °C = 4400 J (to 2 significant figures)

93.   Table 3.2 gives the specific heat capacity of aluminum as 0.89 J/g °C.

Temperature increase = 85.2 − 22.1 = 63.1 °F.

63.1 °F × (100/180) = 35.1 °C.   37.5 lb = 1.70 × 10^4 g

Heat required = 1.70 × 10^4 g × 0.89 J/g °C × 35.1 °C = 5.3 × 10^5 J

94.   For any substance, $Q = m \times s \times \Delta T$. The basic calculation for each of the substances is the same (specific heat capacities are found in Table 3.2)

Heat required = 150. g × (specific heat capacity) × 11.2 °C

Substance	Specific Heat Capacity	Heat Required
water (*l*)	4.184 J/g °C	7.03 × 10^3 J
water (*s*)	2.03 J/g °C	3.41 × 10^3 J
water (*g*)	2.0 J/g °C	3.4 × 10^3 J
aluminum	0.89 J/g °C	1.5 × 10^3 J
iron	0.45 J/g °C	7.6 × 10^2 J
mercury	0.14 J/g °C	2.4 × 10^2 J
carbon	0.71 J/g °C	1.2 × 10^3 J
silver	0.24 J/g °C	4.0 × 10^2 J
gold	0.13 J/g °C	2.2 × 10^2 J

95.   Since, for any substance, $Q = m \times s \times \Delta T$, we can solve this equation for the temperature change, ΔT The results are tabulated:

Substance	Specific Heat Capacity	Temperature Change
water (*l*)	4.184 J/g °C	23.9 °C
water (*s*)	2.03 J/g °C	49.3 °C
water (*g*)	2.0 J/g °C	50. °C
aluminum	0.89 J/g °C	1.1 × 10^2 °C
iron	0.45 J/g °C	2.2 × 10^2 °C
mercury	0.14 J/g °C	7.1 × 10^2 °C
carbon	0.71 J/g °C	1.4 × 10^2 °C
silver	0.24 J/g °C	4.2 × 10^2 °C
gold	0.13 J/g °C	7.7 × 10^2 °C

96.   Heat = mass × specific heat capacity × temperature change

The temperature change is 112.1 − 25.0 = 87.1 °C

1.351 kJ = 1351 J

$$s = \frac{1351 \text{ J}}{125 \text{ g} \times 87.1 \text{ °C}} = 0.124 \text{ J/g °C}$$

Cumulative Review: Chapters 1, 2, and 3

1.   Obviously, this answer depends on your own experiences in studying and learning about chemistry. We hope that by now you have at least gotten over any "fear" of chemistry you may have started out with. Perhaps you have begun to appreciate why one leading chemical manufacturer has as its corporate slogan "better living through chemistry".

2.   By now, after having covered three chapters in this book, it is hoped that you have adopted an "active" approach to your study of chemistry. You may have discovered (perhaps through a disappointing grade on a quiz (though we hope not), that you really have to get involved with chemistry. You can't just sit and take notes, or just look over the solved examples in the textbook. You have to learn to solve problems. You have to learn how to interpret problems, and how to reduce them to the simple mathematical relationships you have studied. Whereas in some courses you might get by on just giving back on exams the facts or ideas presented in class, in chemistry you have to be able to extend and synthesize what has been discussed, and to apply the material to new situations. Don't get discouraged if this is difficult at first: it's difficult for everyone at first.

3.   The steps of the scientific method, in brief, are: (1) make observations of the system and state the problem clearly; (2) formulate an explanation or hypothesis to try to explain your observations; and (3) perform one or more experiments to test the validity of your hypothesis. For the case of the liquid material, we first have to state the problem: we have a sample of clear liquid which may be either a pure compound or a mixture, and we want to determine which of these is correct. The liquid is completely homogeneous, so we can't tell anything just by looking at it.
    If the unknown liquid is a mixture, we should be able to separate the components of the mixture by distillation (see Chapter 3). If the liquid is a mixture of two pure liquids, the liquids should boil at their characteristic temperatures during distillation. If the liquid is a solution of a solid material, then the liquid portion should boil off, leaving a solid residue behind. If the unknown liquid is a pure substance, rather than a mixture, it should boil away at a constant, uniform temperature. Let's hypothesize that the liquid is a mixture.
    Now we perform the experiment: we begin heating the liquid in a distillation apparatus, monitoring the temperature with a thermometer. At 65°C, the liquid begins to boil, and a clear, sweet-smelling liquid begins to collect in the receiving container. The temperature remains at 65°C until approximately half the liquid has distilled, whereupon the temperature rises suddenly to 100°C. At this point, we change receiving flasks. The temperature remains at 100°C until the remainder of the liquid boils. We notice that this second fraction of liquid collected has no odor.
    Based on the observations that two separate fractions were collected, which had different boiling points, and that only one of the fractions had a noticeable odor, we can conclude that our hypothesis that the unknown liquid was a mixture is correct.

4.   It is difficult sometimes for students (especially beginning students) to understand why certain subjects are required for a given college major. The faculty of your major department, however, have collectively many years of experience in the subject in which you have chosen to specialize. They really do know what courses will be helpful to you in the future. They may have had trouble with the same courses that now give you trouble, but they realize that all the work will be worth it in the end. Some courses you take, particularly in your major field itself, have obvious and immediate utility. Other courses, often times chemistry included, are provided to give you a general background knowledge, which may prove useful in understanding your own major or other subjects related to your major. In perhaps a burst of bravado, chemistry has been called "the central science" by one team of textbook authors. This moniker is very true however: in order to understand biology, physics, nutrition, farming, home economics, or whatever(it helps to have a general background in chemistry.

5.   *Physical Quantity*   *Basic SI Units*

mass	kilogram
distance	meter
time	second
temperature	kelvin

Commonly Used Prefixes in the Metric System

Prefix	Meaning	Power of Ten
mega-	million	10^6
kilo-	thousand	10^3
deci-	tenth	10^{-1}
centi-	hundredth	10^{-2}
milli-	thousandth	10^{-3}
nano-	billionth	10^{-9}

The metric system is in use in most of the world because its system of units and multiples is simple to remember, and the system permits easy conversion between units. The various multiples and subdivisions of the basic units are based on factors of *ten*, which is also the basis for our number system. The United States uses a historical system in which there is no simple relationship between most units. Although several attempts have been made to gradually change the United States over to the metric system, no widespread support for the program has been achieved. Although 2-liter soda bottles were accepted without too much complaint (since they replaced a similar-sized 2-quart bottle, the thought of having an size 85 waist (in cm) may be repugnant to too many Americans! There obviously also would be a great cost to industry to retool all machinery and measurement devices in metric units.

6.   Whenever a scientific measurement is made, we always employ the instrument or measuring device we are using to the limits of its precision. On a practical basis, this usually means that we *estimate* our

reading of the last significant figure of the measurement. An example of the uncertainty in the last significant figure is given for measuring the length of a pin in the text in Figure 2.5. Scientists appreciate the limits of experimental techniques and instruments, and always assume that the last digit in a number representing a measurement has been estimated. Since the last significant figure in every measurement is assumed to be estimated, it is never possible to exclude uncertainty from measurements. The best we can do is to try to improve our techniques and instruments so that we get more significant figures for our measurements.

7.   Scientists are careful about reporting their measurements to the appropriate number of significant figures so as to indicate to their colleagues the precision with which experiments were performed. That is, the number of significant figures reported indicates how "carefully" measurements were made. Suppose you were considering buying a new home, and the real estate agent told you that a prospective new house was "between 1000-2000 square feet of space" and had "five or six rooms, more or less" and stood on "maybe an acre or two of land". Would you buy the house or would you look for another real estate agent? When a scientist says that a sample of material "has a mass of 3.126 grams" he or she is narrowing down the limits as to the actual, true mass of the sample: the mass is clearly slightly more than half way between 3.12 and 3.13 grams.

    The rules for significant figures are covered in Section 2.5 of the text. In brief, these rules for experimentally measured numbers are as follows: (1) nonzero integers are *always* significant; (2) leading zeroes are *never* significant, captive zeroes are *always* significant, and trailing zeroes *may* be significant (if a decimal point is indicated); (3) exact numbers (e.g., definitions) have an infinite number of significant figures.

    When we have to round off an answer to the correct number of significant figures (as limited by whatever measurement was least precise), we do this in a particular manner. If the digit to be removed is equal to or greater than 5, the preceding digit is increased by 1. If the digit to be removed is less than 5, the preceding digit is not changed. If you are going to perform a series of calculations involving a set of data, hold on to the digits in the intermediate calculations until you arrive at the final answer, and then round off the final answer to the appropriate number of significant figures.

    When doing arithmetic with experimentally determined numbers, the final answer is determined by the least precise measurement. In doing multiplication or division calculations, the number of significant figures in the result should be the same as the measurement with the fewest significant figures. In performing addition or subtraction, the number of significant figures in the result is limited by the measurement with the fewest decimal places.

8.   Dimensional analysis is a method of problem solving which pays particular attention to the units of measurements and uses these units as if they were algebraic symbols that multiply, divide, and cancel. Consider the following example. A dozen of eggs costs $1.25. Suppose we

want to know how much one egg costs, and also how much three dozens of eggs will cost. To solve these problems, we need to make use of two equivalence statements:

$$1 \text{ dozen of eggs} = 12 \text{ eggs}$$

$$1 \text{ dozen of eggs} = \$1.25$$

The first of these equivalence statements is obvious: everyone knows that 12 eggs is "equivalent" to one dozen. The second statement also expresses an equivalence: if you give the grocer $1.25, he or she will give you a dozen of eggs. From these equivalence statements, we can construct the conversion factors we need to answer the two questions. For the first question (what does one egg cost) we can set up the calculation as follows

$$\frac{\$1.25}{12 \text{ eggs}} = \$0.104 = \$0.10$$

as the cost of one egg. Similarly, for the second question (the cost of 3 dozens of eggs), we can set up the conversion as follows

$$3 \text{ dozens} \times \frac{\$1.25}{1 \text{ dozen}} = \$3.75$$

as the cost of three dozens of eggs. See section 2.6 of the text for how we construct conversion factors from equivalence statements.

9.   The Fahrenheit (°F) temperature scale is defined so that an ice/water bath has an equilibrium temperature of 32°F, and a boiling water bath a temperature of 212°F, under normal atmospheric pressure. There are 180 degree divisions between these two reference points. The Celsius (°C) temperature scale is defined so that an ice/water bath has a temperature of 0°C, whereas a boiling water bath has a temperature of 100°C, with 100 degree divisions between these reference points. Both the Fahrenheit and Celsius temperature scales are human inventions which choose convenient, stable, reproducible reference points as their definitions. The Kelvin (K) or Absolute temperature scale is based on a fundamental property of matter itself: the zero and lowest point (Absolute Zero) on the Kelvin temperature scale is the lowest possible temperature that can exist, and represents the temperature at which atoms and molecules are in their lowest possible energy states. All other temperatures on the Kelvin scale are positive relative to this. Since only this one reference point is used to define the Kelvin scale, the size of the Kelvin degree relative to this point was chosen to be the same size as the Celsius degree for convenience. The temperature of an ice/water bath is 273 K, and the temperature of a boiling water bath is 373 K.

10.   Defining what scientists mean by "matter" often seems circular to students. Scientists say that matter is something that "has mass and occupies space", without ever really explaining what it means to "have mass" or to "occupy space"! The concept of matter is so basic and

fundamental, that it becomes difficult to give a good textbook definition other than to say that matter is the "stuff" of which everything is made. Matter can be classified and subdivided in many ways, depending on what we are trying to demonstrate.

On the most fundamental basis, all matter is composed of tiny particles (such as protons, electrons, neutrons, and the other subatomic particles). On one higher level, these tiny particles are combined in a systematic manner into units called atoms. Atoms in turn may be combined to constitute molecules. And finally, large groups of molecules may be placed together to form a bulk sample of substance that we can see.

Matter can also be classified as to the physical state a particular substance happens to take. Some substances are solids, some are liquids, and some are gases. Matter can also be classified as to whether it is a pure substance (one type of molecule) or a mixture (more than one type of molecule), and furthermore whether a mixture is homogeneous or heterogeneous.

11.   The physical properties of a substance are the inherent characteristics of the substance, which result in no change in the composition of the substance when we measure or study these properties. Such properties include color, odor, physical state, density, solubility, melting point, boiling point, etc. The chemical properties of a given substance indicate how that substance reacts with other substances. For example, when we say that sodium is a grayish-white, soft, low-density metal, we are describing some of sodium's physical properties. When we say that sodium metal reacts with chlorine gas to form sodium chloride, we are describing a chemical property of sodium.

A physical change for a substance is a change in the substance that does not alter the identity or composition of the substance; physical changes typically represent changes in only the physical state (solid, liquid, vapor) of the substance. A chemical change for a substance results in the substance being converted into another substance or substances. For example, when we heat a piece of sodium metal in a sealed tube in a burner flame, the sodium melts and then vaporizes: the liquid and vapor are still sodium, however, and only physical changes have occurred. On the other hand, if we heat a piece of sodium in an open flame, the sodium reacts with oxygen in the air and is converted to a mixture of sodium oxides. The pure elemental substance sodium is converted into compounds and has undergone a chemical change.

12.   Chemists tend to give a functional definition of what they mean by an "element": an element is a fundamental substance that cannot be broken down into any simpler substances by chemical methods. Compounds, on the other hand, can be broken down into simpler substances (the elements of which the compound is composed). For example, sulfur and oxygen are both elements (sulfur occurs as S_8 molecules and oxygen as O_2 molecules). When sulfur and oxygen are placed together and heated, the compound sulfur dioxide (SO_2) forms. When we analyze the sulfur dioxide produced, we notice that each and every molecule consists of one sulfur atom and two oxygen atoms, and on a mass basis, consists of 50% each of sulfur and oxygen. We describe this by saying that sulfur dioxide has a constant composition. The fact that a given compound has constant

composition is usually expressed in terms of the mass percentages of the elements present in the compound, but realize that the reason the mass percentages are constant is because of a constant number of atoms of each type present in the compound's molecules. If a scientist anywhere in the universe analyzed sulfur dioxide, he or she would find the same composition: if a scientist finds something that does not have the same composition, then the substance cannot be sulfur dioxide.

13.   A mixture is a combination of two or more substances which may be varied in its composition. Most commonly in chemistry, a mixture is a combination of two or more pure substances (either elements or compounds). A solution is a particular type of mixture which appears completely homogeneous throughout. Although a solution is homogeneous in appearance, realize, however, that a solution is still a mixture of two or more pure substances: if it were possible to see the individual particles of a solution, we would notice that their were different types of molecules present.

   In a sample of a pure substance, there is only one type of molecule present. There are two types of pure substances: elemental substances and compound substances. In an elemental substance, not only are all the molecules the same type, but all the atoms within those molecules are the same type. For example, the pure elemental substance oxygen consists of O_2 molecules (with no other type of molecule present). In addition, each O_2 molecule contains only one type of atom (O). In a sample of a compound substance, all the molecules are of the same type, but within each molecule are found atoms of different elements. For example, the pure compound substance water consists of H_2O molecules (with no other type of molecule present). Within each H_2O molecule, however, are found two different types of atoms (H and O). A compound is not a mixture, however, because the atoms of the different elements are chemically bonded (not just physically mixed), and the composition of the compound is not variable as to the relative amounts of each element present.

   Two methods for separating mixtures are described in the text: filtration and distillation. Filtration can be used to separate a solid from a liquid. Distillation can be used to separate two liquids, or a dissolved solid from a liquid. There are many other separation methods beyond the scope of this text.

14.   Scientists define energy as "the capacity to do work". As with trying to define "matter" earlier in this chapter, energy is such a fundamental concept that it is hard to define (what is "work"?). Although the *SI* unit of energy is the *joule*, until relatively recently, energies were more commonly given in terms of the *calorie*: one calorie is defined to be the amount of heat required to raise the temperature of one gram of water by one Celsius degree. The calorie is a "working" definition, and we can more easily appreciate this amount of energy. In terms of the *SI* unit, 1 calorie = 4.184 joule, so it takes 4.184 J to raise the temperature of one gram of water by one Celsius degree.

   The specific heat capacity of a substance, in general, is the amount of energy required to raise the temperature of one gram of a substance by one Celsius degree. Therefore, the specific heat capacity of water must be 1.000 cal/g°C or 4.184 J/g°C. To see how specific heat capacities may be used to calculate the energy change for a process, consider this example: How much energy is required to warm 25.0 g of water from 15.1°C to 35.2°C? The specific heat capacity of water is 1.000 cal/g°C: this is the quantity of energy required to raise the temperature of only *one* gram of water by only *one* Celsius degree. In this example, we are raising the temperature of 25.0 g of water, and we are raising the temperature by (35.2 - 15.1) = 20.1°C. So, using the specific heat capacity as a conversion factor, we can say

$$\text{energy required} = \left(\frac{1.00 \text{ cal}}{g \ °C}\right) \times (25.0 \text{ g}) \times (20.1°C) = 503 \text{ cal}$$

Notice how the units of g and °C cancel, leaving the answer in energy units only. This sort of calculation of energy change can be done for any substance, using the substance's own specific heat capacity (see Table 3.2).

15.   a. $122.4 \times 10^5 = (1.224 \times 10^2) \times 10^5 = 1.224 \times 10^7$

   b. $5.993 \times 10^{-4} = 0.0005993$

   c. $0.0004321 \times 10^4 = (4.321 \times 10^{-4}) \times 10^4 = 4.321 \times 10^0 = 4.321$

   d. $5.241 \times 10^2 = 524.1$

   e. $0.0000009814 = 9.814 \times 10^{-7}$

   f. $14.2 \times 10^0 = 14.2$

16.   a. $6.0 \text{ pt} \times \dfrac{1 \text{ qt}}{2 \text{ pt}} \times \dfrac{1 \text{ L}}{1.0567 \text{ qt}} = 2.8 \text{ L}$

   b. $6.0 \text{ pt} \times \dfrac{1 \text{ qt}}{2 \text{ pt}} \times \dfrac{1 \text{ gal}}{4 \text{ qt}} = 0.75 \text{ gal}$

   c. $5.91 \text{ yd} \times \dfrac{1 \text{ m}}{1.0936 \text{ yd}} = 5.40 \text{ m}$

   d. $16.0 \text{ L} \times \dfrac{1 \text{ qt}}{0.94633 \text{ L}} \times \dfrac{32 \text{ fl. oz.}}{1 \text{ qt}} = 541 \text{ fl. oz.}$

   e. $5.25 \text{ L} \times \dfrac{1 \text{ gal}}{3.7854 \text{ L}} = 1.39 \text{ gal}$

   f. $62.5 \text{ mi} \times \dfrac{1 \text{ km}}{0.62137 \text{ mi}} = 101 \text{ km}$

   g. $8.25 \text{ m} \times \dfrac{1.0936 \text{ yd}}{1 \text{ m}} \times \dfrac{36 \text{ in}}{1 \text{ yd}} = 325 \text{ in}$

h. $4.25 \text{ kg} \times \dfrac{2.2046 \text{ lb}}{1 \text{ kg}} = 9.37 \text{ lb}$

i. $88.5 \text{ cm} \times \dfrac{10 \text{ mm}}{1 \text{ cm}} = 885 \text{ mm}$

j. $4.21 \text{ in} \times \dfrac{2.54 \text{ cm}}{1 \text{ in}} = 10.7 \text{ cm}$

17. a. $10.20 + 4.1 + 26.001 + 2.4 = 42.701 = 42.7$ (one decimal place)

b. $[1.091 - 0.991] + 1.2 = 1.3$ (one decimal place)

c. $(4.06 + 5.1)(2.032 - 1.02) = (9.16)(1.012) = (9.2)(1.01) = 9.3$

d. $(67.21)(1.003)(2.4) = 161.8 = 1.6 \times 10^2$ (only 2 significant figures)

e. $[(7.815 + 2.01)(4.5)]/(1.9001) = [(9.825)(4.5)]/(1.9001)$

$= [(9.825)(4.5)]/(1.9001)$

$= 23.27$

$= 23$ (only 2 significant figures)

f. $(1.67 \times 10^{-9})(1.1 \times 10^{-4}) = 1.837 \times 10^{-13} = 1.8 \times 10^{-13}$

g. $(4.02 \times 10^{-4})(2.91 \times 10^3)/(9.102 \times 10^{-1}) = 1.29$

h. $(1.04 \times 10^2 + 2.1 \times 10^1)/(4.51 \times 10^3)$

$= (10.4 \times 10^1 + 2.1 \times 10^1)/(4.51 \times 10^3)$

$= (12.5 \times 10^1)/(4.51 \times 10^3) = 2.77 \times 10^{-2}$

i. $(1.51 \times 10^{-3})^2/(1.074 \times 10^{-7}) = (2.2801 \times 10^{-6})/(1.074 \times 10^{-7})$

$= 21.2$ (only 3 significant figures)

j. $(1.89 \times 10^2)/[(7.01 \times 10^{-3})(4.1433 \times 10^4)]$

$= (1.89 \times 10^2)/[290.45]$

$= 0.651$ (only 3 significant figures)

18. $t_F = 1.80(t_C) + 32 \qquad t_C = (t_F - 32)/1.80 \qquad t_K = t_C + 273$

a. $1.80(-50.1°C) + 32 = -58.2°F$

b. $(-30.7°C - 32)/1.80 = -34.8°C$

c. $541 \text{ K} - 273 = 268°C$

d.   221°C + 273 = 494 K

e.   351 K - 273 = 78°C

     1.80(78°C) + 32 = 172.4 = 172°F

f.   (72°F - 32)/1.80 = 22.2°C

     22.2°C + 273 = 295.2 = 295 K

19.   *density = mass/volume   mass = volume × density   volume = mass/density*

a.   density = 121.4 g/42.4 cm^3 = 2.86 g/cm^3

b.   0.721 lb = 327 g

     density = 327 g/241 cm^3 = 1.36 g/cm^3

c.   mass = 124.1 mL × 0.821 g/mL = 102 g

d.   4.51 L = 4,510 cm^3

     mass = 4,510 cm^3 × 1.15 g/cm^3 = 5.19 × 10^3 g

e.   volume = 142.4 g/0.915 g/mL = 156 mL

f.   4.2 lb = 1.9 × 10^3 g

     volume = 1.9 × 10^3 g/3.75 g/cm^3 = 507 cm^3 = 5.1 × 10^2 cm^3

20.   a.   459 J × $\dfrac{1 \text{ cal}}{4.184 \text{ J}}$ = 109.7 = 110. cal

b.   7,031 cal × $\dfrac{4.184 \text{ J}}{1 \text{ cal}}$ × $\dfrac{1 \text{ kJ}}{1000 \text{ J}}$ = 29.42 kJ

c.   55.31 kJ = 55,310 J = 5.531 × 10^4 J

d.   78.3 kcal × $\dfrac{4.184 \text{ kJ}}{1 \text{ kcal}}$ = 327.6 = 328 kJ

e.   4,541 cal = 4.541 kcal

f.   84.1 kJ × $\dfrac{1 \text{ kcal}}{4.184 \text{ kJ}}$ = 20.1 kcal

21.   In general, heat required = mass × specific heat capacity × temp. change

     a.   temperature change = 27 °C

         mass = 1000 J/(4.184 J/g °C)(27 °C) = 8.9 g

     b.   temperature change = 100. °C

         mass = 1000 J/(0.45 J/g °C)(100. °C) = 22 g

     c.   temperature change = 57 °C

         mass = 1000 J/(0.71 J/g °C)(57 °C) = 25 g

     d.   56 °F = 13.3 °C   75 °F = 23.9 °C

         temperature change = 23.9 -13.3 = 10.6 °C

         mass = 1000 J/(0.13 J/g °C)(10.6 °C) = 7.3×10^2 g

     e.   temperature change = 385 K - 289 K = 96 K = 96 °C

         mass = 1000 J/(0.24 J/g °C)(96 °C) = 43 g

     f.   85 °F = 29.4 °C

         temperature change = 29.4 °C - -10 °C = 39.4 °C

         mass = 1000 J(0.89 J/g °C)(39.4 °C) = 29 g

Chapter 4   Chemical Foundations: Elements, Atoms, and Ions

1. Although the number and nature of the elementary substances postulated by the ancient Greeks were incorrect, their idea that the matter we encounter in everyday life is composed of a few *simpler* substances is very similar to our modern concepts. Also, the idea that the simpler substances *combine* with each other in regular, fixed manners compares well with the modern theory of matter.

2. The alchemists discovered several previously unknown elements (mercury, sulfur, antimony) and were the first to prepare several common acids.

3. Boyle's most important contribution was his insistence that science should be firmly grounded in *experiment*. Boyle tried to limit the influence of any preconceptions about science, and only accepted as fact what could be demonstrated.

4. There are 112 elements presently known; of these 88 occur naturally and 24 are manmade. Table 4.1 lists the most common elements on the earth.

5. Oxygen is found in great abundance in the oceans (combined with hydrogen in water molecules) and in the earth itself (most rocks and minerals are oxygen compounds). Oxygen is found more commonly in compounds.

6. The four most abundant elements in living creatures are, respectively, oxygen, carbon, hydrogen, and nitrogen (see Table 4.2). In the nonliving world, the most abundant elements are, respectively, oxygen, silicon, aluminum, and iron (see Table 4.1).

7. B (boron)

    C (carbon)

    F (fluorine)

    H (hydrogen)

    I (iodine)

    K (potassium)

    N (nitrogen)

    O (oxygen)

    P (phosphorus)

    S (sulfur)

    U (uranium)

    V (vanadium)

    W (tungsten)

    Y (yttrium)

8. Sb (antimony)

    Cu (copper)

Au (gold)

Pb (lead)

Hg (mercury)

K (potassium)

Ag (silver)

Na (sodium)

Sn (tin)

W (tungsten)

Fe (iron)

9.   a.   Ne

b.   Ni

c.   K

d.   Si

e.   Ba

f.   Ag

10.   a.   Al

b.   Fe

c.   F

d.   Ca

e.   Au

f.   Hg

11.   *Symbol*   *Name*

Fe   iron
Cl   chlorine
S   sulfur
U   uranium
Ne   neon
K   potassium

12.   Ir   iridium

Ta   tantalum

Bi   bismuth

Pu   plutonium

Fr   francium

At   astatine

13. a.   potassium

     b.   germanium

     c.   phosphorus

     d.   carbon

     e.   nitrogen

     f.   sodium

     g.   neon

     h.   iodine

14. a.   copper

     b.   cobalt

     c.   calcium

     d.   carbon

     e.   chromium

     f.   cesium

     g.   chlorine

     h.   cadmium

15. a.   False; most materials occur as mixtures of compounds.

     b.   False; a given compound *always* contains the same relative number of atoms of its various elements.

     c.   False; molecules are made up of tiny particles called atoms.

16. According to Dalton, a given compound is always made up of the same number and type of atoms, and so the composition of the compound on a mass percentage basis will always be the same, no matter what the source of the compound is. For example, water molecules from the Atlantic Ocean and the Pacific Ocean all contain two hydrogen atoms bonded to one oxygen atom.

17. A compound is a distinct substance that is composed of two or more elements and always contains exactly the same relative masses of those elements.

18. According to Dalton, all atoms of the same element are *identical*; in particular, every atom of a given element has the same *mass* as every other atom of that element. If a given compound always contains the *same relative numbers* of atoms of each kind, and those atoms always have the *same masses*, then it follows that the compound made from those elements would always contain the same relative masses of its elements.

19. a. PCl_3

    b. B_2H_6

    c. $CaCl_2$

    d. CBr_4

    e. Fe_2O_3

    f. H_3PO_4

20. a. C_6H_6

    b. N_2O_4

    c. $CaCl_2$

    d. $FeBr_3$

    e. $NaNO_3$

    f. Ca_3N_2

21. a.   False; Thomson obtained beams of *identical* particles whose nature did *not* depend on what gas was used to generate them.

    b.   True

    c.   False; the atom was envisioned as a sphere of *positive* charge in which *negatively* charged electrons were randomly distributed.

22. a.   False; Rutherford's bombardment experiments with metal foil suggested that the alpha particles were being deflected by coming near a *dense, positively charged* atomic nucleus.

    b.   False; The proton and the electron have opposite charges, but the mass of the electron is *much smaller* than the mass of the proton.

    c.   True

23. neutrons

24. protons

25. The proton and the neutron have similar (but not identical) masses. Either of these particles has a mass approximately 2000 times greater than that of an electron. The combination of the protons and the neutrons make up the bulk of the mass of an atom, but the electrons make the greatest contribution to the chemical properties of the atom.

26. neutron; electron

27. 10^{-13} cm = 10^{-15} m

28. electrons

29.   False; atoms that have the same number of *protons*, with different numbers of *neutrons*, represent isotopes.

30.   False; the mass number represents the total number of protons and neutrons in the nucleus.

31.   the same

32.   mass

33.   Dalton's original theory proposed that all atoms of a given element were *identical*. We now realize that different atoms of the same element must have a particular number of protons and electrons (the atomic number), but may have different numbers of neutrons (leading to different mass numbers).

34.   Atoms of the same element (i.e., atoms with the same number of protons in the nucleus) may have different numbers of neutrons, and so will have different masses.

35.   a.   24

b.   13

c.   34

d.   18

e.   55

f.   7

g.   26

h.   17

36.   a.   32

b.   30

c.   24

d.   74

e.   38

f.   27

g.   4

h.   3

37.   a. $^{17}_{8}O$

b. $^{37}_{17}Cl$

c. $^{60}_{27}\text{Co}$

d. $^{57}_{26}\text{Fe}$

e. $^{131}_{53}\text{I}$

f. $^{7}_{3}\text{Li}$

38.   a. $^{12}_{5}\text{B}$

b. $^{15}_{7}\text{N}$

c. $^{35}_{17}\text{Cl}$

d. $^{235}_{92}\text{U}$

e. $^{14}_{6}\text{C}$

f. $^{31}_{15}\text{P}$

39.   a.   94 protons, 150 neutrons, 94 electrons

b.   95 protons, 146 neutrons, 95 electrons

c.   89 protons, 138 neutrons, 89 electrons

d.   55 protons, 78 neutrons, 55 electrons

e.   77 protons, 116 neutrons, 77 electrons

f.   25 protons, 31 neutrons, 25 electrons

40.   a.   6 protons, 6 neutrons, 6 electrons

b.   27 protons, 33 neutrons, 27 electrons

c.   17 protons, 20 neutrons, 17 electrons

d.   55 protons, 77 neutrons, 55 electrons

e.   92 protons, 146 neutrons, 92 electrons

f.   26 protons, 30 neutrons, 26 electrons

41.

element	symbol	atomic number	mass number	number of neutrons
sodium	$^{23}_{11}$Na	11	23	12
nitrogen	$^{15}_{7}$N	7	15	8
barium	$^{136}_{56}$Ba	56	136	80
lithium	$^{9}_{3}$Li	3	9	6
boron	$^{11}_{5}$B	5	11	6

42.

element	neutrons	atomic number	mass number	symbol
nitrogen	6	7	13	$^{13}_{7}$N
nitrogen	7	7	14	$^{14}_{7}$N
lead	124	82	206	$^{206}_{82}$Pb
iron	31	26	57	$^{57}_{26}$Fe
krypton	48	36	84	$^{84}_{36}$Kr

43.   The elements are listed in the periodic table in order of increasing atomic number (number of protons in the nucleus). The periodic table originally was arranged on the basis of mass.

44.   Elements with similar chemical properties are aligned *vertically* in families known as *groups*.

45.   Metals are excellent conductors of heat and electricity, and are malleable, ductile, and generally shiny (lustrous) when a fresh surface is exposed.

46.   Metallic elements are found towards the *left* and *bottom* of the periodic table; there are far more metallic elements than there are nonmetals.

47.   Mercury is a liquid at room temperature.

48.   hydrogen, nitrogen, oxygen, fluorine, chlorine, plus all the group 8 elements (noble gases)

49.   The only metal which ordinarily occurs as a liquid is mercury. The only nonmetallic element which occurs as a liquid at room temperature is bromine (elements such as oxygen and nitrogen are frequently obtainable as liquids, but these result from compression of the gases into cylinders at very low temperatures).

50.   The metalloids are the elements found on either side of the "stairstep" region that is marked on most periodic tables. The metalloid elements show some properties of both metals and nonmetals.

51.   a.   Group 1; alkali metals

       b.   Group 2; alkaline earth elements

       c.   Group 8; noble gases

       d.   Group 7; halogens

       e.   Group 2; alkaline earth elements

       f.   Group 8; noble gases

       g.   Group 1; alkali metals

52.   a.   Group 7; halogens

       b.   Group 2; alkaline earth elements

       c.   Group 1; alkali metals

       d.   Group 1; alkali metals

       e.   Group 8; noble gases

       f.   Group 1; alkali metals

       g.   Group 8; noble gases

53.   a.   Sr; $Z = 38$; Group 2; metal

       b.   I; $Z = 53$; Group 7; nonmetal

       c.   Si; $Z = 14$; Group 4; metalloid

       d.   Cs; $Z = 55$; Group 1; metal

       e.   S; $Z = 16$; Group 6; nonmetal

54.

name	symbol	atomic number	group number	metal/nonmetal
rubidium	Rb	37	1	metal
germanium	Ge	32	4	metalloid
magnesium	Mg	12	2	metal
titanium	Ti	22	-	transition metal
iodine	I	53	7	nonmetal

55.   compounds (and mixtures of compounds)

56.   Most of the elements are too reactive to be found in the uncombined form in nature, and are found only in compounds.

57.   argon

58.   These elements are found *uncombined* in nature and do not readily react with other elements. For many years it was thought that these elements formed no compounds at all, although this has now been shown to be untrue.

59.   diatomic

60.   Diatomic gases: H_2, N_2, O_2, Cl_2, and F_2

Monatomic gases: He, Ne, Kr, Xe, Rn, and Ar

61.   electricity

62.   chlorine

63.   liquids: bromine, mercury, gallium
gases: hydrogen, nitrogen, oxygen, fluorine, chlorine, and the noble gases (helium, neon, argon, krypton, xenon, radon)

64.   diamond

65.   zero

66.   electrons

67.   1+

68.   2+

69.   cations, anions

70.   *-ide*

71.   metallic

72.   nonmetallic

73.   [1]   b

[2]   d

[3]   b

[4]   h

[5]   f

[6]   e

[7]   a

[8]   c

[9]   g

[10]   i

74.   a. Co^{2+}:   27 protons   25 electrons CoO

b. Co^{3+}:   27 protons   24 electrons Co_2O_3

c. Cl^-:   17 protons   18 electrons $CaCl_2$

d. K^+:   19 protons   18 electrons K_2O

e. S^{2-}:   16 protons   18 electrons CaS

f. Sr^{2+}:   38 protons   36 electrons SrO

g. Al^{3+}:   13 protons   10 electrons Al_2O_3

h. P^{3-}:   15 protons   18 electrons Ca_3P_2

75.   a.   Ca: 20 protons, 20 electrons Ca^{2+}: 20 protons, 18 electrons

b.   P: 15 protons, 15 electrons P^{3-}: 15 protons, 18 electrons

c.   Br: 35 protons, 35 electrons Br^-: 35 protons, 36 electrons

d.   Fe: 26 protons, 26 electrons Fe^{3+}: 26 protons, 23 electrons

e.   Al: 13 protons, 13 electrons Al^{3+}: 13 protons, 10 electrons

f.   N: 7 protons, 7 electrons N^{3-}: 7 protons, 10 electrons

76.   a. $2e^-$

b. $2e^-$

c. $2e^-$

d. $3e^-$

e. $1e^-$

f. $3e^-$

77.   a. I^-

      b. Sr^{2+}

      c. Cs^+

      d. Ra^{2+}

      e. F^-

      f. Al^{3+}

78.   a. Ra^{2+} (element 88, Ra, is in Group 2)

      b. Te^{2-} (element 52, Te, is in Group 6)

      c. I^- (element 53, I, is in Group 7)

      d. Fr^+ (element 87, Fr, is in Group 1)

      e. At^- (element 85, At, is in Group 7)

      f.   no ion is likely   (element 86, Rn, is a noble gas)

79.   A compound which has a high melting point (many hundreds of degrees) and which conducts an electrical current when melted or dissolved in water almost certainly consists of ions.

80.   Sodium chloride is an *ionic* compound, consisting of Na^+ and Cl^- *ions*. When NaCl is dissolved in water, these ions are *set free*, and can move independently to conduct the electrical current. Sugar crystals, although they may visually *appear* similar contain *no* ions. When sugar is dissolved in water, it dissolves as uncharged *molecules*. There are no electrically charged species present in a sugar solution to carry the electrical current.

81.   In the solid state, although ions are present, they are rigidly held in fixed positions in the crystal of the substance. In order for ionic substances to be able to pass an electrical current, the ions must be able to *move*, which is possible when the solid is converted to the liquid state.

82.   The total number of positive charges must equal the total number of negative charges so that there will be *no net charge* on the crystals of an ionic compound. A macroscopic sample of compound must ordinarily not have any net charge.

83.   a.   One 3- ion is needed to balance one 3+ ion: FeP

      b.   The smallest common multiple of 3 and 2 is 6; three 2- ions are required to balance two 3+ ions: Fe_2S_3

      c.   Three 1- ions are required to balance one 3+ ion: $FeCl_3$

      d.   Two 1- ions are required to balance one 2+ ion: $MgCl_2$

e. One 2- ion balances one 2+ ion: MgO

f. The smallest common multiple of 2 and 3 is 6; two 3- ions are required to balance three 2+ ions: Mg_3N_2

g. Three 1+ ions are required to balance one 3- ion: Na_3P

h. Two 1+ ions are required to balance one 2- ion: Na_2S

84. a. One 2+ ion is exactly balanced by one 2- ion: BaO

b. Three 1+ ions are needed to balance one 3- ion: K_3P

c. Two 2+ ions are required to balance one 4- ion: Ca_2C

d. The smallest common multiple of 3 and 2 is 6; two 3+ ions are balanced by three 2- ions: Al_2S_3

e. The smallest common multiple of 2 and 3 is 6; three 2+ ions are balanced by two 3- ions: Sr_3P_2

f. One 1+ ion is balanced by one 1- ion: NaI

g. One 3+ ion is balanced by three 1- ions: $CoCl_3$

h. One 4+ ion is balanced by four 1- ions: $SnBr_4$

85. a. At; $Z = 85$

b. Xe; $Z = 54$

c. Ra; $Z = 88$

d. Sr; $Z = 38$

e. Pb; $Z = 82$

f. Se; $Z = 34$

g. Ar; $Z = 18$

h. Cs; $Z = 55$

86. a. 7; halogens

b. 8; noble gases

c. 2; alkaline earth elements

d. 2; alkaline earth elements

e. 4

f. 6; (the members of group 6 are sometimes called the chalcogens)

g. 8; noble gases

h. 1; alkali metals

87.   *Group 1*

element	symbol	atomic number
hydrogen	H	1
lithium	Li	3
sodium	Na	11
potassium	K	19

Group 2

beryllium	Be	4
magnesium	Mg	12
calcium	Ca	20
strontium	Sr	38

Group 6

oxygen	O	8
sulfur	S	16
selenium	Se	34
tellurium	Te	52

Group 7

fluorine	F	9
chlorine	Cl	17
bromine	Br	35
iodine	I	53

88.   *Group 3*

element	symbol	atomic number
boron	B	5
aluminum	Al	13
gallium	Ga	31
indium	In	49

Group 5

nitrogen	N	7
phosphorus	P	15
arsenic	As	33
antimony	Sb	51

Group 8

helium	He	2
neon	Ne	10
argon	Ar	18
krypton	Kr	36

89.   The atomic number represents the number of protons in the nucleus of an
atom. The mass number represents the total number of protons and
neutrons. No two different elements have the same atomic number. If the

total number of protons and neutrons happens to be the same for two atoms then the atoms will have the same mass number.

90. Most of the mass of an atom is concentrated in the nucleus: the *protons* and *neutrons* which constitute the nucleus have similar masses, and these particles are nearly two thousand times heavier than electrons. The chemical properties of an atom depend on the number and location of the *electrons* it possesses. Electrons are found in the outer regions of the atom, and are the particles most likely to be involved in interactions between atoms.

91. Yes. For example, carbon and oxygen form carbon monoxide (CO) and carbon dioxide (CO_2). The existence of more than one compound between the same elements does not in any way contradict Dalton's theory. For example, the relative mass of carbon in different samples of CO is always the same, and the relative mass of carbon in different samples of CO_2 is also always the same. Dalton did not say, however, that two different compounds would have to have the same relative masses of the elements present. In fact, Dalton said that two different compounds of the same elements would have to have different relative masses of the elements.

92. $C_6H_{12}O_6$

93. FeO and Fe_2O_3

94. a.   29 protons; 34 neutrons; 29 electrons

    b.   35 protons; 45 neutrons; 35 electrons

    c.   12 protons; 12 neutrons; 12 electrons

95.

mass number	symbol	number of neutrons
24	$^{24}_{13}Al$	11
25	$^{25}_{13}Al$	12
26	$^{26}_{13}Al$	13
28	$^{28}_{13}Al$	15
29	$^{29}_{13}Al$	16
30	$^{30}_{13}Al$	17

These are all considered to be aluminum atoms because they all have 13 protons in the nucleus.

96. The chief use of gold in ancient times was as *ornamentation*, whether in statuary or in jewelry. Gold possesses an especially beautiful luster, and since it is relatively soft and malleable, it could be worked finely by artisans; among the metals, gold is particularly inert to attack by most substances in the environment.

97. Boyle defined a substance as an element if it could not be broken down into simpler substances by chemical means.

98. a.   I

     b.   Si

     c.   W

     d.   Fe

     e.   Cu

     f.   Co

99. a.   Ca

     b.   K

     c.   Cs

     d.   Pb

     e.   Pt

     f.   Au

100. a.   Br

     b.   Bi

     c.   Hg

     d.   V

     e.   F

     f.   Ca

101. a.   Ag

     b.   Al

     c.   Cd

     d.   Sb

     e.   Sn

     f.   As

102. a.   osmium

    b.   zirconium

    c.   rubidium

    d.   radon

    e.   uranium

    f.   manganese

    g.   nickel

    h.   bromine

103. a.   tellurium

    b.   palladium

    c.   zinc

    d.   silicon

    e.   cesium

    f.   bismuth

    g.   fluorine

    h.   titanium

104. a. CO_2

    b. $AlCl_3$

    c. $HClO_4$

    d. SCl_6

105. a.   nitrogen, N

    b.   neon, Ne

    c.   sodium, Na

    d.   nickel, Ni

    e.   titanium, Ti

    f.   argon, Ar

    g.   krypton, Kr

    h.   xenon, Xe

106. a. $^{13}_{6}\text{C}$

    b. $^{13}_{6}\text{C}$

    c. ^{13}C

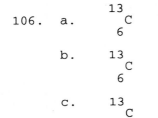

6

d. $^{44}_{19}\text{K}$

e. $^{41}_{20}\text{Ca}$

f. $^{35}_{19}\text{K}$

107. a. 22 protons, 19 neutrons, 22 electrons

b. 30 protons, 34 neutrons, 30 electrons

c. 32 protons, 44 neutrons, 32 electrons

d. 36 protons, 50 neutrons, 36 electrons

e. 33 protons, 42 neutrons, 33 electrons

f. 19 protons, 22 neutrons, 19 electrons

108.

	symbol	*number of protons*	*number of neutrons*	*mass number*
a.	$^{41}_{20}\text{Ca}$	20	21	41
b.	$^{55}_{25}\text{Mn}$	25	30	55
c.	$^{109}_{47}\text{Ag}$	47	62	109
d.	$^{45}_{21}\text{Sc}$	21	24	45

109. a. C; Z = 6; nonmetal

b. Se; Z = 34; nonmetal

c. Rn; Z = 86; nonmetal; noble gases

d. Be; Z = 4; metal; alkaline earth elements

Chapter 5   Nomenclature

1.   A *binary* compound is one that contains only two elements. Examples are sodium chloride, water, and carbon dioxide.

2.   compounds that contain a metal and a nonmetal; compounds containing two nonmetals

3.   cation, anion

4.   cation

5.   positive ion (cation)

6.   The substance "sodium chloride" consists of an extended lattice array of sodium ions, Na^+, and chloride ions, Cl^-. Each sodium ion is surrounded by several chloride ions, and each chloride ion is surrounded by several sodium ions. We write the formula as NaCl to indicate the relative number of each ion in the substance.

7.   *-ous*

8.   Roman numeral

9.   a.   sodium iodide

      b.   calcium fluoride

      c.   aluminum sulfide

      d.   calcium bromide

      e.   strontium oxide

      f.   silver chloride [silver(I) chloride]

      g.   cesium iodide

      h.   lithium oxide

10.   a.   potassium chloride

      b.   barium oxide

      c.   rubidium sulfide

      d.   sodium phosphide

      e.   aluminum fluoride

      f.   magnesium nitride

      g.   calcium iodide

      h.   radium chloride

11. a.   incorrect; BaH_2 is barium hydride

     b.   incorrect; Na_2O is sodium oxide

     c.   correct

     d.   incorrect; SiO_2 is silicon dioxide

     e.   correct

12. a.   incorrect; silver chloride is $AgCl$

     b.   correct

     c.   incorrect; sodium oxide would be Na_2O

     d.   incorrect; barium chloride is $BaCl_2$

     e.   incorrect; strontium oxide is SrO

13. a.   Since the bromide ion has a 1- charge, the tin ion must have a 2+ charge: the name is tin(II) bromide.

     b.   Since the iodide ion has a 1- charge, the tin ion must have a 4+ charge: the name is tin(IV) iodide.

     c.   Since the oxide ion has a 2- charge, the chromium ion must have a 2+ charge: the name is chromium(II) oxide.

     d.   Since the oxide ion has a 2- charge, each chromium ion must have a 3+ charge: the name is chromium(III) oxide.

     e.   Since the iodide ion has a 1- charge, each mercury ion must have a 1+ charge: the name is mercury(I) iodide.

     f.   Since the iodide ion has a 1- charge, the mercury ion must have a 2+ charge: the name is mercury(II) iodide.

14. a.   Since each iodide ion has a 1- charge, the iron ion must have a 3+ charge: the name is iron(III) iodide.

     b.   Since each chloride ion has a 1- charge, the manganese must have a 2+ charge: the name is manganese(II) chloride.

     c.   Since the oxide ion has a 2- charge, the mercury ion must have a 2+ charge: mercury(II) oxide.

     d.   Since the oxide ion has a 2- charge, the copper atoms must each have a 1+ charge: the name is copper(I) oxide.

     e.   Since the oxide ion has a 2- charge, the copper ion must have a 2+ charge: copper(II) oxide.

f.   Since each bromide ion has a 1– charge, the tin ion must have a 4+ charge: tin(IV) bromide.

15.   a.   Since each chloride ion has a 1– charge, the cobalt ion must have a 2+ charge: cobalt*ous* chloride.

b.   Since each bromide ion has a 1– charge, the chromium ion must have a 3+ charge: the name is chrom*ic* bromide.

c.   Since the oxide ion has a 2– charge, the lead ion must have a 2+ charge: the name is plumb*ous* oxide.

d.   Since each oxide ion has a 2– charge, the tin ion must have a 4+ charge: the name is stann*ic* oxide.

e.   Since each oxide ion has a 2– charge, the iron ion must have a 3+ charge: the name is ferr*ic* oxide.

f.   Since each chloride ion has a 1– charge, the iron ion must have a 3+ charge: the name is ferr*ic* chloride.

16.   a.   Since oxide ions have a 2– charge the lead ion must have a 4+ charge: the name is plumb*ic* oxide.

b.   Since bromide ions have a 1– charge, the tin ion must have a 2+ charge: the name is stann*ous* bromide.

c.   Since the sulfide ion has a 2– charge, the two copper ions must each have a 1+ charge: the name is cupr*ous* sulfide.

d.   Since the iodide ion has a 1– charge, the copper ion must have a 1+ charge: the name is cupr*ous* iodide.

e.   Since iodide ions have a 1– charge, each mercury must have a 1+ charge: the name is mercur*ous* iodide.

f.   Since fluoride ions have a 1– charge, the chromium ion must have a 3+ charge: the name is chrom*ic* fluoride.

17.   Remember that for this type of compound of nonmetals, numerical prefixes are used to indicate how many of each type of atom is present. However, if only one atom of the first element mentioned in the compound is present in a molecule, the prefix *mono-* is not needed.

a.   iodine pentafluoride

b.   arsenic trichloride

c.   selenium monoxide

d.   xenon tetrafluoride

    e.   nitrogen triiodide

    f.   diboron trioxide

18.   a.   germanium tetrahydride

    b.   dinitrogen tetrabromide

    c.   diphosphorus pentasulfide

    d.   selenium dioxide

    e.   ammonia (nitrogen trihydride)

    f.   silicon dioxide

19.   a.   tin(IV) bromide, stannic bromide - ionic

    b.   aluminum hydride - ionic

    c.   iron(II) oxide, ferrous oxide - ionic

    d.   copper(II) iodide, cupric iodide - ionic

    e.   oxygen difluoride - nonionic

    f.   xenon hexafluoride - nonionic

20.   a.   diboron hexahydride - nonionic (common name: *diborane*)

    b.   calcium nitride - ionic

    c.   carbon tetrabromide - nonionic

    d.   silver sulfide - ionic

    e.   copper(II) chloride, cupric chloride - ionic

    f.   chlorine monofluoride - nonionic

21.   a.   magnesium sulfide - ionic

    b.   aluminum chloride - ionic

    c.   phosphorus trihydride (the common name *phosphine* is always used)

    d.   chlorine monobromide - nonionic

    e.   lithium oxide - ionic

    f.   tetraphosphorus decoxide - nonionic

22.   a.   radium chloride - ionic

    b.   selenium dichloride - nonionic

    c.   phosphorus trichloride - nonionic

    d.   sodium phosphide - ionic

    e.   manganese(II) fluoride - ionic

    f.   zinc oxide - ionic

23.   polyatomic

24.   An oxyanion is a polyatomic anion containing oxygen combined with another element. The following oxyanions of bromine illustrate the nomenclature

    BrO^- hypobromite
    BrO_2^- bromite
    BrO_3^- bromate
    BrO_4^- perbromate

25.   one fewer oxygen atom

26.   perchlorate, ClO_4^-

27. ClO_4^- perchlorate

    ClO^- hypochlorite

    ClO_3^- chlorate

    ClO_2^- chlorite

28.   hypobromite

    IO_3^-

    periodate

    OI^- or IO^-

29.   a. P^{3-}

    b. PO_4^{3-}

    c. PO_3^{3-}

    d. HPO_4^{2-}

30.   a. NO_3^-

    b. NO_2^-

    c. NH_4^+

    d. CN^-

31.   a. Cl^-

    b. ClO^-

     c. ClO_3^-

     d. ClO_4^-

32.   a. $MgCl_2$

     b. $Ca(ClO)_2$

     c. $KClO_3$

     d. $Ba(ClO_4)_2$

33.   a.   permanganate

     b.   peroxide

     c.   chromate

     d.   dichromate

     e.   nitrate

     f.   sulfite

34.   a.   ammonium

     b.   dihydrogen phosphate

     c.   sulfate

     d.   hydrogen sulfite (also called *bi*sulfite)

     e.   perchlorate

     f.   iodate

35.   a.   iron(III) nitrate, ferric nitrate

     b.   cobalt(II) phosphate, cobaltous phosphate

     c.   chromium(III) cyanide, chromic cyanide

     d.   aluminum sulfate

     e.   chromium(II) acetate, chromous acetate

     f.   ammonium sulfite

36.   a.   ammonium sulfate

     b.   potassium perchlorate

     c.   iron(III) sulfate, ferric sulfate

     d.   calcium phosphate

     e.   calcium hydroxide

     f.   potassium carbonate

37.   An acid is a substance which produces hydrogen ions, H^+, when dissolved in water.

38.   oxygen (commonly referred to as *oxy*acids)

39.   a.   hydrochloric acid

       b.   sulfuric acid

       c.   nitric acid

       d.   hydroiodic acid

       e.   nitrous acid

       f.   chloric acid

       g.   hydrobromic acid

       h.   hydrofluoric acid

       i.   acetic acid

40.   a.   hypochlorous acid

       b.   sulfurous acid

       c.   bromic acid

       d.   hypoiodous acid

       e.   perbromic acid

       f.   hydrosulfuric acid

       g.   hydroselenic acid

       h.   phosphorous acid

41.   a. Li_2O

       b. AlI_3

       c. Ag_2O

       d. K_3N

       e. Ca_3P_2

       f. MgF_2

       g. Na_2S

       h. BaH_2

42.   a. PbO_2

       b. $SnBr_2$

       c. CuS

       d. CuI

   e. Hg_2Cl_2

   f. CrF_3

43.   a. PI_3

   b. $SiCl_4$

   c. N_2O_5

   d. IBr

   e. B_2O_3

   f. N_2O_4

   g. CO

44.   a. CO_2

   b. SO_2

   c. N_2Cl_4

   d. CI_4

   e. PF_5

   f. P_2O_5

45.   a. NH_4NO_3

   b. $Mg(C_2H_3O_2)_2$

   c. CaO_2

   d. $KHSO_4$

   e. $FeSO_4$

   f. $KHCO_3$

   g. $CoSO_4$

   h. $LiClO_4$

46.   a. $Ca_3(PO_4)_2$

   b. NH_4NO_3

   c. $Al(HSO_4)_3$

   d. $BaSO_4$

   e. $Fe(NO_3)_3$

   f. $CuOH$

47.   a. H_2S

   b. $HBrO_4$

c. $HC_2H_3O_2$

d.   HBr

e. $HClO_2$

f. H_2Se

g. H_2SO_3

h. $HBrO_2$

48.   a.   HCN

b. HNO_3

c. H_2SO_4

d. H_3PO_4

e.   HClO or HOCl

f.   HBr

g. $HBrO_2$

h.   HF

49.   a.   LiCl

b. Cu_2CO_3

c.   HBr

d. $Ca(NO_3)_2$

e. $NaClO_4$

f. $Al(OH)_3$

g. $Ba(HCO_3)_2$

h. $FeSO_4$

i. B_2Cl_6

j. PBr_5

k. K_2SO_3

l. $Ba(C_2H_3O_2)_2$

50.   a. $Mg(HSO_4)_2$

b. $CsClO_4$

c.   FeO

d. H_2Te

e. $Sr(NO_3)_2$

f. $Sn(C_2H_3O_2)_4$

g. $MnSO_4$

h. N_2O_4

i. Na_2HPO_4

j. Li_2O_2

k. HNO_2

l. $Co(NO_3)_3$

51.   Ionic compounds have a strong resistance to melting (compared to covalent compounds like sucrose) because of the strong *electrical* attraction of the positive ions for the negative ions in the crystal of ionic compound (each positive ion is surrounded by several negative ions and *vice versa*).

52.   A moist paste of NaCl would contain Na^+ and Cl^- ions in solution, and would serve as a *conductor* of electrical impulses.

53.   A *binary* compound is a compound containing two and only two elements. A *polyatomic* anion is several atoms bonded together which, as a whole, carries a negative electrical charge. An *oxyanion* is a negative ion containing a particular element and one or more oxygen atoms.

54. $H \rightarrow H^+$ (hydrogen ion: a cation) $+ e^-$

$H + e^- \rightarrow H^-$ (hydr*ide* ion: an anion)

55.   hydrogen

56.   missing oxyanions: IO_3^-; ClO_2^-

missing oxyacids: $HClO_4$; $HClO$; $HBrO_2$

57.   a.   calcium acetate

b.   phosphorus trichloride

c.   copper(II) permanganate, cupric permanganate

d.   iron(III) carbonate, ferric carbonate

e.   lithium hydrogen carbonate, lithium bicarbonate

f.   chromium(III) sulfide, chromic sulfide

g.   calcium cyanide

58.   a.   gold(III) bromide, auric bromide

b.   cobalt(III) cyanide, cobaltic cyanide

c.   magnesium hydrogen phosphate

d.   diboron hexahydride (diborane is its common name)

    e.   ammonia

    f.   silver(I) sulfate (usually called silver sulfate)

    g.   beryllium hydroxide

59.   a.   chloric acid

    b.   cobalt(III) chloride; cobaltic chloride

    c.   diboron trioxide

    d.   water

    e.   acetic acid

    f.   iron(III) nitrate; ferric nitrate

    g.   copper(II) sulfate; cupric sulfate

60.   a.   ammonium carbonate

    b.   ammonium hydrogen carbonate, ammonium bicarbonate

    c.   calcium phosphate

    d.   sulfurous acid

    e.   manganese(IV) oxide

    f.   iodic acid

    g.   potassium hydride

61.   a. K_2O

    b. MgO

    c. FeO

    d. Fe_2O_3

    e. ZnO

    f. PbO

    g. Al_2O_3

62.   a. $M(C_2H_3O_2)_4$

    b. $M(MnO_4)_4$

    c. MO_2

    d. $M(HPO_4)_2$

    e. $M(OH)_4$

    f. $M(NO_2)_4$

63.   Answers are given, respectively, for the M^{1+}, M^{2+}, and M^{3+} ions:

   a. M_2CrO_4, $MCrO_4$, $M_2(CrO_4)_3$

   b. $M_2Cr_2O_7$, MCr_2O_7, $M_2(Cr_2O_7)_3$

   c. M_2S, MS, M_2S_3

   d. MBr, MBr_2, MBr_3

   e. $MHCO_3$, $M(HCO_3)_2$, $M(HCO_3)_3$

   f. M_2HPO_4, $MHPO_4$, $M_2(HPO_4)_3$

64. M^+ compounds: MD, M_2E, M_3F

   M^{2+} compounds: MD_2, ME, M_3F_2

   M^{3+} compounds: MD_3, M_2E_3, MF

65. Fe^{2+}: $FeCO_3$ iron(II) carbonate; ferrous carbonate
             $Fe(BrO_3)_2$ iron(II) bromate; ferrous bromate
             $Fe(C_2H_3O_2)_2$ iron(II) acetate; ferrous acetate
             $Fe(OH)_2$ iron(II) hydroxide; ferrous hydroxide
             $Fe(HCO_3)_2$ iron(II) bicarbonate; ferrous bicarbonate
             $Fe_3(PO_4)_2$ iron(II) phosphate; ferrous phosphate
             $FeSO_3$ iron(II) sulfite; ferrous sulfite
             $Fe(ClO_4)_2$ iron(II) perchlorate; ferrous perchlorate
             $FeSO_4$ iron(II) sulfate; ferrous sulfate
             FeO iron(II) oxide; ferrous oxide
             $FeCl_2$ iron(II) chloride; ferrous chloride

   Al^{3+}: $Al_2(CO_3)_3$ aluminum carbonate
             $Al(BrO_3)_3$ aluminum bromate
             $Al(C_2H_3O_2)_3$ aluminum acetate
             $Al(OH)_3$ aluminum hydroxide
             $Al(HCO_3)_3$ aluminum bicarbonate
             $AlPO_4$ aluminum phosphate
             $Al_2(SO_3)_3$ aluminum sulfite
             $Al(ClO_4)_3$ aluminum perchlorate
             $Al_2(SO_4)_3$ aluminum sulfate
             Al_2O_3 aluminum oxide
             $AlCl_3$ aluminum chloride

   Na^+: Na_2CO_3 sodium carbonate
             $NaBrO_3$ sodium bromate
             $NaC_2H_3O_2$ sodium acetate
             $NaOH$ sodium hydroxide

$NaHCO_3$ sodium bicarbonate
Na_3PO_4 sodium phosphate
Na_2SO_3 sodium sulfite
$NaClO_4$ sodium perchlorate
Na_2SO_4 sodium sulfate
Na_2O sodium oxide
$NaCl$ sodium chloride

Ca^{2+}: $CaCO_3$ calcium carbonate
$Ca(BrO_3)_2$ calcium bromate
$Ca(C_2H_3O_2)_2$ calcium acetate
$Ca(OH)_2$ calcium hydroxide
$Ca(HCO_3)_2$ calcium bicarbonate
$Ca_3(PO_4)_2$ calcium phosphate
$CaSO_3$ calcium sulfite
$Ca(ClO_4)_2$ calcium perchlorate
$CaSO_4$ calcium sulfate
CaO calcium oxide
$CaCl_2$ calcium chloride

NH_4^+: $(NH_4)_2CO_3$ ammonium carbonate
NH_4BrO_3 ammonium bromate
$NH_4C_2H_3O_2$ ammonium acetate
NH_4OH ammonium hydroxide
NH_4HCO_3 ammonium bicarbonate
$(NH_4)_3PO_4$ ammonium phosphate
$(NH_4)_2SO_3$ ammonium sulfite
NH_4ClO_4 ammonium perchlorate
$(NH_4)_2SO_4$ ammonium sulfate
$(NH_4)_2O$ ammonium oxide
NH_4Cl ammonium chloride

Fe^{3+}: $Fe_2(CO_3)_3$ iron(III) carbonate
$Fe(BrO_3)_3$ iron(III) bromate
$Fe(C_2H_3O_2)_3$ iron(III) acetate
$Fe(OH)_3$ iron(III) hydroxide
$Fe(HCO_3)_3$ iron(III) bicarbonate
$FePO_4$ iron(III) phosphate
$Fe_2(SO_3)_3$ iron(III) sulfite
$Fe(ClO_4)_3$ iron(III) perchlorate
$Fe_2(SO_4)_3$ iron(III) sulfate
Fe_2O_3 iron(III) oxide
$FeCl_3$ iron(III) chloride

Ni^{2+}: $NiCO_3$ nickel(II) carbonate
         $Ni(BrO_3)_2$ nickel(II) bromate
         $Ni(C_2H_3O_2)_2$ nickel(II) acetate
         $Ni(OH)_2$ nickel(II) hydroxide
         $Ni(HCO_3)_2$ nickel(II) bicarbonate
         $Ni_3(PO_4)_2$ nickel(II) phosphate
         $NiSO_3$ nickel(II) sulfite
         $Ni(ClO_4)_2$ nickel(II) perchlorate
         $NiSO_4$ nickel(II) sulfate
         NiO nickel(II) oxide
         $NiCl_2$ nickel(II) chloride

Hg_2^{2+}: Hg_2CO_3 mercury(I) carbonate
         $Hg_2(BrO_3)_2$ mercury(I) bromate
         $Hg_2(C_2H_3O_2)_2$ mercury(I) acetate
         $Hg_2(OH)_2$ mercury(I) hydroxide
         $Hg_2(HCO_3)_2$ mercury(I) bicarbonate
         $(Hg_2)_3(PO_4)_2$ mercury(I) phosphate
         Hg_2SO_3 mercury(I) sulfite
         $Hg_2(ClO_4)_2$ mercury(I) perchlorate
         Hg_2SO_4 mercury(I) sulfate
         Hg_2O mercury(I) oxide
         Hg_2Cl_2 mercury(I) chloride

Hg^{2+}: $HgCO_3$ mercury(II) carbonate
         $Hg(BrO_3)_2$ mercury(II) bromate
         $Hg(C_2H_3O_2)_2$ mercury(II) acetate
         $Hg(OH)_2$ mercury(II) hydroxide
         $Hg(HCO_3)_2$ mercury(II) bicarbonate
         $Hg_3(PO_4)_2$ mercury(II) phosphate
         $HgSO_3$ mercury(II) sulfite
         $Hg(ClO_4)_2$ mercury(II) perchlorate
         $HgSO_4$ mercury(II) sulfate
         HgO mercury(II) oxide
         $HgCl_2$ mercury(II) chloride

66. $Ca(NO_3)_2$ $CaSO_4$ $Ca(HSO_4)_2$ $Ca(H_2PO_4)_2$ CaO $CaCl_2$
     $Sr(NO_3)_2$ $SrSO_4$ $Sr(HSO_4)_2$ $Sr(H_2PO_4)_2$ SrO $SrCl_2$
     NH_4NO_3 $(NH_4)_2SO_4$ NH_4HSO_4 $NH_4H_2PO_4$ $(NH_4)_2O$ NH_4Cl
     $Al(NO_3)_3$ $Al_2(SO_4)_3$ $Al(HSO_4)_3$ $Al(H_2PO_4)_3$ Al_2O_3 $AlCl_3$
     $Fe(NO_3)_3$ $Fe_2(SO_4)_3$ $Fe(HSO_4)_3$ $Fe(H_2PO_4)_3$ Fe_2O_3 $FeCl_3$

$Ni(NO_3)_2$	$NiSO_4$	$Ni(HSO_4)_2$	$Ni(H_2PO_4)_2$	NiO	$NiCl_2$
$AgNO_3$	Ag_2SO_4	$AgHSO_4$	AgH_2PO_4	Ag_2O	$AgCl$
$Au(NO_3)_3$	$Au_2(SO_4)_3$	$Au(HSO_4)_3$	$Au(H_2PO_4)_3$	Au_2O_3	$AuCl_3$
KNO_3	K_2SO_4	$KHSO_4$	KH_2PO_4	K_2O	KCl
$Hg(NO_3)_2$	$HgSO_4$	$Hg(HSO_4)_2$	$Hg(H_2PO_4)_2$	HgO	$HgCl_2$
$Ba(NO_3)_2$	$BaSO_4$	$Ba(HSO_4)_2$	$Ba(H_2PO_4)_2$	BaO	$BaCl_2$

67. unreactive

68. helium

69. two

70. iodine (solid), bromine (liquid), fluorine and chlorine (gases)

71. 2-

72. 1-

73. 3+

74. 1-

75. [1]   e

   [2]   a

   [3]   a

   [4]   g

   [5]   g

   [6]   f

   [7]   g

   [8]   a

   [9]   e

   [10]   j

76. a. $Al(13e^-) \rightarrow Al^{3+}(10e^-) + 3e^-$

   b. $S(16e^-) + 2e^- \rightarrow S^{2-}(18e^-)$

   c. $Cu(29e^-) \rightarrow Cu^+(28e^-) + e^-$

   d. $F(9e^-) + e^- \rightarrow F^-(10e^-)$

   e. $Zn(30e^-) \rightarrow Zn^{2+}(28e^-) + 2e^-$

f. $P(15e^-) + 3e^- \rightarrow P^{3-}(18e^-)$

77.   a.   none likely (element 36, Kr, is a noble gas)

b. Ga^{3+} (element 31, Ga, is in Group 3)

c. Te^{2-} (element 52, Te, is in Group 6)

d. Tl^{3+} (element 81, Tl, is in Group 3)

e. Br^- (element 35, Br, is in Group 7)

f. Fr^+ (element 87, Fr, is in Group 1)

78.   a.   Two 1+ ions are needed to balance a 2- ion, so the formula must have two Na^+ ions for each S^{2-} ion: Na_2S.

b.   One 1+ ion exactly balances a 1- ion, so the formula should have an equal number of K^+ and Cl^- ions: KCl.

c.   One 2+ ion exactly balances a 2- ion, so the formula must have an equal number of Ba^{2+} and O^{2-} ions: BaO.

d.   One 2+ ion exactly balances a 2- ion, so the formula must have an equal number of Mg^{2+} and Se^{2-} ions: MgSe.

e.   One 2+ ion requires two 1- ions to balance charge, so the formula must have twice as many Br^- ions as Cu^{2+} ions: $CuBr_2$.

f.   One 3+ ion requires three 1- ions to balance charge, so the formula must have three times as many I^- ions as Al^{3+} ions: AlI_3.

g.   Two 3+ ions give a total of 6+, whereas three 2- ions will give a total of 6-. The formula then should contain two Al^{3+} ions and three O^{2-} ions: Al_2O_3.

h.   Three 2+ ions are required to balance two 3- ions, so the formula must contain three Ca^{2+} ions for every two N^{3-} ions: Ca_3N_2.

79.   a.   beryllium oxide

b.   magnesium iodide

c.   sodium sulfide

d.   aluminum oxide

e.   hydrogen chloride (gaseous); hydrochloric acid (aqueous)

f.   lithium fluoride

g.   silver(I) sulfide; usually called silver sulfide

h.   calcium hydride

80. a.   incorrect. Si is the element silicon, not silver.

     b.   incorrect. Co is the symbol for cobalt, not copper.

     c.   incorrect. Hydrogen exists as the hydride ion in this compound.

     d.   correct

     e.   incorrect. P is just "phosphorus" not "phosphoric".

81. a.   Since the bromide ion must have a 1- charge, the iron ion must be
           in the 2+ state: the name is iron(II) bromide.

     b.   Since sulfide ion always has a 2- charge, the cobalt ion must be
           in the 2+ state: the name is cobalt(II) sulfide.

     c.   Since sulfide ion always has a 2- charge, and since there are
           three sulfide ions present, each cobalt ion must be in the 3+
           state: the name is cobalt(III) sulfide.

     d.   Since oxide ion always has a 2- charge, the tin ion must be in the
           4+ state: the name is tin(IV) oxide.

     e.   Since chloride ion always has a 1- charge, each mercury ion must
           be in the 1+ state: the name is mercury(I) chloride.

     f.   Since chloride ion always has a 1- charge, the mercury ion must be
           in the 2+ state: the name is mercury(II) chloride.

82. a.   Since bromide ions always have a 1- charge, the cobalt ion must
           have a 3+ charge: the name is cobalt*ic* bromide.

     b.   Since iodide ions always have a 1- charge, the lead ion must have
           a 4+ charge: the name is plumb*ic* iodide.

     c.   Since oxide ions always have a 2- charge, and since there are
           three oxide ions, each iron ion must have a 3+ charge: the name is
           fer*ric* oxide.

     d.   Since sulfide ions always have a 2- charge, the iron ion must have
           a 2+ charge: the name is ferr*ous* sulfide.

     e.   Since chloride ions always have a 1- charge, the tin ion must have
           a 4+ charge: the name is stann*ic* chloride.

     f.   Since oxide ions always have a 2- charge, the tin ion must have a
           2+ charge: the name is stann*ous* oxide.

83. a.   xenon hexafluoride

     b.   oxygen difluoride

    c.   arsenic triiodide

    d.   dinitrogen tetraoxide (tetroxide)

    e.   dichlorine monoxide

    f.   sulfur hexafluoride

84.   a.   iron(III) acetate, ferric acetate

    b.   bromine monofluoride

    c.   potassium peroxide

    d.   silicon tetrabromide

    e.   copper(II) permanganate, cupric permanganate

    f.   calcium chromate

85.   nitrate (the ending -*ate* always implies the larger number of oxygen atoms)

86.   a. CO_3^{2-}

    b. HCO_3^-

    c. $C_2H_3O_2^-$

    d. CN^-

87.   a. Cr^{2+}

    b. CrO_4^{2-}

    c. Cr^{3+}

    d. $Cr_2O_7^{2-}$

88.   a.   carbonate

    b.   chlorate

    c.   sulfate

    d.   phosphate

    e.   perchlorate

    f.   permanganate

89.   a.   lithium dihydrogen phosphate

    b.   copper(II) cyanide

    c.   lead(II) nitrate

    d.   sodium hydrogen phosphate

e.   sodium chlorite

f.   cobalt(III) sulfate

90.   a. $CaCl_2$

b. Ag_2O

c. Al_2S_3

d. $BeBr_2$

e. H_2S

f.   KH

g. MgI_2

h.   CsF

91.   a. SO_2

b. N_2O

c. XeF_4

d. P_4O_{10}

e. PCl_5

f. SF_6

g. NO_2

92.   a. NaH_2PO_4

b. $LiClO_4$

c. $Cu(HCO_3)_2$

d. $KC_2H_3O_2$

e. BaO_2

f. Cs_2SO_3

93.   a. $AgClO_4$

b. $Co(OH)_3$

c.   NaClO or NaOCl

d. $K_2Cr_2O_7$

e. NH_4NO_2

f. $Fe(OH)_3$

g. NH_4HCO_3

h. $KBrO_4$

Cumulative Review: Chapters 4 and 5

1.   An element is a pure substance which cannot be broken down into simpler substances by chemical means. There are presently 112 elements recognized, of which 88 occur in nature (the remaining 24 have been synthesized by nuclear processes). The most abundant elements (by mass) on the earth are oxygen (49.2%), silicon (25.7%), and aluminum (7.50%), with less than 5% of each the other elements present. A table of elemental abundances is given in the text as Table 4.1

2.   How many elements could you name? While you certainly don't have to memorize all the elements, you should at least be able to give the symbol or name for the most common elements (listed in Table 4.3).

3.   The symbols for some elements may refer to an archaic name for the element, or to the element's name in a modern language other than English. Here are some examples:

Element	English Name	Derivation of Name
Na	sodium	Latin: *natrium*
K	potassium	Latin: *kalium*
Fe	iron	Latin: *ferrum*
W	tungsten	German: *wolfram*

4.   Dalton's atomic theory as presented in this text consists of five main postulates. Realize that although Dalton's theory was exceptional scientific thinking for its time, some of the postulates have been modified as our scientific instruments and calculational methods have become increasingly more sophisticated. The main postulates of Dalton's theory are as follows: (1) Elements are made up of tiny particles called atoms; (2) all atoms of a given element are identical; (3) although all atoms of a given element are identical, these atoms are different from the atoms of all other elements; (4) atoms of one element can combine with atoms of another element to form a compound, and such a compound will always have the same relative numbers and types of atoms for its composition; (5) atoms are merely rearranged into new groupings during an ordinary chemical reaction, and no atom is ever destroyed and no new atom is ever created during such a reaction.

5.   A compound is a distinct, pure substance that is composed of two or more elements held together by chemical bonds. In addition, a given compound always contains exactly the same relative masses of its constituent elements. This latter statement is termed the law of constant composition. The law of constant composition is a result of the fact that a given compound is made up of molecules containing a particular type and number of each constituent atom. For example, water's composition by mass (88.8% oxygen, 11.2% hydrogen) is a result of the fact that each and every water molecule contains one oxygen atom (relative mass 16.0) and two hydrogen atoms (relative mass 1.008 each). The law of constant composition is important to our study of chemistry because it means that we can always assume that any sample of a given pure substance, from whatever source, will be identical to any other sample.

6.   The expression *nuclear* atom indicates that we view the atom as having a
       dense center of positive charge (called the nucleus) around which the
       electrons move through primarily empty space. Rutherford's experiment
       involved shooting a beam of particles at a thin sheet of metal foil.
       According to the then current "plum pudding" model of the atom, most of
       these positively charged particles should have passed right through the
       foil. However, Rutherford detected that a significant number of
       particles effectively bounced off something and were deflected backwards
       to the source of particles, and that other particles were deflected
       from the foil at large angles. Rutherford realized that his observations
       could be explained if the atoms of the metal foil had a small, dense,
       positively charged nucleus, with a significant amount of empty space
       between nuclei. The empty space between nuclei would allow most of the
       particles to pass through the atom. However, if an particle hit a
       nucleus head-on, it would be deflected backwards at the source. If a
       positively-charged particle passed near a positively charged nucleus
       (but did not hit the nucleus head-on), then the particle would be
       deflected by the repulsive forces between the positive charges.
       Rutherford's experiment conclusively disproved the "plum pudding" model
       for the atom, which envisioned the atom as a uniform sphere of positive
       charge, with enough negatively charged electrons scattered through the
       atom to balance out the positive charge.

7.   The three fundamental particles from which atoms are composed are
       electrons, protons, and neutrons. The properties of these particles are
       summarized below:

Particle	Relative Mass	Relative Charge	Location
proton	1836	1+	nucleus
neutron	1839	none	nucleus
electron	1	1-	outside nucleus

       It is the number and arrangement of the *electrons* in an atom which is
       responsible for the chemical behavior of the atom. The electrons are
       found in nearly the entire region of space occupied by an atom, from
       just outside the nucleus all the way out to the outermost *edge* of the
       atom. When two atoms approach each other in space prior to a reaction
       taking place, it is the electrons which "see" the electrons of the other
       atom. The nucleus is so small, compared to the overall size of the atom,
       that the particles are too far away from the outside of the atom to
       interact with other atoms.

8.   Isotopes represent atoms of the same element which have different atomic
       masses. Isotopes are a result of the fact that atoms of a given element
       may have different numbers of neutrons in their nuclei. Isotopes have
       the same atomic number (number of protons in the nucleus) but have
       different mass numbers (total number of protons and neutrons in the
       nucleus). The different isotopes of an atom are indicated by symbolism
       of the form $^A_Z X$ in which Z represents the atomic number, and A the mass
       number, of element X. For example, $^{13}_{6}C$ represents a nuclide of carbon
       with atomic number 6 (6 protons in the nucleus) and mass number 13

(reflecting 6 protons plus 7 neutrons in the nucleus). The various isotopes of an element have identical chemical properties since the chemical properties of an atom are a function of the electrons in the atom (*not* the nucleus). The physical properties of the isotopes of an element (and compounds containing those isotopes) may differ because of the difference in mass of the isotopes.

9. The periodic table arranges the elements in order of increasing atomic number (from $Z = 1$ to $Z = 112$). The table is further arranged by placing elements with similar electronic structure (and hence similar chemical properties) into the same vertical column (group), beginning with each period a new principal energy shell. Based on this arrangement by electronic structure, the metallic elements tend to be towards the left-hand side of the chart, while the non-metallic elements are found towards the right-hand, upper side. Since metallic nature increases going downward within any vertical column (as the outermost shell gets farther from the nucleus), there are also some metallic elements among the lower members of groups at the right-hand side of the table (many periodic tables indicate the dividing line between metallic and nonmetallic elements with a colored "stairstep". Some of the groups have been given common names; these are listed below:

Group	Family Name
1	Alkali Metals
2	Alkaline Earth Elements
6	Chalcogens (not used very commonly)
7	Halogens
8	Noble Gases

10. Most elements are too reactive to be found in nature in other than the combined form. Aside from the noble metals gold, silver, and platinum, the only other elements commonly found in nature in the uncombined state are some of the gaseous elements (such as O_2, N_2, He, Ar, etc.), and the solid nonmetals carbon and sulfur.

11. Ions are electrically charged particles formed from atoms or molecules which have gained or lost one or more electrons. Isolated atoms typically do not form ions on their own, but are induced to gain or lose electrons by some other species (which loses or gains the electrons). Positively charged ions are called *cations*, while negative ions are termed *anions*. A positive ion forms when an atom or molecule *loses* one or more of its electrons (negative charges). For example, sodium atoms and magnesium atoms form ions as indicated below

$$Na(atom) \rightarrow Na^+(ion) + e^-$$

$$Mg(atom) \rightarrow Mg^{2+}(ion) + 2e^-$$

The resulting ions contain the same number of protons and neutrons in their nuclei as do the atoms from which they are formed, since the only change that has taken place involves the electrons (which are not in the nucleus). These ions obviously contain fewer electrons than the atoms from which they are formed, however. A negative ion forms when an atom or molecule *gains* one or more electrons from an outside source (another atom or molecule). For example, chlorine atoms and oxygen atoms form ions as indicated below:

$$Cl(atom) + e^- \rightarrow Cl^-(ion)$$

$$O(atom) + 2e^- \rightarrow O^{2-}(ion)$$

Since the periodic table is arranged in terms of the electronic structure of the elements, in particular with the elements in the same vertical column having *similar* electronic structures, the mere *location* of an element in the periodic table can be an indication of what simple ions the element forms. For example, the Group 1 elements all form 1+ ions (Li^+, Na^+, K^+, Rb^+, Cs^+), while the Group 7 elements all form 1- ions (F^-, Cl^-, Br^-, I^-). You will learn more about how the charge of an ion is related to an atom's electronic structure in a later chapter. For now, concentrate in learning the material shown in Figure 4.19.

12. Ionic compounds typically are hard, crystalline solids with high melting and boiling points. Ionic substances like sodium chloride, when dissolved in water or when melted, conduct electrical currents: chemists have taken this evidence to mean that ionic substances consist of positively and negatively charged particles (ions). Although an ionic substance is made up of positively and negatively charged particles, there is no net electrical charge on a sample of such a substance because the total number of positive charges is balanced by an equal number of negative charges. An ionic compound could not possibly exist of just cations or just anions: there must be a balance of charge or the compound would be very unstable (like charges repel each other).

13. The principle we use when writing the formula of an ionic compound is sometimes called the "principle of electroneutrality". This is just a long word that means that a chemical compound must have an overall net electrical charge of *zero*. For ionic compounds, this means that the total number of positive charges on the positive ions present must *equal* the total number of negative charges on the negative ions present. For example, with sodium chloride, if we realize that an individual sodium ion has a 1+ charge, and that an individual chloride ion has a 1- charge, then if we combine one of each of these ions, the compound will have an overall net charge of zero: (1+) + (1-) = 0. On the other hand for magnesium iodide, when we realize that an individual magnesium ion has a 2+ charge, then clearly one iodide ion with its 1- charge will not lead to a compound with an overall charge of zero: we would need *two* iodide ions, each with its 1- charge, to balance the 2+ charge of the magnesium ion: (2+) + 2(1-) = 0. If we considered magnesium oxide, however, we would need only one oxide ion, with its 2- charge, to balance with one magnesium with its 2+ charge [(2+) + (2-) = 0], and so the formula of magnesium oxide is just MgO.

14. When naming ionic compounds, we name the positive ion (cation) first. For simple binary Type I ionic compounds, the ending *-ide* is added to the root name of the element which is the negative ion (anion). For example, for the Type I ionic compound formed between potassium and sulfur, K_2S, the name would be potassium sulfide: potassium is the cation, sulfur is the anion (with the suffix *-ide* added). Type II compounds are named by either of two systems, the "*ous-ic*" system (which is falling out of use), and the "Roman numeral" system which is preferred by most chemists. Type II compounds involve elements which form more than one stable ion, and so it is necessary to specify *which* ion is present in a given compound. For example, iron forms two types of stable ion: Fe^{2+} and Fe^{3+}. Iron can react with oxygen to form either of two stable oxides, FeO or Fe_2O_3, depending on which cation is involved. Under the Roman numeral naming system, FeO would be named iron(II) oxide to show that it contains Fe^{2+} ions; Fe_2O_3 would be named iron(III) oxide to indicate that it contains Fe^{3+} ions. The Roman numeral used in a name corresponds to the charge of the specific ion present in the compound. Under the less-favored "*ous-ic*" system, for an element that forms two stable ions, the ending *-ous* is used to indicated the lower-charged ion, whereas the ending *-ic* is used to indicate the higher-charged ion. FeO and Fe_2O_3 would thus be named ferr*ous* oxide and ferr*ic* oxide, respectively. The "*ous-ic*" system has fallen out of favor since it does not indicate the actual charge on the ion, but only that it is the lower or higher charged of the two. This can lead to confusion: for example Fe^{2+} is called ferrous ion in this system, but Cu^{2+} is called cupric ion (since there is also a Cu^+ stable ion).

15. Type III binary compounds represent compounds involving only nonmetallic elements. In writing the name for such compounds, the element listed first in the formula is named first (using the full name of the element), and then the second element in the formula is named as though it were an anion (with the *-ide* ending). This is similar, thus far, to the method used for naming ionic compounds (Type I). Since there often may be more than one compound possible involving the same two nonmetallic elements, the naming system for Type III compounds goes one step further than the system for ionic compounds, by explicitly stating (by means of a numerical prefix) the number of atoms of each of the nonmetallic elements present in the molecules of the compound. For example, carbon and oxygen (both nonmetals) form two common compounds, CO and CO_2. To indicate clearly which compound is being discussed, the names of these compounds indicate explicitly the number of oxygen atoms present by using a numerical prefix.

CO   carbon *mon*oxide   (*mon* or *mono* is the prefix meaning "one")

CO_2 carbon *di*oxide   (*di* is the prefix meaning "two")

The prefix *mono* is not normally used for the first element named in a compound if there is only one atom of the element present, but numerical prefixes are used for the first element if there is more than one atom of that element present. For example, nitrogen and oxygen form many binary compounds. Study closely how the examples following are named:

NO   nitrogen *mon*oxide

NO_2 nitrogen *di*oxide

N_2O *di*nitrogen *mon*oxide

N_2O_4 *di*nitrogen *tetr*oxide   (*tetra* or *tetr* means "four")

16. A polyatomic ion is an ion containing more than one atom. Some common polyatomic ions you should be familiar with are listed in Table 5.4. Parentheses are used in writing formulas containing polyatomic ions to indicate unambiguously how many of the polyatomic ion are present in the formula, to make certain that there is no mistake as to what is meant by the formula. For example, consider the substance calcium phosphate. The correct formula for this substance is $Ca_3(PO_4)_2$, which indicates that three calcium ions are combined for every two phosphate ions (check the total number of positive and negative charges to see why this is so). If we did not write the parenthesis around the formula for the phosphate ion, that is, if we had written Ca_3PO_{42}, people reading this formula might think that there were 42 oxygen atoms present!

17. Several families of polyatomic anions contain an atom of a given element, combined with differing numbers of oxygen atoms. Such anions are called "*oxyanions*". For example, sulfur forms two common oxyanions, $SO_3{}^{2-}$ and $SO_4{}^{2-}$. When there are two oxyanions in such a series (as for sulfur), the name of the anion with fewer oxygen atoms ends in -*ite* and the name of the anion with more oxygen atoms ends in -*ate*. Under this method, $SO_3{}^{2-}$ is named sulf*ite* and $SO_4{}^{2-}$ is named sulf*ate*. When there are more than two members of such a series, the prefixes *hypo-* and *per-* are used to indicate the members of the series with the *fewest* and *largest* number of oxygen atoms. For example, bromine forms four common oxyanions. The formulas and names of these oxyanions are listed below.

Formula	*Name*
BrO^-	*hypo*brom*ite* (fewest number of oxygens)
$BrO_2{}^-$	brom*ite*
$BrO_3{}^-$	brom*ate*
$BrO_4{}^-$	*per*brom*ate* (largest number of oxygens)

18. Acids, in general, are substances which produce protons (H^+ ions) when dissolved in water. For acids which do not contain oxygen, the prefix *hydro-* and the suffix -*ic* are used with the root name of the element present in the acid (for example: HCl, hydrochloric acid; H_2S, hydrosulfuric acid; HF, hydrofluoric acid). The nomenclature of acids whose anions contain oxygen is more complicated. A series of prefixes and suffixes is used with the name of the non-oxygen atom in the anion of the acid: these prefixes and suffixes indicate the relative (not actual) number of oxygen atoms present in the anion. Most of the elements that form oxyanions form two such anions: for example, sulfur forms sulfite ion ($SO_3{}^{2-}$) and sulfate ion ($SO_4{}^{2-}$), and nitrogen forms nitrite ion ($NO_2{}^-$) and nitrate ion ($NO_3{}^-$). For an element that forms two

oxyanions, the acid containing the anions will have the ending *-ous* if the anion is the *-ite* anion and the ending *-ic* if the anion is the *-ate* anion. For example, HNO_2 is nitr*ous* acid and HNO_3 is nitr*ic* acid; H_2SO_3 is sulfur*ous* acid and H_2SO_4 is sulfur*ic* acid. The halogen elements (Group 7) each form four oxyanions, and consequently, four oxyacids. The prefix *hypo-* is used for the oxyacid that contains fewer oxygen atoms than the *-ite* anion, and the prefix *per-* is used for the oxyacid that contains more oxygen atoms than the *-ate* anion. For example,

acid	*name*	*anion*	*anion name*
$HBrO$	*hypo*brom*ous* acid	BrO^-	*hypo*brom*ite*
$HBrO_2$	brom*ous* acid	BrO_2^-	brom*ite*
$HBrO_3$	brom*ic* acid	BrO_3^-	brom*ate*
$HBrO_4$	*per*brom*ic* acid	BrO_4^-	*per*brom*ate*

19.

Name	*Symbol*	*Atomic Number*
magnesium	Mg	12
tin	Sn	50
lead	Pb	82
sodium	Na	11
hydrogen	H	1
chlorine	Cl	17
silver	Ag	47
potassium	K	19
calcium	Ca	20
bromine	Br	35
neon	Ne	10
aluminum	Al	13
gold	Au	79
mercury	Hg	80
iodine	I	53

20.

	Formula	Name	Atomic Number
a.	He	helium	2
b.	B	boron	5
c.	C	carbon	6
d.	F	fluorine	9
e.	S	sulfur	16
f.	Ba	barium	56
g.	Be	beryllium	4
h.	O	oxygen	8
i.	P	phosphorus	15
j.	Si	silicon	14

21.

	Atomic Number	Name	Symbol
a.	19	potassium	K
b.	12	magnesium	Mg
c.	36	krypton	Kr
d.	92	uranium	U
e.	1	hydrogen	H
f.	6	carbon	C
g.	15	phosphorus	P
h.	20	calcium	Ca
i.	79	gold	Au
j.	82	lead	Pb
k.	29	copper	Cu
l.	35	bromine	Br
m.	2	helium	He
n.	8	oxygen	O

22.

		protons	neutrons	electrons
a.	$^{4}_{2}He$	2	2	2
b.	$^{37}_{17}Cl$	17	20	17
c.	$^{79}_{35}Br$	35	44	35

d.	$^{41}_{20}\text{Ca}$	20	21	20
e.	$^{40}_{20}\text{Ca}$	20	20	20
f.	$^{238}_{92}\text{U}$	92	146	92
g.	$^{235}_{92}\text{U}$	92	143	92
h.	$^{1}_{1}\text{H}$	1	0	1

23.

	Atom	*Simple Ion*
a.	Mg	Mg^{2+}
b.	F	F^-
c.	Ag	Ag^+
d.	Al	Al^{3+}
e.	O	O^{2-}
f.	Ba	Ba^{2+}
g.	Na	Na^+
h.	Br	Br^-
i.	K	K^+
j.	Ca	Ca^{2+}
k.	S	S^{2-}
l.	Li	Li^+
m.	Cl	Cl^-

24.   a. K^+ (19 protons, 18 electrons)

b. Ca^{2+} (20 protons, 18 electrons)

c. N^{3-} (7 protons, 10 electrons)

d. Br^- (35 protons, 36 electrons)

e. Al^{3+} (13 protons, 10 electrons)

f. Ag^+ (47 protons, 46 electrons)

g. Cl^- (17 protons, 18 electrons)

h. H^+ (1 proton, 0 electrons)

i. H^- (1 proton, 2 electrons)

j. Na^+ (11 protons, 10 electrons)

k. O^{2-} (8 protons, 10 electrons)

l. I^- (53 protons, 54 electrons)

25. K_3N (potassium nitride); KBr (potassium bromide); KCl (potassium chloride); KH (potassium hydride); K_2O (potassium oxide); KI (potassium iodide)

Ca_3N_2 (calcium nitride); $CaBr_2$ (calcium bromide); $CaCl_2$ (calcium chloride); CaH_2 (calcium hydride); CaO (calcium oxide); CaI_2 (calcium iodide)

AlN (aluminum nitride); $AlBr_3$ (aluminum bromide); $AlCl_3$ (aluminum chloride); AlH_3 (aluminum hydride); Al_2O_3 (aluminum oxide); AlI_3 (aluminum iodide)

Ag_3N (silver nitride); AgBr (silver bromide); AgCl (silver chloride); AgH (silver hydride); Ag_2O (silver oxide); AgI (silver iodide)

Realize that most of the hydrogen compounds of the nonmetallic elements which are given as ions in this question are, in fact, covalently bonded compounds (not ionic compounds): H_3N (NH_3, ammonia); HBr (hydrogen bromide); HCl (hydrogen chloride); H_2 (elemental hydrogen); H_2O (water); HI (hydrogen iodide)

Na_3N (sodium nitride); NaBr (sodium bromide); NaCl (sodium chloride); NaH (sodium hydride); Na_2O (sodium oxide); NaI (sodium iodide).

26.   a. $FeCl_3$, iron(III) chloride, ferric chloride

b. Cu_2S, copper(I) sulfide, cuprous sulfide

c. $CoBr_2$, cobalt(II) bromide, cobaltous bromide

d. Fe_2O_3, iron(III) oxide, ferric oxide

e. AuI_3, gold(III) iodide, auric iodide

f. Cr_2S_3, chromium(III) sulfide, chromic sulfide

g. MnO_2, manganese(IV) oxide, manganese dioxide (archaic)

h.   CuO, copper(II) oxide, cupric oxide

i.   NiS, nickel(II) sulfide, nickelous sulfide

27.   a.   NaS is incorrect (Na_2S is correct)

b. K_2S is correct

c. Rb_3N is correct

d. $CaBr_3$ is incorrect ($CaBr_2$ is correct)

e. AlI_3 is correct

f. $NaCl_2$ is incorrect ($NaCl$ is correct)

g. Cs_3Cl_2 is incorrect ($CsCl$ is correct)

28.   a. NH_4^+, ammonium ion   b. SO_3^{2-}, sulfite ion

c. NO_3^-, nitrate ion   d. SO_4^{2-}, sulfate ion

e. NO_2^-, nitrite ion   f. CN^-, cyanide ion

g. OH^-, hydroxide ion   h. ClO_4^-, perchlorate ion

i. ClO^-, hypochlorite ion   j. PO_4^{3-}, phosphate ion

29. Na_2SO_3, $CaSO_3$, $Al_2(SO_3)_3$ $NaNO_3$, $Ca(NO_3)_2$, $Al(NO_3)_3$

Na_2SO_4, $CaSO_4$, $Al_2(SO_4)_3$ $NaNO_2$, $Ca(NO_2)_2$, $Al(NO_2)_3$

$NaCN$, $Ca(CN)_2$, $Al(CN)_3$ $NaOH$, $Ca(OH)_2$, $Al(OH)_3$

$NaClO_4$, $Ca(ClO_4)_2$, $Al(ClO_4)_3$ $NaClO$, $Ca(ClO)_2$, $Al(ClO)_3$

Na_3PO_4, $Ca_3(PO_4)_2$, $AlPO_4$

30.   a. B_2O_3, diboron trioxide

b. NO_2, nitrogen dioxide

c. PCl_5, phosphorus trichloride

d. N_2O_4, dinitrogen tetroxide

e. P_2O_5, diphosphorus pentoxide

f. ICl, iodine monochloride

g. SF_6, sulfur hexafluoride

h. N_2O_3, dinitrogen trioxide

31.   a. K_2S b. NaH

c. $HCl(aq)$ d. N_2O_4

e. $Al(NO_3)_3$ f. $CaSO_4$

g. $H_2S(aq)$ h. $NH_4C_2H_3O_2$

i. $Mg(ClO_4)_2$ j. P_2O_5

k. $HNO_3(aq)$ l. Ag_2SO_3

m. $CuBr_2$ n. $Ba_3(PO_4)_2$

o. $AuCl_3$ p. $MnCl_2$

Chapter 6   Chemical Reactions: An Introduction

1.   The types of evidence for a chemical reaction mentioned in the text are: a change in color, formation of a solid, evolution of a gas, and absorption or evolution of heat. Other bits of evidence that might also be observed include appearance or disappearance of a characteristic odor, or separation of the reaction mixture into layers of visibly different composition.

2.   The fact that there is a decrease in mass is the best evidence for reaction. If mass has been lost, then it is likely that a gaseous substance, which has escaped into the environment has been produced by the heating. The fact that the chalk crumbles into a powder may be taken as secondary evidence that the chalk has been converted into something which does not stick together well.

3.   The fact that the material in the drain, which did *not* dissolve in water, dissolves when the drain cleaner is added, suggests that rather than simple dissolving, the material in the drain has undergone a chemical change which makes it soluble. You may also have noticed that the drain cleaner evolved *heat* when added to the drain: evolution or absorption of heat is also often a sign of a chemical reaction.

4.   Hair certainly is not ordinarily soluble in water, yet when the depilatory is added, the hair dissolves and washes away.

5.   The container of a flashlight battery usually consists of zinc, which is one of the substances involved in the chemical reaction in the battery which generates the electricity. The fact that the zinc decays until the battery leaks is a sign that a chemical reaction has taken place.

6.   The alcohol in the wine is converted by wild yeasts in the air into acetic acid (vinegar). The observation that the odor of the wine has changed to the odor of vinegar indicates that a new substance has been produced. This is a chemical reaction.

7.   reactants, products

8.   atoms

9.   the same

10.   the same

11.   gaseous

12.   water

13. $CaCO_3(s) \rightarrow CaO(s) + CO_2(g)$

14. $C_3H_8(g) + O_2(g) \rightarrow CO_2(g) + H_2O(g)$

15. $H_2(g) + O_2(g) \rightarrow H_2O(g)$

16. $(NH_4)_2CO_3(s) \rightarrow NH_3(g) + CO_2(g) + H_2O(g)$

17. $Ag_2O(s) \rightarrow Ag(s) + O_2(g)$

18. $CO(g) + H_2(g) \rightarrow CH_3OH(l)$

19. $B_2O_3(s) + Mg(s) \rightarrow B(g) + MgO(s)$

20. $Ca(s) + H_2O(l) \rightarrow Ca(OH)_2(s) + H_2(g)$

21. $P_4(s) + Cl_2(g) \rightarrow PCl_3(s)$

22. $Mg(OH)_2(s) + HCl(aq) \rightarrow MgCl_2(aq) + H_2O(l)$

23. $NH_4NO_3(s) \rightarrow N_2O(g) + H_2O(g)$

24. $H_2S(g) + O_2(g) \rightarrow SO_2(g) + H_2O(g)$

25. $C_2H_2(g) + O_2(g) \rightarrow CO_2(g) + H_2O(g)$

26. $Fe_2O_3(s) + CO(g) \rightarrow Fe(l) + CO_2(g)$

27. $BaO(s) + Al(s) \rightarrow Ba(s) + Al_2O_3(s)$

$CaO(s) + Al(s) \rightarrow Ca(s) + Al_2O_3(s)$

$SrO(s) + Al(s) \rightarrow Sr(s) + Al_2O_3(s)$

28. $O_2(g) \rightarrow O_3(g)$

29. $CH_4(g) + Cl_2(g) \rightarrow CCl_4(l) + HCl(g)$

30. $NH_3(g) + HNO_3(aq) \rightarrow NH_4NO_3(s)$

31. $PbS(s) + O_2(g) \rightarrow PbO(s) + SO_2(g)$

$PbO(s) + C(s) \rightarrow Pb(l) + CO_2(g)$

32. $Xe(g) + F_2(g) \rightarrow XeF_4(s)$

33. $NH_4NO_3(s) \rightarrow N_2(g) + O_2(g) + H_2O(g)$

34. $Ag(s) + HNO_3(aq) \rightarrow AgNO_3(aq) + H_2(g)$

35. formula

36. whole numbers

37.
a. $FeCl_3 + KOH \rightarrow Fe(OH)_3 + KCl$

   Balance chlorine: $FeCl_3 + KOH \rightarrow Fe(OH)_3 + \mathbf{3}KCl$

   Balance potassium: $FeCl_3 + \mathbf{3}KOH \rightarrow Fe(OH)_3 + 3KCl$

   Balanced equation: $FeCl_3(aq) + 3KOH(aq) \rightarrow Fe(OH)_3(s) + 3KCl(aq)$

b. $Pb(C_2H_3O_2)_2 + KI \rightarrow PbI_2 + KC_2H_3O_2$

   Balance iodine: $Pb(C_2H_3O_2)_2 + \mathbf{2}KI \rightarrow PbI_2 + KC_2H_3O_2$

   Balance potassium: $Pb(C_2H_3O_2)_2 + 2KI \rightarrow PbI_2 + \mathbf{2}KC_2H_3O_2$

   Balanced equation: $Pb(C_2H_3O_2)_2(aq) + 2KI(aq) \rightarrow PbI_2(s) + \mathbf{2}KC_2H_3O_2(aq)$

c. $P_4O_{10} + H_2O \rightarrow H_3PO_4$

   Balance phosphorus: $P_4O_{10} + H_2O \rightarrow \mathbf{4}H_3PO_4$

   Balance hydrogen: $P_4O_{10} + \mathbf{6}H_2O \rightarrow 4H_3PO_4$

   Balanced equation: $P_4O_{10}(s) + 6H_2O(l) \rightarrow 4H_3PO_4(aq)$

d. $Li_2O + H_2O \rightarrow LiOH$

Balance lithium: $Li_2O + H_2O \rightarrow$ **2**$LiOH$

Balanced equation: $Li_2O(s) + H_2O(l) \rightarrow 2LiOH(aq)$

e. $MnO_2 + C \rightarrow Mn + CO_2$ This equation is already balanced!

f. $Sb + Cl_2 \rightarrow SbCl_3$

This equation is more difficult to balance than it may appear. The problem arises in the fact that there are two Cl atoms on the left side of the equation, whereas there are three Cl atoms on the right side of the equation. To balance the chlorine atoms, we need to know the smallest whole number into which both 2 and 3 divide. This number is 6: we need to adjust the coefficients of Cl_2 and $SbCl_3$ so that there will be 6 chlorine atoms on each side of the equation.

Balance chlorine: $Sb + $**3**$Cl_2 \rightarrow $**2**$SbCl_3$

Balance antimony: **2**$Sb + 3Cl_2 \rightarrow 2SbCl_3$

Balanced equation: **2**$Sb(s) + 3Cl_2(g) \rightarrow 2SbCl_3(s)$

g. $CH_4 + H_2O \rightarrow CO + H_2$

Balance hydrogen: $CH_4 + H_2O \rightarrow CO + $**3**$H_2$

Balanced equation: $CH_4(g) + H_2O(g) \rightarrow CO(g) + 3H_2(g)$

h. $FeS + HCl \rightarrow FeCl_2 + H_2S$

Balance chlorine: $FeS + $**2**$HCl \rightarrow FeCl_2 + H_2S$

Balanced equation: $FeS(s) + 2HCl(aq) \rightarrow FeCl_2(aq) + H_2S(g)$

38.   a. $H_2O_2 \rightarrow H_2O + O_2$

Balance oxygen: **2**$H_2O_2 \rightarrow $**2**$H_2O + O_2$

Balanced equation: **2**$H_2O_2(aq) \rightarrow $**2**$H_2O(l) + O_2(g)$

b. $Ag + H_2S \rightarrow Ag_2S + H_2$

Balance silver: **2**$Ag + H_2S \rightarrow Ag_2S + H_2$

Balanced equation: $2Ag(s) + H_2S(g) \rightarrow Ag_2S(s) + H_2(g)$

c. $FeO + C \rightarrow Fe + CO_2$

Balance oxygen: **2**$FeO + C \rightarrow Fe + CO_2$

Balance iron: $2FeO + C \rightarrow $**2**$Fe + CO_2$

Balanced equation: $2FeO(s) + C(s) \rightarrow 2Fe(l) + CO_2(g)$

d. $Cl_2 + KI \rightarrow KCl + I_2$

Balance chlorine: $Cl_2 + KI \rightarrow $**2**$KCl + I_2$

Balance iodine: $Cl_2 + $**2**$KI \rightarrow 2KCl + I_2$

Balanced equation: $Cl_2(g) + 2KI(aq) \rightarrow 2KCl(aq) + I_2(s)$

e. $Na_2B_4O_7 + H_2SO_4 + H_2O \rightarrow H_3BO_3 + Na_2SO_4$

Balance boron: $Na_2B_4O_7 + H_2SO_4 + H_2O \rightarrow \mathbf{4}H_3BO_3 + Na_2SO_4$

Balance hydrogen: $Na_2B_4O_7 + H_2SO_4 + \mathbf{5}H_2O \rightarrow 4H_3BO_3 + Na_2SO_4$

Balanced equation: $Na_2B_4O_7(s) + H_2SO_4(aq) + 5H_2O(l)$
$\rightarrow 4H_3BO_3(s) + Na_2SO_4(aq)$

f. $CaC_2 + H_2O \rightarrow Ca(OH)_2 + C_2H_2$

Balance oxygen: $CaC_2 + \mathbf{2}H_2O \rightarrow Ca(OH)_2 + C_2H_2$

Balanced equation: $CaC_2(s) + 2H_2O(l) \rightarrow Ca(OH)_2(s) + C_2H_2(g)$

g. $NaCl + H_2SO_4 \rightarrow HCl + Na_2SO_4$

Balance sodium: $\mathbf{2}NaCl + H_2SO_4 \rightarrow HCl + Na_2SO_4$

Balance chlorine: $2NaCl + H_2SO_4 \rightarrow \mathbf{2}HCl + Na_2SO_4$

Balanced equation: $2NaCl(s) + H_2SO_4(l) \rightarrow 2HCl(g) + Na_2SO_4(s)$

h. $SiO_2 + C \rightarrow Si + CO$

Balance oxygen: $SiO_2 + C \rightarrow Si + \mathbf{2}CO$

Balance carbon: $SiO_2 + \mathbf{2}C \rightarrow Si + 2CO$

Balanced equation: $SiO_2(s) + 2C(s) \rightarrow Si(l) + 2CO(g)$

39.   a. $Cl_2 + KI \rightarrow I_2 + KCl$

Balance chlorine: $Cl_2 + KI \rightarrow I_2 + \mathbf{2}KCl$

Balance iodine: $Cl_2 + \mathbf{2}KI \rightarrow I_2 + 2KCl$

Balanced equation: $Cl_2(g) + 2KI(aq) \rightarrow I_2(s) + 2KCl(aq)$

b. $Co + P_4 \rightarrow Co_3P_2$

Balance phosphorus: $Co + P_4 \rightarrow \mathbf{2}Co_3P_2$

Balance cobalt: $\mathbf{6}Co + P_4 \rightarrow 2Co_3P_2$

Balanced equation: $6Co(s) + P_4(s) \rightarrow 2Co_3P_2(s)$

c. $Zn + HNO_3 \rightarrow Zn(NO_3)_2 + H_2$

Balance hydrogen: $Zn + 2HNO_3 \rightarrow Zn(NO_3)_2 + H_2$

Balanced equation: $Zn(s) + 2HNO_3(aq) \rightarrow Zn(NO_3)_2(aq) + H_2(g)$

d. $C_5H_{12} + O_2 \rightarrow CO_2 + H_2O$

Balance carbon: $C_5H_{12} + O_2 \rightarrow \mathbf{5}CO_2 + H_2O$

Balance hydrogen: $C_5H_{12} + O_2 \rightarrow 5CO_2 + \mathbf{6}H_2O$

Balance oxygen: $C_5H_{12} + \mathbf{8}O_2 \rightarrow 5CO_2 + 6H_2O$

Balanced equation: $C_5H_{12}(l) + 8O_2(g) \rightarrow 5CO_2(g) + 6H_2O(g)$

e. $TiBr_4 + H_2 \rightarrow Ti + HBr$

Balance bromine: $TiBr_4 + H_2 \rightarrow Ti + \mathbf{4}HBr$

Balance hydrogen: $TiBr_4$ + **2**H_2 → Ti + $4HBr$

Balanced equation: $TiBr_4(g)$ + $2H_2(g)$ → $Ti(s)$ + $4HBr(g)$

f. SiH_4 + NH_3 → Si_3N_4 + H_2

Balance silicon: **3**SiH_4 + NH_3 → Si_3N_4 + H_2

Balance nitrogen: $3SiH_4$ + **4**NH_3 → Si_3N_4 + H_2

Balance hydrogen: $3SiH_4$ + $4NH_3$ → Si_3N_4 + **12**H_2

Balanced equation: $3SiH_4(g)$ + $4NH_3(g)$ → $Si_3N_4(s)$ + $12H_2(g)$

g. NO + H_2 → N_2 + H_2O

Balance nitrogen: **2**NO + H_2 → N_2 + H_2O

Balance oxygen: $2NO$ + H_2 → N_2 + **2**H_2O

Balance hydrogen: $2NO$ + **2**H_2 → N_2 + $2H_2O$

Balanced equation: $2NO(g)$ + $2H_2(g)$ → $N_2(g)$ + $2H_2O(l)$

h. Cu_2S → Cu + S

Balance copper: Cu_2S → **2**Cu + S

Balanced equation: $Cu_2S(s)$ → $2Cu(s)$ + $S(g)$

40.   a. CaF_2 + H_2SO_4 → $CaSO_4$ + HF

Balance fluorine: CaF_2 + H_2SO_4 → $CaSO_4$ + **2**HF

Balanced equation: $CaF_2(s)$ + $H_2SO_4(l)$ → $CaSO_4(s)$ + $2HF(g)$

b. KBr + H_3PO_4 → K_3PO_4 + HBr

Balance potassium: **3**KBr + H_3PO_4 → K_3PO_4 + HBr

Balance bromine: $3KBr$ + H_3PO_4 → K_3PO_4 + **3**HBr

Balanced equation: $3KBr(s)$ + $H_3PO_4(aq)$ → $K_3PO_4(aq)$ + $3HBr(g)$

c. $TiCl_4$ + Na → $NaCl$ + Ti

Balance chlorine: $TiCl_4$ + Na → **4**$NaCl$ + Ti

Balance sodium: $TiCl_4$ + **4**Na → $4NaCl$ + Ti

Balanced equation: $TiCl_4(l)$ + $4Na(s)$ → $4NaCl(s)$ + $Ti(s)$

d. K_2CO_3 → K_2O + CO_2 This equation is already balanced!

e. KO_2 + H_2O → KOH + O_2

Balance hydrogen: KO_2 + H_2O → **2**KOH + O_2

Balance potassium: **2**KO_2 + H_2O → $2KOH$ + O_2

At this point, we have balanced potassium and hydrogen atoms, but now it becomes difficult to balance oxygen since it occurs in each of the reactants and products. There is no systematic way to balance oxygen at this point (you will learn a special method in a later chapter for oxidation-reduction reactions such as this). We need one more oxygen atom on the right side of the equation to balance it: if we could just have an extra half of an O_2 molecule (that is, $1.5O_2$) the equation would be balanced. That is

Balance using non-integer: $2KO_2 + H_2O \rightarrow 2KOH + \mathbf{1.5}O_2$

Although this equation is balanced, we can't really have 1.5 molecules. If we multiply everything in this equation by 2, however, we will get whole number coefficients.

Balanced equation: $4KO_2(s) + 2H_2O(l) \rightarrow 4KOH(aq) + 3O_2(g)$

f. $Na_2O_2 + H_2O + CO_2 \rightarrow NaHCO_3 + O_2$

Balance sodium: $Na_2O_2 + H_2O + CO_2 \rightarrow \mathbf{2}NaHCO_3 + O_2$

Balance carbon: $Na_2O_2 + H_2O + \mathbf{2}CO_2 \rightarrow 2NaHCO_3 + O_2$

Again we are left with the difficulty of balancing oxygen when it occurs in all the reactants and products. Right now, there are 7 oxygen atoms on the left side of the equation, but there are 8 oxygen atoms on the right side. If we could have just half an O_2 molecule (instead of one entire molecule) things would work out.

Balance using non-integer: $Na_2O_2 + H_2O + 2CO_2 \rightarrow 2NaHCO_3 + \mathbf{0.5}O_2$

Although this equation is balanced, we can't really have half a molecule. If we multiply everything in the equation by 2, however, we'll get whole numbers.

Balanced: $2Na_2O_2(s) + 2H_2O(g) + 4CO_2(g) \rightarrow 4NaHCO_3(s) + O_2(g)$

g. $KNO_2 + C \rightarrow K_2CO_3 + CO + N_2$

Balance nitrogen: $\mathbf{2}KNO_2 + C \rightarrow K_2CO_3 + CO + N_2$

Balance carbon: $2KNO_2 + \mathbf{2}C \rightarrow K_2CO_3 + CO + N_2$

Balanced equation: $2KNO_2(s) + 2C(s) \rightarrow K_2CO_3(s) + CO(g) + N_2(g)$

h. $BaO + Al \rightarrow Ba + Al_2O_3$

Balance aluminum: $BaO + \mathbf{2}Al \rightarrow Ba + Al_2O_3$

Balance oxygen: $\mathbf{3}BaO + 2Al \rightarrow Ba + Al_2O_3$

Balance barium: $3BaO + 2Al \rightarrow \mathbf{3}Ba + Al_2O_3$

Balanced equation: $3BaO(s) + 2Al(s) \rightarrow 3Ba(s) + Al_2O_3(s)$

41.   a. $2Li(s) + Cl_2(g) \rightarrow 2LiCl(s)$

b. $3Ba(s) + N_2(g) \rightarrow Ba_3N_2(s)$

c. $2NaHCO_3(s) \rightarrow Na_2CO_3(s) + CO_2(g) + H_2O(g)$

d. $2Al(s) + 6HCl(aq) \rightarrow 2AlCl_3(aq) + 3H_2(g)$

e. $2NiS(s) + 3O_2(g) \rightarrow 2NiO(s) + 2SO_2(g)$

f. $CaH_2(s) + 2H_2O(l) \rightarrow Ca(OH)_2(s) + 2H_2(g)$

g. $2H_2(g) + CO(g) \rightarrow CH_3OH(l)$

h. $2B_2O_3(s) + 6C(s) \rightarrow B_4C_3(s) + 3CO_2(g)$

42.   a. $SiI_4(s) + 2Mg(s) \rightarrow Si(s) + 2MgI_2(s)$

b. $MnO_2(s) + 2Mg(s) \rightarrow Mn(s) + 2MgO(s)$

c. $8Ba(s) + S_8(s) \rightarrow 8BaS(s)$

d. $4NH_3(g) + 3Cl_2(g) \rightarrow 3NH_4Cl(s) + NCl_3(g)$

e. $8Cu_2S(s) + S_8(s) \rightarrow 16CuS(s)$

f. $2Al(s) + 3H_2SO_4(aq) \rightarrow Al_2(SO_4)_3(aq) + 3H_2(g)$

g. $2NaCl(s) + H_2SO_4(l) \rightarrow 2HCl(g) + Na_2SO_4(s)$

h. $2CO(g) + O_2(g) \rightarrow 2CO_2(g)$

43.   a. $4KO_2(s) + 6H_2O(l) \rightarrow 4KOH(aq) + O_2(g) + 4H_2O_2(aq)$

b. $Fe_2O_3(s) + 6HNO_3(aq) \rightarrow 2Fe(NO_3)_3(aq) + 3H_2O(l)$

c. $4NH_3(g) + 5O_2(g) \rightarrow 4NO(g) + 6H_2O(g)$

d. $PCl_5(l) + 4H_2O(l) \rightarrow H_3PO_4(aq) + 5HCl(g)$

e. $C_2H_5OH(l) + 3O_2(g) \rightarrow 2CO_2(g) + 3H_2O(l)$

f. $2CaO(s) + 5C(s) \rightarrow 2CaC_2(s) + CO_2(g)$

g. $2MoS_2(s) + 7O_2(g) \rightarrow 2MoO_3(s) + 4SO_2(g)$

h. $FeCO_3(s) + H_2CO_3(aq) \rightarrow Fe(HCO_3)_2(aq)$

44.   a. $Ba(NO_3)_2(aq) + Na_2CrO_4(aq) \rightarrow BaCrO_4(s) + 2NaNO_3(aq)$

b. $PbCl_2(aq) + K_2SO_4(aq) \rightarrow PbSO_4(s) + 2KCl(aq)$

c. $C_2H_5OH(l) + 3O_2(g) \rightarrow 2CO_2(g) + 3H_2O(l)$

d. $CaC_2(s) + 2H_2O(l) \rightarrow Ca(OH)_2(s) + C_2H_2(g)$

e. $Sr(s) + 2HNO_3(aq) \rightarrow Sr(NO_3)_2(aq) + H_2(g)$

f. $BaO_2(s) + H_2SO_4(aq) \rightarrow BaSO_4(s) + H_2O_2(aq)$

g. $2AsI_3(s) \rightarrow 2As(s) + 3I_2(s)$

h. $2CuSO_4(aq) + 4KI(s) \rightarrow 2CuI(s) + I_2(s) + 2K_2SO_4(aq)$

45. $NaCl(aq) + NH_3(aq) + CO_2(g) + H_2O(l) \rightarrow NaHCO_3(s) + NH_4Cl(aq)$

46. $Al(s) + O_2(g) \rightarrow Al_2O_3(s)$

47. $KNO_3(s) + C(s) \rightarrow K_2CO_3(s) + CO(g) + N_2(g)$

48. $C_{12}H_{22}O_{11}(aq) + H_2O(l) \rightarrow 4C_2H_5OH(aq) + 4CO_2(g)$

49. $2H_2(g) + CO(g) \rightarrow CH_3OH(l)$

50. $2Al_2O_3(s) + 3C(s) \rightarrow 4Al(s) + 3CO_2(g)$

51. $Fe_3O_4(s) + 4H_2(g) \rightarrow 3Fe(s) + 4H_2O(g)$

$Fe_3O_4(s) + 4CO(g) \rightarrow 3Fe(s) + 4CO_2(g)$

52. $2Li(s) + S(s) \rightarrow Li_2S(s)$

$2Na(s) + S(s) \rightarrow Na_2S(s)$

$2K(s) + S(s) \rightarrow K_2S(s)$

$2Rb(s) + S(s) \rightarrow Rb_2S(s)$

$2Cs(s) + S(s) \rightarrow Cs_2S(s)$

$2Fr(s) + S(s) \rightarrow Fr_2S(s)$

53. $Fe(s) + O_2(g) \rightarrow FeO(s)$
$Fe(s) + O_2(g) \rightarrow Fe_2O_3(s)$

54. $BaO_2(s) + H_2O(l) \rightarrow BaO(s) + H_2O_2(aq)$

55. $4B(s) + 3O_2(g) \rightarrow 2B_2O_3(s)$
$B_2O_3(s) + 3H_2O(l) \rightarrow 2B(OH)_3(s)$

56. $2KClO_3(s) \rightarrow 2KCl(s) + 3O_2(g)$

57. $2H_2O_2(aq) \rightarrow 2H_2O(g) + O_2(g)$

58. $NH_3(g) + HCl(g) \rightarrow NH_4Cl(s)$

59. $CaSiO_3(s) + 6HF(g) \rightarrow CaF_2(aq) + SiF_4(g) + 3H_2O(l)$

60.   The "charring" represents the conversion of the carbohydrates (starch) in the muffin to elemental carbon.

61.   Many over-the-counter antacids contain either carbonate ion (CO_3^{2-}) or hydrogen carbonate ion (HCO_3^-). When either of these encounter stomach acid (primarily HCl), carbon dioxide gas is released.

62. $Fe(s) + S(s) \rightarrow FeS(s)$

63. $Na(s) + Cl_2(g) \rightarrow NaCl(s)$

64. $K_2CrO_4(aq) + BaCl_2(aq) \rightarrow BaCrO_4(s) + 2KCl(aq)$

65. $H_2S(g) + Pb(NO_3)_2(aq) \rightarrow PbS(s) + HNO_3(aq)$

66. $2NaCl(aq) + 2H_2O(l) \rightarrow 2NaOH(aq) + H_2(g) + Cl_2(g)$
$2NaBr(aq) + 2H_2O(l) \rightarrow 2NaOH(aq) + H_2(g) + Br_2(g)$
$2NaI(aq) + 2H_2O(l) \rightarrow 2NaOH(aq) + H_2(g) + I_2(g)$

67. $Mg(s) + O_2(g) \rightarrow MgO(s)$

68. $CaC_2(s) + 2H_2O(l) \rightarrow Ca(OH)_2(s) + C_2H_2(g)$

69. $P_4(s) + O_2(g) \rightarrow P_4O_{10}(g)$

70. $CuO(s) + H_2SO_4(aq) \rightarrow CuSO_4(aq) + H_2O(l)$

71. $PbS(s) + O_2(g) \rightarrow PbO(s) + SO_2(g)$

72. $Na_2SO_3(aq) + S(s) \rightarrow Na_2S_2O_3(aq)$

73.   a. $Cl_2(g) + 2KBr(aq) \rightarrow Br_2(l) + 2KCl(aq)$

b. $2Cr(s) + 3O_2(g) \rightarrow 2Cr_2O_3(s)$

c. $P_4(s) + 6H_2(g) \rightarrow 4PH_3(g)$

d. $2Al(s) + 3H_2SO_4(aq) \rightarrow Al_2(SO_4)_3(aq) + 3H_2(g)$

e. $PCl_3(l) + 3H_2O(l) \rightarrow H_3PO_3(aq) + 3HCl(aq)$

f. $2SO_2(g) + O_2(g) \rightarrow 2SO_3(g)$

g. $C_7H_{16}(l) + 11O_2(g) \rightarrow 7CO_2(g) + 8H_2O(g)$

h. $2C_2H_6(g) + 7O_2(g) \rightarrow 4CO_2(g) + 6H_2O(g)$

74.   a. $ZnCl_2(aq) + Na_2CO_3(aq) \rightarrow ZnCO_3(s) + 2NaCl(aq)$

b. $2Al(s) + 3H_2SO_4(aq) \rightarrow Al_2(SO_4)_3(aq) + 3H_2(g)$

c. $Mn(s) + 2S(s) \rightarrow MnS_2(s)$

d. $C_5H_{12}(l) + 8O_2(g) \rightarrow 5CO_2(g) + 6H_2O(g)$

e. $H_2O(l) + Br_2(l) \rightarrow HBr(aq) + HOBr(aq)$

f. $MnS_2(s) + 3O_2(g) \rightarrow MnO_2(s) + 2SO_2(g)$

g. $PbCl_2(aq) + K_2CrO_4(aq) \rightarrow PbCrO_4(s) + 2KCl(aq)$

h. $2AgNO_3(aq) + H_2SO_4(aq) \rightarrow Ag_2SO_4(s) + 2HNO_3(aq)$

75.   a. $SiCl_4(l) + 2Mg(s) \rightarrow Si(s) + 2MgCl_2(s)$

b. $2NO(g) + Cl_2(g) \rightarrow 2NOCl(g)$

c. $3MnO_2(s) + 4Al(s) \rightarrow 3Mn(s) + 2Al_2O_3(s)$

d. $16Cr(s) + 3S_8(s) \rightarrow 8Cr_2S_3(s)$

e. $4NH_3(g) + 3F_2(g) \rightarrow 3NH_4F(s) + NF_3(g)$

f. $Ag_2S(s) + H_2(g) \rightarrow 2Ag(s) + H_2S(g)$

g. $3O_2(g) \rightarrow 2O_3(g)$

h. $8Na_2SO_3(aq) + S_8(s) \rightarrow 8Na_2S_2O_3(aq)$

76.   a. $Pb(NO_3)_2(aq) + K_2CrO_4(aq) \rightarrow PbCrO_4(s) + 2KNO_3(aq)$

b. $BaCl_2(aq) + Na_2SO_4(aq) \rightarrow BaSO_4(s) + 2NaCl(aq)$

c. $2CH_3OH(l) + 3O_2(g) \rightarrow 2CO_2(g) + 4H_2O(g)$

d. $Na_2CO_3(aq) + S(s) + SO_2(g) \rightarrow CO_2(g) + Na_2S_2O_3(aq)$

e. $Cu(s) + 2H_2SO_4(aq) \rightarrow CuSO_4(aq) + SO_2(g) + 2H_2O(l)$

f. $MnO_2(s) + 4HCl(aq) \rightarrow MnCl_2(aq) + Cl_2(g) + 2H_2O(l)$

g. $As_2O_3(s) + 6KI(aq) + 6HCl(aq) \rightarrow 2AsI_3(s) + 6KCl(aq) + 3H_2O(l)$

h. $2Na_2S_2O_3(aq) + I_2(aq) \rightarrow Na_2S_4O_6(aq) + 2NaI(aq)$

Chapter 7   Reactions in Aqueous Solutions

1.   Water is the most universal of all liquids. Water has a relatively large
      heat capacity, and a relatively large liquid range, which means it can
      absorb the heat liberated by many reactions while still remaining in the
      liquid state. Water is very polar and dissolves well both ionic solutes
      and solutes with which it can hydrogen bond (this is especially
      important to the biochemical reactions of the living cell).

2.   Driving forces are types of *changes* in a system which pull a reaction in
      the *direction of product formation*; driving forces discussed in Chapter
      Seven include: formation of a *solid*, formation of *water*, formation of a
      gas, transfer of electrons.

3.   A *precipitate* is a solid which forms during a chemical reaction between
      aqueous solutions. A chemical reaction which results in the formation of
      a precipitate is called a *precipitation* reaction.

4.   The net charge of a precipitate must be *zero*. The total number of
      positive charges equals the total number of negative charges.

5.   When an electrolyte such as NaCl (sodium chloride) is dissolved in
      water, the resulting solution consists of separate, individual, discrete
      sodium ions (Na^+) and separate, individual, discrete chloride ions
      (Cl^-). There are no identifiable NaCl units in such a solution.

6.   ions

7.   A substance is said to be a strong electrolyte if *each* unit of the
      substance produces separated, distinct ions when the substance is
      dissolved in water. NaCl and KNO_3 are both strong electrolytes.

8.   Chemists know that a solution contains separated ions because such a
      solution will readily allow an electrical current to pass through it.
      The simplest experiment that demonstrates this uses the sort of
      apparatus described in Figure 7.2: if the light bulb glows strongly,
      then the solution contains a strong electrolyte.

9. $NaNO_3$ must be soluble in water.

10.   For most practical purposes, "insoluble" and "slightly" soluble mean the
      same thing. The difference between "insoluble" and "slightly soluble"
      could be crucial if, for example, a substance were highly toxic and were
      found in a water supply.

11.   a.   soluble (Rule 3: most chloride salts are soluble)

      b.   soluble (Rules 1 and 2: most nitrate and ammonium salts are
            soluble)

      c.   insoluble (Rule 5: most hydroxide compounds are insoluble)

      d.   soluble (Rule 4: most sulfate salts are soluble)

      e.   insoluble (Rule 6: most phosphate salts are insoluble)

f.   insoluble (Rule 6: most sulfide salts are insoluble)

g.   insoluble (Rule 3: one of the exceptions for chloride salts)

12.   a.   soluble (Rule 1: most nitrate salts are soluble)

b.   soluble (Rule 2: most potassium salts are soluble)

c.   soluble (Rule 2: most sodium salts are soluble)

d.   insoluble (Rule 5: most hydroxide compounds are insoluble)

e.   insoluble (Rule 3: exception for chloride salts)

f.   soluble (Rule 2: most ammonium salts are soluble)

g.   insoluble (Rule 6: most sulfide salts are insoluble)

h.   insoluble (Rule 4: exception for sulfate salts)

13.   a.   Rule 6: most sulfide salts are only slightly soluble

b.   Rule 5: most hydroxide compounds are only slightly soluble

c.   Rule 6: most carbonate salts are only slightly soluble

d.   Rule 6: most phosphate salts are only slightly soluble

14.   a.   Rule 5: most hydroxides are only slightly soluble

b.   Rule 6: most carbonates are only slightly soluble

c.   Rule 6: most phosphates are only slightly soluble

d.   Rule 3: exception to the rule for chlorides

15.   a. $FePO_4$. Rule 6: most phosphate salts are only slightly soluble.

b. $BaSO_4$. Rule 4: exception to the rule for sulfates

c.   no precipitate is likely: rules 2, 3, and 4

d. $PbCl_2$. Rule 3: $PbCl_2$ is a listed exception.

e.   no precipitate is likely: rules 1, 2, and 3

f.   CuS. Rule 6: most sulfide salts are only slightly soluble.

16.   a. $CaSO_4$. Rule 4: exception to the rule for sulfates

b.   AgI. Rule 3: although the text does not mention it explicitly, as you might expect from your knowledge of the periodic table, bromide and iodide compounds of Ag^+, Pb^{2+}, and Hg_2^{2+} are insoluble

c. $Pb_3(PO_4)_2$. Rule 6: most phosphate salts are only slightly soluble

d. $Fe(OH)_3$. Rule 5: most hydroxides are only slightly soluble

e.   no precipitate is likely: rules 1, 2, and 4

f. $BaCO_3$. Rule 6: most carbonate salts are only slightly soluble.

17.   The precipitates are marked in boldface type.

a.   no precipitate: both $(NH_4)_2SO_4$ and HCl are soluble

$NH_4Cl(aq) + H_2SO_4(aq) \rightarrow$ no precipitate

b.   Rule 6: most carbonate salts are only slightly soluble

$2K_2CO_3(aq) + SnCl_4(aq) \rightarrow \textbf{Sn(CO}_3\textbf{)}_2(s) + 4KCl(aq)$

c.   Rule 3: exception to rule for chlorides

$2NH_4Cl(aq) + Pb(NO_3)_2(aq) \rightarrow \textbf{PbCl}_2(s) + 2NH_4NO_3(aq)$

d.   Rule 5: most hydroxide compounds are only slightly soluble

$CuSO_4(aq) + 2KOH(aq) \rightarrow \textbf{Cu(OH)}_2(s) + K_2SO_4(aq)$

e.   Rule 6: most phosphate salts are only slightly soluble

$Na_3PO_4(aq) + CrCl_3(aq) \rightarrow \textbf{CrPO}_4(s) + 3NaCl(s)$

f.   Rule 6: most sulfide salts are only slightly soluble

$3(NH_4)_2S(aq) + 2FeCl_3(aq) \rightarrow \textbf{Fe}_2\textbf{S}_3(s) + 6NH_4Cl(aq)$

18.   The precipitates are marked in boldface type.

a.   No precipitate: $Ba(NO_3)_2$ and HCl are each soluble.

b.   Rule 6: most sulfide salts are insoluble.

$(NH_4)_2S(aq) + CoCl_2(aq) \rightarrow \textbf{CoS}(s) + 2NH_4Cl(aq)$

c.   Rule 4: lead sulfate is a listed exception.

$H_2SO_4(aq) + Pb(NO_3)_2(aq) \rightarrow \textbf{PbSO}_4(s) + 2HNO_3(aq)$

d.   Rule 6: most carbonate salts are insoluble.

$CaCl_2(aq) + K_2CO_3(aq) \rightarrow \textbf{CaCO}_3(s) + 2KCl(aq)$

e.   No precipitate: $NaNO_3$ and $NH_4C_2H_3O_2$ are each soluble.

f.   Rule 6: most phosphate salts are insoluble

$Na_3PO_4(aq) + CrCl_3(aq) \rightarrow 3NaCl(aq) + \textbf{CrPO}_4(s)$

19.   Hint: when balancing equations involving polyatomic ions, especially in precipitation reactions, balance the polyatomic ions as a *unit*, not in terms of the atoms the polyatomic ions contain (e.g., treat nitrate ion, NO_3^- as a single entity, not as one nitrogen and three oxygen atoms). When finished balancing, however, do be sure to count the individual number of atoms of each type on each side of the equation.

a. $H_2SO_4(aq) + Ba(NO_3)_2(aq) \rightarrow BaSO_4(s) + HNO_3(aq)$

Balance nitrate: $H_2SO_4(aq) + Ba(NO_3)_2(aq) \rightarrow BaSO_4(s) + \textbf{2}HNO_3(aq)$

Balanced equation: $H_2SO_4(aq) + Ba(NO_3)_2(aq) \rightarrow BaSO_4(s) + 2HNO_3(aq)$

b. $Pb(C_2H_3O_2)_2(aq) + HCl(aq) \rightarrow PbCl_2(s) + HC_2H_3O_2(aq)$

Balance acetate: $Pb(C_2H_3O_2)_2(aq) + HCl(aq) \rightarrow PbCl_2(s) + \mathbf{2}HC_2H_3O_2(aq)$

Balance chloride: $Pb(C_2H_3O_2)_2(aq) + \mathbf{2}HCl(aq) \rightarrow PbCl_2(s) + 2HC_2H_3O_2(aq)$

Balanced equation: $Pb(C_2H_3O_2)_2(aq) + 2HCl(aq) \rightarrow PbCl_2(s) + 2HC_2H_3O_2(aq)$

c. $NaOH(aq) + AlCl_3(aq) \rightarrow Al(OH)_3(s) + NaCl(aq)$

Balance hydroxide: $\mathbf{3}NaOH(aq) + AlCl_3(aq) \rightarrow Al(OH)_3(s) + NaCl(aq)$

Balance sodium: $3NaOH(aq) + AlCl_3(aq) \rightarrow Al(OH)_3(s) + \mathbf{3}NaCl(aq)$

Balanced equation: $3NaOH(aq) + AlCl_3(aq) \rightarrow Al(OH)_3(s) + 3NaCl(aq)$

20.   Hint: when balancing equations involving polyatomic ions, especially in precipitation reactions, balance the polyatomic ions as a *unit*, not in terms of the atoms the polyatomic ions contain (e.g., treat nitrate ion, NO_3^- as a single entity, not as one nitrogen and three oxygen atoms). When finished balancing, however, do be sure to count the individual number of atoms of each type on each side of the equation.

a. $AgNO_3(aq) + H_2SO_4(aq) \rightarrow Ag_2SO_4(s) + HNO_3(aq)$

Balance silver: $\mathbf{2}AgNO_3(aq) + H_2SO_4(aq) \rightarrow Ag_2SO_4(s) + HNO_3(aq)$

Balance nitrate: $2AgNO_3(aq) + H_2SO_4(aq) \rightarrow Ag_2SO_4(s) + \mathbf{2}HNO_3(aq)$

Balanced equation: $2AgNO_3(aq) + H_2SO_4(aq) \rightarrow Ag_2SO_4(s) + 2HNO_3(aq)$

b. $Ca(NO_3)_2(aq) + H_2SO_4(aq) \rightarrow CaSO_4(s) + HNO_3(aq)$

Balance nitrate: $Ca(NO_3)_2(aq) + H_2SO_4(aq) \rightarrow CaSO_4(s) + \mathbf{2}HNO_3(aq)$

Balanced equation: $Ca(NO_3)_2(aq) + H_2SO_4(aq) \rightarrow CaSO_4(s) + 2HNO_3(aq)$

c. $Pb(NO_3)_2(aq) + H_2SO_4(aq) \rightarrow PbSO_4(s) + HNO_3(aq)$

Balance nitrate: $Pb(NO_3)_2(aq) + H_2SO_4(aq) \rightarrow PbSO_4(s) + \mathbf{2}HNO_3(aq)$

Balanced equation: $Pb(NO_3)_2(aq) + H_2SO_4(aq) \rightarrow PbSO_4(s) + 2HNO_3(aq)$

21.   The products are determined by having the ions "switch partners." For example, for a general reaction AB + CD →, the possible products are AD and CB if the ions switch partners. If either AD or CB is insoluble, then a precipitation reaction has occurred. In the following reaction, the formula of the precipitate is given in boldface type.

a. $Na_2SO_4(aq) + BaCl_2(aq) \rightarrow \mathbf{BaSO_4}(s) + 2NaCl(aq)$

Rule 4: $BaSO_4$ is a listed exception.

b. $2H_3PO_4(aq) + 3CuSO_4(aq) \rightarrow \mathbf{Cu_3(PO_4)_2}(s) + 3H_2SO_4(aq)$

Rule 6: most phosphate salts are only slightly soluble

c. $2AgNO_3(aq) + NiCl_2(aq) \rightarrow Ni(NO_3)_2(aq) + \mathbf{2AgCl}(s)$

Rule 3: AgCl is a listed exception.

22.   The products are determined by having the ions "switch partners." For example, for a general reaction AB + CD →, the possible products are AD and CB if the ions switch partners. If either AD or CB is insoluble, then a precipitation reaction has occurred. In the following reaction, the formula of the precipitate is given in boldface type.

   a. $(NH_4)_2S(aq)$ + $CoCl_2(aq)$ → **CoS**(s) + $2NH_4Cl(aq)$

          Rule 6: most sulfide salts are only slightly soluble

   b. $FeCl_3(aq)$ + $3NaOH(aq)$ → **Fe(OH)$_3$**(s) + $3NaCl(aq)$

          Rule 5: Most hydroxide compounds are only slightly soluble

   c. $CuSO_4(aq)$ + $Na_2CO_3(aq)$ → **CuCO$_3$**(s) + $Na_2SO_4(aq)$

          Rule 6: most carbonate salts are only slightly soluble.

23.   The *net ionic equation* for a reaction in solution indicates only those components that are directly involved in the reaction. Other ions which may be present to balance charge, but which do not actively participate in the reaction are called *spectator ions* and are not indicated when writing the chemical equation for the reaction.

24.   spectator

25.   The net ionic equation for a reaction indicates *only those ions that form the precipitate*, and does not show the spectator ions present in the solutions mixed. The identity of the precipitate is determined from the Solubility Rules (Table 7.1).

   a. $Ag^+(aq)$ + $Cl^-(aq)$ → $AgCl(s)$

          Rule 3: AgCl is listed as an insoluble exception

   b. $Ba^{2+}(aq)$ + $SO_4^{2-}(aq)$ → $BaSO_4(s)$

          Rule 4: $BaSO_4$ is listed as an insoluble exception

   c. $3Ca^{2+}(aq)$ + $2PO_4^{3-}(aq)$ → $Ca_3(PO_4)_2(s)$

          Rule 6: most phosphate salts are only slightly soluble

   d.   both KF and H_2SO_4 are soluble; no precipitate

   e. $Ca^{2+}(aq)$ + $SO_4^{2-}(aq)$ → $CaSO_4(s)$

          Rule 4: $CaSO_4$ is listed as an insoluble exception

   f. $Pb^{2+}(aq)$ + $2Cl^-(aq)$ → $PbCl_2(s)$

          Rule 3: $PbCl_2$ is listed as an insoluble exception

26.   The net ionic equation for a reaction indicates *only those ions that go to form the precipitate*, and does not show the spectator ions present in the solutes mixed. The identity of the precipitate is determined from the Solubility Rules (Table 7.1).

a. $Ca^{2+}(aq) + SO_4^{2-}(aq) \rightarrow CaSO_4(s)$

Rule 4: exception to rule about sulfate salts.

b. $2Fe^{3+}(aq) + 3CO_3^{2-}(aq) \rightarrow Fe_2(CO_3)_3(s)$

Rule 6: most carbonate salts are only slightly soluble.

c. $Ag^+(aq) + I^-(aq) \rightarrow AgI(s)$

Rule 3: AgI, like AgCl, is insoluble.

d. $3Co^{2+}(aq) + 3PO_4^{3-}(aq) \rightarrow Co_3(PO_4)_2(s)$

Rule 6: most phosphate salts are only slightly soluble.

e. $Hg_2^{2+}(aq) + 2Cl^-(aq) \rightarrow Hg_2Cl_2(s)$

Rule 3: listed exception to the general rule about chlorides.

f. $Pb^{2+}(aq) + 2Br^-(aq) \rightarrow PbBr_2(s)$

Rule 3: like $PbCl_2$, $PbBr_2$ and PbI_2 are also insoluble.

27. $Ag^+(aq) + Cl^-(aq) \rightarrow AgCl(s)$

$Ag^+(aq) + Br^-(aq) \rightarrow AgBr(s)$

$Ag^+(aq) + I^-(aq) \rightarrow AgI(s)$

28. $Ag^+(aq) + Cl^-(aq) \rightarrow AgCl(s)$

$Pb^{2+}(aq) + 2Cl^-(aq) \rightarrow PbCl_2(s)$

$Hg_2^{2+}(aq) + 2Cl^-(aq) \rightarrow Hg_2Cl_2(s)$

29. $Ca^{2+}(aq) + C_2O_4^{2-}(aq) \rightarrow CaC_2O_4(s)$

30. $Co^{2+}(aq) + S^{2-}(aq) \rightarrow CoS(s)$

$2Co^{3+}(aq) + 3S^{2-}(aq) \rightarrow Co_2S_3(s)$

$Fe^{2+}(aq) + S^{2-}(aq) \rightarrow FeS(s)$

$2Fe^{3+}(aq) + 3S^{2-}(aq) \rightarrow Fe_2S_3(s)$

31.   Strong acids are acids that ionize completely in water. The strong acids are also strong electrolytes.

32.   Strong bases are bases that fully produce hydroxide ions when dissolved in water. The strong bases are also strong electrolytes.

33. $H^+(aq) + OH^-(aq) \rightarrow H_2O$; formation of a water molecule

34.   acids: HCl, H_2SO_4, HNO_3, $HClO_4$, HBr
bases: NaOH, KOH, RbOH, CsOH

35.   1000; 1000

36.   salt

37. $HBr(aq) \rightarrow H^+(aq) + Br^-(aq)$ $HClO_4(aq) \rightarrow H^+(aq) + ClO_4^-(aq)$

38. $RbOH(s) \rightarrow Rb^+(aq) + OH^-(aq)$

       $CsOH(s) \rightarrow Cs^+(aq) + OH^-(aq)$

39.   The formulas of the salts are marked in boldface type. Remember that in
       an acid/base reaction in aqueous solution, *water* is always one of the
       products: keeping this in mind makes predicting the formula of the *salt*
       produced easy to do.

       a. $HCl(aq) + RbOH(aq) \rightarrow H_2O(l) + \textbf{RbCl}(aq)$

       b. $HClO_4(aq) + NaOH(aq) \rightarrow H_2O(l) + \textbf{NaClO}_4(aq)$

       c. $HBr(aq) + NaOH(aq) \rightarrow H_2O(l) + \textbf{NaBr}(aq)$

       d. $H_2SO_4(aq) + 2CsOH(aq) \rightarrow 2H_2O(l) + \textbf{Cs}_2\textbf{SO}_4(aq)$

40.   In general, the salt formed in an aqueous acid-base reaction consists of
       the *positive ion of the base* involved in the reaction, combined with the
       negative ion of the acid. The hydrogen ion of the strong acid combines
       with the hydroxide ion of the strong base to produce water, which is the
       other product of the acid-base reactions.

       a. $2NaOH(aq) + H_2SO_4(aq) \rightarrow 2H_2O(l) + Na_2SO_4(aq)$

       b. $RbOH(aq) + HNO_3(aq) \rightarrow H_2O(l) + RbNO_3(aq)$

       c. $KOH(aq) + HClO_4(aq) \rightarrow H_2O(l) + KClO_4(aq)$

       d. $KOH(aq) + HCl(aq) \rightarrow H_2O(l) + KCl(aq)$

41.   An oxidation-reduction reaction is one in which one species loses
       electrons (oxidation) and another species gains electrons (reduction).
       Electrons are transferred from the species being oxidized to the species
       being reduced.

42.   transfer

43.   A driving force, in general, is an event which tends to help to convert
       the reactants of a process into the products. Some elements (metals)
       tend to lose electrons, while other elements (nonmetals) tend to gain
       electrons. A *transfer* of electrons from atoms of a metal to atoms of a
       nonmetal would be favorable, and would result in a chemical reaction. A
       simple example of such a process is the reaction of sodium with
       chlorine: sodium atoms tend to each lose one electron (to form Na^+),
       whereas chlorine atoms tend to each gain one electron (to form Cl^-). The
       reaction of sodium metal with chlorine gas represents a transfer of
       electrons from sodium atoms to chlorine atoms to form sodium chloride.

44.   The metallic element *loses* electrons and the nonmetallic element *gains*
       electrons.

45.   Each potassium atom would lose one electron to become a K^+ ion. Each sulfur atoms would gain two electrons to become a S^{2-} ion. Two potassium atoms would have to be oxidized to provided the two electrons needed to reduce on sulfur atom.

46.   Each nitrogen atom would gain three electrons to become an N^{3-} ion. Each nitrogen atom would gain three electrons, which means that an N_2 molecule would gain six electrons.

47. $FeCl_3$ is made up of Fe^{3+} ions and Cl^- ions. Iron atoms each lose three electrons to become Fe^{3+} ions. Chlorine atoms each gain one electron to become Cl^- ions (so each Cl_2 molecule gains two electrons to become two Cl^- ions).

48. $AlBr_3$ is made up of Al^{3+} ions and Br^- ions. Aluminum atoms each lose three electrons to become Al^{3+} ions. Bromine atoms each gain one electron to become Br^- ions (so each Br_2 molecule gains two electrons to become two Br^- ions).

49.   a. $K + F_2 \rightarrow KF$

        Balance fluorine: $K + F_2 \rightarrow \mathbf{2}KF$

        Balance potassium: $\mathbf{2}K + F_2 \rightarrow 2KF$

        Balanced equation: $2K(s) + F_2(g) \rightarrow 2KF(s)$

        b. $K + O_2 \rightarrow K_2O$

        Balance oxygen: $K + O_2 \rightarrow \mathbf{2}K_2O$

        Balance potassium: $\mathbf{4}K + O_2 \rightarrow 2K_2O$

        Balanced equation: $4K(s) + O_2(g) \rightarrow 2K_2O(s)$

        c. $K + N_2 \rightarrow K_3N$

        Balance nitrogen: $K + N_2 \rightarrow \mathbf{2}K_3N$

        Balance potassium: $\mathbf{6}K + N_2 \rightarrow 2K_3N$

        Balanced equation: $6K(s) + N_2(g) \rightarrow 2K_3N(s)$

        d. $K + C \rightarrow K_4C$

        Balance potassium: $\mathbf{4}K + C \rightarrow K_4C$

        Balanced equation: $4K(s) + C(s) \rightarrow K_4C(s)$

50.   a. $Fe(s) + S(s) \rightarrow Fe_2S_3(s)$

        Balance iron: $\mathbf{2}Fe + S \rightarrow Fe_2S_3$

        Balance sulfur: $2Fe + \mathbf{3}S \rightarrow Fe_2S_3$

        Balanced equation: $2Fe(s) + 3S(s) \rightarrow Fe_2S_3(s)$

b. $Zn(s) + HNO_3(aq) \rightarrow Zn(NO_3)_2(aq) + H_2(g)$

Balance nitrate ions: $Zn + \mathbf{2}HNO_3 \rightarrow Zn(NO_3)_2 + H_2$

Balanced equation: $Zn(s) + 2HNO_3(aq) \rightarrow Zn(NO_3)_2(aq) + H_2(g)$

c. $Sn(s) + O_2(g) \rightarrow SnO(s)$

Balance oxygen: $Sn + O_2 \rightarrow \mathbf{2}SnO$

Balance tin: $\mathbf{2}Sn + O_2 \rightarrow 2SnO$

Balanced equation: $2Sn(s) + O_2(g) \rightarrow 2SnO(s)$

d. $K(s) + H_2(g) \rightarrow KH(s)$

Balance hydrogen: $K + H_2 \rightarrow \mathbf{2}KH$

Balance potassium: $\mathbf{2}K + H_2 \rightarrow 2KH$

Balanced equation: $2K(s) + H_2(g) \rightarrow 2KH(s)$

e. $Cs(s) + H_2O(l) \rightarrow CsOH(aq) + H_2(g)$

Balance hydrogen: $Cs + \mathbf{2}H_2O \rightarrow \mathbf{2}CsOH + H_2$

Balance cesium: $\mathbf{2}Cs + 2H_2O \rightarrow 2CsOH + H_2$

Balanced equation: $2Cs(s) + 2H_2O(l) \rightarrow 2CsOH(aq) + H_2(g)$

51.   A double-displacement reaction has the form AB + CD → AD + CB. In a double-displacement reaction, when two solutions of ionic solutes are mixed, the positive ions of the two solutes exchange anions (this presupposes that some driving force is present which causes a detectable reaction to occur). Two examples are:

$Pb(NO_3)_2(aq) + 2HCl(aq) \rightarrow PbCl_2(s) + 2HNO_3(aq)$

$BaCl_2(aq) + Na_2SO_4(aq) \rightarrow BaSO_4(s) + 2NaCl(aq)$

A single-displacement reaction has the form A + BC → AC + B. In a single displacement reaction, a new element replaces a less active element in its compound. Two examples are:

$Zn(s) + 2HCl(aq) \rightarrow ZnCl_2(aq) + H_2(g)$

$Cu(s) + 2AgNO_3(aq) \rightarrow Cu(NO_3)_2(aq) + 2Ag(s)$

52.   examples of formation of water:

$HCl(aq) + NaOH(aq) \rightarrow H_2O(l) + NaCl(aq)$

$H_2SO_4(aq) + 2KOH(aq) \rightarrow 2H_2O(l) + K_2SO_4(aq)$

examples of formation of a gaseous product

$Mg(s) + 2HCl(aq) \rightarrow MgCl_2(aq) + H_2(g)$

$2KClO_3(s) \rightarrow 2KCl(s) + 3O_2(g)$

53.   For each reaction, the type of reaction is first identified, followed by some of the reasoning that leads to this choice (there may be more than one way in which you can recognize a particular type of reaction).

   a.   precipitation (from Table 7.1, $BaSO_4$ is insoluble).

   b.   oxidation-reduction (Zn changes from the elemental to the combined state; hydrogen changes from the combined to the elemental state).

   c.   precipitation (from Table 7.1, AgCl is insoluble).

   d.   acid-base (HCl is an acid; KOH is a base; water and a salt are produced).

   e.   oxidation-reduction (Cu changes from the combined to the elemental state; Zn changes from the elemental to the combined state).

   f.   acid-base (the $H_2PO_4^-$ ion behaves as an acid; NaOH behaves as a base; a salt and water are produced).

   g.   precipitation (From Table 7.1, $CaSO_4$ is insoluble); acid-base [$Ca(OH)_2$ is a base; H_2SO_4 is an acid; a salt and water are produced].

   h.   oxidation-reduction (Mg changes from the elemental to the combined state; Zn changes from the combined to the elemental state).

   i.   precipitation (From Table 7.1, $BaSO_4$ is insoluble).

54.   For each reaction, the type of reaction is first identified, followed by some of the reasoning that leads to this choice (there may be more than one way in which you can recognize a particular type of reaction).

   a.   oxidation-reduction (oxygen changes from the combined state to the elemental state)

   b.   oxidation-reduction (copper changes from the elemental to the combined state; hydrogen changes from the combined to the elemental state)

   c.   acid-base (H_2SO_4 is a strong acid and NaOH is a strong base; water and a salt are formed)

   d.   acid-base, precipitation (H_2SO_4 is a strong acid, and $Ba(OH)_2$ is a base; water and a salt are formed; an insoluble product forms)

   e.   precipitation (from the Solubility Rules of Table 7.1, AgCl is only slightly soluble)

   f.   precipitation (from the Solubility Rules of Table 7.1, $Cu(OH)_2$ is only slightly soluble)

g.   oxidation-reduction (chlorine and fluorine change from the elemental to the combined state)

h.   oxidation-reduction (oxygen changes from the elemental to the combined state)

i.   acid-base (HNO_3 is a strong acid and $Ca(OH)_2$ is a strong base; a salt and water are formed)

55.   combustion

56.   oxidation-reduction

57.   A synthesis reaction represents the production of a given compound from simpler substances (either elements or simpler compounds). For example,

$$O_2(g) + 2F_2(g) \rightarrow 2OF_2(g)$$

represents a simple synthesis reaction. Synthesis reactions may often (but not necessarily always) also be classified in other ways. For example, the reaction

$$C(s) + O_2(g) \rightarrow CO_2(g)$$

could also be classified as an oxidation-reduction reaction, or as a combustion reaction (a special sub-classification of oxidation-reduction reaction that produces a flame). As another example, the reaction

$$2Fe(s) + 3Cl_2(g) \rightarrow 2FeCl_3(s)$$

is a synthesis reaction that also is an oxidation-reduction reaction.

58.   A decomposition reaction is one in which a given compound is broken down into simpler compounds or constituent elements. The reactions

$$CaCO_3(s) \rightarrow CaO(s) + CO_2(g)$$

$$2HgO(s) \rightarrow 2Hg(l) + O_2(g)$$

both represent decomposition reactions. Such reactions often (but not necessarily always) may be classified in other ways. For example, the reaction of $HgO(s)$ is also an oxidation-reduction reaction.

59.   Compounds like those in this problem, containing only carbon and hydrogen, are called *hydrocarbons*. When a hydrocarbon is reacted with oxygen (O_2), the hydrocarbon is almost always converted to carbon dioxide and water vapor. Since water molecules contain an odd number of oxygen atoms, whereas O_2 contains an even number of oxygen atoms, it is often difficult to balance such equations. For this reason, it is simpler to balance the equation using fractional coefficients if necessary, and then to multiply by a factor that will give whole number coefficients for the final balanced equation.

a. $C_2H_6 + O_2 \rightarrow CO_2 + H_2O$

Balance carbon: $C_2H_6 + O_2 \rightarrow \mathbf{2}CO_2 + H_2O$

Balance hydrogen: $C_2H_6 + O_2 \rightarrow 2CO_2 + \mathbf{3}H_2O$

Balance oxygen: $C_2H_6 + \mathbf{(7/2)}O_2 \rightarrow 2CO_2 + 3H_2O$

Balanced equation: $2C_2H_6(g) + 7O_2(g) \rightarrow 4CO_2(g) + 6H_2O(g)$

b. $C_4H_{10} + O_2 \rightarrow CO_2 + H_2O$

Balance carbon: $C_4H_{10} + O_2 \rightarrow \mathbf{4}CO_2 + H_2O$

Balance hydrogen: $C_4H_{10} + O_2 \rightarrow 4CO_2 + \mathbf{5}H_2O$

Balance oxygen: $C_4H_{10} + \mathbf{(13/2)}O_2 \rightarrow 4CO_2 + 5H_2O$

Balanced equation: $2C_4H_{10}(g) + 13O_2(g) \rightarrow 8CO_2(g) + 10H_2O(g)$

c. $C_6H_{14} + O_2 \rightarrow CO_2 + H_2O$

Balance carbon: $C_6H_{14} + O_2 \rightarrow \mathbf{6}CO_2 + H_2O$

Balance hydrogen: $C_6H_{14} + O_2 \rightarrow 6CO_2 + \mathbf{7}H_2O$

Balance oxygen: $C_6H_{14} + \mathbf{(19/2)}O_2 \rightarrow 6CO_2 + 7H_2O$

Balanced equation: $2C_6H_{14}(g) + 19O_2(g) \rightarrow 12CO_2(g) + 14H_2O(g)$

60.   Compounds like those in parts b and c of this problem, containing only carbon and hydrogen, are called *hydrocarbons*. When a hydrocarbon is reacted with oxygen (O_2), the hydrocarbon is almost always converted to carbon dioxide and water vapor. Since water molecules contain an odd number of oxygen atoms, whereas O_2 contains an even number of oxygen atoms, it is often difficult to balance such equations. For this reason, it is simpler to balance the equation using fractional coefficients if necessary, and then to multiply by a factor that will give whole number coefficients for the final balanced equation.

a. $C_2H_5OH(l) + O_2(g) \rightarrow CO_2(g) + H_2O(g)$

Balance carbon: $C_2H_5OH(l) + O_2(g) \rightarrow \mathbf{2}CO_2(g) + H_2O(g)$

Balance hydrogen: $C_2H_5OH(l) + O_2(g) \rightarrow 2CO_2(g) + \mathbf{3}H_2O(g)$

Balance oxygen: $C_2H_5OH(l) + \mathbf{3}O_2(g) \rightarrow 2CO_2(g) + 3H_2O(g)$

Balanced equation: $C_2H_5OH(l) + 3O_2(g) \rightarrow 2CO_2(g) + 3H_2O(g)$

b. $C_6H_{14}(l) + O_2(g) \rightarrow CO_2(g) + H_2O(g)$

Balance carbon: $C_6H_{14}(l) + O_2(g) \rightarrow \mathbf{6}CO_2(g) + H_2O(g)$

Balance hydrogen: $C_6H_{14}(l) + O_2(g) \rightarrow 6CO_2(g) + \mathbf{7}H_2O(g)$

Balance oxygen: $C_6H_{14}(l) + \mathbf{(19/2)}O_2(g) \rightarrow 6CO_2(g) + 7H_2O(g)$

Balanced equation: $2C_6H_{14}(l) + 19O_2(g) \rightarrow 12CO_2(g) + 14H_2O(g)$

c. $C_6H_{12}(l) + O_2(g) \rightarrow CO_2(g) + H_2O(g)$

Balance carbon: $C_6H_{12}(l) + O_2(g) \rightarrow \textbf{6}CO_2(g) + H_2O(g)$

Balance hydrogen: $C_6H_{12}(l) + O_2(g) \rightarrow 6CO_2(g) + \textbf{6}H_2O(g)$

Balanced equation: $C_6H_{12}(l) + 9O_2(g) \rightarrow 6CO_2(g) + 6H_2O(g)$

61.   a. $C_2H_2 + O_2 \rightarrow CO_2 + H_2O$

Balance carbon: $C_2H_2 + O_2 \rightarrow \textbf{2}CO_2 + H_2O$

Balance hydrogen: $C_2H_2 + O_2 \rightarrow 2CO_2 + H_2O$

Balance oxygen: $C_2H_2 + \textbf{(5/2)}O_2 \rightarrow 2CO_2 + H_2O$

Balanced equation: $2C_2H_2(g) + 5O_2(g) \rightarrow 4CO_2(g) + \textbf{2}H_2O(g)$

b. $C_3H_8 + O_2 \rightarrow CO_2 + H_2O$

Balance carbon: $C_3H_8 + O_2 \rightarrow \textbf{3}CO_2 + H_2O$

Balance hydrogen: $C_3H_8 + O_2 \rightarrow 3CO_2 + \textbf{4}H_2O$

Balance oxygen: $C_3H_8 + \textbf{5}O_2 \rightarrow 3CO_2 + 4H_2O$

Balanced equation: $C_3H_8(g) + 5O_2(g) \rightarrow 3CO_2(g) + 4H_2O(g)$

c. $C_2H_4O_2 + O_2 \rightarrow CO_2 + H_2O$

Balance carbon: $C_2H_4O_2 + O_2 \rightarrow \textbf{2}CO_2 + H_2O$

Balance hydrogen: $C_2H_4O_2 + O_2 \rightarrow 2CO_2 + \textbf{2}H_2O$

Balance oxygen: $C_2H_4O_2 + \textbf{2}O_2 \rightarrow 2CO_2 + 2H_2O$

Balanced equation: $C_2H_4O_2(l) + 2O_2(g) \rightarrow 2CO_2(g) + 2H_2O(g)$

62.   a. $C_2H_6(g) + O_2(g) \rightarrow CO_2(g) + H_2O(g)$

Balance carbon: $C_2H_6(g) + O_2(g) \rightarrow \textbf{2}CO_2(g) + H_2O(g)$

Balance hydrogen: $C_2H_6(g) + O_2(g) \rightarrow 2CO_2(g) + \textbf{3}H_2O(g)$

Balance oxygen: $C_2H_6(g) + \textbf{(7/2)}O_2(g) \rightarrow 2CO_2(g) + 3H_2O(g)$

Balanced equation: $2C_2H_6(g) + 7O_2(g) \rightarrow 4CO_2(g) + 6H_2O(g)$

b. $C_2H_6O(l) + O_2(g) \rightarrow CO_2(g) + H_2O(g)$

Balance carbon: $C_2H_6O(l) + O_2(g) \rightarrow \textbf{2}CO_2(g) + H_2O(g)$

Balance hydrogen: $C_2H_6O(l) + O_2(g) \rightarrow 2CO_2(g) + \textbf{3}H_2O(g)$

Balance oxygen: $C_2H_6O(l) + \textbf{3}O_2(g) \rightarrow 2CO_2(g) + 3H_2O(g)$

Balanced equation: $C_2H_6O(l) + 3O_2(g) \rightarrow 2CO_2(g) + 3H_2O(g)$

c. $C_2H_6O_2(l) + O_2(g) \rightarrow CO_2(g) + H_2O(g)$

Balance carbon: $C_2H_6O_2(l) + O_2(g) \rightarrow \textbf{2}CO_2(g) + H_2O(g)$

Balance hydrogen: $C_2H_6O_2(l) + O_2(g) \rightarrow 2CO_2(g) + \textbf{3}H_2O(g)$

Balance oxygen: $C_2H_6O_2(l) + (5/2)O_2(g) \rightarrow 2CO_2(g) + 3H_2O(g)$

Balanced equation: $2C_2H_6O_2(l) + 5O_2(g) \rightarrow 4CO_2(g) + 6H_2O(g)$

63. a. $Ni(s) + 4CO(g) \rightarrow Ni(CO)_4(g)$

  b. $2Al(s) + 3S(s) \rightarrow Al_2S_3(s)$

  c. $Na_2SO_3(aq) + S(s) \rightarrow Na_2S_2O_3(aq)$

  d. $2Fe(s) + 3Br_2(l) \rightarrow 2FeBr_3(s)$

  e. $2Na(s) + O_2(g) \rightarrow Na_2O_2(s)$

64. a. $2Co(s) + 3S(s) \rightarrow Co_2S_3(s)$

  b. $2NO(g) + O_2(g) \rightarrow 2NO_2(g)$

  c. $FeO(s) + CO_2(g) \rightarrow FeCO_3(s)$

  d. $2Al(s) + 3F_2(g) \rightarrow 2AlF_3(s)$

  e. $2NH_3(g) + H_2CO_3(aq) \rightarrow (NH_4)_2CO_3(s)$

65. a. $CaSO_4(s) \rightarrow CaO(s) + SO_3(g)$

  b. $Li_2CO_3(s) \rightarrow Li_2O(s) + CO_2(g)$

  c. $2LiHCO_3(s) \rightarrow Li_2CO_3(s) + H_2O(g) + CO_2(g)$

  d. $C_6H_6(l) \rightarrow 6C(s) + 3H_2(g)$

  e. $4PBr_3(l) \rightarrow P_4(s) + 6Br_2(l)$

66. a. $2NI_3(s) \rightarrow N_2(g) + 3I_2(s)$

  b. $BaCO_3(s) \rightarrow BaO(s) + CO_2(g)$

  c. $C_6H_{12}O_6(s) \rightarrow 6C(s) + 6H_2O(g)$

  d. $Cu(NH_3)_4SO_4(s) \rightarrow CuSO_4(s) + 4NH_3(g)$

  e. $3NaN_3(s) \rightarrow Na_3N(s) + 4N_2(g)$

67. A *molecular equation* uses the normal, uncharged formulas for the compounds involved. The *complete ionic equation* shows the compounds involved broken up into their respective ions (*all* ions present are shown). The *net ionic equation* shows only those ions which combine to form a precipitate, a gas, or a nonionic product such as water. The net ionic equation shows most clearly the species that are combining with each other.

68. In several cases, the given ion may be precipitated by *many* reactants. The following are only three of the possible examples.

  a.   chloride ion would precipitate when treated with solutions containing silver ion, lead(II) ion, or mercury(I) ion.

  $Ag^+(aq) + Cl^-(aq) \rightarrow AgCl(s)$

$$Pb^{2+}(aq) + 2Cl^-(aq) \rightarrow PbCl_2(s)$$

$$Hg_2^{2+}(aq) + 2Cl^-(aq) \rightarrow Hg_2Cl_2(s)$$

b.   calcium ion would precipitate when treated with solutions containing sulfate ion, carbonate ion, and phosphate ion.

$$Ca^{2+}(aq) + SO_4^{2-}(aq) \rightarrow CaSO_4(s)$$

$$Ca^{2+}(aq) + CO_3^{2-}(aq) \rightarrow CaCO_3(s)$$

$$3Ca^{2+}(aq) + 2PO_4^{3-}(aq) \rightarrow Ca_3(PO_4)_2(s)$$

c.   iron(III) ion would precipitate when treated with solutions containing hydroxide, sulfide, or carbonate ions.

$$Fe^{3+}(aq) + 3OH^-(aq) \rightarrow Fe(OH)_3(s)$$

$$2Fe^{3+}(aq) + 3S^{2-}(aq) \rightarrow Fe_2S_3(s)$$

$$2Fe^{3+}(aq) + 3CO_3^{2-}(aq) \rightarrow Fe_2(CO_3)_3(s)$$

d.   sulfate ion would precipitate when treated with solutions containing barium ion, calcium ion, or lead(II) ion.

$$Ba^{2+}(aq) + SO_4^{2-}(aq) \rightarrow BaSO_4(s)$$

$$Ca^{2+}(aq) + SO_4^{2-}(aq) \rightarrow CaSO_4(s)$$

$$Pb^{2+}(aq) + SO_4^{2-}(aq) \rightarrow PbSO_4(s)$$

e.   mercury(I) ion would precipitate when treated with solutions containing chloride ion, sulfide ion, or carbonate ion.

$$Hg_2^{2+}(aq) + 2Cl^-(aq) \rightarrow Hg_2Cl_2(s)$$

$$Hg_2^{2+}(aq) + S^{2-}(aq) \rightarrow Hg_2S(s)$$

$$Hg_2^{2+}(aq) + CO_3^{2-}(aq) \rightarrow Hg_2CO_3(s)$$

f.   silver ion would precipitate when treated with solutions containing chloride ion, sulfide ion, or carbonate ion.

$$Ag^+(aq) + Cl^-(aq) \rightarrow AgCl(s)$$

$$2Ag^+(aq) + S^{2-}(aq) \rightarrow Ag_2S(s)$$

$$2Ag^+(aq) + CO_3^{2-}(aq) \rightarrow Ag_2CO_3(s)$$

69.   a. $2Fe^{3+}(aq) + 3CO_3^{2-}(aq) \rightarrow Fe_2(CO_3)_3(s)$

b. $Hg_2^{2+}(aq) + 2\ Cl^-(aq) \rightarrow Hg_2Cl_2(s)$

c.   no precipitate

d. $Cu^{2+}(aq) + S^{2-}(aq) \rightarrow CuS(s)$

e. $Pb^{2+}(aq) + 2Cl^-(aq) \rightarrow PbCl_2(s)$

f. $Ca^{2+}(aq) + CO_3^{2-}(aq) \rightarrow CaCO_3(s)$

g. $Au^{3+}(aq) + 3OH^-(aq) \rightarrow Au(OH)_3(s)$

70.   The formulas of the salts are indicated in boldface type.

a. $HNO_3(aq) + KOH(aq) \rightarrow H_2O(l) + \mathbf{KNO_3}(aq)$

b. $H_2SO_4(aq) + Ba(OH)_2(aq) \rightarrow 2H_2O(l) + \mathbf{BaSO_4}(s)$

c. $HClO_4(aq) + NaOH(aq) \rightarrow H_2O(l) + \mathbf{NaClO_4}(aq)$

d. $2HCl(aq) + Ca(OH)_2(aq) \rightarrow 2H_2O(l) + \mathbf{CaCl_2}(aq)$

71.   For each cation, the precipitates that form with the anions listed in the right-hand column are given below. If no formula is listed, it should be assumed that that anion does *not* form a precipitate with the particular cation. See Table 7.1 for the Solubility Rules.

Ag^+ ion: $AgCl$, Ag_2CO_3, $AgOH$, Ag_3PO_4, Ag_2S, Ag_2SO_4

Ba^{2+} ion: $BaCO_3$, $Ba(OH)_2$, $Ba_3(PO_4)_2$, BaS, $BaSO_4$

Ca^{2+} ion: $CaCO_3$, $Ca(OH)_2$, $Ca_3(PO_4)_2$, CaS, $CaSO_4$

Fe^{3+} ion: $Fe_2(CO_3)_3$, $Fe(OH)_3$, $FePO_4$, Fe_2S_3

Hg_2^{2+} ion: Hg_2Cl_2, Hg_2CO_3, $Hg_2(OH)_2$, $(Hg_2)_3(PO_4)_2$, Hg_2S

Na^+ ion: all common salts are soluble

Ni^{2+} ion: $NiCO_3$, $Ni(OH)_2$, $Ni_3(PO_4)_2$, NiS

Pb^{2+} ion: $PbCl_2$, $PbCO_3$, $Pb(OH)_2$, $Pb_3(PO_4)_2$, PbS, $PbSO_4$

72.   a.   soluble (Rule 2: most potassium salts are soluble)

b.   soluble (Rule 2: most ammonium salts are soluble)

c.   insoluble (Rule 6: most carbonate salts are only slightly soluble)

d.   insoluble (Rule 6: most phosphate salts are only slightly soluble)

e.   soluble (Rule 2: most sodium salts are soluble)

f.   insoluble (Rule 6: most carbonate salts are only slightly soluble)

g.   soluble (Rule 3: most chloride salts are soluble)

73.   a.   iron(III) hydroxide, $Fe(OH)_3$. Rule 5: most hydroxide salts are only slightly soluble

b.   nickel(II) sulfide, NiS. Rule 6: most sulfide salts are only slightly soluble

c.   silver chloride, AgCl. Rule 3: Although most chloride salts are soluble, AgCl is a listed exception

d.   barium carbonate, $BaCO_3$. Rule 6: most carbonate salts are only slightly soluble

e.   mercury(I) chloride or mercurous chloride, Hg_2Cl_2. Rule 3: Although most chloride salts are soluble, Hg_2Cl_2 is a listed exception

f.   barium sulfate, $BaSO_4$. Rule 4: Although most sulfate salts are soluble, $BaSO_4$ is a listed exception

74.   The precipitates are marked in boldface type.

a.   Rule 3: AgCl is listed as an exception

$$AgNO_3(aq) + HCl(aq) \rightarrow \textbf{AgCl}(s) + HNO_3(aq)$$

b.   Rule 6: most cabonate salts are only slightly soluble

$$CuSO_4(aq) + (NH_4)_2CO_3(aq) \rightarrow \textbf{CuCO}_3(s) + (NH_4)_2SO_4(aq)$$

c.   Rule 6: most carbonate salts are only slightly soluble.

$$FeSO_4(aq) + K_2CO_3(aq) \rightarrow \textbf{FeCO}_3(s) + K_2SO_4(aq)$$

d.   no reaction

e.   Rule 6: most carbonate salts are only slightly soluble

$$Pb(NO_3)_2(aq) + Li_2CO_3(aq) \rightarrow \textbf{PbCO}_3(s) + 2LiNO_3(aq)$$

f.   Rule 5: most hydroxide compounds are only slightly soluble

$$SnCl_4(aq) + 4NaOH(aq) \rightarrow \textbf{Sn(OH)}_4(s) + 4NaCl(aq)$$

75.   a.   Rule 3: $Ag^+(aq) + Cl^-(aq) \rightarrow AgCl(s)$

b.   Rule 6: $3Ca^{2+}(aq) + 2PO_4^{3-}(aq) \rightarrow Ca_3(PO_4)_2(s)$

c.   Rule 3: $Pb^{2+}(aq) + 2Cl^-(aq) \rightarrow PbCl_2(s)$

d.   Rule 6: $Fe^{3+}(aq) + 3OH^-(aq) \rightarrow Fe(OH)_3(s)$

76. $Fe^{2+}(aq) + S^{2-}(aq) \rightarrow FeS(s)$

$2Cr^{3+}(aq) + 3S^{2-}(aq) \rightarrow Cr_2S_3(s)$

$Ni^{2+}(aq) + S^{2-}(aq) \rightarrow NiS(s)$

77.   a.   potassium hydroxide and perchloric acid
b.   cesium hydroxide and nitric acid
c.   potassium hydroxide and hydrochloric acid
d.   sodium hydroxide and sulfuric acid

78.   These anions tend to form insoluble precipitates with *many* metal ions. The following are illustrative for cobalt(II) chloride, tin(II) chloride, and copper(II) nitrate reacting with the sodium salts of the given anions.

a. $CoCl_2(aq) + Na_2S(aq) \rightarrow CoS(s) + 2NaCl(aq)$

$SnCl_2(aq) + Na_2S(aq) \rightarrow SnS(s) + 2NaCl(aq)$

$Cu(NO_3)_2(aq) + Na_2S(aq) \rightarrow CuS(s) + 2NaNO_3(aq)$

b. $CoCl_2(aq) + Na_2CO_3(aq) \rightarrow CoCO_3(s) + 2NaCl(aq)$

$SnCl_2(aq) + Na_2CO_3(aq) \rightarrow SnCO_3(s) + 2NaCl(aq)$

$Cu(NO_3)_2(aq) + Na_2CO_3(aq) \rightarrow CuCO_3(s) + 2NaNO_3(aq)$

c. $CoCl_2(aq) + 2NaOH(aq) \rightarrow Co(OH)_2(s) + 2NaCl(aq)$

$SnCl_2(aq) + 2NaOH(aq) \rightarrow Sn(OH)_2(s) + 2NaCl(aq)$

$Cu(NO_3)_2(aq) + 2NaOH(aq) \rightarrow Cu(OH)_2(s) + 2NaNO_3(aq)$

d. $3CoCl_2(aq) + 2Na_3PO_4(aq) \rightarrow Co_3(PO_4)_2(s) + 6NaCl(aq)$

$3SnCl_2(aq) + 2Na_3PO_4(aq) \rightarrow Sn_3(PO_4)_2(s) + 6NaCl(aq)$

$3Cu(NO_3)_2(aq) + 2Na_3PO_4(aq) \rightarrow Cu_3(PO_4)_2(s) + 6NaNO_3(aq)$

79. Fe_2S_3 is made up of Fe^{3+} and S^{2-} ions. Iron atoms each lose three electrons to become Fe^{3+} ions. Sulfur atoms each gain two electrons to become S^{2-} ions.

80.   a. $Na + O_2 \rightarrow Na_2O_2$

Balance sodium: $\mathbf{2}Na + O_2 \rightarrow Na_2O_2$

Balanced equation: $2Na(s) + O_2(g) \rightarrow Na_2O_2(s)$

b. $Fe(s) + H_2SO_4(aq) \rightarrow FeSO_4(aq) + H_2(g)$

Equation is already balanced!

c. $Al_2O_3 \rightarrow Al + O_2$

Balance oxygen: $\mathbf{2}Al_2O_3 \rightarrow Al + \mathbf{3}O_2$

Balance aluminum: $2Al_2O_3 \rightarrow \mathbf{4}Al + 3O_2$

Balanced equation: $2Al_2O_3(s) \rightarrow 4Al(s) + 3O_2(g)$

d. $Fe + Br_2 \rightarrow FeBr_3$

Balance bromine: $Fe + \mathbf{3}Br_2 \rightarrow \mathbf{2}FeBr_3$

Balance iron: $\mathbf{2}Fe + 3Br_2 \rightarrow 2FeBr_3$

Balanced equation: $2Fe(s) + 3Br_2(l) \rightarrow 2FeBr_3(s)$

e. $Zn + HNO_3 \rightarrow Zn(NO_3)_2 + H_2$

Balance nitrate ions: $Zn + \mathbf{2}HNO_3 \rightarrow Zn(NO_3)_2 + H_2$

Balanced equation: $Zn(s) + 2HNO_3(aq) \rightarrow$

$$Zn(NO_3)_2(aq) + H_2(g)$$

81.   For each reaction, the type of reaction is first identified, followed by some of the reasoning that leads to this choice (there may be more than one way in which you can recognize a particular type of reaction).

a. oxidation-reduction (Fe changes from the elemental state to the combined state in $Fe_3(SO_4)_2$; hydrogen changes from the combined to the elemental state).

b. acid-base ($HClO_4$ is a strong acid and RbOH is a strong base; water and a salt are produced).

c. oxidation-reduction (both Ca and O_2 change from the elemental to the combined state).

d. acid-base (H_2SO_4 is a strong acid and NaOH is a strong base; water and a salt are produced).

e. precipitation (from the Solubility Rules of Table 7.1, $PbCO_3$ is insoluble).

f. precipitation (from the Solubility Rules of Table 7.1, $CaSO_4$ is insoluble).

g. acid-base (HNO_3 is a strong acid and KOH is a strong base; water and a salt are produced).

h. precipitation (from the Solubility Rules of Table 7.1, NiS is insoluble).

i. oxidation-reduction (both Ni and Cl_2 change from the elemental to the combined state).

82. a. $2C_4H_{10}(l) + 13O_2(g) \rightarrow 8CO_2(g) + 10H_2O(g)$

b. $C_4H_{10}O(l) + 6O_2(g) \rightarrow 4CO_2(g) + 5H_2O(g)$

c. $2C_4H_{10}O_2(l) + 11O_2(g) \rightarrow 8CO_2(g) + 10H_2O(g)$

83. a. $4FeO(s) + O_2(g) \rightarrow 2Fe_2O_3(s)$

b. $2CO(g) + O_2(g) \rightarrow 2CO_2(g)$

c. $H_2(g) + Cl_2(g) \rightarrow 2HCl(g)$

d. $16K(s) + S_8(s) \rightarrow 8K_2S(s)$

e. $6Na(s) + N_2(g) \rightarrow 2Na_3N(s)$

84. a. $2NaHCO_3(s) \rightarrow Na_2CO_3(s) + H_2O(g) + CO_2(g)$

b. $2NaClO_3(s) \rightarrow 2NaCl(s) + 3O_2(g)$

c. $2HgO(s) \rightarrow 2Hg(l) + O_2(g)$

d. $C_{12}H_{22}O_{11}(s) \rightarrow 12C(s) + 11H_2O(g)$

e. $2H_2O_2(l) \rightarrow 2H_2O(l) + O_2(g)$

85. For simplicity, the physical states of the substances are omitted.

$2Ba + O_2 \rightarrow 2BaO$ $Ba + S \rightarrow BaS$

$Ba + Cl_2 \rightarrow BaCl_2$ $3Ba + N_2 \rightarrow Ba_3N_2$

$Ba + Br_2 \rightarrow BaBr_2$

$2K + S \rightarrow K_2S$

$6K + N_2 \rightarrow 2K_3N$

$2Mg + O_2 \rightarrow 2MgO$

$Mg + Cl_2 \rightarrow MgCl_2$

$Mg + Br_2 \rightarrow MgBr_2$

$2Rb + S \rightarrow Rb_2S$

$6Rb + N_2 \rightarrow 2Rb_3N$

$2Ca + O_2 \rightarrow 2CaO$

$Ca + Cl_2 \rightarrow CaCl_2$

$Ca + Br_2 \rightarrow CaBr_2$

$2Li + S \rightarrow Li_2S$

$6Li + N_2 \rightarrow 2Li_3N$

$4K + O_2 \rightarrow 2K_2O$

$2K + Cl_2 \rightarrow 2KCl$

$2K + Br_2 \rightarrow 2KBr$

$Mg + S \rightarrow MgS$

$3Mg + N_2 \rightarrow Mg_3N_2$

$4Rb + O_2 \rightarrow 2Rb_2O$

$2Rb + Cl_2 \rightarrow 2RbCl$

$2Rb + Br_2 \rightarrow 2RbBr$

$Ca + S \rightarrow CaS$

$3Ca + N_2 \rightarrow Ca_3N_2$

$4Li + O_2 \rightarrow 2Li_2O$

$2Li + Cl_2 \rightarrow 2LiCl$

$2Li + Br_2 \rightarrow 2LiBr$

86. $Fe(s) + H_2SO_4(aq) \rightarrow FeSO_4(aq) + H_2(g)$

$Zn(s) + H_2SO_4(aq) \rightarrow ZnSO_4(aq) + H_2(g)$

$Mg(s) + H_2SO_4(aq) \rightarrow MgSO_4(aq) + H_2(g)$

$Co(s) + H_2SO_4(aq) \rightarrow CoSO_4(aq) + H_2(g)$

$Ni(s) + H_2SO_4(aq) \rightarrow NiSO_4(aq) + H_2(g)$

87.   For simplicity, the physical states of the substances are omitted.

$Mg + Cl_2 \rightarrow MgCl_2$

$Ca + Cl_2 \rightarrow CaCl_2$

$Sr + Cl_2 \rightarrow SrCl_2$

$Ba + Cl_2 \rightarrow BaCl_2$

$Mg + Br_2 \rightarrow MgBr_2$

$Ca + Br_2 \rightarrow CaBr_2$

$Sr + Br_2 \rightarrow SrBr_2$

$Ba + Br_2 \rightarrow BaBr_2$

$2Mg + O_2 \rightarrow 2MgO$

$2Ca + O_2 \rightarrow 2CaO$

$2Sr + O_2 \rightarrow 2SrO$

$2Ba + O_2 \rightarrow 2BaO$

88.   a.   one

       b.   one

       c.   two

       d.   two

       e.   three

89.   a.   two; $O + 2e^- \rightarrow O^{2-}$

       b.   one; $F + e^- \rightarrow F^-$

       c.   three; $N + 3e^- \rightarrow N^{3-}$

       d.   one; $Cl + e^- \rightarrow Cl^-$

       e.   two; $S + 2e^- \rightarrow S^{2-}$

90.   A very simple example which fits the bill is: $C(s) + O_2(g) \rightarrow CO_2(g)$

91.   a. $2I_4O_9(s) \rightarrow 2I_2O_6(s) + 2I_2(s) + 3O_2(g)$

              oxidation-reduction, decomposition

       b. $Mg(s) + 2AgNO_3(aq) \rightarrow Mg(NO_3)_2(aq) + 2Ag(s)$

              oxidation-reduction, single-displacement

       c. $SiCl_4(l) + 2Mg(s) \rightarrow 2MgCl_2(s) + Si(s)$

              oxidation-reduction, single-displacement

       d. $CuCl_2(aq) + 2AgNO_3(aq) \rightarrow Cu(NO_3)_2(aq) + 2AgCl(s)$

              precipitation, double-displacement

       e. $2Al(s) + 3Br_2(l) \rightarrow 2AlBr_3(s)$

              oxidation-reduction, synthesis

92.   a. $2C_3H_8O(l) + 9O_2(g) \rightarrow 6CO_2(g) + 8H_2O(g)$

              oxidation-reduction, combustion

       b. $HCl(aq) + AgC_2H_3O_2(aq) \rightarrow AgCl(s) + HC_2H_3O_2(aq)$

              precipitation, double-displacement

       c. $3HCl(aq) + Al(OH)_3(s) \rightarrow AlCl_3(aq) + 3H_2O(l)$

              acid-base, double-displacement

       d. $2H_2O_2(aq) \rightarrow 2H_2O(l) + O_2(g)$

              oxidation-reduction, decomposition

       e. $N_2H_4(l) + O_2(g) \rightarrow N_2(g) + 2H_2O(g)$

              oxidation-reduction, combustion

93. $2Zn(s) + O_2(g) \rightarrow 2ZnO(s)$
       $4Al(s) + 3O_2(g) \rightarrow 2Al_2O_3(s)$

$2Fe(s) + O_2(g) \rightarrow 2FeO(s)$; $4Fe(s) + 3O_2(g) \rightarrow 2Fe_2O_3(s)$

$2Cr(s) + O_2(g) \rightarrow 2CrO(s)$; $4Cr(s) + 3O_2(g) \rightarrow 2Cr_2O_3(s)$

$2Ni(s) + O_2(g) \rightarrow 2NiO(s)$

94. $2Na(s) + Cl_2(g) \rightarrow 2NaCl(s)$

$2Al(s) + 3Cl_2(g) \rightarrow 2AlCl_3(s)$

$Zn(s) + Cl_2(g) \rightarrow ZnCl_2(s)$

$Ca(s) + Cl_2(g) \rightarrow CaCl_2(s)$

$2Fe(s) + 3Cl_2(g) \rightarrow 2FeCl_3(s)$; $Fe(s) + Cl_2(g) \rightarrow FeCl_2(s)$

Cumulative Review: Chapters 6 and 7

1.   There are numerous ways we can recognize that a chemical reaction has taken place.

   In some reactions there may be a *color change*. For example, the ions of many of the transition metals are brightly colored in aqueous solution. If one of these ions undergoes a reaction in which the oxidation state changes, however, the characteristic color of the ion may be changed. For example, when a piece of zinc is added to an aqueous copper(II) ion solution (which is bright blue), the Cu^{2+} ions are reduced to copper metal, and the blue color of the solution fades as the reaction takes place.

$$Zn(s) + Cu^{2+}(aq) \rightarrow Zn^{2+}(aq) + Cu(s)$$

       blue   red/black
       solution   solid

   In many reactions of ionic solutes, a solid *precipitate* may form when the ions are combined. For example, when a clear, colorless aqueous solution of sodium chloride is added to a clear, colorless solution of silver nitrate, a white solid of silver chloride forms and settles out of the mixture.

$$AgNO_3(aq) + NaCl(aq) \rightarrow NaNO_3(aq) + AgCl(s)$$

   In some reactions, *bubbles of a gaseous product* may form. For example, if a piece of magnesium metal is added to a solution of hydrochloric acid, bubbles of hydrogen gas form at the surface of the magnesium.

$$Mg(s) + 2HCl(aq) \rightarrow MgCl_2(aq) + H_2(g)$$

   In some reactions, particularly in the combustion of organic chemical substances with oxygen gas, heat, light, and a flame may be produced. For example, when methane (natural gas) is burned in oxygen, a luminous flame is produced and heat energy is released:

$$CH_4(g) + 2O_2 \rightarrow CO_2(g) + 2H_2O(g) + energy$$

All chemical reactions do produce some evidence that the reaction has occurred, but sometimes this evidence may *not* be visual, and may not be very obvious. For example, when very dilute aqueous solutions of acids and bases are mixed, the neutralization reaction

$$H^+(aq) + OH^-(aq) \rightarrow H_2O(l)$$

takes place. However, the only evidence for this reaction is the release of heat energy, which should be evident as a temperature change for the mixture. Since water has a relatively high specific heat capacity, however, if the acid and base solutions are very dilute, the temperature may only change by a fraction of a degree and may not be noticed.

2.   A chemical equation indicates the substances necessary for a chemical reaction to take place, as well as what is produced by that chemical reaction. The substances to the left of the arrow in a chemical equation are called the reactants; those to the right of the arrow are referred to as the products. In addition, if a chemical equation has been balanced, then the equation indicates the relative proportions in which the reactant molecules combine to form the product molecules.

3.   When we "balance" a chemical equation, we adjust the *coefficients* of the reactants and products in the equation so that the same total numbers of atoms of each element are present both before and after the reaction has taken place. Balancing chemical equations is so important because a balanced chemical equation shows us not only the identities of the reactants and products, but also the relative numbers of each involved in the process: this information is necessary if we are to do any sort of calculation involving the amounts of reactants required for a process or are to calculate the yield expected from a process. When we say that atoms must be *conserved* when writing a balanced chemical equations, we mean that the number of atoms of each element must be the same after the reaction is complete as before the reaction was attempted: no atoms are created or destroyed during a chemical reaction, they are just arranged into new combinations. We often indicate the physical states of the reactants and products for a chemical reaction, because sometimes the physical state is important for the reaction to be successful. The phyiscal states are indicated by using letters in parentheses after the formula: (*s*), (*l*), (*g*), or (*aq*).For example, magnesium metal does not react to any appreciable extent with solid water (ice) or with liquid water at room temperature, but does react readily with gaseous water (steam) above 100°C.

$$Mg(s) + H_2O(s \text{ or } l) \rightarrow \quad \text{no reaction}$$

$$Mg(s) + 2H_2O(g) \rightarrow Mg(OH)_2(s) + H_2(g)$$

The amount of energy consumed or released by a chemical reaction is also strongly dependent on the physical states of the reactants and products.

4.   It is *never* permissible to change the subscripts of a formula when balancing a chemical equation: changing the subscripts changes the *identity* of a substance from one chemical to another. For example, consider the unbalanced chemical equation

$$H_2(g) + O_2(g) \rightarrow H_2O(l)$$

If you changed the *formula* of the product from $H_2O(l)$ to $H_2O_2(l)$, the equation would appear to be "balanced". However, H_2O is water, whereas H_2O_2 is hydrogen peroxide--a completely different chemical substance (which is not prepared by reaction of the elements hydrogen and oxygen).
        When we balance a chemical equation, it is permitted only to adjust the *coefficients* of a formula, since changing a coefficient merely changes the number of molecules of a substance being used in the reaction, without changing the identity of the substance. For the example

above, we can balance the equation by putting coefficients of 2 in front of the formulas of H_2 and H_2O: these coefficients do not change the nature of what is reacting and what product is formed.

$$2H_2(g) + O_2(g) \rightarrow 2H_2O(l)$$

5.   The concept of a "driving force" for chemical reactions, at this point, is a rather nebulous idea. Clearly there must be some reason why certain substances react when combined, and why other substances can be combined without anything happening. If you go on with further studies in chemistry, you will learn that there is a mathematical thermodynamic function which can be used to predict exactly what will happen when a given set of reactants is combined. Even at this point, however, we can use some generalizations about what sorts of events tend to make a reaction take place. A reaction is likely to occur if any of the following things occur as a result of the reaction: formation of a solid, formation of water (or another nonionized molecule), formation of a gas, or the transfer of electrons from one species to another. Here are examples of reactions illustrating each of these:

formation of a solid:

$$BaCl_2(aq) + K_2CrO_4(aq) \rightarrow 2KCl(aq) + BaCrO_4(s)$$
$$Pb(NO_3)_2(aq) + 2NaCl(aq) \rightarrow PbCl_2(s) + 2NaNO_3(aq)$$

formation of water:

$$HCl(aq) + NaOH(aq) \rightarrow NaCl(aq) + H_2O(l)$$
$$CH_3COOH(aq) + KOH(aq) \rightarrow KCH_3COO(aq) + H_2O(l)$$

formation of a gas:

$$2NI_3(s) \rightarrow N_2(g) + 3I_2(s)$$
$$CaCO_3(s) \rightarrow CaO(s) + CO_2(g)$$

transfer of electrons

$$Zn(s) + 2Ag^+(aq) \rightarrow Zn^{2+}(aq) + 2Ag(s)$$
$$Mg(s) + Cu^{2+}(aq) \rightarrow Mg^{2+}(aq) + Cu(s)$$

6.   A precipitation reaction is one in which a *solid* forms when the reactants are combined: the solid is called a precipitate. If you were to perform such a reaction, the mixture would turn cloudy as the reactants are combined, and a solid would eventually settle from the mixture on standing. There are many examples of such precipitation reactions: consult the solubility rules in Table 7.1 if you need help. One example would be to combine barium nitrate and sodium carbonate solutions: a precipitate of barium carbonate would form.

$$Ba(NO_3)_2(aq) + Na_2CO_3(aq) \rightarrow BaCO_3(s) + 2NaNO_3(aq)$$

7.   A strong electrolyte is one which completely dissociates into ions when dissolved in water: that is, each unit of the substance that dissolves in water produces separated, free ions. Ionic compounds, since they already consist of ions in the solid state, are strong electrolytes if they are soluble in water. Certain acids and bases also behave as strong electrolytes. A solution of a strong electrolyte actually consists of free, separated ions moving through the solvent independently of one another (there are no molecules or clusters of combined positive and negative ions). An apparatus for experimentally determining whether or not a substance is an electrolyte is shown in Figure 7.2 in the text.

8.   In summary, nearly all compounds containing the nitrate, sodium, potassium, and ammonium ions are soluble in water. Most salts containing the chloride and sulfate ions are soluble in water, with specific exceptions (see Table 7.1 for these exceptions). Most compounds containing the hydroxide, sulfide, carbonate, and phosphate ions are not soluble in water, unless the compound also contains one of the cations mentioned above (Na^+, K^+, NH_4^+).

The solubility rules are phrased as if you had a sample of a given solute and wanted to see if you could dissolve it in water. These rules can also be applied, however, to predict the identity of the solid produced in a precipitation reaction: a given combination of ions will not be soluble in water whether you take a pure compound out of a reagent bottle or if you generate the insoluble combination of ions during a chemical reaction. For example, the solubility rules say that $BaSO_4$ is not soluble in water. This means not only that a pure sample of $BaSO_4$ taken from a reagent bottle will not dissolve in water, but also that if Ba^{2+} ion and SO_4^{2-} ion end up together in the same solution, they will precipitate as $BaSO_4$. If we were to combine barium chloride and sulfuric acid solutions

$$BaCl_2(aq) + H_2SO_4(aq) \rightarrow BaSO_4(s) + 2HCl(aq)$$

then, because barium sulfate is not soluble in water, a precipitate of $BaSO_4(s)$ would form. Since a precipitate of $BaSO_4(s)$ would form no matter what barium compound or what sulfate compound were mixed, we can write the net ionic equation for the reaction as

$$Ba^{2+}(aq) + SO_4^{2-}(aq) \rightarrow BaSO_4(s)$$

Thus if, for example, barium nitrate solution were combined with sodium sulfate solution, a precipitate of $BaSO_4$ would form. Barium sulfate is insoluble in water regardless of its source.

9.   The spectator ions in a precipitation reaction are, basically, the ions in the solution that do *not* precipitate. Since we take the actual chemical reaction in a precipitation process to be the formation of the solid, and since the spectator ions are are not found in and do not participate in the formation of the solid, we leave them out of the net ionic equation for the reaction. Not including the spectator ions in the net ionic equation for a precipitation reaction also has another important

implication: if we write the net ionic equation for the formation of silver chloride

$$Ag^+(aq) + Cl^-(aq) \rightarrow AgCl(s)$$

we are indicating that it is these specific ions that will combine to form silver chloride, regardless of where they come from. If any soluble silver salt is combined with any soluble chloride, we should get a precipitate of silver chloride. For example, silver nitrate (a common soluble silver salt) reacts in exactly the same manner with NaCl, KCl, NH$_4$Cl, and HCl which are all soluble compounds containing the chloride ion.

Just because we leave the spectator ions out when writing a net ionic equation for a reaction does not mean that the spectator ions do not have to be present: the spectator ions are needed to provide a balance of charge in the reactant compounds for the ions which combine to form the precipitate. For the reaction above in which silver chloride is formed, it would not be possible to have a reagent bottle containing just silver ion (there would have to be some negative ion present) or just chloride ion (there would have to be some positive ion present).

10. Acids (such as the citric acid found in citrus fruits and the acetic acid found in vinegar) were first noted primarily because of their sour taste. The first bases noted were characterized by their bitter taste and slippery feel on the skin. Acids and bases chemically react with (neutralize) each other forming water: the net ionic equation is

$$H^+(aq) + OH^-(aq) \rightarrow H_2O(l)$$

The *strong* acids and bases are those which fully ionize when they dissolve in water: since these substances fully ionize, they are strong electrolytes. The common strong acids are HCl(hydrochloric), HNO$_3$(nitric), H$_2$SO$_4$(sulfuric), and HClO$_4$(perchloric). The most common strong bases are the alkali metal hydroxides, particularly NaOH(sodium hydroxide) and KOH(potassium hydroxide).

11. A salt is basically any ionic compound that contains any ions other than H$^+$ and OH$^-$ (compounds containing these ions are called acids and bases, respectively). In particular, a salt is formed in the neutralization reaction between an acid and a base. Your textbook describes acid-base neutralization reactions as reactions that result in the formation of water: the water results from the combination of the H$^+$(aq) ion from the acid with the OH$^-$(aq) ion from the base

$$H^+(aq) + OH^-(aq) \rightarrow H_2O(l)$$

However, the H$^+$ ion must have been paired with some negative ion in the original acid solution, and the OH$^-$ ion must have been paired with some positive ion in the original base solution. These counter-ions to the acid-base ions are what constitute the salt that is formed during the neutralization. Below are three acid-base neutralization reactions, with the salts that are formed indicated:

$$HCl(aq) + NaOH(aq) \rightarrow H_2O(l) + NaCl(aq)$$
acid   base   water   a salt

$$HNO_3(aq) + KOH(aq) \rightarrow H_2O(l) + KNO_3(aq)$$
acid   base   water   a salt

$$HC_2H_3O_2(aq) + NaOH(aq) \rightarrow H_2O(l) + NaC_2H_3O_2(aq)$$
acid   base   water   a salt

12. Oxidation-reduction reactions are electron-transfer reactions. Oxidation represents a loss of electrons by an atom, molecule, or ion, whereas reduction is the gain of electrons by such a species. Since an oxidation-reduction process represents the transfer of electrons between species, you can't have one without the other also taking place: the electrons lost by one species must be gained by some other species. An example of a simple oxidation reduction reaction between a metal and a nonmetal could be the following

$$Mg(s) + F_2(g) \rightarrow MgF_2(s)$$

In this process, Mg atoms lose two electrons each to become Mg^{2+} ions in MgF_2: Mg is oxidized. Each F atom of F_2 gains one electron to become an F^- ion, for a total of two electrons gained for each F_2 molecule: F_2 is reduced.

$$Mg \rightarrow Mg^{2+} + 2e^- \qquad 2(F + e^- \rightarrow F^-)$$

13. Combustion reactions represent processes involving oxygen gas that release energy rapidly enough that a flame is produced. Combustion reactions are a special sub-class of oxidation-reduction reactions (the fact that elemental oxygen gas is a reactant but combined oxygen is a product shows this). The most common combustion reactions are those we make use of through the burning of petroleum products as sources of heat, light, or other forms of energy. For example, the burning of methane (natural gas) is shown below

$$CH_4(g) + 2O_2(g) \rightarrow CO_2(g) + 2H_2O(g) + energy$$

Combustion reactions of other types of substances are also possible, however. For example, magnesium metal burns in oxygen gas (with a very bright, intense flame) to produce magnesium oxide.

$$2Mg(s) + O_2(g) \rightarrow 2MgO(s) + energy$$

14. In general, a synthesis reaction represents the reaction of elements or simple compounds to produce more complex substances. There are many examples of synthesis reactions, for example

$$N_2(g) + 3H_2(g) \rightarrow 2NH_3(g)$$

$$NaOH(aq) + CO_2(g) \rightarrow NaHCO_3(s)$$

Decomposition reactions represent the breakdown of a more complex substance into simpler substances. There are many examples of decomposition reactions, for example

$$2H_2O_2(aq) \rightarrow 2H_2O(l) + O_2(g)$$

Synthesis and decomposition reactions are very often also oxidation-reduction reactions, especially if an elemental substance reacts or is generated. It is not necessary, however, for synthesis and decomposition reactions to always involve oxidation-reduction. For example, the reaction between NaOH and CO_2 given as an example of a synthesis reaction does *not* represent oxidation-reduction.

15. The different ways of classifying chemical reactions that have been discussed in the text are listed below, along with an example of each type of reaction:

formation of a solid (precipitation):

$$FeCl_3(aq) + 3NaOH(aq) \rightarrow Fe(OH)_3(s) + 3NaCl(aq)$$

formation of water (acid-base)

$$H_2SO_4(aq) + 2NaOH(aq) \rightarrow Na_2SO_4(aq) + 2H_2O(l)$$

transfer of electrons (oxidation-reduction):

$$2Na(s) + Cl_2(g) \rightarrow 2NaCl(s)$$

combustion:

$$2C_2H_6(g) + 7O_2(g) \rightarrow 4CO_2(g) + 6H_2O(g) + energy$$

synthesis (combination):

$$Ca(s) + Cl_2(g) \rightarrow CaCl_2(s)$$

decomposition:

$$2HgO(s) \rightarrow 2Hg(l) + O_2(g)$$

single displacement

$$Mg(s) + 2AgNO_3(aq) \rightarrow Mg(NO_3)_2(aq) + 2Ag(s)$$

double displacement

$$Na_2SO_4(aq) + BaCl_2(aq) \rightarrow 2NaCl(aq) + BaSO_4(s)$$

16. a. $2Na(s) + 2H_2O(l) \rightarrow 2NaOH(aq) + H_2(g)$

   $2K(s) + 2H_2O(l) \rightarrow 2KOH(aq) + H_2(g)$

   b. $2Na(s) + Cl_2(g) \rightarrow 2NaCl(s)$

   $2K(s) + Cl_2(g) \rightarrow 2KCl(s)$

   c. $3Na(s) + P(s) \rightarrow Na_3P(s)$

   $3K(s) + P(s) \rightarrow K_3P(s)$

   d. $6Na(s) + N_2(g) \rightarrow 2Na_3N(s)$

   $6K(s) + N_2(g) \rightarrow 2K_3N(s)$

   e. $2Na(s) + H_2(g) \rightarrow 2NaH(s)$

   $2K(s) + H_2(g) \rightarrow 2KH(s)$

17. a. $FeCl_3(aq) + 3KOH(s) \rightarrow Fe(OH)_3(s) + 3KCl(aq)$

   b. $AgC_2H_3O_2(aq) + HCl(aq) \rightarrow AgCl(s) + HC_2H_3O_2(aq)$

   c. $2Na_2O_2(s) + 2H_2O(l) \rightarrow 4NaOH(aq) + O_2(g)$

   d. $2SnO(s) + C(s) \rightarrow 2Sn(s) + CO_2(g)$

   e. $2Fe(s) + 3Br_2(l) \rightarrow 2FeBr_3(s)$

   f. $Na_2S(s) + 2HCl(aq) \rightarrow 2NaCl(aq) + H_2S(g)$

   g. $K_2O(s) + H_2O(l) \rightarrow 2KOH(aq)$

   h. $H_2SO_4(l) + 2NaCl(s) \rightarrow Na_2SO_4(s) + 2HCl(g)$

   i. $N_2(g) + 3I_2(s) \rightarrow 2NI_3(s)$

18. a. $Ba(NO_3)_2(aq) + K_2CrO_4(aq) \rightarrow BaCrO_4(s) + 2KNO_3(aq)$

   b. $NaOH(aq) + CH_3COOH(aq) \rightarrow H_2O(l) + NaCH_3COO(aq)$
   (then evaporate the water from the solution)

   c. $AgNO_3(aq) + NaCl(aq) \rightarrow AgCl(s) + NaNO_3(aq)$

   d. $Pb(NO_3)_2(aq) + H_2SO_4(aq) \rightarrow PbSO_4(s) + 2HNO_3(aq)$

   e. $2NaOH(aq) + H_2SO_4(aq) \rightarrow Na_2SO_4(aq) + 2H_2O(l)$
   (then evaporate the water from the solution)

   f. $Ba(NO_3)_2(aq) + Na_2CO_3(aq) \rightarrow BaCO_3(s) + 2NaNO_3(aq)$

19. $HCl(aq) + NaOH(aq) \rightarrow NaCl(aq) + H_2O(l)$

   $HNO_3(aq) + NaOH(aq) \rightarrow NaNO_3(aq) + H_2O(l)$

   $H_2SO_4(aq) + 2NaOH(aq) \rightarrow Na_2SO_4(aq) + 2H_2O(l)$

   $HCl(aq) + KOH(aq) \rightarrow KCl(aq) + H_2O(l)$

$HNO_3(aq) + KOH(aq) \rightarrow KNO_3(aq) + H_2O(l)$

$H_2SO_4(aq) + 2KOH(aq) \rightarrow K_2SO_4(aq) + 2H_2O(l)$

20.   a. $FeO(s) + 2HNO_3(aq) \rightarrow Fe(NO_3)_2(aq) + H_2O(l)$
acid-base, double-displacement

b. $2Mg(s) + 2CO_2(g) + O_2(g) \rightarrow 2MgCO_3(s)$
synthesis; oxidation-reduction

c. $2NaOH(s) + CuSO_4(aq) \rightarrow Cu(OH)_2(s) + Na_2SO_4(aq)$
precipitation, double-displacement

d. $HI(aq) + KOH(aq) \rightarrow KI(aq) + H_2O(l)$
acid-base, double-displacement

e. $C_3H_8(g) + 5O_2(g) \rightarrow 3CO_2(g) + 4H_2O(g)$
combustion; oxidation-reduction

f. $Co(NH_3)_6Cl_2(s) \rightarrow CoCl_2(s) + 6NH_3(g)$
decomposition

g. $2HCl(aq) + Pb(C_2H_3O_2)_2(aq) \rightarrow 2HC_2H_3O_2(aq) + PbCl_2(s)$
precipitation, double-displacement

h. $C_{12}H_{22}O_{11}(s) \rightarrow 12C(s) + 11H_2O(g)$
decomposition; oxidation-reduction

i. $2Al(s) + 6HNO_3(aq) \rightarrow 2Al(NO_3)_3(aq) + 3H_2(g)$
oxidation-reduction; single-displacement

j. $4B(s) + 3O_2(g) \rightarrow 2B_2O_3(s)$
synthesis; oxidation-reduction

Chapter 8   Chemical Composition

1. $100 \text{ washers} \times \dfrac{0.110 \text{ g}}{1 \text{ washer}} = 11.0 \text{ g}$ (assuming 100 washers is exact).

$100. \text{ g} \times \dfrac{1 \text{ washer}}{0.110 \text{ g}} = 909 \text{ washers}$

2. $500. \text{ g} \times \dfrac{1 \text{ cork}}{1.63 \text{ g}} = 306.7 = 307 \text{ corks}$

$500. \text{ g} \times \dfrac{1 \text{ stopper}}{4.31 \text{ g}} = 116 \text{ stoppers}$

1 kg (1000 g) of corks contains $\left(1000 \text{ g} \times \dfrac{1 \text{ cork}}{1.63 \text{ g}}\right) = 613.49 = 613 \text{ corks}$

613 stoppers would weigh $\left(613 \text{ stoppers} \times \dfrac{4.31 \text{ g}}{1 \text{ stopper}}\right) = 2644 \text{ g} = 2640 \text{ g}$

The ratio of the mass of a stopper to the mass of a cork is (4.31 g/1.63 g). So the mass of stoppers that contains the same number of stoppers as there are corks in 1000 g of corks is

$1000 \text{ g} \times \dfrac{4.31 \text{ g}}{1.63 \text{ g}} = 2644 \text{ g} = 2640 \text{ g}$

3.   The *atomic mass unit* (amu) is a unit of mass defined by scientists to more simply describe relative masses on an atomic or molecular scale. One amu is equivalent to 1.66×10^{-24} g.

4.   We use the average atomic mass of an element when performing calculations because the average mass takes into account the individual masses and relative abundances of all the isotopes of an element.

5.   a. $635 \text{ H atoms} \times \dfrac{1.008 \text{ amu}}{1 \text{ H atom}} = 640. \text{ amu}$

b. $1.261 \times 10^4 \text{ W atoms} \times \dfrac{183.9 \text{ amu}}{1 \text{ W atom}} = 2.319 \times 10^6 \text{ amu}$

c. $42 \text{ K atoms} \times \dfrac{39.10 \text{ amu}}{1 \text{ K atom}} = 1642 \text{ amu}$

d. $7.213 \times 10^{23} \text{ N atoms} \times \dfrac{14.01 \text{ amu}}{1 \text{ N atom}} = 1.011 \times 10^{25} \text{ amu}$

e. $891 \text{ Fe atoms} \times \dfrac{55.85 \text{ amu}}{1 \text{ Fe atom}} = 4.976 \times 10^4 \text{ amu}$

6.   a. $10.81 \text{ amu} \times \dfrac{1 \text{ B atom}}{10.81 \text{ amu}} = 1.000 \text{ atom} = 1 \text{ B atom}$

b. $320.7 \text{ amu} \times \dfrac{1 \text{ S atom}}{32.07 \text{ amu}} = 10 \text{ S atoms}$

c. $19{,}691 \text{ amu} \times \dfrac{1 \text{ Au atom}}{197.97 \text{ amu}} = 100.00 \text{ Au atoms} = 100 \text{ Au atoms}$

d. $19{,}695 \text{ amu} \times \dfrac{1 \text{ Xe atom}}{131.3 \text{ amu}} = 150.0 \text{ Xe atoms} = 150 \text{ Xe atoms}$

e. $3588.3 \text{ amu} \times \dfrac{1 \text{ Al atom}}{26.98 \text{ amu}} = 133.0 \text{ Al atoms} = 133 \text{ Al atoms}$

7. $8274 \text{ amu} \times \dfrac{1 \text{ S atom}}{32.07 \text{ amu}} = 258 \text{ S atoms}$

$5.213 \times 10^{24} \text{ S atoms} \times \dfrac{32.07 \text{ amu}}{1 \text{ S atom}} = 1.672 \times 10^{26} \text{ amu}$

8. $1.00 \times 10^{4} \text{ atoms} \times \dfrac{196.97 \text{ amu}}{1 \text{ Au atom}} = 1.97 \times 10^{6} \text{ amu}$

$2.955 \times 10^{5} \text{ amu} \times \dfrac{1 \text{ Au atom}}{196.97 \text{ amu}} = 1500. \text{ Au atoms}$

9. 1.205×10^{24}

10.   Avogadro's number (6.022×10^{23})

11.   The ratio of the atomic mass of Ca to the atomic mass of Mg is (40.08 amu/24.31 amu), and the masses of calcium are given by

$12.16 \text{ g Mg} \times \dfrac{40.08 \text{ amu}}{24.31 \text{ amu}} = 20.05 \text{ g Ca}$

$24.31 \text{ g Mg} \times \dfrac{40.08 \text{ amu}}{24.31 \text{ amu}} = 40.08 \text{ g Ca}$

12.   The ratio of the atomic mass of Fe to the atomic mass of N is (55.85 amu/14.01 amu), and the mass of iron is given by

$14.01 \text{ g} \times \dfrac{55.85 \text{ amu}}{14.01 \text{ amu}} = 55.85 \text{ g Fe}$

13.   The ratio of the atomic mass of H to the atomic mass of N is (1.008 amu/14.01 amu), and the mass of hydrogen is given by

$7.00 \text{ g N} \times \dfrac{1.008 \text{ amu}}{14.01 \text{ amu}} = 0.504 \text{ g H}$

14.   The ratio of the atomic mass of Co to the atomic mass of F is (58.93 amu/19.00 amu), and the mass of cobalt is given by

$$57.0 \text{ g} \times \frac{58.93 \text{ amu}}{19.00 \text{ amu}} = 177 \text{ g Co}$$

15. $$3.817 \times 10^{-23} \text{ g Na} \times \frac{24.31 \text{ amu}}{22.99 \text{ amu}} = 4.036 \times 10^{-23} \text{ g Mg}$$

$$3.817 \times 10^{-23} \text{ g Na} \times \frac{39.10 \text{ amu}}{22.99 \text{ amu}} = 6.492 \times 10^{-23} \text{ g K}$$

16. $$1 \text{ mol O} = 16.00 \text{ g O} = 6.02 \times 10^{23} \text{ O atoms}$$

$$1 \text{ O atom} \times \frac{16.00 \text{ g O}}{6.022 \times 10^{23} \text{ O atoms}} = 2.66 \times 10^{-23} \text{ g}$$

17.   1 mol of He atoms = 4.003 g

$$4 \text{ mol of H atoms} \times \frac{1.008 \text{ g H}}{1 \text{ mol}} = 4.032 \text{ g}$$

4 mol of H atoms has a mass slightly larger than 1 mol of He atoms.

18. $$0.50 \text{ mol O atoms} \times \frac{16.00 \text{ g}}{1 \text{ mol}} = 8.0 \text{ g O}$$

$$4 \text{ mol H atoms} \times \frac{1.008 \text{ g}}{1 \text{ mol}} = 4 \text{ g H}$$

Half a mole of O atoms weighs more than 4 moles of H atoms.

19.   a. $$6.22 \text{ g Al} \times \frac{1 \text{ mol}}{26.98 \text{ g}} = 0.231 \text{ mol Al}$$

b. $$52.1 \text{ kg C} \times \frac{1000 \text{ g}}{1 \text{ kg}} \times \frac{1 \text{ mol}}{12.01 \text{ g}} = 4.34 \times 10^{3} \text{ mol C}$$

c. $$1.26 \text{ mg Au} \times \frac{1 \text{ g}}{1000 \text{ mg}} \times \frac{1 \text{ mol}}{197.0 \text{ g}} = 6.40 \times 10^{-6} \text{ mol Au}$$

d. $$2.16 \text{ lb Fe} \times \frac{453.59 \text{ g}}{1.000 \text{ lb}} \times \frac{1 \text{ mol}}{55.85 \text{ g}} = 17.5 \text{ mol Fe}$$

e. $$3.71 \text{ g W} \times \frac{1 \text{ mol}}{183.9 \text{ g}} = 2.02 \times 10^{-2} \text{ mol W}$$

f. $$8.99 \text{ g O} \times \frac{1 \text{ mol}}{16.00 \text{ g}} = 0.562 \text{ mol O}$$

g. $$0.000375 \text{ g F} \times \frac{1 \text{ mol}}{19.00 \text{ g}} = 1.97 \times 10^{-5} \text{ mol F}$$

20. a. $26.2 \text{ g Au} \times \dfrac{1 \text{ mol Au}}{197.0 \text{ g}} = 0.133 \text{ mol Au}$

  b. $41.5 \text{ g Ca} \times \dfrac{1 \text{ mol Ca}}{40.08 \text{ g}} = 1.04 \text{ mol Ca}$

  c. $335 \text{ mg Ba} \times \dfrac{1 \text{ g}}{10^3 \text{ mg}} \times \dfrac{1 \text{ mol Ba}}{137.3 \text{ g}} = 2.44 \times 10^{-3} \text{ mol Ba}$

  d. $1.42 \times 10^{-3} \text{ g Pd} \times \dfrac{1 \text{ mol Pd}}{106.4 \text{ g}} = 1.33 \times 10^{-5} \text{ mol Pd}$

  e. $3.05 \times 10^{-5} \text{ } \mu\text{g Ni} \times \dfrac{1 \text{ g}}{10^6 \text{ } \mu\text{g}} \times \dfrac{1 \text{ mol Ni}}{58.70 \text{ g}} = 5.20 \times 10^{-13} \text{ mol Ni}$

  f. $1.00 \text{ lb Fe} \times \dfrac{453.59 \text{ g}}{1 \text{ lb}} \times \dfrac{1 \text{ mol Fe}}{55.85 \text{ g}} = 8.12 \text{ mol Fe}$

  g. $12.01 \text{ g C} \times \dfrac{1 \text{ mol C}}{12.01 \text{ g}} = 1.000 \text{ mol C}$

21. a. $0.000221 \text{ mol C} \times \dfrac{12.01 \text{ g}}{1 \text{ mol}} = 2.65 \times 10^{-3} \text{ g C}$

  b. $7.04 \text{ mol K} \times \dfrac{39.10 \text{ g}}{1 \text{ mol}} = 275 \text{ g K}$

  c. $2.71 \times 10^6 \text{ mol O} \times \dfrac{16.00 \text{ g}}{1 \text{ mol}} = 4.34 \times 10^7 \text{ g O}$

  d. $1.05 \text{ mol Ag} \times \dfrac{107.9 \text{ g}}{1 \text{ mol}} = 113 \text{ g Ag}$

  e. $0.00141 \text{ mol Cd} \times \dfrac{112.4 \text{ g}}{1 \text{ mol}} = 0.158 \text{ g Cd}$

  f. $1.25 \times 10^{-6} \text{ mol Br} \times \dfrac{79.90 \text{ g}}{1 \text{ mol}} = 9.99 \times 10^{-5} \text{ g Br}$

  g. $9.09 \text{ mol Co} \times \dfrac{58.93 \text{ g}}{1 \text{ mol}} = 536 \text{ g Co}$

22. a. $2.00 \text{ mol Fe} \times \dfrac{55.85 \text{ g}}{1 \text{ mol}} = 112 \text{ g Fe}$

  b. $0.521 \text{ mol Ni} \times \dfrac{58.70 \text{ g}}{1 \text{ mol}} = 30.6 \text{ g Ni}$

  c. $1.23 \times 10^{-3} \text{ mol Pt} \times \dfrac{195.1 \text{ g}}{1 \text{ mol}} = 0.240 \text{ g Pt}$

d.   72.5 mol Pb $\times \dfrac{207.2 \text{ g}}{1 \text{ mol}}$ = 1.50 $\times$ 10^4 g Pb

e.   0.00102 mol Mg $\times \dfrac{24.31 \text{ g}}{1 \text{ mol}}$ = 0.0248 g Mg

f.   4.87 $\times$ 10^3 mol Al $\times \dfrac{26.98 \text{ g}}{1 \text{ mol}}$ = 1.31 $\times$ 10^5 g Al

g.   211.5 mol Li $\times \dfrac{6.941 \text{ g}}{1 \text{ mol}}$ = 1468 g Li

h.   1.72 $\times$ 10^{-6} mol Na $\times \dfrac{22.99 \text{ g}}{1 \text{ mol}}$ = 3.95 $\times$ 10^{-5} g Na

23.   a.   1.50 g Ag $\times \dfrac{6.022 \times 10^{23} \text{ Ag atoms}}{107.9 \text{ g Ag}}$ = 8.37 $\times$ 10^{21} Ag atoms

b.   0.0015 mol Cu $\times \dfrac{6.022 \times 10^{23} \text{ Cu atoms}}{1 \text{ mol}}$ = 9.0 $\times$ 10^{20} Cu atoms

c.   0.0015 g Cu $\times \dfrac{6.022 \times 10^{23} \text{ Cu atoms}}{63.55 \text{ g Cu}}$ = 1.4 $\times$ 10^{19} Cu atoms

d.   2.00 kg = 2.00 $\times$ 10^3 g

2.00 $\times$ 10^3 g Mg $\times \dfrac{6.022 \times 10^{23} \text{ Mg atoms}}{24.31 \text{ g Mg}}$ = 4.95 $\times$ 10^{25} Mg atoms

e.   1.000 oz = 28.35 g

2.34 oz Ca $\times \dfrac{28.35 \text{ g}}{1.000 \text{ oz}} \times \dfrac{6.022 \times 10^{23} \text{ Ca atoms}}{40.08 \text{ g Ca}}$ = 9.97 $\times$ 10^{23} Ca atoms

f.   2.34 g Ca $\times \dfrac{6.022 \times 10^{23} \text{ Ca atoms}}{40.08 \text{ g Ca}}$ = 3.52 $\times$ 10^{22} Ca atoms

g.   2.34 mol Ca $\times \dfrac{6.022 \times 10^{23} \text{ Ca atoms}}{1 \text{ mol}}$ = 1.41 $\times$ 10^{24} Ca atoms

24.   a.   0.00103 g Co $\times \dfrac{6.022 \times 10^{23} \text{ Co atoms}}{58.93 \text{ g Co}}$ = 1.05 $\times$ 10^{19} Co atoms

b.   0.00103 mol Co $\times \dfrac{6.022 \times 10^{23} \text{ Co atoms}}{1 \text{ mol}}$ = 6.20 $\times$ 10^{20} Co atoms

c.   2.75 g cobalt $\times \dfrac{1 \text{ mol}}{58.93 \text{ g Co}}$ = 0.0467 mol Co

d.   5.99 $\times$ 10^{21} Co atoms $\times \dfrac{1 \text{ mol}}{6.022 \times 10^{23} \text{ Co atoms}}$ = 0.00995 mol Co

e. $4.23 \text{ mol Co} \times \dfrac{58.93 \text{ g Co}}{1 \text{ mol Co}} = 249 \text{ g Co}$

f. $4.23 \text{ mol Co} \times \dfrac{6.022 \times 10^{23} \text{ Co atoms}}{1 \text{ mol Co}} = 2.55 \times 10^{24} \text{ Co atoms}$

g. $4.23 \text{ g Co} \times \dfrac{6.022 \times 10^{23} \text{ Co atoms}}{58.93 \text{ g Co}} = 4.32 \times 10^{22} \text{ Co atoms}$

25.   molar mass

26.   adding together (summing)

27.   a.   mass of 1 mol Mg =   24.31 g =   24.31 g

mass of 2 mol N =   2(14.01 g) =   28.02 g

mass of 4 mol O =   4(16.00 g) =   64.00 g

molar mass of $Mg(NO_2)_2$ =   116.33 g

b.   mass of 1 mol Na =   22.99 g =   22.99 g

mass of 1 mol Cl =   35.45 g =   35.45 g

mass of 4 mol O =   4(16.00 g) =   64.00 g

molar mass of $NaClO_4$ =   122.44 g

c.   mass of 1 mol Na =   22.99 g =   22.99 g

mass of 1 mol Mn =   54.94 g =   54.94 g

mass of 4 mol O =   4(16.00) g =   64.00 g

molar mass of $NaMnO_4$ =   141.93 g

d.   mass of 1 mol Li =   6.941 g =   6.941 g

mass of 1 mol Cl =   35.45 g =   35.45 g

molar mass of LiCl =   42.39 g

e.   mass of 1 mol Fe =   55.85 g =   55.85 g

mass of 1 mol S =   32.07 g =   32.07 g

mass of 4 mol O =   4(16.00 g) =   64.00 g

molar mass of $FeSO_4$ =   151.92 g

f.   mass of 1 mol Cu =   63.55 g =   63.55 g

mass of 1 mol Cl =   35.45 g =   35.45 g

molar mass of CuCl =   99.00 g

28.   a.   mass of 3 mol Na =   3(22.99 g) =   68.97 g

mass of 1 mol N = 1(14.01 g) =   14.01 g

molar mass of Na_3N =   82.98 g

b.   mass of 1 mol C =   12.01 g =   12.01 g

mass of 2 mol S =   2(32.07 g) =   64.14 g
_____
molar mass of CS_2 =   76.15 g

c.   mass of 1 mol N =   14.01 g =   14.01 g

mass of 4 mol H =   4(1.008 g) =   4.032 g

mass of 1 mol Br =   79.90 g =   79.90 g
_____
molar mass of NH_4Br =   97.942 g = 97.94 g

d.   mass of 2 mol C =   2(12.01 g) =   24.02 g

mass of 6 mol H =   6(1.008 g) =   6.048 g

mass of 1 mol O =   16.00 g =   16.00 g
_____
molar mass of C_2H_6O =   46.07 g

e.   mass of 2 mol H =   2(1.008 g) =   2.016 g

mass of 1 mol S =   32.07 g =   32.07 g

mass of 3 mol O =   3(16.00 g) =   48.00 g
_____
molar mass of H_2SO_3 =   82.086 g = 82.09 g

f.   mass of 2 mol H =   2(1.008 g) =   2.016 g

mass of 1 mol S =   32.07 g =   32.07 g

mass of 4 mol O =   4(16.00 g) =   64.00 g
_____
molar mass of H_2SO_4 =   98.086 g = 98.09 g

29.   a.   mass of 1 mol Ba =   137.3 g =   137.3 g

mass of 2 mol Cl =   2(35.45 g) =   70.90 g

mass of 8 mol O =   8(16.00 g) =   128.0 g
_____
molar mass of $Ba(ClO_4)_2$ =   336.2 g

b.   mass of 1 mol Mg =   24.31 g =   24.31 g

mass of 1 mol S =   32.07 g =   32.07 g

mass of 4 mol O =   4(16.00 g) =   64.00 g
_____
molar mass of $MgSO_4$ =   120.38 g

c.   mass of 1 mol Pb =   207.2 g =   207.2 g

mass of 2 mol Cl = 2(35.45 g) = 79.90 g
_____

molar mass of $PbCl_2$ =   278.1 g

d.   mass of 1 mol Cu =   63.55 g =   63.55 g

mass of 2 mol N =   2(14.01 g) =   28.02 g

mass of 6 mol O =   6(16.00 g) =   96.00 g
_____

molar mass of $Cu(NO_3)_2$ =   187.57 g

e.   mass of 1 mol Sn =   118.7 g =   118.7 g

mass of 4 mol Cl = 4(35.45 g) = 141.80
_____

molar mass of $SnCl_4$ =   260.5 g

f.   mass of 6 mol C =   6(12.01 g) = 72.06 g

mass of 6 mol H =   6(1.008 g) =   6.048 g

mass of 1 mol O =   16.00 g =   16.00 g
_____

molar mass of = C_6H_6O 94.11 g

30. a.   mass of 2 mol N =   2(14.01 g) =   28.02 g

mass of 8 mol H =   8(1.008 g) =   8.064 g

mass of 1 mol S =   32.07 g =   32.07 g
_____

molar mass of $(NH_4)_2S$ =   68.154 g = 68.15 g

b.   mass of 6 mol C =   6(12.01 g) =   72.06 g

mass of 4 mol H =   4(1.008 g) =   4.032 g

mass of 1 mol O =   16.00 g =   16.00 g

mass of 2 mol Cl = 2(35.45 g) =   70.90 g
_____

molar mass of $C_6H_4OCl_2$ =   162.992 g = 162.99 g

c.   mass of 1 mol Ba =   137.33 g =   137.33 g

mass of 2 mol H =   2(1.008 g) = 2.016 g
_____

molar mass of BaH_2 =   139.346 g = 139.35 g

d.   mass of 1 mol K =   39.10 g =   39.10 g

mass of 2 mol H =   2(1.008 g) =   2.016 g

mass of 1 mol P =   30.97 g =   30.97 g

mass of 4 mol O =   4(16.00 g) =   64.00 g
_____

molar mass of KH_2PO_4 =   136.086 g = 136.09 g

e.   mass of 2 mol K =   2(39.10 g) =   78.20 g

mass of 1 mol H =   1.008 g =   1.008 g

mass of 1 mol P =   30.97 g =   30.97 g

mass of 4 mol O =   4(16.00 g) =   64.00 g
_____

molar mass of K_2HPO_4 =   174.178 g = 174.18 g

f.   mass of 3 mol K =   3(39.10 g) = 117.3 g

mass of 1 mol P =   30.97 g =   30.97 g

mass of 4 mol O =   4(16.00 g) =   64.00 g
_____

molar mass of K_3PO_4 =   212.27 g = 212.3 g

31. a.   molar mass of $AuCl_3$ = 303.4 g

$$5.25 \text{ g AuCl}_3 \times \frac{1 \text{ mol}}{303.4 \text{ g}} = 1.73 \times 10^{-2} \text{ mol AuCl}_3$$

b.   molar mass of SnO = 134.7 g

$$10.2 \text{ g SnO} \times \frac{1 \text{ mol}}{134.7 \text{ g}} = 7.57 \times 10^{-2} \text{ mol SnO}$$

c.   molar mass of $(NH_4)_2Cr_2O_7$ = 252.1 g

$$96.2 \text{ mg} \times \frac{1 \text{ g}}{1000 \text{ mg}} \times \frac{1 \text{ mol}}{252.1 \text{ g}} = 3.82 \times 10^{-4} \text{ mol } (NH_4)_2Cr_2O_7$$

d.   molar mass of $KMnO_4$ = 158.0 g

$$8.91 \text{ g KMnO}_4 \times \frac{1 \text{ mol}}{158.0 \text{ g}} = 5.64 \times 10^{-2} \text{ mol KMnO}_4$$

e.   molar mass of $Al_2(SO_4)_3$ = 342.2 g

$$125 \text{ } \mu g \times \frac{1 \text{ g}}{10^6 \text{ } \mu g} \times \frac{1 \text{ mol}}{342.2 \text{ g}} = 3.65 \times 10^{-7} \text{ mol Al}_2(SO_4)_3$$

32.   **a.**   molar mass of SO_3 = 80.07 g

$$49.2 \text{ mg } SO_3 \times \frac{1 \text{ g}}{1000 \text{ mg}} \times \frac{1 \text{ mol}}{80.07 \text{ g}} = 6.14 \times 10^{-4} \text{ mol } SO_3$$

b.   molar mass of PbO_2 = 239.2 g

$$7.44 \times 10^4 \text{ kg } PbO_2 \times \frac{1000 \text{ g}}{1 \text{ kg}} \times \frac{1 \text{ mol}}{239.2 \text{ g}} = 3.11 \times 10^5 \text{ mol } PbO_2$$

c.   molar mass of $CHCl_3$ 119.37 g

$$59.1 \text{ g } CHCl_3 \times \frac{1 \text{ mol}}{119.37 \text{ g}} = 0.495 \text{ mol } CHCl_3$$

d.   molar mass of $C_2H_3Cl_3$ = 133.39 g

$$3.27 \text{ } \mu g \times \frac{1 \text{ g}}{10^6 \text{ } \mu g} \times \frac{1 \text{ mol}}{133.39 \text{ g}} = 2.45 \times 10^{-8} \text{ mol } C_2H_3Cl_3$$

e.   molar mass of LiOH = 23.95 g

$$4.01 \text{ g LiOH} \times \frac{1 \text{ mol}}{23.95 \text{ g}} = 0.167 \text{ mol LiOH}$$

33.   **a.**   molar mass of $C_6H_{12}O_6$ = 180.16 g

$$18.0 \text{ g} \times \frac{1 \text{ mol}}{180.16 \text{ g}} = 0.0999 \text{ mol } C_6H_{12}O_6$$

b.   molar mass of N_2O = 44.02 g

$$21.94 \text{ g} \times \frac{1 \text{ mol}}{44.02 \text{ g}} = 0.4984 \text{ mol } N_2O$$

c.   molar mass of NO = 30.01 g

$$21.94 \text{ g} \times \frac{1 \text{ mol}}{30.01 \text{ g}} = 0.7311 \text{ mol NO}$$

d.   1 oz = 28.35 g

molar mass of $Au(C_2H_3O_2)_3$ = 374.1 g

$$1.24 \text{ oz} \times \frac{28.35 \text{ g}}{1 \text{ oz}} \times \frac{1 \text{ mol}}{374.1 \text{ g}} = 0.0940 \text{ mol } Au(C_2H_3O_2)_3$$

e.   molar mass of $(NH_4)_2Cr_2O_7$ = 252.1 g

$$44.2 \text{ g} \times \frac{1 \text{ mol}}{252.1 \text{ g}} = 0.175 \text{ mol } (NH_4)_2Cr_2O_7$$

34. a.   molar mass of NaH_2PO_4 = 120.0 g

$$4.26 \times 10^{-3} \text{ g } NaH_2PO_4 \times \frac{1 \text{ mol}}{120.0 \text{ g}} = 3.55 \times 10^{-5} \text{ mol } NaH_2PO_4$$

  b.   molar mass of CuCl = 99.00 g

$$521 \text{ g CuCl} \times \frac{1 \text{ mol}}{99.00 \text{ g}} = 5.26 \text{ mol CuCl}$$

  c.   molar mass of Fe = 55.85 g

$$151 \text{ kg Fe} \times \frac{1000 \text{ g}}{1 \text{ kg}} \times \frac{1 \text{ mol}}{55.85 \text{ g}} = 2.70 \times 10^3 \text{ mol Fe}$$

  d.   molar mass of SrF_2 = 125.6 g

$$8.76 \text{ g } SrF_2 \times \frac{1 \text{ mol}}{125.6 \text{ g}} = 0.0697 \text{ mol } SrF_2$$

  e.   molar mass of Al = 26.98 g

$$1.26 \times 10^4 \text{ g Al} \times \frac{1 \text{ mol}}{26.98 \text{ g}} = 467 \text{ mol Al}$$

35. a.   molar mass of K_2CrO_4 = 194.2 g

$$0.251 \text{ mol} \times \frac{194.2 \text{ g}}{1 \text{ mol}} = 48.7 \text{ g } K_2CrO_4$$

  b.   molar mass of $LiClO_4$ = 106.4 g

$$1.51 \text{ mol} \times \frac{106.4 \text{ g}}{1 \text{ mol}} = 161 \text{ g } LiClO_4$$

  c.   molar mass of PbO = 223.2 g

$$2.52 \times 10^4 \text{ mol} \times \frac{223.2 \text{ g}}{1 \text{ mol}} = 5.62 \times 10^6 \text{ g PbO}$$

  d.   molar mass of $PbCl_4$ = 349.0 g

$$1.74 \times 10^{-3} \text{ mol} \times \frac{349.0 \text{ g}}{1 \text{ mol}} = 0.607 \text{ g}$$

  e.   molar mass of SnF_2 = 156.7 g

$$0.00205 \text{ mol} \times \frac{156.7 \text{ g}}{1 \text{ mol}} = 0.321 \text{ g } SnF_2$$

36. a.   molar mass of AlI_3 = 407.7 g

$$1.50 \text{ mol } AlI_3 \times \frac{407.7 \text{ g}}{1 \text{ mol}} = 612 \text{ g } AlI_3$$

b.   molar mass of C_6H_6 = 78.11 g

$$1.91 \times 10^{-3} \text{ mol } C_6H_6 \times \frac{78.11 \text{ g}}{1 \text{ mol}} = 0.149 \text{ g } C_6H_6$$

c.   molar mass of $C_6H_{12}O_6$ = 180.2 g

$$4.00 \text{ mol } C_6H_{12}O_6 \times \frac{180.2 \text{ g}}{1 \text{ mol}} = 721 \text{ g } C_6H_{12}O_6$$

d.   molar mass of C_2H_5OH = 46.07 g

$$4.56 \times 10^5 \text{ mol } C_2H_5OH \times \frac{46.07 \text{ g}}{1 \text{ mol}} = 2.10 \times 10^7 \text{ g } C_2H_5OH$$

e.   molar mass of $Ca(NO_3)_2$ = 164.1 g

$$2.27 \text{ mol } Ca(NO_3)_2 \times \frac{164.1 \text{ g}}{1 \text{ mol}} = 373 \text{ g } Ca(NO_3)_2$$

37. a.   molar mass of C_2H_6O = 46.07 g

$$0.251 \text{ mol } \times \frac{46.07 \text{ g}}{1 \text{ mol}} = 11.6 \text{ g } C_2H_6O$$

b.   molar mass of CO_2 = 44.01 g

$$1.26 \text{ mol } \times \frac{44.01 \text{ g}}{1 \text{ mol}} = 55.5 \text{ g } CO_2$$

c.   molar mass of $AuCl_3$ = 303.4 g

$$9.31 \times 10^{-4} \text{ mol } \times \frac{303.4 \text{ g}}{1 \text{ mol}} = 0.282 \text{ g } AuCl_3$$

d.   molar mass of $NaNO_3$ = 85.00 g

$$7.74 \text{ mol } \times \frac{85.00 \text{ g}}{1 \text{ mol}} = 658 \text{ g } NaNO_3$$

e.   molar mass of Fe = 55.85 g

$$0.000357 \text{ mol } \times \frac{55.85 \text{ g}}{1 \text{ mol}} = 0.0199 \text{ g Fe}$$

38. a.   molar mass of CO_2 = 44.01 g

$$1.27 \text{ mmol} \times \frac{1 \text{ mol}}{10^3 \text{ mmol}} \times \frac{44.01 \text{ g}}{1 \text{ mol}} = 0.0559 \text{ g } CO_2$$

  b.   molar mass of NCl_3 = 120.4 g

$$4.12 \times 10^3 \text{ mol } NCl_3 \times \frac{120.4 \text{ g}}{1 \text{ mol}} = 4.96 \times 10^5 \text{ g } NCl_3$$

  c.   molar mass of NH_4NO_3 = 80.05 g

$$0.00451 \text{ mol } NH_4NO_3 \times \frac{80.05 \text{ g}}{1 \text{ mol}} = 0.361 \text{ g } NH_4NO_3$$

  d.   molar mass of H_2O = 18.02 g

$$18.0 \text{ mol } H_2O \times \frac{18.02 \text{ g}}{1 \text{ mol}} = 324 \text{ g } H_2O$$

  e.   molar mass of $CuSO_4$ = 159.6 g

$$62.7 \text{ mol } CuSO_4 \times \frac{159.6 \text{ g}}{1 \text{ mol}} = 1.00 \times 10^4 \text{ g } CuSO_4$$

39. a.   4.75 millimol = 0.00475 mol

$$0.00475 \text{ mol} \times \frac{6.022 \times 10^{23} \text{ molecules}}{1 \text{ mol}} = 2.86 \times 10^{21} \text{ molecules}$$

  b.   molar mass of PH_3 = 33.99 g

$$4.75 \text{ g} \times \frac{6.022 \times 10^{23} \text{ molecules}}{33.99 \text{ g}} = 8.42 \times 10^{22} \text{ molecules}$$

  c.   molar mass of $Pb(C_2H_3O_2)_2$ = 325.3 g

$$1.25 \times 10^{-2} \text{ g} \times \frac{6.022 \times 10^{23} \text{ form. units}}{325.3 \text{ g}} = 2.31 \times 10^{19} \text{ form. units}$$

  d. $$1.25 \times 10^{-2} \text{ mol} \times \frac{6.022 \times 10^{23} \text{ form. units}}{1 \text{ mol}}$$

$$= 7.53 \times 10^{21} \text{ form. units}$$

  e.   If the sample contains a total of 5.40 mol of carbon, then since each benzene contains 6 carbons, there must be (5.40/6) = 0.900 mol of benzene present.

$$0.900 \text{ mol} \times \frac{6.022 \times 10^{23} \text{ molecules}}{1 \text{ mol}} = 5.42 \times 10^{23} \text{ molecules}$$

40. a. $$6.37 \text{ mol } CO \times \frac{6.022 \times 10^{23} \text{ molecules}}{1 \text{ mol}} = 3.84 \times 10^{24} \text{ molecules } CO$$

b.   molar mass of CO = 28.01 g

$$6.37 \text{ g} \times \frac{1 \text{ mol}}{28.01 \text{ g}} \times \frac{6.022 \times 10^{23} \text{ molec.}}{1 \text{ mol}} = 1.37 \times 10^{23} \text{ molecules CO}$$

c.   molar mass of H_2O = 18.02 g

$$2.62 \times 10^{-6} \text{ g} \times \frac{6.022 \times 10^{23} \text{ molecules}}{18.02 \text{ g}} = 8.76 \times 10^{16} \text{ molecules } H_2O$$

d. $2.62 \times 10^{-6} \text{ g} \times \dfrac{6.022 \times 10^{23} \text{ molecules}}{1 \text{ mol}} = 1.58 \times 10^{18} \text{ molecules } H_2O$

e.   molar mass of C_6H_6 = 78.11 g

$$5.23 \text{ g} \times \frac{6.022 \times 10^{23} \text{ molecules}}{78.11 \text{ g}} = 4.03 \times 10^{22} \text{ molecules } C_6H_6$$

41.   a.   molar mass of C_2H_6O = 46.07 g

$$1.271 \text{ g} \times \frac{1 \text{ mol}}{46.07 \text{ g}} = 0.02759 \text{ mol } C_2H_6O$$

$$0.02759 \text{ mol } C_2H_6O \times \frac{2 \text{ mol C}}{1 \text{ mol } C_2H_6O} = 0.05518 \text{ mol C}$$

b.   molar mass of $C_6H_4Cl_2$ = 147.0 g

$$3.982 \text{ g} \times \frac{1 \text{ mol}}{147.0 \text{ g}} = 0.027088 \text{ mol } C_6H_4Cl_2$$

$$0.027088 \text{ mol } C_6H_4Cl_2 \times \frac{6 \text{ mol C}}{1 \text{ mol } C_6H_4Cl_2} = 0.1625 \text{ mol C}$$

c.   molar mass of C_3O_2 = 68.03 g

$$0.4438 \text{ g} \times \frac{1 \text{ mol}}{68.03 \text{ g}} = 0.0065236 \text{ mol } C_3O_2$$

$$0.0065236 \text{ mol } C_3O_2 \times \frac{3 \text{ mol C}}{1 \text{ mol } C_3O_2} = 0.01957 \text{ mol C}$$

d.   molar mass of CH_2Cl_2 = 84.93 g

$$2.910 \text{ g} \times \frac{1 \text{ mol}}{84.93 \text{ g}} = 0.034264 \text{ mol } CH_2Cl_2$$

$$0.034264 \text{ mol } CH_2Cl_2 \times \frac{1 \text{ mol C}}{1 \text{ mol } CH_2Cl_2} = 0.03426 \text{ mol C}$$

42.   a.   molar mass of Na_2SO_4 = 142.1 g

$$2.01 \text{ g } Na_2SO_4 \times \frac{1 \text{ mol } Na_2SO_4}{142.1 \text{ g}} \times \frac{1 \text{ mol S}}{1 \text{ mol } Na_2SO_4} = 0.0141 \text{ mol S}$$

b.   molar mass of Na_2SO_3 = 126.1 g

$$2.01 \text{ g } Na_2SO_3 \times \frac{1 \text{ mol } Na_2SO_3}{126.1 \text{ g}} \times \frac{1 \text{ mol S}}{1 \text{ mol } Na_2SO_3} = 0.0159 \text{ mol S}$$

c.   molar mass of Na_2S = 78.05 g

$$2.01 \text{ g } Na_2S \times \frac{1 \text{ mol } Na_2S}{78.05 \text{ g}} \times \frac{1 \text{ mol S}}{1 \text{ mol } Na_2S} = 0.0258 \text{ mol S}$$

d.   molar mass of $Na_2S_2O_3$ = 158.1 g

$$2.01 \text{ g } Na_2S_2O_3 \times \frac{1 \text{ mol } Na_2S_2O_3}{158.1 \text{ g}} \times \frac{2 \text{ mol S}}{1 \text{ mol } Na_2S_2O_3} = 0.0254 \text{ mol S}$$

43.   molar

44.   less than

45.   a.   mass of Mg present =   1(24.31 g) =   24.31 g

mass of N present =   2(14.01 g) =   28.02 g

mass of O present =   6(16.00 g) =   96.00 g
———
molar mass of $Mg(NO_3)_2$ =   148.33 g

$$\% \text{ Mg} = \frac{24.31 \text{ g Mg}}{148.33 \text{ g}} \times 100 = 16.39\% \text{ Mg}$$

$$\% \text{ N} = \frac{28.02 \text{ g N}}{148.33 \text{ g}} \times 100 = 18.89\% \text{ N}$$

$$\% \text{ O} = \frac{96.00 \text{ g O}}{148.33 \text{ g}} \times 100 = 64.72\% \text{ O}$$

b.   mass of Ca present =   1(40.08 g) =   40.08 g

mass of Cl present =   2(35.45 g) =   70.90 g
———
molar mass of $CaCl_2$ =   110.98 g

$$\% \text{ Ca} = \frac{40.08 \text{ g Ca}}{110.98 \text{ g}} \times 100 = 36.11\% \text{ Ca}$$

$$\% \text{ Cl} = \frac{70.90 \text{ g Cl}}{110.98 \text{ g}} \times 100 = 63.89\% \text{ Cl}$$

c.   mass of C present =   1(12.01 g) =   12.01 g

mass of Br present =   4(79.90 g) = 319.6 g
———
molar mass of CBr_4 =   331.6 g

$$\% \text{ C} = \frac{12.01 \text{ g C}}{331.6 \text{ g}} \times 100 = 3.622\% \text{ C}$$

$$\% \ Br = \frac{319.6 \text{ g Br}}{331.6 \text{ g}} \times 100 = 96.38\% \ Br$$

d.   mass of Na present =   2(22.99 g) =   45.98 g

mass of S present =   1(32.07 g) =   32.07 g

mass of O present =   3(16.00 g) =   48.00 g

molar mass of Na_2SO_3 =   126.05 g

$$\% \ Na = \frac{45.98 \text{ g Na}}{126.05 \text{ g}} \times 100 = 36.48\% \ Na$$

$$\% \ S = \frac{32.07 \text{ g S}}{126.05 \text{ g}} \times 100 = 25.44\% \ S$$

$$\% \ O = \frac{48.00 \text{ g O}}{126.05 \text{ g}} \times 100 = 38.08\% \ O$$

e.   mass of Na present =   2(22.99 g) =   45.98 g

mass of S present =   1(32.07 g) =   32.07 g

mass of O present =   4(16.00 g) =   64.00 g

molar mass of Na_2SO_4 =   142.05 g

$$\% \ Na = \frac{45.98 \text{ g Na}}{142.05 \text{ g}} \times 100 = 32.37\% \ Na$$

$$\% \ S = \frac{32.07 \text{ g S}}{142.05 \text{ g}} \times 100 = 22.58\% \ S$$

$$\% \ O = \frac{64.00 \text{ g O}}{142.05 \text{ g}} \times 100 = 45.05\% \ O$$

f.   mass of Na present =   2(22.99) =   45.98 g

mass of S present =   1(32.07 g)   32.07 g

molar mass of Na_2S =   78.05 g

$$\% \ Na = \frac{45.98 \text{ g Na}}{78.05 \text{ g}} \times 100 = 58.91\% \ Na$$

$$\% \ S = \frac{32.07 \text{ g C}}{78.05 \text{ g}} \times 100 = 41.09\% \ S$$

g.   mass of Na present =   1(22.99 g) =   22.99 g

mass of H present =   1(1.008 g) =   1.008 g

mass of S present =   1(32.07 g) =   32.07 g

mass of O present =   4(16.00 g) =   64.00 g

molar mass of $NaHSO_4$ =   120.07 g

$$\% \text{ Na} = \frac{22.99 \text{ g Na}}{120.07 \text{ g}} \times 100 = 19.15\% \text{ Na}$$

$$\% \text{ H} = \frac{1.008 \text{ g H}}{120.07 \text{ g}} \times 100 = 0.8395\% \text{ H}$$

$$\% \text{ S} = \frac{32.07 \text{ g S}}{120.07 \text{ g}} \times 100 = 26.71\% \text{ S}$$

$$\% \text{ O} = \frac{64.00 \text{ g O}}{120.07 \text{ g}} \times 100 = 53.30\% \text{ O}$$

h. mass of Na present =   1(22.99 g) = 22.99 g

mass of H present =   1(1.008 g) = 1.008 g

mass of S present =   1(32.07 g) = 32.07 g

mass of O present =   3(16.00 g) = 48.00 g

molar mass of $NaHSO_3$ =   104.07 g

$$\% \text{ Na} = \frac{22.99 \text{ g Na}}{104.07 \text{ g}} \times 100 = 22.09\% \text{ Na}$$

$$\% \text{ H} = \frac{1.008 \text{ g H}}{104.07 \text{ g}} \times 100 = 0.9686\% \text{ H}$$

$$\% \text{ S} = \frac{32.07 \text{ g S}}{104.07 \text{ g}} \times 100 = 30.82\% \text{ S}$$

$$\% \text{ O} = \frac{48.00 \text{ g O}}{104.07 \text{ g}} \times 100 = 46.12\% \text{ O}$$

46. a. mass of Na present =   2(22.99 g) = 45.98 g

mass of S present =   32.07 g = 32.07 g

mass of O present =   4(16.00 g) = 64.00 g

molar mass of Na_2SO_4 =   142.05 g

$$\% \text{Na} = \frac{45.98 \text{ g Na}}{142.05 \text{ g}} \times 100 = 32.37\% \text{ Na}$$

$$\% \text{S} = \frac{32.07 \text{ g S}}{142.05 \text{ g}} \times 100 = 22.58\% \text{ S}$$

$$\% \text{O} = \frac{64.00 \text{ g O}}{142.05 \text{ g}} \times 100 = 45.05\% \text{ O}$$

b. mass of Na present =   2(22.99 g) = 45.98 g

mass of S present =   32.07 g = 32.07 g

mass of O present =   3(16.00 g) = 48.00 g

molar mass of Na_2SO_3 =   126.05 g

$$\%Na = \frac{45.98 \text{ g Na}}{126.05 \text{ g}} \times 100 = 36.48\% \text{ Na}$$

$$\%S = \frac{32.07 \text{ g S}}{126.05 \text{ g}} \times 100 = 25.44\% \text{ S}$$

$$\%O = \frac{48.00 \text{ g O}}{126.05 \text{ g}} \times 100 = 38.08\% \text{ O}$$

c. mass of Na present =   2(22.99 g) =   45.98 g

mass of S present =   32.07 g =   32.07 g

molar mass of Na_2S =   78.05 g

$$\%Na = \frac{45.98 \text{ g Na}}{78.05 \text{ g}} \times 100 = 58.91\% \text{ Na}$$

$$\%S = \frac{32.07 \text{ g S}}{78.05 \text{ g}} \times 100 = 41.09\% \text{ S}$$

d. mass of Na present =   2(22.99 g) =   45.98 g

mass of S present =   2(32.07 g) =   64.14 g

mass of O present =   3(16.00 g) =   48.00 g

molar mass of $Na_2S_2O_3$ =   158.12 g

$$\%Na = \frac{45.98 \text{ g Na}}{158.12 \text{ g}} \times 100 = 29.08\% \text{ Na}$$

$$\%S = \frac{64.14 \text{ g S}}{158.12 \text{ g}} \times 100 = 40.56\% \text{ S}$$

$$\%O = \frac{48.00 \text{ g O}}{158.12 \text{ g}} \times 100 = 30.36\% \text{ O}$$

e. mass of K present =   3(39.10 g) = 117.3 g

mass of P present =   30.97 g =   30.97 g

mass of O present =   4(16.00 g) =   64.00 g

molar mass of K_3PO_4 =   212.3 g

$$\%K = \frac{117.3 \text{ g K}}{212.3 \text{ g}} \times 100 = 55.25\% \text{ K}$$

$$\%P = \frac{30.97 \text{ g P}}{212.3 \text{ g}} \times 100 = 14.59\% \text{ P}$$

$$\%O = \frac{64.00 \text{ g O}}{212.3 \text{ g}} \times 100 = 30.15\% \text{ O}$$

f. mass of K present =   2(39.10 g) = 78.20 g
    mass of H present =   1.008 g =   1.008 g
    mass of P present =   30.97 g =   30.97 g
    mass of O present =   4(16.00 g) = 64.00 g
    _____
    molar mass of K_2HPO_4 =   174.178 g = 174.18 g

$$\%K = \frac{78.20 \text{ g K}}{174.18 \text{ g}} \times 100 = 44.90\% \text{ K}$$

$$\%H = \frac{1.008 \text{ g H}}{174.18 \text{ g}} \times 100 = 0.5787\% \text{ H}$$

$$\%P = \frac{30.97 \text{ g P}}{174.18 \text{ g}} \times 100 = 17.78\% \text{ P}$$

$$\%O = \frac{64.00 \text{ g O}}{174.18 \text{ g}} * 100 = 36.74\% \text{ O}$$

g. mass of K present =   39.10 g =   39.10 g
    mass of H present =   2(1.008 g) =   2.016 g
    mass of P present =   30.97 g =   30.97 g
    mass of O present =   4(16.00 g) = 64.00 g
    _____
    molar mass of KH_2PO_4 =   136.09 g

$$\%K = \frac{39.10 \text{ g K}}{136.09 \text{ g}} \times 100 = 28.73\% \text{ K}$$

$$\%H = \frac{2.016 \text{ g H}}{136.09 \text{ g}} \times 100 = 1.481\% \text{ H}$$

$$\%P = \frac{30.97 \text{ g P}}{136.09 \text{ g}} \times 100 = 22.76\% \text{ P}$$

$$\%O = \frac{64.00 \text{ g O}}{136.09 \text{ g}} \times 100 = 47.03\% \text{ O}$$

h. mass of K present =   3(39.10 g) = 117.3 g
    mass of P present =   30.97 g =   30.97 g
    _____
    molar mass of K_3P =   148.27 g = 148.3 g

$$\%K = \frac{117.3 \text{ g K}}{148.3 \text{ g}} \times 100 = 79.10\% \text{ K}$$

$$\%P = \frac{30.97 \text{ g P}}{148.3 \text{ g}} \times 100 = 20.88\% \text{ P}$$

47. a.   molar mass of CH_4 = 16.04 g

$$\% \text{ C} = \frac{12.01 \text{ g C}}{16.04 \text{ g}} \times 100 = 74.88\% \text{ C}$$

b.   molar mass $NaNO_3$ = 85.00 g

$$\% \text{ Na} = \frac{22.99 \text{ g Na}}{85.00 \text{ g}} \times 100 = 27.05\% \text{ Na}$$

c.   molar mass of CO = 28.01 g

$$\% \text{ C} = \frac{12.01 \text{ g C}}{28.01 \text{ g}} \times 100 = 42.88\% \text{ C}$$

d.   molar mass of NO_2 = 46.01 g

$$\% \text{ N} = \frac{14.01 \text{ g N}}{46.01 \text{ g}} \times 100 = 30.45\% \text{ N}$$

e.   molar mass of $C_8H_{18}O$ = 130.2 g

$$\% \text{ C} = \frac{96.08 \text{ g C}}{130.2 \text{ g}} \times 100 = 73.79\% \text{ C}$$

f.   molar mass of $Ca_3(PO_4)_2$ = 310.1 g

$$\% \text{ Ca} = \frac{120.2 \text{ g Ca}}{310.1 \text{ g}} \times 100 = 38.76\% \text{ Ca}$$

g.   molar mass of $C_{12}H_{10}O$ = 170.2 g

$$\% \text{ C} = \frac{144.1 \text{ g C}}{170.2 \text{ g}} \times 100 = 84.67\% \text{ C}$$

h.   molar mass of $Al(C_2H_3O_2)_3$ = 204.1 g

$$\% \text{ Al} = \frac{26.98 \text{ g Al}}{204.1 \text{ g}} \times 100 = 13.22\% \text{ Al}$$

48. a.   molar mass of $CuBr_2$ = 223.4

$$\% \text{ Cu} = \frac{63.55 \text{ g Cu}}{223.4 \text{ g}} \times 100 = 28.45\% \text{ Cu}$$

b.   molar mass of CuBr = 143.5 g

$$\% \text{ Cu} = \frac{63.55 \text{ g Cu}}{143.5 \text{ g}} \times 100 = 44.29\% \text{ Cu}$$

c.   molar mass of $FeCl_2$ = 126.75 g

$$\% \text{ Fe} = \frac{55.85 \text{ g Fe}}{126.75 \text{ g}} \times 100 = 44.06\% \text{ Fe}$$

d.   molar mass of $FeCl_3$ = 162.2 g

$$\% \text{ Fe} = \frac{55.85 \text{ g Fe}}{162.2 \text{ g}} \times 100 = 34.43\% \text{ Fe}$$

e.   molar mass of CoI_2 = 312.7 g

$$\% \text{ Co} = \frac{58.93 \text{ g Co}}{312.7 \text{ g}} \times 100 = 18.85\% \text{ Co}$$

f.   molar mass of CoI_3 = 439.6 g

$$\% \text{ Co} = \frac{58.93 \text{ g Co}}{439.6 \text{ g}} \times 100 = 13.41\% \text{ Co}$$

g.   molar mass of SnO = 134.7 g

$$\% \text{ Sn} = \frac{118.7 \text{ g Sn}}{134.7 \text{ g}} \times 100 = 88.12\% \text{ Sn}$$

h.   molar mass of SnO_2 = 150.7 g

$$\% \text{ Sn} = \frac{118.7 \text{ g Sn}}{150.7 \text{ g}} \times 100 = 78.77\% \text{ Sn}$$

49.   a.   molar mass of $C_6H_{10}O_4$ = 146.1 g

$$\% \text{ C} = \frac{72.06 \text{ g C}}{146.1 \text{ g}} \times 100 = 49.32\% \text{ C}$$

b.   molar mass of NH_4NO_3 = 80.05 g

$$\% \text{ N} = \frac{28.02 \text{ g N}}{80.05 \text{ g}} \times 100 = 35.00\% \text{ N}$$

c.   molar mass of $C_8H_{10}N_4O_2$ = 194.2 g

$$\% \text{ C} = \frac{96.08 \text{ g C}}{194.2 \text{ g}} \times 100 = 49.47\% \text{ C}$$

d.   molar mass of ClO_2 = 67.45 g

$$\% \text{ Cl} = \frac{35.45 \text{ g Cl}}{67.45 \text{ g}} \times 100 = 52.56\% \text{ Cl}$$

e.   molar mass of $C_6H_{11}OH$ = 100.2 g

$$\% \text{ C} = \frac{72.06 \text{ g C}}{100.2 \text{ g}} \times 100 = 71.92\% \text{ C}$$

f.   molar mass of $C_6H_{12}O_6$ = 180.2 g

$$\% \text{ C} = \frac{72.06 \text{ g C}}{180.2 \text{ g}} \times 100 = 39.99\% \text{ C}$$

g.   molar mass of $C_{20}H_{42}$ = 282.5 g

$$\% \text{ C} = \frac{240.2 \text{ g C}}{282.5 \text{ g}} \times 100 = 85.03\% \text{ C}$$

h.   molar mass of C_2H_5OH = 46.07 g

$$\% \ C = \frac{24.02 \ g \ C}{46.07 \ g} \times 100 = 52.14\% \ C$$

50.   a.   molar mass of $FeCl_3$ = 162.2 g

$$\%Fe = \frac{55.85 \ g \ Fe}{162.2 \ g} \times 100 = 34.43\% \ Fe$$

b.   molar mass of OF_2 = 54.00 g

$$\%O = \frac{16.00 \ g \ O}{54.00 \ g} \times 100 = 29.63\% \ O$$

c.   molar mass of C_6H_6 = 78.11 g

$$\%C = \frac{72.06 \ g \ C}{78.11 \ g} \times 100 = 92.25\% \ C$$

d.   molar mass of NH_4ClO_4 = 117.5 g

$$\%N = \frac{14.01 \ g \ N}{117.5 \ g} \times 100 = 11.92\% \ N$$

e.   molar mass of Ag_2O = 231.8 g

$$\%Ag = \frac{215.8 \ g \ Ag}{231.8 \ g} \times 100 = 93.10\% \ Ag$$

f.   molar mass of $CoCl_2$ = 129.83 g

$$\%Co = \frac{58.93 \ g \ Co}{129.83 \ g} \times 100 = 45.39\% \ Co$$

g.   molar mass of N_2O_4 = 92.02 g

$$\%N = \frac{28.02 \ g \ N}{92.02 \ g} \times 100 = 30.45\% \ N$$

h.   molar mass of $MnCl_2$ = 125.84 g

$$\%Mn = \frac{54.94 \ g \ Mn}{125.8 \ g} \times 100 = 43.66\% \ Mn$$

51.   a.   molar mass of NH_4I = 144.94 g

$$4.25 \ g \times \frac{1 \ mol \ NH_4I}{144.94 \ g} \times \frac{1 \ mol \ NH_4^+}{1 \ mol \ NH_4I} = 0.0293 \ mol \ NH_4^+$$

molar mass of NH_4^+ = 18.04 g

$$0.0293 \ mol \ NH_4^+ \times \frac{18.04 \ g \ NH_4^+}{1 \ mol \ NH_4^+} = 0.529 \ g \ NH_4^+$$

b. $6.31 \text{ mol } (NH_4)_2S \times \dfrac{2 \text{ mol } NH_4^+}{1 \text{ mol } (NH_4)_2S} = 12.6 \text{ mol } NH_4^+$

molar mass of NH_4^+ = 18.04 g

$12.6 \text{ mol } NH_4^+ \times \dfrac{18.04 \text{ g } NH_4^+}{1 \text{ mol } NH_4^+} = 227 \text{ g } NH_4^+ \text{ ion}$

c.   molar mass of Ba_3P_2 = 473.8 g

$9.71 \text{ g } \times \dfrac{1 \text{ mol } Ba_3P_2}{473.8 \text{ g}} \times \dfrac{3 \text{ mol } Ba^{2+}}{1 \text{ mol } Ba_3P_2} = 0.0615 \text{ mol } Ba^{2+}$

molar mass of Ba^{2+} = 137.3 g

$0.0615 \text{ mol } Ba^{2+} \times \dfrac{137.3 \text{ g } Ba^{2+}}{1 \text{ mol } Ba^{2+}} = 8.44 \text{ g } Ba^{2+}$

d. $7.63 \text{ mol } Ca_3(PO_4)_2 \times \dfrac{3 \text{ mol } Ca^{2+}}{1 \text{ mol } Ca_3(PO_4)_2} = 22.9 \text{ mol } Ca^{2+}$

molar mass of Ca^{2+} = 40.08 g

$22.9 \text{ mol } Ca^{2+} \times \dfrac{40.08 \text{ g } Ca^{2+}}{1 \text{ mol } Ca^{2+}} = 918 \text{ g } Ca^{2+}$

52.   a.   molar mass of NH_4Cl = 53.49 g

molar mass of NH_4^+ ion = 18.04 g

$\% \, NH_4^+ = \dfrac{18.04 \text{ g } NH_4^+}{53.49 \text{ g}} \times 100 = 33.73\% \, NH_4^+$

b.   molar mass of $CuSO_4$ = 159.62 g

molar mass of Cu^{2+} = 63.55 g

$\% \, Cu^{2+} = \dfrac{63.55 \text{ g } Cu^{2+}}{159.62 \text{ g}} \times 100 = 39.81\% \, Cu^{2+}$

c.   molar mass of $AuCl_3$ = 303.4 g

molar mass of Au^{3+} ion = 197.0 g

$\% \, Au^{3+} = \dfrac{197.0 \text{ g } Au^{3+}}{303.4 \text{ g}} \times 100 = 64.93\% \, Au^{3+}$

d.   molar mass of $AgNO_3$ = 169.9 g

molar mass of Ag^+ ion = 107.9 g

$\% \, Ag^+ = \dfrac{107.9 \text{ g } Ag^+}{169.9 \text{ g}} \times 100 = 63.51\% \, Ag^+$

53.   To determine the *empirical* formula of a new compound, the composition of the compound by mass must be known. To determine the *molecular* formula of the compound, the molar mass of the compound must also be known.

54.   The empirical formula represents the smallest whole number ratio of the elements present in a compound. The molecular formula indicates the actual number of atoms of each element found in a molecule of the substance.

55.   a.   NaO

　　　　b. $C_4H_3O_2$

　　　　c. $C_{12}H_{12}N_2O_3$ is already the empirical formula

　　　　d. C_2H_3Cl

56.   a   yes (each of these has empirical formula CH)

　　　　b.   no (the number of hydrogen atoms is wrong)

　　　　c.   yes (both have empirical formula NO_2)

　　　　d.   no (the number of hydrogen and oxygen atoms is wrong)

57. $0.1929 \text{ g C} \times \dfrac{1 \text{ mol C}}{12.01 \text{ g C}} = 0.01606 \text{ mol C}$

　　　　$0.01079 \text{ g H} \times \dfrac{1 \text{ mol H}}{1.008 \text{ g H}} = 0.01070 \text{ mol H}$

　　　　$0.08566 \text{ g O} \times \dfrac{1 \text{ mol O}}{16.00 \text{ g O}} = 0.005354 \text{ mol O}$

　　　　$0.1898 \text{ g Cl} \times \dfrac{1 \text{ mol Cl}}{35.45 \text{ g Cl}} = 0.005354 \text{ mol Cl}$

Dividing each number of moles by the smallest number of moles gives

$\dfrac{0.01606 \text{ mol C}}{0.005354} = 3.000 \text{ mol C}$

$\dfrac{0.01070 \text{ mol H}}{0.005354} = 1.999 \text{ mol H}$

$\dfrac{0.005354 \text{ mol O}}{0.005354} = 1.000 \text{ mol O}$

$\dfrac{0.005354 \text{ mol Cl}}{0.005354} = 1.000 \text{ mol Cl}$

The empirical formula is C_3H_2OCl

58. $2.514 \text{ g Ca} \times \dfrac{1 \text{ mol}}{40.08 \text{ g Ca}} = 0.06272 \text{ mol Ca}$

The increase in mass represents the oxygen with which the calcium reacted:

$$1.004 \text{ g O} \times \frac{1 \text{ mol}}{16.00 \text{ g O}} = 0.06275 \text{ mol O}$$

Since we have effectively the same number of moles of Ca and O, the empirical formula must be CaO.

59. $$0.2322 \text{ g C} \times \frac{1 \text{ mol C}}{12.01 \text{ g C}} = 0.01933 \text{ mol C}$$

$$0.05848 \text{ g H} \times \frac{1 \text{ mol H}}{1.008 \text{ mol H}} = 0.05802 \text{ mol H}$$

$$0.3091 \text{ g O} \times \frac{1 \text{ mol O}}{16.00 \text{ g O}} = 0.01932 \text{ mol O}$$

Dividing each number of moles by the smallest number of moles (0.01932 mol C) gives

$$\frac{0.01933 \text{ mol C}}{0.01932} = 1.001 \text{ mol C}$$

$$\frac{0.05802 \text{ mol H}}{0.01932} = 3.003 \text{ mol H}$$

$$\frac{0.01932 \text{ mol O}}{0.01932} = 1.000 \text{ mol O}$$

The empirical formula is CH_3O.

60.   Consider having 100.0 g of the compound. Then the percentages of the elements present are numerically equal to their masses in grams.

$$58.84 \text{ g Ba} \times \frac{1 \text{ mol}}{137.3 \text{ g Ba}} = 0.4286 \text{ mol Ba}$$

$$13.74 \text{ g S} \times \frac{1 \text{ mol}}{32.07 \text{ g S}} = 0.4284 \text{ mol S}$$

$$27.43 \text{ g O} \times \frac{1 \text{ mol}}{16.00 \text{ g O+}} = 1.714 \text{ mol O}$$

Dividing each number of moles by the smallest number of moles (0.4284 mol S) gives

$$\frac{0.4286 \text{ mol Ba}}{0.4284} = 1.000 \text{ mol Ba}$$

$$\frac{0.4284 \text{ mol S}}{0.4284} = 1.000 \text{ mol S}$$

$$\frac{1.714 \text{ mol O}}{0.4284} = 4.001 \text{ mol O}$$

The empirical formula is $BaSO_4$.

61. The mass of chlorine involved in the reaction is 6.280 − 1.271 = 5.009 g Cl

$$1.271 \text{ g Al} \times \frac{1 \text{ mol Al}}{26.98 \text{ g Al}} = 0.04711 \text{ mol Al}$$

$$5.009 \text{ g Cl} \times \frac{1 \text{ mol Cl}}{35.45 \text{ g Cl}} = 0.1413 \text{ mol Cl}$$

Dividing each of these number of moles by the smaller (0.04711 mol Al) shows that the empirical formula is $AlCl_3$

62. Consider 100.0 g of the compound.

$$29.16 \text{ g N} \times \frac{1 \text{ mol}}{14.01 \text{ g N}} = 2.081 \text{ mol N}$$

$$8.392 \text{ g H} \times \frac{1 \text{ mol}}{1.008 \text{ g H}} = 8.325 \text{ mol H}$$

$$12.50 \text{ g C} \times \frac{1 \text{ mol}}{12.01 \text{ g C}} = 1.041 \text{ mol C}$$

$$49.95 \text{ g O} \times \frac{1 \text{ mol}}{16.00 \text{ g O}} = 3.122 \text{ mol O}$$

Dividing each number of moles by the smallest (1.041 mol C) gives

$$\frac{2.081 \text{ mol N}}{1.041} = 1.999 \text{ mol N}$$

$$\frac{8.325 \text{ mol H}}{1.041} = 7.997 \text{ mol H}$$

$$\frac{1.041 \text{ mol C}}{1.041} = 1.000 \text{ mol C}$$

$$\frac{3.121 \text{ mol O}}{1.041} = 2.998 \text{ mol O}$$

The empirical formula is $N_2H_8CO_3$ [i.e, $(NH_4)_2CO_3$].

63.
$$3.269 \text{ g Zn} \times \frac{1 \text{ mol Zn}}{65.38 \text{ g Zn}} = 0.05000 \text{ mol Zn}$$

$$0.800 \text{ g O} \times \frac{1 \text{ mol O}}{16.00 \text{ g O}} = 0.0500 \text{ mol O}$$

Since the two components are present in equal amounts on a molar basis, the empirical formula must be simply ZnO.

64.   Consider 100.0 g of the compound.

$$55.06 \text{ g Co} \times \frac{1 \text{ mol}}{58.93 \text{ g Co}} = 0.9343 \text{ mol Co}$$

If the sulfide of cobalt is 55.06% Co, then it is 44.94% S by mass.

$$44.94 \text{ g S} \times \frac{1 \text{ mol}}{32.07 \text{ g S}} = 1.401 \text{ mol S}$$

Dividing each number of moles by the smaller (0.9343 mol Co) gives

$$\frac{0.9343 \text{ mol Co}}{0.9343} = 1.000 \text{ mol Co}$$

$$\frac{1.401 \text{ mol S}}{0.9343} = 1.500 \text{ mol S}$$

Multiplying by two, to convert to whole numbers of moles, gives the empirical formula for the compound as Co_2S_3.

65.
$$2.461 \text{ g Ca} \times \frac{1 \text{ mol Ca}}{40.08 \text{ g Ca}} = 0.06140 \text{ mol Ca}$$

$$4.353 \text{ g Cl} \times \frac{1 \text{ mol Cl}}{35.45 \text{ g Cl}} = 0.1228 \text{ mol Cl}$$

Dividing each of the number of moles by the smaller (0.06140 mol Ca) shows that the empirical formula is $CaCl_2$

66. $$10.00 \text{ g Cu} \times \frac{1 \text{ mol}}{63.55 \text{ g Cu}} = 0.1574 \text{ mol Cu}$$

$$2.52 \text{ g O} \times \frac{1 \text{ mol}}{16.00 \text{ g O}} = 0.158 \text{ mol O}$$

The numbers of moles are almost equal: the empirical formula is just CuO.

67.   Consider 100.0 g of the compound.

$$67.61 \text{ g U} \times \frac{1 \text{ mol U}}{238.0 \text{ g U}} = 0.2841 \text{ mol U}$$

$$32.39 \text{ g F} \times \frac{1 \text{ mol F}}{19.00 \text{ g F}} = 1.705 \text{ mol F}$$

Dividing each number of moles by the smaller number of moles (0.2841 mol U) gives

$$\frac{0.2841 \text{ mol U}}{0.2841} = 1.000 \text{ mol U}$$

$$\frac{1.705 \text{ mol F}}{0.2841} = 6.000 \text{ mol F}$$

The empirical formula is UF_6

68.   Consider 100.0 g of the compound.

$$32.13 \text{ g Al} \times \frac{1 \text{ mol}}{26.98 \text{ g Al}} = 1.191 \text{ mol Al}$$

$$67.87 \text{ g F} \times \frac{1 \text{ mol}}{19.00 \text{ g F}} = 3.572 \text{ mol F}$$

Dividing each number of moles by the smaller number (1.191 mol Al) gives

$$\frac{1.191 \text{ mol Al}}{1.191} = 1.000 \text{ mol Al}$$

$$\frac{3.572 \text{ mol F}}{1.191} = 2.999 \text{ mol F}$$

The empirical formula is AlF_3

69.   Consider 100.0 g of the compound.

$$33.88 \text{ g Cu} \times \frac{1 \text{ mol Cu}}{63.55 \text{ g Cu}} = 0.5331 \text{ mol Cu}$$

$$14.94 \text{ g N} \times \frac{1 \text{ mol N}}{14.01 \text{ g N}} = 1.066 \text{ mol N}$$

$$51.18 \text{ g} \times \frac{1 \text{ mol O}}{16.00 \text{ g O}} = 3.199 \text{ mol O}$$

Dividing each number of moles by the smaller number of moles (0.5331 mol Cu) gives

$$\frac{0.5331 \text{ mol Cu}}{0.5331} = 1.000 \text{ mol Cu}$$

$$\frac{1.066 \text{ mol N}}{0.5331} = 2.000 \text{ mol N}$$

$$\frac{3.199 \text{ mol O}}{0.5331} = 6.001 \text{ mol O}$$

The empirical formula is CuN_2O_6 [i.e., $Cu(NO_3)_2$]

70.   Consider 100.0 g of the compound.

$$59.78 \text{ g Li} \times \frac{1 \text{ mol Li}}{6.941 \text{ g Li}} = 8.613 \text{ mol Li}$$

$$40.22 \text{ g N} \times \frac{1 \text{ mol N}}{14.01 \text{ g N}} = 2.871 \text{ mol N}$$

Dividing each number of moles by the smaller number of moles (2.871 mol N) gives

$$\frac{8.613 \text{ mol Li}}{2.871} = 3.000 \text{ mol Li}$$

$$\frac{2.871 \text{ mol N}}{2.871} = 1.000 \text{ mol N}$$

The empirical formula is Li_3N.

71.   Consider 100.0 g of the compound.

$$66.75 \text{ g Cu} \times \frac{1 \text{ mol Cu}}{63.55 \text{ g Cu}} = 1.050 \text{ mol Cu}$$

$$10.84 \text{ g P} \times \frac{1 \text{ mol P}}{30.97 \text{ g P}} = 0.3500 \text{ mol P}$$

$$22.41 \text{ g O} \times \frac{1 \text{ mol O}}{16.00 \text{ g O}} = 1.401 \text{ mol O}$$

Dividing each number of moles by the smallest number of moles (0.3500 mol P) gives

$$\frac{1.050 \text{ mol Cu}}{0.3500} = 3.000 \text{ mol Cu}$$

$$\frac{0.3500 \text{ mol P}}{0.3500} = 1.000 \text{ mol P}$$

$$\frac{1.401 \text{ mol O}}{0.3500} = 4.003 \text{ mol O}$$

The empirical formula is thus Cu_3PO_4

72.   Consider 100.0 g of the compound.

$$15.77 \text{ g Al} \times \frac{1 \text{ mol Al}}{26.98 \text{ g Al}} = 0.5845 \text{ mol Al}$$

$$28.11 \text{ g S} \times \frac{1 \text{ mol S}}{32.07 \text{ g S}} = 0.8765 \text{ mol S}$$

$$56.12 \text{ g O} \times \frac{1 \text{ mol O}}{16.00 \text{ g O}} = 3.508 \text{ mol O}$$

Dividing each number of moles by the smallest number of moles (0.5845 mol Al) gives

$$\frac{0.5845 \text{ mol Al}}{0.5845} = 1.000 \text{ mol Al}$$

$$\frac{0.8765 \text{ mol S}}{0.5845} = 1.500 \text{ mol S}$$

$$\frac{3.508 \text{ mol O}}{0.5845} = 6.002 \text{ mol O}$$

Multiplying these relative numbers of moles by 2 to give whole numbers gives the empirical formula as $Al_2S_3O_{12}$ [i.e., $Al_2(SO_4)_3$].

73.   Consider 100.0 g of the compound.

$$80.69 \text{ g Hg} \times \frac{1 \text{ mol Hg}}{200.6 \text{ g Hg}} = 0.4022 \text{ mol Hg}$$

$$6.436 \text{ g S} \times \frac{1 \text{ mol S}}{32.07 \text{ g S}} = 0.2007 \text{ mol S}$$

$$12.87 \text{ g O} \times \frac{1 \text{ mol O}}{16.00 \text{ g O}} = 0.8044 \text{ mol O}$$

Dividing each number of moles by the smallest number of moles (0.2007 mol S) gives

$$\frac{0.4022 \text{ mol Hg}}{0.2007} = 2.004 \text{ mol Hg}$$

$$\frac{0.2007 \text{ mol S}}{0.2007} = 1.000 \text{ mol S}$$

$$\frac{0.8044 \text{ mol O}}{0.2007} = 4.008 \text{ mol O}$$

The empirical formula of the compound is Hg_2SO_4

74.   Compound 1: Assume 100.0 g of the compound.

$$83.12 \text{ g Na} \times \frac{1 \text{ mol Na}}{22.99 \text{ g Na}} = 3.615 \text{ mol Na}$$

$$16.88 \text{ g N} \times \frac{1 \text{ mol N}}{14.01 \text{ g N}} = 1.205 \text{ mol Na}$$

Dividing each number of moles by the smaller (1.205 mol Na) indicates that the formula of Compound 1 is Na_3N.

Compound 2: Assume 100.0 g of the compound.

$$35.36 \text{ g Na} \times \frac{1 \text{ mol Na}}{22.99 \text{ g Na}} = 1.538 \text{ mol Na}$$

$$64.64 \text{ g N} \times \frac{1 \text{ mol N}}{14.01 \text{ g N}} = 4.614 \text{ mol N}$$

Dividing each number of moles by the smaller (1.538 mol Na) indicates that the formula of Compound 2 is NaN_3

75. The *empirical formula* of a compound represents only the smallest whole number relationship between the number and type of atoms in a compound, whereas the *molecular formula* represents the actual number of atoms of each type in a true molecule of the substance. Many compounds (for example, H_2O) may have the same empirical and molecular formulas.

76. If only the empirical formula is known, the molar mass of the substance must be determined before the molecular formula can be calculated.

77. empirical formula mass of CH_2O = 30 g

$$n = \frac{\text{molar mass}}{\text{empirical formula mass}} = \frac{90 \text{ g}}{30 \text{ g}} = 3$$

molecular formula is $(CH_2O)_3 = C_3H_6O_3$.

78. empirical formula mass of CH = 13 g

$$n = \frac{\text{molar mass}}{\text{empirical formula mass}} = \frac{78 \text{ g}}{13 \text{ g}} = 6$$

The molecular formula is $(CH)_6$ or C_6H_6.

79. empirical formula mass of CH_2 = 14

$$n = \frac{\text{molar mass}}{\text{empirical formula mass}} = \frac{84 \text{ g}}{14 \text{ g}} = 6$$

molecular formula is $(CH_2)_6 = C_6H_{12}$.

80. empirical formula mass of CH_4O = 32.04 g

$$n = \frac{\text{molar mass}}{\text{empirical formula mass}} = \frac{192 \text{ g}}{32.04 \text{ g}} = 6$$

molecular formula is $(CH_4O)_6 = C_6H_{24}O_6$

81.   Consider 100.0 g of the compound.

$$42.87 \text{ g C} \times \frac{1 \text{ mol C}}{12.01 \text{ g C}} = 3.570 \text{ mol C}$$

$$3.598 \text{ g H} \times \frac{1 \text{ mol H}}{1.008 \text{ g H}} = 3.569 \text{ mol H}$$

$$28.55 \text{ g O} \times \frac{1 \text{ mol O}}{16.00 \text{ g O}} = 1.784 \text{ mol O}$$

$$25.00 \text{ g N} \times \frac{1 \text{ mol N}}{14.01 \text{ g N}} = 1.784 \text{ mol N}$$

Dividing each number of moles by the smallest number of moles (1.784   mol O) gives

$$\frac{3.570 \text{ mol C}}{1.784} = 2.001 \text{ mol C}$$

$$\frac{3.569 \text{ mol H}}{1.784} = 2.001 \text{ mol H}$$

$$\frac{1.784 \text{ mol O}}{1.784} = 1.000 \text{ mol O}$$

$$\frac{1.784 \text{ mol N}}{1.784} = 1.000 \text{ mol N}$$

The empirical formula of the compound is C_2H_2ON empirical formula mass of C_2H_2ON = 56

$$n = \frac{\text{molar mass}}{\text{empirical formula mass}} = \frac{168 \text{ g}}{56 \text{ g}} = 3$$

The molecular formula is $(C_2H_2ON)_3 = C_6H_6O_3N_3$.

82.   Consider 100.0 g of the compound.

$$65.45 \text{ g C} \times \frac{1 \text{ mol C}}{12.01 \text{ g C}} = 5.450 \text{ mol C}$$

$$5.492 \text{ g H} \times \frac{1 \text{ mol H}}{1.008 \text{ g H}} = 5.448 \text{ mol H}$$

$$29.06 \text{ g O} \times \frac{1 \text{ mol O}}{16.00 \text{ g O}} = 1.816 \text{ mol O}$$

Dividing each number of moles by the smallest number of moles (1.816 mol O) gives

$$\frac{5.450 \text{ mol C}}{1.816} = 3.001 \text{ mol C}$$

$$\frac{5.448 \text{ mol H}}{1.816} = 3.000 \text{ mol H}$$

$$\frac{1.816 \text{ mol O}}{1.816} = 1.000 \text{ mol O}$$

The empirical formula is C_3H_3O, and the empirical formula mass is approximately 55 g.

$$n = \frac{\text{molar mass}}{\text{empirical formula mass}} = \frac{110 \text{ g}}{55 \text{ g}} = 2$$

The molecular formula is $(C_3H_3O)_2 = C_6H_6O_2$.

83. [1] c   [6] d

  [2] e   [7] a

  [3] j   [8] g

  [4] h   [9] i

  [5] b   [10] f

84. 5.00 g Al   0.185 mol 1.12×10^{23} atoms

  0.140 g Fe   0.00250 mol 1.51×10^{21} atoms

  2.7×10^2 g Cu   4.3 mol 2.6×10^{24} atoms

  0.00250 g Mg 1.03×10^{-4} mol 6.19×10^{19} atoms

  0.062 g Na 2.7×10^{-3} mol 1.6×10^{21} atoms

  3.95×10^{-18} g U 1.66×10^{-20} mol 1.00×10^4 atoms

85. 4.24 g   0.0543 mol 3.27×10^{22} molec. 3.92×10^{23} atoms

  4.04 g   0.224 mol 1.35×10^{23} molec. 4.05×10^{23} atoms

  1.98 g   0.0450 mol 2.71×10^{22} molec. 8.13×10^{22} atoms

  45.9 g   1.26 mol 7.59×10^{23} molec. 1.52×10^{24} atoms

  126 g   6.99 mol 4.21×10^{24} molec. 1.26×10^{25} atoms

  0.297 g   0.00927 mol 5.58×10^{21} molec. 3.35×10^{22} atoms

86. mass of 2 mol X =   2(41.2 g) =   82.4 g

  mass of 1 mol Y =   57.7 g =   57.7 g

  mass of 3 mol Z =   3(63.9 g) =   191.7 g

  ──

  molar mass of X_2YZ_3 =   331.8 g

$$\% \ X = \frac{82.4 \text{ g}}{331.8 \text{ g}} \times 100 = 24.8\% \ \ X$$

$$\% \ Y = \frac{57.7 \text{ g}}{331.8 \text{ g}} \times 100 = 17.4\% \ \ Y$$

$$\% \ Z = \frac{191.7 \text{ g}}{331.8 \text{ g}} \times 100 = 57.8\% \ \ Z$$

If the molecular formula were actually $X_4Y_2Z_6$, the percentage composition would be the same, and the *relative* mass of each element present would not change. The molecular formula is always a whole number multiple of the empirical formula.

87.   magnesium/nitrogen compound:

mass of nitrogen contained = 1.2791 g – 0.9240 = 0.3551 g N

$$0.9240 \text{ g Mg} \times \frac{1 \text{ mol Mg}}{24.31 \text{ g Mg}} = 0.03801 \text{ mol Mg}$$

$$0.3551 \text{ g N} \times \frac{1 \text{ mol N}}{14.01 \text{ g N}} = 0.02535 \text{ mol N}$$

Dividing each number of moles by the smaller number of moles gives

$$\frac{0.03801 \text{ mol Mg}}{0.02535} = 1.499 \text{ mol Mg}$$

$$\frac{0.02535 \text{ mol N}}{0.02535} = 1.000 \text{ mol N}$$

Multiplying by two, to convert to whole numbers, gives the empirical formula as Mg_3N_2

magnesium/oxygen compound:

Consider 100.0 g of the compound.

$$60.31 \text{ g Mg} \times \frac{1 \text{ mol Mg}}{24.31 \text{ g Mg}} = 2.481 \text{ mol Mg}$$

$$39.69 \text{ g O} \times \frac{1 \text{ mol O}}{16.00 \text{ g O}} = 2.481 \text{ mol O}$$

Since the numbers of moles are the same, the compound contains the same relative number of Mg and O atoms: the empirical formula is MgO.

88.   For the first compound (*restricted* amount of oxygen)

$$2.118 \text{ g Cu} \times \frac{1 \text{ mol Cu}}{63.54 \text{ g Cu}} = 0.03333 \text{ mol Cu}$$

$$0.2666 \text{ g O} \times \frac{1 \text{ mol O}}{16.00 \text{ g O}} = 0.01666 \text{ mol O}$$

Since the number of moles of Cu (0.03333 mol) is twice the number of moles of O (0.01666 mol), the empirical formula is Cu_2O.

For the second compound (stream of pure oxygen)

$$2.118 \text{ g Cu} \times \frac{1 \text{ mol Cu}}{63.54 \text{ g Cu}} = 0.03333 \text{ mol Cu}$$

$$0.5332 \text{ g O} \times \frac{1 \text{ mol O}}{16.00 \text{ g O}} = 0.03333 \text{ mol O}$$

Since the numbers of moles are the same, the empirical formula is CuO.

89.

compound	molar mass	% H
HF	20.01 g	5.037%
HCl	36.46 g	2.765%
HBr	80.91 g	1.246%
HI	127.9 g	0.7881%

90.   a.   molar mass H_2O = 18.02 g

$$4.21 \text{ g} \times \frac{1 \text{ mol}}{18.02 \text{ g}} \times \frac{6.022 \times 10^{23} \text{ molecules}}{1 \text{ mol}} = 1.41 \times 10^{23} \text{ molecules}$$

The sample contains 1.41×10^{23} oxygen atoms and $2(1.41 \times 10^{23})$ = 2.82×10^{23} hydrogen atoms

b.   molar mass CO_2 = 44.01 g

$$6.81 \text{ g} \times \frac{1 \text{ mol}}{44.01 \text{ g}} \times \frac{6.022 \times 10^{23} \text{ molecules}}{1 \text{ mol}} = 9.32 \times 10^{22} \text{ molecules}$$

The sample contains 9.32×10^{22} carbon atoms and $2(9.32 \times 10^{22})$ = 1.86×10^{23} oxygen atoms.

c.   molar mass C_6H_6 = 78.11 g

$$0.000221 \text{ g} \times \frac{1 \text{ mol}}{78.11 \text{ g}} \times \frac{6.022 \times 10^{23} \text{ molecules}}{1 \text{ mol}} = 1.70 \times 10^{18} \text{ molec.}$$

The sample contains $6(1.70 \times 10^{18})$ = 1.02×10^{19} atoms of each element.

d. $2.26 \text{ mol} \times \dfrac{6.022 \times 10^{23} \text{ molecules}}{1 \text{ mol}} = 1.36 \times 10^{24} \text{ molecules}$

atoms C = 12(1.36 × 10²⁴) = 1.63 × 10²⁵ atoms
atoms H = 22(1.36 × 10²⁴) = 2.99 × 10²⁵ atoms
atoms O = 11(1.36 × 10²⁴) = 1.50 × 10²⁵ atoms

91.   a.   Assuming 10,000,000,000 = 1.0×10^{10}

$1.0 \times 10^{10} \text{ molecules} \times \dfrac{28.02 \text{ g N}_2}{6.022 \times 10^{23} \text{ molecules}} = 4.7 \times 10^{-13} \text{ g N}_2$

b. $2.49 \times 10^{20} \text{ molecules} \times \dfrac{44.01 \text{ g CO}_2}{6.022 \times 10^{23} \text{ molecules}} = 0.0182 \text{ g CO}_2$

c. $7.0983 \text{ mol NaCl} \times \dfrac{58.44 \text{ g NaCl}}{1 \text{ mol NaCl}} = 414.8 \text{ g NaCl}$

d. $9.012 \times 10^{-6} \text{ mol C}_2\text{H}_4\text{Cl}_2 \times \dfrac{98.95 \text{ g C}_2\text{H}_4\text{Cl}_2}{1 \text{ mol C}_2\text{H}_4\text{Cl}_2} = 8.918 \times 10^{-4} \text{ g C}_2\text{H}_4\text{Cl}_2$

92.   a.   molar mass of C_3O_2 = 3(12.01 g) + 2(16.00 g) = 68.03 g

$\% \text{ C} = \dfrac{36.03 \text{ g}}{68.03 \text{ g}} = 52.96\% \text{ C}$

$7.819 \text{ g C}_3\text{O}_2 \times \dfrac{52.96 \text{ g C}}{100.0 \text{ g C}_3\text{O}_2} = 4.141 \text{ g C}$

$4.141 \text{ g C} \times \dfrac{6.022 \times 10^{23} \text{ C atoms}}{12.01 \text{ g C}} = 2.076 \times 10^{23} \text{ C atoms}$

b.   molar mass of CO = 12.01 g + 16.00 g = 28.01 g

$\% \text{ C} = \dfrac{12.01 \text{ g}}{28.01 \text{ g}} \times 100 = 42.88\% \text{ C}$

$1.53 \times 10^{21} \text{ molecules CO} \times \dfrac{1 \text{ C atom}}{1 \text{ molecule CO}} = 1.53 \times 10^{21} \text{ C atoms}$

$1.53 \times 10^{21} \text{ C atoms} \times \dfrac{12.01 \text{ g C}}{6.022 \times 10^{23} \text{ C atoms}} = 0.0305 \text{ g C}$

c.   molar mass of C_6H_6O = 6(12.01 g) + 6(1.008 g) + 16.00 g = 94.11 g

$\% \text{ C} = \dfrac{72.06 \text{ g}}{94.11 \text{ g}} \times 100 = 76.57\% \text{ C}$

$$0.200 \text{ mol } C_6H_6O \times \frac{6 \text{ mol C}}{1 \text{ mol } C_6H_6O} = 1.20 \text{ mol C}$$

$$1.20 \text{ mol C} \times \frac{12.01 \text{ g C}}{1 \text{ mol C}} = 14.4 \text{ g C}$$

$$14.4 \text{ g C} \times \frac{6.022 \times 10^{23} \text{ C atoms}}{12.01 \text{ g C}} = 7.22 \times 10^{23} \text{ C atoms}$$

93. [1] g   [6] i
     [2] c   [7] f
     [3] b   [8] h
     [4] a   [9] e
     [5] j   [10] d

94. $$2.24 \text{ g Co} \times \frac{55.85 \text{ g Fe}}{58.93 \text{ g Co}} = 2.12 \text{ g Fe}$$

95. $$2.24 \text{ g Fe} \times \frac{58.93 \text{ g Co}}{55.85 \text{ g Fe}} = 2.36 \text{ g Co}$$

96. $$5.00 \text{ g Te} \times \frac{200.6 \text{ g Hg}}{127.6 \text{ g Te}} = 7.86 \text{ g Hg}$$

97. $1.00 \text{ kg} = 1.00 \times 10^3 \text{ g}$

$$1.00 \times 10^3 \text{ g Zr} \times \frac{6.941 \text{ g Li}}{91.22 \text{ g Zr}} = 76.1 \text{ g Li}$$

98. $153.8 \text{ g } CCl_4 = 6.022 \times 10^{23} \text{ molecules } CCL_4$

$$1 \text{ molecule} \times \frac{153.8 \text{ g}}{6.022 \times 10^{23} \text{ molecules}} = 2.554 \times 10^{-22} \text{ g}$$

99. a.   molar mass of C_6H_6 = 78.11 g

$$2.500 \text{ g} \times \frac{6.048 \text{ g H}}{78.11 \text{ g}} = 0.1936 \text{ g H}$$

     b.   molar mass of CaH_2 = 42.10 g

$$2.500 \text{ g} \times \frac{2.016 \text{ g H}}{42.10 \text{ g}} = 0.1197 \text{ g H}$$

     c.   molar mass of C_2H_5OH = 46.07 g

$$2.500 \text{ g} \times \frac{6.048 \text{ g H}}{46.07 \text{ g}} = 0.3282 \text{ g H}$$

d.   molar mass of $C_3H_7O_3N$ = 105.1 g

$$2.500 \text{ g} \times \frac{7.056 \text{ g H}}{105.1 \text{ g}} = 0.1678 \text{ g H}$$

100. a.   molar mass of $C_2H_5O_2N$ = 75.07 g

mass fraction N = $\dfrac{14.01 \text{ g}}{75.07 \text{ g}}$

$$5.000 \text{ g} \times \frac{14.01 \text{ g}}{75.07 \text{ g}} = 0.9331 \text{ g N}$$

b.   molar mass of Mg_3N_2 = 3(24.31 g) + 2(14.01 g) = 100.95 g

mass fraction N = $\dfrac{28.02 \text{ g}}{100.95 \text{ g}}$

$$5.000 \text{ g} \times \frac{28.02 \text{ g}}{100.95 \text{ g}} = 1.388 \text{ g N}$$

c.   molar mass of $Ca(NO_3)_2$ =

40.08 g + 2(14.01 g) + 6(16.00 g) = 164.10 g

mass fraction N = $\dfrac{28.02 \text{ g}}{164.10 \text{ g}}$

$$5.000 \text{ g} \times \frac{28.02 \text{ g}}{164.10 \text{ g}} = 0.8537 \text{ g N}$$

d.   molar mass of N_2O_4 = 2(14.01 g) + 4(16.00 g) = 92.02 g

mass fraction N = $\dfrac{28.02 \text{ g}}{92.02 \text{ g}}$

$$5.000 \text{ g} \times \frac{28.02 \text{ g}}{92.02 \text{ g}} = 1.522 \text{ g N}$$

101. Consider 100.0 g of the compound.

$$25.45 \text{ g Cu} \times \frac{1 \text{ mol Cu}}{63.55 \text{ g Cu}} = 0.4005 \text{ mol Cu}$$

$$12.84 \text{ g S} \times \frac{1 \text{ mol S}}{32.07 \text{ g S}} = 0.4004 \text{ mol S}$$

$$4.036 \text{ g H} \times \frac{1 \text{ mol H}}{1.008 \text{ g H}} = 4.004 \text{ mol H}$$

$$57.67 \text{ g O} \times \frac{1 \text{ mol O}}{16.00 \text{ g O}} = 3.604 \text{ mol O}$$

Dividing each number of moles by the smallest number of moles gives

$$\frac{0.4005 \text{ mol Cu}}{0.4004} = 1.000 \text{ mol Cu}$$

$$\frac{0.4004 \text{ mol S}}{0.4004} = 1.000 \text{ mol S}$$

$$\frac{4.004 \text{ mol H}}{0.4004} = 10.00 \text{ mol H}$$

$$\frac{3.604 \text{ mol O}}{0.4004} = 9.001 \text{ mol O}$$

The empirical formula is $CuSH_{10}O_9$ (which is usually written as $CuSO_4 \cdot 5H_2O$).

102. Consider 100.0 g of the compound.

$$16.39 \text{ g Mg} \times \frac{1 \text{ mol Mg}}{24.31 \text{ g Mg}} = 0.6742 \text{ mol Mg}$$

$$18.89 \text{ g N} \times \frac{1 \text{ mol N}}{14.01 \text{ g N}} = 1.348 \text{ mol N}$$

$$64.72 \text{ g O} \times \frac{1 \text{ mol O}}{16.00 \text{ g O}} = 4.045 \text{ mol O}$$

Dividing each number of moles by the smallest number of moles

$$\frac{0.6742 \text{ mol Mg}}{0.6742} = 1.000 \text{ mol Mg}$$

$$\frac{1.348 \text{ mol N}}{0.6742} = 1.999 \text{ mol N}$$

$$\frac{4.045 \text{ mol O}}{0.6742} = 5.999 \text{ mol O}$$

The empirical formula is MgN_2O_6 [i.e., $Mg(NO_3)_2$].

103. atomic mass unit (amu)

104. We use the *average* mass because this average is a *weighted average* and takes into account both the masses and the relative abundances of the various isotopes.

105. a. $160,000 \text{ amu} \times \frac{1 \text{ O atom}}{16.00 \text{ amu}} = 1.0 \times 10^4$ O atoms (assuming exact)

b. $8139.81 \text{ amu} \times \frac{1 \text{ N atom}}{14.01 \text{ amu}} = 581$ N atoms

c. $13,490 \text{ amu} \times \frac{1 \text{ Al atom}}{26.98 \text{ amu}} = 500$ Al atoms

d. $5040 \text{ amu} \times \dfrac{1 \text{ H atom}}{1.008 \text{ amu}} = 5.00 \times 10^3 \text{ H atoms}$

e. $367{,}495.15 \text{ amu} \times \dfrac{1 \text{ Na atom}}{22.99 \text{ amu}} = 1.599 \times 10^4 \text{ Na atoms}$

106. $1.98 \times 10^{13} \text{ amu} \times \dfrac{1 \text{ Na atom}}{22.99 \text{ amu}} = 8.61 \times 10^{11} \text{ Na atoms}$

$3.01 \times 10^{23} \text{ Na atoms} \times \dfrac{22.99 \text{ amu}}{1 \text{ Na atom}} = 6.92 \times 10^{24} \text{ amu}$

107.   a. $1.5 \text{ mg} = 0.0015 \text{ g}$

$0.0015 \text{ g Cr} \times \dfrac{1 \text{ mol}}{52.00 \text{ g}} = 2.9 \times 10^{-5} \text{ mol Cr}$

b. $2.0 \times 10^{-3} \text{ g Sr} \times \dfrac{1 \text{ mol}}{87.62 \text{ g}} = 2.3 \times 10^{-5} \text{ mol Sr}$

c. $4.84 \times 10^4 \text{ g B} \times \dfrac{1 \text{ mol}}{10.81 \text{ g}} = 4.48 \times 10^3 \text{ mol B}$

d. $3.6 \times 10^{-6} \ \mu\text{g} = 3.6 \times 10^{-12} \text{ g}$

$3.6 \times 10^{-12} \text{ g Cf} \times \dfrac{1 \text{ mol}}{251 \text{ g}} = 1.4 \times 10^{-14} \text{ mol Cf}$

e. $2000 \text{ lb} \times \dfrac{454 \text{ g}}{1 \text{ lb}} = 9.1 \times 10^5 \text{ g}$

$9.1 \times 10^5 \text{ g Fe} \times \dfrac{1 \text{ mol}}{55.85 \text{ g}} = 1.6 \times 10^4 \text{ mol Fe}$

f. $20.4 \text{ g Ba} \times \dfrac{1 \text{ mol}}{137.3 \text{ g}} = 0.149 \text{ mol Ba}$

g. $62.8 \text{ g Co} \times \dfrac{1 \text{ mol}}{58.93 \text{ g}} = 1.07 \text{ mol Co}$

108.   a. $5.0 \text{ mol K} \times \dfrac{39.10 \text{ g}}{1 \text{ mol}} = 195 \text{ g} = 2.0 \times 10^2 \text{ g K}$

b. $0.000305 \text{ mol Hg} \times \dfrac{200.6 \text{ g}}{1 \text{ mol}} = 0.0612 \text{ g Hg}$

c. $2.31 \times 10^{-5} \text{ mol Mn} \times \dfrac{54.94 \text{ g}}{1 \text{ mol}} = 1.27 \times 10^{-3} \text{ g Mn}$

d. $10.5 \text{ mol P} \times \dfrac{30.97 \text{ g}}{1 \text{ mol}} = 325 \text{ g P}$

e. 4.9×10^4 mol Fe $\times \dfrac{55.85 \text{ g}}{1 \text{ mol}} = 2.7 \times 10^6$ g Fe

f.   125 mol Li $\times \dfrac{6.941 \text{ g}}{1 \text{ mol}} = 868$ g Li

g.   0.01205 mol F $\times \dfrac{19.00 \text{ g}}{1 \text{ mol}} = 0.2290$ g F

109. a.   2.89 g Au $\times \dfrac{6.022 \times 10^{23} \text{ Au atoms}}{197.0 \text{ g Au}} = 8.83 \times 10^{21}$ Au atoms

      b.   0.000259 mol Pt $\times \dfrac{6.022 \times 10^{23} \text{ Pt atoms}}{1 \text{ mol}} = 1.56 \times 10^{20}$ Pt atoms

      c.   0.000259 g Pt $\times \dfrac{6.022 \times 10^{23} \text{ Pt atoms}}{195.1 \text{ g Pt}} = 7.99 \times 10^{17}$ Pt atoms

      d.   2.0 lb $\times \dfrac{454 \text{ g}}{1 \text{ lb}} = 908$ g

            908 g Mg $\times \dfrac{6.022 \times 10^{23} \text{ Mg atoms}}{24.31 \text{ g Mg}} = 2.2 \times 10^{25}$ Mg atoms

      e.   1.90 mL $\times \dfrac{13.6 \text{ g}}{1 \text{ mL}} = 25.8$ g Hg

            25.8 g Hg $\times \dfrac{6.022 \times 10^{23} \text{ Hg atoms}}{200.6 \text{ g Hg}} = 7.75 \times 10^{22}$ Hg atoms

      f.   4.30 mol W $\times \dfrac{6.022 \times 10^{23} \text{ W atoms}}{1 \text{ mol}} = 2.59 \times 10^{24}$ W atoms

      g.   4.30 g W $\times \dfrac{6.022 \times 10^{23} \text{ W atoms}}{183.9 \text{ g W}} = 1.41 \times 10^{22}$ W atoms

110. a.   mass of 1 mol Fe = 1(55.85 g) =   55.85 g

            mass of 1 mol S =   1(32.07 g) =   32.07 g

            mass of 4 mol O =   4(16.00 g) =   64.00 g
            _____
            molar mass of $FeSO_4$ =   151.92 g

      b.   mass of 1 mol Hg = 1(200.6 g) =   200.6 g

            mass of 2 mol I = 2(126.9 g) =   253.8 g
            _____
            molar mass of HgI_2 =   454.4 g

c.   mass of 1 mol Sn = 1(118.7 g) =   118.7 g

    mass of 2 mol O =   2(16.00 g) =   32.00 g

    molar mass of SnO_2 =   150.7 g

d.   mass of 1 mol Co = 1(58.93 g) =   58.93 g

    mass of 2 mol Cl = 2(35.45 g) =   70.90 g

    molar mass of $CoCl_2$ =   129.83 g

e.   mass of 1 mol Cu = 1(63.55 g) =   63.55 g

    mass of 2 mol N =   2(14.01 g) =   28.02 g

    mass of 6 mol O =   6(16.00 g) =   96.00 g

    molar mass of $Cu(NO_3)_2$ =   187.57 g

111. a.   mass of 6 mol C =   6(12.01 g) =   72.06 g

    mass of 10 mol H = 10(1.008 g) = 10.08 g

    mass of 4 mol O =   4(16.00 g) =   64.00 g

    molar mass of $C_6H_{10}O_4$ =   146.14 g

b.   mass of 8 mol C =   8(12.01 g) =   96.08 g

    mass of 10 mol H = 10(1.008 g) = 10.08 g

    mass of 4 mol N =   4(14.01 g) =   56.04 g

    mass of 2 mol O =   1(16.00 g) =   32.00 g

    molar mass of $C_8H_{10}N_4O_2$ =   194.20 g

c.   mass of 20 mol C = 20(12.01 g) = 240.2 g

    mass of 42 mol H = 42(1.008 g) = 42.34 g

    molar mass of $C_{20}H_{42}$ =   282.5 g

d.   mass of 6 mol C =   6(12.01 g) =   72.06 g

    mass of 12 mol H = 12(1.008 g) = 12.10 g

    mass of 1 mol O =   16.00 g =   16.00 g

    molar mass of $C_6H_{11}OH$ =   100.16 g

e.   mass of 4 mol C =   4(12.01 g) =   48.04 g

mass of 6 mol H =   6(1.008 g) =   6.048 g

mass of 2 mol O =   2(16.00 g) =   32.00 g

molar mass of $C_4H_6O_2$ =   86.09 g

f.   mass of 6 mol C =   6(12.01 g) =   72.06 g

mass of 12 mol H =   12(1.008 g) = 12.10 g

mass of 6 mol O =   6(16.00 g) =   96.00 g

molar mass of $C_6H_{12}O_6$ =   180.16 g

112. a.   molar mass of $(NH_4)_2S$ = 68.15 g

$$21.2 \text{ g} \times \frac{1 \text{ mol}}{68.15 \text{ g}} = 0.311 \text{ mol } (NH_4)_2S$$

b.   molar mass of $Ca(NO_3)_2$ = 164.1 g

$$44.3 \text{ g} \times \frac{1 \text{ mol}}{164.1 \text{ g}} = 0.270 \text{ mol } Ca(NO_3)_2$$

c.   molar mass of Cl_2O = 86.9 g

$$4.35 \text{ g} \times \frac{1 \text{ mol}}{86.9 \text{ g}} = 0.0501 \text{ mol } Cl_2O$$

d.   1.0 lb = 454 g

molar mass of $FeCl_3$ = 162.2

$$454 \text{ g} \times \frac{1 \text{ mol}}{162.2 \text{ g}} = 2.8 \text{ mol } FeCl_3$$

e.   1.0 kg = 1.0×10^3 g

molar mass of $FeCl_3$ = 162.2 g

$$1.0 \times 10^3 \text{ g} \times \frac{1 \text{ mol}}{162.2 \text{ g}} = 6.2 \text{ mol } FeCl_3$$

113. a.   molar mass of $FeSO_4$ = 151.92 g

$$1.28 \text{ g} \times \frac{1 \text{ mol}}{151.92 \text{ g}} = 8.43 \times 10^{-3} \text{ mol } FeSO_4$$

b.   5.14 mg = 0.00514 g

molar mass of HgI_2 = 454.4 g

$$0.00514 \text{ g} \times \frac{1 \text{ mol}}{454.4 \text{ g}} = 1.13 \times 10^{-5} \text{ mol HgI}_2$$

c. $9.21 \ \mu g = 9.21 \times 10^{-6} \text{ g}$

molar mass of SnO_2 = 150.7 g

$$9.21 \times 10^{-6} \text{ g} \times \frac{1 \text{ mol}}{150.7 \text{ g}} = 6.11 \times 10^{-8} \text{ mol SnO}_2$$

d.   1.26 lb = 1.26(453.59 g) = 572 g

molar mass of $CoCl_2$ = 129.83 g

$$572 \text{ g} \times \frac{1 \text{ mol}}{129.83 \text{ g}} = 4.41 \text{ mol CoCl}_2$$

e.   molar mass of $Cu(NO_3)_2$ = 187.57 g

$$4.25 \text{ g} \times \frac{1 \text{ mol}}{187.57 \text{ g}} = 2.27 \times 10^{-2} \text{ mol Cu(NO}_3)_2$$

114. a.   molar mass of $CuSO_4$ = 159.62 g

$$2.6 \times 10^{-2} \text{ mol} \times \frac{159.62 \text{ g}}{1 \text{ mol}} = 4.2 \text{ g CuSO}_4$$

b.   molar mass of C_2F_4 = 100.0 g

$$3.05 \times 10^3 \text{ mol} \times \frac{100.0 \text{ g}}{1 \text{ mol}} = 3.05 \times 10^5 \text{ g C}_2\text{F}_4$$

c.   7.83 mmol = 0.00783 mol

molar mass of C_5H_8 = 68.11 g

$$0.00783 \text{ mol} \times \frac{68.11 \text{ g}}{1 \text{ mol}} = 0.533 \text{ g C}_5\text{H}_8$$

d.   molar mass of $BiCl_3$ = 315.3 g

$$6.30 \text{ mol} \times \frac{315.3 \text{ g}}{1 \text{ mol}} = 1.99 \times 10^3 \text{ g BiCl}_3$$

e.   molar mass of $C_{12}H_{22}O_{11}$ = 342.3 g

$$12.2 \text{ mol} \times \frac{342.3 \text{ g}}{1 \text{ mol}} = 4.18 \times 10^3 \text{ g C}_{12}\text{H}_{22}\text{O}_{11}$$

115. a.   molar mass of $(NH_4)_2CO_3$ = 96.09 g

$$3.09 \text{ mol} \times \frac{96.09 \text{ g}}{1 \text{ mol}} = 297 \text{ g (NH}_4)_2\text{CO}_3$$

b.   molar mass of $NaHCO_3$ = 84.01 g

$$4.01 \times 10^{-6} \text{ mol} \times \frac{84.01 \text{ g}}{1 \text{ mol}} = 3.37 \times 10^{-4} \text{ g } NaHCO_3$$

c.   molar mass of CO_2 = 44.01 g

$$88.02 \text{ mol} \times \frac{44.01 \text{ g}}{1 \text{ mol}} = 3874 \text{ g } CO_2$$

d.   1.29 mmol = 0.00129 mol

molar mass of $AgNO_3$ = 169.9 g

$$0.00129 \text{ mol} \times \frac{169.9 \text{ g}}{1 \text{ mol}} = 0.219 \text{ g } AgNO_3$$

e.   molar mass of $CrCl_3$ = 158.4 g

$$0.0024 \text{ mol} \times \frac{158.4 \text{ g}}{1 \text{ mol}} = 0.38 \text{ g } CrCl_3$$

116. a.   molar mass of $C_6H_{12}O_6$ = 180.2 g

$$3.45 \text{ g} \times \frac{6.022 \times 10^{23} \text{ molecules}}{180.2 \text{ g}} = 1.15 \times 10^{22} \text{ molecules } C_6H_{12}O_6$$

b. $$3.45 \text{ mol} \times \frac{6.022 \times 10^{23} \text{ molecules}}{1 \text{ mol}} = 2.08 \times 10^{24} \text{ molecules } C_6H_{12}O_6$$

c.   molar mass of ICl_5 = 304.2 g

$$25.0 \text{ g} \times \frac{6.022 \times 10^{23} \text{ molecules}}{304.2 \text{ g}} = 4.95 \times 10^{22} \text{ molecules } ICl_5$$

d.   molar mass of B_2H_6 = 27.67 g

$$1.00 \text{ g} \times \frac{6.022 \times 10^{23} \text{ molecules}}{27.67 \text{ g}} = 2.18 \times 10^{22} \text{ molecules } B_2H_6$$

e.   1.05 mmol = 0.00105 mol

$$0.00105 \text{ mol} \times \frac{6.022 \times 10^{23} \text{ form. units}}{1 \text{ mol}} = 6.32 \times 10^{20} \text{ form. units}$$

117. a.   molar mass of NH_3 = 17.03 g

$$2.71 \text{ g} \times \frac{1 \text{ mol}}{17.03 \text{ g}} = 0.159 \text{ mol } NH_3$$

mol H = 3(0.159 mol) = 0.477 mol H

b.   mol H = 2(0.824 mol) = 1.648 mol H = 1.65 mol

c.   6.25 mg = 0.00625 g

molar mass of H_2SO_4 = 98.09 g

$0.00625 \text{ g} \times \dfrac{1 \text{ mol}}{98.09 \text{ g}}$ = 6.37×10^{-5} mol H_2SO_4

mol H = $2(6.37 \times 10^{-5}$ mol$)$ = 1.27×10^{-4} mol H

d.   molar mass of $(NH_4)_2CO_3$ = 96.09 g

$451 \text{ g} \times \dfrac{1 \text{ mol}}{96.09 \text{ g}}$ = 4.69 mol $(NH_4)_2CO_3$

mol H = 8(4.69 mol) = 37.5 mol H

118. a.   mass of Ca present =   3(40.08 g) =   120.24 g

mass of P present =   2(30.97 g) =   61.94 g

mass of O present =   8(16.00 g) =   128.00 g
_____

molar mass of $Ca_3(PO_4)_2$ =   310.18 g

% Ca = $\dfrac{120.24 \text{ g Ca}}{310.18 \text{ g}}$ × 100 = 38.76% Ca

% P = $\dfrac{61.94 \text{ g P}}{310.18 \text{ g}}$ × 100 = 19.97% P

% O = $\dfrac{128.00 \text{ g O}}{310.18 \text{ g}}$ × 100 = 41.27% O

b.   mass of Cd present =   112.4 g =   112.4 g

mass of S present =   32.07 g =   32.07 g

mass of O present =   4(16.00 g) =   64.00 g
_____

molar mass of $CdSO_4$ =   208.5 g

% Cd = $\dfrac{112.4 \text{ g Cd}}{208.5 \text{ g}}$ × 100 = 53.91% Cd

% S = $\dfrac{32.07 \text{ g S}}{208.5 \text{ g}}$ × 100 = 15.38% S

% O = $\dfrac{64.00 \text{ g O}}{208.5 \text{ g}}$ × 100 = 30.70% O

c.   mass of Fe present =   2(55.85 g) =   111.7 g

mass of S present =   3(32.07 g) =   96.21 g

mass of O present =   12(16.00 g) =   192.0 g
_____

molar mass of $Fe_2(SO_4)_3$ =   399.9 g

$$\% \text{ Fe} = \frac{111.7 \text{ g Fe}}{399.9 \text{ g}} \times 100 = 27.93\% \text{ Fe}$$

$$\% \text{ S} = \frac{96.21 \text{ g S}}{399.9 \text{ g}} \times 100 = 24.06\% \text{ S}$$

$$\% \text{ O} = \frac{192.0 \text{ g O}}{399.9 \text{ g}} \times 100 = 48.01\% \text{ O}$$

d. mass of Mn present =   54.94 g =   54.94 g

mass of Cl present =   2(35.45 g) =   70.90 g

molar mass of $MnCl_2$ =   125.84 g

$$\% \text{ Mn} = \frac{54.94 \text{ g Mn}}{125.84 \text{ g}} \times 100 = 43.66\% \text{ Mn}$$

$$\% \text{ Cl} = \frac{70.90 \text{ g Cl}}{125.84 \text{ g}} \times 100 = 56.34\% \text{ Cl}$$

e. mass of N present =   2(14.01 g) =   28.02 g

mass of H present =   8(1.008 g) =   8.064 g

mass of C present =   12.01 g =   12.01 g

mass of O present =   3(16.00 g) =   48.00 g

molar mass of $(NH_4)_2CO_3$ =   96.09 g

$$\% \text{ N} = \frac{28.02 \text{ g N}}{96.09 \text{ g}} \times 100 = 29.16\% \text{ N}$$

$$\% \text{ H} = \frac{8.064 \text{ g H}}{96.09 \text{ g}} \times 100 = 8.392\% \text{ H}$$

$$\% \text{ C} = \frac{12.01 \text{ g C}}{96.09 \text{ g}} \times 100 = 12.50\% \text{ C}$$

$$\% \text{ O} = \frac{48.00 \text{ g O}}{96.09 \text{ g}} \times 100 = 49.95\% \text{ O}$$

f. mass of Na present =   22.99 g =   22.99 g

mass of H present =   1.008 g =   1.008 g

mass of C present =   12.01 g =   12.01 g

mass of O present =   3(16.00 g) =   48.00 g

molar mass of $NaHCO_3$ =   84.01 g

$$\% \text{ Na} = \frac{22.99 \text{ g Na}}{84.01 \text{ g}} \times 100 = 27.37\% \text{ Na}$$

$$\% \ H = \frac{1.008 \ g \ H}{84.01 \ g} \times 100 = 1.200\% \ H$$

$$\% \ C = \frac{12.01 \ g \ C}{84.01 \ g} \times 100 = 14.30\% \ C$$

$$\% \ O = \frac{48.00 \ g \ O}{84.01 \ g} \times 100 = 57.14\% \ O$$

g.
mass of C present = 12.01 g = 12.01 g

mass of O present = 2(16.00 g) = 32.00 g

molar mass of CO_2 = 44.01 g

$$\% \ C = \frac{12.01 \ g \ C}{44.01 \ g} \times 100 = 27.29\% \ C$$

$$\% \ O = \frac{32.00 \ g \ O}{44.01 \ g} \times 100 = 72.71\% \ O$$

h.
mass of Ag present = 107.9 g = 107.9 g

mass of N present = 14.01 g = 14.01 g

mass of O present = 3(16.00 g) = 48.00 g

molar mass of $AgNO_3$ = 169.9 g

$$\% \ Ag = \frac{107.9 \ g \ Ag}{169.9 \ g} \times 100 = 63.51\% \ Ag$$

$$\% \ N = \frac{14.01 \ g \ N}{169.9 \ g} \times 100 = 8.246\% \ N$$

$$\% \ O = \frac{48.00 \ g \ O}{169.9 \ g} \times 100 = 28.25\% \ O$$

119. a.   molar mass of NaN_3 = 65.02 g

$$\% \ Na = \frac{22.99 \ g \ Na}{65.02 \ g} \times 100 = 35.36\% \ Na$$

b.   molar mass of $CuSO_4$ = 159.62 g

$$\% \ Cu = \frac{63.55 \ g \ Cu}{159.62 \ g} \times 100 = 39.81\% \ Cu$$

c.   molar mass of $AuCl_3$ = 303.4 g

$$\% \ Au = \frac{197.0 \ g \ Au}{303.4 \ g} \times 100 = 64.93\% \ Au$$

d.   molar mass of $AgNO_3$ = 169.9 g

$$\% \text{ Ag} = \frac{107.9 \text{ g Ag}}{169.9 \text{ g}} \times 100 = 63.51\% \text{ Ag}$$

e.   molar mass of Rb_2SO_4 = 267.0 g

$$\% \text{ Rb} = \frac{170.9 \text{ g Rb}}{267.0 \text{ g}} \times 100 = 64.01\% \text{ Rb}$$

f.   molar mass of $NaClO_3$ = 106.44 g

$$\% \text{ Na} = \frac{22.99 \text{ g Na}}{106.44 \text{ g}} \times 100 = 21.60\% \text{ Na}$$

g.   molar mass of NI_3 = 394.7 g

$$\% \text{ N} = \frac{14.01 \text{ g N}}{394.7 \text{ g}} \times 100 = 3.550\% \text{ N}$$

h.   molar mass of CsBr = 212.8 g

$$\% \text{ Cs} = \frac{132.9 \text{ g Cs}}{212.8 \text{ g}} \times 100 = 62.45\% \text{ Cs}$$

120. a. $$\% \text{ Fe} = \frac{55.85 \text{ g Fe}}{151.92 \text{ g}} \times 100 = 36.76\% \text{ Fe}$$

b. $$\% \text{ Ag} = \frac{215.8 \text{ g Ag}}{231.8 \text{ g}} \times 100 = 93.10\% \text{ Ag}$$

c. $$\% \text{ Sr} = \frac{87.62 \text{ g Sr}}{158.5 \text{ g}} \times 100 = 55.28\% \text{ Sr}$$

d. $$\% \text{ C} = \frac{48.04 \text{ g C}}{86.09 \text{ g}} \times 100 = 55.80\% \text{ C}$$

e. $$\% \text{ C} = \frac{12.01 \text{ g C}}{32.04 \text{ g}} \times 100 = 37.48\% \text{ C}$$

f. $$\% \text{ Al} = \frac{53.96 \text{ g Al}}{101.96 \text{ g}} \times 100 = 52.92\% \text{ Al}$$

g. $$\% \text{ K} = \frac{39.10 \text{ g K}}{106.55 \text{ g}} \times 100 = 36.70\% \text{ K}$$

h. $$\% \text{ K} = \frac{39.10 \text{ g K}}{74.55 \text{ g}} \times 100 = 52.45\% \text{ K}$$

121. $$0.7238 \text{ g C} \times \frac{1 \text{ mol C}}{12.01 \text{ g C}} = 0.06027 \text{ mol C}$$

$$0.07088 \text{ g H} \times \frac{1 \text{ mol H}}{1.008 \text{ g H}} = 0.07032 \text{ mol H}$$

$$0.1407 \text{ g N} \times \frac{1 \text{ mol N}}{14.01 \text{ g N}} = 0.01004 \text{ mol N}$$

$$0.3214 \text{ g O} \times \frac{1 \text{ mol O}}{16.00 \text{ g O}} = 0.02009 \text{ mol O}$$

Dividing each number of moles by the smallest number of moles (0.01004 mol N) gives

$$\frac{0.06027 \text{ mol C}}{0.01004} = 6.003 \text{ mol C}$$

$$\frac{0.07032 \text{ mol H}}{0.01004} = 7.004 \text{ mol H}$$

$$\frac{0.01004 \text{ mol N}}{0.01004} = 1.000 \text{ mol N}$$

$$\frac{0.02009 \text{ mol O}}{0.01004} = 2.001 \text{ mol O}$$

The empirical formula is $C_6H_7NO_2$

122. $$0.2990 \text{ g C} \times \frac{1 \text{ mol C}}{12.01 \text{ g C}} = 0.02490 \text{ mol C}$$

$$0.05849 \text{ g H} \times \frac{1 \text{ mol H}}{1.008 \text{ g H}} = 0.05803 \text{ mol H}$$

$$0.2318 \text{ g N} \times \frac{1 \text{ mol N}}{14.01 \text{ g N}} = 0.01655 \text{ mol N}$$

$$0.1328 \text{ g O} \times \frac{1 \text{ mol O}}{16.00 \text{ g O}} = 0.008300 \text{ mol O}$$

Dividing each number of moles by the smallest number of moles (0.008300 mol O) gives

$$\frac{0.02490 \text{ mol C}}{0.008300} = 3.000 \text{ mol C}$$

$$\frac{0.05803 \text{ mol H}}{0.008300} = 6.992 \text{ mol H}$$

$$\frac{0.01655 \text{ mol N}}{0.008300} = 1.994 \text{ mol N}$$

$$\frac{0.008300 \text{ mol O}}{0.008300} = 1.000 \text{ mol O}$$

The empirical formula is $C_3H_7N_2O$.

123. $2.004 \text{ g Ca} \times \dfrac{1 \text{ mol Ca}}{40.08 \text{ g Ca}} = 0.05000 \text{ mol Ca}$

$0.4670 \text{ g N} \times \dfrac{1 \text{ mol Cl}}{14.01 \text{ g N}} = 0.03333 \text{ mol N}$

Dividing each number of moles by the smaller number of moles gives

$\dfrac{0.05000 \text{ mol Ca}}{0.03333} = 1.500 \text{ mol Ca}$ $\dfrac{0.03333 \text{ mol N}}{0.03333} = 1.000 \text{ mol N}$

Multiplying these relative numbers of moles by 2 to give whole numbers gives the empirical formula as Ca_3N_2.

124.   Mass of oxygen in compound = 4.33 g – 4.01 g = 0.32 g O

$4.01 \text{ g Hg} \times \dfrac{1 \text{ mol Hg}}{200.6 \text{ g Hg}} = 0.0200 \text{ mol Hg}$

$0.32 \text{ g O} \times \dfrac{1 \text{ mol O}}{16.00 \text{ g O}} = 0.020 \text{ mol O}$

Since the numbers of moles are equal, the empirical formula is HgO.

125.   Mass of chlorine in compound = 3.045 g – 1.00 g = 2.045 g Cl

$1.00 \text{ g Cr} \times \dfrac{1 \text{ mol Cr}}{52.00 \text{ g Cr}} = 0.0192 \text{ mol Cr}$

$2.045 \text{ g Cl} \times \dfrac{1 \text{ mol Cl}}{35.45 \text{ g Cl}} = 0.0577 \text{ mol Cl}$

Dividing each number of moles by the smaller number of moles

$\dfrac{0.0192 \text{ mol Cr}}{0.0192} = 1.00 \text{ mol Cr}$ $\dfrac{0.0577 \text{ mol Cl}}{0.0192} = 3.01 \text{ mol Cl}$

The empirical formula is $CrCl_3$.

126.   Assume we have 100.0 g of the compound.

$65.95 \text{ g Ba} \times \dfrac{1 \text{ mol Ba}}{137.3 \text{ g Ba}} = 0.4803 \text{ mol Ba}$

$34.05 \text{ g Cl} \times \dfrac{1 \text{ mol Cl}}{35.45 \text{ g Cl}} = 0.9605 \text{ mol Cl}$

Dividing each of these number of moles by the smaller number gives

$$\frac{0.4803 \text{ mol Ba}}{0.4803} = 1.000 \text{ mol Ba}$$

$$\frac{0.9605 \text{ mol Cl}}{0.4803} = 2.000 \text{ mol Cl}$$

The empirical formula is then $BaCl_2$.

Chapter 9   Chemical Quantities

1. The coefficients of the balanced chemical equation for a reaction give the *relative numbers of molecules* of reactants and products that are involved in the reaction.

2. The coefficients of the balanced chemical equation for a reaction indicate the *relative numbers of moles* of each reactant that combine during the process, as well as the number of moles of each product formed.

3. Although we define mass as the "amount of matter in a substance," the *units* in which we measure mass are a human invention. Atoms and molecules react on an individual particle-by-particle basis, and we have to count individual particles when doing chemical calculations.

4. Balanced chemical equations tell us in what proportions *on a mole basis* substances combine; since the molar masses of $C(s)$ and $O_2(g)$ are different, 1 g of O_2 could not represent the same number of moles as 1 g of C.

5. a. $2NO(g) + O_2(g) \rightarrow 2NO_2(g)$

    Two molecules of nitrogen monoxide combine with one molecule of oxygen gas, producing two molecules of nitrogen dioxide. Two moles of gaseous nitrogen monoxide combine with one mole of gaseous oxygen, producing two moles of gaseous nitrogen dioxide.

    b. $2AgC_2H_3O_2(aq) + CuSO_4(aq) \rightarrow Ag_2SO_4(s) + Cu(C_2H_3O_2)_2(aq)$

    Note: The term "formula unit" is used in the following statement because the substances involved in the above reaction are *ionic*, and do not contain true molecules. Two molecules (formula units) of silver acetate will react with one molecule (formula unit) of copper(II) sulfate, precipitating one molecule (formula unit) of silver sulfate and leaving one molecule (formula unit) of copper(II) acetate in solution. Two moles of aqueous silver acetate react with one mole of aqueous copper(II) sulfate, to produce one mole of solid silver sulfate as a precipitate, and leaving one mole of copper(II) acetate in solution.

    c. $PCl_3(l) + 3H_2O(l) \rightarrow H_3PO_3(l) + 3HCl(g)$

    One molecule of phosphorus trichloride reacts with three molecules of water, producing one molecule of phosphorous acid and three molecules of hydrogen chloride. One mole of liquid phosphorus trichloride reacts with three moles of liquid water, producing one mole of liquid phosphorous acid and three moles of gaseous hydrogen chloride.

    d. $C_2H_6(g) + Cl_2(g) \rightarrow C_2H_5Cl(g) + HCl(g)$

    One molecule of ethane (C_2H_6) reacts with one molecule of chlorine, producing one molecule of chloroethane (C_2H_5Cl) and one molecule of hydrogen chloride. One mole of gaseous ethane combines with one mole of chlorine gas, giving one mole of gaseous chloroethane and one mole of gaseous hydrogen chloride.

6.   a. $3MnO_2(s) + 4Al(s) \rightarrow 3Mn(s) + 2Al_2O_3(s)$

Three formula units of manganese(IV) oxide react with four aluminum atoms, producing three manganese atoms and two formula units of aluminum oxide. Three moles of solid manganese(IV) oxide react with four moles of solid aluminum, to produce three moles of solid manganese and two moles of solid aluminum oxide.

b. $B_2O_3(s) + 3CaF_2(s) \rightarrow 2BF_3(g) + 3CaO(s)$

One molecule of diboron trioxide reacts with three formula units of calcium fluoride, producing two molecules of boron trifluoride and three formula units of calcium oxide. One mole of solid diboron trioxide reacts with three moles of solid calcium fluoride, to give two moles of gaseous boron trifluoride and three moles of solid calcium oxide.

c. $3NO_2(g) + H_2O(l) \rightarrow 2HNO_3(aq) + NO(g)$

Three molecules of nitrogen dioxide [nitrogen(IV) oxide] react with one molecule of water, to produce two molecules of nitric acid and one molecule of nitrogen monoxide [nitrogen(II) oxide]. Three moles of gaseous nitrogen dioxide react with one mole of liquid water, to produce two moles of aqueous nitric acid and one mole of nitrogen monoxide gas.

d. $C_6H_6(g) + 3H_2(g) \rightarrow C_6H_{12}(g)$

One molecule of C_6H_6 (which is named benzene) reacts with three molecules of hydrogen, producing just one molecule of C_6H_{12} (which is named cyclohexane). One mole of gaseous benzene reacts with three moles of hydrogen gas, giving one mole of gaseous cyclohexane.

7.   False. The coefficients of the balanced chemical equation represent the ratios on a *mole* basis by which hydrogen peroxide decomposes.

8.   False. Reactions take place on a *mole* basis: one *mole* of nitrogen gas would react with three *moles* of iodine, giving two *moles* of nitrogen triiodide.

9.   For converting from a given number of moles of CH_4 to the number of moles of oxygen needed for reaction, the correct mole ratio is

$$\frac{2 \text{ mol } O_2}{1 \text{ mol } CH_4}$$

For converting from a given number of moles of CH_4 to the number of moles of product produced, the ratios are

$$\frac{1 \text{ mol } CO_2}{1 \text{ mol } CH_4} \qquad \text{and} \qquad \frac{2 \text{ mol } H_2O}{1 \text{ mol } CH_4}$$

10. $2Ag(s) + H_2S(g) \rightarrow Ag_2S(s) + H_2(g)$

$$\frac{1 \text{ mol } Ag_2S}{2 \text{ mol } Ag} \qquad \text{and} \qquad \frac{1 \text{ mol } H_2}{2 \text{ mol } Ag}$$

11.   a. $2Mg(s) + O_2(g) \rightarrow 2MgO(s)$

$$0.15 \text{ mol } Mg \times \frac{2 \text{ mol } MgO}{2 \text{ mol } Mg} = 0.15 \text{ mol } MgO$$

b. $2Mg(s) + O_2(g) \rightarrow 2MgO(s)$

$$0.15 \text{ mol } O_2 \times \frac{2 \text{ mol } MgO}{1 \text{ mol } O_2} = 0.30 \text{ mol } MgO$$

c. $4Fe(s) + 3O_2(g) \rightarrow 2Fe_2O_3(s)$

$$0.15 \text{ mol } Fe \times \frac{2 \text{ mol } Fe_2O_3}{4 \text{ mol } Fe} = 0.075 \text{ mol } Fe_2O_3$$

d. $4Fe(s) + 3O_2(g) \rightarrow 2Fe_2O_3(s)$

$$0.15 \text{ mol } O_2 \times \frac{2 \text{ mol } Fe_2O_3}{3 \text{ mol } O_2} = 0.10 \text{ mol } Fe_2O_3$$

12.   a. $2FeO(s) + C(s) \rightarrow 2Fe(l) + CO_2(g)$

$$0.125 \text{ mol } FeO \times \frac{2 \text{ mol } Fe}{2 \text{ mol } FeO} = 0.125 \text{ mol } Fe$$

$$0.125 \text{ mol } FeO \times \frac{1 \text{ mol } CO_2}{2 \text{ mol } FeO} = 0.0625 \text{ mol } CO_2$$

b. $Cl_2(g) + 2KI(aq) \rightarrow 2KCl(aq) + I_2(s)$

$$0.125 \text{ mol } KI \times \frac{2 \text{ mol } KCl}{2 \text{ mol } KI} = 0.125 \text{ mol } KCl$$

$$0.125 \text{ mol } KI \times \frac{1 \text{ mol } I_2}{2 \text{ mol } KI} = 0.0625 \text{ mol } I_2$$

c. $Na_2B_4O_7(s) + H_2SO_4(aq) + 5H_2O(l) \rightarrow 4H_3BO_3(s) + Na_2SO_4(aq)$

$$0.125 \text{ mol } Na_2B_4O_7 \times \frac{4 \text{ mol } H_3BO_3}{1 \text{ mol } Na_2B_4O_7} = 0.500 \text{ mol } H_3BO_3$$

$$0.125 \text{ mol } Na_2B_4O_7 \times \frac{1 \text{ mol } Na_2SO_4}{1 \text{ mol } Na_2B_4O_7} = 0.125 \text{ mol } Na_2SO_4$$

d. $CaC_2(s) + 2H_2O(l) \rightarrow Ca(OH)_2(s) + C_2H_2(g)$

$$0.125 \text{ mol CaC}_2 \times \frac{1 \text{ mol Ca(OH)}_2}{1 \text{ mol CaC}_2} = 0.125 \text{ mol Ca(OH)}_2$$

$$0.125 \text{ mol CaC}_2 \times \frac{1 \text{ mol C}_2\text{H}_2}{1 \text{ mol CaC}_2} = 0.125 \text{ mol C}_2\text{H}_2$$

13.   a. $C_2H_5OH(l) + 3O_2(g) \rightarrow 2CO_2(g) + 3H_2O(g)$

$$1.25 \text{ mol C}_2\text{H}_5\text{OH} \times \frac{2 \text{ mol CO}_2}{1 \text{ mol C}_2\text{H}_5\text{OH}} = 2.50 \text{ mol CO}_2$$

$$1.25 \text{ mol C}_2\text{H}_5\text{OH} \times \frac{3 \text{ mol H}_2\text{O}}{1 \text{ mol C}_2\text{H}_5\text{OH}} = 3.75 \text{ mol H}_2\text{O}$$

b. $N_2(g) + O_2(g) \rightarrow 2NO(g)$

$$1.25 \text{ mol N}_2 \times \frac{2 \text{ mol NO}}{1 \text{ mol N}_2} = 2.50 \text{ mol NO}$$

c. $2NaClO_2(s) + Cl_2(g) \rightarrow 2ClO_2(g) + 2NaCl(s)$

$$1.25 \text{ mol NaClO}_2 \times \frac{2 \text{ mol ClO}_2}{2 \text{ mol NaClO}_2} = 1.25 \text{ mol ClO}_2$$

$$1.25 \text{ mol NaClO}_2 \times \frac{2 \text{ mol NaCl}}{2 \text{ mol NaClO}_2} = 1.25 \text{ mol NaCl}$$

d. $3H_2(g) + N_2(g) \rightarrow 2NH_3(g)$

$$1.25 \text{ mol H}_2 \times \frac{2 \text{ mol NH}_3}{3 \text{ mol H}_2} = 0.833 \text{ mol NH}_3$$

14.   a. $NH_3(g) + HCl(g) \rightarrow NH_4Cl(s)$
molar mass of NH_4Cl, 53.49 g

$$0.50 \text{ mol NH}_3 \times \frac{1 \text{ mol NH}_4\text{Cl}}{1 \text{ mol NH}_3} = 0.50 \text{ mol NH}_4\text{Cl}$$

$$0.50 \text{ mol NH}_4\text{Cl} \times \frac{53.49 \text{ g NH}_4\text{Cl}}{1 \text{ mol NH}_4\text{Cl}} = 27 \text{ g NH}_4\text{Cl}$$

b. $CH_4(g) + 4S(g) \rightarrow CS_2(l) + 2H_2S(g)$
molar masses: CS_2, 76.15 g; H_2S, 34.09 g

$$0.50 \text{ mol S} \times \frac{1 \text{ mol CS}_2}{4 \text{ mol S}} = 0.125 \text{ mol CS}_2 \ (= 0.13 \text{ mol CS}_2)$$

$$0.125 \text{ mol CS}_2 \times \frac{76.15 \text{ g CS}_2}{1 \text{ mol CS}_2} = 9.5 \text{ g CS}_2$$

$$0.50 \text{ mol S} \times \frac{2 \text{ mol H}_2\text{S}}{4 \text{ mol S}} = 0.25 \text{ mol H}_2\text{S}$$

$$0.25 \text{ mol } H_2S \times \frac{34.09 \text{ g } H_2S}{1 \text{ mol } H_2S} = 8.5 \text{ g } H_2S$$

c. $PCl_3(l) + 3H_2O(l) \rightarrow H_3PO_3(aq) + 3HCl(aq)$

molar masses: H_3PO_3, 81.99 g; HCl, 36.46 g

$$0.50 \text{ mol } PCl_3 \times \frac{1 \text{ mol } H_3PO_3}{1 \text{ mol } PCl_3} = 0.50 \text{ mol } H_3PO_3$$

$$0.50 \text{ mol } H_3PO_3 \times \frac{81.99 \text{ g } H_3PO_3}{1 \text{ mol } H_3PO_3} = 41 \text{ g } H_3PO_3$$

$$0.50 \text{ mol } PCl_3 \times \frac{3 \text{ mol } HCl}{1 \text{ mol } PCl_3} = 1.5 \text{ mol } HCl$$

$$1.5 \text{ mol } HCl \times \frac{36.46 \text{ g } HCl}{1 \text{ mol } HCl} = 54.7 = 55 \text{ g } HCl$$

d. $NaOH(s) + CO_2(g) \rightarrow NaHCO_3(s)$

molar mass of $NaHCO_3$ = 84.01 g

$$0.50 \text{ mol } NaOH \times \frac{1 \text{ mol } NaHCO_3}{1 \text{ mol } NaOH} = 0.50 \text{ mol } NaHCO_3$$

$$0.50 \text{ mol } NaHCO_3 \times \frac{84.01 \text{ g } NaHCO_3}{1 \text{ mol } NaHCO_3} = 42 \text{ g } NaHCO_3$$

15.   a. $Cl_2(g) + 2KI(aq) \rightarrow 2KCl(aq) + I_2(s)$

$$0.275 \text{ mol } Cl_2 \times \frac{2 \text{ mol } KI}{1 \text{ mol } Cl_2} = 0.550 \text{ mol } KI$$

b. $6Co(s) + P_4(s) \rightarrow 2Co_3P_2(s)$

$$0.275 \text{ mol } Co \times \frac{1 \text{ mol } P_4}{6 \text{ mol } Co} = 0.0458 \text{ mol } P_4$$

c. $Zn(s) + 2HNO_3(aq) \rightarrow Zn(NO_3)_2(aq) + H_2(g)$

$$0.275 \text{ mol } Zn \times \frac{2 \text{ mol } HNO_3}{1 \text{ mol } Zn} = 0.550 \text{ mol } HNO_3$$

d. $C_5H_{12}(l) + 8O_2(g) \rightarrow 5CO_2(g) + 6H_2O(g)$

$$0.275 \text{ mol } C_5H_{12} \times \frac{8 \text{ mol } O_2}{1 \text{ mol } C_5H_{12}} = 2.20 \text{ mol } O_2$$

16.   Before doing the calculations, the equations must be *balanced*.

a. $4KO_2(s) + 2H_2O(l) \rightarrow 3O_2(g) + 4KOH(s)$

$$0.625 \text{ mol } KOH \times \frac{3 \text{ mol } O_2}{4 \text{ mol } KOH} = 0.469 \text{ mol } O_2$$

b. $SeO_2(g) + 2H_2Se(g) \rightarrow 3Se(s) + 2H_2O(g)$

$$0.625 \text{ mol } H_2O \times \frac{3 \text{ mol Se}}{2 \text{ mol } H_2O} = 0.938 \text{ mol Se}$$

c. $2CH_3CH_2OH(l) + O_2(g) \rightarrow 2CH_3CHO(aq) + 2H_2O(l)$

$$0.625 \text{ mol } H_2O \times \frac{2 \text{ mol } CH_3CHO}{2 \text{ mol } H_2O} = 0.625 \text{ mol } CH_3CHO$$

d. $Fe_2O_3(s) + 2Al(s) \rightarrow 2Fe(l) + Al_2O_3(s)$

$$0.625 \text{ mol } Al_2O_3 \times \frac{2 \text{ mol Fe}}{1 \text{ mol } Al_2O_3} = 1.25 \text{ mol Fe}$$

17.   the molar mass of the substance

18.   Stoichiometry is the process of using a chemical equation to calculate the relative masses of reactants and products involved in a reaction.

19.   a.   molar mass Ag = 107.9 g

$$14.2 \text{ g Ag} \times \frac{1 \text{ mol Au}}{107.9 \text{ g Ag}} = 0.132 \text{ mol Ag}$$

b.   molar mass $CoCl_2$ = 129.8 g

$$7.29 \text{ g } CoCl_2 \times \frac{1 \text{ mol } CoCl_2}{129.8 \text{ g } CoCl_2} = 0.0562 \text{ mol } CoCl_2$$

c.   molar mass Li_2CO_3 = 73.89 g

$$4.16 \text{ g } Li_2CO_3 \times \frac{1 \text{ mol } Li_2CO_3}{73.89 \text{ g } Li_2CO_3} = 0.0563 \text{ mol } Li_2CO_3$$

d.   molar mass $PbSO_4$ = 303.3 g

1.25 mg = 1.25×10^{-3} g

$$1.25 \times 10^{-3} \text{ g } PbSO_4 \times \frac{1 \text{ mol } PbSO_4}{303.3 \text{ g } PbSO_4} = 4.12 \times 10^{-6} \text{ mol } PbSO_4$$

e.   molar mass K = 39.10 g

$$0.104 \text{ g K} \times \frac{1 \text{ mol K}}{39.1 \text{ g K}} = 2.66 \times 10^{-3} \text{ mol K}$$

f.   molar mass Fe = 55.85 g

1.12 lb = 1.12×453.59 = 508 g

$$508 \text{ g Fe} \times \frac{1 \text{ mol Fe}}{55.85 \text{ g Fe}} = 9.10 \text{ mol Fe}$$

g.   molar mass MgO = 40.31 g

$$62.4 \text{ g MgO} \times \frac{1 \text{ mol MgO}}{40.31 \text{ g MgO}} = 1.55 \text{ mol MgO}$$

20. a.   molar mass of Ag = 107.9 g

$$2.01 \times 10^{-2} \text{ g Ag} \times \frac{1 \text{ mol}}{107.9 \text{ g}} = 1.86 \times 10^{-4} \text{ mol Ag}$$

b.   molar mass of $(NH_4)_2S$ = 68.15 g

$$45.2 \text{ mg } (NH_4)_2S \times \frac{1 \text{ g}}{1000 \text{ mg}} \times \frac{1 \text{ mol}}{68.15 \text{ g}} = 6.63 \times 10^{-4} \text{ mol } (NH_4)_2S$$

c.   molar mass of uranium = 238.0 g

$$61.7 \text{ }\mu g \text{ U} \times \frac{1 \text{ g}}{10^6 \text{ }\mu g} \times \frac{1 \text{ mol}}{238.0 \text{ g}} = 2.59 \times 10^{-7} \text{ mol U}$$

d.   molar mass of SO_2 = 64.07 g

$$5.23 \text{ kg } SO_2 \times \frac{1000 \text{ g}}{1 \text{ kg}} \times \frac{1 \text{ mol}}{64.07 \text{ g}} = 81.6 \text{ mol } SO_2$$

e.   molar mass of $Fe(NO_3)_3$ = 241.9 g

$$272 \text{ g } Fe(NO_3)_3 \times \frac{1 \text{ mol}}{241.9 \text{ g}} = 1.12 \text{ mol } Fe(NO_3)_3$$

f.   molar mass of $FeSO_4$ = 151.9 g

$$12.7 \text{ mg } FeSO_4 \times \frac{1 \text{ g}}{1000 \text{ mg}} \times \frac{1 \text{ mol}}{151.9 \text{ g}} = 8.36 \times 10^{-5} \text{ mol } FeSO_4$$

g.   molar mass of LiOH = 23.95 g

$$6.91 \times 10^3 \text{ g LiOH} \times \frac{1 \text{ mol}}{23.95 \text{ g}} = 288.5 = 289 \text{ mol LiOH}$$

21. a.   molar mass $PtCl_4$ = 336.9 g

$$1.25 \text{ mol } PtCl_4 \times \frac{336.9 \text{ g } PtCl_4}{1 \text{ mol } PtCl_4} = 421 \text{ g } PtCl_4$$

b.   molar mass CuO = 79.55 g

$$0.00255 \text{ mol CuO} \times \frac{79.55 \text{ g CuO}}{1 \text{ mol CuO}} = 0.203 \text{ g CuO}$$

c.   molar mass C_2H_6 = 30.07 g

$$1.89 \times 10^{-4} \text{ mol } C_2H_6 \times \frac{30.07 \text{ g } C_2H_6}{1 \text{ mol } C_2H_6} = 5.68 \times 10^{-3} \text{ g } C_2H_6$$

d.   molar mass Be = 9.012 g

$$55.56 \text{ mol Be} \times \frac{9.012 \text{ g Be}}{1 \text{ mol Be}} = 500.7 \text{ g Be}$$

e.   molar mass B_2O_3 = 69.62 g

$$2.6 \times 10^7 \text{ mol } B_2O_3 \times \frac{69.62 \text{ g } B_2O_3}{1 \text{ mol } B_2O_3} = 1.8 \times 10^9 \text{ g } B_2O_3$$

f.   molar mass NaF = 41.99 g

$$0.45 \text{ mol NaF} \times \frac{41.99 \text{ g NaF}}{1 \text{ mol NaF}} = 19 \text{ g NaF}$$

g.   molar mass $Ca(NO_3)_2$ = 164.1 g

$$0.00115 \text{ mol } Ca(NO_3)_2 \times \frac{164.1 \text{ g } Ca(NO_3)_2}{1 \text{ mol } Ca(NO_3)_2} = 0.189 \text{ g } Ca(NO_3)_2$$

22.   a.   molar mass of $CaCO_3$ = 100.1 g

$$2.21 \times 10^{-4} \text{ mol } CaCO_3 \times \frac{100.1 \text{ g}}{1 \text{ mol}} = 0.0221 \text{ g } CaCO_3$$

b.   molar mass of He = 4.003 g

$$2.75 \text{ mol He} \times \frac{4.003 \text{ g}}{1 \text{ mol}} = 11.0 \text{ g He}$$

c.   molar mass of O_2 = 32.00 g

$$0.00975 \text{ mol } O_2 \times \frac{32.00 \text{ g}}{1 \text{ mol}} = 0.312 \text{ g } O_2$$

d.   molar mass of CO_2 = 44.01 g

7.21 millimol = 0.00721 mol

$$0.00721 \text{ mol} \times \frac{44.01 \text{ g}}{1 \text{ mol}} = 0.317 \text{ g } CO_2$$

e.   molar mass of FeS = 87.92 g

$$0.835 \text{ mol FeS} \times \frac{87.92 \text{ g}}{1 \text{ mol}} = .73.4 \text{ g FeS}$$

f.   molar mass of KOH = 56.11 g

$$4.01 \text{ mol KOH} \times \frac{56.11 \text{ g}}{1 \text{ mol}} = 225 \text{ g KOH}$$

g.   molar mass of H_2 = 2.016 g

$$0.0219 \text{ mol } H_2 \times \frac{2.016 \text{ g}}{1 \text{ mol}} = 0.0442 \text{ g } H_2$$

23.   Before any calculations are done, the equations must be *balanced*.

a. $2LiOH(s) + CO_2(g) \rightarrow Li_2CO_3(s) + H_2O(l)$

molar mass CO_2 = 44.01 g

$$1.00 \text{ g } CO_2 \times \frac{1 \text{ mol } CO_2}{44.01 \text{ g } CO_2} = 0.0227 \text{ mol } CO_2$$

$$0.0227 \text{ mol } CO_2 \times \frac{1 \text{ mol } Li_2CO_3}{1 \text{ mol } CO_2} = 0.0227 \text{ mol } Li_2CO_3$$

$$0.0227 \text{ mol } CO_2 \times \frac{1 \text{ mol } H_2O}{1 \text{ mol } CO_2} = 0.0227 \text{ mol } H_2O$$

b. $Ba(OH)_2(s) \rightarrow BaO(s) + H_2O(g)$ (already balanced)

molar mass $Ba(OH)_2$ = 171.3 g

$$1.00 \text{ g } Ba(OH)_2 \times \frac{1 \text{ mol } Ba(OH)_2}{171.3 \text{ g } Ba(OH)_2} = 0.00584 \text{ mol } Ba(OH)_2$$

$$0.00584 \text{ mol } Ba(OH)_2 \times \frac{1 \text{ mol } BaO}{1 \text{ mol } Ba(OH)_2} = 0.00584 \text{ mol } BaO$$

$$0.00584 \text{ mol } Ba(OH)_2 \times \frac{1 \text{ mol } H_2O}{1 \text{ mol } Ba(OH)_2} = 0.00584 \text{ mol } H_2O$$

c. $C_2H_4(g) + Cl_2(g) \rightarrow C_2H_4Cl_2(l)$ (already balanced)

molar mass Cl_2 = 70.90 g

$$1.00 \text{ g } Cl_2 \times \frac{1 \text{ mol } Cl_2}{70.90 \text{ g } Cl_2} = 0.0141 \text{ mol } Cl_2$$

$$0.0141 \text{ mol } Cl_2 \times \frac{1 \text{ mol } C_2H_4Cl_2}{1 \text{ mol } Cl_2} = 0.0141 \text{ mol } C_2H_4Cl_2$$

d. $H_2SO_4(aq) + 2NaOH(aq) \rightarrow Na_2SO_4(aq) + 2H_2O(l)$

molar mass NaOH = 40.00 g

$$1.00 \text{ g NaOH} \times \frac{1 \text{ mol NaOH}}{40.00 \text{ g NaOH}} = 0.0250 \text{ mol NaOH}$$

$$0.0250 \text{ mol NaOH} \times \frac{1 \text{ mol } Na_2SO_4}{2 \text{ mol NaOH}} = 0.0125 \text{ mol } Na_2SO_4$$

$$0.0250 \text{ mol NaOH} \times \frac{2 \text{ mol } H_2O}{2 \text{ mol NaOH}} = 0.0250 \text{ mol } H_2O$$

24.   Before any calculations are done, the equations must be *balanced*.

a. $Mg(s) + CuCl_2(aq) \rightarrow MgCl_2(aq) + Cu(s)$

molar mass of Mg = 24.31 g

$$25.0 \text{ g Mg} \times \frac{1 \text{ mol}}{24.31 \text{ g}} = 1.03 \text{ mol Mg}$$

$$1.03 \text{ mol Mg} \times \frac{1 \text{ mol CuCl}_2}{1 \text{ mol Mg}} = 1.03 \text{ mol CuCl}_2$$

b.　$2AgNO_3(aq) + NiCl_2(aq) \rightarrow 2AgCl(s) + Ni(NO_3)_2(aq)$

molar mass of $AgNO_3$ = 169.9 g

$$25.0 \text{ g AgNO}_3 \times \frac{1 \text{ mol}}{169.9 \text{ g}} = 0.147 \text{ mol AgNO}_3$$

$$0.147 \text{ mol AgNO}_3 \times \frac{1 \text{ mol NiCl}_2}{2 \text{ mol AgNO}_3} = 0.0735 \text{ mol NiCl}_2$$

c.　$NaHSO_3(aq) + NaOH(aq) \rightarrow Na_2SO_3(aq) + H_2O(l)$

molar mass of $NaHSO_3$ = 104.1 g

$$25.0 \text{ g NaHSO}_3 \times \frac{1 \text{ mol}}{104.1 \text{ g}} = 0.240 \text{ mol NaHSO}_3$$

$$0.240 \text{ mol NaHSO}_3 \times \frac{1 \text{ mol NaOH}}{1 \text{ mol NaHSO}_3} = 0.240 \text{ mol NaOH}$$

d.　$KHCO_3(aq) + HCl(aq) \rightarrow KCl(aq) + H_2O(l) + CO_2(g)$

molar mass of $KHCO_3$ = 100.1 g

$$25.0 \text{ g KHCO}_3 \times \frac{1 \text{ mol}}{100.1 \text{ g}} = 0.250 \text{ mol KHCO}_3$$

$$0.250 \text{ mol KHCO}_3 \times \frac{1 \text{ mol HCl}}{1 \text{ mol KHCO}_3} = 0.250 \text{ mol HCl}$$

25.　Before any calculations are done, the equations must be *balanced*.

a.　$TiBr_4(g) + 2H_2(g) \rightarrow Ti(s) + 4HBr(g)$

molar mass H_2 = 2.016 g

$$12.5 \text{ g H}_2 \times \frac{1 \text{ mol H}_2}{2.016 \text{ g H}_2} = 6.20 \text{ mol H}_2$$

$$6.20 \text{ mol H}_2 \times \frac{1 \text{ mol Ti}}{2 \text{ mol H}_2} = 3.10 \text{ mol Ti}$$

molar mass Ti = 47.90 g

$$3.10 \text{ mol Ti} \times \frac{47.90 \text{ g Ti}}{1 \text{ mol Ti}} = 148 \text{ g Ti}$$

$$6.20 \text{ mol H}_2 \times \frac{4 \text{ mol HBr}}{2 \text{ mol H}_2} = 12.4 \text{ mol HBr}$$

molar mass of HBr = 80.91 g

$$12.4 \text{ mol HBr} \times \frac{80.91 \text{ g HBr}}{1 \text{ mol HBr}} = 1.00 \times 10^3 \text{ g HBr}$$

b. $3SiH_4(g) + 4NH_3(g) \rightarrow Si_3N_4(s) + 12H_2(g)$

molar mass SiH_4 = 32.12 g

$$12.5 \text{ g SiH}_4 \times \frac{1 \text{ mol SiH}_4}{32.12 \text{ g SiH}_4} = 0.389 \text{ mol SiH}_4$$

$$0.389 \text{ mol SiH}_4 \times \frac{1 \text{ mol Si}_3N_4}{3 \text{ mol SiH}_4} = 0.130 \text{ mol Si}_3N_4$$

molar mass Si_3N_4 = 140.3 g

$$0.130 \text{ mol Si}_3N_4 \times \frac{140.3 \text{ g Si}_3N_4}{1 \text{ mol Si}_3N_4} = 18.2 \text{ g Si}_3N_4$$

$$0.389 \text{ mol SiH}_4 \times \frac{12 \text{ mol H}_2}{3 \text{ mol SiH}_4} = 1.56 \text{ mol H}_2$$

molar mass H_2 = 2.016 g

$$1.56 \text{ mol H}_2 \times \frac{2.016 \text{ mol H}_2}{1 \text{ mol H}_2} = 3.14 \text{ g H}_2$$

c. $2NO(g) + 2H_2(g) \rightarrow N_2(g) + 2H_2O(l)$

molar mass H_2 = 2.016 g

$$12.5 \text{ g H}_2 \times \frac{1 \text{ mol H}_2}{2.016 \text{ g H}_2} = 6.20 \text{ mol H}_2$$

$$6.20 \text{ mol H}_2 \times \frac{1 \text{ mol N}_2}{2 \text{ mol H}_2} = 3.10 \text{ mol N}_2$$

molar mass N_2 = 28.02 g

$$3.10 \text{ mol N}_2 \times \frac{28.02 \text{ g N}_2}{1 \text{ mol N}_2} = 86.9 \text{ g N}_2$$

$$6.20 \text{ mol H}_2 \times \frac{2 \text{ mol H}_2O}{2 \text{ mol H}_2} = 6.20 \text{ mol H}_2O$$

molar mass H_2O = 18.02 g

$$6.20 \text{ mol H}_2O \times \frac{18.02 \text{ g H}_2O}{1 \text{ mol H}_2O} = 112 \text{ g H}_2O$$

d. $Cu_2S(s) \rightarrow 2Cu(s) + S(g)$

molar mass Cu_2S = 159.2 g

$$12.5 \text{ g Cu}_2S \times \frac{1 \text{ mol Cu}_2S}{159.2 \text{ g Cu}_2S} = 0.0785 \text{ mol Cu}_2S$$

$$0.0785 \text{ mol } Cu_2S \times \frac{2 \text{ mol } Cu}{1 \text{ mol } Cu_2S} = 0.157 \text{ mol } Cu$$

molar mass Cu = 63.55 g

$$0.157 \text{ mol } Cu \times \frac{63.55 \text{ g } Cu}{1 \text{ mol } Cu} = 9.98 \text{ g } Cu$$

$$0.0785 \text{ mol } Cu_2S \times \frac{1 \text{ mol } S}{1 \text{ mol } Cu_2S} = 0.0785 \text{ mol } S$$

molar mass S = 32.07 g

$$0.0785 \text{ mol } S \times \frac{32.07 \text{ g } S}{1 \text{ mol } S} = 2.52 \text{ g } S$$

26.   Before any calculations are done, the equations must be *balanced*. Since the given and required quantities in this question are given in *milligrams*, it is most convenient to perform the calculations in terms of *millimoles* of the substances involved. One millimole of a substance represents the molar mass of the substance expressed in milligrams.

a. $FeSO_4(aq) + K_2CO_3(aq) \rightarrow FeCO_3(s) + K_2SO_4(aq)$

millimolar masses: $FeSO_4$, 151.9 mg; $FeCO_3$, 115.9 mg; K_2SO_4, 174.3 mg

$$10.0 \text{ mg } FeSO_4 \times \frac{1 \text{ mmol } FeSO_4}{151.9 \text{ mg } FeSO_4} = 0.0658 \text{ mmol } FeSO_4$$

$$0.0658 \text{ mmol } FeSO_4 \times \frac{1 \text{ mmol } FeCO_3}{1 \text{ mmol } FeSO_4} \times \frac{115.9 \text{ mg } FeCO_3}{1 \text{ mmol } FeCO_3} = 7.63 \text{ mg } FeCO_3$$

$$0.0658 \text{ mmol } FeSO_4 \times \frac{1 \text{ mmol } K_2SO_4}{1 \text{ mmol } FeSO_4} \times \frac{174.3 \text{ mg } K_2SO_4}{1 \text{ mmol } K_2SO_4} = 11.5 \text{ mg } K_2SO_4$$

b. $4Cr(s) + 3SnCl_4(l) \rightarrow 4CrCl_3(s) + 3Sn(s)$

millimolar masses: Cr, 52.00 mg; $CrCl_3$, 158.4 mg; Sn, 118.7 mg

$$10.0 \text{ mg } Cr \times \frac{1 \text{ mmol } Cr}{52.00 \text{ mg } Cr} = 0.192 \text{ mmol } Cr$$

$$0.192 \text{ mmol } Cr \times \frac{4 \text{ mmol } CrCl_3}{4 \text{ mmol } Cr} \times \frac{158.4 \text{ mg } CrCl_3}{1 \text{ mmol } CrCl_3} = 30.4 \text{ mg } CrCl_3$$

$$0.192 \text{ mmol } Cr \times \frac{3 \text{ mmol } Sn}{4 \text{ mmol } Cr} \times \frac{118.7 \text{ mg } Sn}{1 \text{ mmol } Sn} = 17.1 \text{ mg } Sn$$

c. $16Fe(s) + 3S_8(s) \rightarrow 8Fe_2S_3(s)$

millimolar masses: S_8, 256.6 mg; Fe_2S_3, 207.9 mg

$$10.0 \text{ mg } S_8 \times \frac{1 \text{ mmol } S_8}{256.6 \text{ mg } S_8} = 0.0390 \text{ mmol } S_8$$

$$0.0390 \text{ mmol } S_8 \times \frac{8 \text{ mmol } Fe_2S_3}{3 \text{ mmol } S_8} \times \frac{207.9 \text{ mg } Fe_2S_3}{1 \text{ mmol } Fe_2S_3} = 21.6 \text{ mg } Fe_2S_3$$

d. $3Ag(s) + 4HNO_3(aq) \rightarrow 3AgNO_3(aq) + 2H_2O(l) + NO(g)$

millimolar masses: HNO_3, 63.0 mg; $AgNO_3$, 169.9 mg
H_2O, 18.0 mg;   NO, 30.0 mg

$$10.0 \text{ mg } HNO_3 \times \frac{1 \text{ mmol } HNO_3}{63.0 \text{ mg } HNO_3} = 0.159 \text{ mmol } HNO_3$$

$$0.159 \text{ mmol } HNO_3 \times \frac{3 \text{ mmol } AgNO_3}{4 \text{ mmol } HNO_3} \times \frac{169.9 \text{ mg } AgNO_3}{1 \text{ mmol } AgNO_3} = 20.3 \text{ mg } AgNO_3$$

$$0.159 \text{ mmol } HNO_3 \times \frac{2 \text{ mmol } H_2O}{4 \text{ mmol } HNO_3} \times \frac{18.0 \text{ mg } H_2O}{1 \text{ mmol } H_2O} = 1.43 \text{ mg } H_2O$$

$$0.159 \text{ mmol } HNO_3 \times \frac{1 \text{ mmol } NO}{4 \text{ mmol } HNO_3} \times \frac{30.0 \text{ mg } NO}{1 \text{ mmol } NO} = 1.19 \text{ mg } NO$$

27. $2H_2(g) + O_2(g) \rightarrow 2H_2O$

molar masses: H_2, 2.016 g; H_2O, 18.02 g

$$56.0 \text{ g } H_2 \times \frac{1 \text{ mol } H_2}{2.016 \text{ g } H_2} = 27.77 \text{ mol } H_2$$

$$27.77 \text{ mol } H_2 \times \frac{2 \text{ mol } H_2O}{2 \text{ mol } H_2} = 27.77 \text{ mol } H_2O$$

$$27.77 \text{ mol } H_2O \times \frac{18.02 \text{ g } H_2O}{1 \text{ mol } H_2O} = 500. \text{ g } H_2O$$

28. $2H_2(g) + O_2(g) \rightarrow 2H_2O(g)$

molar masses of O_2 = 32.00 g

$$0.0275 \text{ mol } H_2 \times \frac{1 \text{ mol } O_2}{2 \text{ mol } H_2} = 0.01375 = 0.0138 \text{ mol } O_2$$

$$0.01375 \text{ mol } O_2 \times \frac{32.00 \text{ g } O_2}{1 \text{ mol } O_2} = 0.440 \text{ g } O_2$$

29.   molar masses: C, 12.01 g; CO, 28.01 g; CO_2, 44.01 g

$$5.00 \text{ g } C \times \frac{1 \text{ mol } C}{12.01 \text{ g } C} = 0.4163 \text{ mol } C$$

carbon dioxide: $C(s) + O_2(g) \rightarrow CO_2(g)$

$$0.4163 \text{ mol } C \times \frac{1 \text{ mol } CO_2}{1 \text{ mol } C} = 0.4163 \text{ mol } CO_2$$

$$0.4163 \text{ mol } CO_2 \times \frac{44.01 \text{ g } CO_2}{1 \text{ mol } CO_2} = 18.3 \text{ g } CO_2$$

carbon monoxide: $2C(s) + O_2(g) \rightarrow 2CO(g)$

$$0.4163 \text{ mol } C \times \frac{2 \text{ mol } CO}{2 \text{ mol } C} = 0.4163 \text{ mol } CO$$

$$0.4163 \text{ mol } CO \times \frac{28.01 \text{ g } CO}{1 \text{ mol } CO} = 11.7 \text{ g } CO$$

30. $Cl_2(g) + 2KI(aq) \rightarrow I_2(s) + 2KCl(aq)$

molar masses: Cl_2, 70.90 g; I_2, 253.8 g

$$2.55 \text{ g } Cl_2 \times \frac{1 \text{ mol } Cl_2}{70.90 \text{ g } Cl_2} = 0.0360 \text{ mol } Cl_2$$

$$0.0360 \text{ mol } Cl_2 \times \frac{1 \text{ mol } I_2}{1 \text{ mol } Cl_2} = 0.0360 \text{ mol } I_2$$

$$0.0360 \text{ mol } I_2 \times \frac{253.8 \text{ g } I_2}{1 \text{ mol } I_2} = 9.13 \text{ g } I_2$$

31. $2Fe(s) + 3Cl_2(g) \rightarrow 2FeCl_3(s)$

millimolar masses: iron, 55.85 mg; $FeCl_3$, 162.2 mg

$$15.5 \text{ mg } Fe \times \frac{1 \text{ mmol } Fe}{55.85 \text{ mg } Fe} = 0.2775 \text{ mmol } Fe$$

$$0.2775 \text{ mmol } Fe \times \frac{2 \text{ mmol } FeCl_3}{2 \text{ mmol } Fe} = 0.2775 \text{ mmol } FeCl_3$$

$$0.2775 \text{ mmol } FeCl_3 \times \frac{162.2 \text{ mg } FeCl_3}{1 \text{ mmol } FeCl_3} = 45.0 \text{ mg } FeCl_3$$

32. $C_2H_5OH(l) + 3O_2(g) \rightarrow 2CO_2(g) + 3H_2O(l)$

molar masses: C_2H_5OH, 46.07 g; CO_2, 44.01 g

$$25.0 \text{ g } C_2H_5OH \times \frac{1 \text{ mol}}{46.07 \text{ g}} = 0.543 \text{ mol } C_2H_5OH$$

$$0.543 \text{ mol } C_2H_5OH \times \frac{2 \text{ mol } CO_2}{1 \text{ mol } C_2H_5OH} = 1.086 \text{ mol } CO_2$$

$$1.086 \text{ mol } CO_2 \times \frac{44.01 \text{ g}}{1 \text{ mol}} = 47.8 \text{ g } CO_2$$

33. $2H_2O_2(aq) \rightarrow 2H_2O(l) + O_2(g)$

molar masses: H_2O_2, 34.02 g; O_2, 32.00 g

$$10.00 \text{ g H}_2\text{O}_2 \times \frac{1 \text{ mol H}_2\text{O}_2}{34.02 \text{ g H}_2\text{O}_2} = 0.2939 \text{ mol H}_2\text{O}_2$$

$$0.2939 \text{ mol H}_2\text{O}_2 \times \frac{1 \text{ mol O}_2}{2 \text{ mol H}_2\text{O}_2} = 0.1470 \text{ mol O}_2$$

$$0.1470 \text{ mol O}_2 \times \frac{32.00 \text{ g O}_2}{1 \text{ mol O}_2} = 4.704 \text{ g O}_2$$

34. $Cl_2(g) + F_2(g) \rightarrow 2ClF(g)$

molar masses: Cl_2, 70.90 g; F_2, 38.00 g

$$5.00 \text{ mg F}_2 \times \frac{1 \text{ g}}{10^3 \text{ mg}} \times \frac{1 \text{ mol F}_2}{38.00 \text{ g F}_2} = 1.316 \times 10^{-4} \text{ mol F}_2$$

$$1.316 \times 10^{-4} \text{ mol F}_2 \times \frac{1 \text{ mol Cl}_2}{1 \text{ mol F}_2} \times \frac{70.90 \text{ g Cl}_2}{1 \text{ mol Cl}_2} = 9.33 \times 10^{-3} \text{ g Cl}_2$$

35. $CaCO_3(s) + 2HCl(aq) \rightarrow CaCl_2(aq) + H_2O(l) + CO_2(g)$

molar masses: $CaCO_3$, 100.1 g; HCl, 36.46 g

500 mg = 0.500 g

$$0.500 \text{ g CaCO}_3 \times \frac{1 \text{ mol CaCO}_3}{100.1 \text{ g CaCO}_3} = 0.004995 \text{ mol CaCO}_3$$

$$0.004995 \text{ mol CaCO}_3 \times \frac{2 \text{ mol HCl}}{1 \text{ mol CaCO}_3} = 0.009990 \text{ mol HCl}$$

$$0.009990 \text{ mol HCl} \times \frac{36.46 \text{ g HCl}}{1 \text{ mol HCl}} = 0.364 \text{ g HCl}$$

36. $Cu(s) + S(s) \rightarrow CuS(s)$

molar masses: Cu, 63.55 g; S, 32.07 g

$$1.25 \text{ g Cu} \times \frac{1 \text{ mol}}{63.55 \text{ g}} = 1.97 \times 10^{-2} \text{ mol Cu}$$

$$1.97 \times 10^{-2} \text{ mol Cu} \times \frac{1 \text{ mol S}}{1 \text{ mol Cu}} = 1.97 \times 10^{-2} \text{ mol S}$$

$$1.97 \times 10^{-2} \text{ mol S} \times \frac{32.07 \text{ g}}{1 \text{ mol}} = 0.631 \text{ g S}$$

37. $2NH_4NO_3(s) \rightarrow 2N_2(g) + O_2(g) + 4H_2O(g)$

molar masses: NH_4NO_3, 80.05 g; N_2, 28.02 g; O_2, 32.00 g; H_2O, 18.02 g

$$1.25 \text{ g NH}_4\text{NO}_3 \times \frac{1 \text{ mol NH}_4\text{NO}_3}{80.05 \text{ g NH}_4\text{NO}_3} = 0.0156 \text{ mol NH}_4\text{NO}_3$$

$$0.0156 \text{ mol } NH_4NO_3 \times \frac{2 \text{ mol } N_2}{2 \text{ mol } NH_4NO_3} = 0.0156 \text{ mol } N_2$$

$$0.0156 \text{ mol } N_2 \times \frac{28.02 \text{ g } N_2}{1 \text{ mol } N_2} = 0.437 \text{ g } N_2$$

$$0.0156 \text{ mol } NH_4NO_3 \times \frac{1 \text{ mol } O_2}{2 \text{ mol } NH_4NO_3} = 0.00780 \text{ mol } O_2$$

$$0.00780 \text{ mol } O_2 \times \frac{32.00 \text{ g } O_2}{1 \text{ mol } O_2} = 0.250 \text{ g } O_2$$

$$0.0156 \text{ mol } NH_4NO_3 \times \frac{4 \text{ mol } H_2O}{2 \text{ mol } NH_4NO_3} = 0.0312 \text{ mol } H_2O$$

$$0.0312 \text{ mol } H_2O \times \frac{18.02 \text{ g } H_2O}{1 \text{ mol } H_2O} = 0.562 \text{ g } H_2O$$

As a check, note that 0.437 g + 0.250 g + 0.562 g = 1.249 g = 1.25 g.

38. $2NaOH(aq) + CO_2(g) \rightarrow Na_2CO_3(aq) + H_2O(l)$

molar masses: NaOH, 40.00 g; CO_2, 44.01 g

$$5.00 \text{ g NaOH} \times \frac{1 \text{ mol}}{40.00 \text{ g}} = 0.125 \text{ mol NaOH}$$

$$0.125 \text{ mol NaOH} \times \frac{1 \text{ mol } CO_2}{2 \text{ mol NaOH}} = 6.25 \times 10^{-2} \text{ mol } CO_2$$

$$6.25 \times 10^{-2} \text{ mol } CO_2 \times \frac{44.01 \text{ g}}{1 \text{ mol}} = 2.75 \text{ g } CO_2$$

39. $SOCl_2(l) + H_2O(l) \rightarrow SO_2(g) + 2HCl(g)$

molar masses: $SOCl_2$, 119.0 g; H_2O, 18.02 g

$$35.0 \text{ g } SOCl_2 \times \frac{1 \text{ mol } SOCl_2}{119.0 \text{ g } SOCl_2} = 0.294 \text{ mol } SOCl_2$$

$$0.294 \text{ mol } SOCl_2 \times \frac{1 \text{ mol } H_2O}{1 \text{ mol } SOCl_2} = 0.294 \text{ mol } H_2O$$

$$0.294 \text{ mol } H_2O \times \frac{18.02 \text{ g } H_2O}{1 \text{ mol } H_2O} = 5.30 \text{ g } H_2O$$

40. $2Mg(s) + O_2(g) \rightarrow 2MgO(s)$

molar masses: Mg, 24.31 g; MgO, 40.31 g

$$1.25 \text{ g Mg} \times \frac{1 \text{ mol}}{24.31 \text{ g}} = 5.14 \times 10^{-2} \text{ mol Mg}$$

$$5.14 \times 10^{-2} \text{ mol Mg} \times \frac{2 \text{ mol MgO}}{2 \text{ mol Mg}} = 5.14 \times 10^{-2} \text{ mol MgO}$$

$$5.14 \times 10^{-2} \text{ mol MgO} \times \frac{40.31 \text{ g}}{1 \text{ mol}} = 2.07 \text{ g MgO}$$

41. The limiting reactant is the reactant which limits the amounts of products that can form in a chemical reaction. *All* given reactants are necessary for the production of products: if the limiting reactant has been consumed, then there is none of this reactant present for reaction.

42. To determine the limiting reactant, first calculate the number of moles of each reactant present. Then determine how these numbers of moles correspond to the stoichiometric ratio indicated by the balanced chemical equation for the reaction.

43. The theoretical yield of a reaction represents the stoichiometric amount of product that should form if the limiting reactant for the process is completely consumed.

44. A reactant is present *in excess* if there is more of that reactant present than is needed to combine with the limiting reactant for the process. By definition, the limiting reactant cannot be present in excess. An excess of any reactant does not affect the theoretical yield for a process: the theoretical yield is determined by the limiting reactant.

45. a. $Na_2B_4O_7(s) + H_2SO_4(aq) + 5H_2O(l) \rightarrow 4H_3BO_3(s) + Na_2SO_4(aq)$

    molar masses: $Na_2B_4O_7$, 201.2 g; H_2SO_4, 98.08 g; H_2O, 18.02 g

$$5.00 \text{ g Na}_2B_4O_7 \times \frac{1 \text{ mol}}{201.2 \text{ g}} = 0.0249 \text{ mol Na}_2B_4O_7$$

$$5.00 \text{ g H}_2SO_4 \times \frac{1 \text{ mol}}{98.09 \text{ g}} = 0.0510 \text{ mol H}_2SO_4$$

$$5.00 \text{ g H}_2O \times \frac{1 \text{ mol}}{18.02 \text{ g}} = 0.277 \text{ mol H}_2O$$

$Na_2B_4O_7$ is the limiting reactant.

mol H_2SO_4 remaining unreacted = 0.0510 − 0.0249 = 0.0261 mol

mol H_2O remaining unreacted = 0.277 − 5(0.0249) = 0.153 mol

$$\text{mass of H}_2SO_4 \text{ remaining} = 0.0261 \text{ mol} \times \frac{98.08 \text{ g}}{1 \text{ mol}} = 2.56 \text{ g H}_2SO_4$$

$$\text{mass of H}_2O \text{ remaining} = 0.153 \text{ mol} \times \frac{18.02 \text{ g}}{1 \text{ mol}} = 2.76 \text{ g H}_2O$$

b. $CaC_2(s) + 2H_2O(l) \rightarrow Ca(OH)_2(s) + C_2H_2(g)$

molar masses: CaC_2, 64.10 g; H_2O, 18.02 g

$$5.00 \text{ g } CaC_2 \times \frac{1 \text{ mol}}{64.10 \text{ g}} = 0.0780 \text{ mol } CaC_2$$

$$5.00 \text{ g } H_2O \times \frac{1 \text{ mol}}{18.02 \text{ g}} = 0.277 \text{ mol } H_2O$$

CaC_2 is the limiting reactant; water is present in excess.

mol of H_2O remaining = 0.277 - 2(0.0780) = 0.121 mol H_2O

mass of H_2O remaining = 0.121 mol $\times \dfrac{18.02 \text{ g}}{1 \text{ mol}}$ = 2.18 g H_2O

c. $2NaCl(s) + H_2SO_4(l) \rightarrow 2HCl(g) + Na_2SO_4(s)$

molar masses: NaCl, 58.44 g; H_2SO_4, 98.09 g

$$5.00 \text{ g NaCl} \times \frac{1 \text{ mol}}{58.44 \text{ g}} = 0.0856 \text{ mol NaCl}$$

$$5.00 \text{ g } H_2SO_4 \times \frac{1 \text{ mol}}{98.09 \text{ g}} = 0.0510 \text{ mol } H_2SO_4$$

NaCl is the limiting reactant; H_2SO_4 is present in excess.

mol H_2SO_4 that reacts = 0.5(0.0856) = 0.0428 mol H_2SO_4

mol H_2SO_4 remaining = 0.0510 - 0.0428 = 0.0082 mol

mass of H_2SO_4 remaining = 0.0082 mol $\times \dfrac{98.09 \text{ g}}{1 \text{ mol}}$ = 0.80 g H_2SO_4

d. $SiO_2(s) + 2C(s) \rightarrow Si(l) + 2CO(g)$

molar masses: SiO_2, 60.09 g; C, 12.01 g

$$5.00 \text{ g } SiO_2 \times \frac{1 \text{ mol}}{60.09 \text{ g}} = 0.0832 \text{ mol } SiO_2$$

$$5.00 \text{ g C} \times \frac{1 \text{ mol}}{12.01 \text{ g}} = 0.416 \text{ mol C}$$

SiO_2 is the limiting reactant; C is present in excess.

mol C remaining = 0.416 - 2(0.0832) = 0.250 mol

mass of C remaining = 0.250 mol $\times \dfrac{12.01 \text{ g}}{1 \text{ mol}}$ = 3.00 g C

46.   a. $2Al(s) + 6HCl(aq) \rightarrow 2AlCl_3(aq) + 3H_2(g)$

Molar masses: Al, 26.98 g; HCl, 36.46 g; $AlCl_3$, 133.3 g; H_2, 2.016 g

$$15.0 \text{ g Al} \times \frac{1 \text{ mol}}{26.98 \text{ g}} = 0.556 \text{ mol Al}$$

$$15.0 \text{ g HCl} \times \frac{1 \text{ mol}}{36.46 \text{ g}} = 0.411 \text{ mol HCl}$$

Since HCl is needed to react with Al in a 6:2 (i.e., 3:1) molar ratio, it seems pretty certain that HCl is the limiting reactant. To prove this, we can calculate the quantity of Al that would react with the given number of moles of HCl.

$$0.411 \text{ mol HCl} \times \frac{2 \text{ mol Al}}{6 \text{ mol HCl}} = 0.137 \text{ mol Al}$$

By this calculation we have shown that *all* the HCl present will be needed to react with only 0.137 mol Al (out of the 0.556 mol Al present). Therefore HCl is the limiting reactant, and Al is present in excess. The calculation of the masses of products produced is based on the number of moles of the limiting reactant.

$$0.411 \text{ mol HCl} \times \frac{2 \text{ mol AlCl}_3}{6 \text{ mol HCl}} \times \frac{133.3 \text{ g}}{1 \text{ mol}} = 18.3 \text{ g AlCl}_3$$

$$0.411 \text{ mol HCl} \times \frac{3 \text{ mol H}_2}{6 \text{ mol HCl}} \times \frac{2.016 \text{ g}}{1 \text{ mol}} = 0.414 \text{ g H}_2$$

b. $2NaOH(aq) + CO_2(g) \rightarrow Na_2CO_3(aq) + H_2O(l)$

molar masses: NaOH, 40.00 g; CO_2, 44.01 g; Na_2CO_3, 105.99 g; H_2O, 18.02 g

$$15.0 \text{ g NaOH} \times \frac{1 \text{ mol}}{40.00 \text{ g}} = 0.375 \text{ mol NaOH}$$

$$15.0 \text{ g CO}_2 \times \frac{1 \text{ mol}}{44.01 \text{ g}} = 0.341 \text{ mol CO}_2$$

For the 0.375 mol NaOH, let's calculate if there is enough CO_2 present to react:

$$0.375 \text{ mol NaOH} \times \frac{1 \text{ mol CO}_2}{2 \text{ mol NaOH}} = 0.1875 \text{ mol CO}_2 \ (0.188 \text{ mol})$$

We have present *more* CO_2 (0.341 mol) than is needed to react with the given quantity of NaOH. NaOH is therefore the limiting reactant, and CO_2 is present in excess. The quantities of products resulting are based on the complete conversion of the limiting reactant (0.375 mol NaOH):

$$0.375 \text{ mol NaOH} \times \frac{1 \text{ mol Na}_2\text{CO}_3}{2 \text{ mol NaOH}} \times \frac{105.99 \text{ g}}{1 \text{ mol}} = 19.9 \text{ g Na}_2\text{CO}_3$$

$$0.375 \text{ mol NaOH} \times \frac{1 \text{ mol } H_2O}{2 \text{ mol NaOH}} \times \frac{18.02 \text{ g}}{1 \text{ mol}} = 3.38 \text{ g } H_2O$$

c. $Pb(NO_3)_2(aq) + 2HCl(aq) \rightarrow PbCl_2(s) + 2HNO_3(aq)$

Molar masses: $Pb(NO_3)_2$, 331.2 g; HCl, 36.46 g; $PbCl_2$, 278.1 g
HNO_3, 63.02 g

$$15.0 \text{ g } Pb(NO_3)_2 \times \frac{1 \text{ mol}}{331.2 \text{ g}} = 0.0453 \text{ mol } Pb(NO_3)_2$$

$$15.0 \text{ g HCl} \times \frac{1 \text{ mol}}{36.46 \text{ g}} = 0.411 \text{ mol}$$

With such a large disparity between the numbers of moles of the reactants, it's probably a sure bet that $Pb(NO_3)_2$ is the limiting reactant. To confirm this, we can calculate how many mol of HCl are needed to react with the given amount of $Pb(NO_3)_2$.

$$0.0453 \text{ mol } Pb(NO_3)_2 \times \frac{2 \text{ mol HCl}}{1 \text{ mol } Pb(NO_3)_2} = 0.0906 \text{ mol HCl}$$

We have considerably more HCl present than is needed to react completely with the $Pb(NO_3)_2$. Therefore $Pb(NO_3)_2$ is the limiting reactant, and HCl is present in excess. The quantities of products produced are based on the limiting reactant being completely consumed.

$$0.0453 \text{ mol } Pb(NO_3)_2 \times \frac{1 \text{ mol } PbCl_2}{1 \text{ mol } Pb(NO_3)_2} \times \frac{278.1 \text{ g}}{1 \text{ mol}} = 12.6 \text{ g } PbCl_2$$

$$0.0453 \text{ mol } Pb(NO_3)_2 \times \frac{2 \text{ mol } HNO_3}{1 \text{ mol } Pb(NO_3)_2} \times \frac{63.02 \text{ g}}{1 \text{ mol}} = 5.71 \text{ g } HNO_3$$

d. $2K(s) + I_2(s) \rightarrow 2KI(s)$

Molar masses: K, 39.10 g; I_2, 253.8 g; KI, 166.0 g

$$15.0 \text{ g K} \times \frac{1 \text{ mol}}{39.10 \text{ g}} = 0.384 \text{ mol K}$$

$$15.0 \text{ g } I_2 \times \frac{1 \text{ mol}}{253.8 \text{ g}} = 0.0591 \text{ mol } I_2$$

Since, from the balanced chemical equation, we need twice as many moles of K as moles of I_2, and since there is so little I_2 present, it's a safe bet that I_2 is the limiting reactant. To confirm this, we can calculate how many moles of K are needed to react with the given amount of I_2 present:

$$0.0591 \text{ mol } I_2 \times \frac{2 \text{ mol K}}{1 \text{ mol } I_2} = 0.1182 \text{ mol K}$$

Clearly we have more potassium present than is needed to react with the small amount of I_2 present. I_2 is therefore the limiting reactant, and potassium is present in excess. The amount of product produced is calculated from the number of moles of the limiting reactant present:

$$0.0591 \text{ mol } I_2 \times \frac{2 \text{ mol KI}}{1 \text{ mol } I_2} \times \frac{166.0 \text{ g}}{1 \text{ mol}} = 19.6 \text{ g KI}$$

47.   Before any calculations are attempted, the equations must be balanced.

a. $C_3H_8(g) + 5O_2(g) \rightarrow 3CO_2(g) + 4H_2O(g)$

molar masses: C_3H_8, 44.09 g; O_2, 32.00 g;

CO_2, 44.01 g; H_2O, 18.02 g

$$10.0 \text{ g } C_3H_8 \times \frac{1 \text{ mol } C_3H_8}{44.09 \text{ g } C_3H_8} = 0.2268 \text{ mol } C_3H_8$$

$$10.0 \text{ g } O_2 \times \frac{1 \text{ mol } O_2}{32.00 \text{ g } O_2} = 0.3125 \text{ mol } O_2$$

For 0.2268 mol C_3H_8, the amount of O_2 that would be needed is

$$0.2268 \text{ mol } C_3H_8 \times \frac{5 \text{ mol } O_2}{1 \text{ mol } C_3H_8} = 1.134 \text{ mol } O_2$$

Since we do not have this amount of O_2, then O_2 is the limiting reactant.

$$0.3125 \text{ mol } O_2 \times \frac{3 \text{ mol } CO_2}{5 \text{ mol } O_2} = 0.1875 \text{ mol } CO_2$$

$$0.1875 \text{ mol } CO_2 \times \frac{44.01 \text{ g } CO_2}{1 \text{ mol } CO_2} = 8.25 \text{ g } CO_2$$

$$0.3125 \text{ mol } O_2 \times \frac{4 \text{ mol } H_2O}{5 \text{ mol } O_2} = 0.2500 \text{ mol } H_2O$$

$$0.2500 \text{ mol } H_2O \times \frac{18.02 \text{ g } H_2O}{1 \text{ mol } H_2O} = 4.51 \text{ g } H_2O$$

b. $2Al(s) + 3Cl_2(g) \rightarrow 2AlCl_3(s)$

molar masses: Al, 26.98 g; Cl_2, 70.90 g; $AlCl_3$, 133.3 g

$$10.0 \text{ g Al} \times \frac{1 \text{ mol Al}}{26.98 \text{ g Al}} = 0.3706 \text{ mol Al}$$

$$10.0 \text{ g } Cl_2 \times \frac{1 \text{ mol } Cl_2}{70.90 \text{ g } Cl_2} = 0.1410 \text{ mol } Cl_2$$

For 0.1410 mol $Cl_2(g)$, the amount of $Al(s)$ required is

$$0.1410 \text{ mol Cl}_2 \times \frac{2 \text{ mol Al}}{3 \text{ mol Cl}_2} = 0.09400 \text{ mol Al}$$

We have far more than this amount of Al(*s*) present, so Cl_2(*g*) must be the limiting reactant which will control the amount of $AlCl_3$ which forms.

$$0.1410 \text{ mol Cl}_2 \times \frac{2 \text{ mol AlCl}_3}{3 \text{ mol Cl}_2} = 0.09400 \text{ mol AlCl}_3$$

$$0.09400 \text{ mol AlCl}_3 \times \frac{133.3 \text{ g AlCl}_3}{1 \text{ mol AlCl}_3} = 12.5 \text{ g AlCl}_3$$

c. $2NaOH(s) + CO_2(g) \rightarrow Na_2CO_3(s) + H_2O(l)$

molar masses: NaOH, 40.00 g; CO_2, 44.01 g;

Na_2CO_3, 106.0 g; H_2O, 18.02 g

$$10.0 \text{ g NaOH} \times \frac{1 \text{ mol NaOH}}{40.00 \text{ g NaOH}} = 0.2500 \text{ mol NaOH}$$

$$10.0 \text{ g CO}_2 \times \frac{1 \text{ mol CO}_2}{44.01 \text{ g CO}_2} = 0.2272 \text{ mol CO}_2$$

Without having to calculate, according to the balanced chemical equation, we would need *twice* as many moles of NaOH as CO_2 for complete reaction. For the amounts calculated above, there is not nearly enough NaOH present for the amount of Cl_2 used: NaOH is the limiting reactant.

$$0.2500 \text{ mol NaOH} \times \frac{1 \text{ mol Na}_2\text{CO}_3}{2 \text{ mol NaOH}} = 0.1250 \text{ mol Na}_2\text{CO}_3$$

$$0.1250 \text{ mol Na}_2\text{CO}_3 \times \frac{106.0 \text{ g Na}_2\text{CO}_3}{1 \text{ mol Na}_2\text{CO}_3} = 13.3 \text{ g Na}_2\text{CO}_3$$

$$0.2500 \text{ mol NaOH} \times \frac{1 \text{ mol H}_2\text{O}}{2 \text{ mol NaOH}} = 0.1250 \text{ mol H}_2\text{O}$$

$$0.1250 \text{ mol H}_2\text{O} \times \frac{18.02 \text{ g H}_2\text{O}}{1 \text{ mol H}_2\text{O}} = 2.25 \text{ g H}_2\text{O}$$

d. $NaHCO_3(s) + HCl(aq) \rightarrow NaCl(aq) + H_2O(l) + CO_2(g)$

molar masses: $NaHCO_3$, 84.01 g; HCl, 36.46 g; NaCl, 58.44 g

H_2O, 18.02 g; CO_2, 44.01 g

$$10.0 \text{ g NaHCO}_3 \times \frac{1 \text{ mol NaHCO}_3}{84.01 \text{ g NaHCO}_3} = 0.1190 \text{ mol NaHCO}_3$$

$$10.0 \text{ g HCl} \times \frac{1 \text{ mol HCl}}{36.46 \text{ g HCl}} = 0.2742 \text{ mol HCl}$$

Since the coefficients of $NaHCO_3(s)$ and $HCl(aq)$ are both *one* in the balanced chemical equation for the reaction, there is not enough $NaHCO_3$ present to react with the amount of HCl present: the 0.1190 mol $NaHCO_3$ present is the limiting reactant. Since all the coefficients of the products are also each *one*, then if 0.1190 mol $NaHCO_3$ reacts completely (with 0.1190 mol HCl), then 0.1190 mol of each product will form.

$$0.1190 \text{ mol NaCl} \times \frac{58.44 \text{ g NaCl}}{1 \text{ mol NaCl}} = 6.95 \text{ g NaCl}$$

$$0.1190 \text{ mol H}_2\text{O} \times \frac{18.02 \text{ g H}_2\text{O}}{1 \text{ mol H}_2\text{O}} = 2.14 \text{ g H}_2\text{O}$$

$$0.1190 \text{ mol CO}_2 \times \frac{44.01 \text{ g CO}_2}{1 \text{ mol CO}_2} = 5.24 \text{ g CO}_2$$

48.   a. $2NH_3(g) + 2Na(s) \rightarrow 2NaNH_2(s) + H_2(g)$

Molar masses: NH_3, 17.03 g; Na, 22.99 g; $NaNH_2$, 39.02 g

$$50.0 \text{ g NH}_3 \times \frac{1 \text{ mol}}{17.03 \text{ g}} = 2.94 \text{ mol NH}_3$$

$$50.0 \text{ g Na} \times \frac{1 \text{ mol}}{22.99 \text{ g}} = 2.17 \text{ mol Na}$$

Since the coefficients of NH_3 and Na are the *same* in the balanced chemical equation for the reaction, the two reactants combine in a 1:1 molar ratio. Therefore Na is the limiting reactant, which will control the amount of product produced.

$$2.17 \text{ mol Na} \times \frac{2 \text{ mol NaNH}_2}{2 \text{ mol Na}} \times \frac{39.02 \text{ g}}{1 \text{ mol}} = 84.7 \text{ g NaNH}_2$$

b. $BaCl_2(aq) + Na_2SO_4(aq) \rightarrow BaSO_4(s) + 2NaCl(aq)$

Molar masses: $BaCl_2$, 208.2 g; Na_2SO_4, 142.1 g; $BaSO_4$, 233.4 g

$$50.0 \text{ g BaCl}_2 \times \frac{1 \text{ mol}}{208.2 \text{ g}} = 0.240 \text{ mol BaCl}_2$$

$$50.0 \text{ g Na}_2\text{SO}_4 \times \frac{1 \text{ mol}}{142.1 \text{ g}} = 0.352 \text{ mol Na}_2\text{SO}_4$$

Since the coefficients of $BaCl_2$ and Na_2SO_4 are the *same* in the balanced chemical equation for the reaction, the reactant having the smaller number of moles present ($BaCl_2$) must be the limiting reactant, which will control the amount of product produced.

$$0.240 \text{ mol BaCl}_2 \times \frac{1 \text{ mol BaSO}_4}{1 \text{ mol BaCl}_2} \times \frac{233.4 \text{ g}}{1 \text{ mol}} = 56.0 \text{ g BaSO}_4$$

c. $SO_2(g) + 2NaOH(aq) \rightarrow Na_2SO_3(aq) + H_2O(l)$

Molar masses: SO_2, 64.07 g; NaOH, 40.00 g; Na_2SO_3, 126.1 g

$$50.0 \text{ g } SO_2 \times \frac{1 \text{ mol}}{64.07 \text{ g}} = 0.780 \text{ mol } SO_2$$

$$50.0 \text{ g NaOH} \times \frac{1 \text{ mol}}{40.00 \text{ g}} = 1.25 \text{ mol NaOH}$$

From the balanced chemical equation for the reaction, every time one mol of SO_2 reacts, two mol of NaOH are needed. For 0.780 mol of SO_2, 2(0.780 mol) = 1.56 mol of NaOH would be needed. We do not have sufficient NaOH to react with the SO_2 present: therefore, NaOH is the limiting reactant, and controls the amount of product obtained.

$$1.25 \text{ mol NaOH} \times \frac{1 \text{ mol } Na_2SO_3}{2 \text{ mol NaOH}} \times \frac{126.1 \text{ g}}{1 \text{ mol}} = 78.8 \text{ g } Na_2SO_3$$

d. $2Al(s) + 3H_2SO_4(l) \rightarrow Al_2(SO_4)_3(s) + 3H_2(g)$

Molar masses: Al, 26.98 g; H_2SO_4, 98.09 g; $Al_2(SO_4)_3$, 342.2 g

$$50.0 \text{ g Al} \times \frac{1 \text{ mol}}{26.98 \text{ g}} = 1.85 \text{ mol Al}$$

$$50.0 \text{ g } H_2SO_4 \times \frac{1 \text{ mol}}{98.09 \text{ g}} = 0.510 \text{ mol } H_2SO_4$$

Since the amount of H_2SO_4 present is smaller than the amount of Al, let's see if H_2SO_4 is the limiting reactant, by calculating how much Al would react with the given amount of H_2SO_4.

$$0.510 \text{ mol } H_2SO_4 \times \frac{2 \text{ mol Al}}{3 \text{ mol } H_2SO_4} = 0.340 \text{ mol Al}$$

Since all the H_2SO_4 present would react with only a small portion of the Al present, H_2SO_4 is therefore the limiting reactant and will control the amount of product obtained.

$$0.510 \text{ mol } H_2SO_4 \times \frac{1 \text{ mol } Al_2(SO_4)_3}{3 \text{ mol } H_2SO_4} \times \frac{342.2 \text{ g}}{1 \text{ mol}} = 58.2 \text{ g } Al_2(SO_4)_3$$

49.   a. $UO_2(s) + 4HF(aq) \rightarrow UF_4(aq) + 2H_2O(l)$

UO_2 is the limiting reactant; 1.16 g UF_4, 0.133 g H_2O

b. $2NaNO_3(aq) + H_2SO_4(aq) \rightarrow Na_2SO_4(aq) + 2HNO_3(aq)$

$NaNO_3$ is the limiting reactant; 0.836 g Na_2SO_4; 0.741 g HNO_3

c. $Zn(s) + 2HCl(aq) \rightarrow ZnCl_2(aq) + H_2(g)$

HCl is the limiting reactant; 1.87 g $ZnCl_2$; 0.0276 g H_2

d. $B(OH)_3(s) + 3CH_3OH(l) \rightarrow B(OCH_3)_3(s) + 3H_2O(l)$

CH_3OH is the limiting reactant; 1.08 g $B(OCH_3)_3$; 0.562 g H_2O

50.   a. $CO(g) + 2H_2(g) \rightarrow CH_3OH(l)$

CO is the limiting reactant; 11.4 mg CH_3OH

b. $2Al(s) + 3I_2(s) \rightarrow 2AlI_3(s)$

I_2 is the limiting reactant; 10.7 mg AlI_3

c. $Ca(OH)_2(aq) + 2HBr(aq) \rightarrow CaBr_2(aq) + 2H_2O(l)$

HBr is the limiting reactant; 12.4 mg $CaBr_2$; 2.23 mg H_2O

d. $2Cr(s) + 2H_3PO_4(aq) \rightarrow 2CrPO_4(s) + 3H_2(g)$

H_3PO_4 is the limiting reactant; 15.0 mg $CrPO_4$; 0.309 mg H_2

51. $Cl_2(g) + 2NaI(aq) \rightarrow 2NaCl(aq) + I_2(s)$
$Br_2(l) + 2NaI(aq) \rightarrow 2NaBr(aq) + I_2(s)$

molar masses: Cl_2, 70.90 g; Br_2, 159.8 g; I_2, 253.8 g; NaI, 149.9 g

$$5.00 \text{ g } Cl_2 \times \frac{1 \text{ mol } Cl_2}{70.90 \text{ g } Cl_2} = 0.0705 \text{ mol } Cl_2$$

$$25.0 \text{ g NaI} \times \frac{1 \text{ mol NaI}}{149.9 \text{ g NaI}} = 0.167 \text{ mol NaI}$$

Since we would need 2(0.0705) = 0.141 mol of NaI for the Cl_2 to react completely, and we have more than this amount of NaI, then Cl_2 must be the limiting reactant.

$$0.0705 \text{ mol } Cl_2 \times \frac{1 \text{ mol } I_2}{1 \text{ mol } Cl_2} = 0.0705 \text{ mol } I_2$$

$$0.0705 \text{ mol } I_2 \times \frac{253.8 \text{ g } I_2}{1 \text{ mol } I_2} = 17.9 \text{ g } I_2$$

$$5.00 \text{ g } Br_2 \times \frac{1 \text{ mol } Br_2}{159.8 \text{ g } Br_2} = 0.0313 \text{ mol } Br_2$$

$$25.0 \text{ g NaI} \times \frac{1 \text{ mol NaI}}{149.9 \text{ g NaI}} = 0.167 \text{ mol NaI}$$

Since we would need 2(0.0313) = 0.0626 mol of NaI for the Br_2 to react completely, and we have more than this amount of NaI, then Br_2 must be the limiting reactant.

$$0.0313 \text{ mol } Br_2 \times \frac{1 \text{ mol } I_2}{1 \text{ mol } Br_2} = 0.0313 \text{ mol } I_2$$

$$0.0313 \text{ mol } I_2 \times \frac{253.8 \text{ g } I_2}{1 \text{ mol } I_2} = 7.94 \text{ g } I_2$$

52. $2NH_3(g) + CO_2(g) \rightarrow CN_2H_4O(s) + H_2O(l)$

molar masses: NH_3, 17.03 g; CO_2, 44.01 g; CN_2H_4O, 60.06 g

$$100. \text{ g } NH_3 \times \frac{1 \text{ mol } NH_3}{17.03 \text{ g } NH_3} = 5.872 \text{ mol } NH_3$$

$$100. \text{ g } CO_2 \times \frac{1 \text{ mol } CO_2}{44.01 \text{ g } CO_2} = 2.272 \text{ mol } CO_2$$

See if CO_2 is the limiting reactant.

$$2.272 \text{ mol } CO_2 \times \frac{2 \text{ mol } NH_3}{1 \text{ mol } CO_2} = 4.544 \text{ mol } NH_3$$

CO_2 is indeed the limiting reactant.

$$2.272 \text{ mol } CO_2 \times \frac{1 \text{ mol } CN_2H_4O}{1 \text{ mol } CO_2} = 2.272 \text{ mol } CN_2H_4O$$

$$2.272 \text{ mol } CN_2H_4O \times \frac{60.06 \text{ g } CN_2H_4O}{1 \text{ mol } CN_2H_4O} = 136 \text{ g } CN_2H_4O$$

53. $NH_3(g) + HCl(g) \rightarrow NH_4Cl(s)$

millimolar masses: NH_3, 17.03 mg; HCl, 36.46 mg; NH_4Cl, 53.49 mg

$$125 \text{ mg } NH_3 \times \frac{1 \text{ mmol } NH_3}{17.03 \text{ mg } NH_3} = 7.340 \text{ mmol}$$

$$190. \text{ mg } HCl \times \frac{1 \text{ mmol } HCl}{36.46 \text{ mg } HCl} = 5.211 \text{ mmol } HCl$$

HCl is the limiting reactant.

$$5.211 \text{ mmol } HCl \times \frac{1 \text{ mmol } NH_4Cl}{1 \text{ mmol } HCl} \times \frac{53.49 \text{ mg } NH_4Cl}{1 \text{ mmol } NH_4Cl} = 279 \text{ mg } NH_4Cl$$

54. $4Fe(s) + 3O_2(g) \rightarrow 2Fe_2O_3(s)$

Molar masses: Fe, 55.85 g; Fe_2O_3, 159.7 g

$$1.25 \text{ g } Fe \times \frac{1 \text{ mol}}{55.85 \text{ g}} = 0.0224 \text{ mol } Fe \text{ present}$$

Calculate how many mol of O_2 are required to react with this amount of Fe

$$0.0224 \text{ mol Fe} \times \frac{3 \text{ mol O}_2}{4 \text{ mol Fe}} = 0.0168 \text{ mol O}_2$$

Since we have more O_2 than this, Fe must be the limiting reactant.

$$0.0224 \text{ mol Fe} \times \frac{2 \text{ mol Fe}_2O_3}{4 \text{ mol Fe}} = 0.0112 \text{ mol Fe}_2O_3$$

$$0.0112 \text{ mol Fe}_2O_3 \times \frac{159.7 \text{ g Fe}_2O_3}{1 \text{ mol Fe}_2O_3} = 1.79 \text{ g Fe}_2O_3$$

55. $Ca^{2+}(aq) + Na_2C_2O_4(aq) \rightarrow CaC_2O_4(s) + 2Na^+(aq)$

molar masses: Ca^{2+}, 40.08 g; $Na_2C_2O_4$, 134.0 g

$$15 \text{ g Ca}^{2+} \times \frac{1 \text{ mol Ca}^{2+}}{40.08 \text{ g Ca}^{2+}} = 0.37 \text{ mol Ca}^{2+}$$

$$15 \text{ g Na}_2C_2O_4 \times \frac{1 \text{ mol Na}_2C_2O_4}{134.0 \text{ g Na}_2C_2O_4} = 0.11 \text{ mol Na}_2C_2O_4$$

Since the balanced chemical equation tells us that one oxalate ion is needed to precipitate each calcium ion, from the number of moles calculated to be present, it should be clear that not nearly enough sodium oxalate ion has been added to precipitate all the calcium ion in the sample.

56. $2CuSO_4(aq) + 5KI(aq) \rightarrow 2CuI(s) + KI_3(aq) + 2K_2SO_4(aq)$

Molar masses: $CuSO_4$, 159.6 g; KI, 166.0 g; CuI, 190.5 g; KI_3, 419.8 g; K_2SO_4, 174.3 g

$$0.525 \text{ g CuSO}_4 \times \frac{1 \text{ mol}}{159.6 \text{ g}} = 3.29 \times 10^{-3} \text{ mol CuSO}_4$$

$$2.00 \text{ g KI} \times \frac{1 \text{ mol}}{166.0 \text{ g}} = 0.0120 \text{ mol KI}$$

To determine the limiting reactant, let's calculate what amount of KI would be needed to react with the given amount of $CuSO_4$ present

$$3.29 \times 10^{-3} \text{ mol CuSO}_4 \times \frac{5 \text{ mol KI}}{2 \text{ mol CuSO}_4} = 8.23 \times 10^{-3} \text{ mol KI}$$

Since we have more KI present than the amount required to react with the $CuSO_4$ present, $CuSO_4$ must be the limiting reactant, which will control the amounts of products produced.

$$3.29 \times 10^{-3} \text{ mol CuSO}_4 \times \frac{2 \text{ mol Cu I}}{2 \text{ mol CuSO}_4} \times \frac{190.5 \text{ g}}{1 \text{ mol}} = 0.627 \text{ g CuI}$$

$$3.29 \times 10^{-3} \text{ mol CuSO}_4 \times \frac{1 \text{ mol KI}_3}{2 \text{ mol CuSO}_4} \times \frac{419.8 \text{ g}}{1 \text{ mol}} = 0.691 \text{ g KI}_3$$

$$3.29 \times 10^{-3} \text{ mol CuSO}_4 \times \frac{2 \text{ mol K}_2\text{SO}_4}{2 \text{ mol CuSO}_4} \times \frac{174.3 \text{ g}}{1 \text{ mol}} = 0.573\text{g K}_2\text{SO}_4$$

57. $BaO_2(s) + 2HCl(aq) \rightarrow H_2O_2(aq) + BaCl_2(aq)$

molar masses: BaO_2, 169.3 g; HCl, 36.46 g; H_2O_2, 34.02 g

$$1.50 \text{ g BaO}_2 \times \frac{1 \text{ mol BaO}_2}{169.3 \text{ g BaO}_2} = 8.860 \times 10^{-3} \text{ mol BaO}_2$$

$$25.0 \text{ mL solution} \times \frac{0.0272 \text{ g HCl}}{1 \text{ mL solution}} = 0.680 \text{ g HCl}$$

$$0.680 \text{ g HCl} \times \frac{1 \text{ mol HCl}}{36.46 \text{ g HCl}} = 1.865 \times 10^{-2} \text{ mol HCl}$$

BaO_2 is the limiting reactant.

$$8.860 \times 10^{-3} \text{ mol BaO}_2 \times \frac{1 \text{ mol H}_2\text{O}_2}{1 \text{ mol BaO}_2} = 8.860 \times 10^{-3} \text{ mol H}_2\text{O}_2$$

$$8.860 \times 10^{-3} \text{ mol H}_2\text{O}_2 \times \frac{34.02 \text{ g H}_2\text{O}_2}{1 \text{ mol H}_2\text{O}_2} = 0.301 \text{ g H}_2\text{O}_2$$

58. $SiO_2(s) + 3C(s) \rightarrow 2CO(g) + SiC(s)$

molar masses: SiO_2, 60.09 g; SiC, 40.10 g

$1.0 \text{ kg} = 1.0 \times 10^3 \text{ g}$

$$1.0 \times 10^3 \text{ g SiO}_2 \times \frac{1 \text{ mol SiO}_2}{60.09 \text{ g SiO}_2} = 16.64 \text{ mol SiO}_2$$

From the balanced chemical equation, if 16.64 mol of SiO_2 were to react completely (an excess of carbon is present), then 16.64 mol of SiC should be produced (the coefficients of SiO_2 and SiC are the same).

$$16.64 \text{ mol SiC} \times \frac{40.01 \text{ g SiC}}{1 \text{ mol SiC}} = 6.7 \times 10^2 \text{ g SiC} = 0.67 \text{ kg SiC}$$

59. The actual yield for a reaction is the quantity of product *actually isolated* from the reaction vessel. The theoretical yield represents the mass of products that should be produced by the reaction if the limiting reactant is fully consumed. The percent yield represents what *fraction* of the amount of product that *should* have been collected was *actually* collected.

60. If the reaction is performed in a solvent, the product may have a substantial solubility in the solvent; the reaction may come to equilibrium before the full yield of product is achieved (see Chapter 16); loss of product may occur through operator error.

61. $\text{Percent yield} = \dfrac{\text{actual yield}}{\text{theoretical yield}} \times 100 = \dfrac{1.23 \text{ g}}{1.44 \text{ g}} \times 100 = 85.4\%$

62. $$\text{Percent yield} = \frac{\text{actual yield}}{\text{theoretical yield}} \times 100 = \frac{1.279 \text{ g}}{1.352 \text{ g}} \times 100 = 94.60\%$$

63. $S_8(s) + 8Na_2SO_3(aq) + 40H_2O(l) \rightarrow 8Na_2S_2O_3 \cdot 5H_2O$

    molar masses: S_8, 256.6 g; Na_2SO_3, 126.1 g; $Na_2S_2O_3 \cdot 5H_2O$, 248.2 g

    $$3.25 \text{ g } S_8 \times \frac{1 \text{ mol } S_8}{256.6 \text{ g } S_8} = 0.01267 \text{ mol } S_8$$

    $$13.1 \text{ g } Na_2SO_3 \times \frac{1 \text{ mol } Na_2SO_3}{126.1 \text{ g } Na_2SO_3} = 0.1039 \text{ mol } Na_2SO_3$$

    S_8 is the limiting reactant.

    $$0.01267 \text{ mol } S_8 \times \frac{8 \text{ mol } Na_2S_2O_3 \cdot 5H_2O}{1 \text{ mol } S_8} = 0.1014 \text{ mol } Na_2S_2O_3 \cdot 5H_2O$$

    $$0.1014 \text{ mol } Na_2S_2O_3 \cdot 5H_2O \times \frac{248.2 \text{ g } Na_2S_2O_3 \cdot 5H_2O}{1 \text{ mol } Na_2S_2O_3 \cdot 5H_2O} = 25.2 \text{ g } Na_2S_2O_3 \cdot 5H_2O$$

    $$\text{Percent yield} = \frac{\text{actual yield}}{\text{theoretical yield}} \times 100 = \frac{5.26 \text{ g}}{25.2 \text{ g}} \times 100 = 20.9\%$$

64. $2LiOH(s) + CO_2(g) \rightarrow Li_2CO_3(s) + H_2O(g)$

    molar masses: LiOH, 23.95 g; CO_2, 44.01 g

    $$155 \text{ g LiOH} \times \frac{1 \text{ mol LiOH}}{23.95 \text{ g LiOH}} \times \frac{1 \text{ mol } CO_2}{2 \text{ mol LiOH}} \times \frac{44.01 \text{ g } CO_2}{1 \text{ mol } CO_2} = 142 \text{ g } CO_2$$

    Since the cartridge has only absorbed 102 g CO_2 out of a total capacity of 142 g CO_2, the cartridge has absorbed

    $$\frac{102 \text{ g}}{142 \text{ g}} \times 100 = 71.8\% \text{ of its capacity}$$

65. $Xe(g) + 2F_2(g) \rightarrow XeF_4(s)$

    molar masses: Xe, 131.3 g; F_2, 38.00 g; XeF_4, 207.3 g

    $$130. \text{ g Xe} \times \frac{1 \text{ mol Xe}}{131.3 \text{ g Xe}} = 0.9901 \text{ mol Xe}$$

    $$100. \text{ g } F_2 \times \frac{1 \text{ mol } F_2}{38.00 \text{ g } F_2} = 2.632 \text{ mol } F_2$$

    Xe is the limiting reactant.

    $$0.9901 \text{ mol Xe} \times \frac{1 \text{ mol } XeF_4}{1 \text{ mol Xe}} = 0.9901 \text{ mol } XeF_4$$

    $$0.9901 \text{ mol } XeF_4 \times \frac{207.3 \text{ g } XeF_4}{1 \text{ mol } XeF_4} = 205 \text{ g } XeF_4$$

$$\text{Percent yield} = \frac{\text{actual yield}}{\text{theoretical yield}} \times 100 = \frac{145 \text{ g}}{205 \text{ g}} \times 100 = 70.7\%$$

66. $CaCO_3(s) + 2HCl(g) \rightarrow CaCl_2(s) + CO_2(g) + H_2O(g)$

molar masses: $CaCO_3$, 100.1 g; HCl, 36.46 g; $CaCl_2$, 111.0 g

$$155 \text{ g } CaCO_3 \times \frac{1 \text{ mol } CaCO_3}{100.1 \text{ g } CaCO_3} = 1.548 \text{ mol } CaCO_3$$

$$250. \text{ g HCl} \times \frac{1 \text{ mol HCl}}{36.46 \text{ g HCl}} = 6.857 \text{ mol HCl}$$

$CaCO_3$ is the limiting reactant.

$$1.548 \text{ mol } CaCO_3 \times \frac{1 \text{ mol } CaCl_2}{1 \text{ mol } CaCO_3} = 1.548 \text{ mol } CaCl_2$$

$$1.548 \text{ mol } CaCl_2 \times \frac{111.0 \text{ g } CaCl_2}{1 \text{ mol } CaCl_2} = 172 \text{ g } CaCl_2$$

$$\text{Percent yield} = \frac{\text{actual yield}}{\text{theoretical yield}} \times 100 = \frac{142 \text{ g}}{172 \text{ g}} \times 100 = 82.6\%$$

67. millimolar masses: $Ca(HCO_3)_2$, 162.1 mg; $CaCO_3$, 100.1 mg

$$2.0 \times 10^{-3} \text{ mg } Ca(HCO_3)_2 \times \frac{1 \text{ mmol } Ca(HCO_3)_2}{162.1 \text{ mg } Ca(HCO_3)_2} = 1.23 \times 10^{-5} \text{ mmol } Ca(HCO_3)_2$$

$$1.23 \times 10^{-5} \text{ mmol } Ca(HCO_3)_2 \times \frac{1 \text{ mmol } CaCO_3}{1 \text{ mmol } Ca(HCO_3)_2} = 1.23 \times 10^{-5} \text{ mmol } CaCO_3$$

$$1.23 \times 10^{-5} \text{ mmol} \times \frac{100.1 \text{ mg } CaCO_3}{1 \text{ mmol } CaCO_3} = 1.2 \times 10^{-3} \text{ mg} = 1.2 \times 10^{-6} \text{ g } CaCO_3$$

68. $NaCl(aq) + NH_3(aq) + H_2O(l) + CO_2(s) \rightarrow NH_4Cl(aq) + NaHCO_3(s)$

molar masses: NH_3, 17.03 g; CO_2, 44.01 g; $NaHCO_3$, 84.01 g

$$10.0 \text{ g } NH_3 \times \frac{1 \text{ mol } NH_3}{17.03 \text{ g } NH_3} = 0.5872 \text{ mol } NH_3$$

$$15.0 \text{ g } CO_2 \times \frac{1 \text{ mol } CO_2}{44.01 \text{ g } CO_2} = 0.3408 \text{ mol } CO_2$$

CO_2 is the limiting reactant.

$$0.3408 \text{ mol } CO_2 \times \frac{1 \text{ mol } NaHCO_3}{1 \text{ mol } CO_2} = 0.3408 \text{ mol } NaHCO_3$$

$$0.3408 \text{ mol } NaHCO_3 \times \frac{84.01 \text{ g } NaHCO_3}{1 \text{ mol } NaHCO_3} = 28.6 \text{ g } NaHCO_3$$

69. $Fe(s) + S(s) \rightarrow FeS(s)$

molar masses: Fe, 55.85 g; S, 32.07 g; FeS, 87.92 g

$$5.25 \text{ g Fe} \times \frac{1 \text{ mol Fe}}{55.85 \text{ g Fe}} = 0.0940 \text{ mol Fe}$$

$$12.7 \text{ g S} \times \frac{1 \text{ mol S}}{32.07 \text{ g S}} = 0.396 \text{ mol S}$$

Fe is the limiting reactant.

$$0.0940 \text{ mol Fe} \times \frac{1 \text{ mol FeS}}{1 \text{ mol Fe}} \times \frac{87.92 \text{ g FeS}}{1 \text{ mol FeS}} = 8.26 \text{ g FeS produced}$$

70. $C_6H_{12}O_6(s) + 6O_2(g) \rightarrow 6CO_2(g) + 6H_2O(g)$

molar masses: glucose, 180.2 g; CO_2, 44.01 g

$$1.00 \text{ g glucose} \times \frac{1 \text{ mol glucose}}{180.2 \text{ g glucose}} = 5.549 \times 10^{-3} \text{ mol glucose}$$

$$5.549 \times 10^{-3} \text{ mol glucose} \times \frac{6 \text{ mol } CO_2}{1 \text{ mol glucose}} = 3.33 \times 10^{-2} \text{ mol } CO_2$$

$$3.33 \times 10^{-2} \text{ mol } CO_2 \times \frac{44.01 \text{ g } CO_2}{1 \text{ mol } CO_2} = 1.47 \text{ g } CO_2$$

71. $Cu(s) + S(s) \rightarrow CuS(s)$

molar masses: Cu, 63.55 g; S, 32.07 g; CuS, 95.62 g

$$31.8 \text{ g Cu} \times \frac{1 \text{ mol Cu}}{63.55 \text{ g Cu}} = 0.5004 \text{ mol Cu}$$

$$50.0 \text{ g S} \times \frac{1 \text{ mol S}}{32.07 \text{ g S}} = 1.559 \text{ mol S}$$

Cu is the limiting reactant.

$$0.5004 \text{ mol Cu} \times \frac{1 \text{ mol CuS}}{1 \text{ mol Cu}} = 0.5004 \text{ mol CuS}$$

$$0.5004 \text{ mol CuS} \times \frac{95.62 \text{ g CuS}}{1 \text{ mol CuS}} = 47.8 \text{ g CuS}$$

$$\% \text{ yield} = \frac{40.0 \text{ g}}{47.8 \text{ g}} \times 100 = 83.7\%$$

72. $Ba^{2+}(aq) + SO_4^{2-}(aq) \rightarrow BaSO_4(s)$

millimolar ionic masses: Ba^{2+}, 137.3 mg; SO_4^{2-}, 96.07 mg; $BaCl_2$, 208.2 mg

$$150 \text{ mg } SO_4^{2-} \times \frac{1 \text{ mmol } SO_4^{2-}}{96.07 \text{ mg } SO_4^{2-}} = 1.56 \text{ millimol } SO_4^{2-}$$

Since barium ion and sulfate ion react on a 1:1 stoichiometric basis, then 1.56 millimol of barium ion is needed, which corresponds to 1.56 millimol of $BaCl_2$

$$1.56 \text{ millimol } BaCl_2 \times \frac{208.2 \text{ mg } BaCl_2}{1 \text{ millimol } BaCl_2} = 325 \text{ milligrams } BaCl_2 \text{ needed}$$

73.   mass of Cl^- present = $1.054 \text{ g sample} \times \dfrac{10.3 \text{ g } Cl^-}{100.0 \text{ sample}} = 0.1086 \text{ g } Cl^-$

molar masses: Cl^-, 35.45 g; $AgNO_3$, 169.9 g; AgCl, 143.4 g

$$0.1086 \text{ g } Cl^- \times \frac{1 \text{ mol } Cl^-}{35.45 \text{ g } Cl^-} = 3.063 \times 10^{-3} \text{ mol } Cl^-$$

$$3.063 \times 10^{-3} \text{ mol } Cl^- \times \frac{1 \text{ mol } AgNO_3}{1 \text{ mol } Cl^-} = 3.063 \times 10^{-3} \text{ mol } AgNO_3$$

$$3.063 \times 10^{-3} \text{ mol } AgNO_3 \times \frac{169.9 \text{ g } AgNO_3}{1 \text{ mol } AgNO_3} = 0.520 \text{ g } AgNO_3 \text{ required}$$

$$3.063 \times 10^{-3} \text{ mol } Cl^- \times \frac{1 \text{ mol AgCl}}{1 \text{ mol } Cl^-} = 3.063 \times 10^{-3} \text{ mol AgCl}$$

$$3.063 \times 10^{-3} \text{ mol AgCl} \times \frac{143.4 \text{ g AgCl}}{1 \text{ mol AgCl}} = 0.439 \text{ g AgCl produced}$$

74.   a. $UO_2(s) + 4HF(aq) \rightarrow UF_4(aq) + 2H_2O(l)$

One molecule (formula unit) of uranium(IV) oxide will combine with four molecules of hydrofluoric acid, producing one uranium(IV) fluoride molecule and two water molecules. One mole of uranium(IV) oxide will combine with four moles of hydrofluoric acid to produce one mole of uranium(IV) fluoride and two moles of water.

b. $2NaC_2H_3O_2(aq) + H_2SO_4(aq) \rightarrow Na_2SO_4(aq) + 2HC_2H_3O_2(aq)$

Two molecules (formula units) of sodium acetate react exactly with one molecule of sulfuric acid, producing one molecule (formula unit) of sodium sulfate and two molecules of acetic acid. Two moles of sodium acetate will combine with one mole of sulfuric acid, producing one mole of sodium sulfate and two moles of acetic acid.

c. $Mg(s) + 2HCl(aq) \rightarrow MgCl_2(aq) + H_2(g)$

One magnesium atom will react with two hydrochloric acid molecules (formula units) to produce one molecule (formula unit) of magnesium chloride and one molecule of hydrogen gas. One mole of magnesium will combine with two moles of hydrochloric acid, producing one mole of magnesium chloride and one mole of gaseous hydrogen.

d. $B_2O_3(s) + 3H_2O(l) \rightarrow 2B(OH)_3(aq)$

One molecule of diboron trioxide will react exactly with three molecules of water, producing two molecules of boron trihydroxide (boric acid). One mole of diboron trioxide will combine with three moles of water to produce two moles of boron trihydroxide (boric acid).

75.   False. For 0.40 mol of $Mg(OH)_2$ to react, 0.80 mol of HCl will be needed. According to the balanced equation, for a given amount of $Mg(OH)_2$, *twice* as many moles of HCl is needed.

76.   For O_2: $\dfrac{5 \text{ mol } O_2}{1 \text{ mol } C_3H_8}$ For CO_2: $\dfrac{3 \text{ mol } CO_2}{1 \text{ mol } C_3H_8}$ For H_2O: $\dfrac{4 \text{ mol } H_2O}{1 \text{ mol } C_3H_8}$

77.   a. $2H_2O_2(l) \rightarrow 2H_2O(l) + O_2(g)$

$0.50 \text{ mol } H_2O_2 \times \dfrac{2 \text{ mol } H_2O}{2 \text{ mol } H_2O_2} = 0.50 \text{ mol } H_2O$

$0.50 \text{ mol } H_2O_2 \times \dfrac{1 \text{ mol } O_2}{2 \text{ mol } H_2O_2} = 0.25 \text{ mol } O_2$

b. $2KClO_3(s) \rightarrow 2KCl(s) + 3O_2(g)$

$0.50 \text{ mol } KClO_3 \times \dfrac{2 \text{ mol } KCl}{2 \text{ mol } KClO_3} = 0.50 \text{ mol } KCl$

$0.50 \text{ mol } KClO_3 \times \dfrac{3 \text{ mol } O_2}{2 \text{ mol } KClO_3} = 0.75 \text{ mol } O_2$

c. $2Al(s) + 6HCl(aq) \rightarrow 2AlCl_3(aq) + 3H_2(g)$

$0.50 \text{ mol } Al \times \dfrac{2 \text{ mol } AlCl_3}{2 \text{ mol } Al} = 0.50 \text{ mol } AlCl_3$

$0.50 \text{ mol } Al \times \dfrac{3 \text{ mol } H_2}{2 \text{ mol } Al} = 0.75 \text{ mol } H_2$

d. $C_3H_8(g) + 5O_2(g) \rightarrow 3CO_2(g) + 4H_2O(l)$

$0.50 \text{ mol } C_3H_8 \times \dfrac{3 \text{ mol } CO_2}{1 \text{ mol } C_3H_8} = 1.5 \text{ mol } CO_2$

$0.50 \text{ mol } C_3H_8 \times \dfrac{4 \text{ mol } H_2O}{1 \text{ mol } C_3H_8} = 2.0 \text{ mol } H_2O$

78.   a. $NH_3(g) + HCl(g) \rightarrow NH_4Cl(s)$

molar mass of NH_3 = 17.0 g

$1.00 \text{ g } NH_3 \times \dfrac{1 \text{ mol } NH_3}{17.0 \text{ g } NH_3} = 0.0588 \text{ mol } NH_3$

$$0.0588 \text{ mol NH}_3 \times \frac{1 \text{ mol NH}_4\text{Cl}}{1 \text{ mol NH}_3} = 0.0588 \text{ mol NH}_4\text{Cl}$$

b. $\text{CaO}(s) + \text{CO}_2(g) \rightarrow \text{CaCO}_3(s)$

molar mass CaO = 56.1 g

$$1.00 \text{ g CaO} \times \frac{1 \text{ mol CaO}}{56.1 \text{ g CaO}} = 0.0178 \text{ mol CaO}$$

$$0.0178 \text{ mol CaO} \times \frac{1 \text{ mol CaCO}_3}{1 \text{ mol CaO}} = 0.0178 \text{ mol CaCO}_3$$

c. $4\text{Na}(s) + \text{O}_2(g) \rightarrow 2\text{Na}_2\text{O}(s)$

molar mass Na = 22.99 g

$$1.00 \text{ g Na} \times \frac{1 \text{ mol Na}}{22.99 \text{ g Na}} = 0.0435 \text{ mol Na}$$

$$0.0435 \text{ mol Na} \times \frac{2 \text{ mol Na}_2\text{O}}{4 \text{ mol Na}} = 0.0217 \text{ mol Na}_2\text{O}$$

d. $2\text{P}(s) + 3\text{Cl}_2(g) \rightarrow 2\text{PCl}_3(l)$

molar mass P = 30.97 g

$$1.00 \text{ g P} \times \frac{1 \text{ mol P}}{30.97 \text{ g P}} = 0.0323 \text{ mol P}$$

$$0.0323 \text{ mol P} \times \frac{2 \text{ mol PCl}_3}{2 \text{ mol P}} = 0.0323 \text{ mol PCl}_3$$

79.   a.   molar mass CuSO_4 = 159.6 g

$$4.21 \text{ g CuSO}_4 \times \frac{1 \text{ mol CuSO}_4}{159.6 \text{ g CuSO}_4} = 0.0264 \text{ mol CuSO}_4$$

b.   molar mass $\text{Ba(NO}_3)_2$ = 261.3 g

$$7.94 \text{ g Ba(NO}_3)_2 \times \frac{1 \text{ mol Ba(NO}_3)_2}{261.3 \text{ g Ba(NO}_3)_2} = 0.0304 \text{ mol Ba(NO}_3)_2$$

c.   molar mass water = 18.02 g; 1.24 mg = 0.00124 g

$$0.00124 \text{ g} \times \frac{1 \text{ mol H}_2\text{O}}{18.02 \text{ g H}_2\text{O}} = 6.88 \times 10^{-5} \text{ mol H}_2\text{O}$$

d.   molar mass W = 183.9 g

$$9.79 \text{ g W} \times \frac{1 \text{ mol W}}{183.9 \text{ g W}} = 5.32 \times 10^{-2} \text{ mol W}$$

e.   molar mass S = 32.07 g; 1.45 lb = 1.45(453.59) = 658 g

$$658 \text{ g S} \times \frac{1 \text{ mol S}}{32.07 \text{ g S}} = 20.5 \text{ mol S}$$

f.   molar mass C_2H_5OH = 46.07 g

$$4.65 \text{ g } C_2H_5OH \times \frac{1 \text{ mol } C_2H_5OH}{46.07 \text{ g } C_2H_5OH} = 0.101 \text{ mol } C_2H_5OH$$

g.   molar mass C = 12.01 g

$$12.01 \text{ g C} \times \frac{1 \text{ mol C}}{12.01 \text{ g C}} = 1.00 \text{ mol C}$$

80.   a.   molar mass HNO_3 = 63.0 g

$$5.0 \text{ mol } HNO_3 \times \frac{63.0 \text{ g } HNO_3}{1 \text{ mol } HNO_3} = 3.2 \times 10^2 \text{ g } HNO_3$$

b.   molar mass Hg = 200.6 g

$$0.000305 \text{ mol Hg} \times \frac{200.6 \text{ g Hg}}{1 \text{ mol Hg}} = 0.0612 \text{ g Hg}$$

c.   molar mass K_2CrO_4 = 194.2 g

$$2.31 \times 10^{-5} \text{ mol } K_2CrO_4 \times \frac{194.2 \text{ g } K_2CrO_4}{1 \text{ mol } K_2CrO_4} = 4.49 \times 10^{-3} \text{ g } K_2CrO_4$$

d.   molar mass $AlCl_3$ = 133.3 g

$$10.5 \text{ mol } AlCl_3 \times \frac{133.3 \text{ g } AlCl_3}{1 \text{ mol } AlCl_3} = 1.40 \times 10^3 \text{ g } AlCl_3$$

e.   molar mass SF_6 = 146.1 g

$$4.9 \times 10^4 \text{ mol } SF_6 \times \frac{146.1 \text{ g } SF_6}{1 \text{ mol } SF_6} = 7.2 \times 10^6 \text{ g } SF_6$$

f.   molar mass NH_3 = 17.0 g

$$125 \text{ mol } NH_3 \times \frac{17.0 \text{ g } NH_3}{1 \text{ mol } NH_3} = 2.13 \times 10^3 \text{ g } NH_3$$

g.   molar mass Na_2O_2 = 77.98 g

$$0.01205 \text{ mol } Na_2O_2 \times \frac{77.98 \text{ g } Na_2O_2}{1 \text{ mol } Na_2O_2} = 0.9397 \text{ g } Na_2O_2$$

81.   Before any calculations are done, the equations must be *balanced*.

a. $BaCl_2(aq) + H_2SO_4(aq) \rightarrow BaSO_4(s) + 2HCl(aq)$

$$0.145 \text{ mol } BaCl_2 \times \frac{1 \text{ mol } H_2SO_4}{1 \text{ mol } BaCl_2} = 0.145 \text{ mol } H_2SO_4$$

b. $AgNO_3(aq) + NaCl(aq) \rightarrow AgCl(s) + NaNO_3(aq)$

$$0.145 \text{ mol AgNO}_3 \times \frac{1 \text{ mol NaCl}}{1 \text{ mol AgNO}_3} = 0.145 \text{ mol NaCl}$$

c. $Pb(NO_3)_2(aq) + Na_2CO_3(aq) \rightarrow PbCO_3(s) + 2NaNO_3(aq)$

$$0.145 \text{ mol Pb(NO}_3)_2 \times \frac{1 \text{ mol Na}_2CO_3}{1 \text{ mol Pb(NO}_3)_2} = 0.145 \text{ mol Na}_2CO_3$$

d. $C_3H_8(g) + 5O_2(g) \rightarrow 3CO_2(g) + 4H_2O(g)$

$$0.145 \text{ mol C}_3H_8 \times \frac{5 \text{ mol O}_2}{1 \text{ mol C}_3H_8} = 0.725 \text{ mol O}_2$$

82. $2SO_2(g) + O_2(g) \rightarrow 2SO_3(g)$

molar masses: SO_2, 64.07 g; SO_3, 80.07 g

$150 \text{ kg} = 1.5 \times 10^5 \text{ g}$

$$1.5 \times 10^5 \text{ g SO}_2 \times \frac{1 \text{ mol SO}_2}{64.07 \text{ g SO}_2} = 2.34 \times 10^3 \text{ mol SO}_2$$

$$2.34 \times 10^3 \text{ mol SO}_2 \times \frac{2 \text{ mol SO}_3}{2 \text{ mol SO}_2} = 2.34 \times 10^3 \text{ mol SO}_3$$

$$2.34 \times 10^3 \text{ mol SO}_3 \times \frac{80.07 \text{ g SO}_3}{1 \text{ mol SO}_3} = 1.9 \times 10^5 \text{ g SO}_3 = 1.9 \times 10^2 \text{ kg SO}_3$$

83. $2ZnS(s) + 3O_2(g) \rightarrow 2ZnO(s) + 2SO_2(g)$

molar masses: ZnS, 97.45 g; SO_2, 64.07 g

$1.0 \times 10^2 \text{ kg} = 1.0 \times 10^5 \text{ g}$

$$1.0 \times 10^5 \text{ g ZnS} \times \frac{1 \text{ mol ZnS}}{97.45 \text{ g ZnS}} = 1.026 \times 10^3 \text{ mol ZnS}$$

$$1.026 \times 10^3 \text{ mol ZnS} \times \frac{2 \text{ mol SO}_2}{2 \text{ mol ZnS}} = 1.026 \times 10^3 \text{ mol SO}_2$$

$$1.026 \times 10^3 \text{ mol SO}_2 \times \frac{64.07 \text{ g SO}_2}{1 \text{ mol SO}_2} = 6.6 \times 10^4 \text{ g SO}_2 = 66 \text{ kg SO}_2$$

84. $2Na_2O_2(s) + 2H_2O(l) \rightarrow 4NaOH(aq) + O_2(g)$

molar masses: Na_2O_2, 77.98 g; O_2, 32.00 g

$$3.25 \text{ g Na}_2O_2 \times \frac{1 \text{ mol Na}_2O_2}{77.98 \text{ g Na}_2O_2} = 0.0417 \text{ mol Na}_2O_2$$

$$0.0417 \text{ mol Na}_2O_2 \times \frac{1 \text{ mol O}_2}{2 \text{ mol Na}_2O_2} = 0.0209 \text{ mol O}_2$$

$$0.0209 \text{ mol O}_2 \times \frac{32.00 \text{ g O}_2}{1 \text{ mol O}_2} = 0.669 \text{ g O}_2$$

85. $Cu(s) + 2AgNO_3(aq) \rightarrow Cu(NO_3)_2(aq) + 2Ag(s)$

millimolar masses: Cu, 63.55 mg; $AgNO_3$, 169.9 mg

$$1.95 \text{ mg AgNO}_3 \times \frac{1 \text{ mmol AgNO}_3}{169.9 \text{ mg AgNO}_3} = 0.01148 \text{ mmol AgNO}_3$$

$$0.01148 \text{ mmol AgNO}_3 \times \frac{1 \text{ mmol Cu}}{2 \text{ mmol AgNO}_3} = 0.005740 \text{ mmol Cu}$$

$$0.005740 \text{ mmol Cu} \times \frac{63.55 \text{ mg Cu}}{1 \text{ mmol Cu}} = 0.365 \text{ mg Cu}$$

86. $Zn(s) + 2HCl(aq) \rightarrow ZnCl_2(aq) + H_2(g)$

molar masses: Zn, 65.38 g; H_2, 2.016 g

$$2.50 \text{ g Zn} \times \frac{1 \text{ mol Zn}}{65.38 \text{ g Zn}} = 0.03824 \text{ mol Zn}$$

$$0.03824 \text{ mol Zn} \times \frac{1 \text{ mol H}_2}{1 \text{ mol Zn}} = 0.03824 \text{ mol H}_2$$

$$0.03824 \text{ mol H}_2 \times \frac{2.016 \text{ g H}_2}{1 \text{ mol H}_2} = 0.0771 \text{ g H}_2$$

87. $2C_2H_2(g) + 5O_2(g) \rightarrow 4CO_2(g) + 2H_2O(g)$

molar masses: C_2H_2, 26.04 g; O_2, 32.00 g

$150 \text{ g} = 1.5 \times 10^2 \text{ g}$

$$1.5 \times 10^2 \text{ g C}_2\text{H}_2 \times \frac{1 \text{ mol C}_2\text{H}_2}{26.04 \text{ g C}_2\text{H}_2} = 5.760 \text{ mol C}_2\text{H}_2$$

$$5.760 \text{ mol C}_2\text{H}_2 \times \frac{5 \text{ mol O}_2}{2 \text{ mol C}_2\text{H}_2} = 14.40 \text{ mol O}_2$$

$$14.40 \text{ mol O}_2 \times \frac{32.00 \text{ g O}_2}{1 \text{ mol O}_2} = 4.6 \times 10^2 \text{ g O}_2$$

88.   a. $2Na(s) + Br_2(l) \rightarrow 2NaBr(s)$

molar masses: Na, 22.99 g; Br_2, 159.8 g; NaBr, 102.9 g

$$5.0 \text{ g Na} \times \frac{1 \text{ mol Na}}{22.99 \text{ g Na}} = 0.2175 \text{ mol Na}$$

$$5.0 \text{ g Br}_2 \times \frac{1 \text{ mol Br}_2}{159.8 \text{ g Br}_2} = 0.03129 \text{ mol Br}_2$$

Intuitively, we would suspect that Br_2 is the limiting reactant, since there is much less Br_2 than Na on a mole basis. To *prove* that Br_2 is the limiting reactant, the following calculation is needed:

$$0.03129 \text{ mol } Br_2 \times \frac{2 \text{ mol Na}}{1 \text{ mol } Br_2} = 0.06258 \text{ mol Na}$$

Clearly, there is more Na than this present, so Br_2 limits the reaction extent and the amount of NaBr formed.

$$0.03129 \text{ mol } Br_2 \times \frac{2 \text{ mol NaBr}}{1 \text{ mol } Br_2} = 0.06258 \text{ mol NaBr}$$

$$0.06258 \text{ mol NaBr} \times \frac{102.9 \text{ g NaBr}}{1 \text{ mol NaBr}} = 6.4 \text{ g NaBr}$$

b. $Zn(s) + CuSO_4(aq) \rightarrow ZnSO_4(aq) + Cu(s)$

molar masses: Zn, 65.38 g; Cu, 63.55 g;

$ZnSO_4$, 161.5 g; $CuSO_4$, 159.6 g

$$5.0 \text{ g Zn} \times \frac{1 \text{ mol Zn}}{65.38 \text{ g Zn}} = 0.07648 \text{ mol Zn}$$

$$5.0 \text{ g } CuSO_4 \times \frac{1 \text{ mol } CuSO_4}{159.6 \text{ g } CuSO_4} = 0.03132 \text{ mol } CuSO_4$$

Since the coefficients of Zn and $CuSO_4$ are the *same* in the balanced chemical equation, an equal number of moles of Zn and $CuSO_4$ would be needed for complete reaction. Since there is less $CuSO_4$ present, $CuSO_4$ must clearly be the limiting reactant.

$$0.03132 \text{ mol } CuSO_4 \times \frac{1 \text{ mol } ZnSO_4}{1 \text{ mol } CuSO_4} = 0.03132 \text{ mol } ZnSO_4$$

$$0.03132 \text{ mol } ZnSO_4 \times \frac{161.5 \text{ g } ZnSO_4}{1 \text{ mol } ZnSO_4} = 5.1 \text{ g } ZnSO_4$$

$$0.03132 \text{ mol } CuSO_4 \times \frac{1 \text{ mol Cu}}{1 \text{ mol } CuSO_4} = 0.03132 \text{ mol Cu}$$

$$0.03132 \text{ mol Cu} \times \frac{63.55 \text{ g Cu}}{1 \text{ mol Cu}} = 2.0 \text{ g Cu}$$

c. $NH_4Cl(aq) + NaOH(aq) \rightarrow NH_3(g) + H_2O(l) + NaCl(aq)$

molar masses: NH_4Cl, 53.49 g; NaOH, 40.00 g; NH_3, 17.03 g

H_2O, 18.02 g; NaCl, 58.44 g

$$5.0 \text{ g } NH_4Cl \times \frac{1 \text{ mol } NH_4Cl}{53.49 \text{ g } NH_4Cl} = 0.09348 \text{ mol } NH_4Cl$$

$$5.0 \text{ g NaOH} \times \frac{1 \text{ mol NaOH}}{40.00 \text{ g NaOH}} = 0.1250 \text{ mol NaOH}$$

Since the coefficients of NH_4Cl and NaOH are both *one* in the balanced chemical equation for the reaction, an equal number of moles of NH_4Cl and NaOH would be needed for complete reaction. Since there is less NH_4Cl present, NH_4Cl must be the limiting reactant.

Since the coefficients of the products in the balanced chemical equation are also all *one*, if 0.09348 mol of NH_4Cl (the limiting reactant) reacts completely, then 0.09348 mol of each product will be formed.

$$0.09348 \text{ mol } NH_3 \times \frac{17.03 \text{ g } NH_3}{1 \text{ mol } NH_3} = 1.6 \text{ g } NH_3$$

$$0.09348 \text{ mol } H_2O \times \frac{18.02 \text{ g } H_2O}{1 \text{ mol } H_2O} = 1.7 \text{ g } H_2O$$

$$0.09348 \text{ mol } NaCl \times \frac{58.44 \text{ g } NaCl}{1 \text{ mol } NaCl} = 5.5 \text{ g } NaCl$$

d. $Fe_2O_3(s) + 3CO(g) \rightarrow 2Fe(s) + 3CO_2(g)$

molar masses: Fe_2O_3, 159.7 g; CO, 28.01 g

Fe, 55.85 g; CO_2, 44.01 g

$$5.0 \text{ g } Fe_2O_3 \times \frac{1 \text{ mol } Fe_2O_3}{159.7 \text{ g } Fe_2O_3} = 0.03131 \text{ mol } Fe_2O_3$$

$$5.0 \text{ g CO} \times \frac{1 \text{ mol CO}}{28.01 \text{ g CO}} = 0.1785 \text{ mol CO}$$

Because there is considerably less Fe_2O_3 than CO on a mole basis, let's see if Fe_2O_3 is the limiting reactant.

$$0.03131 \text{ mol } Fe_2O_3 \times \frac{3 \text{ mol CO}}{1 \text{ mol } Fe_2O_3} = 0.09393 \text{ mol CO}$$

Since there is 0.1785 mol of CO present, but we have determined that only 0.09393 mol CO would be needed to react with all the Fe_2O_3 present, then Fe_2O_3 must be the limiting reactant. CO is present in excess.

$$0.03131 \text{ mol } Fe_2O_3 \times \frac{2 \text{ mol Fe}}{1 \text{ mol } Fe_2O_3} = 0.06262 \text{ mol Fe}$$

$$0.06262 \text{ mol Fe} \times \frac{55.85 \text{ g Fe}}{1 \text{ mol Fe}} = 3.5 \text{ g Fe}$$

$$0.03131 \text{ mol } Fe_2O_3 \times \frac{3 \text{ mol } CO_2}{1 \text{ mol } Fe_2O_3} = 0.09393 \text{ mol } CO_2$$

$$0.09393 \text{ mol } CO_2 \times \frac{44.01 \text{ g } CO_2}{1 \text{ mol } CO_2} = 4.1 \text{ g } CO_2$$

89.   a. $C_2H_5OH(l) + 3O_2(g) \rightarrow 2CO_2(g) + 3H_2O(l)$

molar masses: C_2H_5OH, 46.07 g; O_2, 32.00 g; CO_2, 44.01 g

$$25.0 \text{ g } C_2H_5OH \times \frac{1 \text{ mol } C_2H_5OH}{46.07 \text{ g } C_2H_5OH} = 0.5427 \text{ mol } C_2H_5OH$$

$$25.0 \text{ g } O_2 \times \frac{1 \text{ mol } O_2}{32.00 \text{ g } O_2} = 0.7813 \text{ mol } O_2$$

Since there is less C_2H_5OH present on a mole basis, see if this substance is the limiting reactant.

$$0.5427 \text{ mol } C_2H_5OH \times \frac{3 \text{ mol } O_2}{1 \text{ mol } C_2H_5OH} = 1.6281 \text{ mol } O_2$$

From the above calculation, C_2H_5OH must *not* be the limiting reactant (even though there is a smaller number of moles of C_2H_5OH present) since more oxygen than is present would be required to react completely with the C_2H_5OH present. Oxygen is the limiting reactant.

$$0.7813 \text{ mol } O_2 \times \frac{2 \text{ mol } CO_2}{3 \text{ mol } O_2} = 0.5209 \text{ mol } CO_2$$

$$0.5209 \text{ mol } CO_2 \times \frac{44.01 \text{ g } CO_2}{1 \text{ mol } CO_2} = 22.9 \text{ g } CO_2$$

b. $N_2(g) + O_2(g) \rightarrow 2NO(g)$

molar masses: N_2, 28.02 g; O_2, 32.00 g; NO, 30.01 g

$$25.0 \text{ g } N_2 \times \frac{1 \text{ mol } N_2}{28.02 \text{ g } N_2} = 0.8922 \text{ mol } N_2$$

$$25.0 \text{ g } O_2 \times \frac{1 \text{ mol } O_2}{32.00 \text{ g } O_2} = 0.7813 \text{ mol } O_2$$

Since the coefficients of N_2 and O_2 are the *same* in the balanced chemical equation for the reaction, an equal number of moles of each substance would be necessary for complete reaction. Since there is less O_2 present on a mole basis, O_2 must be the limiting reactant.

$$0.7813 \text{ mol } O_2 \times \frac{2 \text{ mol NO}}{1 \text{ mol } O_2} = 1.5626 \text{ mol NO}$$

$$1.5626 \text{ mol NO} \times \frac{30.01 \text{ g NO}}{1 \text{ mol NO}} = 46.9 \text{ g NO}$$

c. $2NaClO_2(aq) + Cl_2(g) \rightarrow 2ClO_2(g) + 2NaCl(aq)$

molar masses: $NaClO_2$, 90.44 g; Cl_2, 70.90 g; NaCl, 58.44 g

$$25.0 \text{ g } NaClO_2 \times \frac{1 \text{ mol } NaClO_2}{90.44 \text{ g } NaClO_2} = 0.2764 \text{ mol } NaClO_2$$

$$25.0 \text{ g Cl}_2 \times \frac{1 \text{ mol Cl}_2}{70.90 \text{ g Cl}_2} = 0.3526 \text{ mol Cl}_2$$

See if $NaClO_2$ is the limiting reactant.

$$0.2764 \text{ mol NaClO}_2 \times \frac{1 \text{ mol Cl}_2}{2 \text{ mol NaClO}_2} = 0.1382 \text{ mol Cl}_2$$

Since 0.2764. mol of $NaClO_2$ would require only 0.1382 mol Cl_2 to react completely (and since we have more than this amount of Cl_2), then $NaClO_2$ must indeed be the limiting reactant.

$$0.2764 \text{ mol NaClO}_2 \times \frac{2 \text{ mol NaCl}}{2 \text{ mol NaClO}_2} = 0.2764 \text{ mol NaCl}$$

$$0.2764 \text{ mol NaCl} \times \frac{58.44 \text{ g NaCl}}{1 \text{ mol NaCl}} = 16.2 \text{ g NaCl}$$

d. $3H_2(g) + N_2(g) \rightarrow 2NH_3(g)$

molar masses: H_2, 2.016 g; N_2, 28.02 g; NH_3, 17.03 g

$$25.0 \text{ g H}_2 \times \frac{1 \text{ mol H}_2}{2.016 \text{ g H}_2} = 12.40 \text{ mol H}_2$$

$$25.0 \text{ g N}_2 \times \frac{1 \text{ mol N}_2}{28.02 \text{ g N}_2} = 0.8922 \text{ mol N}_2$$

See if N_2 is the limiting reactant.

$$0.8922 \text{ mol N}_2 \times \frac{3 \text{ mol H}_2}{1 \text{ mol N}_2} = 2.677 \text{ mol H}_2$$

N_2 is clearly the limiting reactant, since there is 12.40 mol H_2 present (a large excess).

$$0.8922 \text{ mol N}_2 \times \frac{2 \text{ mol NH}_3}{1 \text{ mol N}_2} = 1.784 \text{ mol NH}_3$$

$$1.784 \text{ mol NH}_3 \times \frac{17.03 \text{ g NH}_3}{1 \text{ mol NH}_3} = 30.4 \text{ g NH}_3$$

90. $N_2H_4(l) + O_2(g) \rightarrow N_2(g) + 2H_2O(g)$

molar masses: N_2H_4, 32.05 g; O_2, 32.00 g; N_2, 28.02 g; H_2O, 18.02 g

$$20.0 \text{ g N}_2H_4 \times \frac{1 \text{ mol N}_2H_4}{32.05 \text{ g N}_2H_4} = 0.624 \text{ mol N}_2H_4$$

$$20.0 \text{ g O}_2 \times \frac{1 \text{ mol O}_2}{32.00 \text{ g O}_2} = 0.625 \text{ mol O}_2$$

The two reactants are present in nearly the required ratio for complete reaction (due to the 1:1 stoichiometry of the reaction and the very similar molar masses of the substances). We will consider N_2H_4 as the limiting reactant in the following calculations.

$$0.624 \text{ mol } N_2H_4 \times \frac{1 \text{ mol } N_2}{1 \text{ mol } N_2H_4} = 0.624 \text{ mol } N_2$$

$$0.624 \text{ mol } N_2 \times \frac{28.02 \text{ g } N_2}{1 \text{ mol } N_2} = 17.5 \text{ g } N_2$$

$$0.624 \text{ mol } N_2H_4 \times \frac{2 \text{ mol } H_2O}{1 \text{ mol } N_2H_4} = 1.248 \text{ mol } H_2O = 1.25 \text{ mol } H_2O$$

$$1.248 \text{ mol } H_2O \times \frac{18.02 \text{ g } H_2O}{1 \text{ mol } H_2O} = 22.5 \text{ g } H_2O$$

91.   Total quantity of $H_2S = 50. \text{ L} \times \dfrac{1.5 \times 10^{-5} \text{ g}}{1 \text{ L}} = 7.5 \times 10^{-4} \text{ g } H_2S$

$8H_2S(aq) + 8Cl_2(aq) \rightarrow 16HCl(aq) + S_8(s)$

molar masses: H_2S, 34.09 g; Cl_2, 70.90 g; S_8, 256.6 g

$$7.5 \times 10^{-4} \text{ g } H_2S \times \frac{1 \text{ mol } H_2S}{34.09 \text{ g } H_2S} = 2.20 \times 10^{-5} \text{ mol } H_2S$$

$$1.0 \text{ g } Cl_2 \times \frac{1 \text{ mol } Cl_2}{70.90 \text{ g } Cl_2} = 1.41 \times 10^{-2} \text{ mol } Cl_2$$

There is a large excess of chlorine present, compared to the amount of Cl_2 that would be needed to react with all the H_2S present in the water sample: H_2S is the limiting reactant for the process.

$$2.20 \times 10^{-5} \text{ mol } H_2S \times \frac{1 \text{ mol } S_8}{8 \text{ mol } H_2S} = 2.75 \times 10^{-6} \text{ mol } S_8$$

$$2.75 \times 10^{-6} \text{ mol } S_8 \times \frac{256.6 \text{ g } S_8}{1 \text{ mol } S_8} = 7.1 \times 10^{-4} \text{ g } S_8 \text{ removed}$$

92. $12.5 \text{ g theory} \times \dfrac{40 \text{ g actual}}{100 \text{ g theory}} = 5.0 \text{ g}$

Cumulative Review: Chapters 8 and 9

1.   The average atomic mass of an element represents the weighted average mass, on the relative atomic scale, of all the isotopes of an element. Average atomic masses are usually given in terms of atomic mass units (1 amu = 1.66×10^{-24} g). For example, the average atomic mass of sodium is 22.99 amu, which represents the average mass of all the sodium atoms in the world (including all the various isotopes and their relative abundances). So that we will be able to use the mass of a sample of sodium to count the number of atoms of sodium present in the sample, we consider that every sodium atom in a sample has exactly the same mass (the *average* atomic mass). The average atomic mass of an element is typically *not* a whole number of amu because of the presence of the different isotopes of the element, each with its own relative abundance. Since the relative abundance of an element can be any random number, when the weighted average atomic mass of the element is calculated, the average is unlikely to be a whole number.

2.   On a microscopic basis, one mole of a substance represents Avogadro's number (6.022×10^{23}) of individual units (atoms or molecules) of the substance. On a macroscopic, more practical basis, one mole of a substance represents the amount of substance present when the molar mass of the substance in grams is taken (for example 12.01 g of carbon will be one mole of carbon). Chemists have chosen these definitions so that there will be a simple relationship between measurable amounts of substances (grams) and the actual number of atoms or molecules present, and so that the number of particles present in samples of *different* substances can easily be compared. For example, it is known that carbon and oxygen react by the reaction

$$C(s) + O_2(g) \rightarrow CO_2(g)$$

Chemists understand this equation to mean that one carbon atom reacts with one oxygen molecule to produce one molecule of carbon dioxide, and also that one mole (12.01 g) of carbon will react with one mole (32.00 g) of oxygen to produce one mole (44.01 g) of carbon dioxide.

3.   It's all relative! The mass of each substance mentioned in this question happens to be the molar mass of that substance. Each of the three samples of elemental substances mentioned (O, C, and Na) contains Avogadro's number (6.022×10^{23}) of atoms of its respective element. For the compound Na_2CO_3 given, since each unit of Na_2CO_3 contains two sodium atoms, one carbon atom, and three oxygen atoms, then it's not surprising that a sample having a mass equal to the molar mass of Na_2CO_3 should contain one molar mass of carbon, two molar masses of sodium, and three molar masses of oxygen: 12.01 g + 2(22.99 g) + 3(16.00 g) = 106.0 g.

4.   The molar mass of a compound is the mass in grams of one mole of the compound (6.022×10^{23} molecules of the compound), and is calculated by summing the average atomic masses of all the atoms present in a molecule of the compound. For example, a molecule of the compound H_3PO_4 contains three hydrogen atoms, one phosphorus atom, and four oxygen atom: the

molar mass is obtained by adding up the average atomic masses of these atoms: molar mass H_3PO_4 = 3(1.008 g) + 1(30.97 g) + 4(16.00 g) = 97.99 g

5.   The percentage composition (by mass) of a compound shows the relative amount of each element present in the compound on a mass basis. For compounds whose formulas are known (and whose molar masses are therefore known), the percentage of a given element present in the compound is given by

$$\frac{\text{mass of the element present in 1 mol of the compound}}{\text{mass of 1 mol of the compound}} \times 100$$

When a new compound is prepared, whose formula is not known, the percentage composition must be determined on an experimental basis. An elemental analysis must be done of a sample of the new compound to see what mass of each element is present in the sample. For example, if a 1.000 g sample of a hydrocarbon is analyzed, and it is found that the sample contains 0.7487 g of C, then the percentage by mass of carbon present in the compound is

$$\frac{0.7487 \text{ g C}}{1.000 \text{ g sample}} \times 100 = 74.87 \text{ \%C}$$

Since we can use the formula of a known compound to calculate the percentage composition by mass of the compound, it is perhaps not surprising that, from experimentally-determined percentage compositions for an unknown compound, we can calculate the formula of the compound (see questions 7 and 8).

6.   The empirical formula of a compound represents the lowest ratio of the relative number of atoms of each type present in a molecule of the compound, whereas the molecular formula represents the actual number of atoms of each type present in a real molecule of the compound. For example, both acetylene (molecular formula C_2H_2) and benzene (molecular formula C_6H_6) have the same relative number of carbon and hydrogen atoms (one hydrogen for each carbon atom), and so have the same empirical formula (CH). Once the empirical formula of a compound has been determined, it is also necessary to determine the molar mass of the compound before the actual molecular formula can be calculated. Since real molecules cannot contain fractional parts of atoms, the molecular formula is always a whole number multiple of the empirical formula. For the examples above, the molecular formula of acetylene is twice the empirical formula, and the molecular formula of benzene is six times the empirical formula (both factors are integers).

7.   For our example, let's use the "known" compound phosphoric acid, H_3PO_4. First we will calculate the percentage composition (by mass) for H_3PO_4, and then we will use our results to calculate back the empirical formula!

Molar mass = 3(1.008 g) + 1(30.97 g) + 4(16.00 g) = 97.99 g

$$\%H = \frac{3(1.008 \text{ g H})}{97.99 \text{ g}} \times 100 = 3.086 \ \%H$$

$$\%P = \frac{30.97 \text{ g P}}{97.99 \text{ g}} \times 100 = 31.60 \ \%P$$

$$\%O = \frac{4(16.00 \text{ g O})}{97.99 \text{ g}} \times 100 = 65.31 \ \%O$$

Now we will use this percentage composition data to calculate back the empirical formula. We will pretend that we did not know the formula, and were just presented with a question of the type: "a compound contains 3.086 % hydrogen, 31.60 % phosphorus, and 65.31 % oxygen; calculate the empirical formula."

Let's go! First, we will assume, as usual, that we have 100.0 g of the compound, so that the percentages turn into masses in grams. So our sample will contain 3.086 g H, 31.60 g P, and 65.31 g O. Next, we can calculate the number of moles of each element these masses represent.

$$\text{mol H} = 3.086 \text{ g H} \times \frac{1 \text{ mol H}}{1.008 \text{ g H}} = 3.062 \text{ mol H}$$

$$\text{mol P} = 31.60 \text{ g P} \times \frac{1 \text{ mol P}}{30.97 \text{ g P}} = 1.020 \text{ mol P}$$

$$\text{mol O} = 65.31 \text{ g O} \times \frac{1 \text{ mol O}}{16.00 \text{ g O}} = 4.082 \text{ mol O}$$

To get the empirical formula, divide each of these numbers of moles by the smallest number of moles: this puts things on a relative basis.

$$\frac{3.062 \text{ mol H}}{1.020} = 3.002 \text{ mol H}$$

$$\frac{1.020 \text{ mol P}}{1.020} = 1.000 \text{ mol P}$$

$$\frac{4.082 \text{ mol O}}{1.020} = 4.002 \text{ mol O}$$

which gives us as the empirical formula--H_3PO_4!

8.   In question 7, we chose to calculate the percentage composition of phosphoric acid, H_3PO_4: 3.086% H, 31.60% P, 65.31% O. We could convert this percentage composition data into "experimental" data by first choosing a mass of sample to be "analyzed", and then calculating what mass of each element is present in this size sample using the percentage of

each element. For example, suppose we choose our sample to have a mass of 2.417 g. Then the masses of H, P, and O present in this sample would be given by the following

$$g\ H\ =\ (2.417\ g\ sample)\ \times\ \frac{3.086\ g\ H}{100.0\ g\ sample}\ =\ 0.07459\ g\ H$$

$$g\ P\ =\ (2.417\ g\ sample)\ \times\ \frac{31.60\ g\ P}{100.0\ g\ sample}\ =\ 0.7638\ g\ P$$

$$g\ O\ =\ (2.417\ g\ sample)\ \times\ \frac{65.31\ g\ O}{100.0\ g\ sample}\ =\ 1.579\ g\ O$$

Note that (0.07459 g + 0.7638 g + 1.579 g) = 2.41739 = 2.417 g.

So our new problem could be worded as follows: "A 2.417-g sample of a compound has been analyzed and was found to contain 0.07459 g H, 0.7638 g of P, and 1.579 g of oxygen. Calculate the empirical formula of the compound".

$$mol\ H\ =\ (0.07459\ g\ H)\ \times\ \frac{1\ mol\ H}{1.008\ g\ H}\ =\ 0.07400\ mol\ H$$

$$mol\ P\ =\ (0.7638\ g\ P)\ \times\ \frac{1\ mol\ P}{30.97\ g\ P}\ =\ 0.02466\ mol\ P$$

$$mol\ O\ =\ (1.579\ g\ O)\ \times\ \frac{1\ mol\ O}{16.00\ g\ O}\ =\ 0.09869\ mol\ O$$

Dividing each of these numbers of moles by the smallest number of moles (0.02466 mol P) gives the following

$$\frac{0.07400\ mol\ H}{0.02466}\ =\ 3.001\ mol\ H$$

$$\frac{0.02466\ mol\ P}{0.02466}\ =\ 1.000\ mol\ P$$

$$\frac{0.09869\ mol\ O}{0.02466}\ =\ 4.002\ mol\ O$$

and the empirical formula is (not surprisingly) just H_3PO_4!

9.   You could, of course, have chosen practically any reaction as your example. For this discussion, let's keep it simple and use the equation

$$2H_2O_2\,(aq)\ \rightarrow\ 2H_2O\,(l)\ +\ O_2\,(g)$$

which describes the decomposition reaction of hydrogen peroxide.

Microscopic: Two molecules of hydrogen peroxide (in aqueous solution) decompose to produce two molecules of liquid water and one molecule of oxygen gas.

Macroscopic: Two moles of hydrogen peroxide (present in aqueous solution) decompose to produce two moles of liquid water and one mole of oxygen **gas**.

10. The mole ratios for a reaction are based on the *coefficients* of the balanced chemical equation for the reaction: these coefficients show in what proportions molecules (or moles of molecules) combine. For a given amount of C_2H_5OH, the following mole ratios could be constructed, which would enable you to calculate the number of moles of each product, or of the second reactant, that would be involved.

$$C_2H_5OH(l) + 3O_2(g) \rightarrow 2CO_2(g) + 3H_2O(g)$$

to calculate mol CO_2 produced: $\dfrac{2 \text{ mol } CO_2}{1 \text{ mol } C_2H_5OH}$

to calculate mol H_2O produced: $\dfrac{3 \text{ mol } H_2O}{1 \text{ mol } C_2H_5OH}$

to calculate mol O_2 required: $\dfrac{3 \text{ mol } O_2}{1 \text{ mol } C_2H_5OH}$

We could then calculate the numbers of moles of the other substances if 0.65 mol of C_2H_5OH were to be combusted as follows:

mol CO_2 produced = (0.65 mol C_2H_5OH) × $\dfrac{2 \text{ mol } CO_2}{1 \text{ mol } C_2H_5OH}$ = 1.3 mol CO_2

mol H_2O produced = (0.65 mol C_2H_5OH) × $\dfrac{3 \text{ mol } H_2O}{1 \text{ mol } C_2H_5OH}$ = 1.95 = 2.0 mol H_2O

mol O_2 required = (0.65 mol C_2H_5OH × $\dfrac{3 \text{ mol } O_2}{1 \text{ mol } C_2H_5OH}$ = 1.95 = 2.0 mol O_2

11. Let's consider this simple reaction showing the decomposition of calcium carbonate, producing calcium oxide and carbon dioxide.

$$CaCO_3(s) \rightarrow CaO(s) + CO_2(g)$$

Let's suppose that 50.0 g of $CaCO_3$ is to be decomposed.

In any calculation of yield for a reaction, the molar masses of the reactants and products are almost certainly going to be needed, so let's write these down now.

Molar masses: $CaCO_3$, 100.09 g; CaO, 56.08 g; CO_2, 44.01 g

$$\text{mol CaCO}_3 = 50.0 \text{ g} \times \frac{1 \text{ mol}}{100.09 \text{ g}} = 0.4995 \text{ mol CaCO}_3$$

$$\text{mol CaO} = 0.4995 \text{ mol CaCO}_3 \times \frac{1 \text{ mol CaO}}{1 \text{ mol CaCO}_3} = 0.4995 \text{ mol CaO}$$

$$\text{mass CaO} = 0.4995 \text{ mol CaO} \times \frac{56.08 \text{ g}}{1 \text{ mol}} = 28.0 \text{ g CaO}$$

$$\text{mol CO}_2 = 0.4995 \text{ mol CaCO}_3 \times \frac{1 \text{ mol CO}_2}{1 \text{ mol CaCO}_3} = 0.4995 \text{ mol CO}_2$$

$$\text{mass CO}_2 = 0.4995 \text{ mol CO}_2 \times \frac{44.01 \text{ g}}{1 \text{ mol}} = 22.0 \text{ g CO}_2$$

Although this example was especially simple, since the coefficients of the balanced chemical equation were all unity, the results illustrate an important point: the sum of the masses of the two products (28.0 g + 22.0 g) equals the mass of the reactant (50.0 g).

12. Although we can calculate specifically the exact amounts of each reactant needed for a chemical reaction, oftentimes reaction mixtures are prepared using more or less arbitrary amounts of the reagents. However, regardless of how much of each reagent may be used for a reaction, the substances still react stoichiometrically, according to the mole ratios derived from the balanced chemical equation for the reaction. When arbitrary amounts of reactants are used, there will be one reactant which, stoichiometrically, is present in the least amount. This substance is called the *limiting reactant* for the experiment. It is the limiting reactant that controls how much product is formed, regardless of how much of the other reactants are present. ·
The limiting reactant limits the amount of product that can form in the experiment, because once the limiting reactant has reacted completely, the reaction must stop. We say that the other reactants in the experiment are present in excess, which means that a portion of these reactants will still be present unchanged after the reaction has ended and the limiting reactant has been used up completely.

13. For our discussion, let's use the simple balanced chemical equation

$$2H_2(g) + O_2(g) \rightarrow 2H_2O(l)$$

Molar masses: H_2, 2.016 g; O_2, 32.00 g

To determine which reactant is limiting, we first need to realize that the masses of the reactants (25.0 g of each) tell us nothing: we need to calculate how many *moles* of each reactant is present.

$$\text{mol H}_2 = 25.0 \text{ g H}_2 \times \frac{1 \text{ mol H}_2}{2.016 \text{ g H}_2} = 12.40 \text{ mol H}_2$$

$$\text{mol O}_2 = 25.0 \text{ g O}_2 \times \frac{1 \text{ mol O}_2}{32.00 \text{ g O}_2} = 0.7813 \text{ mol O}_2$$

Considering now these numbers of moles, it is clear that there is considerably more hydrogen present than oxygen. Chances are, the hydrogen is present in excess, and oxygen is the limiting reactant. We need to *prove* this, however, by calculation. If we consider that the 0.7813 mol of oxygen may be the limiting reactant, we can calculate how much hydrogen would be needed for complete reaction: this requires the mole ratio as determined by the coefficients of the balanced chemical equation.

$$0.7813 \text{ mol O}_2 \times \frac{2 \text{ mol H}_2}{1 \text{ mol O}_2} = 1.56 \text{ mol H}_2 \text{ required for reaction}$$

Since only 1.56 mol of H_2 is required to react with 0.7813 mol of O_2, and since we have considerably more hydrogen present in our sample than this amount, then clearly hydrogen is present in excess and oxygen is, indeed, the limiting reactant.

Suppose we had not initially considered that oxygen was the limiting reactant (because there is so much less oxygen present on a mole basis) and had wondered if H_2 was the limiting reactant. For the given amount of H_2 (12.40 mol), we could calculate how much oxygen would be required to react

$$12.40 \text{ mol H}_2 \times \frac{1 \text{ mol O}_2}{2 \text{ mol H}_2} = 6.20 \text{ mol O}_2 \text{ would be required}$$

Since we do not have 6.20 mol of O_2 (we have only 0.7813 mol O_2), then clearly there is not enough oxygen present to react with all the hydrogen, and we would conclude again that oxygen must be the limiting reactant.

14. The *theoretical yield* for an experiment is the mass of product calculated based on the limiting reactant for the experiment being completely consumed. The *actual yield* for an experiment is the mass of product actually collected by the experimenter. Obviously, any experiment is restricted by the skills of the experimenter and by the inherent limitations of the experimental method being used. For these reasons, the actual yield is often *less* than the theoretical yield (most scientific writers report the actual or percentage yield for their experiments as an indication of the usefulness of their experiments). Although one would expect that the actual yield should never be more than the theoretical yield, in real experiments, sometimes this happens: however, an actual yield greater than a theoretical yield is usually taken to mean that something is *wrong* in either the experiment (for example, impurities may be present, or the reaction may not occur as envisioned) or in the calculations.

15. a. Cu (molar mass = 63.55 g)

$$\text{mol Cu} = 5.00 \text{ g} \times \frac{1 \text{ mol}}{63.55 \text{ g}} = 0.0787 \text{ mol}$$

$$\text{atoms Cu} = 0.0787 \text{ mol} \times \frac{6.022 \times 10^{23} \text{ atoms}}{1 \text{ mol}} = 4.74 \times 10^{24} \text{ atoms}$$

b. NH_3 (molar mass = 17.03 g

$$\text{mol } NH_3 = 5.00 \text{ g} \times \frac{1 \text{ mol}}{17.03 \text{ g}} = 0.294 \text{ mol}$$

$$\text{molecules } NH_3 = 0.294 \text{ mol} \times \frac{6.022 \times 10^{23} \text{ molecules}}{1 \text{ mol}}$$

$$= 1.77 \times 10^{23} \text{ molecules}$$

$$\text{atoms N} = 1.77 \times 10^{23} \text{ molecules} \times \frac{1 \text{ N atom}}{1 \text{ molecule}} = 1.77 \times 10^{23} \text{ atoms N}$$

$$\text{atoms H} = 1.77 \times 10^{23} \text{ molecules} \times \frac{3 \text{ H atom}}{1 \text{ molecule}} = 5.31 \times 10^{23} \text{ atoms H}$$

c. SiH_4 (molar mass = 32.12 g)

$$\text{mol } SiH_4 = 5.00 \text{ g} \times \frac{1 \text{ mol}}{32.12 \text{ g}} = 0.156 \text{ mol } SiH_4$$

$$\text{molecules } SiH_4 = 0.156 \text{ mol} \times \frac{6.022 \times 10^{23} \text{ molecules}}{1 \text{ mol}}$$

$$= 9.39 \times 10^{22} \text{ molecules } SiH_4$$

$$\text{atoms Si} = 9.39 \times 10^{22} \text{ molecules} \times \frac{1 \text{ Si atom}}{1 \text{ molecule}} = 9.39 \times 10^{22} \text{ atoms Si}$$

$$\text{atoms H} = 9.39 \times 10^{22} \text{ molecules} \times \frac{4 \text{ H atoms}}{1 \text{ molecule}} = 3.76 \times 10^{23} \text{ atoms H}$$

d. K_2CrO_4 (molar mass = 194.2 g)

$$\text{mol } K_2CrO_4 = 5.00 \text{ g} \times \frac{1 \text{ mol}}{194.2 \text{ g}} = 0.0257 \text{ mol } K_2CrO_4$$

$$\text{formula units } K_2CrO_4 = 0.0257 \text{ mol} \times \frac{6.022 \times 10^{23} \text{ forumla units}}{1 \text{ mol}}$$

$$= 1.55 \times 10^{22} \text{ formula units } K_2CrO_4$$

$$\text{atoms K} = 1.55 \times 10^{22} \text{ form. un.} \times \frac{2 \text{ K atoms}}{1 \text{ form. un.}} = 3.10 \times 10^{22} \text{ atoms K}$$

$$\text{atoms Cr} = 1.55 \times 10^{22} \text{ form. un.} \times \frac{1 \text{ Cr atom}}{1 \text{ form. un.}} = 1.55 \times 10^{22} \text{ atoms Cr}$$

$$\text{atoms O} = 1.55 \times 10^{22} \text{ form. un.} \times \frac{4 \text{ O atoms}}{1 \text{ form. un.}} = 6.20 \times 10^{22} \text{ atoms O}$$

e. O_2 (molar mass = 32.00 g)

$$\text{mol } O_2 = 5.00 \text{ g} \times \frac{1 \text{ mol}}{32.00 \text{ g}} = 0.156 \text{ mol } O_2$$

$$\text{molecules} = 0.156 \text{ mol} \times \frac{6.022 \times 10^{23} \text{ molecules}}{1 \text{ mol}}$$

$$= 9.39 \times 10^{22} \text{ molecules } O_2$$

$$\text{atoms O} = 9.39 \times 10^{22} \text{ molecules} \times \frac{2 \text{ O atoms}}{1 \text{ molecule}} = 1.88 \times 10^{23} \text{ atoms O}$$

f. O_3 (molar mass = 48.00 g)

$$\text{mol } O_3 = 5.00 \text{ g} \times \frac{1 \text{ mol}}{48.00 \text{ g}} = 0.104 \text{ mol } O_3$$

$$\text{molecules } O_3 = 0.104 \text{ mol} \times \frac{6.022 \times 10^{23} \text{ molecules}}{1 \text{ mol}}$$

$$= 6.26 \times 10^{22} \text{ molecules } O_3$$

$$\text{atoms O} = 6.26 \times 10^{22} \text{ molecules} \times \frac{3 \text{ O atoms}}{1 \text{ molecule}} = 1.88 \times 10^{23} \text{ atoms O}$$

g. I_2 (molar mass = 253.8 g)

$$\text{mol } I_2 = 5.00 \text{ g} \times \frac{1 \text{ mol}}{253.8 \text{ g}} = 0.0197 \text{ mol } I_2$$

$$\text{molecules } I_2 = 0.0197 \text{ mol } I_2 \times \frac{6.022 \times 10^{23} \text{ molecules}}{1 \text{ mol}}$$

$$= 1.19 \times 10^{22} \text{ molecules } I_2$$

$$\text{atoms I} = 1.19 \times 10^{22} \text{ molecules} \times \frac{2 \text{ I atoms}}{1 \text{ molecule}} = 2.38 \times 10^{22} \text{ atoms I}$$

h. $AuCl_3$ (molar mass = 303.4 g)

$$\text{mol } AuCl_3 = 5.00 \text{ g} \times \frac{1 \text{ mol}}{303.4 \text{ g}} = 0.0165 \text{ mol } AuCl_3$$

$$\text{formula units } AuCl_3 = 0.0165 \text{ mol} \times \frac{6.022 \times 10^{23} \text{ form. units}}{1 \text{ mol}}$$

$$= 9.94 \times 10^{21} \text{ formula units } AuCl_3$$

$$\text{atoms Au} = 9.94 \times 10^{21} \text{ form. un.} \times \frac{1 \text{ Au atom}}{1 \text{ form. un.}} = 9.94 \times 10^{21} \text{ atoms Au}$$

$$\text{atoms Cl} = 9.94 \times 10^{21} \text{ form. un.} \times \frac{3 \text{ Cl atoms}}{1 \text{ form. un.}} = 2.98 \times 10^{22} \text{ atoms Cl}$$

i. $KMnO_4$ (molar mass = 158.0 g)

$$\text{mol } KMnO_4 = 5.00 \text{ g} \times \frac{1 \text{ mol}}{158.0 \text{ g}} = 0.0316 \text{ mol } KMnO_4$$

$$\text{formula units } KMnO_4 = 0.0316 \text{ mol} \times \frac{6.022 \times 10^{23} \text{ formula units}}{1 \text{ mol}}$$

$$= 1.90 \times 10^{22} \text{ formula units } KMnO_4$$

$$\text{atoms K} = 1.90 \times 10^{22} \text{ form. un.} \times \frac{1 \text{ K atom}}{1 \text{ form. un.}} = 1.90 \times 10^{22} \text{ atoms K}$$

$$\text{atoms Mn} = 1.90 \times 10^{22} \text{ form. un.} \times \frac{1 \text{ Mn atom}}{1 \text{ form. un.}} = 1.90 \times 10^{22} \text{ atoms Mn}$$

$$\text{atoms O} = 1.90 \times 10^{22} \text{ form. un.} \times \frac{4 \text{ O atoms}}{1 \text{ form. un.}} = 7.60 \times 10^{22} \text{ atoms O}$$

j. $KClO_3$ (molar mass = 122.6 g)

$$\text{mol } KClO_3 = 5.00 \text{ g} \times \frac{1 \text{ mol}}{122.6 \text{ g}} = 0.0408 \text{ mol } KClO_3$$

$$\text{formula units } KClO_3 = 0.0408 \text{ mol} \times \frac{6.022 \times 10^{23} \text{ form. units}}{1 \text{ mol}}$$

$$= 2.46 \times 10^{22} \text{ formula units } KClO_3$$

$$\text{atoms K} = 2.46 \times 10^{22} \text{ form. un.} \times \frac{1 \text{ K atom}}{1 \text{ form. un.}} = 2.46 \times 10^{22} \text{ atoms K}$$

$$\text{atoms Cl} = 2.46 \times 10^{22} \text{ form. un.} \times \frac{1 \text{ Cl atom}}{1 \text{ form. un.}} = 2.46 \times 10^{22} \text{ atoms Cl}$$

$$\text{atoms O} = 2.46 \times 10^{22} \text{ form. units} \times \frac{3 \text{ O atoms}}{1 \text{ form. un.}} = 7.38 \times 10^{22} \text{ atoms O}$$

16. NH_3: $\%N = \dfrac{14.01 \text{ g N}}{17.03 \text{ g}} \times 100 = 82.27\% \text{ N}$

$\%H = \dfrac{3(1.008 \text{ g H})}{17.03 \text{ g}} \times 100 = 17.76\% \text{ H}$

SiH_4: $\%Si = \dfrac{28.09 \text{ g Si}}{32.12 \text{ g}} \times 100 = 87.45\% \text{ Si}$

$\%H = \dfrac{4(1.008 \text{ g H})}{32.12 \text{ g}} \times 100 = 12.55\% \text{ H}$

K_2CrO_4:

$$\%K = \frac{2(39.10 \text{ g K})}{194.2 \text{ g}} \times 100 = 40.27\% \text{ K}$$

$$\%Cr = \frac{52.00 \text{ g Cr}}{194.2 \text{ g}} \times 100 = 26.78\% \text{ Cr}$$

$$\%O = \frac{4(16.00 \text{ g O})}{194.2 \text{ g}} \times 100 = 32.96\% \text{ O}$$

$AuCl_3$:

$$\%Au = \frac{197.0 \text{ g Au}}{303.4 \text{ g}} \times 100 = 64.93\% \text{ Au}$$

$$\%Cl = \frac{3(35.45 \text{ g Cl})}{303.4 \text{ g}} \times 100 = 35.05\% \text{ Cl}$$

$KMnO_4$:

$$\%K = \frac{39.10 \text{ g K}}{158.0 \text{ g}} \times 100 = 24.75\% \text{ K}$$

$$\%Mn = \frac{54.94 \text{ g Mn}}{158.0 \text{ g}} \times 100 = 34.77\% \text{ Mn}$$

$$\%O = \frac{4(16.00 \text{ g O})}{158.0 \text{ g}} \times 100 = 40.51\% \text{ O}$$

$KClO_3$:

$$\%K = \frac{39.10 \text{ g K}}{122.5 \text{ g}} \times 100 = 31.92\% \text{ K}$$

$$\%Cl = \frac{35.45 \text{ g Cl}}{122.5 \text{ g}} \times 100 = 28.94\% \text{ Cl}$$

$$\%O = \frac{3(16.00 \text{ g O})}{122.5 \text{ g}} \times 100 = 39.18\% \text{ O}$$

17. $$\text{millimol C} = 82.80 \text{ mg} \times \frac{1 \text{ millimol}}{12.01 \text{ mg}} = 6.894 \text{ millimol C}$$

$$\text{millimol H} = 13.90 \text{ mg} \times \frac{1 \text{ millimol}}{1.008 \text{ mg}} = 13.79 \text{ millimol H}$$

$$\text{millimol O} = 55.15 \text{ mg} \times \frac{1 \text{ millimol}}{16.00 \text{ g}} = 3.447 \text{ millimol O}$$

Dividing each of these numbers of millimols by the smallest number of millimols (3.447 millimol O) gives the empirical formula as C_2H_4O.

18. a. $2AgNO_3(aq) + CaSO_4(aq) \rightarrow Ag_2SO_4(s) + Ca(NO_3)_2(aq)$

Molar masses: $AgNO_3$, 169.9 g; Ag_2SO_4, 311.9 g; $Ca(NO_3)_2$, 164.1 g

$$25.0 \text{ g AgNO}_3 \times \frac{1 \text{ mol}}{169.9 \text{ g}} = 0.147 \text{ mol AgNO}_3$$

$$0.147 \text{ mol AgNO}_3 \times \frac{1 \text{ mol Ag}_2\text{SO}_4}{2 \text{ mol AgNO}_3} = 0.0735 \text{ mol Ag}_2\text{SO}_4$$

$$0.0735 \text{ mol Ag}_2\text{SO}_4 \times \frac{311.9 \text{ g}}{1 \text{ mol}} = 22.9 \text{ g Ag}_2\text{SO}_4$$

$$0.147 \text{ mol AgNO}_3 \times \frac{1 \text{ mol Ca(NO}_3)_2}{2 \text{ mol AgNO}_3} = 0.0735 \text{ mol Ca(NO}_3)_2$$

$$0.0735 \text{ mol Ca(NO}_3)_2 \times \frac{164.1 \text{ g}}{1 \text{ mol}} = 12.1 \text{ g Ca(NO}_3)_2$$

b. $2\text{Al}(s) + 6\text{HNO}_3(aq) \rightarrow 2\text{Al(NO}_3)_3(aq) + 3\text{H}_2(g)$

Molar masses: Al, 26.98 g; $\text{Al(NO}_3)_3$, 213.0 g; H_2, 2.016 g

$$25.0 \text{ g Al} \times \frac{1 \text{ mol}}{26.98 \text{ g}} = 0.927 \text{ mol Al}$$

$$0.927 \text{ mol Al} \times \frac{2 \text{ mol Al(NO}_3)_3}{2 \text{ mol Al}} = 0.927 \text{ mol Al(NO}_3)_3$$

$$0.927 \text{ mol Al(NO}_3)_3 \times \frac{213.0 \text{ g}}{1 \text{ mol}} = 197 \text{ g Al(NO}_3)_3$$

$$0.927 \text{ mol Al} \times \frac{3 \text{ mol H}_2}{2 \text{ mol Al}} = 1.39 \text{ mol H}_2$$

$$1.39 \text{ mol H}_2 \times \frac{2.016 \text{ g}}{1 \text{ mol}} = 2.80 \text{ g H}_2$$

c. $\text{H}_3\text{PO}_4(aq) + 3\text{NaOH}(aq) \rightarrow \text{Na}_3\text{PO}_4(aq) + 3\text{H}_2\text{O}(l)$

Molar masses: H_3PO_4, 97.99 g; Na_3PO_4, 163.9 g; H_2O, 18.02 g

$$25.0 \text{ g H}_3\text{PO}_4 \times \frac{1 \text{ mol}}{97.99 \text{ g}} = 0.255 \text{ mol H}_3\text{PO}_4$$

$$0.255 \text{ mol H}_3\text{PO}_4 \times \frac{1 \text{ mol Na}_3\text{PO}_4}{1 \text{ mol H}_3\text{PO}_4} = 0.255 \text{ mol Na}_3\text{PO}_4$$

$$0.255 \text{ mol Na}_3\text{PO}_4 \times \frac{163.9 \text{ g}}{1 \text{ mol}} = 41.8 \text{ g Na}_3\text{PO}_4$$

$$0.255 \text{ mol H}_3\text{PO}_4 \times \frac{3 \text{ mol H}_2\text{O}}{1 \text{ mol H}_3\text{PO}_4} = 0.765 \text{ mol H}_2\text{O}$$

$$0.765 \text{ mol H}_2\text{O} \times \frac{18.02 \text{ g}}{1 \text{ mol}} = 13.8 \text{ g H}_2\text{O}$$

d. $CaO(s) + 2HCl(aq) \rightarrow CaCl_2(aq) + H_2O(l)$

Molar masses: CaO, 56.08 g; $CaCl_2$, 111.0 g; H_2O, 18.02 g

$$25.0 \text{ g CaO} \times \frac{1 \text{ mol}}{56.08 \text{ g}} = 0.446 \text{ mol CaO}$$

$$0.446 \text{ mol CaO} \times \frac{1 \text{ mol } CaCl_2}{1 \text{ mol CaO}} = 0.446 \text{ mol } CaCl_2$$

$$0.446 \text{ mol } CaCl_2 \times \frac{111.0 \text{ g}}{1 \text{ mol}} = 49.5 \text{ g } CaCl_2$$

$$0.446 \text{ mol CaO} \times \frac{1 \text{ mol } H_2O}{1 \text{ mol CaO}} = 0.446 \text{ mol } H_2O$$

$$0.446 \text{ mol } H_2O \times \frac{18.02 \text{ g}}{1 \text{ mol}} = 8.04 \text{ g } H_2O$$

19.   a. $2AgNO_3(aq) + CaSO_4(aq) \rightarrow Ag_2SO_4(s) + Ca(NO_3)_2(aq)$

Molar masses: $AgNO_3$, 169.9 g; $CaSO_4$, 136.2 g
                     Ag_2SO_4, 311.9 g; $Ca(NO_3)_2$, 164.1 g

$$12.5 \text{ g } AgNO_3 \times \frac{1 \text{ mol}}{169.9 \text{ g}} = 0.0736 \text{ mol } AgNO_3$$

$$10.0 \text{ g } CaSO_4 \times \frac{1 \text{ mol}}{136.2 \text{ g}} = 0.0734 \text{ mol } CaSO_4$$

$AgNO_3$ is the limiting reactant

$$0.0736 \text{ mol } AgNO_3 \times \frac{1 \text{ mol } Ag_2SO_4}{2 \text{ mol } AgNO_3} \times \frac{311.9 \text{ g } Ag_2SO_4}{1 \text{ mol } Ag_2SO_4} = 11.5 \text{ g } Ag_2SO_4$$

$$0.0736 \text{ mol } AgNO_3 \times \frac{1 \text{ mol } Ca(NO_3)_2}{2 \text{ mol } AgNO_3} \times \frac{164.1 \text{ g}}{1 \text{ mol}} = 6.04 \text{ g } Ca(NO_3)_2$$

b. $2Al(s) + 6HNO_3(aq) \rightarrow 2Al(NO_3)_3(aq) + 3H_2(g)$

Molar masses: Al, 26.98 g; HNO_3, 63.02 g
                     $Al(NO_3)_3$, 213.0 g; H_2, 2.016 g

$$12.5 \text{ g Al} \times \frac{1 \text{ mol}}{26.98 \text{ g}} = 0.463 \text{ mol Al}$$

$$10.0 \text{ g } HNO_3 \times \frac{1 \text{ mol}}{63.02 \text{ g}} = 0.159 \text{ mol } HNO_3$$

HNO_3 is the limiting reactant

$$0.159 \text{ mol HNO}_3 \times \frac{2 \text{ mol Al(NO}_3)_3}{6 \text{ mol HNO}_3} \times \frac{213.0 \text{ g}}{1 \text{ mol}} = 11.3 \text{ g Al(NO}_3)_3$$

$$0.159 \text{ mol HNO}_3 \times \frac{3 \text{ mol H}_2}{6 \text{ mol HNO}_3} \times \frac{2.016 \text{ g}}{1 \text{ mol}} = 0.160 \text{ g H}_2$$

c. $H_3PO_4(aq) + 3NaOH(aq) \rightarrow Na_3PO_4(aq) + 3H_2O(l)$

Molar masses: H_3PO_4, 97.99 g; NaOH, 40.00 g
Na_3PO_4, 163.9 g; H_2O, 18.02 g

$$12.5 \text{ g H}_3PO_4 \times \frac{1 \text{ mol}}{97.99 \text{ g}} = 0.128 \text{ mol H}_3PO_4$$

$$10.0 \text{ g NaOH} \times \frac{1 \text{ mol}}{40.00 \text{ g}} = 0.250 \text{ mol NaOH}$$

NaOH is the limiting reactant

$$0.250 \text{ mol NaOH} \times \frac{1 \text{ mol Na}_3PO_4}{3 \text{ mol NaOH}} \times \frac{163.9 \text{ g}}{1 \text{ mol}} = 13.7 \text{ g Na}_3PO_4$$

$$0.250 \text{ mol NaOH} \times \frac{3 \text{ mol H}_2O}{3 \text{ mol NaOH}} \times \frac{18.02 \text{ g}}{1 \text{ mol}} = 4.51 \text{ g H}_2O$$

d. $CaO(s) + 2HCl(aq) \rightarrow CaCl_2(aq) + H_2O(l)$

Molar masses: CaO, 56.08 g; HCl, 36.46 g
$CaCl_2$, 111.0 g; H_2O, 18.02 g

$$12.5 \text{ g CaO} \times \frac{1 \text{ mol}}{56.08 \text{ g}} = 0.223 \text{ mol CaO}$$

$$10.0 \text{ g HCl} \times \frac{1 \text{ mol}}{36.46 \text{ g}} = 0.274 \text{ mol HCl}$$

HCl is the limiting reactant

$$0.274 \text{ mol HCl} \times \frac{1 \text{ mol CaCl}_2}{2 \text{ mol HCl}} \times \frac{111.0 \text{ g}}{1 \text{ mol}} = 15.2 \text{ g CaCl}_2$$

$$0.274 \text{ mol HCl} \times \frac{1 \text{ mol H}_2O}{2 \text{ mol HCl}} \times \frac{18.02 \text{ g}}{1 \text{ mol}} = 2.47 \text{ g H}_2O$$

20.   For potassium: $2K(s) + Cl_2(g) \rightarrow 2KCl(s)$

Molar masses: K, 39.10 g; Cl_2, 70.90 g; KCl, 74.55 g

$$25.0 \text{ g K} \times \frac{1 \text{ mol}}{39.10 \text{ g}} = 0.639 \text{ mol K}$$

$$50.0 \text{ g Cl}_2 \times \frac{1 \text{ mol}}{70.90 \text{ g}} = 0.705 \text{ mol Cl}_2$$

K is the limiting reactant

$$0.639 \text{ mol K} \times \frac{2 \text{ mol KCl}}{2 \text{ mol K}} \times \frac{74.55 \text{ g}}{1 \text{ mol}} = 47.6 \text{ g KCl}$$

For calcium: $Ca(s) + Cl_2(g) \rightarrow CaCl_2(s)$

Molar masses: Ca, 40.08 g; Cl_2, 70.90 g; $CaCl_2$, 111.0 g

$$25.0 \text{ g Ca} \times \frac{1 \text{ mol}}{40.08 \text{ g}} = 0.624 \text{ mol Ca}$$

$$50.0 \text{ g Cl}_2 \times \frac{1 \text{ mol}}{70.90 \text{ g}} = 0.705 \text{ mol Cl}_2$$

Ca is the limiting reactant

$$0.624 \text{ mol Ca} \times \frac{1 \text{ mol CaCl}_2}{1 \text{ mol Ca}} \times \frac{111.0 \text{ g}}{1 \text{ mol}} = 69.3 \text{ g CaCl}_2$$

For aluminum: $2Al(s) + 3Cl_2(g) \rightarrow 2AlCl_3(s)$

Molar masses: Al, 26.98 g; Cl_2 70.90 g; $AlCl_3$, 133.3 g

$$25.0 \text{ g Al} \times \frac{1 \text{ mol}}{26.98 \text{ g}} = 0.927 \text{ mol Al}$$

$$50.0 \text{ g Cl}_2 \times \frac{1 \text{ mol}}{70.90 \text{ g}} = 0.705 \text{ mol Cl}_2$$

Cl_2 is the limiting reactant

$$0.705 \text{ mol Cl}_2 \times \frac{2 \text{ mol AlCl}_3}{3 \text{ mol Cl}_2} \times \frac{133.3 \text{ g}}{1 \text{ mol}} = 62.7 \text{ g AlCl}_3$$

Chapter 10   Modern Atomic Theory

1. Electromagnetic radiation is radiant energy that travels through space with wavelike behavior. There are many examples of electromagnetic radiation: light, radio/television signals, microwaves, heat, X-rays, cosmic rays, etc.

2. The different forms of electromagnetic radiation are similar in that they all exhibit the same type of wave-like behavior and are propagated through space at the same speed (the speed of light). The types of electromagnetic radiation differ in their frequency (and wavelength) and in the resulting amount of energy carried per photon.

3. The *wavelength* represents the distance between two corresponding points (peaks, troughs, etc.) on successive cycles of a wave. Figure 10.1 in the text illustrates a typical wave. The *frequency* of electromagnetic radiation represents how many complete cycles of the wave pass a given point per second. The wavelength and frequency are related, however, since obviously a longer wave will take more time to pass a given point in space than a shorter wave, if the two waves are propagated at the same speed.

4. The *speed* of electromagnetic radiation represents how fast a given wave moves through space. The *frequency* of electromagnetic radiation represents how many complete cycles of the wave pass a given point per second. For example, your favorite radio station broadcasts waves of a particular frequency that distinguishes it, but how long those waves take to reach you depends on their speed through space.

5. photon

6. Although electromagnetic radiation exhibits characteristic wave-like properties, such radiation also demonstrates a particle-like nature. For example, when an excited atom emits radiation, the radiation demonstrates wave properties, but occurs in discrete particle-like bundles (photons). The wave-particle nature of light refers to the fact that a beam of electromagnetic energy can be considered not only as a continuous wave, but also as a stream of discrete packets of energy moving through space.

7. An atom is said to be in an excited state when it possesses more than its minimum energy (its ground state). An atom is promoted from its ground state to an excited state by the absorption of energy, and returns to its ground state by the emission of the excess energy.

8. A photon having an energy corresponding to the energy difference between the two states is emitted by an atom in an excited state when it returns to its ground state.

9. larger ($E = hc/\lambda$)

10. smaller ($E = h\nu$)

11. The emission of light by excited atoms has been the key interconnection between the macroscopic world we can observe and measure, and with what

is happening on a microscopic basis within an atom. Excited atoms emit light (which we can measure) because of changes in the microscopic structure of the atom. By studying the emissions of atoms we can trace back to what happened inside the atom.

12. When excited hydrogen atoms emit their excess energy, the photons of radiation emitted are always of exactly the same wavelength and energy. We consider this to mean that the hydrogen atom possesses only certain allowed energy states, and that the photons emitted correspond to the atom changing from one of these allowed energy states to another of the allowed energy state. The energy of the photon emitted corresponds to the energy difference in the allowed states. If the hydrogen atom did not possess discrete energy levels, then we would expect the photons emitted to have random wavelengths and energies.

13. transitions of electrons

14. difference

15. Hydrogen always emits light at exactly the same wavelengths, corresponding to transitions of the electron between the fixed energy states within the atom.

16. The ground state of an atom is its lowest possible energy state.

17. Bohr pictured electrons moving in circular orbits corresponding to the various allowed energy levels. He suggested that the electron could jump to a different orbit by absorbing or emitting a photon of light with exactly the correct energy content (corresponding to the difference in energy between the orbits).

18. According to Bohr, electrons move in discrete, fixed circular *orbits* around the nucleus. If the wavelength of the applied energy corresponds to the *difference in energy* between the two orbits, the atom absorbs a photon and the electron moves to a larger orbit.

19. Bohr suggested that the electron could jump to a different orbit by absorbing or emitting a photon of light with exactly the correct energy content (corresponding to the difference in energy between the orbits). Since the energy levels of a given atom were fixed and definite, then the atom should always emit energy at the same discrete wavelengths.

20. Bohr's theory *explained* the experimentally *observed* line spectrum of hydrogen *exactly*. Bohr's theory was ultimately discarded because when attempts were made to extend the theory to atoms other than hydrogen, the calculated properties did *not* correspond closely to experimental measurements.

21. Schrödinger and de Broglie reasoned that, since light seems to have both wave and particle characteristics (it behaves simultaneously as a wave and as if it were a stream of particles), that perhaps the electron might exhibit both of these characteristics. That is, although the

electron behaves as a discrete particle, perhaps the properties of the electron in the atom could be treated as if they were wavelike.

22.   An orbit represents a definite, exact circular pathway around the nucleus in which an electron can be found. An orbital represents a region of space in which there is a high probability of finding the electron.

23.   Schrödinger's mathematical treatment could only describe the movement of the electron through the atom in terms of the *probability* of finding the electron in given regions of space within the atom, but not at a particular point within the atom at a particular time. Any attempt to determine the exact position of the electron within an atom experimentally would, in fact, disturb the electron from wherever it had been.

24.   Any experiment which sought to measure the exact location of an electron (such as shooting a beam of light at it) would cause the electron to move. Any measurement made would necessitate the application or removal of energy, which would disturb the electron from where it had been before the measurement.

25.   Chemists arbitrarily *defined* an orbital to represent a 90% probability of finding the electron with this region. Orbitals represent mathematical functions and have no distinct outer edge (so they are drawn to appear "fuzzy": they are *not* hard-edged capsules enclosing the electron, but merely represent the most likely region where an electron may be found.

26.   Pictures we draw to represent orbitals should only be interpreted as probability maps. They are not meant to represent that the electron moves only on the surface of, or within, the region drawn in the picture. Since the mathematical probability of finding the electron never actually becomes zero on moving outward from the nucleus, scientists have decided that pictures of orbitals should represent a 90% probability that the electron will be found inside the region depicted in the drawing (for 100% probability, the orbital would have to encompass all space).

27.   The 2*s* orbital is similar in shape to the 1*s* orbital, but is larger.

28.   The *p* orbitals, in general, have two lobes and are sometimes described as having a "dumbbell" shape. The 2*p* and 3*p* orbitals are similar in shape, and in the fact that there are three equivalent 2*p* or 3*p* orbitals in the 2*p* or 3*p* subshell. The orbitals differ in size, mean distance from the nucleus, and energy.

29.   The higher the principal energy level (*n*), the farther from the nucleus, on average, the electron will be.

30.   increases; the energy of an electron increases with its principal quantum number.

31. The other orbitals serve as the excited states of the hydrogen atom. When energy of the right frequency is applied to the hydrogen atom, the electron can move from its normal orbital (ground state) to one of the other orbitals (excited states). Later on, the electron can move back to its normal orbital and release the absorbed energy as light.

32. The fourth principal energy level is divided into four sublevels: these sublevels are given the designations 4*s*, 4*p*, 4*d*, and 4*f*. The fifth principal energy level is divided into five sublevers: these are given the designations 5*s*, 5*p*, 5*d*, 5*f*, and 5*g*.

33. When we say that an electron has its own intrinsic spin, we mean that, in addition to moving around the nucleus of the atom, the electron is also spinning on its own axis.

34. The Pauli exclusion principle states that an orbital can hold a maximum of two electrons, and those two electrons must have opposite spins.

35. The higher the value of the principal quantum number, *n*, the higher the energy of the principal energy level.

36. increases; as you move out from the nucleus, there is more space and room for more sublevels.

37. two

38. opposite

39. a.   correct (the *n* = 2 shell contains *s* and *p* subshells)

     b.   incorrect (the *n* = 1 shell consists only of 1*s* orbitals)

     c.   incorrect (the *n* = 3 shell contains 3*s*, 3*p*, and 3*d* orbitals)

     d.   correct (the *n* = 4 shell contains *s*, *p*, *d*, and *f* subshells)

40. a.   incorrect (the *n* = 1 shell has only the 1*s* subshell)

     b.   incorrect (the *n* = 2 shell has only 2*s* and 2*p* subshells)

     c.   correct (the *n* = 4 shell contains *s*, *p*, *d* and *f* subshells)

     d.   correct (the *n* = 5 shell contains *s*, *p*, *d*, *f*, and *g* subshells)

41. The 1*s* orbital is closest to the nucleus and lowest in energy, so it is always filled first.

42. When a hydrogen atom is in its ground state, the electron is found in the 1*s* orbital. The 1*s* orbital has the lowest energy of all the possible hydrogen orbitals.

43.   Valence electrons are those in the outermost (highest) principal energy
       level of an atom. These electrons are especially important because they
       are at the "outside edge" of an atom, and are those electrons which are
       "seen" by other atoms and which can interact with the electrons of another
       atom in a chemical reaction.

44.   The elements in a given vertical column of the periodic table have the
       same valence electron configuration. Having the same valence electron
       configuration causes the elements in a given group to have similar
       chemical properties.

45.   a. $1s^2\ 2s^2\ 2p^4$

       b. $1s^2\ 2s^1$

       c. $1s^2\ 2s^2\ 2p^6\ 3s^2\ 3p^5$

       d. $1s^2\ 2s^2\ 2p^6$

46.   a. $1s^2\ 2s^2\ 2p^6\ 3s^2\ 3p^6\ 4s^2\ 3d^{10}\ 4p^6\ 5s^2$

       b. $1s^2\ 2s^2\ 2p^6\ 3s^2\ 3p^6\ 4s^2\ 3d^{10}$

       c. $1s^2$

       d. $1s^2\ 2s^2\ 2p^6\ 3s^2\ 3p^6\ 4s^2\ 3d^{10}\ 4p^5$

47.   a. $1s^2\ 2s^2\ 2p^6\ 3s^1$

       b. $1s^2\ 2s^2\ 2p^6\ 3s^2\ 3p^6\ 4s^2\ 3d^{10}\ 4p^6\ 5s^2\ 4d^{10}\ 5p^6\ 6s^1$

       c. $1s^2\ 2s^2\ 2p^3$

       d. $1s^2\ 2s^2$

48.   a. $1s^2\ 2s^2\ 2p^6\ 3s^2\ 3p^6\ 4s^2$

       b. $1s^2\ 2s^2\ 2p^6\ 3s^2\ 3p^6\ 4s^1$

       c. $1s^2\ 2s^2\ 2p^5$

       d. $1s^2\ 2s^2\ 2p^6\ 3s^2\ 3p^6\ 4s^2\ 3d^{10}\ 4p^6$

49.   a.   (↑↓) (↑↓) (↑↓)(↑↓)(↑↓) (↑↓)

             1s   2s   2p   3s

       b.   (↑↓) (↑↓) (↑↓)(↑↓)(↑↓) (↑↓) (↑↓)(↑↓)(↑↓) (↑)

             1s   2s   2p   3s   3p   4s

c.   (↑↓) (↑↓) (↑↓)(↑↓)(↑↓) (↑↓) (↑↓)(↑↓)(↑↓) (↑↓)

      1s   2s   2p   3s   3p   4s

      (↑↓)(↑↓)(↑↓)(↑↓)(↑↓) (↑↓)(↑↓)(↑↓)

      3d   4p

d.   (↑↓) (↑↓) (↑↓)(↑↓)(↑↓) (↑↓) (↑)( )( )

      1s   2s   2p   3s   3p

50.   a.   (↑↓) (↑↓) (↑↓)(↑↓)(↑↓) (↑↓) (↑)( )( )

            1s   2s   2p   3s   3p

      b.   (↑↓) (↑↓) (↑↓)(↑↓)(↑↓) (↑↓) (↑)(↑)(↑)

            1s   2s   2p   3s   3p

      c.   (↑↓) (↑↓) (↑↓)(↑↓)(↑↓) (↑↓) (↑↓)(↑↓)(↑↓) (↑↓)

            1s   2s   2p   3s   3p   4s

            (↑↓)(↑↓)(↑↓)(↑↓)(↑↓) (↑↓)(↑↓)(↑)

                  3d   4p

      d.   (↑↓) (↑↓) (↑↓)(↑↓)(↑↓) (↑↓) (↑↓)(↑↓)(↑↓)

            1s   2s   2p   3s   3p

51.   For the representative elements (those filling *s* and *p* subshells), the group number gives the number of valence electrons.

      a.   one (2*s*)

      b.   three (2*s*, 2*p*)

      c.   eight (3*s*, 3*p*)

      d.   five (3*s*, 3*p*)

52.   For the representative elements (those filling *s* and *p* subshells), the group number gives the number of valence electrons.

      a.   one (3*s*)

      b.   two (4*s*)

      c.   seven (5*s*, 5*p*)

      d.   five (2*s*, 2*p*)

53.   This belief is based on the *experimental properties* of K and Ca. The physical and chemical properties of K are like those of the other Group 1 elements; Ca's properties are similar to the other Group 2 elements.

54.   The properties of Rb and Sr suggest that they are members of Groups 1 and 2, respectively, and so must be filling the 5s orbital. The 5s orbital is lower in energy (and fills before) the 4d orbitals.

55.   a.   [Kr] $5s^2$

       b.   [Xe] $6s^2$

       c.   [Ne] $3s^2\ 3p^4$

       d.   [Xe] $6s^1$

56.   a.   [Ar] $4s^2$

       b.   [Rn] $7s^1$

       c.   [Kr] $5s^2\ 4d^1$

       d.   [Xe] $6s^2\ 4f^1\ 5d^1$

57.   a.   [Ar] $4s^2\ 3d^1$

       b.   [Kr] $5s^2\ 4d^1$

       c.   [Xe] $6s^2\ 5d^1$

       d.   [Rn] $7s^2\ 6d^1$

58.   a.   [Ne] $3s^2\ 3p^3$

       b.   [Ne] $3s^2\ 3p^5$

       c.   [Ne] $3s^2$

       d.   [Ar] $4s^2\ 3d^{10}$

59.   a.   one

       b.   five (configuration is $4s^1\ 3d^5$ rather than $4s^2\ 3d^4$)

       c.   ten

       d.   two

60.   a.   one

       b.   two

       c.   zero

       d.   ten

61. The *position* of the element (both in terms of the vertical column and the horizontal row) tells you which set of orbitals is being filled last. See Figure 10.27 for details.

   a. $5d$

   b. $3d$

   c. $4f$

   d. $4f$

62. Figure 10.27 shows the orbitals being filled as a function of location in the periodic table.

   a. $5f$

   b. $5f$

   c. $4f$

   d. $6p$

63. Figure 10.30 shows partial electronic configurations.

   a.   [Xe] $4f^{14}\ 5d^2\ 6s^2$

   b.   [Rn] $7s^2$

   c.   [Kr] $4d^{10}\ 5s^2\ 5p^3$

   d.   [Xe] $4f^{14}\ 5d^{10}\ 6s^2\ 6p^2$

64. Figure 10.30 shows partial electronic configurations.

   a.   [Rn] $7s^2\ 5f^3\ 6d^1$

   b.   [Ar] $4s^2\ 3d^5$

   c.   [Xe] $6s^2\ 4f^{14}\ d^{10}$

   d.   [Rn] $7s^1$

65. Some typical properties of metals are: a lustrous appearance, the ability to be pounded into sheets (malleability) or pulled into wires (ductility), and the ability to conduct heat and electricity. Nonmetals typically have a non-shiny appearance, are brittle, and do not conduct heat or electricity well. There are exceptions to these general properties: for example, graphite (a form of the nonmetal carbon) conducts electricity well.

66. The metallic elements *lose* electrons and form *positive* ions (cations); the nonmetallic elements *gain* electrons and form *negative* ions (anions). Remember that the electron itself is *negatively* charged.

67. The Group 1 metals are all highly reactive, and all form 1+ ions almost exclusively when they react. Physically, these metals are soft (they can

be cut with a knife) and very low in density. Because of their high reactivity, these metals tend to be found with a coating of the metal oxide which hides their metallic luster (which can be seen, however, if a fresh surface of the metal is exposed).

68.   All exist as *diatomic* molecules (F_2, Cl_2, Br_2, I_2); all are *nonmetals*; all have relatively high electronegativities; all form 1- ions in reacting with metallic elements.

69.   The elements toward the *bottom* of a given group (vertical column) lose electrons more easily than the elements toward the top of the group. Elements at the bottom of a group have their valence electrons in an energy level that is far from the nucleus: the nuclear attraction is less as the electrons are farther from the nucleus.

70.   Elements at the *left* of a period (horizontal row) lose electrons more readily; at the left of a period (given principal energy level) the nuclear charge is the smallest and the electrons are least tightly held.

71.   The nonmetallic elements are clustered at the upper right side of the periodic table. These elements are effective at pulling electrons from metallic elements for several reasons. First, these elements have little tendency to lose electrons themselves (they have high ionization energies). Secondly, the atoms of these elements tend to be small in size, which means that electrons can be pulled in strongly since they can get closer to the nucleus. Finally, if these atoms gain electrons, they can approach the electronic configuration of the following noble gas elements (see Chapter 12 for why the electronic configuration of the noble gases are desirable for other atoms to attain).

72.   The elements of a given period (horizontal row) have valence electrons in the same principal energy level. Nuclear charge, however, increases across a period going from left to right. Atoms at the left side have smaller nuclear charges, and hold onto their valence electrons less tightly.

73.   All atoms within a given group have the same number of valence electrons, and these valence electrons occur in the same type of subshell. However, at the bottom of a group, the valence electrons are in a higher *principal* energy level. The principal energy levels increase in distance from the nucleus as the principal quantum number, *n*, increases.

74.   The *nuclear charge* increases from left to right within a period, pulling progressively more tightly on the valence electrons.

75.   For most elements, the chemical activity is reflected in the ease with which the element gains or loses electrons

    a.   Na (the less reactive metals are further up in a group)
    b.   Be (the less reactive metals are further up in a group)
    c.   Br (the less reactive nonmetals are at the bottom of a group)
    d.   Te (the less reactive nonmetals are at the bottom of a group)

76. Ionization energies decrease in going from top to bottom within a vertical group; ionization energies increase in going from left to right within a horizontal period.

    a.   Li

    b.   Ca

    c.   Cl

    d.   S

77. Atomic size increases in going from top to bottom within a vertical group; atomic size decreases in going from left to right within a horizontal period.

    a.   Xe < Sn < Sr < Rb

    b.   He < Kr < Xe < Rn

    c.   At < Pb < Ba < Cs

78. Atomic size increases in going from top to bottom within a vertical group; atomic size decreases in going from left to right within a horizontal period.

    a.   Na

    b.   S

    c.   N

    d.   F

79. wavelength

80. speed of light

81. visible

82. photons

83. ground

84. quantized

85. orbits

86. orbital

87. valence

88. transition metal

89.   frequency

90.   spins

91.   a.   [Ne] (↑↓) (↑)(↑)(↑)

   $\quad\quad\quad\quad\quad\quad$ 3s $\quad\quad$ 3p

   P is expected to be paramagnetic; three unpaired 3p electrons

   b.   [Kr] (↑↓) (↑↓)(↑↓)(↑↓)(↑↓)(↑↓) (↑↓)(↑↓)(↑)

   $\quad\quad\quad\quad\quad$ 5s $\quad\quad\quad\quad$ 4d $\quad\quad\quad\quad\quad$ 5p

   I is expected to be paramagnetic; one unpaired 5p electron

   c.   [Ar] (↑↓) (↑↓)(↑↓)(↑↓)(↑↓)(↑↓) (↑)(↑)(   )

   $\quad\quad\quad\quad\quad$ 4s $\quad\quad\quad\quad$ 3d $\quad\quad\quad\quad\quad$ 4p

   Ge is expected to be paramagnetic; two unpaired 4p electrons

92.   a. $1s^2\ 2s^2\ 2p^6\ 3s^2\ 3p^6\ 4s^1$ $\quad\quad\quad\quad\quad\quad$ [Ar] $4s^1$

   (↑↓) (↑↓) (↑↓)(↑↓)(↑↓) (↑↓) (↑↓)(↑↓)(↑↓) (↑)
   1s $\quad$ 2s $\quad\quad$ 2p $\quad\quad$ 3s $\quad\quad$ 3p $\quad\quad$ 4s

   b. $1s^2\ 2s^2\ 2p^6\ 3s^2\ 3p^6\ 4s^2\ 3d^2$ $\quad\quad\quad$ [Ar] $4s^2\ 3d^2$

   (↑↓) (↑↓) (↑↓)(↑↓)(↑↓) (↑↓) (↑↓)(↑↓)(↑↓) (↑↓) (↑)(↑)(   )(   )(   )
   1s $\quad$ 2s $\quad\quad$ 2p $\quad\quad$ 3s $\quad\quad$ 3p $\quad\quad$ 4s $\quad\quad\quad$ 3d

   c. $1s^2\ 2s^2\ 2p^6\ 3s^2\ 3p^2$ $\quad\quad\quad\quad\quad\quad$ [Ne] $3s^2\ 3p^2$

   (↑↓) (↑↓) (↑↓)(↑↓)(↑↓) (↑↓) (↑)(↑)(   )
   1s $\quad$ 2s $\quad\quad$ 2p $\quad\quad$ 3s $\quad\quad$ 3p

   d. $1s^2\ 2s^2\ 2p^6\ 3s^2\ 3p^6\ 4s^2\ 3d^6$ $\quad\quad\quad$ [Ar] $4s^2\ 3d^6$

   (↑↓) (↑↓) (↑↓)(↑↓)(↑↓) (↑↓) (↑↓)(↑↓)(↑↓) (↑↓) (↑↓)(↑)(↑)(↑)(↑)
   1s $\quad$ 2s $\quad\quad$ 2p $\quad\quad$ 3s $\quad\quad$ 3p $\quad\quad$ 4s $\quad\quad\quad$ 3d

   e. $1s^2\ 2s^2\ 2p^6\ 3s^2\ 3p^6\ 4s^2\ 3d^{10}$ $\quad\quad\quad$ [Ar] $4s^2\ 3d^{10}$

   (↑↓) (↑↓) (↑↓)(↑↓)(↑↓) (↑↓) (↑↓)(↑↓)(↑↓) (↑↓) (↑↓)(↑↓)(↑↓)(↑↓)(↑↓)
   1s $\quad$ 2s $\quad\quad$ 2p $\quad\quad$ 3s $\quad\quad$ 3p $\quad\quad$ 4s $\quad\quad\quad$ 3d

93.   a. $1s^2\ 2s^2\ 2p^6\ 3s^2\ 3p^6\ 4s^2\ 3d^1$

   (↑↓) (↑↓) (↑↓)(↑↓)(↑↓) (↑↓) (↑↓)(↑↓)(↑↓) (↑↓) (↑)(   )(   )(   )(   )

   1s $\quad$ 2s $\quad\quad$ 2p $\quad\quad$ 3s $\quad\quad$ 3p $\quad\quad$ 4s $\quad\quad\quad$ 3d

   [Ar] $4s^2\ 3d^1$

b. $1s^2\ 2s^2\ 2p^6\ 3s^2\ 3p^3$

(↑↓) (↑↓) (↑↓)(↑↓)(↑↓) (↑↓) (↑)(↑)(↑)

   1s   2s   2p   3s   3p

[Ne] $3s^2\ 3p^3$

c. $1s^2\ 2s^2\ 2p^6\ 3s^2\ 3p^6\ 4s^2\ 3d^{10}\ 4p^6$

(↑↓) (↑↓) (↑↓)(↑↓)(↑↓) (↑↓) (↑↓)(↑↓)(↑↓) (↑↓)

   1s   2s   2p   3s   3p   4s

(↑↓)(↑↓)(↑↓)(↑↓)(↑↓) (↑↓)(↑↓)(↑↓)

         3d   4p

[Kr] is itself a noble gas

d. $1s^2\ 2s^2\ 2p^6\ 3s^2\ 3p^6\ 4s^2\ 3d^{10}\ 4p^6\ 5s^2$

(↑↓) (↑↓) (↑↓)(↑↓)(↑↓) (↑↓) (↑↓)(↑↓)(↑↓) (↑↓)

   1s   2s   2p   3s   3p   4s

(↑↓)(↑↓)(↑↓)(↑↓)(↑↓) (↑↓)(↑↓)(↑↓) (↑↓)

         3d   4p   5s

[Kr] $5s^2$

e. $1s^2\ 2s^2\ 2p^6\ 3s^2\ 3p^6\ 4s^2\ 3d^{10}$

(↑↓) (↑↓) (↑↓)(↑↓)(↑↓) (↑↓) (↑↓)(↑↓)(↑↓) (↑↓) (↑↓)(↑↓)(↑↓)(↑↓)(↑↓)

   1s   2s   2p   3s   3p   4s   3d

[Ar] $4s^2\ 3d^{10}$

94. a. ns^2 b. $ns^2\ np^5$

     c. $ns^2\ np^4$ d. ns^1

     e. $ns^2\ np^4$

95. a.   four (two if the d electrons are not counted as valence electrons)
     b.   seven
     c.   two
     d.   seven (two if the d electrons are not counted as valence electrons)

96. a. $\lambda = \dfrac{h}{mv}$

          $\lambda = \dfrac{6.63 \times 10^{-34}\ J\ s}{(9.11 \times 10^{-31}\ kg)[0.90(3.00 \times 10^8\ m\ s^{-1})]}$

$$\lambda = 2.7 \times 10^{-12} \text{ m } (0.0027 \text{ nm})$$

b. 4.4×10^{-34} m

c. 2×10^{-35} m

The wavelengths for the ball and the person are *infinitesimally small*, whereas the wavelength for the electron is nearly the same order of magnitude as the diameter of a typical atom.

97. 3.00×10^8 m/sec

98.   Light is emitted from the hydrogen atom only at certain fixed wavelengths. If the energy levels of hydrogen were *continuous*, a hydrogen atom would emit energy at all possible wavelengths.

99.   As an electron moves to a higher-number principal energy level, the electron's mean distance from the nucleus increases, thereby decreasing the attractive force between the electron and the nucleus.

100.   The third principal energy level of hydrogen is divided into *three* sublevels ($3s$, $3p$, and $3d$); there is a *single* $3s$ orbital; there is a set of *three* $3p$ orbitals; there is a set of *five* $3d$ orbitals. See Figures 10.21-10.24 for the shapes of these orbitals.

101.   Orbitals in the $1s$ and $2s$ subshells can only contain two electrons.

102.   a.   incorrect; the $n = 1$ energy shell has only the $1s$ subshell

       b.   correct

       c.   incorrect; the $n = 3$ energy shell has only $3s$. $3p$, and $3d$ subshells

       d.   correct

       e.   correct

       f.   correct

103.   The three $2p$ orbitals of carbon are of the *same energy*; by occupying different orbitals of the same energy, repulsion between electrons is minimized.

104.   a. $1s^2 \, 2s^2 \, 2p^6 \, 3s^2 \, 3p^6 \, 4s^2 \, 3d^{10} \, 4p^5$

       b. $1s^2 \, 2s^2 \, 2p^6 \, 3s^2 \, 3p^6 \, 4s^2 \, 3d^{10} \, 4p^6 \, 5s^2 \, 4d^{10} \, 5p^6$

       c. $1s^2 \, 2s^2 \, 2p^6 \, 3s^2 \, 3p^6 \, 4s^2 \, 3d^{10} \, 4p^6 \, 5s^2 \, 4d^{10} \, 5p^6 \, 6s^2$

       d. $1s^2 \, 2s^2 \, 2p^6 \, 3s^2 \, 3p^6 \, 4s^2 \, 3d^{10} \, 4p^4$

105.   a.   (↑↓) (↑↓) (↑↓)(↑↓)(↑↓) (↑↓) (↑↓)(↑↓)(↑↓) (↑↓) (↑)( )( )( )( )
             $1s$ $2s$ $2p$ $3s$ $3p$ $4s$ $3d$

b.   (↑↓) (↑↓) (↑↓)(↑↓)(↑↓) (↑↓) (↑↓)(↑)(↑)

1s   2s   2p   3s   3p

c.   (↑↓) (↑↓) (↑↓)(↑↓)(↑↓) (↑↓) (↑↓)(↑↓)(↑↓) (↑)

1s   2s   2p   3s   3p   4s

d.   (↑↓) (↑↓) (↑)(↑)(↑)

1s   2s   2p

106. a.   five (2s, 2p)

b.   seven (3s, 3p)

c.   one (3s)

d.   three (3s, 3p)

107. transition metals

108. a.   [Kr] $5s^2$ $4d^2$ b.   [Kr] $5s^2$ $4d^{10}$ $5p^5$

c.   [Ar] $4s^2$ $3d^{10}$ $4p^2$ d.   [Xe] $6s^1$

109. a.   [Ar] $4s^2$ $3d^2$ b.   [Ar] $4s^2$ $3d^{10}$ $4p^4$

c.   [Kr] $5s^2$ $4d^{10}$ $5p^3$ d.   [Kr] $5s^2$

110. The *position* of the element (both in terms of the vertical column and the horizontal row) tells you which set of orbitals is being filled last. See Figure 10.27 for details.

a.   3d   b.   4d

c.   5f   d.   4p

111. a.   [Ar] $4s^2$ $3d^8$

b.   [Kr] $5s^2$ $4d^3$ (actually [Kr] $5s^1$ $4d^4$ for reasons beyond text)

c.   [Xe] $6s^2$ $4f^{14}$ $5d^2$

d.   [Xe] $6s^2$ $4f^{14}$ $5d^{10}$ $6p^5$

112. metals, low; nonmetals, high

113. a.   B and Al are both very reactive

b.   Na

c.   F

114.   Atomic size increases in going from top to bottom within a vertical group; atomic size decreases in going from left to right within a horizontal period.

   a.   Ca

   b.   P

   c.   K

Chapter 11   Chemical Bonding

1. A chemical bond represents a force which holds groups of two or more atoms together and makes them function as a unit.

2. The strength of a chemical bond is characterized by the bond energy (the amount of energy required to break the bond).

3. An ionic compound results when a metallic element reacts with a nonmetallic element. An example is the reaction of the metal sodium with the nonmetal chlorine: $2Na(s) + Cl_2(g) \rightarrow 2Na^+Cl^-(s)$

4. *Ionic* bonding results from the complete transfer of an electron from one atom to another, whereas *covalent* bonding exists when two atoms share pairs of electrons.

5. The H_2 molecule contains two atoms of the same element. When two hydrogen atoms are brought close together, each hydrogen atom contributes its electron to the formation of a covalent bond, with the resulting pair of electrons shared equally by the two hydrogen atoms. An H_2 molecule is more stable than two separated hydrogen atoms. The pair of electrons is simultaneously attracted by the two nuclei.

6. The HF molecule contains atoms of two different elements. In bonding with each other, these atoms share a pair of valence electrons, but they do not share them equally. The bonding in HF is described as polar covalent, which indicates that although valence electron pairs are shared between atoms, the electron pair is attracted more strongly by one of the atoms than the other. Nonetheless, an HF molecule is more stable in energy than are separated H and F atoms.

7. Electronegativity is the ability of an atom to attract a shared pair of electrons toward itself in forming a chemical bond. If we postulate a bond forming between two atoms, the relative electronegativies of the atoms will tell us what type of chemical bond is likely to be formed.

8. A polar covalent bond results when one atom of the bond attracts electrons more strongly toward itself than does the second atom of the bond. A polar covalent bond results when the atoms forming the covalent bond have different electronegativities. The fact that the bonds in a molecule are polar does *not* necessarily mean that the overall molecule itself will be polar: the overall polarity of the molecule also depends on the geometry of the molecule.

9. separate (i.e., the centers of charge do not coincide)

10. electronegativity

11.   In general, an element farther to the right in a given period or an element closer to the top of a given group is more electronegative. The elements below are ranked in order of increasing electronegativity.

    a.   Mg < Si < S

    b.   Bi < As < N

    c.   Li < Be < F

12.   In each case, the element higher up within a given group of the periodic table, or to the right within a period, has the higher electronegativity.

    a.   K< Ca < Sc

    b.   At < Br < F

    c.   C < N < O

13.   Generally, covalent bonds between atoms of *different* elements are *polar*.

    a.   covalent (nonpolar)

    b.   polar covalent

    c.   polar covalent

    d.   polar covalent

14.   Generally, covalent bonds between atoms of *different* elements are *polar*.

    a.   covalent

    b.   polar covalent

    c.   polar covalent

    d.   ionic

15.   For a bond to be polar covalent, the atoms involved in the bond must have different electronegativities (must be of different elements).

    a.   *non*polar covalent (atoms of the same element)

    b.   *non*polar covalent (atoms of the same element)

    c.   *non*polar covalent (atoms of the same element)

    d.   polar covalent (atoms of different elements)

16.   For a bond to be polar covalent, the atoms involved in the bond must have different electronegativities (must be of different elements).

    a.   covalent (atoms of the same element)

    b.   covalent (atoms of the same element)

c.   polar covalent (different elements)

d.   polar covalent (different elements)

17.   The *degree* of polarity of a polar covalent bond is indicated by the magnitude of the difference in electronegativities of the elements involved: the larger the difference in electronegativity, the more polar is the bond. Electronegativity differences are given in parentheses below:

a.   H-F (1.9); H-Cl (0.9); the H-F bond is more polar

b.   H-Cl (0.9); H-I (0.4); the H-Cl bond is more polar

c.   H-Br (0.7); H-Cl (0.9); the H-Cl bond is more polar

d.   H-I (0.4); H-Br (0.7); the H-Br bond is more polar

18.   The *degree* of polarity of a polar covalent bond is indicated by the magnitude of the difference in electronegativities of the elements involved: the larger the difference in electronegativity, the more polar is the bond. Electronegativity differences are given in parentheses below:

a.   H-O (1.4); H-N (0.9); the H-O bond is more polar.

b.   H-N (0.9); H-F (1.9); the H-F bond is more polar.

c.   H-O (1.4); H-F (1.9); the H-F bond is more polar.

d.   H-O (1.4); H-Cl (0.9); the H-O bond is more polar.

19.   The larger the difference in electronegativity between two atoms, the more polar will be the bond between those atoms. Electronegativity differences are given in parentheses.

a.   H-S (0.4); H-F (1.9); the H-F bond is more polar

b.   O-S (1.0); O-F (0.5); the O-S bond is more polar

c.   N-S (0.5); N-Cl(0); the N-S bond is more polar

d.   C-S (0); C-Cl (0.5); the C-Cl bond is more polar

20.   The greater the electronegativity difference between two atoms, the more ionic will be the bond between those two atoms. Electronegativity differences are given in parentheses.

a.   Na-O (2.6) has more ionic character than Na-N (2.1)

b.   K-S (1.7) has more ionic character than K-P (1.3)

c.   K-Cl (2.2) has more ionic character than Na-Cl (2.1)

d.   Na-Cl (2.1) has more ionic character than Mg-Cl (1.8)

21.   A dipole moment is an electrical effect that occurs in a molecule that has separate centers of positive and negative charge. The simplest examples of molecules with dipole moments would be diatomic molecules involving two different elements. For example:

δ+ C→O δ–   δ+ N→O δ–   δ+ Cl→F δ–   δ+ Br→Cl δ–

22.   The presence of strong bond dipoles and a large overall dipole moment in water make it a very polar substance overall. Among those properties of water that are dependent on its dipole moment are its freezing point, melting point, vapor pressure, and its ability to dissolve many substances.

23.   In a diatomic molecule containing two different elements, the more electronegative atom will be the negative end of the molecule, and the *less* electronegative atom will be the positive end.

   a.   chlorine

   b.   oxygen

   c.   fluorine

24.   In a diatomic molecule containing two different elements, the more electronegative atom will be the negative end of the molecule, and the *less* electronegative atom will be the positive end.

   a.   H

   b.   Cl

   c.   I

25.   In the figures, the arrow points toward the more electronegative atom.

   a.   δ+   Cl→O   δ–

   b.   δ+   O→F   δ–

   c.   δ+   S→O   δ–

   d.   δ+   N→O   δ–

26.   In the figures, the arrow points toward the more electronegative atom.

   a.   δ+   P→F   δ–

   b.   δ+   P→O   δ–

   c.   δ+   P→C   δ–

   d.   P and H have similar electronegativities.

27. In the figures, the arrow points toward the more electronegative atom.

    a. $\delta+$ Si→H $\delta-$

    b.   P–H   The atoms have very nearly the same electronegativity, so there is a very small, if any, dipole moment.

    c. $\delta+$ H→S $\delta-$

    d. $\delta+$ H→Cl $\delta-$

28. In the figures, the arrow points toward the more electronegative atom.

    a. $\delta+$ P→S $\delta-$

    b. $\delta+$ S→O $\delta-$

    c. $\delta+$ S→N $\delta-$

    d. $\delta+$ S→Cl $\delta-$

29. noble gas

30. previous

31. gaining

32. Atoms in covalent molecules gain a configuration like that of a noble gas by sharing one or more pairs of electrons between atoms: such shared pairs of electrons "belong" to each of the atoms of the bond at the same time. In ionic bonding, one atom completely gives over one or more electrons to another atom, and then the resulting ions behave independently of one another.

33. a.   Na $1s^2\ 2s^2\ 2p^6\ 3s^1$

    Na$^+$ $1s^2\ 2s^2\ 2p^6$

    Ne has the same configuration as Na$^+$

    b.   I $1s^2\ 2s^2\ 2p^6\ 3s^2\ 3p^6\ 4s^2\ 3d^{10}\ 4p^6\ 5s^2\ 4d^{10}\ 5p^5$

    I$^-$ $1s^2\ 2s^2\ 2p^6\ 3s^2\ 3p^6\ 4s^2\ 3d^{10}\ 4p^6\ 5s^2\ 4d^{10}\ 5p^6$

    Xe has the same configuration as I$^-$

    c.   Ca $1s^2\ 2s^2\ 2p^6\ 3s^2\ 3p^6\ 4s^2$

    Ca^{2+} $1s^2\ 2s^2\ 2p^6\ 3s^2\ 3p^6$

    Ar has the same configuration as Ca^{2+}

   d.   N $1s^2\ 2s^2\ 2p^3$

           N^{3-} $1s^2\ 2s^2\ 2p^6$

           Ne has the same configuration as N^{3-}

   e.   F $1s^2\ 2s^2\ 2p^5$

           F^- $1s^2\ 2s^2\ 2p^6$

           Ne has the same configuration as F^-

34. a.   Li $1s^2\ 2s^1$

           Li^+ $1s^2$

           He has the same configuration as Li^+

   b.   Br $1s^2\ 2s^2\ 2p^6\ 3s^2\ 3p^6\ 4s^2\ 3d^{10}\ 4p^5$

           Br^- $1s^2\ 2s^2\ 2p^6\ 3s^2\ 3p^6\ 4s^2\ 3d^{10}\ 4p^6$

           Kr has the same configuration as Br^-

   c.   Cs $1s^2\ 2s^2\ 2p^6\ 3s^2\ 3p^6\ 4s^2\ 3d^{10}\ 4p^6\ 5s^2\ 4d^{10}\ 5p^6\ 6s^1$

           Cs^+ $1s^2\ 2s^2\ 2p^6\ 3s^2\ 3p^6\ 4s^2\ 3d^{10}\ 4p^6\ 5s^2\ 4d^{10}\ 5p^6$

           Xe has the same configuration as Cs^+

   d.   S $1s^2\ 2s^2\ 2p^6\ 3s^2\ 3p^4$

           S^{2-} $1s^2\ 2s^2\ 2p^6\ 3s^2\ 3p^6$

           Ar has the same configuration as S^{2-}

   e.   Mg $1s^2\ 2s^2\ 2p^6\ 3s^2$

           Mg^{2+} $1s^2\ 2s^2\ 2p^6$

           Ne has the same configuration as Mg^{2+}

35. a. Mg^{2+} (Mg has two electrons more than the noble gas Ne)

   b. Al^{3+} (Al has three electrons more than the noble gas Ne)

   c. I^- (I has one electron less than the noble gas Xe)

   d. Ca^{2+} (Ca has two electrons more than the noble gas Ar)

36. a. Ca^{2+} (Ca has two electrons more than the noble gas Ar)

   b. N^{3-} (N has three electrons fewer than the noble gas Ne)

   c. Br^- (Br has one electron fewer than the noble gas Kr)

   d. Mg^{2+} (Mg has two electrons more than the noble gas Ne)

37.   a. Al_2O_3 Al has three electrons more than a noble gas; O has two electrons fewer than a noble gas.

b. Cs_2O Cs has one electron more than a noble gas; O has two electrons fewer than a noble gas.

c. $BaCl_2$ Ba has two electrons more than a noble gas; Cl has one electron less than a noble gas.

d. Fr_2O Fr has one electron more than a noble gas; O has two electrons fewer than a noble gas.

e. $RaCl_2$ Ra has two electrons more than a noble gas; Cl has one electron less than a noble gas.

f.   BaTe   Ba has two electrons more than a noble gas; Te has two electrons fewer than a noble gas.

38.   a. Na_2S Na has one electrone more than a noble gas; S has two electrons fewer than a noble gas.

b.   BaSe   Ba has two electrons more than a noble gas; Se has two electrons fewer than a noble gas.

c. $MgBr_2$ Mg has two electrons more than a noble gas; Br has one electron less than a noble gas.

d. Li_3N Li has one electron more than a noble gas; N has three electrons fewer than a noble gas.

e.   KH   K has one electron more than a noble gas; H has one electron less than a noble gas.

39.   a. Ba^{2+} [Xe]; S^{2-} [Ar]

b. Sr^{2+} [Kr]; F^- [Ne]

c. Mg^{2+} [Ne]; O^{2-} [Ne]

d. Al^{3+} [Ne]; S^{2-} [Ar]

40.   a. Al^{3+}, [Ne]; S^{2-}, [Ar]

b. Mg^{2+}, [Ne]; N^{3-}, [Ne]

c. Rb^+, [Kr]; O^{2-}, [Ne]

d. Cs^+, [Xe]; I^-, [Xe]

41.   The formula of an ionic compound represents only the smallest whole number ratio of the positive and negative ions present (the empirical formula).

42.   An ionic solid such as NaCl basically consists of an array of alternating positively and negatively charged ions: that is, each positive ion has as its nearest neighbors a group of negative ions, and each negative ion has a group of positive ions surrounding it. In most ionic solids, the ions are packed as tightly as possible.

43.   Positive ions are always smaller than the atoms from which they are formed, because in forming the ion, the valence electron shell (or part of it) is "removed" from the atom.

44.   In forming an anion, an atom gains additional electrons in its outermost (valence) shell. Having additional electrons in the valence shell increases the repulsive forces between electrons, and the outermost shell becomes larger to accommodate this.

45.   Relative ionic sizes are indicated in Figure 11.9. Within a given horizontal row of the periodic chart, negative ions tend to be larger than positive ions because the negative ions contain a larger number of electrons in the valence shell. Within a vertical group of the periodic table, ionic size increases from top to bottom. In general, positive ions are smaller than the atoms they come from, whereas negative ions are larger than the atoms they come from.

   a. Na^+

   b.   F

   c. Mg^{2+}

   d.   S

46.   Relative ionic sizes are indicated in Figure 11.9. Within a given horizontal row of the periodic chart, negative ions tend to be larger than positive ions because the negative ions contain a larger number of electrons in the valence shell. Within a vertical group of the periodic table, ionic size increases from top to bottom. In general, positive ions are smaller than the atoms they come from, whereas negative ions are larger than the atoms they come from.

   a. F^-

   b. Cl^-

   c.   Ca

   d. I^-

47.   Relative ionic sizes are indicated in Figure 11.9. Within a given horizontal row of the periodic chart, negative ions tend to be larger than positive ions because the negative ions contain a larger number of electrons in the valence shell. Within a vertical group of the periodic table, ionic size increases from top to bottom. In general, positive ions are smaller than the atoms they come from, whereas negative ions are larger than the atoms they come from.

a. Fe^{3+}

b.   Cl

c. Al^{3+}

48.   Relative ionic sizes are indicated in Figure 11.9. Within a given horizontal row of the periodic chart, negative ions tend to be larger than positive ions because the negative ions contain a larger number of electrons in the valence shell. Within a vertical group of the periodic table, ionic size increases from top to bottom. In general, positive ions are smaller than the atoms they come from, whereas negative ions are larger than the atoms they come from.

a. I^-

b. Cl^-

c. Cl^-

d. S^{2-}

49.   Valence electrons are those found in the outermost principal energy level of the atom. The valence electrons effectively represent the outside edge of the atom, and are the electrons most influenced by the electrons of another atom.

50.   When atoms form covalent bonds, they try to attain a valence electronic configuration similar to that of the following noble gas element. When the elements in the first few horizontal rows of the periodic table form covalent bonds, they will attempt to gain configurations similar to the noble gases helium (2 valence electrons, duet rule), and neon and argon (8 valence electrons, octet rule).

51.   noble gas electronic configuration

52.   These elements attain a total of eight valence electrons, making the valence electron configurations similar to those of the noble gases Ne and Ar.

53.   When two atoms in a molecule are connected by a double bond, we are indicating that the atoms share two pairs of electrons (4 electrons) in completing their outermost shells. A simple molecule containing a double bond is ethene (ethylene), C_2H_4 $H_2C::CH_2$

54.   When two atoms in a molecule are connected by a triple bond, we are indicating that the atoms share three pairs of electrons (6 electrons) in completing their outermost shells. A simple molecule containing a triple bond is acetylene, C_2H_2 $H:C:::C:H$

55.   a. $:\ddot{O}\cdot$

      b. $\cdot\ddot{N}\cdot$

      c. $\ddot{Mg}$

      d. $:\ddot{F}\cdot$

      e. $\ddot{Al}\cdot$

      f. $\ddot{Si}\cdot$

56.   a. 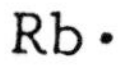 $Rb\cdot$

      b. 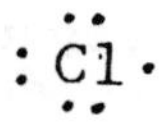 $:\ddot{Cl}\cdot$

      c. 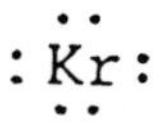 $:\ddot{Kr}:$

      d. 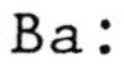 $Ba:$

      e. 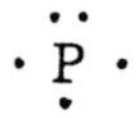 $\cdot\ddot{P}\cdot$

      f. 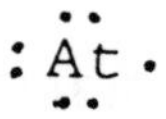 $:\ddot{At}\cdot$

57.   a.   Si provides 4; each H provides 1; total valence electrons = 8

      b.   each H provides 1; S provides 6; each O provides 6: total valence electrons = 32

      c.   C provides 4; each Cl provides 7; total valence electrons = 32

      d.   B provides 3; each F provides 7; total valence electrons = 24

58.   a.   C provides 4; each Br provides 7; total valence electrons = 32

      b.   N provides 5; each O provides 6; total valence electrons = 17

c.   each C provides 4; each H provides 1; total valence electrons = 30

d.   each O provides 6; each H provides 1; total valence electrons = 14

59. a. PH_3 P provides 5 valence electrons.
                              Each H provides 1 valence electron.
                              Total valence electrons = 8

H—P̈—H
     |
     H

b. SF_2 S provides 6 valence electrons.
                              Each F provides 7 valence electrons.
                              Total valence electrons = 20

:F̈—S̈—F̈:

c.   HBr   H provides 1 valence electron.
                              Br provides 7 valence electrons.
                              Total valence electrons = 8

H—B̈r:

d. CCl_4 C provides 4 valence electrons.
                              Each Cl provides 7 valence electrons.
                              Total valence electrons = 32

:C̈l:
          |
:C̈l—C—C̈l:
          |
      :C̈l:

60. a. NH_3 N provides 5 valence electrons.
                              Each H provides 1 valence electron.
                              Total valence electrons = 8

H — N̈ — H
         |
         H

b. CI_4 C provides 4 valence electrons.
                              Each I provides 7 valence electrons.
                              Total valence electrons = 32

:Ï:
           |
:Ï — C — Ï:
           |
       :Ï:

c.   NCl₃   N provides 5 valence electrons.
                      Each Cl provides 7 valence electrons.
                      Total valence electrons = 26.

:C̈l—N̈—C̈l:
   |
  :C̈l:

d.   SiBr₄   Si provides 4 valence electrons.
                      Each Br provides 7 valence electrons.
                      Total valence electrons = 32

:B̈r:
 |
:B̈r—Si—B̈r:
 |
:B̈r:

61.   a.   C₂H₆   Each C provides 4 valence electrons.
                      Each H provides 1 valence electron.
                      Total valence electrons = 14

b.   NF₃   N provides 5 valence electrons.
                      Each F provides 7 valence electrons.
                      Total valence electrons = 26

:F̈—N—F̈:
   |
  :F̈:

c.   C₄H₁₀   Each C provides 4 valence electrons.
                      Each H provides 1 valence electron.
                      Total valence electrons = 26

  H H H H
  | | | |
H—C—C—C—C—H
  | | | |
  H H H H

d.   SiCl₄   Si provides 4 valence electrons.
                      Each Cl provides 7 valence electrons
                      Total valence electrons = 32

:C̈l:
 |
:C̈l—Si—C̈l:
 |
:C̈l:

62. a. H_2S

Each H provides 1 valence electron.
S provides 6 valence electrons.
Total valence electrons = 8

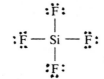

   b. SiF_4

Si provides 4 valence electrons.
Each F provides 7 valence electrons.
Total valence electrons = 32

   c. C_2H_4

Each C provides 4 valence electrons.
Each H provides 1 valence electron.
Total valence electrons = 12

$$
\begin{array}{ccc}
H & & H \\
| & & | \\
C & = & C \\
| & & | \\
H & & H
\end{array}
$$

   d. C_3H_8

Each C provides 4 valence electrons.
Each H provides 1 valence electron.
Total valence electrons = 20

$$
\begin{array}{ccccccc}
 & H & & H & & H & \\
 & | & & | & & | & \\
H- & C & - & C & - & C & -H \\
 & | & & | & & | & \\
 & H & & H & & H &
\end{array}
$$

63. a. Cl_2O

Each Cl provides 7 valence electrons.
O provides 6 valence electrons.
Total valence electrons = 20

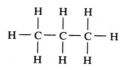

   b. CO_2

C provides 4 valence electrons.
Each O provides 6 valence electrons.
Total valence electrons = 16

$$\ddot{O}=C=\ddot{O}$$

c.   SO₃   S provides 6 valence electrons.
                   Each O provides 2 valence electrons.
                   Total valence electrons = 24

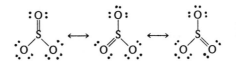

64. a.   NO₂   N provides 5 valence electrons.
                    Each O provides 6 valence electrons.
                    Total valence electrons = 17

Note that there are several Lewis structures possible because of the odd number of electrons (the unpaired electron can be located on different atoms in the Lewis structure).

b.   H₂SO₄   Each H provides 1 valence electron.
                 S provides 6 valence electrons.
                 Each O provides 6 valence electrons.
                 Total valence electrons = 32

c.   N₂O₄   Each N provides 5 valence electrons.
                Each O provides 6 valence electrons.
                Total valence electrons = 34

65. a.   SO₄²⁻   S provides 6 valence electrons.
                      Each O provides 6 valence electrons.
                      The 2- charge means two additional valence electrons.
                      Total valence electrons = 32

b. PO_4^{3-}

P provides 5 valence electrons.
Each O provides 6 valence electrons.
The 3- charge means three additional valence electrons.
Total valence electrons = 32.

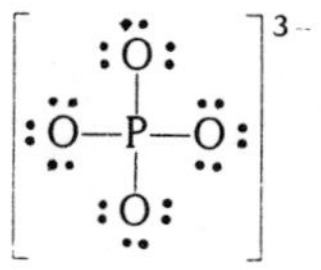

c. SO_3^{2-}

S provides 6 valence electrons.
Each O provides 6 valence electrons.
The 2- charge means two additional valence electrons.
Total valence electrons = 26

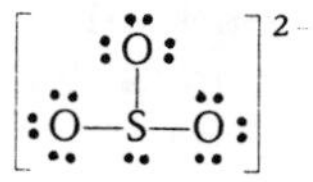

66.   a. ClO_3^-

Cl provides 7 valence electrons.
Each O provides 6 valence electrons.
The 1- charge means 1 additional electron.
Total valence electrons = 26

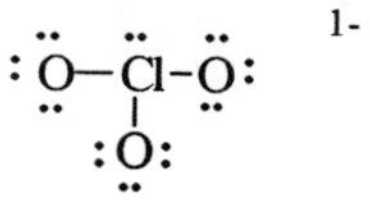

b. O_2^{2-}

Each O provides 6 valence electrons.
The 2- charge means two additional valence electrons.
Total valence electrons = 14

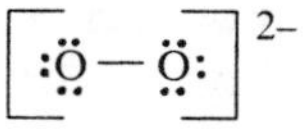

c. $C_2H_3O_2^-$

Each C provides 4 valence electrons.
Each H provides 1 valence electron.
Each O provides 6 valence electrons.
The 1- charge means 1 additional valence electron.
Total valence electrons = 24

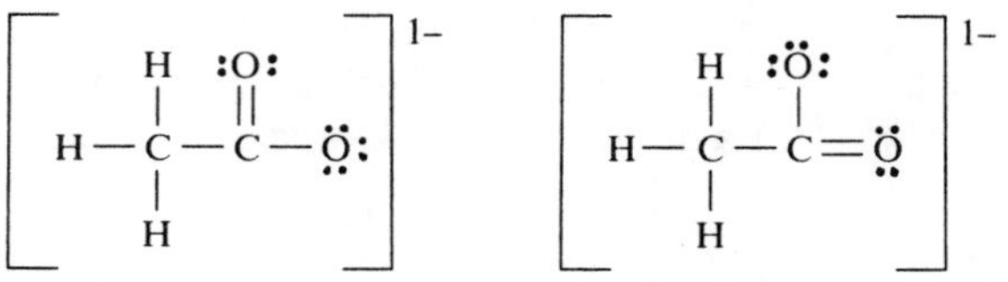

67. a. NO_2^- N provides 5 valence electrons.
                            Each O provides 6 valence electrons.
                            The 1- charge means one additional valence electron.
                            Total valence electrons = 18

$$(\ddot{O}=\ddot{N}-\ddot{\ddot{O}}:) \longleftrightarrow (:\ddot{\ddot{O}}-\ddot{N}=\ddot{O})^-$$

   b. HCO_3^- H provides 1 valence electron.
                            C provides 4 valence electrons.
                            Each O provides 6 valence electrons.
                            The 1- charge means one additional valence electron.
                            Total valence electrons = 24

$$\left(H-\ddot{O}=C\overset{:\ddot{O}:}{-}\ddot{\ddot{O}}:\right)^{2-} \longleftrightarrow \left(H-\ddot{\ddot{O}}-C\overset{:\ddot{O}:}{-}\ddot{\ddot{O}}:\right)^{2-} \longleftrightarrow \left(H-\ddot{\ddot{O}}-C\overset{:\ddot{O}:}{=}\ddot{O}\right)^{2}$$

   c. OH^- O provides 6 valence electrons.
                            H provides 1 valence electron.
                            The 1- charge means one additional valence electron.
                            Total valence electrons = 8

$$(:\ddot{\ddot{O}}-H)^-$$

68. a. HPO_4^{2-} H provides 1 valence electron.
                            P provides 5 valence electrons.
                            Each O provides 6 valence electrons
                            The 2- charge means two additional valence electrons.
                            Total valence electrons = 32

$$H-\ddot{O}-\overset{:\ddot{O}:}{\underset{:\ddot{O}:}{P}}-\ddot{O}: \quad {}^{2-}$$

   b. $H_2PO_4^-$ Each H provides 1 valence electron.
                            P provides 5 valence electrons.
                            Each O provides 6 valence electrons.
                            The 1- charge means one additional valence electron.
                            Total valence electrons = 32

$$H-\ddot{O}-\overset{:\ddot{O}:}{\underset{:\ddot{O}:}{P}}-\ddot{O}-H \quad {}^{1-}$$

c.   PO₄³⁻   P provides 5 valence electrons.
                     Each O provides 6 valence electrons.
                     The 3- charge means three additional valence electrons.
                     Total valence electrons = 32

$$\begin{array}{c} \text{:O:} \\ | \\ \text{:\ddot{O}—P—\ddot{O}:} \\ | \\ \text{:O:} \end{array} \quad 3-$$

69.   The geometric structure of the water molecule is bent (or *V*-shaped).
      There are four pairs of valence electrons on the oxygen atom of water
      (two pairs are bonding pairs, two pairs are non-bonding lone pairs). The
      H–O–H bond angle in water is approximately 106°.

70.   The geometric structure of NH₃ is that of a trigonal pyramid. The
      nitrogen atom of NH₃ is surrounded by four electron pairs (three are
      bonding, one is a lone pair). The H–N–H bond angle is somewhat less than
      109.5° (due to the presence of the lone pair).

71.   BF₃ is described as having a trigonal planar geometric structure. The
      boron atom of BF₃ is surrounded by only three pairs of valence electrons.
      The F–B–F bond angle in BF₃ is 120°.

72.   The geometric structure of CH₄ is that of a tetrahedron. The carbon atom
      of CH₄ is surrounded by four bonding electron pairs. The H–C–H bond angle
      is the characteristic angle of the tetrahedron, 109.5°.

73.   The geometric structure of a molecule plays a very important part in its
      chemistry. For biological molecules, a slight change in the geometric
      structure of the molecule can completely destroy the molecule's
      usefulness to a cell, or can cause a destructive change in the cell.

74.   The general molecular structure of a molecule is determined by *how many
      electron pairs* surround the central atom in the molecule, and by which of
      those electron pairs are used for *bonding* to the other atoms of the
      molecule. Nonbonding electron pairs on the central atom do, however,
      cause minor changes in the bond angles, compared to the ideal regular
      geometric structure.

75.   For a given atom, the positions of the other atoms bonded to the given
      atom are determined by maximizing the angular separation of the valence
      electron pairs on the given atom to mimimize the electron repulsions.

76.   You will remember from high school geometry, that two points in space are
      all that is needed to define a straight line. A diatomic molecule
      represents two points (the nuclei of the atoms) in space.

77.   One of the valence electron pairs of the ammonia molecule is a *lone* pair with no hydrogen atom attached. This lone pair is part of the nitrogen atom and does not enter the description of the molecule's overall shape (aside from influencing the H–N–H bond angles between the remaining valence electron pairs).

78.   In NF_3, the nitrogen atom has *four* pairs of valence electrons, whereas in BF_3, there are only *three* pairs of valence electrons around the boron atom. The nonbonding electron pair on nitrogen in NF_3 pushes the three F atoms out of the plane of the N atom.

79.   If you draw the Lewis structures for these molecules, you will see that each of the nitrogen atoms is surrounded by *four pairs* of electrons with a (distorted) *tetrahedral* orientation of the electron pairs.

80.   If you draw the Lewis structures for these species, you will see that each of the indicated atoms is surrounded by *four pairs* of electrons with a *tetrahedral* orientation. Although the electron pairs are arranged tetrahedrally, realize that the overall geometric shape of the molecules may *not* be tetrahedral, depending on what atoms are *bonded* to the four pairs of electrons on the central atom.

81.   a.   trigonal pyramidal (there is a lone pair on N)

       b.   nonlinear, *V*-shaped (four electron pairs on Se, but only two atoms are attached to Se)

       c.   tetrahedral (four electron pairs on Si, and four atoms attached)

82.   a.   tetrahedral (four electron pairs on C, and four atoms attached)

       b.   nonlinear, *V*-shaped (four electron pairs on S, but only two atoms attached)

       c.   tetrahedral (four electron pairs on Ge, and four atoms attached)

83.   a.   tetrahedral

       b.   tetrahedral

       c.   tetrahedral

84.   a.   basically tetrahedral around the P atom (the hydrogen atoms are attached to two of the oxygen atoms and do not affect greatly the geometrical arrangement of the oxygen atoms around the phosphorus)

       b.   tetrahedral (4 electron pairs on Cl, and 4 atoms attached)

       c.   trigonal pyramidal (4 electron pairs on S, and 3 atoms attached)

85.   a.   <109.5°

b.   <109.5°

c.   109.5°

d.   109.5°

86.   a.   approximately 109.5° (the molecule is *V*-shaped or nonlinear)

b.   approximately 109.5° (the molecule is trigonal pyramidal)

c.   109.5°

d.   approximately 120° (the double bond makes the molecule flat)

87.   The CO_3^{2-} ion is has a trigonal planar geometry, with bond angles of 120° degrees around the carbon atom. The molecule exhibits resonance.

88.   Acetylene is a linear molecule with bond angles of 180°.

89.   Resonance is said to exist when more than one valid Lewis structure can be drawn for a molecule. The actual bonding and structure of such molecules is thought to be somewhere "in between" the various possible Lewis structures. In such molecules, certain electrons are delocalized over more than one bond.

90.   double

91.   repulsion

92.   The bond with the larger electronegativity difference will be the more polar bond. See Figure 11.3 for electronegativities.

a.   S–F

b.   P–O

c.   C–H

93.   The bond with the larger electronegativity difference will be the more polar bond. See Figure 11.3 for electronegativities.

a.   Br–F

b.   As–O

c.   Pb–C

94.   The bond energy of a chemical bond is the quantity of energy required to break the bond and separate the atoms.

95.   covalent

96.   In each case, the element *higher up* within a group of the periodic table has the higher electronegativity.

   a.   Be

   b.   N

   c.   F

97.   For a bond to be polar covalent, the atoms involved in the bond must have different electronegativities (must be of different elements).

   a.   polar covalent

   b.   covalent

   c.   covalent

   d.   polar covalent

98.   For a bond to be polar covalent, the atoms involved in the bond must have different electronegativities (must be of different elements).

   a.   polar covalent (different elements)

   b.   *non*polar covalent (two atoms of the same element)

   c.   polar covalent (different elements)

   d.   *non*polar covalent (atoms of the same element)

99.   Electronegativity differences are given in parentheses.

   a.   N–P (0.9); N–O (0.5); the N–P bond is more polar.

   b.   N–C (0.5); N–O (0.5); the bonds are of the same polarity.

   c.   N–S (0.5); N–C (0.5); the bonds are of the same polarity.

   d.   N–F (1.0); N–S (0.5); the N–F bond is more polar.

100.   In a diatomic molecule containing two different elements, the more electronegative atom will be the negative end of the molecule, and the *less* electronegative atom will be the positive end.

   a.   oxygen

   b.   bromine

   c.   iodine

101.   In the figures, the arrow points toward the more electronegative atom.

   a.   N–Cl The atoms have very nearly the same electronegativity, so there is a very small, if any, dipole moment.

b. $\delta+$ P→N $\delta-$

c. $\delta+$ S→N $\delta-$

d. $\delta+$ C→N $\delta-$

102. a.   Al $1s^2\ 2s^2\ 2p^6\ 3s^2\ 3p^1$

Al^{3+} $1s^2\ 2s^2\ 2p^6$

Ne has the same configuration as Al^{3+}.

b.   Br $1s^2\ 2s^2\ 2p^6\ 3s^2\ 3p^6\ 4s^2\ 3d^{10}\ 4p^5$

Br$^-$ $1s^2\ 2s^2\ 2p^6\ 3s^2\ 3p^6\ 4s^2\ 3d^{10}\ 4p^6$

Kr has the same configuration as Br$^-$.

c.   Ca $1s^2\ 2s^2\ 2p^6\ 3s^2\ 3p^6\ 4s^2$

Ca^{2+} $1s^2\ 2s^2\ 2p^6\ 3s^2\ 3p^6$

Ar has the same configuration as Ca^{2+}.

d.   Li $1s^2\ 2s^1$

Li$^+$ $1s^2$

He has the same configuration as Li$^+$.

e.   F $1s^2\ 2s^2\ 2p^5$

F$^-$ $1s^2\ 2s^2\ 2p^6$

Ne has the same configuration as F$^-$.

103. a.   Na$^+$ e.   S^{2-}

b.   I$^-$ f.   Mg^{2+}

c.   K$^+$ g.   Al^{3+}

d.   Ca^{2+} h.   N^{3-}

104. a.   Na$_2$Se   Na has one electron more than a noble gas; Se has two electrons fewer than a noble gas.

b.   RbF   Rb has one electron more than a noble gas; F has one electron less than a noble gas.

c.   K$_2$Te   K has one electron more than a noble gas; Te has two electrons fewer than a noble gas.

d.   BaSe   Ba has two electrons more than a noble gas; Se has two electrons fewer than a noble gas.

e.   KAt   K has one electron more than a noble gas; At has one electron less than a noble gas.

f.   FrCl   Fr has one electron more than a noble gas; Cl has one electron less than a noble gas.

105.   a. Ca^{2+} [Ar]; Br^- [Kr]

b. Al^{3+} [Ne]; Se^{2-}[Kr]

c. Sr^{2+} [Kr]; O^{2-} [Ne]

d. K^+ [Ar]; S^{2-} [Ar]

106.   Relative ionic sizes are indicated in Figure 11.9.

a. Na^+

b. Al^{3+}

c. F^-

d. Na^+

107.   a.   He:

b.   :$\overset{..}{\underset{..}{Br}}$·

c.   Sr:

d.   :$\overset{..}{\underset{..}{Ne}}$:

e.   :$\overset{..}{\underset{..}{I}}$·

f.   Ra:

108.   a.   H provides 1; N provides 5; each O provides 6; total valence electrons = 24

b.   each H provides 1; S provides 6; each O provides 6; total valence electrons = 32

c.   each H provides 1; P provides 5; each O provides 6; total valence electrons = 32

d.   H provides 1; Cl provides 7; each O provides 6; total valence electrons = 32

109.   a. GeH_4 Ge provides 4 valence electrons.
                            Each H provides 1 valence electron.
                            Total valence electrons = 8

$$\begin{array}{c} H \\ | \\ H—Ge—H \\ | \\ H \end{array}$$

   b.   ICl   I provides 7 valence electrons.
                            Cl provides 7 valence electrons.
                            Total valence electrons = 14

$$:\!\ddot{I}\!—\!\ddot{C}l\!:$$

   c. NI_3 N provides 5 valence electrons.
                            Each I provides 7 valence electrons.
                            Total valence electrons = 26

$$\begin{array}{c} :\!\ddot{I}\!—\!\ddot{N}\!—\!\ddot{I}\!: \\ | \\ :\!\ddot{I}\!: \end{array}$$

   d. PF_3 P provides 5 valence electrons.
                            Each F provides 7 valence electrons.
                            Total valence electrons = 26

$$\begin{array}{c} :\!\ddot{F}\!—\!\ddot{P}\!—\!\ddot{F}\!: \\ | \\ :\!\ddot{F}\!: \end{array}$$

110.   a. N_2H_4 Each N provides 5 valence electrons.
                            Each H provides 1 valence electron.
                            Total valence electrons = 14

$$\begin{array}{c} H—\ddot{N}—\ddot{N}—H \\ | \quad | \\ H \quad H \end{array}$$

   b. C_2H_6 Each C provides 4 valence electrons.
                            Each H provides 1 valence electron.
                            Total valence electrons = 14

$$\begin{array}{c} H \quad H \\ | \quad | \\ H—C—C—H \\ | \quad | \\ H \quad H \end{array}$$

c.   NCl$_3$ N provides 5 valence electrons.
                     Each Cl provides 7 valence electrons.
                     Total valence electrons = 26

$$:\ddot{\underset{..}{Cl}}—\overset{|}{\underset{|}{\ddot{N}}}—\ddot{\underset{..}{Cl}}:$$
$$:\ddot{\underset{..}{Cl}}:$$

d.   SiCl$_4$ Si provides 4 valence electrons.
                     Each Cl provides 7 valence electrons.
                     Total valence electrons = 32

$$:\ddot{\underset{..}{Cl}}:$$
$$:\ddot{\underset{..}{Cl}}—Si—\ddot{\underset{..}{Cl}}:$$
$$:\ddot{\underset{..}{Cl}}:$$

111. a.   SO$_2$ S provides 6 valence electrons.
                     Each O provides 6 valence electrons.
                     Total valence electrons = 18

$$\ddot{\underset{..}{O}}{=}S{—}\ddot{\underset{..}{O}}: \leftrightarrow :\ddot{\underset{..}{O}}{—}S{=}\ddot{\underset{..}{O}}$$

b.   N$_2$O   Each N provides 5 valence electrons.
                     O provides 6 valence electrons.
                     Total valence electrons = 16

$$:N{\equiv}N{—}\ddot{\underset{..}{O}}:$$

c.   O$_3$ Each O provides 6 valence electrons.
                     Total valence electrons = 18

$$\ddot{\underset{..}{O}}{=}O{—}\ddot{\underset{..}{O}}: \leftrightarrow :\ddot{\underset{..}{O}}{—}O{=}\ddot{\underset{..}{O}}$$

112. a. NO_3^- N provides 5 valence electrons.
                            Each O provides 6 valence electrons.
                            The 1– charge means one additional valence electron.
                            Total valence electrons = 24

      b. CO_3^{2-} C provides 4 valence electrons.
                            Each O provides 6 valence electrons.
                            The 2– charge means two additional valence electrons.
                            Total valence electrons = 24

      c. NH_4^+ N provides 5 valence electrons.
                            Each H provides 1 valence electron.
                            The 1+ charge means one *less* valence electron.
                            Total valence electrons = 8

113. Beryllium atoms only have *two* valence electrons. In BeF_2, there are
      single bonds between the beryllium atom and each fluorine atom. The
      beryllium atom of BeF_2 thus has two electron pairs around it, which lie
      180° apart from one another. For the water molecule, in addition to the
      bonding pairs of electrons which attach the hydrogen atoms to the oxygen
      atoms, there are two nonbonding pairs of electrons which affect the H–O–H
      bond angle.

114. a.   four electron pairs arranged tetrahedrally about C

      b.   four electron pairs arranged tetrahedrally about Ge

      c.   three electron pairs arranged trigonally (planar) around B

115. a.   nonlinear (*V*-shaped, due to lone pairs on O)

      b.   nonlinear (*V*-shaped, due to lone pairs on O)

      c.   tetrahedral

116.   a. ClO_3^-, trigonal pyramid (lone pair on Cl)

       b. ClO_2^-, nonlinear (*V*-shaped, two lone pairs on Cl)

       c. ClO_4^-, tetrahedral (all pairs on Cl are bonding)

117.   a.   < 109.5° (molecule is nonlinear, *V*-shaped)

       b.   109.5° (molecule is tetrahedral)

       c.   180° (molecule is linear)

       d.   120° (molecule is trigonal planar)

118.   a.   nonlinear (V-shaped)

       b.   trigonal planar

       c.   basically trigonal planar around the C (the H is attached to one of the O atoms, and distorts the shape around the carbon only slightly)

       d.   linear

119.   a.   trigonal planar

       b.   basically trigonal planar around the N (the H is attached to one of the O atoms, and distorts the shape around the nitrogen only slightly)

       c.   nonlinear (V-shaped)

       d.   linear

120.   Ionic compounds tend to be hard, crystalline substances with relatively high melting and boiling points. Covalently bonded substances tend to be gases, liquids, or relatively soft solids, with much lower melting and boiling points.

121.   In a covalent bond between two atoms of the same element, the electron pair is shared equally and the bond is nonpolar; with a bond between atoms of different elements, the electron pair is unequally shared and the bond is polar (assuming the elements have different electronegativities).

Cumulative Review: Chapters 10 and 11

1.   Electromagnetic radiation represents the propagation of energy through space in the form of waves. Visible light, radio and television transmissions, microwaves, *x*-rays, and radiant heat are all examples of electromagnetic radiation. The waves by which electromagnetic radiation is propagated have several characteristic properties. The wavelength (λ) represents the distance between two corresponding points (peaks or troughs) on consecutive waves, and is measured in units of length (meters, centimeters, etc.). The frequency (ν) of electromagnetic radiation represents how many complete waves pass a given point in space per second and is measured in waves/sec (Hertz). A representative wave is depicted in Figure 10.1 in the text. The speed (c) or propagation velocity of electromagnetic radiation represents how fast a given wave itself moves through space, and is equal to 3×10^8 m/sec in a vacuum. For electromagnetic radiation, these three properties are related by the formula $\lambda \times \nu = c$.

2.   An atom is said to be in its ground state when it is in its lowest possible energy state. When an atom possesses more energy than in its ground state, the atom is said to be in an excited state. An atom is promoted from its ground state to an excited state by absorbing energy; when the atom returns from an excited state to its ground state it emits the excess energy as electromagnetic radiation. Atoms do not gain or emit radiation randomly, but rather do so only in discrete bundles of radiation called photons. The photons of radiation emitted by atoms are characterized by the wavelength (color) of the radiation: longer wavelength photons carry less energy than shorter wavelength photons. The energy of a photon emitted by an atom corresponds exactly to the difference in energy between two allowed energy states in an atom: thus, we can use an observable phenomenon (emission of light by excited atoms), to gain insight into the energy changes taking place within the atom.

3.   Excited atoms definitely do *not* emit their excess energy in a random or continuous manner. Rather, an excited atom of a given element emits only discrete photons of characteristic wavelength and energy when going back to its ground state. Since an excited atom of a given element always emits photons of exactly the same energy, we take this to mean that the internal structure of the atom is such that there are only certain discrete allowed energy states for the electrons in atoms, and that the wavelengths of radiation emitted by an atom correspond to the exact energy differences between these allowed energy states. For example, excited hydrogen atoms always display the visible spectrum shown in Figure 10.7 of the text: we take this spectrum as evidence for the existence of only certain discrete energy levels within the hydrogen atom, and we describe this by saying that the energy levels of hydrogen are quantized. Previously, scientists had thought that atoms emitted energy continuously.

4.   Bohr pictured the electron moving in only certain circular orbits around the nucleus. Each particular orbit (corresponding to a particular distance from the nucleus) had associated with it a particular energy (resulting from the attraction between the nucleus and the electron). When an atom absorbs energy, the electron moves from its ground state in the orbit closest to the nucleus ($n = 1$) to an orbit farther away from the nucleus ($n = 2, 3, 4, \ldots$). When an excited atom returns to its ground state, corresponding to the electron moving from an outer orbit to the orbit nearest the nucleus, the atom emits the excess energy as radiation. Since the Bohr orbits are of fixed distances from the nucleus and from each other, when an electron moves from one fixed orbit to another, the energy change is of a definite amount, which corresponds to a photon being emitted of a particular characteristic wavelength and energy. The original Bohr theory worked very well for hydrogen: Bohr even predicted emission wavelengths for hydrogen which had not yet been seen, which were subsequently found at the exact wavelengths Bohr had calculated. However, when the simple Bohr model for the atom was applied to the emission spectra of other elements, the theory could not predict or explain the observed emission spectra.

5.   De Broglie and Schrodinger took the new idea that electromagnetic radiation behaved as if it were a steam of small particles (photons), as well as a traditional wave, and basically reversed the premise. That is, if something which had previously been considered to be entirely wave-like also had a particle-like nature, then perhaps small particles also have a wave-like nature under some circumstances. The wave-mechanical theory for atomic structure developed by Schrodinger provided an exact model for the structure of the hydrogen atom which was consistent with all the observed properties of the hydrogen atom. Unlike Bohr's theory, however, which failed completely for atoms other than hydrogen, the wave-mechanical model was able to be extended to describe other atoms with considerable success. Rather than the fixed "orbits" which Bohr had postulated, the wave-mechanical model for the atom pictures the electrons of an atom as being distributed in regions of space called orbitals. The wave-mechanical model for the atom does not describe in classical terms the exact motion or trajectory of an electron as it moves around the nucleus, but rather predicts the probability of finding the electron in a particular location within the atom. The orbitals that constitute the solutions to the mathematical formulation of the wave-mechanical model for the atom represent probability contour maps for finding the electrons. When we draw a particular picture of a given orbital, we are saying that there is a 90% probability of finding the electron within the region indicated in the drawing.

6.   The lowest energy hydrogen atomic orbital is called the 1s orbital. The 1s orbital is spherical in shape (that is, the electron density around the nucleus is uniform in all directions from the nucleus). The 1s orbital represents a probability map of electron density around the nucleus for the first principal energy level. The orbital does not have a sharp edge (it appears fuzzy) since the probability of finding the electron does not drop off completely suddenly with distance from the

nucleus. The orbital does not represent just a spherical surface on which the electron moves (this would be similar to Bohr's original theory): when we draw a picture to represent the 1s orbital we are indicating that the probability of finding the electron within this region of space is greater than 90%. We know that the likelihood of finding the electron within this orbital is very high, but we still don't know exactly where in this region the electron is at a given instant in time.

7. When an atom (hydrogen, for example) absorbs energy, the electron moves to a higher energy state, which corresponds in the wave-mechanical model to a different type of orbital. The orbitals are arranged in a hierarchy of principal energy levels, as well as sub-levels of these principal levels. The principal energy levels (for hydrogen) correspond fairly well with the "orbits" of the Bohr theory, and are designated by an integer, n, called the "principal quantum number (n = 1, 2, 3, ...). In the wave-mechanical model, however, these principal energy levels are further subdivided into sets of equivalent orbitals called subshells. For example, the n = 2 principal level of hydrogen is further subdivided into an s and a p subshell (indicated as the 2s and 2p subshells, respectively). Then these subshells, in turn, consist of the individual orbitals in which the electrons reside. The 2s subshell consists of the single, spherically-shaped 2s orbital, while the 2p subshell consists of a set of three equivalent, dumbbell-shaped 2p orbitals (which are often designated as $2p_x$, $2p_y$, and $2p_z$ to indicated their orientation in space). Similarly, the n = 3 principal energy level of hydrogen is subdivided into three subshells: the 3s subshell (1 orbital), the 3p subshell (a set of three orbitals), and the 3d subshell (a set of five orbitals).

8. The third principal energy level of hydrogen is divided into three sublevels, the 3s, 3p, and 3d sublevels. The 3s subshell consists of the single 3s orbital: like the other s orbitals, the 3s orbital is spherical in shape. The 3p subshell consists of a set of three equal-energy 3p orbitals: each of these 3p orbitals has the same shape ("dumbbell"), but each of the 3p orbitals is oriented in a different direction in space. The 3d subshell consists of a set of five 3d orbitals: the 3d orbitals have the shapes indicated in Figure 10.23, and are oriented in different directions around the nucleus (students sometimes say that the 3d orbitals have the shape of a 4-leaf clover). The fourth principal energy level of hydrogen is dived into four sublevels, the 4s, 4p, 4d, and 4f orbitals. The 4s subshell consists of the single 4s orbital. The 4p subshell consists of a set of three 4p orbitals. The 4d subshell consists of a set of five 4d orbitals. The shapes of the 4s, 4p, and 4d orbitals are the same as the shapes of the orbitals of the third principal energy level (the orbitals of the fourth principal energy level are larger and further from the nucleus than the orbitals of the third level, however). The fourth principal energy level, because it is further from the nucleus, also contains a 4f subshell, consisting of seven 4f orbitals (the shapes of the 4f orbitals are beyond the scope of this text).

9.   In simple terms, in addition to moving around the nucleus of the atom, an electron also rotates (spins) on its own axis. There are only two ways a body spinning on its own axis can rotate: in pre-digital watch days, these were often described as "clockwise" and "counter-clockwise" motions, but basically this just means to the right or two the left (for example, the earth is rotating on its axis to the right). Since there are only two possible orientations for an electron's intrinsic spin, this results in a given orbital being only able to accommodate two electrons (one spinning in each direction). The Pauli exclusion principle summarizes our theory about intrinsic electron spin: a given atomic orbital can hold a maximum of two electrons, and those two electrons must have opposite spins.

10.   Atoms have a series of principal energy levels symbolized by the letter n. The $n = 1$ level is the closest to the nucleus, and the energies of the levels increase as the value of n increases going out from the nucleus. Each principal energy level is divided into a set of sublevels of different characteristic shapes (designated by the letters s, p, d, and f). Each sublevel is further subdivided into a set of orbitals: each s subshell consists of a single s orbital; each p subshell consists of a set of three p orbitals; each d subshell consists of a set of five d orbitals; etc. A given orbital can be empty or it can contain one or two electrons, but never more than two electrons (if an orbital contains two electrons, then the electrons must have opposite intrinsic spins). The shape we picture for an orbital represents only a probability map for finding electrons: the shape does not represent a trajectory or pathway for electron movements.

11.   The order in which the orbitals fill with electrons is indicated in Figure 10.28 in the text: this figure is especially useful since it also shows the specific number of orbitals of each type. Since the first principal level consists only of the $1s$ orbital, the $n = 1$ level can contain only two electrons. Since the second principal level consists of the $2s$ orbital and the set of three $2p$ orbitals, the $n = 2$ level can hold a maximum of $[2 + 3(2)] = 8$ electrons. Since any p subshell consists of three orbitals, a given p subshell can hold a maximum of six electrons. A particular p orbital (like any orbital) can hold only two electrons (of opposite spin). Since the three orbitals within a given p subshell are of exactly the same energy, and differ only in their orientation in space, when we write the electron configuration of an element like N or O which has a partially-filled p-subshell, we place the electrons in separate p-orbitals to minimize the interelectronic repulsion. Thus, the configuration of nitrogen is written sometimes as $1s^2\ 2s^2\ 2p_x^1\ 2p_y^1\ 2p_z^1$ to emphasize this.

12.   The valence electrons of an atoms are the electrons in the outermost shell of the atom. The core electrons are those in principal energy levels closer to the nucleus than the outermost shell (the core electrons are the electrons that are not valence electrons). Since the valence electrons are those in the outermost shell of the atom, it is these electrons that are affected by the presence of other atoms, and which are gained, lost, or shared with other atoms. The periodic table

is basically arranged in terms of the valence electronic configurations of the elements (elements in the same vertical group have similar configurations): for example, Group 1 is the first column in the periodic table because all the elements in Group 1 have one valence electron.

13. This general periodic table is shown in the text as Figure 10.27. You do not have to memorize the specifics of exactly where each element is found in the table, but you should notice that the table is arranged basically in terms of the electronic structure of the atoms. For example, the first horizontal row of the table corresponds to the $n = 1$ shell, which consists of only the 1s orbital, and so there are only two elements in the row. However, the second row of the table contains eight elements, since the $n = 2$ shell contains a total of four orbitals (the 2s and the three 2p orbitals).

14. The general periodic table you drew for Question 13 should be similar to that found in Figure 10.27 of the text. Just from the column and row location of an element, you should be able to determine what the valence shell of an element has for its electronic configuration. For example, the element in the third horizontal row, in the second vertical column, has $3s^2$ as its valence configuration. We know that the valence electrons are in the $n = 3$ shell because the element is in the third horizontal row. We know that the valence electrons are s electrons because the first two electrons in a horizontal row are always in an s subshell. We know that there are two electrons because the element is the second element in the horizontal row. As an additional example, the element in the seventh vertical column of the second horizontal row in the periodic table has valence configuration $2s^2 2p^5$.

15. The representative elements are the elements in Groups 1-8 of the periodic table whose valence electrons are in s and p subshells: there are two groups of representative elements at the left side of the periodic table (corresponding to the s subshells) and six groups of representative elements at the right side of the periodic table (corresponding to the p subshells). Metallic character is largest at the left-hand end of any horizontal row of the periodic table, and largest at the bottom of any vertical group. Overall, these two trends mean that the most metallic elements are at the lower left of the periodic table, and the least metallic (i.e., the nonmetals) are at the top right of the periodic table. The metalloids, which have both metallic and nonmetallic properties are found in the "stairstep" region indicated on most periodic tables.

16. The ionization energy of an atom represents the energy required to remove an electron from the atom. As one goes from top to bottom in a vertical group in the periodic table, the ionization energies decrease (it becomes easier to remove an electron). As one goes down within a group, the valence electrons are farther and farther from the nucleus and are less tightly held. The ionization energies increase when going from left to right within a horizontal row within the periodic table. The left-hand side of the periodic table is where the metallic elements

are found, which lose electrons relatively easily. The right-hand side of the periodic table is where the nonmetallic elements are found: rather than losing electrons, these elements tend to gain electrons. Within a given horizontal row in the periodic table, the valence electrons are all in the same principal energy shell: however, as you go from left to right in the horizontal row, the nuclear charge which holds onto the electrons is increasing one unit with each successive element, making it that much more difficult to remove an electron. The relative sizes of atoms also vary systematically with the location of an element in the periodic table. Within a given vertical group, the atoms get progressively larger when going from the top of the group to the bottom: the valence electrons of the atoms are in progressively higher principal energy shells (and are progressively further from the nucleus) as we go down in a group. In going from left to right within a horizontal row in the periodic table, the atoms get progressively smaller. Although all the elements in a given horizontal row in the periodic table have their valence electrons in the same principal energy shell, the nuclear charge is progressively increasing from left to right, making the given valence shell progressively smaller as the electrons are drawn more closely to the nucleus.

17.   A chemical bond is a force which holds two or more atoms together and makes them function as a unit. The strength of a chemical bond is commonly described in terms of the bond energy, which is the quantity of energy required to break the bond. The principal types of chemical bonding are ionic bonding, pure covalent bonding and polar covalent bonding.

18.   Ionic bonding results when elements of very different electro-negativities react with each other. Typically a metallic element reacts with a nonmetallic element, with the metallic element losing electrons and forming forming positive ions and the nonmetallic element gaining electrons and forming negative ions. Sodium chloride, NaCl, is an example of a typical ionic compound. The aggregate form of such a compound consists of a crystal lattice of alternating positively and negatively charged ions. A given positive ion is attracted by several surrounding negatively charged ions, and a given negative ion is attracted by several surrounding positively charged ions. Similar electrostatic attractions go on in three dimensions throughout the crystal of ionic solid, leading to a very stable system (with very high melting and boiling points, for example). We know that ionically bonded solids do not conduct electricity in the solid state (since the ions are held tightly in place by all the attractive forces), but such substances are strong electrolytes when melted or when dissolved in water (either of which process sets the ions free to move around).

19.   A bond between two atoms is, in general, covalent if the atoms share a pair of electrons in mutually completing their valence electron shells. Covalent bonds can be subclassed as to whether they are pure (nonpolar) covalent or are polar covalent. In a nonpolar covalent bond, two atoms of the same electronegativity (often this means the same type of atom) equally share a pair of electrons: the electron cloud of the bond is

symmetrically distributed along the bond axis. In a polar covalent bond, one of the atoms of the bond has a higher electronegativity than the other atom, and draws the shared pair of electrons more closely towards itself (pulling the electron cloud along the bond axis closer to the more electronegative atom). Because the more electronegative atom of a polar covalent bond ends up with a higher electron density than normal, their is a center of partial negative charge at this end of the bond. Conversely, because the less electronegative element of a polar covalent bond has one of its valence electrons pulled partly away from the atom, a center of positive charge develops at this end of the bond. A polar covalent bond, thus, represents a partial transfer of an electron from one atom to another, but with the atoms still held together as a unit. This is in contrast with an ionic bond, in which one atom completely transfers an electron to a more electronegative atom, but with the resulting positive and negative ions able to separate and behave independently of one another (e.g., in solution).

20. Electronegativity represents the relative ability of an atom in a molecule to attract shared electrons towards itself. In order for a bond to be polar, one of the atoms in the bond must attract the shared electron pair towards itself and away from the other atom of the bond: this can only happen if one atom of the bond is more electronegative than the other (that is, that there is a considerable difference in electronegativity for the two atoms of the bond). If two atoms in a bond have the same electronegativity, then the two atoms pull the electron pair equally and the bond is nonpolar covalent. If two atoms sharing a pair of electrons have vastly different electronegativities, the electron pair will be pulled so strongly by the more electronegative atom that a negative ion may be formed (as well as a positive ion for the second atom) and ionic bonding will result. If the difference in electronegativity between two atoms sharing an electron pair is somewhere in between these two extremes (equal sharing of the electron pair and formation of ions), then a polar covalent bond results.

21. A molecule is said to possess an overall dipole moment if the centers of positive and negative charge in the molecule do not coincide. A distinction must be made between whether or not individual bonds within a molecule are polar and whether the molecule overall possess a net dipole moment: sometimes the geometric shape of a molecule is such that individual bond dipoles effectively cancel each other out, leaving the molecule nonpolar overall. For example, compare the two molecules H_2O and CO_2. From Chapter 11, you realize that the water molecule is nonlinear (bent or *V*-shaped), whereas the CO_2 molecule is linear because of the double bonds. Both the O-H and the C-O bonds are themselves polar (since the atoms involved do not have the same electronegativities). However, since the CO_2 molecule is linear, the two individual bond dipoles lie in opposite directions on the same axis and cancel each other out, leaving CO_2 overall as a nonpolar molecule. In water, the two individual bond dipoles lie at an angle, and combine to increase the negative charge on the oxygen atom, leading water to be a very polar molecule. Bond dipoles are in actuality vector quantities, and the overall dipole moment of the molecule represents the resultant of all

the individual bond dipole vectors. The high polarity of the water molecule, combined with the existence of hydrogen bonding among water molecules, is responsible for the fact that water is a liquid at room temperature.

22.   It has been observed over many, many experiments that when an active metal like sodium or magnesium reacts with a nonmetal, the sodium atoms always form Na^+ ions and the magnesium atoms always form Mg^{2+} ions. It has been further observed that aluminum always forms only the Al^{3+} ion, and that when nitrogen, oxygen, or fluorine form simple ions, the ions that are formed are always N^{3-}, O^{2-}, and F^-, respectively. Clearly the facts that these elements always form the same ions and that those ions all contain eight electrons in the outermost shell, led scientists to speculate that there must be something very fundamentally stable about a species that has eight electrons in its outermost shell (like the noble gas neon). The repeated observation that so many elements, when reacting, tend to attain an electronic configuration that is isoelectronic with a noble gas led chemists to speculate that all elements try to attain such a configuration for their outermost shells. In general, when atoms of a metal react with atoms of a nonmetal, the metal atoms lose electrons until they have the configuration of the preceding noble gas, and the nonmetal atoms gain electrons until they have the configuration of the following noble gas. Covalently and polar covalently bonded molecules also strive to attain pseudo-noble gas electronic configurations. For a covalently bonded molecule like F_2, in which neither fluorine atom has a greater tendency than the other to gain or lose electrons completely, each F atom provides one electron of the pair of electrons which constitutes the covalent bond. Each F atom feels also the influence of the other F atom's electron in the shared pair, and each F atom effectively fills its outermost shell. Similarly, in polar covalently bonded molecules like HF or HCl, the shared pair of electrons between the atoms effectively completes the outer electron shell of each atom simultaneously to give each atom a noble gas-like electronic configuration.

23.   The properties of typical ionic substances (hardness, rigidity, high melting and boiling points, etc.) suggest that the ionic bond is a very strong one. The formulas we write for ionic substances are really only empirical formulas, showing the relative numbers of each type of atom present in the substance: for example, when we write $CaCl_2$ as the formula for calcium chloride, we are only saying that there are two chloride ions for each calcium ion in the substance, and not that there are distinct molecules of $CaCl_2$. Ionic substances in the bulk consist of crystals containing an extended lattice array of positive and negative ions, in a more or less alternating pattern (that is, a given positive ion typically has several negative ions as its nearest neighbors in the crystal). A typical ionic crystal lattice is shown as Figure 11.8 in the text. When an atom forms a positive ion (cation), it basically sheds it outermost electron shell (the valence electrons), leaving the resulting positive ion smaller than the atom it was formed from. When an atom forms a negative ion, the atoms takes additional electrons into its outermost shell, which causes the outermost shell to

increase in size because of the additional repulsive forces, which results in the negative ion being larger than the atom from which it was formed. In the case of ionic compounds involving polyatomic ions, more than one type of bonding force is involved. First of all, ionic bonding exists between the positive and negative ion. However, within the polyatomic ions themselves, the atoms which make up the polyatomic ion are held together by polar covalent bonds.

24. Bonding between atoms to form a molecule involves only the valence electrons of the atoms (not the inner core electrons). So when we draw the Lewis structure of a molecule, we show only these valence electrons (both bonding valence electrons and non-bonding valence electrons, however). The most important requisite for the formation of a stable compound, and which we try to demonstrate when we write Lewis structures, is that each atom of a molecule attains a noble gas electron configuration. When we write Lewis structures, we arrange the bonding and nonbonding valence electrons to try to complete the octet (or duet) for as many atoms as is possible.

25. Both the duet and octet rules are simplified statements of our basic guiding principle when discussing how atoms bond with one another to form molecules: when atoms of one element react with atoms of another element to form a compound, as many of the atoms as possible will end up with a noble gas-like electronic configuration in the compound. The "duet" rule applies only for the element hydrogen: when a hydrogen atom forms a bond to another atom, the single electron of the hydrogen atom pairs up with an electron from the other atom to give the shared electron pair that constitutes the covalent bond. By sharing this additional electron, the hydrogen atom attains effectively the $1s^2$ configuration of the noble gas helium. The "octet" rule applies for the representative elements other than hydrogen: when one of these atoms forms bonds to other atoms, the atom shares enough electrons to end up with the ns^2np^6 (i.e., eight electrons--an octet) electron configuration of a noble gas. Bonding electrons are those electrons used in forming a covalent bond between atoms: the bonding electrons in a molecule represent the electrons which are shared between atoms. Nonbonding (or lone pair) electrons are those valence electrons which are not used in covalent bonding, and which "belong" exclusively to one atom in a molecule. For example, in the molecule ammonia (NH_3), the Lewis structure shows that there are three pairs of bonding electrons (each pair constitutes a covalent bond between the nitrogen atom and one of the hydrogen atoms) as well as one nonbonding pair of electrons which belong exclusively to the nitrogen atom. The presence of nonbonding pairs of electrons on an atom in a molecule can have a big effect on the geometric shape of the molecule and on the molecule's properties.

26. Obviously, you could choose practically any molecules for your discussion. Let's illustrate the method for ammonia, NH_3. First count up the total number of valence electrons available in the molecule (without regard to what atom they officially come from); remember that for the representative elements, the number of valence electrons is indicated by what group the element is found in on the periodic table. For NH_3, since

nitrogen is in Group 5, one nitrogen atom would contribute five valence electron. Since hydrogen atoms only have one electron each, the three hydrogen atoms provide an additional three valence electrons, for a total of eight valence electrons overall. Next write down the symbols for the atoms in the molecule, and use one pair of electrons (represented by a line) to form a bond between each pair of bound atoms.

$$H-N-H$$
$$\overset{|}{H}$$

These three bonds use six of the eight valence electrons. Since each hydrogen already has its duet in what we have drawn so far, while the nitrogen atom only has six electrons around it so far, the final two valence electrons must represent a lone pair on the nitrogen.

$$H-\overset{..}{N}-H$$
$$\overset{|}{H}$$

27.   A double bond between two atoms represents the atoms sharing two pairs of electrons (4 electrons) between them. A triple bond represents two atoms sharing three pairs (6 electrons) between them. When writing a Lewis structure for a molecule, if you discover (after writing down a pair of bonding electrons between each of the atoms to be connected) that there do not seem to be enough valence electrons remaining to complete independently the octet (or duet) for each atom, then this strongly suggests that there must be multiple bonding present in the molecule. For example, if a molecule seems to be two electrons short of enough to complete independently the octet, this suggests that there must be a second bond between two of the atoms (a double bond exists between those atoms). If a molecule seems to be four electrons short, this could mean either that a triple bond exists between two of the atoms, or that there are two double bonds present in the molecule. If it is possible to draw more than one valid Lewis structure for a molecule, differing only in the location of the double bonds, we say that the molecule exhibits resonance: the existence of resonance can markedly affect the geometry of the molecule, and its resulting properties.

28.   There are several types of exceptions to the octet rule described in the text. The octet rule is really a "rule of thumb" which we apply to molecules unless we have some evidence that a molecule does not follow the rule. There are some common molecules which, from experimental measurements, we know do not follow the octet rule. Boron and beryllium compounds sometimes do not fit the octet rule. For example, in BF_3, the boron atom only has six valence electrons, whereas in BeF_2, the beryllium atom only has four valence electrons. Other molecules which are exceptions to the octet rule include any molecule with an odd number

of valence electrons (such as NO or NO_2): you can't get an octet (an even number) of electrons around each atom in a molecule with an odd number of valence electrons. Even the oxygen gas we breathe is an exception to the octet rule: although we can write a Lewis structure for O_2 satisfying the octet rule for each oxygen, we know from experiment that O_2 contains unpaired electrons (which would not be consistent with a structure in which all the electrons were paired up.)

29. The general geometric structure of a molecule is determined by *how many electron pairs* surround the central atom in the molecule, and by which of those electron pairs are used for *bonding* to the other atoms of the molecule. Nonbonding electron pairs on the central atom do, however, cause minor changes in the bond angles, compared to the ideal regular geometric structure. As examples, let's show how we would determine the geometric structure of the molecules CH_4, NH_3, and H_2O. First we would draw the Lewis structures for each of these molecules

In each of these structures, the central atom (C, N, or O) is surrounded by four pairs (an octet) of electrons. According to the VSEPR theory, the four pairs of electrons repel each other and orient themselves in space so as to be as far away from each other as possible. This leads to the electron pairs being oriented tetrahedrally, separated by angles of 109.5°. For CH_4, each of the four pairs of electrons around the C atom is a bonding pair. We therefore say that CH_4 itself has a tetrahedral geometry, with H-C-H bond angles of 109.5°. For NH_3, however, although there are four tetrahedrally arranged electron pairs around the nitrogen atom, only three of these pairs are bonding pairs: there is a lone pair on the nitrogen atom. We describe the geometry of NH_3 as a trigonal pyramid: the three hydrogen atoms lie below the nitrogen atom in space as a result of the presence of the lone pair on nitrogen. The H-N-H bond angles are slightly less than the tetrahedral angle of 109.5°. Finally, in H_2O, although we have four pairs of electrons around the oxygen atom, only two of these pairs are bonding pairs: there are two lone electron pairs on the oxygen atom. We describe the geometry of H_2O as bent, V-shaped, or nonlinear: the presence of the lone pairs makes the H-O-H bond angle not 180° (linear) but somewhat less than the tetrahedral angle of 109.5°.

30.

Number of valence pairs	bond angle	example(s)
2	180°	BeF_2, BeH_2
3	120°	BCl_3
4	109.5°	CH_4, CCl_4, GeF_4

31.   In predicting the geometric structure of a molecule, we treat a double (or triple) bond as a single entity (as if it were a single pair of electrons). This approach is reasonable, since all the electrons that bond together two particular atoms must be present in the same region of space between the atoms (whether one, two, or three electron pairs). For example, if we write the Lewis structure of acetylene, C_2H_2

H:C:::C:H

we realize that each carbon atom in the molecule has effectively only two "things" attached to it: a bonding pair of electrons (which bonds the H atom) and a triple bond (which bonds the other C atom). Since there are effectively only two things attached to each carbon atom, we would expect the bond angles for each carbon atom to be 180°, which makes the molecule linear overall.

Chapter 12   Gases

1.   The three states of matter are the solid, liquid, and gaseous states.

   solid   rigid (molecules are not free to move relative to one
                another); definite shape and volume

   liquid   nonrigid (molecules are free to move relative to one
                another, enables liquids to flow); definite volume, but
                takes on the shape of container.

   gas   nonrigid (molecules move freely); mostly empty space
                (molecules are not close to one another); volume depends on
                conditions (pressure and temperature); takes on shape of
                container.

2.   Solids and liquids have essentially fixed volumes and are not able to be
      compressed easily. Gases have volumes that depend on their conditions,
      and can be compressed or expanded by changes in those conditions.
      Although the particles of matter in solids are essentially fixed in
      position (the solid is rigid), the particles in liquids and gases are
      free to move.

3.   The "pressure of the atmosphere" represents the weight of the several-
      mile-thick layer of gases pressing down on every surface of the earth.
      Pressure, in general, represents a force exerted over a particular area,
      and the pressure of the atmosphere corresponds to a pressure of nearly
      15 pounds per square inch on the surface of the earth.

4.   Figure 12.2 in the text shows a simple mercury barometer: a tube filled
      with mercury is inverted over a reservoir containing mercury which is
      open to the atmosphere. When the tube is inverted, the mercury falls to
      a level at which the pressure of the atmosphere is sufficient to support
      the column of mercury. One standard atmosphere of pressure is taken to
      be the pressure capable of supporting a column of mercury to a height of
      760.0 mm above the reservoir level.

5.   101,325 Pa

6.   760 (defined quantity)

7.   a.
      $$657 \text{ mm Hg} \times \frac{1 \text{ atm}}{760 \text{ mm Hg}} = 0.864 \text{ atm}$$

      b.   862 torr = 862 mm Hg

      $$862 \text{ mm Hg} \times \frac{1 \text{ atm}}{760 \text{ mm Hg}} = 1.13 \text{ atm}$$

      c. $117.8 \text{ kPa} \times \frac{1 \text{ atm}}{101.325 \text{ kPa}} = 1.163 \text{ atm}$

      d. $121,500 \text{ Pa} \times \frac{1 \text{ atm}}{101,325 \text{ Pa}} = 1.199 \text{ atm}$

8. a. $105.2 \text{ kPa} \times \dfrac{1 \text{ atm}}{101.325 \text{ kPa}} = 1.038 \text{ atm}$

    b. $75.2 \text{ cm Hg} \times \dfrac{10 \text{ mm Hg}}{1 \text{ cm Hg}} \times \dfrac{1 \text{ atm}}{760 \text{ mm Hg}} = 0.989 \text{ atm}$

    c. $752 \text{ mm Hg} \times \dfrac{1 \text{ atm}}{760 \text{ mm Hg}} = 0.989 \text{ atm}$

    d. $767 \text{ torr} = 767 \text{ mm Hg}$

          $767 \text{ torr} \times \dfrac{1 \text{ atm}}{760 \text{ torr}} = 1.01 \text{ atm}$

9. a. $1.045 \text{ atm} \times \dfrac{760 \text{ mm Hg}}{1 \text{ atm}} = 794.2 \text{ mm Hg}$

    b. $103.2 \text{ kPa} \times \dfrac{760 \text{ mm Hg}}{101.325 \text{ kPa}} = 774.1 \text{ mm Hg}$

    c. $75.2 \text{ cm Hg} = 752 \text{ mm Hg}$

    d. $101,700 \text{ Pa} \times \dfrac{760 \text{ mm Hg}}{101,325 \text{ Pa}} = 762.8 \text{ mm Hg}$

10. a. $0.9975 \text{ atm} \times \dfrac{760 \text{ mm Hg}}{1 \text{ atm}} = 758.1 \text{ mm Hg}$

    b. $225,400 \text{ Pa} \times \dfrac{760 \text{ mm Hg}}{101,325 \text{ Pa}} = 1691 \text{ mm Hg}$

    c. $99.7 \text{ kPa} \times \dfrac{760 \text{ mm Hg}}{101.325 \text{ kPa}} = 748 \text{ mm Hg}$

    d. $1.078 \text{ atm} \times \dfrac{760 \text{ mm Hg}}{1 \text{ atm}} = 819.3 \text{ mm Hg}$

11. a. $774 \text{ torr} \times \dfrac{101,325 \text{ Pa}}{760 \text{ torr}} = 1.03 \times 10^5 \text{ Pa}$

    b. $0.965 \text{ atm} \times \dfrac{101,325 \text{ Pa}}{1 \text{ atm}} = 9.78 \times 10^4 \text{ Pa}$

    c. $112.5 \text{ kPa} = 1.125 \times 10^5 \text{ Pa}$

    d. $801 \text{ mm Hg} \times \dfrac{101,325 \text{ Pa}}{760 \text{ mm Hg}} = 1.07 \times 10^5 \text{ Pa}$

12. a. $2.07 \times 10^6 \text{ Pa} \times \dfrac{1 \text{ kPa}}{10^3 \text{ Pa}} = 2.07 \times 10^3 \text{ kPa}$

b. $795 \text{ mm Hg} \times \dfrac{101,325 \text{ Pa}}{760 \text{ mm Hg}} \times \dfrac{1 \text{ kPa}}{10^3 \text{ Pa}} = 106 \text{ kPa}$

c. $10.9 \text{ atm} \times \dfrac{101,325 \text{ Pa}}{1 \text{ atm}} \times \dfrac{1 \text{ kPa}}{10^3 \text{ Pa}} = 1.10 \times 10^3 \text{ kPa}$

d. $659 \text{ torr} \times \dfrac{101,325 \text{ Pa}}{760 \text{ torr}} \times \dfrac{1 \text{ kPa}}{10^3 \text{ Pa}} = 87.9 \text{ kPa}$

13.   decreased

14.   increases

15.   pressure

16. $PV = k; \qquad P_1 V_1 = P_2 V_2$

17.   a. $P_1 = 785 \text{ mm Hg}$ $\qquad\qquad\qquad\qquad$ $P_2 = 700 \text{ mm Hg}$

$\qquad$ $V_1 = 53.2 \text{ mL}$ $\qquad\qquad\qquad\qquad\quad$ $V_2 = ? \text{ mL}$

$\qquad\qquad$ $V_2 = \dfrac{P_1 V_1}{P_2} = \dfrac{(53.2 \text{ mL})(785 \text{ mm Hg})}{700 \text{ mm Hg}} = 59.7 \text{ mL}$

$\quad$ b. $P_1 = 1.67 \text{ atm}$ $\qquad\qquad\qquad\qquad\quad$ $P_2 = ? \text{ atm}$

$\qquad$ $V_1 = 2.25 \text{ L}$ $\qquad\qquad\qquad\qquad\qquad$ $V_2 = 2.00 \text{ L}$

$\qquad\qquad$ $P_2 = \dfrac{P_1 V_1}{V_2} = \dfrac{(1.67 \text{ atm})(2.25 \text{ L})}{2.00 \text{ L}} = 1.88 \text{ atm}$

$\quad$ c. $P_1 = 695 \text{ mm Hg}$ $\qquad\qquad\qquad\qquad$ $P_2 = 1.51 \text{ atm} = 1148 \text{ mm Hg}$

$\qquad$ $V_1 = 5.62 \text{ L}$ $\qquad\qquad\qquad\qquad\qquad$ $V_2 = ? \text{ L}$

$\qquad\qquad$ $V_2 = \dfrac{P_1 V_1}{P_2} = \dfrac{(695 \text{ mm Hg})(5.62 \text{ L})}{1148 \text{ mm Hg}} = 3.40 \text{ L}$

18.   a. $P_1 = 1.00 \text{ atm}$ $\qquad\qquad\qquad\qquad\qquad$ $P_2 = 699 \text{ torr} = 0.920 \text{ atm}$

$\qquad$ $V_1 = 541 \text{ mL}$ $\qquad\qquad\qquad\qquad\qquad$ $V_2 = ? \text{ mL}$

$\qquad\qquad$ $V_2 = \dfrac{P_1 V_1}{P_2} = \dfrac{(1.00 \text{ atm})(541 \text{ mL})}{(0.920 \text{ atm})} = 588 \text{ mL}$

$\quad$ b. $P_1 = 110.2 \text{ kPa}$ $\qquad\qquad\qquad\qquad$ $P_2 = 0.995 \text{ atm} = 100.8 \text{ kPa}$

$\qquad$ $V_1 = 2.32 \text{ L}$ $\qquad\qquad\qquad\qquad\qquad$ $V_2 = ? \text{ L}$

$\qquad\qquad$ $V_2 = \dfrac{P_1 V_1}{P_2} = \dfrac{(110.2 \text{ kPa})(2.32 \text{ L})}{(100.8 \text{ kPa})} = 2.54 \text{ L}$

$\quad$ c. $P_1 = 135 \text{ atm} = 1.026 \times 10^5 \text{ mm Hg}$ $\qquad$ $P_2 = ? \text{ mm Hg}$

$\qquad$ $V_1 = 4.15 \text{ mL}$ $\qquad\qquad\qquad\qquad\qquad$ $V_2 = 10.0 \text{ mL}$

$$P_2 = \frac{P_1 V_1}{V_2} = \frac{(1.026 \times 10^5 \text{ mm Hg})(4.15 \text{ mL})}{(10.0 \text{ mL})} = 4.26 \times 10^4 \text{ mm Hg}$$

19. a. $P_1 = 102.1$ kPa $P_2 = ?$ kPa

$V_1 = 19.3$ L $V_2 = 10.0$ L

$$P_2 = \frac{P_1 V_1}{V_2} = \frac{(102.1 \text{ kPa})(19.3 \text{ L})}{10.0 \text{ L}} = 197 \text{ kPa}$$

b. $P_1 = 755$ torr $= 755$ mm Hg $P_2 = 761$ mm Hg

$V_1 = 25.7$ mL $V_2 = ?$ mL

$$V_2 = \frac{P_1 V_1}{P_2} = \frac{(755 \text{ mm Hg})(25.7 \text{ mL})}{761 \text{ mm Hg}} = 25.5 \text{ mL}$$

c. $P_1 = 1.05$ atm $P_2 = 112.2$ kPa $= 1.107$ atm

$V_1 = 51.2$ L $V_2 = ?$

$$V_2 = \frac{P_1 V_1}{P_2} = \frac{(1.05 \text{ atm})(51.2 \text{ L})}{1.107 \text{ atm}} = 48.6 \text{ L}$$

20. a. $P_1 = 1.07$ atm $P_2 = 2.14$ atm

$V_1 = 291$ mL $V_2 = ?$ mL

$$V_2 = \frac{P_1 V_1}{P_2} = \frac{(1.07 \text{ atm})(291 \text{ mL})}{(2.14 \text{ atm})} = 146 \text{ mL}$$

b. $P_1 = 755$ mm Hg $P_2 = 3.51$ atm $= 2668$ mm Hg

$V_1 = 1.25$ L $V_2 = ?$ L

$$V_2 = \frac{P_1 V_1}{P_2} = \frac{(755 \text{ mm Hg})(1.25 \text{ L})}{(2668 \text{ mm Hg})} = 0.354 \text{ L}$$

c. $P_1 = 101.4$ kPa $= 760.6$ mm Hg $P_2 = ?$ mm Hg

$V_1 = 2.71$ L $V_2 = 3.00$ L

$$P_2 = \frac{P_1 V_1}{V_2} = \frac{(760.6 \text{ mm Hg})(2.71 \text{ L})}{(3.00 \text{ L})} = 687 \text{ mm Hg}$$

21. $425 \text{ mL} \times \dfrac{855 \text{ mm Hg}}{759 \text{ mm Hg}} = 479 \text{ mL}$

22.   If the pressure exerted on the gas in the balloon is decreased, the volume of the gas in the balloon will increase in inverse proportion to the factor by which the pressure was changed. The factor in this example is (1.01 atm/0.562 atm) = 1.80

23. $759 \text{ mm Hg} \times \dfrac{1.04 \text{ L}}{2.24 \text{ L}} = 352 \text{ mm Hg}$

24. $P_1 = 760$ mm $= 1.00$ atm $P_2 = ?$ atm

$V_1 = 1.00$ L $V_2 = 50.0$ mL $= 0.0500$ L

$$P_2 = \frac{P_1 V_1}{V_2} = \frac{(1.00 \text{ atm})(1.00 \text{ L})}{(0.0500 \text{ L})} = 20.0 \text{ atm}$$

25. Absolute zero is the lowest temperature than can exist. Absolute zero is the temperature at which the volume of an ideal gas sample would be predicted to become zero. Absolute zero is the zero-point on the Kelvin temperature scale (and corresponds to –273 °C).

26. Charles's law states that the volume of an ideal gas sample varies linearly with the absolute temperature of the gas sample. An experiment such as those indicated in Figures 12.7 and 12.8 can be performed to determine absolute zero. The volume of a sample of gas is measured at several convenient temperatures (e.g., between 0° and 100° C) and the data is plotted. The straight line obtained is then extrapolated to the point where the volume of the gas would become zero. The temperature at which the volume of the gas would be predicted to become zero is then absolute zero.

27. directly

28. $V = bT$; $V_1/T_1 = V_2/T_2$

29. $V_1 = 45.0$ mL $V_2 = ?$ mL

$T_1 = 26.5$ °C $= 300$ K $T_2 = 55.2$ °C $= 328$ K

$$V_2 = \frac{V_1 T_2}{T_1} = \frac{(45.0 \text{ mL})(328 \text{ K})}{300 \text{ K}} = 49.2 \text{ mL}$$

30. $V_1 = 525$ mL $V_2 = ?$ mL

$T_1 = 25$ °C $= 298$ K $T_2 = 50$ °C $= 323$ K

$$V_2 = \frac{V_1 T_2}{T_1} = \frac{(525 \text{ mL})(323 \text{ K})}{(298 \text{ K})} = 569 \text{ mL}$$

31. a. $V_1 = 1.14$ L $V_2 = ?$ L

$T_1 = 21$ °C $= 294$ K $T_2 = 42$ °C $= 315$ K

$$V_2 = \frac{V_1 T_2}{T_1} = \frac{(1.14 \text{ L})(315 \text{ K})}{(294 \text{ K})} = 1.22 \text{ L}$$

b. $V_1 = 257$ mL $V_2 = 300$ mL

$T_1 = 45$ °C $= 318$ K $T_2 = ?$ °C

$$T_2 = \frac{V_2 T_1}{V_1} = \frac{(300 \text{ mL})(318 \text{ K})}{(257 \text{ mL})} = 371 \text{ K} = 98 \text{ °C})$$

c. $V_1 = 2.78$ L $V_2 = 5.00$ L

$T_1 = -50$ °C $= 223$ K $T_2 = ?$ °C

$$T_2 = \frac{V_2 T_1}{V_1} = \frac{(5.00 \text{ L})(223 \text{ K})}{(2.78 \text{ L})} = 401 \text{ K} = 128 \text{ °C}$$

32.   a. $V_1 = 25.0$ L $V_2 = 50.0$ L

$T_1 = 0$ °C $= 273$ K $T_2 = ?$ °C

$$T_2 = \frac{V_2 T_1}{V_1} = \frac{(50.0 \text{ L})(273 \text{ K})}{(25.0 \text{ L})} = 546 \text{ K} = 273 \text{ °C}$$

b. $V_1 = 247$ mL $V_2 = 255$ mL

$T_1 = 25$ °C $= 298$ K $T_2 = ?$ °C

$$T_2 = \frac{V_2 T_1}{V_1} = \frac{(255 \text{ mL})(298 \text{ K})}{(247 \text{ mL})} = 308 \text{ K} = 35 \text{ °C}$$

c. $V_1 = 1.00$ mL $V_2 = ?$ mL

$T_1 = -272$ °C $= 1$ K $T_2 = 25$ °C $= 298$ K

$$V_2 = \frac{V_1 T_2}{T_1} = \frac{(1.00 \text{ mL})(298 \text{ K})}{(1 \text{ K})} = 298 \text{ mL}$$

33.   a. $V_1 = 25$ mL $V_2 = ?$ mL

$T_1 = 25$ °C $= 298$ K $T_2 = 0$ °C $= 273$ K

$$V_2 = \frac{V_1 T_2}{T_1} = \frac{(25 \text{ mL})(273 \text{ K})}{298 \text{ K}} = 23 \text{ mL}$$

b. $V_1 = 10.2$ L $V_2 = ?$ L

$T_1 = 100.$ °C $= 373$ K $T_2 = 100.$ K

$$V_2 = \frac{V_1 T_2}{T_1} = \frac{(10.2 \text{ L})(100 \text{ K})}{373 \text{ K}} = 2.73 \text{ L}$$

c. $V_1 = 551$ mL $V_2 = 1.00$ mL

$T_1 = 75$ °C $= 348$ K $T_2 = ?$ °C

$$T_2 = \frac{V_2 T_1}{V_1} = \frac{(1.00 \text{ mL})(348 \text{ K})}{551 \text{ mL}} = 0.632 \text{ K} = -272 \text{ °C}$$

34.   a. $V_1 = 2.01 \times 10^2$ L $V_2 = 5.00$ L

$T_1 = 1150$ °C $= 1423$ K $T_2 = ?$ °C

$$T_2 = \frac{V_2 T_1}{V_1} = \frac{(5.00 \text{ L})(1423 \text{ K})}{(2.01 \times 10^2 \text{ L})} = 35.4 \text{ K} = -238 \text{ °C}$$

b. $V_1 = 44.2$ mL $V_2 = ?$ mL

$T_1 = 298$ K $T_2 = 0$ K

$$V_2 = \frac{V_1 T_2}{T_1} = \frac{(44.2 \text{ mL})(0 \text{ K})}{(298 \text{ K})} = 0 \text{ mL} \quad (0 \text{ K is absolute zero})$$

c. $V_1 = 44.2$ mL $V_2 = ?$ mL

   $T_1 = 298$ K $T_2 = 0$ °C $= 273$ K

$$V_2 = \frac{V_1 T_2}{T_1} = \frac{(44.2 \text{ mL})(273 \text{ K})}{(298 \text{ K})} = 40.5 \text{ mL}$$

35.   24 °C = 297 K   −272 °C = 1 K

$$5.00 \text{ L} \times \frac{1 \text{ K}}{297 \text{ K}} = 0.0168 \text{ L} = 0.02 \text{ L}$$

36.   You should be able to answer these without having to set up a formal
      calculation. Charles's law says that the volume of a gas sample is
      directly proportional to its absolute temperature. So if a sample of
      neon has a volume of 266 mL at 25.2 °C (298 K), then the volume will
      become half as big at half the absolute temperature (149 K, -124 °C).
      The volume of the gas sample will become twice as big at twice the
      absolute temperature (596 K, 323°C).

37.   25°C + 273 = 298 K   54°C + 273 = 327 K

$$500. \text{ mL} \times \frac{327 \text{ K}}{298 \text{ K}} = 549 \text{ mL}$$

38.   One method of solution (using Charles's Law in the form $V_1/T_1 = V_2/T_2$) is
      shown in Example 12.6. A second method might make use of Charles's Law
      in the form $V = kT$. Using the information that the gas thermometer has a
      volume of 135 mL at 11°C (284 K), we can solve for the value of the
      proportionality constant k in the formula, and then use this information
      to calculate the additional temperatures requested.

$V = kT$

$$k = \frac{V}{T} = \frac{135 \text{ mL}}{284 \text{ K}} = 0.4754 \text{ mL/K}$$

$$T = \frac{V}{k} = \frac{V}{0.475 \text{ mL/K}} = 2.104V$$

For 113 mL, $T = 2.104(113) = 238$ K (−35°C)

For 142 mL, $T = 2.104(142) = 299$ K (26°C)

For 155 mL, $T = 2.104(155) = 326$ K (53°C)

For 127 mL, $T = 2.104(127) = 267$ K (−6°C)

39.   directly

40. $V = an;$ $V_1/n_1 = V_2/n_2$

41. V_1 = 652 mL V_2 = ? L

     n_1 = 0.214 mol n_2 = 0.375 mol

     652 mL $\times \dfrac{0.375 \text{ mol}}{0.214 \text{ mol}}$ = 1143 mL = 1.14 L

42. V_1 = 12.0 L V_2 = ? L

     n_1 = 2.01 g = 0.502 mol n_2 = 6.52 g = 1.63 mol

     $V_2 = \dfrac{V_1 n_2}{n_1} = \dfrac{(12.0 \text{ L})(1.63 \text{ mol})}{(0.502 \text{ L})}$ = 39.0 L

43. V_1 = 100. L V_2 = ? L

     n_1 = 3.25 mol n_2 = 14.15 mol

     100. L $\times \dfrac{14.15 \text{ mol}}{3.25 \text{ mol}}$ = 435 L

44. V_1 = 100. L V_2 = ? L

     n_1 = 46.2 g/32.00 g mol^{-1} n_2 = 5.00 g/32.00 g mol^{-1}

     $V_2 = \dfrac{V_1 n_2}{n_1} = \dfrac{(100. \text{ L})(5.00 \text{ g}/32.00 \text{ g mol}^{-1})}{(46.2 \text{ g}/32.00 \text{ g mol}^{-1})}$ = 10.8 L

     Note that the *molar mass* of the O_2 gas cancels out in this calculation. Since the number of moles of Ne (or any gas) present in a sample is *directly proportional* to the mass of the gas sample, the problem could also have been set up directly in terms of the masses.

45. Although the definition may seem a little strange, basically an ideal gas is one which obeys the ideal gas law, *PV = nRT*, exactly. That is, if knowledge of *three* of the properties of a gas (pressure, volume, temperature, and amount) lead to the correct value for the *fourth* property when using this equation, then the gas under study is an ideal gas.

46. Real gases most closely approach ideal gas behavior under conditions of relatively high temperatures (0°C or higher) and relatively low pressures (1 atm or lower).

47. For an ideal gas, *PV = nRT* is true under any conditions. Consider a particular sample of gas (so that *n* remains constant) at a particular fixed temperature (so that *T* remains constant also). Suppose that at pressure P_1 the volume of the gas sample is V_1. Then for this set of conditions, the ideal gas equation would be given by

$$P_1 V_1 = nRT$$

If we then change the pressure of the gas sample to a new pressure P_2, the volume of the gas sample changes to a new volume V_2. For this new set of conditions, the ideal gas equation would be given by

$$P_2V_2 = nRT$$

Since the right-hand sides of these equations are equal to the same quantity (since we defined n and T to be constant), then the left-hand sides of the equations must also be equal, and we obtain the usual form of Boyle's law.

$$P_1V_1 = P_2V_2$$

48.   For an ideal gas, $PV = nRT$ is true under any conditions. Consider a particular sample of gas (so that n remains constant) at a particular fixed pressure (so that P remains constant also). Suppose that at temperature T_1 the volume of the gas sample is V_1. Then for this set of conditions, the ideal gas equation would be given by

$$PV_1 = nRT_1$$

If we then change the temperature of the gas sample to a new temperature T_2, the volume of the gas sample changes to a new volume V_2. For this new set of conditions, the ideal gas equation would be given by

$$PV_2 = nRT_2$$

If we make a ratio of these two expressions for the ideal gas equation for this gas sample, and cancel out terms that are constant for this situation (P, n, and R) we get

$$\frac{PV_1}{PV_2} = \frac{nRT_1}{nRT_2}$$

$$\frac{V_1}{V_2} = \frac{T_1}{T_2}$$

which can be rearranged to the familiar form of Charles's law

$$\frac{V_1}{T_1} = \frac{V_2}{T_2}$$

49. a. $P = 782.4$ mm Hg $= 1.029$ atm

$T = 26.2$ °C $= 299$ K

$$V = nRT/P = \frac{(0.1021 \text{ mol})(0.08206 \text{ L atm mol}^{-1} \text{ K}^{-1})(299 \text{ K})}{(1.029 \text{ atm})} = 2.44 \text{ L}$$

b. $V = 27.5$ mL $= 0.0275$ L

$T = 16.6$°C $= 290$ K

$$P = nRT/V = \frac{(0.007812 \text{ mol})(0.08206 \text{ L atm mol}^{-1} \text{ K}^{-1})(290 \text{ K})}{(0.0275 \text{ L})} = 6.76 \text{ atm}$$

c. $V = 45.2$ mL $= 0.0452$ L

$$T = PV/nR = \frac{(1.045 \text{ atm})(0.0452 \text{ L})}{(0.002241 \text{ mol})(0.08206 \text{ L atm mol}^{-1} \text{ K}^{-1})} = 257 \text{ K}$$

50. a. $P = 782$ mm Hg $= 1.03$ atm

T = 27 °C = 300 K

$$V = \frac{nRT}{P} = \frac{(0.210 \text{ mol})(0.08206 \text{ L atm mol}^{-1} \text{ K}^{-1})(300 \text{ K})}{(1.03 \text{ atm})} = 5.02 \text{ L}$$

b. $V = 644$ mL $= 0.644$ L

$$P = \frac{nRT}{V} = \frac{(0.0921 \text{ mol})(0.08206 \text{ L atm mol}^{-1} \text{ K}^{-1})(303 \text{ K})}{(0.644 \text{ L})} = 3.56 \text{ atm}$$

$P = 3.56$ atm $= 2.70 \times 10^3$ mm Hg

c. $P = 745$ mm $= 0.980$ atm

$$T = \frac{PV}{nR} = \frac{(0.980 \text{ atm})(11.2 \text{ L})}{(0.401 \text{ mol})(0.08206 \text{ L atm mol}^{-1} \text{ K}^{-1})} = 334 \text{ K}$$

51. a. $P = 7.74 \times 10^3$ Pa $= 0.0764$ atm

$V = 12.2$ mL $= 0.0122$ L

$$n = PV/RT = \frac{(0.0764 \text{ atm})(0.0122 \text{ L})}{(0.08206 \text{ L atm mol}^{-1} \text{ K}^{-1})(298 \text{K})} = 3.81 \times 10^{-5} \text{ mol}$$

b. $V = 43.0$ mL $= 0.0430$ L

$$P = nRT/V = \frac{(0.421 \text{ mol})(0.08206 \text{ L atm mol}^{-1} \text{ K}^{-1})(223 \text{ K})}{(0.0430 \text{ L})} = 179 \text{ atm}$$

$P = 1.36 \times 10^5$ mm Hg

c. $P = 455$ mm Hg $= 0.5987$ atm

$T = 331°C + 273 = 604$ K

$$V = nRT/P = \frac{(4.4 \times 10^{-2} \text{ mol})(0.08206 \text{ L atm mol}^{-1} \text{ K}^{-1})(604 \text{ K})}{(0.5987 \text{ atm})}$$

$V = 3.6$ L $= 3.6 \times 10^3$ mL

52. a.   T = 25 °C = 298 K

$$V = \frac{(0.00831 \text{ mol})(0.08206 \text{ L atm mol}^{-1} \text{ K}^{-1})(298 \text{ K})}{(1.01 \text{ atm})} = 0.201 \text{ L}$$

b. $V = 602$ mL $= 0.602$ L

$$P = \frac{(8.01 \times 10^{-3} \text{ mol})(0.08206 \text{ L atm mol}^{-1} \text{ K}^{-1})(310 \text{ K})}{(0.602 \text{ L})} = 0.338 \text{ atm}$$

c. $V = 629 \text{ mL} = 0.629 \text{ L}$

$T = 35 \text{ °C} = 308 \text{ K}$

$$n = \frac{(0.998 \text{ atm})(0.629 \text{ L})}{(0.08206 \text{ L atm mol}^{-1} \text{ K}^{-1})(308 \text{ K})} = 2.48 \times 10^{-2} \text{ mol}$$

53.   molar mass of N_2 = 28.02 g   58.2 °C = 331 K

$$n = 4.24 \text{ g N}_2 \times \frac{1 \text{ mol N}_2}{28.02 \text{ g N}_2} = 0.151 \text{ mol N}_2$$

$$V = nRT/P = \frac{(0.151 \text{ mol})(0.08206 \text{ L atm mol}^{-1} \text{ K}^{-1})(331 \text{ K})}{(2.04 \text{ atm})} = 2.01 \text{ L}$$

54.   Molar mass of O_2 = 32.00 g

$$6.21 \text{ g O}_2 \times \frac{1 \text{ mol}}{32.00 \text{ g}} = 0.194 \text{ mol O}_2$$

$$T = \frac{PV}{nR} = \frac{(5.00 \text{ atm})(10.0 \text{ L})}{(0.194 \text{ mol})(0.08206 \text{ L atm mol}^{-1} \text{ K}^{-1})} = 3140 \text{ K}$$

55. $T = 25\text{°C} + 273 = 298 \text{ K}$

$$n = PV/RT = \frac{(255 \text{ atm})(100.0 \text{ L})}{(0.08206 \text{ L atm mol}^{-1} \text{ K}^{-1})(298 \text{ K})} = 1043 \text{ mol} = 1.04 \times 10^3 \text{ mol}$$

1.04×10^3 mol of either He or O_2 would be needed.

molar masses: He, 4.003 g; O_2, 32.00 g

$$1.04 \times 10^3 \text{ mol He} \times \frac{4.003 \text{ g He}}{1 \text{ mol He}} = 4.16 \times 10^3 \text{ g He}$$

$$1.04 \times 10^3 \text{ mol O}_2 \times \frac{32.00 \text{ g O}_2}{1 \text{ mol O}_2} = 3.33 \times 10^4 \text{ g O}_2$$

56.   The number of moles of *any* ideal gas that can be contained in the tank under the given conditions can first be calculated.

$T = 24 \text{ °C} = 297 \text{ K}$

$$n = \frac{PV}{RT} = \frac{(135 \text{ atm})(200 \text{ L})}{(0.08206 \text{ L atm mol}^{-1} \text{ K}^{-1})(297 \text{ K})} = 1.11 \times 10^3 \text{ mol gas}$$

Molar masses: He, 4.003 g; H_2, 2.016 g

for He: $1.11 \times 10^3 \text{ mol He} \times \dfrac{4.003 \text{ g}}{1 \text{ mol}} = 4.44 \times 10^3 \text{ g He} = 4.44 \text{ kg He}$

for H_2: $1.11 \times 10^3 \text{ mol H}_2 \times \dfrac{2.016 \text{ g}}{1 \text{ mol}} = 2.24 \times 10^3 \text{ g H}_2 = 2.24 \text{ kg H}_2$

57.   molar mass Ne = 20.18 g

$$n = 1.0 \text{ g Ne} \times \frac{1 \text{ mol Ne}}{20.18 \text{ g Ne}} = 0.0496 \text{ mol Ne}$$

$P = 500$ torr = 0.6579 atm

$$T = PV/nR = \frac{(0.6579 \text{ atm})(5.0 \text{ L})}{(0.0496 \text{ mol})(0.08206 \text{ L atm mol}^{-1} \text{ K}^{-1})} = 810 \text{ K}$$

58.   Molar mass of N_2 = 28.02 g

$$16.3 \text{ g N}_2 \times \frac{1 \text{ mol}}{28.02 \text{ g}} = 0.582 \text{ mol N}_2$$

$$T = \frac{PV}{nR} = \frac{(1.25 \text{ atm})(25.0 \text{ L})}{(0.582 \text{ mol})(0.08206 \text{ L atm mol}^{-1} \text{ K}^{-1})} = 654 \text{ K} = 381 \text{ °C}$$

59.   1.0 kg = 1.0×10^3 g

molar mass O_2 = 32.00 g

$$1.0 \times 10^3 \text{ g O}_2 \times \frac{1 \text{ mol O}_2}{32.00 \text{ g O}_2} = 31.3 \text{ mol O}_2$$

$$P = nRT/V = \frac{(31.3 \text{ mol})(0.08206 \text{ L atm mol}^{-1} \text{ K}^{-1})(300. \text{ K})}{(25 \text{ L})} = 31 \text{ atm}$$

60.   Molar mass of O_2 = 32.00 g

56.2 kg = 5.62×10^4 g

$$5.62 \times 10^4 \text{ g} \times \frac{1 \text{ mol}}{32.00 \text{ g}} = 1.76 \times 10^3 \text{ mol}$$

$T = 21$ °C = 294 K

$$P = \frac{nRT}{V} = \frac{(1.76 \times 10^3 \text{ mol})(0.08206 \text{ L atm mol}^{-1} \text{ K}^{-1})(294 \text{ K})}{(125 \text{ L})}$$

$P = 340$ atm

61. P_1 = 1.045 atm P_2 = 2.00 atm

V_1 = 500. mL V_2 = ?

T_1 = 25°C = 298 K T_2 = −40°C = 233 K

$$V_2 = \frac{T_2 P_1 V_1}{T_1 P_2} = \frac{(233 \text{ K})(1.045 \text{ atm})(500. \text{ mL})}{(298 \text{ K})(2.00 \text{ atm})} = 204 \text{ mL}$$

62. P_1 = 0.981 atm P_2 = 1.15 atm

V_1 = 125 mL V_2 = ? mL

T_1 = 100 °C = 373 K T_2 = 25 °C = 298 K

$$V_2 = \frac{P_1 V_1 T_2}{P_2 T_1} = \frac{(0.981 \text{ atm})(125 \text{ mL})(298 \text{ K})}{(1.15 \text{ atm})(373 \text{ K})} = 85.2 \text{ mL}$$

63. $P_1 = 1.05 \text{ atm}$ $P_2 = 0.997 \text{ atm}$

  $V_1 = 459 \text{ mL}$ $V_2 = ? \text{ mL}$

  $T_1 = 27 \text{ °C} = 300. \text{ K}$ $T_2 = 15 \text{ °C} = 288 \text{ K}$

$$V_2 = \frac{P_1 V_1 T_2}{P_2 T_1} = \frac{(1.05 \text{ atm})(459 \text{ mL})(288 \text{ K})}{(0.997 \text{ atm})(300 \text{ K})} = 464 \text{ mL}$$

64. Molar mass of H_2 = 2.016 g

$$5.00 \text{ g } H_2 \times \frac{1 \text{ mol}}{2.016 \text{ g}} = 2.48 \text{ mol } H_2$$

  $P = 761 \text{ mm} = 1.001 \text{ atm}$

$$T = \frac{PV}{nR} = \frac{(1.001 \text{ atm})(50.0 \text{ L})}{(2.48 \text{ mol})(0.08206 \text{ L atm mol}^{-1} \text{ K}^{-1})} = 246 \text{ K} = -27 \text{ °C}$$

65. In deriving the ideal gas law, we assume that the molecules of gas themselves occupy no volume, and that the molecules do not interact with each other. Under these conditions, there is no difference between gas molecules of different substances (other than their masses) as far as the bulk behavior of the gas is concerned. Each gas behaves independently of other gases present, and the overall properties of the sample are determined by the overall quantity of gas present.

  $$P_{\text{total}} = P_1 + P_2 + \ldots P_n \qquad \text{where } n \text{ is the number of individual gases present in the mixture.}$$

66. As a gas is bubbled through water, the bubbles of gas become saturated with water vapor, thus forming a gaseous mixture. The total pressure in a sample of gas which has been collected by bubbling through water is made up of two components: the pressure of the gas of interest and the pressure of water vapor. The partial pressure of the gas of interest is then the total pressure of the sample minus the vapor pressure of water.

67. molar masses: O_2, 32.00 g; He, 4.003 g   65°C + 273 = 338 K

$$4.0 \text{ g } O_2 \times \frac{1 \text{ mol } O_2}{32.0 \text{ g } O_2} = 0.125 \text{ mol } O_2$$

$$4.0 \text{ g He} \times \frac{1 \text{ mol He}}{4.003 \text{ g He}} = 0.999 \text{ mol He}$$

$$P_{\text{oxygen}} = n_{\text{oxygen}} RT/V = \frac{(0.125 \text{ mol})(0.08206 \text{ L atm mol}^{-1} \text{ K}^{-1})(338\text{K})}{(5.0 \text{ L})}$$

$$P_{\text{oxygen}} = 0.693 \text{ atm} = 0.69 \text{ atm}$$

$$P_{helium} = n_{helium}RT/V = \frac{(0.999 \text{ mol})(0.08206 \text{ L atm mol}^{-1} \text{ K}^{-1})(338K)}{(5.0 \text{ L})}$$

P_{helium} = 5.54 atm = 5.5 atm

P_{total} = 0.693 atm + 5.54 atm = 6.233 atm = 6.2 atm

68.   The volume of a sample of an ideal gas (at a given temperature and pressure) depends on the total number of moles of gas present, not on the specific identity of the gas. For a gaseous mixture as in this problem, the volume of the gas will depend on the total *combined* moles of nitrogen, oxygen, and helium.

Molar masses: N_2, 28.02 g; O_2, 32.00 g; He, 4.003 g

T = 28 °C = 301 K

$$6.91 \text{ g N}_2 \times \frac{1 \text{ mol}}{28.02 \text{ g}} = 0.2466 \text{ mol N}_2$$

$$4.71 \text{ g O}_2 \times \frac{1 \text{ mol}}{32.00 \text{ g}} = 0.1472 \text{ mol O}_2$$

$$2.95 \text{ g He} \times \frac{1 \text{ mol}}{4.003 \text{ g}} = 0.7369 \text{ mol He}$$

n_{total} = 0.2466 mol + 0.1472 mol + 0.7369 mol = 1.131 mol

$$V = \frac{nRT}{P} = \frac{(1.131 \text{ mol})(0.08206 \text{ L atm mol}^{-1} \text{ K}^{-1})(301 \text{ K})}{(1.05 \text{ atm})} = 26.6 \text{ L}$$

69.   Total moles of gas = 3.0 mol + 2.0 mol + 1.0 mol = 6.0 mol

$$P_{nitrogen} = 10.0 \text{ atm} \times \frac{3.0 \text{ mol}}{6.0 \text{ mol}} = 5.0 \text{ atm}$$

$$P_{oxygen} = 10.0 \text{ atm} \times \frac{2.0 \text{ mol}}{6.0 \text{ mol}} = 3.3 \text{ atm}$$

$$P_{carbon\ dioxide} = 10.0 \text{ atm} \times \frac{1.0 \text{ mol}}{6.0 \text{ mol}} = 1.7 \text{ atm}$$

70.   Molar masses: O_2, 32.00 g; N_2, 28.02 g

5.21 kg = 5.21 × 10³ g   4.49 kg = 4.49 × 10³ g

$$4.49 \times 10^3 \text{ g O}_2 \times \frac{1 \text{ mol}}{32.00 \text{ g}} = 140. \text{ mol O}_2$$

$$5.21 \times 10^3 \text{ g N}_2 \times \frac{1 \text{ mol}}{28.02 \text{ g}} = 186 \text{ mol N}_2$$

n_{total} = 140. mol + 186 mol = 326 mol

T = 24 °C = 297 K

$$P = \frac{nRT}{V} = \frac{(326 \text{ mol})(0.08206 \text{ L atm mol}^{-1} \text{ K}^{-1})(297 \text{ K})}{(50.0 \text{ L})} = 159 \text{ atm}$$

71. $P_{oxygen} = P_{total} - P_{water\ vapor} = 772 - 26.7 = 745$ torr

72.   The pressures must be expressed in the same units, either mm Hg or atm.

$P_{oxygen} = P_{total} - P_{water\ vapor}$

1.02 atm = 775 mm Hg

$P_{oxygen} = 775$ mm Hg $- 23.756$ mm Hg $= 751.244$ mm $= 751$ mm Hg

73. $P_{oxygen} = P_{total} - P_{water\ vapor} = 755 - 23 = 732$ mm Hg $= 0.9632$ atm

$T = 24°C + 273 = 297$ K

$V = 500.$ mL $= 0.500$ L

$$n = PV/RT = \frac{(0.9632 \text{ atm})(0.500 \text{ L})}{(0.08206 \text{ L atm mol}^{-1} \text{ K}^{-1})(297 \text{ K})} = 1.98 \times 10^{-2} \text{ mol } O_2$$

74.   1.032 atm = 784.3 mm Hg

$P_{hydrogen} = 784.3$ mm Hg $- 32$ mm Hg $= 752.3$ mm Hg $= 0.990$ atm

$V = 240$ mL $= 0.240$ L

$T = 30°C + 273 = 303$ K

$$n_{hydrogen} = P_{hydrogen}V/RT = \frac{(0.990 \text{ atm})(0.240 \text{ L})}{(0.08206 \text{ L atm mol}^{-1} \text{ K}^{-1})(303 \text{ K})} = 0.00956 \text{ mol}$$

0.00956 mol $H_2 \times \dfrac{1 \text{ mol Zn}}{1 \text{ mol } H_2} = 0.00956$ mol of Zn must have reacted

molar mass of Zn = 65.38 g

0.00956 mol Zn $\times \dfrac{65.38 \text{ g Zn}}{1 \text{ mol Zn}} = 0.625$ g Zn must have reacted

75.   A *law* is a statement that precisely expresses generally observed behavior. A *theory* consists of a set of assumptions/hypotheses that is put forth to *explain* the observed behavior of matter. Theories attempt to explain natural laws.

76.   A theory is successful if it explains known experimental observations. Theories which have been successful in the past may not be successful in the future (for example, as technology evolves, more sophisticated experiments may be possible in the future).

77.   We assume that the volume of the molecules themselves in a gas sample is negligible compared to the bulk volume of the gas sample: this helps us to explain why gases are so compressible.

78.   Chemists believe the pressure exerted by a gas sample on the walls of its container arises from collisions between the gas molecules and the walls of the container.

79.   kinetic energy

80.   no

81.   The temperature of a gas reflects, on average, how rapidly the molecules in the gas are moving. At high temperatures, the particles are moving very fast and collide with the walls of the container frequently, whereas at low temperatures, the molecules are moving more slowly and collide with the walls of the container infrequently. The Kelvin temperature is directly proportional to the average kinetic energy of the particles in a gas.

82.   If the temperature of a sample of gas is increased, the average kinetic energy of the particles of gas increases. This means that the speeds of the particles increase. If the particles have a higher speed, they will hit the walls of the container more frequently and with greater force, thereby increasing the pressure.

83.   The molar volume of a gas is the volume occupied by one mole of the gas under a particular set of temperature and pressure conditions (usually STP: 0°C, 1 atm). When measured under the same conditions, all ideal gases have the same molar volume (22.4 L at STP).

84.   Standard Temperature and Pressure, STP = 0 °C, 1 atm pressure. These conditions were chosen because they are easy to attain and reproduce *experimentally*. The barometric pressure within a laboratory is likely to be near 1 atm most days, and 0°C can be attained with a simple ice bath.

85. $CaCO_3(s) \rightarrow CO_2(g) + CaO(s)$

molar mass $CaCO_3$ = 100.1 g

$$15.2 \text{ g } CaCO_3 \times \frac{1 \text{ mol } CaCO_3}{100.1 \text{ g } CaCO_3} = 0.152 \text{ mol } CaCO_3$$

From the balanced chemical equation, if 0.152 mol $CaCO_3$ reacts, 0.152 mol of CO_2 will result.

STP: 1.00 atm, 273 K

$$V = nRT/P = \frac{(0.152 \text{ mol})(0.08206 \text{ L atm mol}^{-1} \text{ K}^{-1})(273 \text{ K})}{1.00 \text{ atm}} = 3.41 \text{ L}$$

86.   Molar mass of P_4 = 123.88 g

$$2.51 \text{ g } P_4 \times \frac{1 \text{ mol}}{123.88 \text{ g}} = 0.02026 \text{ mol } P_4$$

From the balanced chemical equation, the amount of hydrogen needed is

$$0.02026 \text{ mol } P_4 \times \frac{6 \text{ mol } H_2}{1 \text{ mol } P_4} = 0.1216 \text{ mol } H_2$$

$$T = 25 \text{ °C} = 298 \text{ K} \qquad\qquad P = 753 \text{ mm Hg} = 0.991 \text{ atm}$$

$$V = \frac{nRT}{P} = \frac{(0.1216 \text{ mol})(0.08206 \text{ L atm mol}^{-1} \text{ K}^{-1})(298 \text{ K})}{(0.991 \text{ atm})} = 3.00 \text{ L } H_2$$

87. $C_3H_8(g) + 5O_2(g) \rightarrow 3CO_2(g) + 4H_2O(g)$

25°C + 273 = 298 K

molar mass C_3H_8 = 44.09 g

$$5.53 \text{ g } C_6H_6 \times \frac{1 \text{ mol } C_3H_8}{44.09 \text{ g } C_3H_8} = 0.1254 \text{ mol } C_3H_8$$

$$0.1254 \text{ mol } C_3H_8 \times \frac{5 \text{ mol } O_2}{1 \text{ mol } C_3H_8} = 0.6270 \text{ mol } O_2$$

$$V = nRT/P = \frac{(0.6270 \text{ mol } O_2)(0.08206 \text{ L atm mol}^{-1} \text{ K}^{-1})(298 \text{ K})}{(1.04 \text{ atm})} = 14.7 \text{ L } O_2$$

88. Molar mass of Mg = 24.31 g

$$1.02 \text{ g Mg} \times \frac{1 \text{ mol}}{24.31 \text{ g}} = 0.0420 \text{ mol Mg}$$

Since the coefficients for Mg and Cl_2 in the balanced equation are the same, for 0.0420 mol of Mg reacting we will need 0.0420 mol of Cl_2

STP: 1.00 atm, 273 K

$$V = \frac{nRT}{P} = \frac{(0.0420 \text{ mol})(0.08206 \text{ L atm mol}^{-1} \text{ K}^{-1})(273 \text{ K})}{(1.00 \text{ atm})} = 0.941 \text{ L } Cl_2$$

89. 27 °C = 300 K   26 °C = 299 K

$$\text{mol } NH_3 \text{ present} = \frac{(1.02 \text{ atm})(4.21 \text{ L})}{(0.08206 \text{ L atm mol}^{-1} \text{ K}^{-1})(300 \text{ K})} = 0.174 \text{ mol } NH_3$$

$$\text{mol HCl present} = \frac{(0.998 \text{ atm})(5.35 \text{ L})}{(0.08206 \text{ L atm mol}^{-1} \text{ K}^{-1})(299 \text{ K})} = 0.218 \text{ mol HCl}$$

NH_3 and HCl react on a 1:1 basis: NH_3 is the limiting reactant.

molar mass NH_4Cl = 53.49 g

$$0.174 \text{ mol } NH_3 \times \frac{1 \text{ mol } NH_4Cl}{1 \text{ mol } NH_3} \times \frac{53.49 \text{ g } NH_4Cl}{1 \text{ mol } NH_4Cl} = 9.31 \text{ g } NH_4Cl \text{ produced}$$

90.   Molar mass of $CaCO_3$ = 100.08 g

$$4.74 \text{ g } CaCO_3 \times \frac{1 \text{ mol}}{100.08 \text{ g}} = 0.0474 \text{ mol } CaCO_3$$

Since the coefficients of $CaCO_3$ and CO_2 in the balanced chemical equation are the same, when 0.0474 mol $CaCO_3$ is heated, 0.0474 mol CO_2 results.

T = 26 °C = 299 K

$$V = \frac{nRT}{P} = \frac{(0.0474 \text{ mol})(0.08206 \text{ L atm mol}^{-1} \text{ K}^{-1})(299 \text{ K})}{(0.997 \text{ atm})} = 1.17 \text{ L } CO_2$$

91. $CuSO_4 \cdot 5H_2O(s) \rightarrow CuSO_4(s) + 5H_2O(g)$

350°C + 273 = 623 K

molar mass $CuSO_4 \cdot 5H_2O$ = 249.7 g

$$5.00 \text{ g } CuSO_4 \cdot 5H_2O \times \frac{1 \text{ mol } CuSO_4 \cdot 5H_2O}{249.7 \text{ g } CuSO_4 \cdot 5H_2O} = 0.02002 \text{ mol } CuSO_4 \cdot 5H_2O$$

$$0.02002 \text{ mol } CuSO_4 \cdot 5H_2O \times \frac{5 \text{ mol } H_2O}{1 \text{ mol } CuSO_4 \cdot 5H_2O} = 0.1001 \text{ mol } H_2O$$

$$V = nRT/P = \frac{(0.1001 \text{ mol})(0.08206 \text{ L atm mol}^{-1} \text{ K}^{-1})(623 \text{ K})}{(1.04 \text{ atm})} = 4.92 \text{ L } H_2O$$

92.   Molar mass of Mg_3N_2 = 100.95 g

$$10.3 \text{ g } Mg_3N_2 \times \frac{1 \text{ mol}}{100.95 \text{ g}} = 0.102 \text{ mol } Mg_3N_2$$

From the balanced chemical equation, the amount of NH_3 produced will be

$$0.102 \text{ mol } Mg_3N_2 \times \frac{2 \text{ mol } NH_3}{1 \text{ mol } Mg_3N_2} = 0.204 \text{ mol } NH_3$$

T = 24 °C = 297 K P = 752 mm Hg = 0.989 atm

$$V = \frac{nRT}{P} = \frac{(0.204 \text{ mol})(0.08206 \text{ L atm mol}^{-1} \text{ K}^{-1})(297 \text{ K})}{(0.989 \text{ atm})} = 5.03 \text{ L}$$

This assumes that the ammonia was collected dry.

93.   Molar masses: He, 4.003 g; H_2, 2.016 g

$$14.2 \text{ g He} \times \frac{1 \text{ mol He}}{4.003 \text{ g He}} = 3.55 \text{ mol He}$$

$$21.6 \text{ g } H_2 \times \frac{1 \text{ mol } H_2}{2.016 \text{ g } H_2} = 10.7 \text{ mol } H_2$$

total moles = 3.55 mol + 10.7 mol = 14.3 mol

28 °C = 301 K

$$V = \frac{nRT}{P} = \frac{(14.3 \text{ mol})(0.08206 \text{ L atm mol}^{-1} \text{ K}^{-1})(301 \text{ K})}{(0.985 \text{ atm})} = 359 \text{ L}$$

94.   Molar masses: O_2, 32.00 g; N_2, 28.02 g

$$26.2 \text{ g } O_2 \times \frac{1 \text{ mol}}{32.00 \text{ g}} = 0.819 \text{ mol } O_2$$

$$35.1 \text{ g } N_2 \times \frac{1 \text{ mol}}{28.02 \text{ g}} = 1.25 \text{ mol } N_2$$

$n_{total} = 0.819 \text{ mol} + 1.25 \text{ mol} = 2.07 \text{ mol}$

$T = 35 \text{ °C} = 308 \text{ K}$

$P = 755 \text{ mm Hg} = 0.993 \text{ atm}$

$$V = \frac{nRT}{P} = \frac{(2.07 \text{ mol})(0.08206 \text{ L atm mol}^{-1} \text{ K}^{-1})(308 \text{ K})}{(0.993 \text{ atm})} = 52.7 \text{ L}$$

95. $P_1 = 690 \text{ torr} = 0.9079 \text{ atm}$ $P_2 = 1.00 \text{ atm}$

$V_1 = 50. \text{ mL} = 0.050 \text{ L}$ $V_2 = ?$

$T_1 = 100\text{°C} + 273 = 373 \text{ K}$ $T_2 = 273 \text{ K}$

$$V_2 = \frac{T_2 P_1 V_1}{T_1 P_2} = \frac{(273 \text{ K})(0.9079 \text{ atm})(0.050 \text{ L})}{(373 \text{ K})(1.00 \text{ atm})} = 0.033 \text{ L} = 33 \text{ mL}$$

96. $P_1 = 1.47 \text{ atm}$ $P_2 = 1.00 \text{ atm}$ (Standard Pressure)

$V_1 = 145 \text{ mL}$ $V_2 = ? \text{ mL}$

$T_1 = 44 \text{ °C} = 317 \text{ K}$ $T_2 = 0 \text{ °C} = 273 \text{ K}$ (Standard Temperature)

$$V_2 = \frac{P_1 V_1 T_2}{P_2 T_1} = \frac{(1.47 \text{ atm})(145 \text{ mL})(273 \text{ K})}{(1.00 \text{ atm})(317 \text{ K})} = 184 \text{ mL}$$

97.   molar masses: O_2, 32.00 g; N_2, 28.02 g; CO_2, 44.01 g; Ne, 20.18 g

$$5.00 \text{ g } O_2 \times \frac{1 \text{ mol } O_2}{32.00 \text{ g } O_2} = 0.1563 \text{ mol } O_2$$

$$5.00 \text{ g } N_2 \times \frac{1 \text{ mol } N_2}{28.02 \text{ g } N_2} = 0.1784 \text{ mol } N_2$$

$$5.00 \text{ g } CO_2 \times \frac{1 \text{ mol } CO_2}{44.01 \text{ g } CO_2} = 0.1136 \text{ mol } CO_2$$

$$5.00 \text{ g Ne} \times \frac{1 \text{ mol Ne}}{20.18 \text{ g Ne}} = 0.2478 \text{ mol Ne}$$

Total moles of gas = 0.1563 + 0.1784 + 0.1136 + 0.2478 = 0.6961 mol

22.4 L is the volume occupied by one mole of any ideal gas at STP. This would apply even if the gas sample is a *mixture* of individual gases.

$$0.6961 \text{ mol} \times \frac{22.4 \text{ L}}{1 \text{ mol}} = 15.59 \text{ L} = 15.6 \text{ L}$$

The *partial pressure* of each individual gas in the mixture will be related to what *fraction* on a mole basis each gas represents in the mixture.

$$P_{oxygen} = 1.00 \text{ atm} \times \frac{0.1563 \text{ mol O}_2}{0.6961 \text{ mol total}} = 0.225 \text{ atm O}_2$$

$$P_{nitrogen} = 1.00 \text{ atm} \times \frac{0.1784 \text{ mol N}_2}{0.6961 \text{ mol total}} = 0.256 \text{ atm N}_2$$

$$P_{carbon\ dioxide} = 1.00 \text{ atm} \times \frac{0.1136 \text{ mol CO}_2}{0.6961 \text{ mol total}} = 0.163 \text{ atm CO}_2$$

$$P_{neon} = 1.00 \text{ atm} \times \frac{0.2478 \text{ mol Ne}}{0.6961 \text{ mol total}} = 0.356 \text{ atm Ne}$$

98. Molar masses: He, 4.003 g; Ne, 20.18 g

$$6.25 \text{ g He} \times \frac{1 \text{ mol}}{4.003 \text{ g}} = 1.561 \text{ mol He}$$

$$4.97 \text{ g Ne} \times \frac{1 \text{ mol}}{20.18 \text{ g}} = 0.2463 \text{ mol Ne}$$

$$n_{total} = 1.561 \text{ mol} + 0.2463 \text{ mol} = 1.807 \text{ mol}$$

Since 1 mol of an ideal gas occupies 22.4 L at STP, the volume is given by

$$1.807 \text{ mol} \times \frac{22.4 \text{ L}}{1 \text{ mol}} = 40.48 \text{ L} = 40.5 \text{ L}$$

The partial pressure of a given gas in a mixture will be proportional to what *fraction* of the total number of moles of gas the given gas represents

$$P_{He} = \frac{1.561 \text{ mol He}}{1.807 \text{ mol total}} \times 1.00 \text{ atm} = 0.8639 \text{ atm} = 0.864 \text{ atm}$$

$$P_{Ne} = \frac{0.2463 \text{ mol Ne}}{1.807 \text{ mol total}} \times 1.00 \text{ atm} = 0.1363 \text{ atm} = 0.136 \text{ atm}$$

99. $2Na(s) + Cl_2(g) \rightarrow 2NaCl(s)$

molar mass Na = 22.99 g

$$4.81 \times \frac{1 \text{ mol Na}}{22.99 \text{ g Na}} = 0.2092 \text{ mol Na}$$

$$0.2092 \text{ mol Na} \times \frac{1 \text{ mol Cl}_2}{2 \text{ mol Na}} = 0.1046 \text{ mol Cl}_2$$

$$0.1046 \text{ mol Cl}_2 \times \frac{22.4 \text{ L}}{1 \text{ mol}} = 2.34 \text{ L Cl}_2 \text{ at STP}$$

100. Molar mass of N_2 = 28.02 g

$$10.2 \text{ g N}_2 \times \frac{1 \text{ mol}}{28.02 \text{ g}} = 0.364 \text{ mol N}_2$$

$$0.364 \text{ mol N}_2 \times \frac{3 \text{ mol Cl}_2}{1 \text{ mol N}_2} = 1.09 \text{ mol Cl}_2$$

$$1.09 \text{ mol Cl}_2 \times \frac{22.4 \text{ L}}{1 \text{ mol}} = 24.5 \text{ L Cl}_2$$

101. $FeO(s) + CO(g) \rightarrow Fe(s) + CO_2(g)$

molar mass FeO = 71.85 g

$1.45 \text{ kg} = 1.45 \times 10^3 \text{ g}$

$$1.45 \times 10^3 \text{ g FeO} \times \frac{1 \text{ mol FeO}}{71.85 \text{ g FeO}} = 20.18 \text{ mol FeO}$$

Since the coefficients of the balanced equation are all *one*, if 20.18 mol FeO reacts, then 20.18 mol $CO(g)$ is required and 20.18 mol of $CO_2(g)$ is produced.

$$20.18 \text{ mol} \times \frac{22.4 \text{ L}}{1 \text{ mol}} = 452 \text{ L}$$

4.52×10^4 L $CO(g)$ is required for reaction and 4.52×10^4 L $CO_2(g)$ are produced by the reaction.

102. $2K_2MnO_4(aq) + Cl_2(g) \rightarrow 2KMnO_4(s) + 2KCl(aq)$

molar mass $KMnO_4$ = 158.0 g

$$10.0 \text{ g KMnO}_4 \times \frac{1 \text{ mol KMnO}_4}{158.0 \text{ g KMnO}_4} = 0.06329 \text{ mol KMnO}_4$$

$$0.06329 \text{ mol KMnO}_4 \times \frac{1 \text{ mol Cl}_2}{2 \text{ mol KMnO}_4} = 0.03165 \text{ mol Cl}_2$$

$$0.03165 \text{ mol Cl}_2 \times \frac{22.4 \text{ L}}{1 \text{ mol}} = 0.709 \text{ L} = 709 \text{ mL}$$

103. kelvin (absolute)

104. twice

105. Gases consist of tiny particles, which are so small that the fraction of the bulk volume of the gas occupied by the particles is negligible. The particles of a gas are in constant random motion and collide with the walls of the container (giving rise to the *pressure* of the gas). The

particles of a gas do not attract or repel each other. The average kinetic energy of the particles of a gas is reflected in the *temperature* of the gas sample.

106.   a. $PV = k;\ P_1V_1 = P_2V_2$

b. $V = bT;\ V_1/T_1 = V_2/T_2$

c. $V = an;\ V_1/n_1 = V_2/n_2$

d. $PV = nRT$

e. $P_1V_1/T_1 = P_2V_2/T_2$

107.   sum

108.   First determine what volume the helium in the tank would have if it were at a pressure of 755 mm Hg (corresponding to the pressure the gas will have in the balloons).

8.40 atm = 6384 mm Hg

$$V_2 = (25.2\ \text{L}) \times \frac{6384\ \text{mm Hg}}{755\ \text{mm Hg}} = 213\ \text{L}$$

Allowing for the fact that 25.2 L of He will have to remain in the tank, this leaves 213 – 25.2 = 187.8 L of He for filling the balloons.

$$187.8\ \text{L He} \times \frac{1\ \text{balloon}}{1.50\ \text{L He}} = 125\ \text{balloons}$$

109.   A decrease in temperature would tend to make the volume of the weather balloon *decrease*. Since the overall volume of a weather balloon *increases* when it rises to higher altitudes, the contribution to the new volume of the gas from the decrease in pressure must be more important than the decrease in temperature (the temperature change in kelvins is not as dramatic as it seems in degrees Celsius).

110.   According to the balanced chemical equation, when 1 mol of $(NH_4)_2CO_3$ reacts, a total of 4 moles of gaseous substances are produced.

molar mass $(NH_4)_2CO_3$ = 96.09 g

$$52.0\ \text{g} \times \frac{1\ \text{mol}}{96.09\ \text{g}} = 0.541\ \text{mol}$$

Since 0.541 mol of $(NH_4)_2CO_3$ reacts, 4(0.541) = 2.16 mol of gaseous products result.

453 °C = 726 K

$$V = \frac{(2.16\ \text{mol})(0.08206\ \text{L atm/mol}^{-1}\ \text{K}^{-1})(726\ \text{K})}{(1.04\ \text{atm})} = 124\ \text{L}$$

111. $CaCO_3(s) \rightarrow CaO(s) + CO_2(g)$

774 torr = 1.018 atm

55°C + 273 = 328 K

molar mass $CaCO_3$ = 100.1 g

$10.0 \text{ g } CaCO_3 \times \dfrac{1 \text{ mol } CaCO_3}{100.1 \text{ g } CaCO_3} = 0.09990 \text{ mol } CaCO_3$

From the balanced equation, 0.09990 mol CO_2 will be produced

$V = nRT/P = \dfrac{(0.09990 \text{ mol})(0.08206 \text{ L atm mol}^{-1} \text{ K}^{-1})(328 \text{ K})}{(1.018 \text{ atm})} = 2.64 \text{ L } CO_2$

112. $CaCO_3(s) + 2H^+(aq) \rightarrow Ca^{2+}(aq) + H_2O(l) + CO_2(g)$

molar mass $CaCO_3$ = 100.1 g

$10.0 \text{ g } CaCO_3 \times \dfrac{1 \text{ mol } CaCO_3}{100.1 \text{ g } CaCO_3} = 0.0999 \text{ mol } CaCO_3 = 0.0999 \text{ mol } CO_2 \text{ also}$

60°C + 273 = 333 K

$P_{\text{carbon dioxide}} = P_{\text{total}} - P_{\text{water vapor}}$

$P_{\text{carbon dioxide}} = 774 \text{ mm Hg} - 149.4 \text{ mm Hg} = 624.6 \text{ mm Hg} = 0.822 \text{ atm}$

$V_{\text{wet}} = \dfrac{(0.0999 \text{ mol})(0.08206 \text{ L atm mol}^{-1} \text{ K}^{-1})(333 \text{ K})}{(0.822 \text{ atm})} = 3.32 \text{ L wet } CO_2$

$V_{\text{dry}} = 3.32 \text{ L} \times \dfrac{624.6 \text{ mm Hg}}{774 \text{ mm Hg}} = 2.68 \text{ L}$

113. $2S(s) + 3O_2(g) \rightarrow 2SO_3(g)$

350.°C + 273 = 623 K

molar mass S = 32.07 g

$5.00 \text{ g} \times \dfrac{1 \text{ mol S}}{32.07 \text{ g S}} = 0.1559 \text{ mol S}$

$0.1559 \text{ mol S} \times \dfrac{3 \text{ mol } O_2}{2 \text{ mol S}} = 0.2339 \text{ mol } O_2$

$V = nRT/P = \dfrac{(0.2339 \text{ mol})(0.08206 \text{ L atm mol}^{-1} \text{ K}^{-1})(623 \text{ K})}{(5.25 \text{ atm})} = 2.28 \text{ L } O_2$

114. $2KClO_3(s) \rightarrow 2KCl(s) + 3O_2(g)$

molar mass $KClO_3$ = 122.6 g

$50.0 \text{ g } KClO_3 \times \dfrac{1 \text{ mol } KClO_3}{122.6 \text{ g } KClO_3} = 0.408 \text{ mol } KClO_3$

$$0.408 \text{ mol KClO}_3 \times \frac{3 \text{ mol O}_2}{2 \text{ mol KClO}_3} = 0.612 \text{ mol O}_2$$

$$25°C + 273 = 298 \text{ K} \qquad\qquad 630. \text{ torr} = 0.829 \text{ atm}$$

$$V = nRT/P = \frac{(0.612 \text{ mol})(0.08206 \text{ L atm mol}^{-1} \text{ K}^{-1})(298 \text{ K})}{(0.829 \text{ atm})} = 18.1 \text{ L O}_2$$

115.   molar mass He = 4.003 g

$$10.0 \text{ g He} \times \frac{1 \text{ mol He}}{4.003 \text{ g He}} = 2.498 \text{ mol He}$$

$$2.498 \text{ mol} \times \frac{22.4 \text{ L}}{1 \text{ mol}} = 56.0 \text{ L He}$$

116.   a. $752 \text{ mm Hg} \times \dfrac{101,325 \text{ Pa}}{760 \text{ mm Hg}} = 1.00 \times 10^5 \text{ Pa}$

       b. $458 \text{ kPa} \times \dfrac{1 \text{ atm}}{101.325 \text{ kPa}} = 4.52 \text{ atm}$

       c. $1.43 \text{ atm} \times \dfrac{760 \text{ mm Hg}}{1 \text{ atm}} = 1.09 \times 10^3 \text{ mm Hg}$

       d.   842 = 842 mm Hg

117.   a. $0.903 \text{ atm} \times \dfrac{760 \text{ mm Hg}}{1 \text{ atm}} = 686 \text{ mm Hg}$

       b. $2.1240 \times 10^6 \text{ Pa} \times \dfrac{1 \text{ atm}}{101,325 \text{ Pa}} \times \dfrac{760 \text{ mm Hg}}{1 \text{ atm}} = 1.5931 \times 10^4 \text{ mm Hg}$

       c. $445 \text{ kPa} = 445 \times 10^3 \text{ Pa}$

             $445 \times 10^3 \text{ Pa} \times \dfrac{1 \text{ atm}}{101,325 \text{ Pa}} \times \dfrac{760 \text{ mm Hg}}{1 \text{ atm}} = 3.34 \times 10^3 \text{ mm Hg}$

       d.   342 torr = 342 mm Hg

118.   a. $645 \text{ mm Hg} \times \dfrac{1 \text{ atm}}{760 \text{ mm Hg}} \times \dfrac{101,325 \text{ Pa}}{1 \text{ atm}} = 8.60 \times 10^4 \text{ Pa}$

       b. $221 \text{ kPa} = 221 \times 10^3 \text{ Pa} = 2.21 \times 10^5 \text{ Pa}$

       c. $0.876 \text{ atm} \times \dfrac{101,325 \text{ Pa}}{1 \text{ atm}} = 8.88 \times 10^4 \text{ Pa}$

       d. $32 \text{ torr} \times \dfrac{1 \text{ atm}}{760 \text{ torr}} \times \dfrac{101,325 \text{ Pa}}{1 \text{ atm}} = 4.3 \times 10^3 \text{ Pa}$

119. a.   1002 mm Hg = 1.318 atm

$$V = 123 \text{ L} \times \frac{4.56 \text{ atm}}{1.318 \text{ atm}} = 426 \text{ L}$$

   b.   25.2 mm Hg = 0.0332 atm

$$P = 0.0332 \text{ atm} \times \frac{634 \text{ mL}}{166 \text{ mL}} = 0.127 \text{ atm}$$

   c.   511 torr = 6.81×10^4 Pa = 68.1 kPa

$$V = 443 \text{ L} \times \frac{68.1 \text{ kPa}}{1.05 \text{ kPa}} = 2.87 \times 10^4 \text{ L}$$

120. a.   1.00 mm Hg = 1.00 torr

$$V = 255 \text{ mL} \times \frac{1.00 \text{ torr}}{2.00 \text{ torr}} = 128 \text{ mL}$$

   b.   1.0 atm = 101.325 kPa

$$V = 1.3 \text{ L} \times \frac{1.0 \text{ kPa}}{101.325 \text{ kPa}} = 1.3 \times 10^{-2} \text{ L}$$

   c.   1.0 mm Hg = 0.133 kPa

$$V = 1.3 \text{ L} \times \frac{1.0 \text{ kPa}}{0.133 \text{ kPa}} = 9.8 \text{ L}$$

121.   Assume the pressure at sea level to be 1 atm (760 mm Hg). Calculate the volume the balloon would have if it rose to the point where the pressure has dropped to 500 mm Hg. If this calculated volume is greater than the balloon's specified maximum volume (2.5 L) the balloon will burst.

$$2.0 \text{ L} \times \frac{760 \text{ mm Hg}}{500 \text{ mm Hg}} = 3.0 \text{ L} > 2.5 \text{ L}. \text{ The balloon will burst.}$$

122.   1.52 L = 1.52×10^3 mL

$$755 \text{ mm Hg} \times \frac{1.52 \times 10^3 \text{ mL}}{450 \text{ mL}} = 2.55 \times 10^3 \text{ mm Hg}$$

123.   22°C + 273 = 295 K   100°C + 273 = 373 K

$$729 \text{ mL} \times \frac{373 \text{ K}}{295 \text{ K}} = 922 \text{ mL}$$

124. a.   74°C + 273 = 347 K   −74°C + 273 = 199 K

$$100. \text{ mL} \times \frac{199 \text{ K}}{347 \text{ K}} = 57.3 \text{ mL}$$

b.   100°C + 273 = 373 K

$$373 \text{ K} \times \frac{600 \text{ mL}}{500 \text{ mL}} = 448 \text{ K } (175°C)$$

c.   zero (the volume of any gas sample becomes zero at 0 K)

125.   a.   0°C + 273 = 273 K

$$273 \text{ K} \times \frac{44.4 \text{ L}}{22.4 \text{ L}} = 541 \text{ K } (268°C)$$

b.   –272°C + 273 = 1 K   25°C + 273 = 298 K

$$1.0 \times 10^{-3} \text{ mL} \times \frac{298 \text{ K}}{1 \text{ K}} = 0.30 \text{ mL}$$

c.   –40°C + 273 = 233 K

$$233 \text{ K} \times \frac{1000 \text{ L}}{32.3 \text{ L}} = 7.21 \times 10^3 \text{ K } (6940°C)$$

126.   12 °C + 273 = 285 K   192 °C + 273 = 465 K

$$75.2 \text{ mL} \times \frac{465 \text{ K}}{285 \text{ K}} = 123 \text{ mL}$$

127.   5.12 g O_2 = 0.160 mol   25.0 g O_2 = 0.781 mol

$$6.21 \text{ L} \times \frac{0.781 \text{ mol}}{0.160 \text{ mol}} = 30.3 \text{ L}$$

128.   For a given gas, the number of moles present in a sample is directly proportional to the mass of the sample. So the problem can be solved even though the gas is not identified (so that its molar mass is not known).

$$23.2 \text{ g} \times \frac{10.4 \text{ L}}{93.2 \text{ L}} = 2.59 \text{ g}$$

129.   a. V = 142 mL = 0.142 L

$$T = PV/nR = \frac{(21.2 \text{ atm})(0.142 \text{ L})}{(0.432 \text{ mol})(0.08206 \text{ L atm mol}^{-1} \text{ K}^{-1})} = 84.9 \text{ K}$$

b. V = 1.23 mL = 0.00123 L

$$P = nRT/V = \frac{(0.000115 \text{ mol})(0.08206 \text{ L atm mol}^{-1} \text{ K}^{-1})(293 \text{ K})}{(0.00123 \text{ L})}$$

P = 2.25 atm

c. P = 755 mm Hg = 0.993 atm

T = 131°C + 273 = 404 K

$$V = nRT/P = \frac{(0.473 \text{ mol})(0.08206 \text{ L atm mol}^{-1} \text{ K}^{-1})(404 \text{ K})}{(0.993 \text{ atm})} = 15.8 \text{ L}$$

$$15.8 \text{ L} = 1.58 \times 10^4 \text{ mL}$$

130. a. $V = 21.2 \text{ mL} = 0.0212 \text{ L}$

$$T = PV/nR = \frac{(1.034 \text{ atm})(0.0212 \text{ L})}{(0.00432 \text{ mol})(0.08206 \text{ L atm mol}^{-1} \text{ K}^{-1})} = 61.8 \text{ K}$$

b. $V = 1.73 \text{ mL} = 0.00173 \text{ L}$

$$P = nRT/V = \frac{(0.000115 \text{ mol})(0.08206 \text{ L atm mol}^{-1} \text{ K}^{-1})(182 \text{ K})}{(0.00173 \text{ L})}$$

$$P = 0.993 \text{ atm}$$

c. $P = 1.23 \text{ mm Hg} = 0.00162 \text{ atm}$

$T = 152°\text{C} + 273 = 425 \text{ K}$

$$V = nRT/P = \frac{(0.773 \text{ mol})(0.08206 \text{ L atm mol}^{-1} \text{ K}^{-1})(425 \text{ K})}{(0.00162 \text{ atm})}$$

$$V = 1.66 \times 10^4 \text{ L}$$

131. molar mass N_2 = 28.02 g

$$n = 14.2 \text{ g } N_2 \times \frac{1 \text{ mol}}{28.02 \text{ g } N_2} = 0.507 \text{ mol } N_2$$

$T = 26 °\text{C} + 273 = 299 \text{ K}$

$$P = nRT/V = \frac{(0.507 \text{ mol})(0.08206 \text{ L atm mol}^{-1} \text{ K}^{-1})(299 \text{ K})}{(10.0 \text{ L})} = 1.24 \text{ atm}$$

132. $27°\text{C} + 273 = 300 \text{ K}$

The number of moles of gas it takes to fill the 100. L tanks to 120 atm at 27°C is independent of the identity of the gas.

$$n = PV/RT = \frac{(120 \text{ atm})(100. \text{ L})}{(0.08206 \text{ L atm mol}^{-1} \text{ K}^{-1})(300 \text{ K})} = 487 \text{ mol}$$

487 mol of *any* gas will fill the tanks to the required specifications.

molar masses: CH_4, 16.0 g; N_2, 28.0 g; CO_2, 44.0 g

for CH_4: (487 mol)(16.0 g/mol) = 7792 g = 7.79 kg CH_4

for N_2: (487 mol)(28.0 g/mol) = 13,636 g = 13.6 kg N_2

for CO_2: (487 mol)(44.0 g/mol) = 21,428 g = 21.4 kg CO_2

133. molar mass He = 4.003 g

$$n = 4.00 \text{ g He} \times \frac{1 \text{ mol}}{4.003 \text{ g He}} = 0.999 \text{ mol}$$

$$T = PV/nR = \frac{(1.00 \text{ atm})(22.4 \text{ L})}{(0.999 \text{ mol})(0.08206 \text{ L atm mol}^{-1} \text{ K}^{-1})} = 273 \text{ K } (0°C)$$

134. molar mass of O_2 = 32.00 g

55 mg = 0.055 g

$$n = 0.055 \text{ g} \times \frac{1 \text{ mol}}{32.00 \text{ g}} = 0.0017 \text{ mol}$$

V = 100. mL = 0.100 L

T = 26°C + 273 = 299 K

$$P = nRT/V = \frac{(0.0017 \text{ mol})(0.08206 \text{ L atm mol}^{-1} \text{ K}^{-1})(299 \text{ K})}{(0.100 \text{ L})} = 0.42 \text{ atm}$$

135. P_1 = 1.0 atm P_2 = 220 torr = 0.289 atm

V_1 = 1.0 L V_2 = ?

T_1 = 23°C + 273 = 296 K T_2 = –31°C = 242 K

$$V_2 = \frac{T_2 P_1 V_1}{T_1 P_2} = \frac{(242 \text{ K})(1.0 \text{ atm})(1.0 \text{ L})}{(296 \text{ K})(0.289 \text{ atm})} = 2.8 \text{ L}$$

136. P_1 = 1.13 atm P_2 = 1.89 atm

V_1 = 100 mL = 0.100 L V_2 = 500 mL = 0.500 L

T_1 = 300 K T_2 = ?

$$T_2 = \frac{T_1 P_2 V_2}{P_1 V_1} = \frac{(300 \text{ K})(1.89 \text{ atm})(0.500 \text{ L})}{(1.13 \text{ atm})(0.100 \text{ L})} = 2.51 \times 10^3 \text{ K}$$

Note that the calculation could have been carried through with the two volumes expressed in milliliters since the universal gas constant does not appear explicitly in this form of the ideal gas equation.

137. molar mass of O_2 = 32.00 g

$$50. \text{ g } O_2 \times \frac{1 \text{ mol } O_2}{32.00 \text{ g } O_2} = 1.56 \text{ mol } O_2$$

total number of moles of gas = 1.0 mol N_2 + 1.56 mol O_2 = 2.56 mol

25°C + 273 = 298 K

$$P = nRT/V = \frac{(2.56 \text{ mol})(0.08206 \text{ L atm mol}^{-1} \text{ K}^{-1})(298 \text{ K})}{(5.0 \text{ L})} = 13 \text{ atm}$$

138. molar masses: N_2, 28.0 g; He, 4.003 g

$$12.1 \text{ g N}_2 \times \frac{1 \text{ mol N}_2}{28.0 \text{ g N}_2} = 0.432 \text{ mol N}_2$$

$$4.05 \text{ g He} \times \frac{1 \text{ mol He}}{4.003 \text{ g He}} = 1.01 \text{ mol He}$$

Total moles of gas = 0.432 mol + 1.01 mol = 1.44 mol

STP: 1.00 atm, 273 K

$$V = nRT/P = \frac{(1.44 \text{ mol})(0.08206 \text{ L atm mol}^{-1} \text{ K}^{-1})(273 \text{ K})}{(1.00 \text{ atm})} = 32.3 \text{ L}$$

139. The pressures must be expressed in the same units, either mm Hg or atm.

$$P_{\text{hydrogen}} = P_{\text{total}} - P_{\text{water vapor}}$$

1.023 atm = 777.5 mm Hg

$$P_{\text{hydrogen}} = 777.5 \text{ mm Hg} - 42.2 \text{ mm Hg} = 735.3 \text{ mm Hg}$$

42.2 mm Hg = 0.056 atm

$$P_{\text{hydrogen}} = 1.023 \text{ atm} - 0.056 \text{ atm} = 0.967 \text{ atm}$$

140. molar mass of NH_3 = 17.03 g

$$5.00 \text{ g NH}_3 \times \frac{1 \text{ mol NH}_3}{17.03 \text{ g NH}_3} = 0.294 \text{ mol NH}_3 \text{ to be produced}$$

$$N_2(g) + 3H_2(g) \rightarrow 2NH_3(g)$$

$$0.294 \text{ mol NH}_3 \times \frac{1 \text{ mol N}_2}{2 \text{ mol NH}_3} = 0.147 \text{ mol N}_2 \text{ required}$$

$$0.294 \text{ mol NH}_3 \times \frac{3 \text{ mol H}_2}{2 \text{ mol NH}_3} = 0.441 \text{ mol H}_2 \text{ required}$$

11°C + 273 = 284 K

$$V_{\text{nitrogen}} = \frac{(0.147 \text{ mol})(0.08206 \text{ L atm mol}^{-1} \text{ K}^{-1})(284 \text{ K})}{(0.998 \text{ atm})} = 3.43 \text{ L N}_2$$

$$V_{\text{hydrogen}} = \frac{(0.441 \text{ mol})(0.08206 \text{ L atm mol}^{-1} \text{ K}^{-1})(284 \text{ K})}{(0.998 \text{ atm})} = 10.3 \text{ L H}_2$$

141. $C_6H_{12}O_6(s) + 6O_2(g) \rightarrow 6CO_2(g) + 6H_2O(g)$

molar mass of $C_6H_{12}O_6$ = 180. g

$$5.00 \text{ g C}_6\text{H}_{12}\text{O}_6 \times \frac{1 \text{ mol C}_6\text{H}_{12}\text{O}_6}{180. \text{ g C}_6\text{H}_{12}\text{O}_6} = 0.02778 \text{ mol C}_6\text{H}_{12}\text{O}_6$$

$$0.02778 \text{ mol } C_6H_{12}O_6 \times \frac{6 \text{ mol } O_2}{1 \text{ mol } C_6H_{12}O_6} = 0.1667 \text{ mol } O_2$$

$$28°C + 273 = 301 \text{ K}$$

$$V_{\text{oxygen}} = \frac{(0.1667 \text{ mol})(0.08206 \text{ L atm mol}^{-1} \text{ K}^{-1})(301 \text{ K})}{(0.976 \text{ atm})} = 4.22 \text{ L}$$

Because the coefficients of $CO_2(g)$ and $H_2O(g)$ in the balanced chemical equation happen to be the same as the coefficient of $O_2(g)$, the calculations for the volumes of these gases produced are identical: 4.21 L of each gaseous product is produced.

142. $2Cu_2S(s) + 3O_2(g) \rightarrow 2Cu_2O(s) + 2SO_2(g)$

molar mass Cu_2S = 159.2 g

$$25 \text{ g } Cu_2S \times \frac{1 \text{ mol } Cu_2S}{159.2 \text{ g } Cu_2S} = 0.1570 \text{ mol } Cu_2S$$

$$0.1570 \text{ mol } Cu_2S \times \frac{3 \text{ mol } O_2}{2 \text{ mol } Cu_2S} = 0.2355 \text{ mol } O_2$$

$$27.5°C + 273 = 301 \text{ K}$$

$$V_{\text{oxygen}} = \frac{(0.2355 \text{ mol})(0.08206 \text{ L atm mol}^{-1} \text{ K}^{-1})(301 \text{ K})}{(0.998 \text{ atm})} = 5.8 \text{ L } O_2$$

$$0.1570 \text{ mol } Cu_2S \times \frac{2 \text{ mol } SO_2}{2 \text{ mol } Cu_2S} = 0.1570 \text{ mol } SO_2$$

$$V_{\text{sulfur dioxide}} = \frac{(0.1570 \text{ mol})(0.08206 \text{ L atm mol}^{-1} \text{ K}^{-1})(301 \text{ K})}{(0.998 \text{ atm})}$$

$$V_{\text{sulfur dioxide}} = 3.9 \text{ L } SO_2$$

143. $2NaHCO_3(s) \rightarrow Na_2CO_3(s) + H_2O(g) + CO_2(g)$

molar mass $NaHCO_3$ = 84.01 g

$$1.00 \text{ g } NaHCO_3 \times \frac{1 \text{ mol } NaHCO_3}{84.01 \text{ g } NaHCO_3} = 0.01190 \text{ mol } NaHCO_3$$

$$0.01190 \text{ mol } NaHCO_3 \times \frac{1 \text{ mol } H_2O}{2 \text{ mol } NaHCO_3} = 0.00595 \text{ mol } H_2O$$

Because $H_2O(g)$ and $CO_2(g)$ have the same coefficients in the balanced chemical equation for the reaction, if 0.00595 mol H_2O is produced, then 0.00595 mol CO_2 must also be produced. The total number of moles of gaseous substances produced is thus 0.00595 + 0.00595 = 0.0119 mol.

$$29°C + 273 = 302 \text{ K}$$

$$769 \text{ torr} = 1.012 \text{ atm}$$

$$V_{total} = \frac{(0.0119 \text{ mol})(0.08206 \text{ L atm mol}^{-1} \text{ K}^{-1})(302 \text{ K})}{(1.012 \text{ atm})} = 0.291 \text{ L}$$

144. One mole of any ideal gas occupies 22.4 L at STP.

$$35 \text{ mol N}_2 \times \frac{22.4 \text{ L}}{1 \text{ mol}} = 7.8 \times 10^2 \text{ L}$$

145. $P_1 = 0.987$ atm $P_2 = 1.00$ atm

   $V_1 = 125$ L $V_2 = ?$

   $T_1 = 25°C + 273 = 298$ K $T_2 = 273$ K

$$V_2 = \frac{T_2 P_1 V_1}{T_1 P_2} = \frac{(273 \text{ K})(0.987 \text{ atm})(125 \text{ L})}{(298 \text{ K})(1.00 \text{ atm})} = 113 \text{ L}$$

146. molar masses: He, 4.003 g; Ar, 39.95 g; Ne, 20.18 g

$$5.0 \text{ g He} \times \frac{1 \text{ mol He}}{4.003 \text{ g He}} = 1.249 \text{ mol He}$$

$$1.0 \text{ g Ar} \times \frac{1 \text{ mol Ar}}{39.95 \text{ g Ar}} = 0.02503 \text{ mol Ar}$$

$$3.5 \text{ g Ne} \times \frac{1 \text{ mol Ne}}{20.18 \text{ g Ne}} = 0.1734 \text{ mol Ne}$$

Total moles of gas = 1.249 + 0.02503 + 0.1734 = 1.447 mol

22.4 L is the volume occupied by one mole of any ideal gas at STP. This would apply even if the gas sample is a *mixture* of individual gases.

$$1.447 \text{ mol} \times \frac{22.4 \text{ L}}{1 \text{ mol}} = 32 \text{ L total volume for the mixture}$$

The *partial pressure* of each individual gas in the mixture will be related to what *fraction* on a mole basis each gas represents in the mixture.

$$P_{He} = 1.00 \text{ atm} \times \frac{1.249 \text{ mol He}}{1.447 \text{ mol total}} = 0.86 \text{ atm}$$

$$P_{Ar} = 1.00 \text{ atm} \times \frac{0.02503 \text{ mol Ar}}{1.447 \text{ mol total}} = 0.017 \text{ atm}$$

$$P_{Ne} = 1.00 \text{ atm} \times \frac{0.1734 \text{ mol Ne}}{1.447 \text{ mol total}} = 0.12 \text{ atm}$$

147. $CaCO_3(s) \rightarrow CaO(s) + CO_2(g)$

   molar mass of $CaCO_3 = 100.1$ g

$$27.5 \text{ g CaCO}_3 \times \frac{1 \text{ mol CaCO}_3}{100.1 \text{ g CaCO}_3} = 0.275 \text{ mol CaCO}_3$$

From the balanced chemical equation, if 0.275 mol of $CaCO_3$ reacts, then 0.275 mol of $CaCO_3$ will be produced.

$$0.275 \text{ mol } H_2 \times \frac{22.4 \text{ L}}{1 \text{ mol}} = 6.16 \text{ L}$$

148. The solution is only 50% H_2O_2. Therefore 125 g solution = 62.5 g H_2O_2

Molar mass of H_2O_2 = 34.02 g

$$62.5 \text{ g } H_2O_2 \times \frac{1 \text{ mol}}{34.02 \text{ g}} = 1.84 \text{ mol } H_2O_2$$

$$1.84 \text{ mol } H_2O_2 \times \frac{1 \text{ mol } O_2}{2 \text{ mol } H_2O_2} = 0.920 \text{ mol } O_2$$

$T = 27 \text{ °C} = 300 \text{ K}$ $\qquad\qquad$ $P = 764 \text{ mm Hg} = 1.01 \text{ atm}$

$$V = nRT/P = \frac{(0.920)(0.08206 \text{ L atm mol}^{-1} \text{ K}^{-1})(300 \text{ K})}{(1.01 \text{ atm})} = 22.4 \text{ L}$$

Chapter 13   Liquids and Solids

1. Pure water is a colorless, tasteless substance that freezes to form a solid at 0 °C and boils at 100 °C. Water has a relatively large specific heat capacity and is able to absorb massive amounts of energy from the sun, preventing rapid or unusually large changes in temperature in the environment.

2. Water exerts its cooling effect in nature in many ways. Water, as perspiration, helps cool the human body (the evaporation of water from skin is an endothermic process; the heat required for evaporation comes from the body). Large bodies of natural water (e.g., the oceans) have a cooling effect on nearby land masses (the interior of the United States, away from the oceans, tends to be hotter than coastal regions). In industry, water is used as a coolant in *many* situations Some nuclear power plants, for example, use water to cool the reactor core. Many office buildings are air-conditioned in summer by circulating cold water systems.

3. Ice floats because it is less dense than liquid water. Generally, the solid form of an element is *more* dense than the liquid form. Water is an exception to this.

4. The fact that water expands when it freezes often results in broken water pipes during cold weather. The expansion of water when it freezes also makes ice float on liquid water. The expansion of a given mass of water into a larger volume upon freezing lowers the density of ice compared to liquid water. Aquatic life (and probably all life) could not exist if ice sank in water.

5. From room temperature to 100 °C, adding heat to water raises the temperature of the water (as the molecules of water convert the applied heat to kinetic energy, they begin to move faster and faster). At 100°C, the boiling point, water molecules possess enough kinetic energy to escape readily from the liquid's surface (the temperature remains at 100°C until all the liquid water has been converted to steam). If heated above 100°C, steam molecules absorb additional kinetic energy and the temperature of the steam increases.

6. Sloped portions of a heating/cooling curve represent *changes in temperature* as heat is applied or removed; for example, in the cooling/heating curve shown, there are sloped portions representing the heating of ice, the heating of liquid water, and the heating of steam, as heat continues to be applied. Flat portions of such curves represent equilibrium transitions between states; for example, the flat portions in the curve shown represent the solid-liquid (melting-freezing) transition and the liquid-vapor (boiling-condensation) phase transitions.

7. In a solid well below its melting point, the constituent particles are virtually locked in place in a regular lattice array (they can only vibrate somewhat about their mean positions). As heat energy is added to such a solid, the vibrational motions of the particles increase (the heat energy is converted to greater kinetic energies for the particles). Eventually the particles are vibrating so strongly that they are able to

move apart from one another and begin to move in the more random manner of the particles in a liquid.

8. As a liquid is heated, the motions of the molecules increase as the temperature rises. As the liquid reaches its boiling point, bubbles of vapor begin to form in the liquid, which rise to the surface of the liquid and burst. As the liquid remains at its boiling point, the additional heat energy being supplied to the liquid is used to overcome attractive forces among the molecules in the liquid. As heat energy continues to be applied, more and more molecules will be moving in the right direction and with sufficient energy to escape from the liquid.

9. *Intra*molecular forces are the forces *within* a molecule itself (e.g., a covalent bond is an intramolecular force). *Inter*molecular forces are forces between or among *different* molecules. Consider liquid bromine, Br_2. *Intra*molecular forces (a covalent bond) are responsible for the fact that bromine atoms form discrete two-atom units (molecules) within the substance. *Inter*molecular forces between adjacent Br_2 molecules are responsible for the fact that the substance is a liquid at room temperature and pressure.

10. To melt a solid, or to vaporize a liquid, the molecules of the substance must be moved apart: thus, it is the *inter*molecular forces that must be overcome.

11. In ice, water molecules are in more or less regular, fixed positions in the ice crystal; strong hydrogen bonding forces exist within the ice crystal holding the water molecules together. In liquid water, enough heat has been applied that the molecules are no longer fixed in position (but are more free to roam about in the bulk of the liquid); since the water molecules are still relatively close together, strong hydrogen bonding forces still exist, however, which keep the liquid together in one place. In steam, the water molecules possess enough kinetic energy that they have escaped from the liquid; because the water molecules are very far apart in steam, and because the molecules are moving very quickly, they do not exert any forces on each other (each water molecule in steam behaves independently).

12. It takes more heat to vaporize a liquid than to melt the same amount of solid because of the greater degree to which the intermolecular forces must be overcome.

13.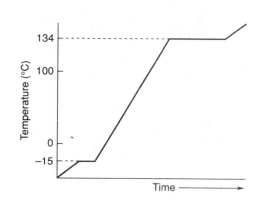

14. $10.0 \text{ g X} \times \dfrac{1 \text{ mol X}}{52 \text{ g X}} = 0.192 \text{ mol X}$

$0.192 \text{ mol} \times \dfrac{2.5 \text{ kJ}}{1 \text{ mol}} = 0.48 \text{ kJ}$

$25.0 \text{ g X} \times \dfrac{1 \text{ mol X}}{52 \text{ g X}} = 0.481 \text{ mol X}$

$0.481 \text{ mol} \times \dfrac{55.3 \text{ kJ}}{1 \text{ mol}} = 27 \text{ kJ}$

15.   molar mass $CHCl_3$ = 119.4 g

melt: $11.5 \text{ g } CHCl_3 \times \dfrac{1 \text{ mol } CHCl_3}{119.4 \text{ g } CHCl_3} \times \dfrac{8.80 \text{ kJ}}{1 \text{ mol } CHCl_3} = 0.848 \text{ kJ} = 848 \text{ J}$

boil: $11.5 \text{ g } CHCl_3 \times \dfrac{1 \text{ mol } CHCl_3}{119.4 \text{ g } CHCl_3} \times \dfrac{31.4 \text{ kJ}}{1 \text{ mol } CHCl_3} = 3.02 \text{ kJ} = 3,020 \text{ J}$

16.   molar mass H_2O = 18.02 g

$25.0 \text{ g } H_2O \times \dfrac{1 \text{ mol } H_2O}{18.02 \text{ g } H_2O} = 1.39 \text{ mol}$

To melt the ice: $1.39 \text{ mol} \times \dfrac{6.02 \text{ kJ}}{1 \text{ mol}} = 8.37 \text{ kJ}$

$37.5 \text{ g } H_2O \times \dfrac{1 \text{ mol } H_2O}{18.02 \text{ g } H_2O} = 2.08 \text{ mol}$

To vaporize the liquid: $2.08 \text{ mol} \times \dfrac{40.6 \text{ kJ}}{1 \text{ mol}} = 84.4 \text{ kJ}$

To heat the liquid: $55.2 \text{ g} \times 4.18 \dfrac{\text{J}}{\text{g °C}} \times 100°C = 23,073 \text{ J} = 23.1 \text{ kJ}$

17. $10.0 \text{ g } H_2O = 0.555 \text{ mol } H_2O$

for steam going from 200° to 100°C:

$Q = 10.0 \text{ g steam} \times \dfrac{2.03 \text{ J}}{\text{g °C}} \times 100°C = 2030 \text{ J} = 2.03 \text{ kJ released}$

to condense the steam: $0.555 \text{ mol steam} \times \dfrac{40.6 \text{ kJ}}{1 \text{ mol}} = 22.5 \text{ kJ}$

for liquid water going from 100° to 0°C:

$10.0 \text{ g } H_2O \times \dfrac{4.184 \text{ J}}{\text{g °C}} \times 100°C = 4184 \text{ J} = 4.184 \text{ kJ}$

to freeze the liquid water: $0.555 \text{ mol } H_2O \times \dfrac{6.02 \text{ kJ}}{1 \text{ mol}} = 3.34 \text{ kJ}$

for ice going from $0°$ to $-50°C$:

$10.0 \text{ g} \times \dfrac{2.06 \text{ J}}{\text{g °C}} \times 50°C = 1030 \text{ J} = 1.03 \text{ kJ}$

Total heat released = $2.03 + 22.5 + 4.184 + 3.34 + 1.03 = 33.1 \text{ kJ}$

18. The *molar* heat of fusion of aluminum is the heat required to melt 1 mol.

$\dfrac{3.95 \text{ kJ}}{1 \text{ g}} \times \dfrac{26.98 \text{ g}}{1 \text{ mol}} = 107 \text{ kJ/mol}$

$10.0 \text{ g} \times \dfrac{3.95 \text{ kJ}}{1 \text{ g}} = 39.5 \text{ kJ required to melt } 10.0 \text{ g Al}$

$10.0 \text{ mol} \times \dfrac{107 \text{ kJ}}{1 \text{ mol}} = 1.07 \times 10^3 \text{ kJ required to melt } 10.0 \text{ mol Al.}$

19. Dipole-dipole interactions occur when molecules possessing dipole moments orient themselves so that the positive and negative ends of adjacent molecules attract each other. *Any* three polar liquids will possess dipole-dipole forces among their molecules [e.g., $CH_3Cl(l)$, $SO_2(l)$, $NO_2(l)$].

20. Dipole-dipole forces are relatively stronger at short distances; they are short-range forces. Molecules must first closely approach one another before dipole-dipole forces can cause attraction between molecules.

21. Hydrogen bonding is a special case of dipole-dipole forces that can come into play in molecules in which hydrogen atoms are directly bonded to highly electronegative atoms (such as nitrogen, oxygen, or fluorine). Such bonds are extremely polar, and because the hydrogen atom is so tiny, the dipoles of different molecules are able to approach each other much more closely. Since dipole-dipole forces are strongly distance-dependent, this makes hydrogen bonding especially strong. Three substances which would be expected to show hydrogen bonding in the liquid state are water, ammonia, and ethyl alcohol (CH_3CH_2-OH).

22. Water molecules are able to form strong *hydrogen bonds* with each other. These bonds are an especially strong form of dipole-dipole forces and are only possible when hydrogen atoms are bonded to the most electronegative elements (N, O, and F). The extra strong intermolecular forces in H_2O require much higher temperatures (high energies) to be overcome in order to permit the liquid to boil. We take the fact that water has a much higher boiling point than the other hydrogen compounds of the Group 6 elements as proof that a special force is at play in water (hydrogen bonding).

23. The magnitude of a dipole-dipole interactions is very strongly dependent on the distance between the dipoles. In the solid and liquid states, the molecular dipoles are quite close together. In the vapor phase (gaseous state), however, the molecules are too far apart from one another for dipole-dipole forces to be very strong.

24. The fact that such nonpolar, monatomic atoms *can* be liquefied and solidified indicates that there must be *some* sort of intermolecular forces possible between atoms in these substances. London dispersion forces arise when a temporary (instantaneous) dipolar arrangement of charge develops as the electrons of an atom move around its nucleus. This instantaneous dipole can induce a similar dipole in a neighboring atom, leading to a momentary attraction.

25. a.   dipole-dipole forces (polar molecules); London dispersion forces

    b.   dipole-dipole forces (polar molecules); London dispersion forces

    c.   London dispersion forces (nonpolar molecules)

    d.   London dispersion forces (nonpolar molecules)

26. a.   London dispersion forces (nonpolar, atoms)

    b.   London dispersion forces (nonpolar molecules)

    c.   dipole-dipole forces; London dispersion forces

    d.   hydrogen bonding (H attached to O); London dispersion forces

27. The boiling points increase with an increase in the molar mass of the noble gas. As the noble gas atoms increase in size, the valence electrons are farther from the nucleus. At greater distance from the nucleus, it is easy for another atom's electrons to momentarily distort the electron cloud of the noble gas atom. As the size of the noble gas atoms increases, so does the magnitude of the London dispersion forces.

28. An increase in the heat of fusion is observed for an increase in the size of the halogen atom involved (the electron cloud of a larger atom is more easily polarized by an approaching dipole, thus giving larger London dispersion forces).

29. Both water and ammonia molecules are capable of hydrogen bonding (H attached to O, and H attached to N, respectively). When ammonia gas is first bubbled into a sample of water, the ammonia molecules begin to hydrogen bond to the water molecules and to draw the water molecules closer together than they would ordinarily be because of the increased intermolecular forces.

30. For a homogeneous mixture to be able to form at all, the forces between molecules of the two substances being mixed must be at least *comparable in magnitude* to the intermolecular forces within each *separate* substance. Apparently in the case of a water-ethanol mixture, the forces that exist when water and ethanol are mixed are stronger than

water-water or ethanol-ethanol forces in the separate substances. This allows ethanol and water molecules to approach each other more closely in the mixture than either substance's molecules could approach a like molecule in the separate substances. There is strong hydrogen bonding in both ethanol and water.

31.   Evaporation represents molecules of a liquid entering the vapor phase, whereas condensation is the reverse of this process. In order to evaporate, molecules must gain sufficient kinetic energy to escape from the liquid. Evaporation therefore requires an external input of energy, whereas condensation releases energy.

32.   Vapor pressure is the pressure of vapor present *at equilibrium* above a liquid in a sealed container at a particular temperature. When a liquid is placed in a closed container, molecules of the liquid evaporate freely into the empty space above the liquid. As the number of molecules present in the vapor state increases with time, vapor molecules begin to rejoin the liquid state (condense). Eventually a dynamic equilibrium is reached between evaporation and condensation in which the net number of molecules present in the vapor phase becomes *constant* with time.

33.   A dynamic equilibrium is the situation in which two opposite processes are going on at the same speed, so that there is no *net* change in the system. When a liquid evaporates into the empty space above it, eventually, as more molecules accumulate in the vapor state, condensation will be occurring at the same rate as further evaporation. When evaporation and condensation are going on at the same rate, a fixed pressure of vapor will have developed, and there will be no further net change in the amount of liquid present.

34.   A method is shown in Figure 13.10. The apparatus consists of basically a barometer into which a volatile liquid may be injected. Since mercury is so much more dense than other liquids, the injected volatile liquid rises to the top of the mercury column in the tube and floats on top of the mercury. Since the space above the mercury is a vacuum, the volatile liquid evaporates into the empty space. As the liquid is converted to the gaseous state, the level of the mercury column drops as the pressure of vapor builds up.

35.   a. H_2S Hydrogen bonding will occur in H_2O, preventing it from evaporating as readily. In H_2S, only the relatively weak dipole-dipole forces can exist.

      b. CH_3OH Both substances are capable of hydrogen bonding, but in H_2O there are two locations where such interactions are possible (making the hydrogen bonding in H_2O stronger than in CH_3OH).

      c. CH_3OH Although both molecules are capable of hydrogen bonding, generally a lighter molecule is more volatile than a heavier molecule.

36. a. HF   Although both substances are capable of hydrogen
                     bonding, water has two O–H bonds which can be involved
                     in hydrogen bonding versus only one F–H bond in HF.

     b. CH_3OCH_3 Since there is no H attached to the O atom, no
                     hydrogen bonding can exist. Since there is no hydrogen
                     bonding possible, the molecule should be relatively
                     more volatile than CH_3CH_2OH even though it contains
                     the same number of atoms of each element.

     c. CH_3SH Hydrogen bonding is not as important for a S–H bond
                     (because S has a lower electronegativity than O).
                     Since there is little hydrogen bonding, the molecule
                     is relatively more volatile than CH_3OH.

37. Hydrogen bonding can occur in *both* molecules. Oxygen atoms are more
     electronegative than nitrogen atoms, however, and the polarity of the
     O–H bond is considerably greater than the polarity of the N–H bond. This
     leads to *stronger* hydrogen bonding in liquid water than in liquid NH_3.

38. Both substances have the same molar mass. However ethyl alcohol contains
     a hydrogen atom directly bonded to an oxygen atom. Therefore, hydrogen
     bonding can exist in ethyl alcohol, whereas only weak dipole-dipole
     forces can exist in dimethyl ether. Dimethyl ether is more volatile;
     ethyl alcohol has a higher boiling point.

39. A crystalline solid is a solid with a regular, repeating microscopic
     arrangement of its components (ions, atoms, or molecules). This
     highly-ordered microscopic arrangement of the components of a
     crystalline solid is frequently reflected macroscopically in beautiful,
     regularly shaped crystals for such solids.

40. *Ionic* solids have as their fundamental particles positive and negative
     ions; a simple example is sodium chloride, in which Na^+ and Cl^- ions are
     held together by strong electrostatic forces.

     Molecular solids have molecules as their fundamental particles, with the
     molecules being held together in the crystal by dipole-dipole forces,
     hydrogen bonding forces, or London dispersion forces (depending on the
     identity of the substance); simple examples of molecular solids include
     ice (H_2O) and ordinary table sugar (sucrose).

     Atomic solids have simple atoms as their fundamental particles, with the
     atoms being held together in the crystal either by covalent bonding (as
     in graphite or diamond) or by metallic bonding (as in copper or other
     metals).

41. The fundamental particles in ionic solids are positive and negative
     ions. For example, the ionic solid sodium chloride consists of an
     alternating, regular array of Na^+ and Cl^- ions. Similarly, an ionic
     solid such as $CaBr_2$ consists of a regular array of Ca^{2+} ions and Br^-
     ions. In ionic crystals, each positive ion is surrounded by and

attracted to a group of negative ions, and each negative ion is surrounded by and attracted to a group of positive ions. The fundamental particles in molecular solids are discrete molecules. Although the atoms in each molecule are held together by strong intramolecular forces (covalent bonds), the intermolecular forces in a molecular solid are not nearly as strong as in an ionic solid, which leads to molecular solids typically having relatively low melting points. Two examples of molecular solids are the common sugars glucose, $C_6H_{12}O_6$, and sucrose, $C_{12}H_{22}O_{11}$.

42.   The interparticle forces in ionic solids (the ionic bond) are much stronger than the interparticle forces in molecular solids (dipole-dipole forces, London forces, etc.). The difference in intermolecular forces is most clearly shown in the great differences in melting points and boiling points between ionic and molecular solids. For example, table salt and ordinary sugar are both crystalline solids that appear very similar. Yet sugar can be melted easily in a saucepan during the making of candy, whereas even the full heat of a stove will not melt salt.

43.   Ionic solids are held together by very strong electrostatic forces between the positive and negative ions. The forces are so strong that it become very difficult to move or displace ions from one another when an outside force is applied to the solid, and so the solid is perceived as being "hard". Molecular solids are held together by much weaker dipole-dipole forces. When an outside force seeking to deform or displace the solid is applied, these weaker forces are much more easy to overcome. The overall magnitude of an electrostatic force is related (in part) to the magnitude of the charges involved. In ionic compounds the charges are "full" ionic charges and the forces are strong; in molecular solids the charges are "partial" and the forces are weaker.

44.   Ionic solids consist of a crystal lattice of basically alternating positively and negatively charged ions. A given ion is surrounded by several ions of the opposite charge, all of which electrostatically attract it strongly. This pattern repeats itself throughout the crystal. The existence of these strong electrostatic forces throughout the crystal means a great deal of energy my be applied to overcome the forces and melt the solid.

45.   Strong electrostatic forces exist between oppositely charged ions in ionic solids (i.e., the attraction of a positive ion by several nearby ions of the opposite charge, and *vice versa*).

46.   Ordinary ice contains nonlinear, highly polar water molecules. In addition, there is extensive, strong hydrogen bonding possible between water molecules in ordinary ice. Dry ice, on the other hand, consists of linear, nonpolar carbon dioxide molecules, and only very weak intermolecular forces are possible.

47.   In solid Kr, the only forces that exist are the very weak London dispersion forces. In diamond, however, each carbon atom is held to its four nearest neighbors by strong covalent bonds.

48.   In a metal, the valence electrons are mobile, and can move throughout the entire metal's crystal lattice. In ionic solids, although there are positive and negative ions present, each ion is held rigidly in place by several ions of the opposite charge.

49.   An alloy represents a mixture of elements that as a whole shows metallic properties. In a substitutional alloy, some of the host metal atoms are *replaced* by other metal atoms (e.g., brass, pewter, plumber's solder). In an interstitial alloy, other small atoms occupy the spaces between the larger host metal atoms (e.g., carbon steel).

50.   Alloys may be of two types: *substitutional* (in which one metal is substituted for another in the regular positions of the crystal lattice) and *interstitial* (in which a second metal's atoms fit into the empty space in a given metal's crystal lattice). The presence of atoms of a second metal in a given metal's crystal lattice changes the properties of the metal: frequently the alloy is stronger than either of the original metals because the irregularities introduced into the crystal lattice by the presence of a second metal's atoms prevent the crystal from being deformed as easily. The properties of iron may be modified by alloying with many different substances, particularly with carbon, nickel, and cobalt. Steels with relatively high carbon content are exceptionally strong, whereas steels with low carbon contents are softer, more malleable, and more ductile. Steels produced by alloying iron with nickel and cobalt are more resistant to corrosion than iron itself.

51.   m

52.   j

53.   g

54.   f

55.   i

56.   d

57.   e

58.   a

59.   c

60.   l

61.   ice: $1.0 \text{ g} \times \dfrac{1 \text{ cm}^3}{0.9168 \text{ g}} = 1.1 \text{ cm}^3$

      liquid: $1.0 \text{ g} \times \dfrac{1 \text{ cm}^3}{0.9971 \text{ g}} = 1.0 \text{ cm}^3$

      steam: $1.0 \text{ g} \times \dfrac{1 \text{ cm}^3}{3.26 \times 10^{-4} \text{ g}} = 3.1 \times 10^3 \text{ cm}^3$

62.   Dimethyl ether has the larger vapor pressure. No hydrogen bonding is possible since the O atom does not have a hydrogen atom attached. Hydrogen bonding can occur *only* when a hydrogen atom is *directly* attached to a strongly electronegative atom (such as N, O, or F). Hydrogen bonding *is* possible in ethanol (ethanol contains an –OH group).

63.   a.   KBr (ionic bonding)

      b.   NaCl (ionic bonding)

      c. H_2O (hydrogen bonding)

64.   a. H_2.   London dispersion forces are the only intermolecular forces present in these nonpolar molecules; typically London forces become larger with increasing atomic size (as the atoms become bigger, the edge of the electron cloud lies farther from the nucleus and becomes more easily distorted).

      b.   Xe.   Only the relatively weak London forces could exist in a crystal of Xe atoms, whereas in NaCl strong ionic forces exist, and in diamond strong covalent bonding exists between carbon atoms.

      c. Cl_2.   Only London forces exist among such nonpolar molecules. London forces become larger with increasing atomic size.

65.   Evaporation of a substance is the *liquid → vapor* change of state. For every substance, a certain amount of energy is required to accomplish this change of state (heat of vaporization). Alcohol is a volatile liquid, with a relatively large heat of vaporization. Applying alcohol to a fever victim's skin causes internal heat from the body to be absorbed as the heat of vaporization of the alcohol.

66.   Steel is a general term applied to alloys consisting primarily of iron, but with small amounts of other substances added. Whereas pure iron itself is relatively soft, malleable, and ductile, steels are typically much stronger and harder, and much less subject to damage.

67.   1.00 mol Al = 27.0 g Al

      a. $27.0 \text{ g Al} \times \dfrac{0.902 \text{ J}}{\text{g °C}} \times 633\text{°C} = 1.54 \times 10^4 \text{ J} = 15.4 \text{ kJ}$

b. $27.0 \text{ g} \times \dfrac{3.95 \text{ kJ}}{\text{g}} = 106.7 \text{ kJ} = 107 \text{ kJ}$

c. $27.0 \text{ g} \times \dfrac{10.52 \text{ kJ}}{\text{g}} = 284 \text{ kJ}$

68.   Water is the solvent in which cellular processes take place in living creatures. Water in the oceans moderates the earth's temperature. Water is used in industry as a cooling agent. Water serves as a means of transportation on the earth's oceans. The liquid range is 0°C to 100°C at 1 atm pressure.

69.   From room temperature to the freezing point (0°C), the average kinetic energy of the molecules in liquid water decreases, and the molecules slow down. At the freezing point, the liquid freezes, with the molecules forming a crystal lattice in which there is much greater order than in the liquid state: molecules no longer move freely, but rather are only able to vibrate somewhat. Below the freezing point, the molecules' vibrations slow down as the temperature is lowered further.

70.   At higher altitudes, the boiling points of liquids, such as water, are lower because there is a lower atmospheric pressure above the liquid. The temperature at which food cooks is determined by the temperature to which the water in the food can be heated before it escapes as steam. Thus, food cooks at a lower temperature at high elevations where the boiling point of water is lowered.

71.   *Intra*molecular forces are the forces that hold the atoms together within a molecule. When a molecular solid is melted, it is the forces between molecules, not within the molecules themselves, that must be overcome. *Intra*molecular forces are typically stronger than *inter*molecular forces.

72.   Heat of fusion (melt); Heat of vaporization (boil).
       The heat of vaporization is always larger, because virtually all of the intermolecular forces must be overcome to form a gas. In a liquid, considerable intermolecular forces remain. Thus going from a solid to liquid requires less energy than going from the liquid to the gas.

73.   molar mass CS_2 = 76.15 g

$1.0 \text{ g } CS_2 \times \dfrac{1 \text{ mol } CS_2}{76.15 \text{ g } CS_2} = 0.0131 \text{ mol } CS_2$

$0.131 \text{ mol} \times \dfrac{28.4 \text{ kJ}}{1 \text{ mol}} = 0.37 \text{ kJ required}$

$50. \text{ g } CS_2 \times \dfrac{1 \text{ mol } CS_2}{76.15 \text{ g } CS_2} = 0.657 \text{ mol } CS_2$

$$0.657 \text{ mol } CS_2 \times \frac{28.4 \text{ kJ}}{1 \text{ mol}} = 19 \text{ kJ evolved } (-19 \text{ kJ})$$

74. Dipole-dipole interactions are typically about 1% as strong as a covalent bond. Dipole-dipole interactions represent electrostatic attractions between portions of molecules which carry only a *partial* positive or negative charge, and such forces require the molecules that are interacting to come *near* enough to each other.

75. Hydrogen bonding is a particularly strong dipole-dipole force arising among molecules in which hydrogen is bonded to a highly electronegative atom, such as N, O, or F. Such bonds are highly polar, and because the H atom is so small, the dipoles of different molecules are able to approach each other much more closely than in other polar molecules. Examples of substances in which hydrogen bonding is important include H_2O, NH_3, and HF.

76. London dispersion forces are relatively weak forces that arise among noble gas atoms and in nonpolar molecules. London forces are due to *instantaneous dipoles* that develop when one atom (or molecule) momentarily distorts the electron cloud of another atom (or molecule). London forces are typically weaker than either permanent dipole-dipole forces or covalent bonds.

77. a.   London dispersion forces (nonpolar molecules)

     b.   hydrogen bonding (H attached to N); London dispersion forces

     c.   London dispersion forces (nonpolar molecules)

     d.   London dispersion forces (nonpolar molecules)

78. For every mole of liquid water that evaporates, several kilojoules of heat must be absorbed to provide kinetic energy to overcome attractive forces among the molecules. This heat is absorbed by the water from its surroundings.

79. A *volatile* liquid is one that evaporates relatively easily. Volatile liquids typically have large vapor pressures because the intermolecular forces that would tend to prevent evaporation are small.

80. In NH_3, strong hydrogen bonding can exist. In CH_4, because the molecule is nonpolar, only the relatively weak London dispersion forces exist.

81. Ionic solids typically have the highest melting points, because the ionic charges and close packing in ionic solids allow for very strong forces among a given ion and its nearest neighbors of the opposite charge.

82. In a crystal of ice, strong *hydrogen bonding* forces are present, while in the crystal of a nonpolar substance like oxygen, only the much weaker *London* forces exist.

83. The electron sea model envisions a metal as a cluster of positive ions through which the valence electrons are able to move freely. An electrical current represents the movement of electrons, for example through a metal wire, and is consistent with a model in which the electrons are free to roam.

Chapter 14   Solutions

1. A homogeneous mixture is a combination of two (or more) pure substances which is uniform in composition and appearance throughout. Examples of homogeneous mixtures in the real world include rubbing alcohol (70% isopropyl alcohol, 30% water) and gasoline (a mixture of hydrocarbons).

2. A heterogeneous mixture does not have a uniform composition: the composition varies in different places within the mixture. Examples of nonhomogeneous mixtures include salad dressing (mixture of oil, vinegar, water, herbs and spices) and granite (combination of minerals).

3. solvent, solute

4. solid

5. When an ionic solute dissolves in water, a given ion is pulled into solution by the attractive ion-dipole force exerted by several water molecules. For example, in dissolving a positive ion, the ion is approached by the negatively charged end of several water molecules: if the attraction of the water molecules for the positive ion is stronger than the attraction of the negative ions near it in the crystal, the ion leaves the crystal and enters solution. After entering solution, the dissolved ion is surrounded completely by water molecules, which tends to prevent the ion from reentering the crystal.

6. One substance will mix with and dissolve in another substance if the intermolecular forces are similar in the two substances, so that when the mixture forms, the forces between particles in the mixture will be similar to the forces present in the separate substances. Sugar and ethyl alcohol molecules both contain polar -OH groups, which are comparable to the polar -OH structure in water. Sugar or ethyl alcohol molecules can hydrogen bond with water molecules and intermingle with them freely to form a solution. Substances like petroleum (whose molecules contain only carbon and hydrogen) are very nonpolar and cannot form interactions with polar water molecules.

7. water molecules

8. independently

9. saturated

10. unsaturated

11. variable

12. large

13. five

14. 100.0

15.   Let NaAc represent sodium acetate ($NaC_2H_3O_2$)

a. $$\frac{5.00 \text{ g NaAc}}{(5.00 \text{ g NaAc} + 25.0 \text{ g H}_2\text{O})} \times 100 = 16.7\% \text{ NaAc}$$

b. $$\frac{10.0 \text{ g NaAc}}{(10.0 \text{ g NaAc} + 25.0 \text{ g H}_2\text{O})} \times 100 = 28.6\% \text{ NaAc}$$

c. $$\frac{15.0 \text{ g NaAc}}{(15.0 \text{ g NaAc} + 25.0 \text{ g H}_2\text{O})} \times 100 = 37.5\% \text{ NaAc}$$

d. $$\frac{20.0 \text{ g NaAc}}{(20.0 \text{ g NaAc} + 25.0 \text{ g H}_2\text{O})} \times 100 = 44.4\% \text{ NaAc}$$

16.   a. $$\frac{5.00 \text{ g CaCl}_2}{(95.0 \text{ g H}_2\text{O} + 5.00 \text{ g CaCl}_2)} \times 100 = 5.00\% \text{ CaCl}_2$$

b. $$\frac{1.00 \text{ g CaCl}_2}{(19.0 \text{ g H}_2\text{O} + 1.00 \text{ g CaCl}_2)} \times 100 = 5.00\% \text{ CaCl}_2$$

c. $$\frac{15.0 \text{ g CaCl}_2}{(285 \text{ g H}_2\text{O}) + 15.0 \text{ g CaCl}_2)} \times 100 = 5.00\% \text{ CaCl}_2$$

d. $$\frac{0.00200 \text{ g CaCl}_2}{(0.0380 \text{ g H}_2\text{O} + 0.00200 \text{ g CaCl}_2)} \times 100 = 5.00\% \text{ CaCl}_2$$

17.   To say that a solution is $x\%$ NaCl means that 100 g of the solution would contain x g of NaCl

a. $11.5 \text{ g solution} \times \dfrac{6.25 \text{ g NaCl}}{100 \text{ g solution}} = 0.719 \text{ g NaCl}$

b. $6.25 \text{ g solution} \times \dfrac{11.5 \text{ g NaCl}}{100 \text{ g solution}} = 0.719 \text{ g NaCl}$

c. $54.3 \text{ g solution} \times \dfrac{0.91 \text{ g NaCl}}{100 \text{ g solution}} = 0.49 \text{ g NaCl}$

d. $452 \text{ g solution} \times \dfrac{12.3 \text{ g NaCl}}{100 \text{ g solution}} = 55.6 \text{ g NaCl}$

18.   To say a solution is 15.0% NaCl by mass means that 100. g of the solution would contain 15.0 g of NaCl.

a. $150. \text{ g solution} \times \dfrac{15.0 \text{ g NaCl}}{100. \text{ g solution}} = 22.5 \text{ g NaCl}$

b. $35.0 \text{ g NaCl} \times \dfrac{100. \text{ g solution}}{15.0 \text{ g NaCl}} = 233 \text{ g solution}$

c. $1000. \text{ g solution} \times \dfrac{15.0 \text{ g NaCl}}{100. \text{ g solution}} = 150. \text{ g NaCl}$

d. $1000. \text{ g solution} \times \dfrac{15.0 \text{ g NaCl}}{100. \text{ g solution}} = 150. \text{ g NaCl}$

Note that the calculation for parts (c) and (d) are identical. These questions are just different ways of asking the same thing: How many g of NaCl are in 1000. g of a 15.0% NaCl solution?

19. $\dfrac{5.34 \text{ g KCl}}{(5.34 \text{ g KCl} + 152 \text{ g H}_2\text{O})} \times 100 = \dfrac{5.34 \text{ g}}{157.34 \text{ g}} \times 100 = 3.39\% \text{ KCl}$

20. $\%\text{Cu} = \dfrac{5.31 \text{ g Cu}}{(5.31 \text{ g Cu} + 4.03 \text{ g Zn} + 145 \text{ g Fe})} \times 100 = \dfrac{5.31 \text{ g}}{154.3 \text{ g}} \times 100 = 3.44\% \text{ Cu}$

$\% \text{ Zn} = \dfrac{4.03 \text{ g Zn}}{(5.31 \text{ g Cu} + 4.03 \text{ g Zn} + 145 \text{ g Fe})} \times 100 = \dfrac{4.03 \text{ g}}{154.3 \text{ g}} \times 100 = 2.61\% \text{ Zn}$

$\% \text{ Fe} = \dfrac{145 \text{ g Fe}}{(5.31 \text{ g Cu} + 4.03 \text{ g Zn} + 145 \text{ g Fe})} \times 100 = \dfrac{145 \text{ g}}{154.3 \text{ g}} \times 100 = 94.0\% \text{ Fe}$

21.   To say that the insecticide consists 5.4% of pyrethrums means that every hundred ounces of the insecticide will contain 5.4 ounces of pyrethrums.

$24.0 \text{ ounces spray} \times \dfrac{5.4 \text{ ounces pyrethrums}}{100 \text{ ounces spray}} = 1.3 \text{ ounces pyrethrums}$

22. $\dfrac{67.1 \text{ g CaCl}_2}{(67.1 \text{ g CaCl}_2 + 275 \text{ g H}_2\text{O})} \times 100 = 19.6\% \text{ CaCl}_2$

23.   To say that the solution to be prepared is 2.2% by mass $NaHCO_3$ means that 2.2 g of $NaHCO_3$ will be contained in every 100 g of the solution.

$45 \text{ g solution} \times \dfrac{2.2 \text{ g NaHCO}_3}{100 \text{ g solution}} = 0.99 \text{ g NaHCO}_3 \text{ is needed}$

24.   To say that the solution is 6.25% KBr by mass, means that 100. g of the solution will contain 6.25 g KBr.

$125 \text{ g solution} \times \dfrac{6.25 \text{ g KBr}}{100. \text{ g solution}} = 7.81 \text{ g KBr}$

25. $285 \text{ g solution} \times \dfrac{5.00 \text{ g NaCl}}{100.0 \text{ g solution}} = 14.3 \text{ g NaCl}$

$$285 \text{ g solution} \times \frac{7.50 \text{ g Na}_2\text{CO}_3}{100.0 \text{ g solution}} = 21.4 \text{ g Na}_2\text{CO}_3$$

26. To say that the solution is to be 1.25% $CuCl_2$ by mass, means that 100. g of the solution will contain 1.25 g $CuCl_2$

$$1250. \text{ g solution} \times \frac{1.25 \text{ g CuCl}_2}{100. \text{ g solution}} = 15.6 \text{ g CuCl}_2$$

27. First find the mass of the solution, since the percentage is by mass.

$$255 \text{ mL solution} \times \frac{1.19 \text{ g solution}}{1 \text{ mL solution}} = 303 \text{ g solution}$$

$$303 \text{ g solution} \times \frac{37.2 \text{ g HCl}}{100 \text{ g solution}} = 113 \text{ g HCl contained}$$

28. $\text{g heptane} = 93 \text{ g solution} \times \dfrac{5.2 \text{ g heptane}}{100. \text{ g solution}} = 4.8 \text{ g heptane}$

$\text{g pentane} = 93 \text{ g solution} \times \dfrac{2.9 \text{ g pentane}}{100. \text{ g solution}} = 2.7 \text{ g pentane}$

$\text{g hexane} = 93 \text{ g solution} - 4.8 \text{ g heptane} - 2.7 \text{ g pentane} = 86 \text{ g hexane}$

29. 0.105

30. $0.221 \text{ mol Ca}^{2+}$; 0.442 mol Cl^-

31. A standard solution is one whose concentration is known very accurately and with high precision. A standard solution is typically prepared by weighing out a precise amount of solute, and then dissolving the solute in a precise amount of solvent, or to a precise final volume using a volumetric flask.

32. To say that a solution has a concentration of 5 *M* means that in 1 L of solution (*not* solvent) there would be 5 mol of solute: to prepare such a solution one would place 5 mol of NaCl in a 1 L flask, and then add whatever amount of water is necessary so that the *total* volume would be 1 L after mixing. The NaCl will occupy some space, so the amount of water to be added will be *less* than 1.00 L.

33. $\text{Molarity} = \dfrac{\text{moles of solute}}{\text{liters of solution}}$

   a. $M = \dfrac{0.50 \text{ mol NaCl}}{0.200 \text{ L solution}} = 2.5 \ M$

   b. $M = \dfrac{0.50 \text{ mol NaCl}}{0.125 \text{ L solution}} = 4.0 \ M$

c.   100. mL = 0.100 L

$$M = \frac{0.25 \text{ mol NaCl}}{0.100 \text{ L solution}} = 2.5 \ M$$

d.   300. mL = 0.300 L

$$M = \frac{0.75 \text{ mol NaCl}}{0.300 \text{ L solution}} = 2.5 \ M$$

34.   Molarity = $\dfrac{\text{moles of solute}}{\text{liters of solution}}$

a.   250 mL = 0.25 L

$$M = \frac{0.50 \text{ mol KBr}}{0.25 \text{ L solution}} = 2.0 \ M$$

b.   500 mL = 0.500 L

$$M = \frac{0.50 \text{ mol KBr}}{0.500 \text{ L solution}} = 1.0 \ M$$

c.   750 mL = 0.75 L

$$M = \frac{0.50 \text{ mol KBr}}{0.75 \text{ L solution}} = 0.67 \ M$$

d. $M = \dfrac{0.50 \text{ mol KBr}}{1.0 \text{ L solution}} = 0.50 \ M$

35.   Molarity = $\dfrac{\text{moles of solute}}{\text{liters of solution}}$

a.   molar mass of $CaCl_2$ = 111.0 g

$$321 \text{ g } CaCl_2 \times \frac{1 \text{ mol}}{111.0 \text{ g}} = 2.89 \text{ mol } CaCl_2$$

$$M = \frac{2.89 \text{ mol } CaCl_2}{1.45 \text{ L solution}} = 1.99 \ M$$

b.   millimolar mass of NaCl = 58.44 mg

$$4.21 \text{ mg NaCl} \times \frac{1 \text{ mmol}}{58.44 \text{ mg}} = 0.0720 \text{ millimol NaCl}$$

$$M = \frac{0.0720 \text{ millimol NaCl}}{1.65 \text{ mL solution}} = 0.0437 \ M$$

c.   125 mL = 0.125 L

molar mass of KBr = 119.0 g

$$6.45 \text{ g KBr} \times \frac{1 \text{ mol}}{119.0 \text{ g}} = 0.0542 \text{ mol KBr}$$

$$M = \frac{0.0542 \text{ mol KBr}}{0.125 \text{ L solution}} = 0.434 \text{ } M$$

d.   molar mass of NH_4NO_3 = 80.05 g

$$62.5 \text{ g } NH_4NO_3 \times \frac{1 \text{ mol}}{80.05 \text{ g}} = 0.781 \text{ mol } NH_4NO_3$$

$$M = \frac{0.781 \text{ mol } NH_4NO_3}{7.25 \text{ L solution}} = 0.108 \text{ } M$$

36.   Molarity = $\dfrac{\text{moles of solute}}{\text{liters of solution}}$

a.   Molar mass of $CuCl_2$ = 134.45 g   125 mL = 0.125 L

$$4.25 \text{ g } CuCl_2 \times \frac{1 \text{ mol}}{134.45 \text{ g}} = 0.0316 \text{ mol } CuCl_2$$

$$M = \frac{0.0316 \text{ mol } CuCl_2}{0.125 \text{ L solution}} = 0.253 \text{ } M$$

b.   Molar mass of $NaHCO_3$ = 84.01 g   11.3 mL = 0.0113 L

$$0.101 \text{ g } NaHCO_3 \times \frac{1 \text{ mol}}{84.01 \text{ g}} = 0.00120 \text{ mol } NaHCO_3$$

$$M = \frac{0.00120 \text{ mol } NaHCO_3}{0.0113 \text{ L solution}} = 0.106 \text{ } M$$

c.   Molar mass of Na_2CO_3 = 105.99 g

$$52.9 \text{ g } Na_2CO_3 \times \frac{1 \text{ mol}}{105.99 \text{ g}} = 0.499 \text{ mol } Na_2CO_3$$

$$M = \frac{0.499 \text{ mol } Na_2CO_3}{1.15 \text{ L solution}} = 0.434 \text{ } M$$

d.   Molar mass of KOH = 56.11 g   1.5 mL = 0.0015 L

$$0.14 \text{ mg KOH} \times \frac{1 \text{ g}}{10^3 \text{ mg}} \times \frac{1 \text{ mol}}{56.11 \text{ g}} = 2.50 \times 10^{-6} \text{ mol KOH}$$

$$M = \frac{2.50 \times 10^{-6} \text{ mol KOH}}{0.0015 \text{ L solution}} = 1.67 \times 10^{-3} \text{ } M = 1.7 \times 10^{-3} \text{ } M$$

37.   molar mass of KNO_3 = 101.1 g   225 mL = 0.225 L

$$45.3 \text{ g } KNO_3 \times \frac{1 \text{ mol}}{101.1 \text{ g}} = 0.448 \text{ mol } KNO_3$$

$$M = \frac{0.448 \text{ mol } KNO_3}{0.225 \text{ L solution}} = 1.99 \text{ } M$$

38.   Molar mass of $CaBr_2$ = 199.9 g

$$4.25 \text{ g } CaBr_2 \times \frac{1 \text{ mol}}{199.9 \text{ g}} = 0.0213 \text{ mol } CaBr_2$$

125 mL = 0.125 L

$$M = \frac{0.0213 \text{ mol } CaBr_2}{0.125 \text{ L solution}} = 0.170 \text{ } M$$

39.   250.0 mL = 0.2500 L

molar mass $CaCO_3$ = 100.1 g

$$1.745 \text{ g } CaCO_3 \times \frac{1 \text{ mol}}{100.1 \text{ g}} = 0.01743 \text{ mol } CaCO_3$$

One mole of $CaCO_3$ contains one mole of Ca^{2+} ion; therefore,

$$M = \frac{0.01743 \text{ mol } Ca^{2+}}{0.2500 \text{ L solution}} = 0.06973 \text{ } M$$

40.   Molar mass of I_2 = 253.8 g

225 mL = 0.225 L

$$5.15 \text{ g } I_2 \times \frac{1 \text{ mol}}{253.8 \text{ g}} = 0.0203 \text{ mol } I_2$$

$$M = \frac{0.0203 \text{ mol } I_2}{0.225 \text{ L solution}} = 0.0902 \text{ } M$$

41.   molar mass of $FeCl_3$ = 162.2 g

$$1.01 \text{ g } FeCl_3 \times \frac{1 \text{ mol } FeCl_3}{162.2 \text{ g } FeCl_3} = 0.00623 \text{ mol } FeCl_3$$

10.0 mL = 0.0100 L

$$M = \frac{0.00623 \text{ mol } FeCl_3}{0.0100 \text{ L solution}} = 0.623 \text{ } M$$

Since one mole of $FeCl_3$ contains one mole of Fe^{3+} and three moles of Cl^-, the solution is 0.623 M in Fe^{3+} and 3(0.623) = 1.87 M in Cl^-

42. a.   Molar mass of NaOH = 40.00 g

$$495 \text{ g NaOH} \times \frac{1 \text{ mol}}{40.00 \text{ g}} = 12.4 \text{ mol NaOH}$$

$$M = \frac{12.4 \text{ mol NaOH}}{20.0 \text{ L solution}} = 0.619 \; M$$

43. Molarity = $\dfrac{\text{moles of solute}}{\text{liters of solution}}$

a. $10.0 \text{ L solution} \times \dfrac{0.550 \text{ mol NaHCO}_3}{1.00 \text{ L solution}} = 5.50 \text{ mol NaHCO}_3$

b. $5.0 \text{ L solution} \times \dfrac{12 \text{ mol HCl}}{1.0 \text{ L solution}} = 60. \text{ mol HCl}$

c.   250. mL = 0.250 L

$$0.250 \text{ L solution} \times \frac{19.4 \text{ mol NaOH}}{1.00 \text{ L solution}} = 4.85 \text{ mol NaOH}$$

d.   125 mL = 0.125 L

$$0.125 \text{ L solution} \times \frac{17.0 \text{ mol HC}_2\text{H}_3\text{O}_2}{1.00 \text{ L solution}} = 2.13 \text{ mol HC}_2\text{H}_3\text{O}_2$$

44. a.   molar mass of HNO_3 = 63.02 g   127 mL = 0.127 L

$$0.127 \text{ L solution} \times \frac{0.105 \text{ mol HNO}_3}{1.00 \text{ L solution}} = 0.0133 \text{ mol HNO}_3$$

$$0.0133 \text{ mol HNO}_3 \times \frac{63.02 \text{ g HNO}_3}{1 \text{ mol HNO}_3} = 0.838 \text{ g HNO}_3$$

b.   molar mass of NH_3 = 17.03 g   155 mL = 0.155 L

$$0.155 \text{ L solution} \times \frac{15.1 \text{ mol NH}_3}{1.00 \text{ L solution}} = 2.34 \text{ mol NH}_3$$

$$2.34 \text{ mol NH}_3 \times \frac{17.03 \text{ g NH}_3}{1 \text{ mol NH}_3} = 39.9 \text{ g NH}_3$$

c.   molar mass KSCN = 97.19 g

$$2.51 \text{ L solution} \times \frac{2.01 \times 10^{-3} \text{ mol KSCN}}{1.00 \text{ L solution}} = 5.05 \times 10^{-3} \text{ mol KSCN}$$

$$5.05 \times 10^{-3} \text{ mol KSCN} \times \frac{97.19 \text{ g KSCN}}{1 \text{ mol KSCN}} = 0.490 \text{ g KSCN}$$

d.   molar mass of HCl = 36.46 g   12.2 mL = 0.0122 L

$$0.0122 \text{ L solution} \times \frac{2.45 \text{ mol HCl}}{1.00 \text{ L solution}} = 0.0299 \text{ mol HCl}$$

$$0.0299 \text{ mol HCl} \times \frac{36.46 \text{ g HCl}}{1 \text{ mol HCl}} = 1.09 \text{ g HCl}$$

45. a. $$2.00 \text{ L solution} \times \frac{1.33 \text{ mol NaCl}}{1.00 \text{ L solution}} = 2.66 \text{ mol NaCl}$$

molar mass NaCl = 58.44 g

$$2.66 \text{ mol NaCl} \times \frac{58.44 \text{ g NaCl}}{1 \text{ mol NaCl}} = 155 \text{ g NaCl}$$

b.   0.050 mL = 0.000050 L

$$0.000050 \text{ L solution} \times \frac{6.0 \text{ mol HCl}}{1.0 \text{ L solution}} = 0.00030 \text{ mol HCl}$$

molar mass HCl = 36.46 g

$$0.00030 \text{ mol HCl} \times \frac{36.46 \text{ g HCl}}{1 \text{ mol HCl}} = 0.011 \text{ g HCl}$$

c.   125 mL = 0.125 L

$$0.125 \text{ L solution} \times \frac{3.05 \text{ mol HNO}_3}{1.00 \text{ L solution}} = 0.3813 \text{ mol HNO}_3$$

molar mass HNO_3 = 63.02 g

$$0.3813 \text{ mol HNO}_3 \times \frac{63.02 \text{ g HNO}_3}{1 \text{ mol HNO}_3} = 24.0 \text{ g HNO}_3$$

d. $$1.25 \text{ L solution} \times \frac{0.503 \text{ mol NaBr}}{1.00 \text{ L solution}} = 0.6288 \text{ mol NaBr}$$

molar mass NaBr = 102.9 g

$$0.6288 \text{ mol NaBr} \times \frac{102.9 \text{ g NaBr}}{1 \text{ mol NaBr}} = 64.7 \text{ g NaBr}$$

46. a.   molar mass of KBr = 119.0 g   173 mL = 0.173 L

$$0.173 \text{ L solution} \times \frac{1.24 \text{ mol KBr}}{1.00 \text{ L solution}} = 0.215 \text{ mol KBr}$$

$$0.215 \text{ mol KBr} \times \frac{119.0 \text{ g}}{1 \text{ mol}} = 25.6 \text{ g KBr}$$

b.   molar mass of HCl = 36.46 g

$$2.04 \text{ L solution} \times \frac{12.1 \text{ mol HCl}}{1.00 \text{ L solution}} = 24.7 \text{ mol HCl}$$

$$24.7 \text{ mol HCl} \times \frac{36.46 \text{ g}}{1 \text{ mol}} = 901 \text{ g HCl}$$

c.   molar mass of NH_3 = 17.03 g   25 mL = 0.025 L

$$0.025 \text{ L solution} \times \frac{3.0 \text{ mol } NH_3}{1.00 \text{ L solution}} = 0.075 \text{ mol } NH_3$$

$$0.075 \text{ mol } NH_3 \times \frac{17.03 \text{ g}}{1 \text{ mol}} = 1.3 \text{ g } NH_3$$

d.   molar mass $CaCl_2$ = 111.0 g   125 mL = 0.125 L

$$0.125 \text{ L solution} \times \frac{0.552 \text{ mol } CaCl_2}{1.00 \text{ L solution}} = 0.0690 \text{ mol } CaCl_2$$

$$0.0690 \text{ mol } CaCl_2 \times \frac{111.0 \text{ g}}{1 \text{ mol}} = 7.66 \text{ g } CaCl_2$$

47.   molar mass of NH_4Cl = 53.49 g   450 mL = 0.450 L

$$0.450 \text{ L solution} \times \frac{0.251 \text{ mol } NH_4Cl}{1 \text{ L solution}} = 0.113 \text{ mol } NH_4Cl$$

$$0.113 \text{ mol } NH_4Cl \times \frac{53.49 \text{ g } NH_4Cl}{1 \text{ mol } NH_4Cl} = 6.04 \text{ g } NH_4Cl$$

48.   Molar mass of NaCl = 58.44 g   1 lb = 453.59 g

$$453.59 \text{ g NaCl} \times \frac{1 \text{ mol}}{58.44 \text{ g}} = 7.76 \text{ mol NaCl}$$

$$7.76 \text{ mol NaCl} \times \frac{1.00 \text{ L solution}}{1.0 \text{ mol NaCl}} = 7.76 \text{ L} = 7.8 \text{ L of solution}$$

49.   a. $$1.00 \text{ L solution} \times \frac{0.251 \text{ mol } Na_2SO_4}{1.00 \text{ L solution}} = 0.251 \text{ mol } Na_2SO_4$$

$$0.251 \text{ mol } Na_2SO_4 \times \frac{2 \text{ mol } Na^+}{1 \text{ mol } Na_2SO_4} = 0.502 \text{ mol } Na^+$$

b. $$5.50 \text{ L solution} \times \frac{0.10 \text{ mol } FeCl_3}{1.00 \text{ L solution}} = 0.550 \text{ mol } FeCl_3$$

$$0.550 \text{ mol } FeCl_3 \times \frac{3 \text{ mol } Cl^-}{1 \text{ mol } FeCl_3} = 1.65 \text{ mol} = 1.7 \text{ mol } Cl^-$$

c.   100. mL = 0.100 L

$$0.100 \text{ L solution} \times \frac{0.55 \text{ mol Ba(NO}_3)_2}{1.00 \text{ L solution}} = 0.0550 \text{ mol Ba(NO}_3)_2$$

$$0.0550 \text{ mol Ba(NO}_3)_2 \times \frac{2 \text{ mol NO}_3^-}{1 \text{ mol Ba(NO}_3)_2} = 0.11 \text{ mol NO}_3^-$$

d.   250. mL = 0.250 L

$$0.250 \text{ L solution} \times \frac{0.350 \text{ mol (NH}_4)_2\text{SO}_4}{1.00 \text{ L solution}} = 0.0875 \text{ mol (NH}_4)_2\text{SO}_4$$

$$0.0875 \text{ mol (NH}_4)_2\text{SO}_4 \times \frac{2 \text{ mol NH}_4^+}{1 \text{ mol (NH}_4)_2\text{SO}_4} = 0.175 \text{ mol NH}_4^+$$

50.   a.   10.2 mL = 0.0102 L

$$0.0102 \text{ L} \times \frac{0.451 \text{ mol AlCl}_3}{1.00 \text{ L}} \times \frac{1 \text{ mol Al}^{3+}}{1 \text{ mol AlCl}_3} = 4.60 \times 10^{-3} \text{ mol Al}^{3+}$$

$$0.0102 \text{ L} \times \frac{0.451 \text{ mol AlCl}_3}{1.00 \text{ L}} \times \frac{3 \text{ mol Cl}^-}{1 \text{ mol AlCl}_3} = 1.38 \times 10^{-2} \text{ mol Cl}^-$$

b. $$5.51 \text{ L} \times \frac{0.103 \text{ mol Na}_3\text{PO}_4}{1.00 \text{ L}} \times \frac{3 \text{ mol Na}^+}{1 \text{ mol Na}_3\text{PO}_4} = 1.70 \text{ mol Na}^+$$

$$5.51 \text{ L} \times \frac{0.103 \text{ mol Na}_3\text{PO}_4}{1.00 \text{ L}} \times \frac{1 \text{ mol PO}_4^{3-}}{1 \text{ mol Na}_3\text{PO}_4} = 0.568 \text{ mol PO}_4^{3-}$$

c.   1.75 mL = 0.00175 L

$$0.00175 \text{ L} \times \frac{1.25 \text{ mol CuCl}_2}{1.00 \text{ L}} \times \frac{1 \text{ mol Cu}^{2+}}{1 \text{ mol CuCl}_2} = 2.19 \times 10^{-3} \text{ mol Cu}^{2+}$$

$$0.00175 \text{ L} \times \frac{1.25 \text{ mol CuCl}_2}{1.00 \text{ L}} \times \frac{2 \text{ mol Cl}^-}{1 \text{ mol CuCl}_2} = 4.38 \times 10^{-3} \text{ mol Cl}^-$$

d.   25.2 mL = 0.0252 L

$$0.0252 \text{ L} \times \frac{0.00157 \text{ mol Ca(OH)}_2}{1.00 \text{ L}} \times \frac{1 \text{ mol Ca}^{2+}}{1 \text{ mol Ca(OH)}_2} = 3.96 \times 10^{-5} \text{ mol Ca}^{2+}$$

$$0.0252 \text{ L} \times \frac{0.00157 \text{ mol Ca(OH)}_2}{1.00 \text{ L}} \times \frac{2 \text{ mol OH}^-}{1 \text{ mol Ca(OH)}_2} = 7.91 \times 10^{-5} \text{ mol OH}^-$$

51.   250. mL = 0.250 L

$$0.250 \text{ L solution} \times \frac{0.100 \text{ mol AgNO}_3}{1.00 \text{ L solution}} = 0.0250 \text{ mol AgNO}_3$$

molar mass AgNO$_3$ = 169.9 g

$$0.0250 \text{ mol AgNO}_3 \times \frac{169.9 \text{ g AgNO}_3}{1 \text{ mol AgNO}_3} = 4.25 \text{ g AgNO}_3$$

52. Molar mass of Na_2CO_3 = 106.0 g   250 mL = 0.250 L

$$0.250 \text{ L} \times \frac{0.0500 \text{ mol Na}_2\text{CO}_3}{1.00 \text{ L}} \times \frac{106.0 \text{ g}}{1 \text{ mol}} = 1.33 \text{ g Na}_2\text{CO}_3$$

53. moles of solute

54. half

55. $M_1 \times V_1 = M_2 \times V_2$

a. $M_1 = 0.105\ M$ $M_2 = ?$

$V_1 = 425$ mL = 0.425 L $V_2 = 1.00$ L

$$M_2 = \frac{(0.105\ M)(0.425\ L)}{(1.00\ L)} = 0.0446\ M$$

b. $M_1 = 12.1\ M$ $M_2 = ?$

$V_1 = 10.5$ mL = 0.0105 L $V_2 = 1.00$ L

$$M_2 = \frac{(12.1\ M)(0.0105\ L)}{(1.00\ L)} = 0.127\ M$$

c. $M_1 = 14.9\ M$ $M_2 = ?$

$V_1 = 25.2$ mL = 0.0252 L $V_2 = 1.00$ L

$$M_2 = \frac{(14.9\ M)(0.0252\ L)}{(1.00\ L)} = 0.375\ M$$

d. $M_1 = 18.0\ M$ $M_2 = ?$

$V_1 = 6.25$ mL = 0.00625 L $V_2 = 1.00$ L

$$M_2 = \frac{(18.0\ M)(0.00625\ L)}{(1.00\ L)} = 0.113\ M$$

56. $M_1 \times V_1 = M_2 \times V_2$

a. $M_1 = 0.251\ M$ $M_2 = ?$

$V_1 = 125$ mL $V_2 = 250. + 125 = 375$ mL

$$M_2 = \frac{(0.251\ M)(125\ mL)}{(375\ mL)} = 0.0837\ M$$

b. $M_1 = 0.499\ M$ $M_2 = ?$

$V_1 = 445$ mL $V_2 = 445 + 250. = 695$ mL

$$M_2 = \frac{(0.499\ M)(445\ mL)}{(695\ mL)} = 0.320\ M$$

c. M_1 = 0.101 M M_2 = ?

  V_1 = 5.25 L V_2 = 5.25 + 0.250 = 5.50 L

$$M_2 = \frac{(0.101\ M)(5.25\ L)}{(5.50\ L)} = 0.0964\ M$$

d. M_1 = 14.5 M M_2 = ?

  V_1 = 11.2 mL V_2 = 11.2 + 250. = 261.2 mL

$$M_2 = \frac{(14.5\ M)(11.2\ mL)}{(261.2\ mL)} = 0.622\ M$$

57. $M_1 \times V_1 = M_2 \times V_2$

  HCl: M_1 = 3.0 M M_2 = 12.1 M

              V_1 = 225 mL V_2 = ?

$$V_2 = \frac{(3.0\ M)(225\ mL)}{(12.1\ M)} = 55.8\ mL = 56\ mL$$

  HNO_3: M_1 = 3.0 M M_2 = 15.9 M

              V_1 = 225 mL V_2 = ?

$$V_2 = \frac{(3.0\ M)(225\ mL)}{(15.9\ M)} = 42.45\ mL = 42\ mL$$

  H_2SO_4: M_1 = 3.0 M M_2 = 18.0 M

              V_1 = 225 mL V_2 = ?

$$V_2 = \frac{(3.0\ M)(225\ mL)}{(18.0\ M)} = 37.5\ mL = 38\ mL$$

  $HC_2H_3O_2$: M_1 = 3.0 M M_2 = 17.5 M

              V_1 = 225 mL V_2 = ?

$$V_2 = \frac{(3.0\ M)(225\ mL)}{(17.5\ M)} = 38.6\ mL = 39\ mL$$

  H_3PO_4: M_1 = 3.0 M M_2 = 14.9 M

              V_1 = 225 mL V_2 = ?

$$V_2 = \frac{(3.0\ M)(225\ mL)}{(14.9\ M)} = 45.3\ mL = 45\ mL$$

58. M_1 = 18.1 M M_2 = 0.100 M

  V_1 = ? mL V_2 = 125 mL

$$M_1 = \frac{(0.100\ M)(125\ mL)}{(18.1\ M)} = 0.691\ mL$$

59. $M_1 \times V_1 = M_2 \times V_2$

$M_1 = 3.02\ M$ $\qquad\qquad M_2 = 0.150\ M$

$V_1 = ?$ $\qquad\qquad V_2 = 125\ \text{mL} = 0.125\ \text{L}$

$$V_1 = \frac{(0.150\ M)(0.125\ \text{L})}{(3.02\ M)} = 0.00621\ \text{L} = 6.21\ \text{mL}$$

The student could prepare her solution by transferring 6.21 mL of the 3.02 *M* NaOH solution from a pipet or buret to a 125-mL volumetric flask, and then adding distilled water to the calibration mark of the flask.

60. $M_1 = 0.211\ M$ $\qquad\qquad M_2 = ?$

$V_1 = 75\ \text{mL}$ $\qquad\qquad V_2 = 125\ \text{mL}$

$$M_2 = \frac{(0.211\ M)(75\ \text{mL})}{(125\ \text{mL})} = 0.127\ M = 0.13\ M$$

61. $M_1 \times V_1 = M_2 \times V_2$

$M_1 = 0.200\ M$ $\qquad\qquad M_2 = 0.150\ M$

$V_1 = 500.\ \text{mL} = 0.500\ \text{L}$ $\qquad\qquad V_2 = ?$

$$V_2 = \frac{(0.200\ M)(0.500\ \text{L})}{(0.150\ M)} = 0.667\ \text{L} = 667\ \text{mL}$$

Therefore 667 - 500. = 167 mL of water must be added.

62. $M_1 = 0.227\ M$ $\qquad\qquad M_2 = 0.105\ M$

$V_1 = 25.0\ \text{mL}$ $\qquad\qquad V_2 = ?$

$$V_2 = \frac{(0.227\ M)(25.0\ \text{mL})}{(0.105\ M)} = 54.0\ \text{mL}$$

So 54.0 - 25.0 = 29.0 mL of water should be added.

63. $27.2\ \text{mL} = 0.0272\ \text{L}$ $\qquad\qquad 25.0\ \text{mL} = 0.0250\ \text{L}$

$$\text{mol AgNO}_3 = 0.0272\ \text{L solution} \times \frac{0.104\ \text{mol AgNO}_3}{1.00\ \text{L solution}} = 0.002829\ \text{mol AgNO}_3$$

$$0.002829\ \text{mol AgNO}_3 \times \frac{1\ \text{mol Cl}^-}{1\ \text{mol AgNO}_3} = 0.002829\ \text{mol Cl}^-$$

$$M = \frac{0.002829\ \text{mol Cl}^-}{0.0250\ \text{L}} = 0.113\ M$$

64. $\text{Ba(NO}_3)_2(aq) + \text{Na}_2\text{SO}_4(aq) \rightarrow \text{BaSO}_4(s) + 2\text{NaNO}_3(aq)$

$12.5\ \text{mL} = 0.0125\ \text{L}$

$$\text{moles Ba(NO}_3)_2 = 0.0125 \text{ L} \times \frac{0.15 \text{ mol Ba(NO}_3)_2}{1.00 \text{ L}} = 1.88 \times 10^{-3} \text{ mol Ba(NO}_3)_2$$

From the balanced chemical equation for the reaction, if 1.88×10^{-3} mol $\text{Ba(NO}_3)_2$ are to be precipitated, then 1.88×10^{-3} mol Na_2SO_4 will be needed.

$$1.88 \times 10^{-3} \text{ mol Na}_2\text{SO}_4 \times \frac{1.00 \text{ L}}{0.25 \text{ mol Na}_2\text{SO}_4} = 0.0075 \text{ L required} = 7.5 \text{ mL}$$

65.   36.2 mL = 0.0362 L   37.5 mL = 0.0375 L

Since each formula unit of CaCO_3 contains one Ca^{2+} ion, and since each Na_2CO_3 formula unit contains one CO_3^{2-} ion, we can say that

$$\text{mol Ca}^{2+} = 0.0362 \text{ L CaCl}_2 \times \frac{0.158 \text{ mol CaCl}_2}{1 \text{ L CaCl}_2} = 0.00572 \text{ mol Ca}^{2+}$$

$$\text{mol CO}_3^{2-} = 0.0375 \text{ L Na}_2\text{CO}_3 \times \frac{0.149 \text{ mol Na}_2\text{CO}_3}{1 \text{ L Na}_2\text{CO}_3} = 0.00559 \text{ mol CO}_3^{2-}$$

Since one Ca^{2+} reacts with one CO_3^{2-}, Na_2CO_3 is the limiting reactant. Since 0.00559 mol CO_3^{2-} reacts, 0.00559 mol of CaCO_3 will form.

molar mass CaCO_3 = 100.1 g

$$0.00559 \text{ mol CaCO}_3 \times \frac{100.1 \text{ g CaCO}_3}{1 \text{ mol CaCO}_3} = 0.560 \text{ g CaCO}_3$$

66.   Molar mass $\text{Na}_2\text{C}_2\text{O}_4$ = 134.0 g   37.5 mL = 0.0375 L

$$\text{moles Ca}^{2+} \text{ ion} = 0.0375 \text{ L} \times \frac{0.104 \text{ mol}}{1.00 \text{ L}} = 0.00390 \text{ mol Ca}^{2+} \text{ ion}$$

$$\text{Ca}^{2+}(aq) + \text{C}_2\text{O}_4^{2-}(aq) \rightarrow \text{CaC}_2\text{O}_4(s)$$

Since the precipitation reaction is of 1:1 stoichiometry, then 0.00390 mol of $\text{C}_2\text{O}_4^{2-}$ ion is needed. And since each formula unit of $\text{Na}_2\text{C}_2\text{O}_4$ contains one $\text{C}_2\text{O}_4^{2-}$ ion, then 0.00390 mol of $\text{Na}_2\text{C}_2\text{O}_4$ is required.

$$0.00390 \text{ mol Na}_2\text{C}_2\text{O}_4 \times \frac{134.0 \text{ g}}{1 \text{ mol}} = 0.523 \text{ g Na}_2\text{C}_2\text{O}_4 \text{ required}$$

67. $\text{Pb(NO}_3)_2(aq) + \text{K}_2\text{CrO}_4(aq) \rightarrow \text{PbCrO}_4(s) + 2\text{KNO}_3(aq)$

molar masses: $\text{Pb(NO}_3)_2$, 331.2 g; PbCrO_4, 323.2 g

$$1.00 \text{ g Pb(NO}_3)_2 \times \frac{1 \text{ mol Pb(NO}_3)_2}{331.2 \text{ g Pb(NO}_3)_2} = 0.003019 \text{ mol Pb(NO}_3)_2$$

25.0 mL = 0.0250 L

$$0.0250 \text{ L solution} \times \frac{1.00 \text{ mol K}_2\text{CrO}_4}{1.00 \text{ L solution}} = 0.0250 \text{ mol K}_2\text{CrO}_4$$

Pb(NO$_3$)$_2$ is the limiting reactant: 0.003019 mol PbCrO$_4$ will form.

$$0.003019 \text{ mol PbCrO}_4 \times \frac{323.2 \text{ g PbCrO}_4}{1 \text{ mol PbCrO}_4} = 0.976 \text{ g PbCrO}_4$$

68. 10.0 mL = 0.0100 L

$$0.0100 \text{ L} \times \frac{0.250 \text{ mol AlCl}_3}{1.00 \text{ L}} = 2.50 \times 10^{-3} \text{ mol AlCl}_3$$

AlCl$_3$(aq) + 3NaOH(s) → Al(OH)$_3$(s) + 3NaCl(aq)

$$2.50 \times 10^{-3} \text{ mol AlCl}_3 \times \frac{3 \text{ mol NaOH}}{1 \text{ mol AlCl}_3} = 7.50 \times 10^{-3} \text{ mol NaOH}$$

molar mass NaOH = 40.0 g

$$7.50 \times 10^{-3} \text{ mol NaOH} \times \frac{40.0 \text{ g NaOH}}{1 \text{ mol}} = 0.300 \text{ g NaOH}$$

69. HCl(aq) + NaOH(aq) → NaCl(aq) + H$_2$O(l)

25.0 mL = 0.0250 L

$$0.0250 \text{ L} \times \frac{0.150 \text{ mol NaOH}}{1.00 \text{ L}} = 0.00375 \text{ mol NaOH}$$

$$0.00375 \text{ mol NaOH} \times \frac{1 \text{ mol HCl}}{1 \text{ mol NaOH}} = 0.00375 \text{ mol HCl}$$

$$0.00375 \text{ mol HCl} \times \frac{1 \text{ L solution}}{0.200 \text{ mol HCl}} = 0.01875 \text{ L} = 18.8 \text{ mL}$$

70. HCl(aq) + NaOH(aq) → NaCl(aq) + H$_2$O(l)

24.9 mL = 0.0249 L

$$0.0249 \text{ L} \times \frac{0.451 \text{ mol NaOH}}{1.00 \text{ L}} = 0.0112 \text{ mol NaOH}$$

$$0.0112 \text{ mol NaOH} \times \frac{1 \text{ mol HCl}}{1 \text{ mol NaOH}} = 0.0112 \text{ mol HCl}$$

$$0.0112 \text{ mol HCl} \times \frac{1.00 \text{ L}}{0.175 \text{ mol HCl}} = 0.0642 \text{ L required} = 64.2 \text{ mL}$$

71. HCl(aq) + NaOH(aq) → NaCl(aq) + H$_2$O(l)

50.0 mL = 0.0500 L   48.7 mL = 0.0487 L

$$0.0500 \text{ L} \times \frac{0.104 \text{ mol HCl}}{1.00 \text{ L solution}} = 0.00520 \text{ mol HCl}$$

$$0.00520 \text{ mol HCl} \times \frac{1 \text{ mol NaOH}}{1 \text{ mol HCl}} = 0.00520 \text{ mol NaOH}$$

$$M = \frac{0.00520 \text{ mol NaOH}}{0.0487 \text{ L}} = 0.107 \; M$$

72. $7.2 \text{ mL} = 0.0072 \text{ L}$

$$0.0072 \text{ L} \times \frac{2.5 \times 10^{-3} \text{ mol NaOH}}{1.00 \text{ L}} = 1.8 \times 10^{-5} \text{ mol NaOH}$$

$$H^+(aq) + OH^-(aq) \rightarrow H_2O(l)$$

$$1.8 \times 10^{-5} \text{ mol OH}^- \times \frac{1 \text{ mol H}^+}{1 \text{ mol OH}^-} = 1.8 \times 10^{-5} \text{ mol H}^+$$

$100 \text{ mL} = 0.100 \text{ L}$

$$M = \frac{1.8 \times 10^{-5} \text{ mol H}^+}{0.100 \text{ L}} = 1.8 \times 10^{-4} \; M \; H^+(aq)$$

73.   a. $NaOH(aq) + HC_2H_3O_2(aq) \rightarrow NaC_2H_3O_2(aq) + H_2O(l)$

$25.0 \text{ mL} = 0.0250 \text{ L}$

$$0.0250 \text{ L} \times \frac{0.154 \text{ mol HC}_2\text{H}_3\text{O}_2}{1.00 \text{ L}} = 0.00385 \text{ mol HC}_2\text{H}_3\text{O}_2$$

$$0.00385 \text{ mol HC}_2\text{H}_3\text{O}_2 \times \frac{1 \text{ mol NaOH}}{1 \text{ mol HC}_2\text{H}_3\text{O}_2} = 0.00385 \text{ mol NaOH}$$

$$0.00385 \text{ mol NaOH} \times \frac{1.00 \text{ L}}{1.00 \text{ mol NaOH}} = 0.00385 \text{ L} = 3.85 \text{ mL NaOH}$$

b. $HF(aq) + NaOH(aq) \rightarrow NaF(aq) + H_2O(l)$

$35.0 \text{ mL} = 0.0350 \text{ L}$

$$0.0350 \text{ L} \times \frac{0.102 \text{ mol HF}}{1.00 \text{ L}} = 0.00357 \text{ mol HF}$$

$$0.00357 \text{ mol HF} \times \frac{1 \text{ mol HF}}{1 \text{ mol NaOH}} = 0.00357 \text{ mol NaOH}$$

$$0.00357 \text{ mol NaOH} \times \frac{1.00 \text{ L}}{1.00 \text{ mol NaOH}} = 0.00357 \text{ L} = 3.57 \text{ mL}$$

c. $H_3PO_4(aq) + 3NaOH(aq) \rightarrow Na_3PO_4(aq) + 3H_2O(l)$

$10.0 \text{ mL} = 0.0100 \text{ L}$

$$0.0100 \text{ L} \times \frac{0.143 \text{ mol H}_3\text{PO}_4}{1.00 \text{ L}} = 0.00143 \text{ mol H}_3\text{PO}_4$$

$$0.00143 \text{ mol } H_3PO_4 \times \frac{3 \text{ mol NaOH}}{1 \text{ mol } H_3PO_4} = 0.00429 \text{ mol NaOH}$$

$$0.00429 \text{ mol NaOH} \times \frac{1.00 \text{ L}}{1.00 \text{ mol NaOH}} = 0.00429 \text{ L} = 4.29 \text{ mL}$$

d. $H_2SO_4(aq) + 2NaOH(aq) \rightarrow Na_2SO_4(aq) + 2H_2O(l)$

35.0 mL = 0.0350 L

$$0.0350 \text{ L} \times \frac{0.220 \text{ mol } H_2SO_4}{1.00 \text{ L}} = 0.00770 \text{ mol } H_2SO_4$$

$$0.00770 \text{ mol } H_2SO_4 \times \frac{2 \text{ mol NaOH}}{1 \text{ mol } H_2SO_4} = 0.0154 \text{ mol NaOH}$$

$$0.0154 \text{ mol NaOH} \times \frac{1.00 \text{ L}}{1.00 \text{ mol NaOH}} = 0.0154 \text{ L} = 15.4 \text{ mL}$$

74.   Experimentally, neutralization reactions are usually performed with volumetric glassware that is calibrated in milliliters rather than liters. For convenience in calculations for such reactions, the arithmetic is often performed in terms of *milli*liters and *milli*moles, rather than in liters and moles. 1 mmol = 0.001 mol. Note that the number of moles of solute per liter of solution, the molarity, is numerically equivalent to the number of *milli*moles of solute per *milli*liter of solution.

a. $HNO_3(aq) + NaOH(aq) \rightarrow NaNO_3(aq) + H_2O(l)$

$$12.7 \text{ mL} \times \frac{0.501 \text{ mmol}}{1 \text{ mL}} = 6.36 \text{ mmol NaOH present in the sample}$$

$$6.36 \text{ mmol NaOH} \times \frac{1 \text{ mmol } HNO_3}{1 \text{ mmol NaOH}} = 6.36 \text{ mmol } HNO_3 \text{ required to react}$$

$$6.36 \text{ mmol } HNO_3 \times \frac{1.00 \text{ mL}}{0.101 \text{ mmol } HNO_3} = 63.0 \text{ mL } HNO_3 \text{ required}$$

b. $2HNO_3(aq) + Ba(OH)_2 \rightarrow Ba(NO_3)_2 + 2H_2O(l)$

$$24.9 \text{ mL} \times \frac{0.00491 \text{ mmol}}{1.00 \text{ mL}} = 0.122 \text{ mmol Ba(OH)}_2 \text{ present in the sample}$$

$$0.122 \text{ mmol Ba(OH)}_2 \times \frac{2 \text{ mmol } HNO_3}{1 \text{ mmol Ba(OH)}_2} = 0.244 \text{ mmol } HNO_3 \text{ required}$$

$$0.244 \text{ mmol } HNO_3 \times \frac{1.00 \text{ mL}}{0.101 \text{ mmol } HNO_3} = 2.42 \text{ mL } HNO_3 \text{ is required}$$

c. $HNO_3(aq) + NH_3(aq) \rightarrow NH_4NO_3(aq)$

$$49.1 \text{ mL} \times \frac{0.103 \text{ mmol}}{1.00 \text{ mL}} = 5.06 \text{ mmol } NH_3 \text{ present in the sample}$$

$$5.06 \text{ mmol } NH_3 \times \frac{1 \text{ mmol } HNO_3}{1 \text{ mmol } NH_3} = 5.06 \text{ mmol } HNO_3 \text{ required}$$

$$5.06 \text{ mmol } HNO_3 \times \frac{1.00 \text{ mL}}{0.101 \text{ mmol } HNO_3} = 50.1 \text{ mL } HNO_3 \text{ required}$$

d. $KOH(aq) + HNO_3(aq) \rightarrow KNO_3(aq) + H_2O(l)$

$$1.21 \text{ L} \times \frac{0.102 \text{ mol}}{1.00 \text{ L}} = 0.123 \text{ mol KOH present in the sample}$$

$$0.123 \text{ mol KOH} \times \frac{1 \text{ mol } HNO_3}{1 \text{ mol KOH}} = 0.123 \text{ mol } HNO_3 \text{ required}$$

$$0.123 \text{ mol } HNO_3 \times \frac{1.00 \text{ L}}{0.101 \text{ mol } HNO_3} = 1.22 \text{ L } HNO_3 \text{ required}$$

75.   equivalent

76.   1 normal

77.   When H_2SO_4 reacts with OH^-, the reaction is

$$H_2SO_4(aq) + 2OH^-(aq) \rightarrow 2H_2O(l) + SO_4^{2-}(aq)$$

Since each mol of H_2SO_4 provides *two* moles of H^+ ion, it is only necessary to take *half* a mole of H_2SO_4 to provide *one* mole of H^+ ion. The equivalent weight of H_2SO_4 is thus half the molar mass.

78.   1.53 equivalents OH^- ion are needed to react with 1.53 equivalents of H^+ ion. By *definition*, one equivalent of OH^- ion exactly neutralizes one equivalent of H^+ ion.

79. $N = \dfrac{\text{number of equivalents of solute}}{\text{number of liters of solution}}$ 225 mL = 0.225 L

a.   equivalent weight HCl = molar mass HCl = 36.46 g

$$0.225 \text{ L} \times \frac{0.124 \text{ equiv HCl}}{1 \text{ L}} = 0.0279 \text{ equiv HCl}$$

$$0.0279 \text{ equiv HCl} \times \frac{36.46 \text{ g HCl}}{1 \text{ equiv HCl}} = 1.02 \text{ g HCl}$$

b.   equivalent weight $H_2SO_4 = \dfrac{\text{molar mass}}{2} = \dfrac{98.09 \text{ g}}{2} = 49.05 \text{ g}$

$$0.225 \text{ L} \times \frac{0.124 \text{ equiv } H_2SO_4}{1 \text{ L}} = 0.0279 \text{ equiv } H_2SO_4$$

$$0.0279 \text{ equiv } H_2SO_4 \times \frac{49.05 \text{ g } H_2SO_4}{1 \text{ equiv } H_2SO_4} = 1.37 \text{ g } H_2SO_4$$

c. $\text{equivalent weight } H_3PO_4 = \dfrac{\text{molar mass}}{3} = \dfrac{98.0 \text{ g}}{3} = 32.7 \text{ g}$

$$0.225 \text{ L} \times \frac{0.124 \text{ equiv } H_3PO_4}{1 \text{ L}} = 0.0279 \text{ equiv } H_3PO_4$$

$$0.0279 \text{ equiv } H_3PO_4 \times \frac{32.7 \text{ g } H_3PO_4}{1 \text{ equiv } H_3PO_4} = 0.912 \text{ g } H_3PO_4$$

80. $N = \dfrac{\text{number of equivalents of solute}}{\text{number of liters of solution}}$

a.   equivalent weight NaOH = molar mass NaOH = 40.00 g

$$0.113 \text{ g NaOH} \times \frac{1 \text{ equiv NaOH}}{40.00 \text{ g}} = 2.83 \times 10^{-3} \text{ equiv NaOH}$$

10.2 mL = 0.0102 L

$$N = \frac{2.83 \times 10^{-3} \text{ equiv}}{0.0102 \text{ L}} = 0.277 \ N$$

b. $\text{equivalent weight } Ca(OH)_2 = \dfrac{\text{molar mass}}{2} = \dfrac{74.10 \text{ g}}{2} = 37.05 \text{ g}$

$$12.5 \text{ mg} \times \frac{1 \text{ g}}{10^3 \text{ mg}} \times \frac{1 \text{ equiv}}{37.05 \text{ g}} = 3.37 \times 10^{-4} \text{ equiv } Ca(OH)_2$$

100. mL = 0.100 L

$$N = \frac{3.37 \times 10^{-3} \text{ equiv}}{0.100 \text{ L}} = 3.37 \times 10^{-3} \ N$$

c. $\text{equivalent weight } H_2SO_4 = \dfrac{\text{molar mass}}{2} = \dfrac{98.09 \text{ g}}{2} = 49.05 \text{ g}$

$$12.4 \text{ g} \times \frac{1 \text{ equiv}}{49.05 \text{ g}} = 0.253 \text{ equiv } H_2SO_4$$

155 mL = 0.155 L

$$N = \frac{0.253 \text{ equiv}}{0.155 \text{ L}} = 1.63 \ N$$

81. a. $0.250 \; M \; \text{HCl} \times \dfrac{1 \; \text{equiv HCl}}{1 \; \text{mol HCl}} = 0.250 \; N \; \text{HCl}$

   b. $0.105 \; M \; H_2SO_4 \times \dfrac{2 \; \text{equiv } H_2SO_4}{1 \; \text{mol } H_2SO_4} = 0.210 \; N$

   c. $5.3 \times 10^{-2} \; M \; H_3PO_4 \times \dfrac{3 \; \text{equiv } H_3PO_4}{1 \; \text{mol } H_3PO_4} = 0.159 \; N = 0.16 \; N$

82. a. $0.134 \; M \; \text{NaOH} \times \dfrac{1 \; \text{equiv NaOH}}{1 \; \text{mol NaOH}} = 0.134 \; N \; \text{NaOH}$

   b. $0.00521 \; M \; Ca(OH)_2 \times \dfrac{2 \; \text{equiv } Ca(OH)_2}{1 \; \text{mol } Ca(OH)_2} = 0.0104 \; N \; Ca(OH)_2$

   c. $4.42 \; M \; H_3PO_4 \times \dfrac{3 \; \text{equiv } H_3PO_4}{1 \; \text{mol } H_3PO_4} = 13.3 \; N \; H_3PO_4$

83. molar mass H_3PO_4 = 98.0 g

   $35.2 \; \text{g } H_3PO_4 \times \dfrac{1 \; \text{mol } H_3PO_4}{98.0 \; \text{g } H_3PO_4} = 0.3592 \; \text{mol } H_3PO_4$

   $M = \dfrac{0.3592 \; \text{mol } H_3PO_4}{1.00 \; \text{L}} = 0.3592 \; M = 0.359 \; M$

   $0.3592 \; M \; H_3PO_4 \times \dfrac{3 \; \text{equiv } H_3PO_4}{1 \; \text{mol } H_3PO_4} = 1.08 \; N$

84. Molar mass of $Ca(OH)_2$ = 74.10 g

   $5.21 \; \text{mg } Ca(OH)_2 \times \dfrac{1 \; \text{g}}{10^3 \; \text{mg}} \times \dfrac{1 \; \text{mol}}{74.10 \; \text{g}} = 7.03 \times 10^{-5} \; \text{mol } Ca(OH)_2$

   1000. mL = 1.000 L (volumetric flask volume: 4 significant figures).

   $M = \dfrac{7.03 \times 10^{-5} \; \text{mol}}{1.000 \; \text{L}} = 7.03 \times 10^{-5} \; M \; Ca(OH)_2$

   $N = 7.03 \times 10^{-5} \; M \; Ca(OH)_2 \times \dfrac{2 \; \text{equiv } Ca(OH)_2}{1 \; \text{mol } Ca(OH)_2} = 1.41 \times 10^{-4} \; N \; Ca(OH)_2$

85. $H_2SO_4(aq) + 2NaOH(aq) \rightarrow Na_2SO_4(aq) + 2H_2O(l)$

   $N_{acid} \times V_{acid} = N_{base} \times V_{base}$

   $(0.35 \; N) \times (15.0 \; \text{mL}) = (0.50 \; N) \times (V_{base})$

   $V_{base} = 10.5 \; \text{mL} = 11 \; \text{mL}$

86. $H_2SO_4(aq) + 2NaOH \rightarrow Na_2SO_4(aq) + 2H_2O(l)$

   $0.145 \; M \; \text{NaOH} = 0.145 \; N \; \text{NaOH}$ 56.2 mL = 0.0562 L

$$0.0562 \text{ L NaOH} \times \frac{0.145 \text{ equiv}}{1.00 \text{ L}} = 0.00815 \text{ equiv NaOH}$$

0.00815 equiv NaOH requires 0.00815 equiv H_2SO_4 to react.

$$0.00815 \text{ equiv } H_2SO_4 \times \frac{1.00 \text{ L}}{0.172 \text{ equiv}} = 0.0474 \text{ L} = 47.4 \text{ mL } H_2SO_4 \text{ solution}$$

87. $2NaOH(aq) + H_2SO_4(aq) \rightarrow Na_2SO_4(aq) + 2 H_2O(l)$

For the 0.125 N H_2SO_4:

$N_{acid} \times V_{acid} = N_{base} \times V_{base}$

$(0.125 \text{ } N) \times (24.2 \text{ mL}) = (0.151 \text{ } N) \times (V_{base})$

V_{base} = 20.0 mL of the 0.151 N NaOH solution needed

For the 0.125 M H_2SO_4:

Since each H_2SO_4 formula unit produces two H^+ ions, the normality of this solution will be twice its molarity

0.125 M H_2SO_4 = 0.250 N H_2SO_4

$N_{acid} \times V_{acid} = N_{base} \times V_{base}$

$(0.250 \text{ } N) \times (24.1 \text{ mL}) = (0.151 \text{ } N) \times (V_{base})$

V_{base} = 39.9 mL of the 0.151 N NaOH solution needed

88. $2NaOH(aq) + H_2SO_4(aq) \rightarrow Na_2SO_4(aq) + 2 H_2O(l)$

$$27.34 \text{ mL NaOH} \times \frac{0.1021 \text{ mmol}}{1.00 \text{ mL}} = 2.791 \text{ mmol NaOH}$$

$$2.791 \text{ mmol NaOH} \times \frac{1 \text{ mmol } H_2SO_4}{2 \text{ mmol NaOH}} = 1.396 \text{ mmol } H_2SO_4$$

$$M = \frac{1.396 \text{ mmol } H_2SO_4}{25.00 \text{ mL}} = 0.05583 \text{ } M \text{ } H_2SO_4 = 0.1117 \text{ } N \text{ } H_2SO_4$$

89.   total mass of solution = 50.0 g + 50.0 g + 5.0 g = 105.0 g

$$\% \text{ ethanol} = \frac{50.0 \text{ g ethanol}}{105.0 \text{ g total}} \times 100 = 47.6\% \text{ ethanol}$$

$$\% \text{ water} = \frac{50.0 \text{ g water}}{105.0 \text{ g total}} \times 100 = 47.6\% \text{ water}$$

$$\% \text{ sugar} = \frac{5.0 \text{ g sugar}}{105.0 \text{ g total}} \times 100 = 4.8\% \text{ sugar}$$

$$1.5 \text{ g sugar} \times \frac{100.0 \text{ g solution}}{4.8 \text{ g sugar}} = 31 \text{ g solution}$$

$$10.0 \text{ g ethanol} \times \frac{100.0 \text{ g solution}}{47.6 \text{ g ethanol}} = 21.0 \text{ g solution}$$

90. Molarity is defined as the number of moles of solute contained in 1 liter of *total* solution volume (solute plus solvent after mixing). In the first case, where 50. g of NaCl is dissolved in 1.0 L of water, the total volume after mixing is *not* known and the molarity cannot be calculated. In the second example, the final volume after mixing is known and the molarity can be calculated simply.

91. millimol $CoCl_2$ = 50.0 mL × 0.250 M $CoCl_2$ = 12.5 millimol $CoCl_2$

    This contains 12.5 millimol Co^{2+} and 25.0 millimol Cl^-

    millimol $NiCl_2$ = 25.0 mL × 0.350 M $NiCl_2$ = 8.75 millimol $NiCl_2$

    This contains 8.75 millimol Ni^{2+} and 17.5 millimol Cl^-

    Total millimol Cl^- after mixing = 25.0 + 17.5 = 42.5 millimol Cl^-

    Total volume after mixing = 50.0 mL + 25.0 mL = 75.0 mL

    $$M_{cobalt(II) \text{ ion}} = \frac{12.5 \text{ millimol } Co^{2+}}{75.0 \text{ mL}} = 0.167 \ M$$

    $$M_{nickel(II) \text{ ion}} = \frac{8.75 \text{ millimol } Ni^{2+}}{75.0 \text{ mL}} = 0.117 \ M$$

    $$M_{chloride \text{ ion}} = \frac{42.5 \text{ millimol } Cl^-}{75.0 \text{ mL}} = 0.567 \ M$$

92. $$75 \text{ g solution} \times \frac{25 \text{ g NaCl}}{100 \text{ g solution}} = 18.75 \text{ g NaCl}$$

    $$new \ \% = \frac{18.75 \text{ g NaCl}}{575 \text{ g solution}} \times 100 = 3.26 = 3.3 \ \%$$

93. $AgNO_3(s)$ + $NaCl(aq)$ → $AgCl(s)$ + $NaNO_3(aq)$

    molar masses: $AgNO_3$, 169.9 g; $AgCl$, 143.4 g

    $$10.0 \text{ g } AgNO_3 \times \frac{1 \text{ mol } AgNO_3}{169.9 \text{ g } AgNO_3} = 0.05886 \text{ mol } AgNO_3$$

    50. mL = 0.050 L

    $$0.050 \text{ L} \times \frac{1.0 \times 10^{-2} \text{ mol NaCl}}{1.00 \text{ L}} = 0.00050 \text{ mol NaCl}$$

    NaCl is the limiting reactant. 0.00050 mol AgCl form.

$$0.00050 \text{ mol AgCl} \times \frac{143.4 \text{ g AgCl}}{1 \text{ mol}} = 0.072 \text{ g AgCl (72 mg)}$$

Since 1 mol $AgNO_3$ contains 1 mol Ag^+, the mol Ag^+ remaining in solution = $0.05886 - 0.00050 = 0.05836$ mol $AgNO_3$

0.05836 mol $AgNO_3$ = 0.05836 mol Ag^+

$$M_{silver \ ion} = \frac{0.05836 \text{ mol Ag}^+}{0.050 \text{ L}} = 1.167 \ M = 1.2 \ M$$

94. $Ba(NO_3)_2(aq) + H_2SO_4(aq) \rightarrow BaSO_4(s) + 2HNO_3(aq)$

37.5 mL = 0.0375 L

$$0.0375 \text{ L} \times \frac{0.221 \text{ mol H}_2\text{SO}_4}{1.00 \text{ L}} = 0.00829 \text{ mol H}_2\text{SO}_4$$

Since the coefficients of $Ba(NO_3)_2$ and H_2SO_4 in the balanced chemical equation for the reaction are both *one*, then 0.00829 mol of Ba^{2+} ion will be precipitated from the solution as $BaSO_4$.

molar mass $BaSO_4$ = 233.4 g

$$0.00829 \text{ mol BaSO}_4 \times \frac{233.4 \text{ g BaSO}_4}{1 \text{ mol BaSO}_4} = 1.93 \text{ g BaSO}_4 \text{ precipitate}$$

95. $NiCl_2(aq) + H_2S(aq) \rightarrow NiS(s) + 2HCl(aq)$

10. mL = 0.010 L

$$0.010 \text{ L} \times \frac{0.050 \text{ mol NiCl}_2}{1.00 \text{ L}} = 0.00050 \text{ mol NiCl}_2$$

From the balanced equation, 0.00050 mol H_2S will be required.

$$0.00050 \text{ mol H}_2\text{S} \times \frac{22.4 \text{ L}}{1 \text{ mol}} = 0.0112 \text{ L} = 11 \text{ mL H}_2\text{S}$$

96.   molar mass H_2O = 18.0 g

1.0 L water = 1.0×10^3 mL water $\approx 1.0 \times 10^3$ g water

$$1.0 \times 10^3 \text{ g H}_2\text{O} \times \frac{1 \text{ mol H}_2\text{O}}{18.0 \text{ g H}_2\text{O}} = 56 \text{ mol H}_2\text{O}$$

97.   100. mL = 0.100 L

$$0.100 \text{ L} \times \frac{14.5 \text{ mol NH}_3}{1.00 \text{ L}} = 1.45 \text{ mol NH}_3$$

$$1.45 \text{ mol NH}_3 \times \frac{22.4 \text{ L}}{1 \text{ mol}} = 32.5 \text{ L}$$

98.   500 mL HCl solution = 0.500 L HCl solution

$$0.500 \text{ L solution} \times \frac{0.100 \text{ mol HCl}}{1.00 \text{ L HCl solution}} = 0.0500 \text{ mol HCl}$$

$$0.0500 \text{ mol HCl} \times \frac{22.4 \text{ L HCl gas at STP}}{1 \text{ mol HCl}} = 1.12 \text{ L HCl gas at STP}$$

99.   When we say "like dissolves like" we mean that two substances will be miscible if they have similar intermolecular forces, so that the forces existing in the mixture will be similar to the forces existing in each separate substance. Molecules do *not* have to be identical to be miscible, but a similarity in structure (e.g., an –OH group) will aid solubility.

100. $$10.0 \text{ g HCl} \times \frac{100. \text{ g solution}}{33.1 \text{ g HCl}} = 30.21 \text{ g solution}$$

$$30.21 \text{ g solution} \times \frac{1.00 \text{ mL solution}}{1.147 \text{ g solution}} = 26.3 \text{ mL solution}$$

101. $$1.00 \text{ g AgNO}_3 \times \frac{100.0 \text{ g solution}}{0.50 \text{ g AgNO}_3} = 200 \text{ g solution} \ (2.0 \times 10^2 \text{ mL solution})$$

102.   molar mass $CaCl_2$ = 111.0 g

$$14.2 \text{ g CaCl}_2 \times \frac{1 \text{ mol CaCl}_2}{111.0 \text{ g CaCl}_2} = 0.128 \text{ mol CaCl}_2$$

50.0 mL = 0.0500 L

$$M = \frac{0.128 \text{ mol CaCl}_2}{0.0500 \text{ L}} = 2.56 \ M$$

103.   0.1 g $CaCl_2$

104.   a. $$\frac{5.0 \text{ g KNO}_3}{(5.0 \text{ g KNO}_3 + 75 \text{ g H}_2\text{O})} \times 100 = \frac{5.0 \text{ g}}{80.0 \text{ g}} \times 100 = 6.3\% \text{ KNO}_3$$

b.   2.5 mg = 0.0025 g

$$\frac{0.0025 \text{ g KNO}_3}{(0.0025 \text{ g KNO}_3 + 1.0 \text{ g H}_2\text{O})} \times 100 = \frac{0.0025 \text{ g}}{1.0025 \text{ g}} \times 100 = 0.25\% \text{ KNO}_3$$

c. $$\frac{11 \text{ g KNO}_3}{(11 \text{ g KNO}_3 + 89 \text{ g H}_2\text{O})} \times 100 = \frac{11 \text{ g}}{100 \text{ g}} \times 100 = 11\% \text{ KNO}_3$$

d. $$\frac{11 \text{ g KNO}_3}{(11 \text{ g KNO}_3 + 49 \text{ g H}_2\text{O})} \times 100 = \frac{11 \text{ g}}{60 \text{ g}} \times 100 = 18\% \text{ KNO}_3$$

105. To say a solution is 15.0% by mass NaCl means that 100.0 g of the solution would contain 15.0 g of NaCl:

   a. $10.0 \text{ g NaCl} \times \dfrac{100 \text{ g solution}}{15.0 \text{ g NaCl}} = 66.7 \text{ g solution}$

   b. $25.0 \text{ g NaCl} \times \dfrac{100 \text{ g solution}}{15.0 \text{ g NaCl}} = 167 \text{ g solution}$

   c. $100.0 \text{ g NaCl} \times \dfrac{100 \text{ g solution}}{15.0 \text{ g NaCl}} = 667 \text{ g solution}$

   d. $1.0 \text{ lb} = 453.59 \text{ g}$

   $453.59 \text{ g NaCl} \times \dfrac{100 \text{ g solution}}{15.0 \text{ g NaCl}} = 3.02 \times 10^3 \text{ g solution}$

106. $\%C = \dfrac{5.0 \text{ g C}}{(5.0 \text{ g C} + 1.5 \text{ g Ni} + 100. \text{ g Fe})} \times 100 = \dfrac{5.0 \text{ g}}{106.5 \text{ g}} \times 100 = 4.7\% \text{ C}$

   $\%Ni = \dfrac{1.5 \text{ g Ni}}{(5.0 \text{ g C} + 1.5 \text{ g Ni} + 100. \text{ g Fe})} \times 100 = \dfrac{1.5 \text{ g}}{106.5 \text{ g}} \times 100 = 1.4\% \text{ Ni}$

   $\%Fe = \dfrac{100. \text{ g Fe}}{(5.0 \text{ g C} + 1.5 \text{ g Ni} + 100. \text{ g Fe})} \times 100 = \dfrac{100. \text{ g}}{106.5 \text{ g}} \times 100 = 93.9\% \text{ Fe}$

107. $25 \text{ g dextrose} \times \dfrac{100 \text{ g solution}}{10 \text{ g dextrose}} = 250 \text{ g solution}$

108. To say that the solution is 5.5% by mass Na_2CO_3 means that 5.5 g of Na_2CO_3 are contained in every 100 g of the solution.

   $500. \text{ g solution} \times \dfrac{5.5 \text{ g } Na_2CO_3}{100 \text{ g solution}} = 28 \text{ g } Na_2CO_3$

109. $125 \text{ g solution} \times \dfrac{1.5 \text{ g } KNO_3}{100 \text{ g solution}} = 1.9 \text{ g } KNO_3$

110. For NaCl: $125 \text{ g solution} \times \dfrac{7.5 \text{ g NaCl}}{100 \text{ g solution}} = 9.4 \text{ g NaCl}$

   For KBr: $125 \text{ g solution} \times \dfrac{2.5 \text{ g KBr}}{100 \text{ g solution}} = 3.1 \text{ g KBr}$

111. $0.0117 \text{ L} \times \dfrac{0.102 \text{ mol } Na_3PO_4}{1 \text{ L}} = 1.19 \times 10^{-4} \text{ mol } Na_3PO_4$

   The sample would contain 1.19×10^{-4} mol of PO_4^{3-} and $3(1.19 \times 10^{-4}) = 3.58 \times 10^{-4}$ mol of Na^+ ion.

112. Molarity = $\dfrac{\text{moles of solute}}{\text{liters of solution}}$

a.   25 mL = 0.025 L

$$M = \frac{0.10 \text{ mol } CaCl_2}{0.025 \text{ L solution}} = 4.0 \ M$$

b. $M = \dfrac{2.5 \text{ mol KBr}}{2.5 \text{ L solution}} = 1.0 \ M$

c.   755 mL = 0.755 L

$$M = \frac{0.55 \text{ mol } NaNO_3}{0.755 \text{ L solution}} = 0.73 \ M$$

d. $M = \dfrac{4.5 \text{ mol } Na_2SO_4}{1.25 \text{ L solution}} = 3.6 \ M$

113. Molarity = $\dfrac{\text{moles of solute}}{\text{liters of solution}}$

a.   molar mass $BaCl_2$ = 208.2 g

$$5.0 \text{ g } BaCl_2 \times \frac{1 \text{ mol}}{208.2 \text{ g}} = 0.0240 \text{ mol } BaCl_2$$

$$M = \frac{0.240 \text{ mol } BaCl_2}{2.5 \text{ L solution}} = 9.6 \times 10^{-3} \ M$$

b.   molar mass KBr = 119.0 g

$$3.5 \text{ g KBr} \times \frac{1 \text{ mol}}{119.0 \text{ g}} = 0.0294 \text{ mol KBr}$$

75 mL = 0.075 L

$$M = \frac{0.0294 \text{ mol KBr}}{0.075 \text{ L solution}} = 0.39 \ M$$

c.   molar mass Na_2CO_3 = 106.0 g

$$21.5 \text{ g } Na_2CO_3 \times \frac{1 \text{ mol}}{106.0 \text{ g}} = 0.2028 \text{ mol } Na_2CO_3$$

175 mL = 0.175 L

$$M = \frac{0.2028 \text{ mol } Na_2CO_3}{0.175 \text{ L solution}} = 1.16 \ M$$

d.   molar mass $CaCl_2$ = 111.0 g

$$55 \text{ g } CaCl_2 \times \frac{1 \text{ mol}}{111.0 \text{ g}} = 0.495 \text{ mol } CaCl_2$$

$$M = \frac{0.495 \text{ mol } CaCl_2}{1.2 \text{ L solution}} = 0.41 \text{ } M$$

114. molar mass $C_{12}H_{22}O_{11}$ = 342.3 g

$$125 \text{ g } C_{12}H_{22}O_{11} \times \frac{1 \text{ mol}}{342.3 \text{ g}} = 0.3652 \text{ mol } C_{12}H_{22}O_{11}$$

450. mL = 0.450 L

$$M = \frac{0.3652 \text{ mol } C_{12}H_{22}O_{11}}{0.450 \text{ L solution}} = 0.812 \text{ } M$$

115. molar mass HCl = 36.46 g

$$439 \text{ g HCl} \times \frac{1 \text{ mol}}{36.46 \text{ g}} = 12.04 \text{ mol HCl}$$

$$M = \frac{12.04 \text{ mol HCl}}{1.00 \text{ L solution}} = 12.0 \text{ } M$$

116. molar mass NaCl = 58.44 g

$$1.5 \text{ g NaCl} \times \frac{1 \text{ mol}}{58.44 \text{ g}} = 0.0257 \text{ mol NaCl}$$

$$M = \frac{0.0257 \text{ mol NaCl}}{1.0 \text{ L solution}} = 0.026 \text{ } M$$

117. Molarity = $\dfrac{\text{moles of solute}}{\text{liters of solution}}$

a. $1.5 \text{ L solution} \times \dfrac{3.0 \text{ mol } H_2SO_4}{1.00 \text{ L solution}} = 4.5 \text{ mol } H_2SO_4$

b.   35 mL = 0.035 L

$$0.035 \text{ L solution} \times \frac{5.4 \text{ mol NaCl}}{1.00 \text{ L solution}} = 0.19 \text{ mol NaCl}$$

c. $5.2 \text{ L solution} \times \dfrac{18 \text{ mol } H_2SO_4}{1.00 \text{ L solution}} = 94 \text{ mol } H_2SO_4$

d. $0.050 \text{ L} \times \dfrac{1.1 \times 10^{-3} \text{ mol NaF}}{1.00 \text{ L solution}} = 5.5 \times 10^{-5} \text{ mol NaF}$

118. a. $4.25 \text{ L solution} \times \dfrac{0.105 \text{ mol KCl}}{1.00 \text{ L solution}} = 0.446 \text{ mol KCl}$

molar mass KCl = 74.6 g

$0.446 \text{ mol KCl} \times \dfrac{74.6 \text{ g KCl}}{1 \text{ mol KCl}} = 33.3 \text{ g KCl}$

b.   15.1 mL = 0.0151 L

$0.0151 \text{ L solution} \times \dfrac{0.225 \text{ mol NaNO}_3}{1.00 \text{ L solution}} = 3.40 \times 10^{-3} \text{ mol NaNO}_3$

molar mass $NaNO_3$ = 85.00 g

$3.40 \times 10^{-3} \text{ mol} \times \dfrac{85.00 \text{ g NaNO}_3}{1 \text{ mol NaNaNO}_3} = 0.289 \text{ g NaNO}_3$

c.   25 mL = 0.025 L

$0.025 \text{ L solution} \times \dfrac{3.0 \text{ mol HCl}}{1.00 \text{ L solution}} = 0.075 \text{ mol HCl}$

molar mass HCl = 36.46 g

$0.075 \text{ mol HCl} \times \dfrac{36.46 \text{ g HCl}}{1 \text{ mol HCl}} = 2.7 \text{ g HCl}$

d.   100. mL = 0.100 L

$0.100 \text{ L solution} \times \dfrac{0.505 \text{ mol H}_2\text{SO}_4}{1.00 \text{ L solution}} = 0.0505 \text{ mol H}_2\text{SO}_4$

molar mass H_2SO_4 = 98.09 g

$0.0505 \text{ mol H}_2\text{SO}_4 \times \dfrac{98.09 \text{ g H}_2\text{SO}_4}{1 \text{ mol H}_2\text{SO}_4} = 4.95 \text{ g H}_2\text{SO}_4$

119. molar mass $AgNO_3$ = 169.9 g

$10. \text{ g AgNO}_3 \times \dfrac{1 \text{ mol AgNO}_3}{169.9 \text{ g AgNO}_3} = 0.0589 \text{ mol AgNO}_3$

$0.0589 \text{ mol AgNO}_3 \times \dfrac{1.00 \text{ L solution}}{0.25 \text{ mol AgNO}_3} = 0.24 \text{ L solution}$

120. a. $1.25 \text{ L} \times \dfrac{0.250 \text{ mol Na}_3\text{PO}_4}{1.00 \text{ L}} = 0.3125 \text{ mol Na}_3\text{PO}_4$

$0.3125 \text{ mol Na}_3\text{PO}_4 \times \dfrac{3 \text{ mol Na}^+}{1 \text{ mol Na}_3\text{PO}_4} = 0.938 \text{ mol Na}^+$

$$0.3125 \text{ mol } Na_3PO_4 \times \frac{1 \text{ mol } PO_4^{3-}}{1 \text{ mol } Na_3PO_4} = 0.313 \text{ mol } PO_4^{3-}$$

b.   3.5 mL = 0.0035 L

$$0.0035 \text{ L} \times \frac{6.0 \text{ mol } H_2SO_4}{1.00 \text{ L}} = 0.021 \text{ mol } H_2SO_4$$

$$0.021 \text{ mol } H_2SO_4 \times \frac{2 \text{ mol } H^+}{1 \text{ mol } H_2SO_4} = 0.042 \text{ mol } H^+$$

$$0.021 \text{ mol } H_2SO_4 \times \frac{1 \text{ mol } SO_4^{2-}}{1 \text{ mol } H_2SO_4} = 0.021 \text{ mol } SO_4^{2-}$$

c.   25 mL = 0.025 L

$$0.025 \text{ L} \times \frac{0.15 \text{ mol } AlCl_3}{1.00 \text{ L}} = 0.00375 \text{ mol } AlCl_3$$

$$0.00375 \text{ mol } AlCl_3 \times \frac{1 \text{ mol } Al^{3+}}{1 \text{ mol } AlCl_3} = 0.0038 \text{ mol } Al^{3+}$$

$$0.00375 \text{ mol } AlCl_3 \times \frac{3 \text{ mol } Cl^-}{1 \text{ mol } AlCl_3} = 0.011 \text{ mol } Cl^-$$

d. $$1.50 \text{ L} \times \frac{1.25 \text{ mol } BaCl_2}{1.00 \text{ L}} = 1.875 \text{ mol } BaCl_2$$

$$1.875 \text{ mol } BaCl_2 \times \frac{1 \text{ mol } Ba^{2+}}{1 \text{ mol } BaCl_2} = 1.88 \text{ mol } Ba^{2+}$$

$$1.875 \text{ mol } BaCl_2 \times \frac{2 \text{ mol } Cl^-}{1 \text{ mol } BaCl_2} = 3.75 \text{ mol } Cl^-$$

121.   500. mL = 0.500 L

$$0.500 \text{ L} \times \frac{0.0200 \text{ mol } CaCO_3}{1.00 \text{ L}} = 0.0100 \text{ mol } CaCO_3 \text{ needed}$$

molar mass $CaCO_3$ = 100.1 g

$$0.0100 \text{ mol } CaCO_3 \times \frac{100.1 \text{ g } CaCO_3}{1 \text{ mol } CaCO_3} = 1.00 \text{ g } CaCO_3$$

122. $M_1 \times V_1 = M_2 \times V_2$

    a. $M_1 = 0.200 \, M$ $M_2 = \, ?$

        $V_1 = 125 \text{ mL}$ $V_2 = 125 + 150. = 275 \text{ mL}$

$$M_2 = \frac{(0.200 \, M)(125 \text{ mL})}{(275 \text{ mL})} = 0.0909 \, M$$

b. $M_1 = 0.250\ M$ $M_2 = ?$

      $V_1 = 155\ mL$ $V_2 = 155 + 150. = 305\ mL$

$$M_2 = \frac{(0.250\ M)(155\ mL)}{(305\ mL)} = 0.127\ M$$

c. $M_1 = 0.250\ M$ $M_2 = ?$

      $V_1 = 0.500\ L = 500.\ mL$ $V_2 = 500. + 150. = 650.\ mL$

$$M_2 = \frac{(0.250\ M)(500.\ mL)}{(650\ mL)} = 0.192\ M$$

d. $M_1 = 18.0\ M$ $M_2 = ?$

      $V_1 = 15\ mL$ $V_2 = 15 + 150. = 165\ mL$

$$M_2 = \frac{(18.0\ M)(15\ mL)}{(165\ mL)} = 1.6\ M$$

123. $M_1 \times V_1 = M_2 \times V_2$

      $M_1 = 18.0\ M$ $M_2 = 0.250\ M$

      $V_1 = ?$ $V_2 = 35.0\ mL$

$$V_1 = \frac{(0.250\ M)(35.0\ mL)}{(18.0\ M)} = 0.486\ mL$$

124. $M_1 \times V_1 = M_2 \times V_2$

      $M_1 = 5.4\ M$ $M_2 = ?$

      $V_1 = 50.\ mL$ $V_2 = 300.\ mL$

$$M_2 = \frac{(5.4\ M)(50.\ mL)}{(300.\ mL)} = 0.90\ M$$

125. $M_1 \times V_1 = M_2 \times V_2$

      $M_1 = 6.0\ M$ $M_2 = ?$

      $V_1 = 3.0\ L$ $V_2 = 10.0 + 3.0 = 13.0\ L$

$$M_2 = \frac{(6.0\ M)(3.0\ L)}{(13.0\ L)} = 1.4\ M$$

126. $25.0\ mL = 0.0250\ L$

$$0.0250\ L\ NiCl_2\ solution \times \frac{0.20\ mol\ NiCl_2}{1.00\ L\ NiCl_2\ solution} = 0.00500\ mol\ NiCl_2$$

$$0.00500\ mol\ NiCl_2 \times \frac{1\ mol\ Na_2S}{1\ mol\ NiCl_2} = 0.00500\ mol\ Na_2S$$

$$0.00500 \text{ mol } Na_2S \times \frac{1.00 \text{ L } Na_2S \text{ solution}}{0.10 \text{ mol } Na_2S} = 0.050 \text{ L} = 50. \text{ mL } Na_2S \text{ solution}$$

127.   15.3 mL = 0.0153 L

$$0.0153 \text{ L} \times \frac{0.139 \text{ mol } H_2SO_4}{1.00 \text{ L}} = 2.127 \times 10^{-3} \text{ mol } H_2SO_4$$

$$2.127 \times 10^{-3} \text{ mol } H_2SO_4 \times \frac{1 \text{ mol } Ba(NO_3)_2}{1 \text{ mol } H_2SO_4} = 2.127 \times 10^{-3} \text{ mol } Ba(NO_3)_2$$

molar mass $Ba(NO_3)_2$ = 261.3 g

$$2.127 \times 10^{-3} \text{ mol } Ba(NO_3)_2 \times \frac{261.3 \text{ g } Ba(NO_3)_2}{1 \text{ mol } Ba(NO_3)_2} = 0.556 \text{ g } Ba(NO_3)_2$$

128. $HNO_3(aq) + NaOH(aq) \rightarrow NaNO_3(aq) + H_2O(l)$

35.0 mL = 0.0350 L

$$0.0350 \text{ L} \times \frac{0.150 \text{ mol } NaOH}{1.00 \text{ L}} = 5.25 \times 10^{-3} \text{ mol } NaOH$$

$$5.25 \times 10^{-3} \text{ mol } NaOH \times \frac{1 \text{ mol } HNO_3}{1 \text{ mol } NaOH} = 5.25 \times 10^{-3} \text{ mol } HNO_3$$

$$5.25 \times 10^{-3} \text{ mol } HNO_3 \times \frac{1.00 \text{ L}}{0.150 \text{ mol } HNO_3} = 0.0350 \text{ L} = 35.0 \text{ mL } HNO_3$$

129.   a. $HCl(aq) + NaOH(aq) \rightarrow NaCl(aq) + H_2O(l)$

25.0 mL = 0.0250 L

$$0.0250 \text{ L} \times \frac{0.103 \text{ mol } NaOH}{1.00 \text{ L}} = 0.02575 \text{ mol } NaOH$$

$$0.02575 \text{ mol } NaOH \times \frac{1 \text{ mol } HCl}{1 \text{ mol } NaOH} = 0.02575 \text{ mol } HCl$$

$$0.02575 \text{ mol } HCl \times \frac{1.00 \text{ L}}{0.250 \text{ mol } HCl} = 0.0103 \text{ L } HCl = 10.3 \text{ mL } HCl$$

b. $2HCl(aq) + Ca(OH)_2(aq) \rightarrow CaCl_2(aq) + 2H_2O(l)$

50.0 mL = 0.0500 L

$$0.0500 \text{ L} \times \frac{0.00501 \text{ mol } Ca(OH)_2}{1.00 \text{ L}} = 2.505 \times 10^{-4} \text{ mol } Ca(OH)_2$$

$$2.505 \times 10^{-4} \text{ mol } Ca(OH)_2 \times \frac{2 \text{ mol } HCl}{1 \text{ mol } Ca(OH)_2} = 5.010 \times 10^{-4} \text{ mol } HCl$$

$$5.010 \times 10^{-4} \text{ mol HCl} \times \frac{1.00 \text{ L}}{0.250 \text{ mol HCl}} = 0.00200 \text{ L} = 2.00 \text{ mL}$$

c. $HCl(aq) + NH_3(aq) \rightarrow NH_4Cl(aq)$

20.0 mL = 0.0200 L

$$0.0200 \text{ L} \times \frac{0.226 \text{ mol NH}_3}{1.00 \text{ L}} = 0.00452 \text{ mol NH}_3$$

$$0.00452 \text{ mol NH}_3 \times \frac{1 \text{ mol HCl}}{1 \text{ mol NH}_3} = 0.00452 \text{ mol HCl}$$

$$0.00452 \text{ mol HCl} \times \frac{1.00 \text{ L}}{0.250 \text{ mol HCl}} = 0.01808 \text{ L} = 18.1 \text{ mL}$$

d. $HCl(aq) + KOH(aq) \rightarrow KCl(aq) + H_2O(l)$

15.0 mL = 0.0150 L

$$0.0150 \text{ L} \times \frac{0.0991 \text{ mol KOH}}{1.00 \text{ L}} = 1.487 \times 10^{-3} \text{ mol KOH}$$

$$1.487 \times 10^{-3} \text{ mol KOH} \times \frac{1 \text{ mol HCl}}{1 \text{ mol KOH}} = 1.487 \times 10^{-3} \text{ mol HCl}$$

$$1.487 \times 10^{-3} \text{ mol HCl} \times \frac{1.00 \text{ L}}{0.250 \text{ mol HCl}} = 0.00595 \text{ L} = 5.95 \text{ mL}$$

130. $N = \dfrac{\text{number of equivalents of solute}}{\text{number of liters of solution}}$

a. equivalent weight HCl = molar mass HCl = 36.46 g

$$15.0 \text{ g HCl} \times \frac{1 \text{ equiv HCl}}{36.46 \text{ g HCl}} = 0.411 \text{ equiv HCl}$$

500. mL = 0.500 L

$$N = \frac{0.411 \text{ equiv}}{0.500 \text{ L}} = 0.822 \ N$$

b. equivalent weight $H_2SO_4 = \dfrac{\text{molar mass}}{2} = \dfrac{98.09 \text{ g}}{2} = 49.05 \text{ g}$

$$49.0 \text{ g H}_2\text{SO}_4 \times \frac{1 \text{ equiv H}_2\text{SO}_4}{49.05 \text{ g H}_2\text{SO}_4} = 0.999 \text{ equiv H}_2\text{SO}_4$$

250. mL = 0.250 L

$$N = \frac{0.999 \text{ equiv}}{0.250 \text{ L}} = 4.00 \ N$$

c.   equivalent weight H_3PO_4 = $\dfrac{\text{molar mass}}{3}$ = $\dfrac{98.0 \text{ g}}{3}$ = 32.67 g

$$10.0 \text{ g } H_3PO_4 \times \dfrac{1 \text{ equiv } H_3PO_4}{32.67 \text{ g } H_3PO_4} = 0.3061 \text{ equiv } H_3PO_4$$

100. mL = 0.100 L

$$N = \dfrac{0.3061 \text{ equiv}}{0.100 \text{ L}} = 3.06 \ N$$

131.   a. $0.50 \ M \ HC_2H_3O_2 \times \dfrac{1 \text{ equiv } HC_2H_3O_2}{1 \text{ mol } HC_2H_3O_2} = 0.50 \ N \ HC_2H_3O_2$

      b. $0.00250 \ M \ H_2SO_4 \times \dfrac{2 \text{ equiv } H_2SO_4}{1 \text{ mol } H_2SO_4} = 0.00500 \ N \ H_2SO_4$

      c. $0.10 \ M \ KOH \times \dfrac{1 \text{ equiv KOH}}{1 \text{ mol KOH}} = 0.10 \ N \ KOH$

132.   molar mass NaH_2PO_4 = 120.0 g

$$5.0 \text{ g } NaH_2PO_4 \times \dfrac{1 \text{ mol } NaH_2PO_4}{120.0 \text{ g } NaH_2PO_4} = 0.04167 \text{ mol } NaH_2PO_4$$

500. mL = 0.500 L

$$M = \dfrac{0.04167 \text{ mol}}{0.500 \text{ L}} = 0.08333 \ M \ NaH_2PO_4 = 0.083 \ M \ NaH_2PO_4$$

$$0.08333 \ M \ NaH_2PO_4 \times \dfrac{2 \text{ equiv } NaH_2PO_4}{1 \text{ mol } NaH_2PO_4} = 0.1667 \ N \ NaH_2PO_4 = 0.17 \ N \ NaH_2PO_4$$

133. $3NaOH(aq) + H_3PO_4(aq) \rightarrow Na_3PO_4(aq) + 3H_2O(l)$

14.2 mL = 0.0142 L

$$0.0142 \text{ L} \times \dfrac{0.141 \text{ mol } H_3PO_4}{1.00 \text{ L}} = 2.00 \times 10^{-3} \text{ mol } H_3PO_4$$

$$2.00 \times 10^{-3} \text{ mol } H_3PO_4 \times \dfrac{3 \text{ mol NaOH}}{1 \text{ mol } H_3PO_4} = 6.00 \times 10^{-3} \text{ mol NaOH}$$

$$6.00 \times 10^{-3} \text{ mol NaOH} \times \dfrac{1.00 \text{ L}}{0.105 \text{ mol NaOH}} = 5.72 \times 10^{-2} \text{ L} = 57.2 \text{ mL}$$

134. $N_{acid} \times V_{acid} = N_{base} \times V_{base}$

$$N_{acid} \times (10.0 \text{ mL}) = (3.5 \times 10^{-2} \ N)(27.5 \text{ mL})$$

$$N_{acid} = 9.6 \times 10^{-2} \ N \ HNO_3$$

Cumulative Review: Chapters 12, 13, and 14

1. Gases have no fixed volume or shape, but rather take on the shape and volume of the container in which they are confined. This is in contrast to solids and liquids: a sample of solid has its own intrinsic volume and shape, and is very incompressible; a sample of liquid has an intrinsic volume, but does take on the shape of its container.

2. The pressure exerted by the atmosphere is due to the several mile thick layer of gases above the surface of the earth pressing down on us. Atmospheric pressure has traditionally been measured with a mercury barometer (see Figure 12.2). A mercury barometer usually consists of a glass tube which is sealed at one end and filled with mercury. The tube is then inverted over an open reservoir also containing mercury. When the tube is inverted, most of the mercury does not fall out of the tube. Since the reservoir of mercury is open to the atmosphere, the atmospheric pressure on the surface of the mercury in the reservoir is enough pressure to hold the bulk of the mercury in the glass tube. The pressure of the atmosphere is sufficient, on average, to support a column of mercury 76 cm (760 mm) high in the tube.

3. The SI unit of pressure is the pascal, but this unit is almost never used in everyday situations because it is too small to be practical. Rather, we tend to use units of pressure that are based on the simple instruments used to measure pressures, the mercury barometer and manometer (see Figures 12.2 and 12.3 in the text). The mercury barometer (Figure 12.2), used for measuring the pressure of the atmosphere, consists of a column of mercury which is held in a vertical glass tube by the atmosphere. The pressure of the atmosphere is then indicated in terms of the height of the surface of the mercury in the long tube (relative to the surface of the mercury in the reservoir). As the atmospheric pressure changes, the height of the mercury column changes. The height of the mercury column is given in radio and TV weather reports in inches in mercury, but most scientific applications would quote the height in millimeters of mercury (mm Hg, torr). Pressures are also quoted in standard atmospheres, where 1 atm is equivalent to a pressure of 760 mm Hg. While the barometer is used to measure atmospheric pressure, a device called a mercury manometer is used to measure the pressure of samples of gas in the laboratory. A manometer consists basically of a *U*-shaped tube filled with mercury, with one arm of the *U* open to the atmosphere and the other arm of the *U* connected to the gas sample to be measured. If the pressure of the gas sample is the same as the pressure of the atmosphere, then the mercury levels will be the same in both sides of the *U*. If the pressure of the gas is not the same as the atmospheric pressure, then the difference in height of the mercury levels can be used to determine by how many mm Hg the pressure of the gas sample differs from atmospheric pressure.

4. Boyle's law basically says that the volume of a gas sample will decrease if you squeeze harder on it. Imagine squeezing hard on a tennis ball with your hand: the ball collapses as the gas inside it is forced into a smaller volume by your hand. Of course, to be perfectly correct, the temperature and amount of gas (moles) must remain the same while you adjust the pressure for Boyle's law to hold true. The first of the two mathematical statements of Boyle's law you should remember is

$P \times V$ = constant

which basically is the definition of Boyle's law (in order for the product ($P \times V$) to remain constant, if one of these terms increases the other must decrease). The second formulation of Boyle's law you have to be able to deal with is the one more commonly used in solving problems,

$P_1 \times V_1 = P_2 \times V_2$

With this second formulation, we can determine pressure-volume information about a given sample under two sets of conditions. These two mathematical formulas are just two different ways of saying the same thing: if the pressure on a sample of gas is increased, the volume of the sample of gas will decrease. A graph of Boyle's law data is given as Figure 12.5: this sort of graph ($xy = k$) is known to mathematicians as a hyperbola.

5.   The qualification is necessary because the volume of a gas sample is dependent on all its properties. The properties of a gas are all inter-related (as shown by the ideal gas law, $PV = nRT$). If we want to use one of the derivative gas laws (Boyle's, Charles's, or Avogadro's gas laws), which isolate how the volume of a gas sample varies with just one of its properties, then we must keep all the other properties constant while that one property is studied.

6.   Charles's law basically says that if you heat a sample of gas, the volume of the sample will increase. That is, when the temperature of a gas is increased, the volume of the gas also increases (assuming the pressure and amount of gas remains the same). Charles's law is a direct proportionality when the temperature is expressed in kelvins (if you increase T, this increases V), whereas Boyle's law is an inverse proportionality (if you increase P, this decreases V). There are two mathematical statements of Charles's law you should be familiar with. The first statement

$V = bT$

is just a definition (the volume of a gas sample is directly related to its Kelvin temperature: if you increase the temperature, the volume increases). The working formulation of Charles's law we use in problem solving is given as

$$\frac{V_1}{T_1} = \frac{V_2}{T_2}$$

With this formulation, we can determine volume-temperature information for a given gas sample under two sets of conditions. Charles's law only holds true if the amount of gas remains the same (obviously the volume of a gas sample would increase if there were more gas present) and also if the pressure remains the same (a change in pressure also changes the volume of a gas sample).

7. The volume of a gas sample changes by the same factor (i.e., linearly) for each degree its temperature is changed (for a fixed amount of gas at a constant pressure). Charles realized that, if a gas were cooled, the volume of a gas sample would decrease by a constant factor for each degree the temperature was lowered. When Charles plotted his experimental data, and extrapolated the linear data to very low temperatures that he could not measure experimentally, he realized that there would be an ultimate temperature where the volume of a gas sample would shrink to zero if the temperature were lowered any further. The same ultimate temperature was calculated no matter what gas sample was used for the experiment. This temperature--where the volume of an ideal gas sample would approach zero as a limit--we refer to as the absolute zero of temperature. Unlike the Fahrenheit and Celsius temperature scales, which were defined by humans with experimentally convenient reference points, the absolute zero of temperature is a fundamental, natural reference point for the measurement of temperatures. The Kelvin or absolute temperature scale is defined with absolute zero as its lowest temperature, with all temperatures positive relative to this point. The size of the Kelvin degree was chosen to be the same size as the Celsius degree. Absolute zero (0 K) corresponds to -273°C.

8. Avogadro's law tells us that, with all other things being equal, two moles of gas is twice as big as one mole of gas! That is, the volume of a sample of gas is directly proportional to the number of moles or molecules of gas present (at constant temperature and pressure). If we want to compare the volumes of two samples of the same gas as an indication of the amount of gas present in the samples, we would have to make certain that the two samples of gas are at the same pressure and temperature: the volume of a sample of gas would vary with either temperature or pressure, or both. Avogadro's law holds true for comparing gas samples that are under the same conditions. Avogadro's law is a direct proportionality: the greater the number of gas molecules you have in a sample, the larger the sample's volume will be.

9. Although it may sound strange, an *ideal gas* is defined to be a gas which obeys the ideal gas law (realize that the ideal gas law is based on the experimental measurement of the properties of gases). Boyle's law tells us that the volume of a gas is inversely proportional to its pressure (at constant temperature for a fixed amount of gas):

$$V = (\text{constant})/P$$

Charles's law indicates that the volume of a gas sample is related to its temperature (at constant pressure for a fixed amount of gas):

$$V = (\text{constant}) \times T$$

Avogadro's law shows that the volume of a gas sample is proportional to the number of moles of gas (at constant pressure and temperature):
$$V = (\text{constant}) \times n$$

If we combine all these relationships (and constants) to show how the volume of a gas is proportional to *all* its properties simultaneously:

$$V = (constant) \times \frac{T \times n}{P}$$

which can be arranged to the familiar form of the ideal gas law:

$$P \times V = n \times R \times T \quad \text{or just} \quad PV = nRT$$

where *R* is the universal gas constant, which has the value

$$R = \frac{0.08206 \text{ L atm}}{\text{mol K}}$$

Although it is always important to pay attention to the units when solving a problem, this is especially important when solving gas problems involving the universal gas constant, *R*. The numerical value of 0.08206 for *R* applies only when the properties of the gas sample are given in the units specified for the constant: the volume in liters (not mL), the pressure in atmospheres (not mm Hg, torr, or Pa), the amount of gas in moles (not g), and the temperature in kelvins (not °F or °C).

10. The "partial" pressure of an individual gas in a mixture of gases represents the pressure the gas would have in the same container at the same temperature if it were the only gas present. The total pressure in a mixture of gases is just the sum of the individual partial pressures of the gases present in the mixture. Because the partial pressures of the gases in a mixture are additive (i.e., the total pressure is the sum of the partial pressures), this suggests that the total pressure in a container is a function really only of the number of molecules present in the same, and not of the identity of the molecules or any other property of the molecules (such as their inherent atomic size).

11. When a gas is collected by displacement of liquid water from a container, the gas becomes saturated with water vapor. The collected gas is, in effect, a mixture of the desired gas and water vapor. To determine the partial pressure of the desired gas in the mixture, it is necessary to subtract off the pressure of water vapor from the total pressure of the sample

$$P_{gas} = P_{total} - P_{water\ vapor}$$

Dalton's law of partial pressures states that the total pressure in a mixture of gases is the sum of the partial pressures of the components of the mixture. Since the saturation pressure of water vapor is a function only of temperature, such water vapor pressures are conveniently tabulated (see Table 12.2 in the text).

12. The main postulates of the kinetic-molecular theory for gases are as follows: (a) gases consist of tiny particles (atoms or molecules), and

the size of these particles themselves is negligible compared to the bulk volume of a gas sample; (b) the particles in a gas are in constant random motion, colliding with each other and with the walls of the container; (c) the particles in a gas sample do not exert any attractive or repulsive forces on one another; (d) the average kinetic energy of the particles in a sample of gas is directly related to the absolute temperature of the gas sample. The pressure exerted by a gas is a result of the molecules colliding with (and pushing on) the walls of the container; the pressure increases with temperature because at a higher temperature, the molecules are moving faster and hit the walls of the container with greater force. A gas fills whatever volume is available to it because the molecules in a gas are in constant random motion: if the motion of the molecules is random, they eventually will move out into whatever volume is available until the distribution of molecules is uniform; at constant pressure, the volume of a gas sample increases as the temperature is increased because with each collision having greater force, the container must expand so that the molecules (and therefore the collisions) are farther apart if the pressure is to remain constant.

13. The abbreviation "STP" stands for "Standard Temperature and Pressure". STP corresponds to a temperature of 0°C and a pressure of 1 atm. These conditions were chosen as STP for comparisons of gas samples because they are easy to reproduce in any laboratory (an equilibrium mixture of ice and water has a temperature of 0°C, and the pressure in most laboratories is very near to 1 atm). One mole of any ideal gas occupies a volume of 22.4 L at STP.

14. Solids and liquids are much more condensed states of matter than are gases: the molecules are much closer together in solids and liquids and interact with each other to a much greater extent. Solids and liquids have much greater densities than do gases, and are much less compressible, because there is so little room between the molecules in the solid and liquid states (solids and liquids effectively have native volumes of their own, and their volumes are not affected nearly as much by the temperature or pressure). Although solids are more rigid than liquids, the solid and liquid state have much more in common with each other than either of these states has with the gaseous state. We know this is true since it typically only takes a few kilojoules of energy to melt 1 mol of a solid (since not much change has to take place in the molecules), whereas it may take 10 times more energy to vaporize a liquid (since there is such a great change between the liquid and gaseous states).

15. Water is a colorless, odorless, tasteless liquid which freezes at 0°C and which boils at 100°C at 1 atm pressure. Water is one of the most important substances on earth. Water forms the solvent for most of the biochemical processes necessary for plant and animal life. Water in the oceans moderates the temperature of the earth. Because of its relatively large specific heat capacity, and its great abundance, water is used as the primary coolant in industrial machinery. Water provides a medium for transportation across vast distances on the earth. Water provides a medium for the smallest plants and animals in many food chains.

16.   The normal boiling point of water, that is, water's boiling point at a pressure of exactly 760 mm Hg, is 100°C (you will recall that the boiling point of water was used to set one of the reference temperatures of the Celsius temperature scale). Water remains at 100°C while boiling, until all the water has boiled away, because the additional heat energy being added to the sample is used to overcome attractive forces among the water molecules as they go from the condensed, liquid state to the gaseous state. The normal (760 mm Hg) freezing point of water is exactly 0°C (again, this property of water was used as one of the reference points for the Celsius temperature scale). A cooling curve for water is given as Figure 13.2: notice how the curve shows that the amount of heat needed to boil the sample is much larger than the amount needed to melt the sample.

17.   Changes in state are only physical changes: no chemical bonds are broken during the change and no new substances result (no changes in the *intra*molecular bonding forces takes place). In order to melt a solid or to boil a liquid, the *inter*molecular forces which hold the molecules together in the solid or liquid must be overcome. The quantity of energy required to melt and to boil 1 mol of a substance are called the substance's *molar heat of fusion* and *molar heat of vaporization*, respectively. The molar heat of vaporization of water (or any substance) is much larger than the molar heat of fusion because in order to form a vapor, the molecules have to be moved much farther apart, and virtually all the intermolecular forces must be overcome (when a solid melts, the intermolecular forces remaining in the liquid are still relatively strong). The boiling point of a liquid decreases with altitude because the atmospheric pressure (against which the vapor must be expanded during boiling) decreases with altitude (the atmosphere is thinner).

18.   Dipole-dipole forces are a type of intermolecular force that can exist between molecules with permanent dipole moments. Molecules with permanent dipole moments try to orient themselves so that the positive end of one polar molecule can attract the negative end of another polar molecule. Dipole-dipole forces are not nearly as strong as ionic or covalent bonding forces (only about 1% strong as covalent bonding forces) since electrostatic attraction is related to the magnitude of the charges of the attracting species. Since polar molecules have only a "partial" charge at each end of the dipole, the magnitude of the attractive force is not as large. The strength of such forces also drops rapidly as molecules become farther apart and is important only in the solid and liquid states (such forces are negligible in the gaseous state since the molecules are too far apart). Hydrogen bonding is an especially strong sort of dipole-dipole attractive force which can exist when hydrogen atoms are directly bonded to the most strongly electronegative atoms (N, O, and F). Because the hydrogen atom is so small, dipoles involving N-H, O-H, and F-H bonds can approach each other much more closely than can dipoles involving other atoms. Since the magnitude of dipole-dipole forces is dependent on distance, unusually strong attractive forces can exist in such molecules. We take the fact that the boiling point of water is so much higher than that of the other covalent hydrogen compounds of the Group 6 elements as evidence for the

special strength of hydrogen bonding (it takes more energy to vaporize water because of the extra strong forces holding together the molecules in the liquid state).

19.   London dispersion are the extremely weak forces which must exist to explain the fact that substances consisting of single atoms or of nonpolar molecules can be liquefied and solidified. London forces are instantaneous dipole forces, which come about as the electrons of an atom move around the nucleus. Although we usually consider that the electrons are uniformly distributed in space around the nucleus, at any given instant there may be more electronic charge on one side of the nucleus than on the other, which results in an instantaneous separation of charge and a small dipole moment. Such an instantaneous dipole may induce a similar instantaneous dipole in a neighboring atom, which then results in an attractive force between the dipoles. Although an instantaneous dipole can arise in any molecule, in most cases other, much stronger intermolecular forces predominate. However, for substances which exist as single atoms (e.g., the noble gases) or which exist as nonpolar molecules (e.g., H_2, O_2), London forces are the only major intermolecular forces existing.

20.   Vaporization of a liquid requires and input of energy because the intermolecular forces which hold the molecules together in the liquid state must be overcome. The high heat of vaporization of water is essential to life on earth since much of the excess energy striking the earth from the sun is dissipated in vaporizing water. Condensation is the opposite process to vaporization: that is, condensation refers to the process by which molecules in the vapor state form a liquid. In a closed container containing a liquid and some empty space above the liquid, an equilibrium is set up between vaporization and condensation. The liquid in such a sealed container never completely evaporates: when the liquid is first placed in the container, the liquid phase begins to evaporate into the empty space. As the number of molecules in the vapor phase begins to get large, however, some of these molecules begin to re-enter the liquid phase. Eventually, every time a molecule of liquid somewhere in the container enters the vapor phase, somewhere else in the container a molecule of vapor re-enters the liquid. There is no further net change in the amount of liquid phase (although molecules are continually moving between the liquid and vapor phases). The pressure of the vapor in such an equilibrium situation is characteristic for the liquid at each particular temperature (for example, the vapor pressures of water are tabulated at different temperatures in Table 12.2). A simple experiment to determine vapor pressure is shown in Figure 13.10: samples of a liquid are injected into a sealed tube containing mercury; since mercury is so dense, the liquids float to the top of the mercury where they evaporate; as the vapor pressures of the liquids develop to the saturation point, the level of mercury in the tube changes as an index of the magnitude of the vapor pressures. Typically, liquids with strong intermolecular forces have small vapor pressures (they have more difficulty in evaporating) than do liquids with very weak intermolecular

forces: for example, the components of gasoline (weak forces) have much higher vapor pressures than does water (strong forces) and evaporate more easily.

21. Crystalline solids consist of a regular lattice array, which extends in three dimensions, of repeating component units (atoms, molecules, or ions): a small portion of a sodium chloride crystal lattice is show in Figure 13.11 in the text. The three important types of crystalline solids are *ionic* solids, *molecular* solids, and *atomic* solids.

Sodium chloride is a typical ionic solid. Its crystals consists of an alternating array of positive Na^+ ions and negative Cl^- ions. Each positive ion is surrounded by several negative ions, and each negative ion is surrounded by several positive ions. The electrostatic forces that develop in such an arrangement are very large, and the resulting substance is very stable, and has very high melting and boiling points.

Ice represents a molecular solid. The crystals consist of polar water molecules arranged in three dimensions so as to maximize dipole-dipole interactions (and hydrogen bonding). Figure 13.14 (b) shows a representation of an ice crystal, showing how the negative end of one water molecule is oriented towards the positive end of another water molecule, and how this arrangement repeats. Since dipole-dipole forces are weaker than ionic bonding forces, substances which exist as molecular solids typically have much lower melting and boiling points.

Atomic solids vary as to how the atoms are held together in the crystal. Substances such as the noble gases are held together in the solid only by very weak London dispersion forces. Such substances have extremely low melting and boiling points because these forces are so weak. In other atomic solids, such as the diamond form of carbon, adjacent atoms may actually form covalent bonds with each other, leading the entire crystal to be one giant molecule. Such atomic solids have much higher boiling and melting points than those substances held together by only London forces, since there is so much energy held in all the covalent bonds that exist in the crystal. Finally, the metallic substances are also atomic solids, in which there is strong, but nondirectional bonding which leads to the properties associated with metals. Metals are envisioned in terms of the "electron sea" model in which a regular array of metal atoms are perfused with a sea of freely moving valence electrons.

22. The simple model we use to explain many properties of metallic elements is called the electron sea model. In this model we picture a regular lattice array of metal cations in sort of a "sea" of mobile valence electrons. The electrons can move easily to conduct heat or electricity through the metal, and the lattice of cations can be deformed fairly easily, allowing the metal to be hammered into a sheet or stretched to make a wire. An alloy is a material that contains a mixture of elements, which overall has metallic properties. Substitutional alloys consist of a host metal in which some of the atoms in the metal's crystalline structure are replaced by atoms of other metallic elements of comparable size to the atoms of the host metal. For example, sterling silver consists of an alloy in which approximately 7% of the silver atoms have been replaced by copper atoms. Brass and pewter are also substitutional

alloys. An interstitial alloy is formed when other smaller atoms enter the interstices (holes) between atoms in the host metal's crystal structure. Steel is an interstitial alloy in which typically carbon atoms enter the interstices of a crystal of iron atoms. The presence of the interstitial carbon atoms markedly changes the properties of the iron, making it much harder, more malleable, and more ductile. Depending on the amount of carbon introduced into the iron crystals, the properties of the steel resulting can be carefully controlled.

23.   A solution is a homogeneous mixture, a mixture in which the components are uniformly intermingled. When an ionic substance is dissolved in water to form a solution, the water plays an essential role in overcoming the strong interparticle forces in the ionic crystal (shown in Figure 14.2 in the text). Water is a highly polar substance: one end of the water molecule dipole is strongly negative, and the other is strongly positive. Consider a crystal of sodium chloride, in which there is a negative chloride ion at one of the corners of the crystal. When this crystal is placed in water, water molecules surround the chloride ion, and orient themselves with the positive end of their dipoles aimed at the negative chloride ion. When enough water molecules have so arranged themselves, the resultant attraction of the several water molecules for the chloride ion becomes stronger than the attractive forces from the positive sodium ions in the crystal, and the chloride ion separates from the crystal and enters solution (still surrounded by the group of water molecules). Similarly, a positive sodium ion in a similar position would be attracted by a group of water molecules arranged with the negative end of their dipoles oriented toward the positive ion, and when enough water molecules had so arranged themselves so as to surpass the attractive forces from negative ions in the crystal, the sodium ion would enter solution. Once the chloride ion and the sodium ion are in solution, they remain surrounded by a layer of water molecules (called a hydration sphere), which diminishes the effective charge each ion would feel from the other, which prevents them from easily recombining. For a molecular solid (such as sugar) to be able to dissolve in a solvent, there must be some portion or portions of the molecule which can be attracted by molecules of solvent. For example, common table sugar (sucrose) contains many hydroxyl groups, -OH. These hydroxyl groups are relatively polar and can be attracted by water molecule dipoles. When enough water molecules have attracted enough hydroxyl groups on a sugar molecule to overcome attractive forces from other sugar molecules within the crystal, the molecule leaves the crystal and enters solution (naturally, the -OH groups can also hydrogen bond with water molecules). In order for a substance to dissolve in water, not only must there be attractive forces possible between water molecules and solute molecules, but these forces must be strong enough to overcome the strong attractive forces that water molecules have for one another. In order for a substance to dissolve, the molecules of substance must be capable of being dispersed among water molecules. If the water-solute interactions are not comparable to the water-water interactions, the substance will not dissolve.

24. A saturated solution is one that contains as much solute as can dissolve at a particular temperature. To say that a solution is saturated doe not necessarily mean that the solute is present at a high concentration: for example, magnesium hydroxide only dissolves to a very small extent before the solution is saturated, whereas it takes a great deal of sugar to form a saturated solution (and the saturated solution is extremely concentrated). A saturated solution is one which is in equilibrium with undissolved solute: as molecules of solute dissolve from the solid in one place in the solution, dissolved molecules rejoin the solid phase in another place in the solution. As with the development of vapor pressure above a liquid (see Question 20 above), formation of a solution reaches a state of dynamic equilibrium: once the rates of dissolving and "undissolving" become equal, there will be no further net change in the concentration of the solution and the solution will be saturated.

25. The mass percent and the molarity are similar in that both methods of expressing the concentration of a solution represent ratios: that is, the both express the amount of solute per unit of solvent. The *mass percent* for a solution represents the number of grams of solute that would be present in 100. g of the solution. Since the mass percent is based only on mass, it is invariant for a given solution under all conditions. The *molarity* of a solution represents the number of moles of solute that would be present in one liter of the solution. Since the volume of a liquid varies somewhat with temperature, the molarity of a solution varies also with temperature.

    If 5.0 g of NaCl were dissolved in 15.0 g of water, the mass percent composition of the solution could be calculated as

$$\frac{5.00 \text{ g NaCl}}{(15.0 \text{ g H}_2\text{O} + 5.0 \text{ g NaCl})} \times 100 = 25\% \text{ NaCl}$$

Since the mass percent is based only on the masses of the components of the solution, the volume of the solution is not needed for this calculation.

    If 5.0 g of NaCl (molar mass 58.4 g) were dissolved in enough water to give a total solution volume of 16.1 mL, the molarity of the solution could be calculated as

$$5.0 \text{ g NaCl} \times \frac{1 \text{ mol}}{58.4 \text{ g}} = 0.0856 \text{ mol NaCl}$$

$$16.1 \text{ mL} = 0.0161 \text{ L}$$

$$M = \frac{0.0856 \text{ mol NaCl}}{0.0161 \text{ L solution}} = 5.3 \text{ } M$$

Since the molarity is based on the amount of solute per liter of solution, the mass of solvent present is not needed for the calculation. If the density (1.24 g/mL) of the solution had been given, rather than the explicit volume, the volume could be calculated as shown

$$V = m/d = \frac{(5.0 \text{ g} + 15.0 \text{ g})}{1.24 \text{ g/mL}} = \frac{20.0 \text{ g}}{1.24 \text{ g/mL}} = 16.1 \text{ mL}$$

26. Adding additional solvent to a solution so as to dilute the solution *does not change* the number of moles of solute present, but only changes the volume in which the solute is dispersed. If we are using the molarity of the solution to describe its concentration, the number of liters is changed when we add solvent, and the number of moles per liter (the molarity) changes, but the actual number of moles of solute does not change. For example, 125 mL of 0.551 M NaCl contains 68.9 millimol of NaCl. The solution will still contain 68.9 millimol of NaCl after the 250 mL of water is added to it, only now the 68.9 millimol of NaCl will be dispersed in a total volume of 375 mL. This gives the new molarity as 68.9 mmol/375 mL = 0.184 M. The volume and the concentration have changed, but the number of moles of solute in the solution has not changed.

27. One equivalent of an acid is the amount of acid that can furnish one mole of H^+ ions; one equivalent of a base is the amount of base that can furnish one mole of OH^- ions. The equivalent weight of an acid or base is the mass of the substance representing one equivalent of the acid or base. The equivalent weight of a substance is determined from the molar mass of the substance, also taking into account how many H^+ or OH^- ions the substance furnishes per molecule. For example, HCl and NaOH have equivalent weights equal to their molar masses, since each of these substances furnishes one H^+ or OH^- ion per molecule, respectively

$$HCl \rightarrow H^+ + Cl^- \qquad\qquad NaOH \rightarrow Na^+ + OH^-$$

However, sulfuric acid (H_2SO_4) has an equivalent weight that is half the molar mass, since each H_2SO_4 molecule can produce *two* H^+ ions: therefore, only half a mole of H_2SO_4 is needed to provide one mole of H^+ ion. Similarly, the equivalent weight of phosphoric acid (H_3PO_4) is one third of its molar mass, since each H_3PO_4 molecule can provide three H^+ ions (and so only one third of a mole of H_3PO_4 is needed to provide one mole of H^+ ions).

$$H_2SO_4 \rightarrow 2H^+ + SO_4^{2-} \qquad\qquad H_3PO_4 \rightarrow 3H^+ + PO_4^{3-}$$

Similarly, bases like $Ca(OH)_2$ and $Mg(OH)_2$ have equivalent weights that are half the molar masses, since each of these substances produces two moles of OH^- ion per mole of base (and so only half a mole of base is needed to provide one mole of OH^-).

The *normality* of a solution is defined to be the number of equivalents of solute contained in one liter of the solution: a 1 *N* solution of an acid contains 1 mole of H^+ per liter; a 1 *N* solution of a base contains 1 mole of OH^- per liter. Since the equivalent weight and the molar mass of a substance are related by small whole numbers (representing the number of H^+ or OH^- a molecule of the substance furnishes), the normality and molarity of a solution are also simply related by these same numbers. In fact, $N = n \times M$ for a solution, where *n* represents the number of H^+ or OH^- ions furnished per molecule of solute. For example, a 0.521 *M* HCl(*aq*) solution is also 0.521 *N*, since each HCl furnishes one H^+ ion. However, a 0.475 *M* H_2SO_4 solution would have a normality equal to

$$N = n \times M = 2 \times 0.475 \ M = 0.950 \ N$$

since each H_2SO_4 molecule furnishes two H^+ ions.

28. $$V_2 = \frac{P_1 \times V_1}{P_2}$$

a. $2.41 \ atm = 1.83 \times 10^3 \ mm \ Hg$

$$V_2 = \frac{(759 \ mm \ Hg)(245 \ mL)}{(1.83 \times 10^3 \ mm \ Hg)} = 102 \ mL$$

b. $$V_2 = \frac{(759 \ mm \ Hg)(2.71 \ L)}{(1104 \ mmHg)} = 1.86 \ L$$

c. $204 \ kPa = 1530 \ mm \ Hg$

$$V_2 = \frac{(759 \ mm \ Hg)(45.2 \ mL)}{(1530 \ mm \ Hg)} = 22.4 \ mL$$

29. $$V_2 = \frac{V_1 \times T_2}{T_1}$$

a. $101 \ °C = 374 \ K \qquad 25 \ °C = 298 \ K$

$$V_2 = \frac{(5.23 \ L)(298 \ K)}{(374 \ K)} = 4.17 \ L$$

b. $101 \ °C = 374 \ K \qquad -25 \ °C = 248 \ K$

$$V_2 = \frac{(125 \ mL)(248 \ K)}{(374 \ K)} = 82.9 \ mL$$

c. $101 \ °C = 374 \ K \qquad -201 \ °C = 72 \ K$

$$V_2 = \frac{(1.58 \ L)(72 \ K)}{(374 \ K)} = 0.304 \ L$$

30. a. $P_1 = 775 \ mm \ Hg \qquad\qquad P_2 = 760 \ mm \ Hg$

$V_1 = 45.1 \ mL \qquad\qquad V_2 = \ ?$

$T_1 = 24.1°C = 297 \ K \qquad\qquad T_2 = 273 \ K$

$$V_2 = \frac{P_1 V_1 T_2}{T_1 P_2} = \frac{(775 \ mm \ Hg)(45.1 \ mL)(273 \ K)}{(297 \ K)(760 \ mm \ Hg)} = 42.3 \ mL$$

b. P_1 = 0.890 atm P_2 = 1.00 atm

      V_1 = 4.31 L V_2 = ?

      T_1 = 72.1°C = 345 K T_2 = 273 K

$$V_2 = \frac{P_1 V_1 T_2}{T_1 P_2} = \frac{(0.890 \text{ atm})(4.31 \text{ L})(273 \text{ K})}{(345 \text{ K})(1.00 \text{ atm})} = 3.03 \text{ L}$$

c. P_1 = 91.2 kPa P_2 = 101.325 kPa

      V_1 = 5.12 mL V_2 = ?

      T_1 = 289 K T_2 = 273 K

$$V_2 = \frac{P_1 V_1 T_2}{T_1 P_2} = \frac{(91.2 \text{ kPa})(5.12 \text{ mL})(273 \text{ K})}{(289 \text{ K})(101.325 \text{ kPa})} = 4.35 \text{ mL}$$

d. P_1 = 1.45 atm P_2 = 1.00 atm

      V_1 = 91.3 L V_2 = ?

      T_1 = 451°C = 724 K T_2 = 273 K

$$V_2 = \frac{P_1 V_1 T_2}{T_1 P_2} = \frac{(1.45 \text{ atm})(91.3 \text{ L})(273 \text{ K})}{(724 \text{ K})(1.00 \text{ atm})} = 49.9 \text{ L}$$

31.   The vapor pressure of water at 24°C is 23.8 mm Hg

The partial pressure of O_2 in the experiment will equal the total pressure *minus* the pressure due to water vapor:

P_{oxygen} = 775 mm Hg - 23.8 mm Hg = 751 mm Hg

We need to use the ideal gas law to calculate the moles of oxygen gas present in the sample

P_{oxygen} = 751 mm Hg = 0.988 atm

V = 158 mL = 0.158 L

T = 24°C = 297 K

$$n = \frac{P\,V}{R\,T} = \frac{(0.988 \text{ atm})(0.158 \text{ L})}{(0.0821 \text{ L atm/mol K})(297 \text{ K})} = 0.00640 \text{ mol } O_2$$

Using the coefficients of the balanced chemical equation, we can determine how many mol of $KClO_3$ would give rise to 0.00640 mol of O_2

$$0.00640 \text{ mol } O_2 \times \frac{2 \text{ mol } KClO_3}{3 \text{ mol } O_2} = 0.00427 \text{ mol } KClO_3$$

From the number of moles of $KClO_3$, and from its molar mass (122.6 g) we can calculate what specific mass of $KClO_3$ was in the sample being heated.

$$0.00427 \text{ mol } KClO_3 \times \frac{122.6 \text{ g}}{1 \text{ mol}} = 0.523 \text{ g } KClO_3$$

Since the original impure sample weighed 1.35 g, and contains 0.523 g of $KClO_3$, the percentage $KClO_3$ is

$$\% \ KClO_3 = \frac{0.523 \text{ g } KClO_3}{1.35 \text{ g sample}} \times 100 = 38.7\% \ KClO_3$$

32. Since we have 100. g of the solution, which is 3.11% by mass H_2O_2, then the sample must contain 3.11 g of H_2O_2

molar mass H_2O_2 = 34.02 g

$$3.11 \text{ g } H_2O_2 \times \frac{1 \text{ mol } H_2O_2}{34.02 \text{ g } H_2O_2} = 0.0914 \text{ mol } H_2O_2$$

$$0.0914 \text{ mol } H_2O_2 \times \frac{1 \text{ mol } O_2}{2 \text{ mol } H_2O_2} = 0.0457 \text{ mol } O_2 \text{ produced}$$

$$\text{At STP, } 0.0457 \text{ mol } O_2 \times \frac{22.4 \text{ L } O_2}{1 \text{ mol } O_2} = 1.02 \text{ L } O_2$$

P_1 = 760 mm Hg $\qquad\qquad$ P_2 = 771 mm Hg

V_1 = 1.02 L $\qquad\qquad$ V_2 = ?

T_1 = 273 K $\qquad\qquad$ T_2 = 297 K

$$V_2 = \frac{P_1 V_1 T_2}{T_1 P_2} = \frac{(760 \text{ mm Hg})(1.02 \text{ L})(297 \text{ K})}{(273 \text{ K})(771 \text{ mm Hg})} = 1.09 \text{ L}$$

33. molar mass H_2O = 18.02 g

Molar heat of fusion of ice = 6.02 kJ/mol

Specific heat capacity of water = 4.184 J/g°C

Molar heat of vaporization of water = 40.6 kJ/mol

Heat required to melt the ice

$$55.1 \text{ g } \times \frac{1 \text{ mol}}{18.02 \text{ g}} \times \frac{6.02 \text{ kJ}}{1 \text{ mol}} = 18.4 \text{ kJ}$$

Heat required to warm the liquid water

$$55.1 \text{ g} \times \frac{4.184 \text{ J}}{\text{g} \, °\text{C}} \times (100°\text{C} - 0°\text{C}) = 23,053 \text{ J} = 23.1 \text{ kJ}$$

Heat required to vaporize the liquid water

$$55.1 \text{ g} \times \frac{1 \text{ mol}}{18.02 \text{ g}} \times \frac{40.6 \text{ kJ}}{1 \text{ mol}} = 124 \text{ kJ}$$

Total heat required = 18.4 kJ + 23.1 kJ + 124 kJ = 166 kJ

34. a.   mass of solution = 4.25 + 7.50 + 52.0 = 63.75 g (63.8 g)

$$\frac{4.25 \text{ g NaCl}}{63.75 \text{ g}} \times 100 = 6.67 \text{ \%NaCl} \qquad \frac{7.50 \text{ g KCl}}{63.75 \text{ g}} \times 100 = 11.8 \text{ \%KCl}$$

b.   mass of solution = 4.25 + 7.50 + 125 = 136.75 g (137 g)

$$\frac{4.25 \text{ g NaCl}}{136.75 \text{ g}} \times 100 = 3.11 \text{ \%NaCl} \qquad \frac{7.50 \text{ g KCl}}{136.75 \text{ g}} \times 100 = 5.48 \text{ \% KCl}$$

c.   mass of solution = 4.25 + 7.50 + 355 = 366.75 g (367 g)

$$\frac{4.25 \text{ g NaCl}}{366.75 \text{ g}} \times 100 = 1.16 \text{ \%NaCl} \qquad \frac{7.50 \text{ g KCl}}{366.75 \text{ g}} \times 100 = 2.04 \text{ \%KCl}$$

35. 500.0 mL = 0.5000 L

a.   molar mass NaCl = 58.44 g

$$4.865 \text{ g NaCl} \times \frac{1 \text{ mol}}{58.44 \text{ g NaCl}} = 0.08325 \text{ mol NaCl}$$

$$M = \frac{0.08325 \text{ mol NaCl}}{0.5000 \text{ L}} = 0.1665 \, M$$

b.   molar mass $AgNO_3$ = 169.9 g

$$78.91 \text{ g AgNO}_3 \times \frac{1 \text{ mol}}{169.9 \text{ g AgNO}_3} = 0.4644 \text{ mol AgNO}_3$$

$$M = \frac{0.4644 \text{ mol AgNO}_3}{0.5000 \text{ L}} = 0.9289 \, M$$

c.   molar mass Na_2CO_3 = 106.0 g

$$121.1 \text{ g Na}_2\text{CO}_3 \times \frac{1 \text{ mol}}{106.0 \text{ g Na}_2\text{CO}_3} = 1.142 \text{ mol Na}_2\text{CO}_3$$

$$M = \frac{1.142 \text{ mol Na}_2\text{CO}_3}{0.5000 \text{ L}} = 2.285 \, M$$

(3.02 *M*)(255 mL)

36. a. $$\frac{}{(255 + 375)\ \text{mL}} = 1.22\ M$$

     b. $$\frac{(1.51\ \%)(75.1\ \text{g})}{(75.1 + 125)\ \text{g}} = 0.567\ \%$$

     c. $$\frac{(12.1\ M)(6.25\ \text{mL})}{(6.25 + 490.)\ \text{mL}} = 0.152\ M$$

37. It would be convenient to first calculate the number of moles of NaOH present in the sample, since this information will be needed for each part of the answer. 36.2 mL = 0.0362 L

$$\text{mol NaOH} = 0.0362\ \text{L} \times \frac{0.259\ \text{mol NaOH}}{1\ \text{L}} = 9.38 \times 10^{-3}\ \text{mol NaOH}$$

     a. $HCl + NaOH \rightarrow NaCl + H_2O$

$$9.38 \times 10^{-3}\ \text{mol NaOH} \times \frac{1\ \text{mol HCl}}{1\ \text{mol NaOH}} = 9.38 \times 10^{-3}\ \text{mol HCl}$$

$$9.38 \times 10^{-3}\ \text{mol HCl} \times \frac{1\ \text{L}}{0.271\ \text{mol HCl}} = 0.0346\ \text{L} = 34.6\ \text{mL}$$

     b. $H_2SO_4 + 2NaOH \rightarrow Na_2SO_4 + 2H_2O$

$$9.38 \times 10^{-3}\ \text{mol NaOH} \times \frac{1\ \text{mol H}_2\text{SO}_4}{2\ \text{mol NaOH}} = 4.69 \times 10^{-3}\ \text{mol H}_2\text{SO}_4$$

$$4.69 \times 10^{-3}\ \text{mol H}_2\text{SO}_4 \times \frac{1\ \text{L}}{0.119\ \text{mol H}_2\text{SO}_4} = 0.0394\ \text{L} = 39.4\ \text{mL}$$

     c. $H_3PO_4 + 3NaOH \rightarrow Na_3PO_4 + 3H_2O$

$$9.38 \times 10^{-3}\ \text{mol H}_3\text{PO}_4 \times \frac{1\ \text{mol H}_3\text{PO}_4}{3\ \text{mol NaOH}} = 3.13 \times 10^{-3}\ \text{mol H}_3\text{PO}_4$$

$$3.13 \times 10^{-3}\ \text{mol H}_3\text{PO}_4 \times \frac{1\ \text{L}}{0.171\ \text{mol H}_3\text{PO}_4} = 0.0183\ \text{L} = 18.3\ \text{mL}$$

38. a. $$\frac{(41.5\ \text{mL})(0.118\ M)(1)}{(0.242\ M)(2)} = 10.1\ \text{mL H}_2\text{SO}_4$$

     b. $$\frac{(27.1\ \text{mL})(0.121\ M)(3)}{(0.242\ M)(2)} = 20.3\ \text{mL H}_2\text{SO}_4$$

Chapter 15   Acids and Bases

1.   Acids were recognized primarily from their sour taste. Bases were recognized from their bitter taste and slippery feel on skin.

2.   In the Arrhenius definition, an acid is a substance which produces hydrogen ions (H^+) when dissolved in water, whereas a base is a substance which produces hydroxide ions (OH^-) in aqueous solution. These definitions proved to be too restrictive since the only base permitted was hydroxide ion, and the only solvent permitted was water.

3.   A Brönsted-Lowry acid is a molecule or ion capable of providing a proton to some other species; acids are *proton donors*. A Brönsted-Lowry base is a molecule or ion capable of receiving a proton from some other species; bases are *proton acceptors*. It is the *transfer of protons* that characterizes the Brönsted-Lowry model for acids and bases.

4.   A conjugate acid-base pair differ from each other by one proton (one hydrogen ion, H^+). For example, CH_3COOH (acetic acid), differs from its conjugate base, CH_3COO^- (acetate ion), by a single H^+ ion.

$$CH_3COOH(aq) \rightarrow CH_3COO^-(aq) + H^+(aq)$$

5.   A Brönsted-Lowry acid converts into its conjugate base in water (aqueous) solution by transferring a proton to a water molecule (forming an H_3O^+ ion). The portion of the original acid molecule or ion that *remains* after the proton leaves is the conjugate base of the original acid. In this process, water behaves as a Brönsted-Lowry base, since it receives a proton from the acid.

6.   When an acid is dissolved in water, the hydronium ion (H_3O^+) is formed. The hydronium ion is the conjugate *acid* of water (H_2O).

7.   a. H_2SO_4 and SO_4^{2-} do *not* represent a conjugate acid-base pair, since they differ from each other by more than one proton. The conjugate base of H_2SO_4 is the HSO_4^- ion; the conjugate acid of SO_4^{2-} is also the HSO_4^- ion.

     b. $H_2PO_4^-$ and HPO_4^{2-} represent a conjugate acid-base pair.

     c. $HClO_4$ and Cl^- are *not* a conjugate acid-base pair since they differ in the number of oxygen atoms present. The perchlorate ion, ClO_4^- is the conjugate base of the acid $HClO_4$; the conjugate acid of Cl^- is HCl.

     d. NH_4^+ and NH_2^- are *not* a conjugate acid-base pair since they differ from each other by more than one proton. NH_3 is the conjugate base of NH_4^+ and also the conjugate acid of NH_2^-.

8.   a. HSO_4^- and SO_4^{2-} represent a conjugate acid-base pair (HSO_4^- is the acid, SO_4^{2-} is the base; they differ by one proton).

     b.   HBr and BrO^- are not a conjugate acid-base pair (Br^- is the conjugate base of HBr; BrO^- is the conjugate base of HBrO).

c. $H_2PO_4^-$ and PO_4^{3-} are not a conjugate acid-base pair; they differ by *two* protons ($H_2PO_4^-$ is the conjugate acid of HPO_4^{2-} and also the conjugate base of H_3PO_4; HPO_4^{2-} is the conjugate acid of PO_4^{3-}).

d. HNO_3 and NO_2^- are not a conjugate acid-base pair; they differ by an oxygen atom as well as a proton (NO_3^- is the conjugate base of HNO_3; NO_2^- is the conjugate base of HNO_2).

9. a. HSO_4^-(acid), H_2O(base); SO_4^{2-}(base), H_3O^+(acid)

b. NH_2^-(base), H_2O(acid); NH_3(acid), OH^-(base)

c. HCl(acid), CH_3OH(base); Cl^-(base), $CH_3OH_2^+$(acid)

10. a. NH_3 (base), H_2O (acid); NH_4^+ (acid), OH^-(base)

b. PO_4^{3-} (base), H_2O (acid); HPO_4^{2-} (acid), OH^- (base)

c. $C_2H_3O_2^-$ (base), H_2O (acid); $HC_2H_3O_2$ (acid), OH^- (base)

11. The conjugate *acid* of the species indicated would have *one additional proton*:

a. H_2SO_4

b. HSO_3^-

c. $HClO_4$

d. H_3PO_4

12. The conjugate *acid* of the species indicated would have *one additional proton*:

a. HSO_4^-

b. HPO_4^{2-}

c. $CH_3NH_3^+$

d. HF

13. The conjugate *bases* of the species indicated would have *one less proton*:

a. HS^-

b. S^{2-}

c. NH_2^-

d. HSO_3^-

14. The conjugate *bases* of the species indicated would have *one less proton*:

a. CO_3^{2-}

b. HPO_4^{2-}

    c. Cl^-

    d. SO_4^{2-}

15.   a. $NH_3^+ + H_2O \rightleftharpoons NH_4^+ + OH^-$

    b. $NH_2^- + H_2O \rightarrow NH_3 + OH^-$

    c. $O^{2-} + H_2O \rightarrow OH^- + OH^-$

    d. $F^- + H_2O \rightleftharpoons HF + OH^-$

16.   a. $HClO_4 + H_2O \rightarrow ClO_4^- + H_3O^+$
    b. $HC_2H_3O_2 + H_2O \rightleftharpoons C_2H_3O_2^- + H_3O^+$
    c. $HSO_3^- + H_2O \rightleftharpoons SO_3^{2-} + OH^-$
    d. $HBr + H_2O \rightarrow Br^- + H_3O^+$

17.   A strong acid is one for which the equilibrium in water lies far to the right. A strong acid is almost completely converted to its conjugate base when dissolved in water. A strong acid's anion (its conjugate base) must be very poor at attracting, or holding onto, protons. A regular arrow ($\rightarrow$) rather than a double arrow ($\rightleftharpoons$) is used when writing an equation for the dissociation of a strong acid to indicate this.

18.   To say that an acid is *weak* in aqueous solution means that the acid does not easily transfer protons to water (and does not fully ionize). If an acid does not lose protons easily, then the acid's anion must be a strong attractor of protons (good at holding on to protons).

19.   If water is a much stronger base than the anion of the acid, then protons will be attracted more strongly to water molecules than to the anions, and the acid will ionize well. If the anion of the acid is a much stronger base than water, then the anions will hold on to their protons (or will attract any protons present in the water), and the acid will ionize poorly.

20.   A strong acid is one which loses its protons easily and fully ionizes in water; this means that the acid's conjugate base must be poor at attracting and holding on to protons, and is therefore a relatively weak base. A weak acid is one which resists loss of its protons and does not ionize well in water; this means that the acid's conjugate base attracts and holds onto protons tightly and is a relatively strong base.

21.   The hydronium ion is H_3O^+. For a general acid HA: $HA + H_2O \rightarrow A^- + H_3O^+$

22. H_2SO_4 (sulfuric): $H_2SO_4 + H_2O \rightarrow HSO_4^- + H_3O^+$

    HCl (hydrochloric): $HCl + H_2O \rightarrow Cl^- + H_3O^+$

    HNO_3 (nitric): $HNO_3 + H_2O \rightarrow NO_3^- + H_3O^+$

    $HClO_4$ (perchloric): $HClO_4 + H_2O \rightarrow ClO_4^- + H_3O^+$

23.   Organic acids are typically characterized by the presence of the *carboxyl* group, –COOH. Organic acids generally are *weak* acids.

24.   oxyacids: $HClO_4$, HNO_3, H_2SO_4, CH_3COOH, etc.

non-oxyacids: HCl, HBr, HF, HI, HCN, etc.

25.   Acids that are *strong* have relatively weak conjugate bases.

a. CH_3COO^- is a relatively strong base; CH_3COOH is a weak acid.

b. F^- is a relatively strong base; HF is a weak acid.

c. HS^- is a relatively strong base; H_2S is a weak acid.

d. Cl^- is a very weak base; HCl is a strong acid.

26.   Bases that are *weak* have relatively strong conjugate acids:

a. SO_4^{2-} is a moderately weak base; HSO_4^- is a moderately strong acid

b. Br^- is a very weak base; HBr is a strong acid

c. CN^- is a fairly strong base; HCN is a weak acid

d. CH_3COO^- is a fairly strong base; CH_3COOH is a weak acid

27.   A substance is said to be amphoteric if it can behave either as an acid or as a base. Water is an example of an amphoteric substance.

water as a base: $HCl + H_2O \rightarrow Cl^- + H_3O^+$

water as an acid: $H_2O + NH_2^- \rightarrow OH^- + NH_3$

28.   For example, HCO_3^- can behave as an acid if it reacts with something that more strongly gains protons than does HCO_3^- itself. For example, HCO_3^- would behave as an acid when reacting with hydroxide ion (a much stronger base).

$$HCO_3^-(aq) + OH^-(aq) \rightarrow CO_3^{2-}(aq) + H_2O(l)$$

On the other hand, HCO_3^- would behave as a base when reacted with something that more readily loses protons than does HCO_3^- itself. For example, HCO_3^- would behave as a base when reacting with hydrochloric acid (a much stronger acid).

$$HCO_3^-(aq) + HCl(aq) \rightarrow H_2CO_3(aq) + Cl^-(aq)$$

For $H_2PO_4^-$, similar equations can be written:

$$H_2PO_4^-(aq) + OH^-(aq) \rightarrow HPO_4^{2-}(aq) + H_2O(l)$$

$$H_2PO_4^-(aq) + H_3O^+(aq) \rightarrow H_3PO_4(aq) + H_2O(l)$$

29. $H_2O + H_2O \rightleftarrows H_3O^+ + OH^-$ $K_w = [H_3O^+][OH^-] = 1.0 \times 10^{-14}$

       $H_2O \rightleftarrows H^+ + OH^-$ $K_w = [H^+][OH^-] = 1.0 \times 10^{-14}$

30.   The hydrogen ion concentration and the hydroxide ion concentration of water are *not* independent of each other: they are related by the equilibrium

$$H_2O(l) \rightleftarrows H^+(aq) + OH^-(aq)$$

for which $K_w = [H^+][OH^-] = 1.0 \times 10^{-14}$ at 25°C.

If the concentration of one of these ions is increased by addition of a reagent producing H^+ or OH^-, then the concentration of the complementary ion will have to decrease so that the value of K_w will hold true. So if an acid is added to a solution, the concentration of hydroxide ion in the solution will decrease to a lower value. Similarly, if a base is added to a solution, then the concentration of hydrogen ion will have to decrease to a lower value.

31. $K_w = [H^+][OH^-] = 1.0 \times 10^{-14}$ at 25°C

$$[H^+] = \frac{1.0 \times 10^{-14}}{[OH^-]}$$

a. $[H^+] = \dfrac{1.0 \times 10^{-14}}{4.51 \times 10^{-7} \ M} = 2.2 \times 10^{-8} \ M;$ solution is basic

b. $[H^+] = \dfrac{1.0 \times 10^{-14}}{6.45 \times 10^{-9} \ M} = 1.6 \times 10^{-6} \ M;$ solution is acidic

c. $[H^+] = \dfrac{1.0 \times 10^{-14}}{7.00 \times 10^{-1} \ M} = 1.4 \times 10^{-14} \ M;$ solution is basic

d. $[H^+] = \dfrac{1.0 \times 10^{-14}}{1.00 \times 10^{-7} \ M} = 1.0 \times 10^{-7} \ M;$ solution is neutral

32. $K_w = [H^+][OH^-] = 1.0 \times 10^{-14}$ at 25°C

$$[H^+] = \frac{1.0 \times 10^{-14}}{[OH^-]}$$

a. $[H^+] = \dfrac{1.0 \times 10^{-14}}{3.99 \times 10^{-5} \ M} = 2.5 \times 10^{-10} \ M;$ solution is basic

b. $[H^+] = \dfrac{1.0 \times 10^{-14}}{2.91 \times 10^{-9} \ M} = 3.4 \times 10^{-6} \ M;$ solution is acidic

c. $[H^+] = \dfrac{1.0 \times 10^{-14}}{7.23 \times 10^{-2} \ M} = 1.4 \times 10^{-13} \ M;$ solution is basic

d. $[H^+] = \dfrac{1.0 \times 10^{-14}}{9.11 \times 10^{-7}\ M} = 1.1 \times 10^{-8}\ M$; solution is basic

33. $[OH^-] = \dfrac{1.0 \times 10^{-14}}{[H^+]}$

a. $[OH^-] = \dfrac{1.0 \times 10^{-14}}{8.89 \times 10^{-7}\ M} = 1.1 \times 10^{-8}\ M$; solution is acidic

b. $[OH^-] = \dfrac{1.0 \times 10^{-14}}{1.19 \times 10^{-7}\ M} = 8.4 \times 10^{-8}\ M$; solution is acidic

c. $[OH^-] = \dfrac{1.0 \times 10^{-14}}{7.00 \times 10^{-7}\ M} = 1.4 \times 10^{-8}\ M$; solution is acidic

d. $[OH^-] = \dfrac{1.0 \times 10^{-14}}{1.00 \times 10^{-7}\ M} = 1.0 \times 10^{-7}\ M$; solution is neutral

34. $[OH^-] = \dfrac{1.0 \times 10^{-14}}{[H^+]}$

a. $[OH^-] = \dfrac{1.0 \times 10^{-14}}{1.00 \times 10^{-7}\ M} = 1.0 \times 10^{-7}\ M$; solution is neutral

b. $[OH^-] = \dfrac{1.0 \times 10^{-14}}{7.00 \times 10^{-7}\ M} = 1.4 \times 10^{-8}\ M$; solution is acidic

c. $[OH^-] = \dfrac{1.0 \times 10^{-14}}{7.00 \times 10^{-1}\ M} = 1.4 \times 10^{-14}\ M$; solution is acidic

d. $[OH^-] = \dfrac{1.0 \times 10^{-14}}{5.99 \times 10^{-6}\ M} = 1.7 \times 10^{-9}\ M$; solution is acidic

35.   a. $[H^+] = 1.2 \times 10^{-3}\ M$ is more acidic

b. $[H^+] = 2.6 \times 10^{-6}\ M$ is more acidic

c. $[H^+] = 0.000010\ M$ is more acidic

36.   a. $[H^+] = 1.04 \times 10^{-8}\ M$ is more basic

b. $[OH^-] = 4.49 \times 10^{-6}\ M$ is more basic

c. $[OH^-] = 6.01 \times 10^{-7}\ M$ is more basic

37.   Because the concentrations of $[H^+]$ and $[OH^-]$ in aqueous solutions tend to be expressed in scientific notation, and since these numbers have negative exponents for their powers of ten, it tends to be clumsy to make comparisons between different concentrations of these ions (see questions 35 and 36 above). The pH scale converts such numbers into "ordinary" numbers between 0 and 14 which can be more easily compared.

The pH of a solution is defined as the *negative* of the base 10 logarithm of the hydrogen ion concentration, pH = $-\log[H^+]$.

38.   household ammonia (pH 12); blood (pH 7-8); milk (pH 6-7); vinegar (pH 3); lemon juice (pH 2-3); stomach acid (pH 2)

39.   Since 2.33×10^{-6} has three significant figures, the pH should be expressed to the third decimal place. The figure *before* the decimal place in a pH is *not* one of the significant digits: the figure before the decimal place is related to the *power of ten* (exponent) of the concentration.

40.   The pH of a solution is defined as the *negative* of the logarithm of the hydrogen ion concentration, pH = $-\log[H^+]$. Mathematically, the *negative sign* in the definition causes the pH to *decrease* as the hydrogen ion concentration *increases*.

41.   pH = $-\log[H^+]$

   a.   pH = $-\log[4.59 \times 10^{-7}\ M]$ = 6.338; solution is acidic

   b.   pH = $-\log[0.251\ M]$ = 0.600; solution is acidic

   c.   pH = $-\log[7.21 \times 10^{-13}\ M]$ = 12.142; solution is basic

   d.   pH = $-\log[2.18 \times 10^{-3}\ M]$ = 2.662; solution is acidic

42.   pH = $-\log[H^+]$

   a.   pH = $-\log[0.0010\ M]$ = 3.000; solution is acidic

   b.   pH = $-\log[2.19 \times 10^{-4}\ M]$ = 3.660; solution is acidic

   c.   pH = $-\log[9.18 \times 10^{-11}\ M]$ = 10.037; solution is basic

   d.   pH = $-\log[4.71 \times 10^{-7}\ M]$ = 6.327; solution is acidic

43.   pOH = $-\log[OH^-]$ pH = 14 - pOH

   a.   pOH = $-\log[7.42 \times 10^{-5}\ M]$ = 4.130

        pH = 14 - 4.130 = 9.870; solution is basic

   b.   pOH = $-\log[0.00151\ M]$ = 2.821

        pH = 14 - 2.821 = 11.179; solution is basic

   c.   pOH = $-\log[3.31 \times 10^{-2}\ M]$ = 1.480

        pH = 14 - 1.480 = 12.520; solution is basic

d. $pOH = -log[9.01 \times 10^{-9} \, M] = 8.045$

$pH = 14 - 8.045 = 5.955$; solution is acidic

44. $pOH = -log[OH^-]$ $pH = 14 - pOH$

a. $pOH = -log[1.00 \times 10^{-7} \, M] = 7.000$

$pH = 14 - 7.000 = 7.000$; solution is neutral

b. $pOH = -log[4.59 \times 10^{-13} \, M] = 12.338$

$pH = 14 - 12.338 = 1.662$; solution is acidic

c. $pOH = -log[1.04 \times 10^{-4} \, M] = 3.983$

$pH = 14 - 3.983 = 10.017$; solution is basic

d. $pOH = -log[7.00 \times 10^{-1} \, M] = 0.155$

$pH = 14 - 0.155 = 13.845$; solution is basic

45. $pH = 14 - pOH$

a. $pH = 14 - 4.32 = 9.68$; solution is basic

b. $pH = 14 - 8.90 = 5.10$; solution is acidic

c. $pH = 14 - 1.81 = 12.19$; solution is basic

d. $pH = 14 - 13.1 = 0.9$; solution is acidic

46. $pOH = 14 - pH$

a. $pOH = 14 - 6.49 = 7.51$; solution is acidic

b. $pOH = 14 - 1.93 = 12.07$; solution is acidic

c. $pOH = 14 - 11.21 = 2.79$; solution is basic

d. $pOH = 14 - 7.00 = 7.00$; solution is neutral

47.   a. $[H^+] = \dfrac{1.0 \times 10^{-14}}{0.0505 \, M} = 1.98 \times 10^{-13} \, M$

$pH = -log[1.98 \times 10^{-13} \, M] = 12.70$

$pOH = 14 - 11.22 = 1.30$

b. $[OH^-] = \dfrac{1.0 \times 10^{-14}}{0.115 \, M} = 8.70 \times 10^{-14} \, M$

$$pOH = -\log[8.70 \times 10^{-14} \ M] = 13.06$$

$$pH = 14 - 13.061 = 0.94$$

c. $$[OH^-] = \frac{1.0 \times 10^{-14}}{1.24 \times 10^{-5} \ M} = 8.06 \times 10^{-10} \ M$$

$$pOH = -\log[8.06 \times 10^{-10} \ M] = 9.09$$

$$pH = 14 - 9.093 = 4.91$$

d. $$[H^+] = \frac{1.0 \times 10^{-14}}{8.99 \times 10^{-12} \ M} = 1.11 \times 10^{-3} \ M$$

$$pH = -\log[1.11 \times 10^{-3} \ M] = 2.95$$

$$pOH = 14 - 12.05 = 11.05$$

48.   a. $$[H^+] = 1.00 \times 10^{-7} \ M$$

$$[OH^-] = \frac{1.0 \times 10^{-14}}{1.00 \times 10^{-7} \ M} = 1.0 \times 10^{-7} \ M$$

$$pH = -\log[1.0 \times 10^{-7} \ M] = 7.00$$

$$pOH = 14 - 7.00 = 7.00$$

b. $$[OH^-] = 4.39 \times 10^{-5} \ M$$

$$[H^+] = \frac{1.0 \times 10^{-14}}{4.39 \times 10^{-5} \ M} = 2.28 \times 10^{-10} \ M = 2.3 \times 10^{-10} \ M$$

$$pH = -\log[2.28 \times 10^{-10} \ M] = 9.64$$

$$pOH = 14 - 9.64 = 4.36$$

c. $$[H^+] = 4.29 \times 10^{-11} \ M$$

$$[OH^-] = \frac{1.0 \times 10^{-14}}{4.29 \times 10^{-11} \ M} = 2.33 \times 10^{-4} \ M = 2.3 \times 10^{-4} \ M$$

$$pH = -\log[4.29 \times 10^{-11} \ M] = 10.37$$

$$pOH = 14 - 10.368 = 3.63$$

d. $$[OH^-] = 7.36 \times 10^{-2} \ M$$

$$[H^+] = \frac{1.0 \times 10^{-14}}{7.36 \times 10^{-2} \ M} = 1.36 \times 10^{-13} \ M = 1.4 \times 10^{-13} \ M$$

$$pH = -\log[1.36 \times 10^{-13} \ M] = 12.87$$

$$pOH = 14 - 12.87 = 1.13$$

49. $$[H^+] = \{inv\}\{log\}[-pH]$$

a. $$[H^+] = \{inv\}\{log\}[-4.32] = 4.8 \times 10^{-5} \ M$$

b. $$[H^+] = \{inv\}\{log\}[-5.93] = 1.2 \times 10^{-6} \ M$$

c. $[H^+] = \{inv\}\{log\}[-1.02] = 9.5 \times 10^{-2}\ M$

d. $[H^+] = \{inv\}\{log\}[-13.1] = 8 \times 10^{-14}\ M$

50. $[H^+] = \{inv\}\{log\}[-pH]$

a. $[H^+] = \{inv\}\{log\}[-1.04] = 9.2 \times 10^{-2}\ M$

b. $[H^+] = \{inv\}\{log\}[-13.1] = 8 \times 10^{-14}\ M$

c. $[H^+] = \{inv\}\{log\}[-5.99] = 1.0 \times 10^{-6}\ M$

d. $[H^+] = \{inv\}\{log\}[-8.62] = 2.4 \times 10^{-9}\ M$

51. $pH = 14 - pOH$ $[H^+] = \{inv\}\{log\}[-pH]$

a. $pH = 14 - 4.95 = 9.05$

$[H^+] = \{inv\}\{log\}[-9.05] = 8.9 \times 10^{-10}\ M$

b. $pH = 14 - 7.00 = 7.00$

$[H^+] = \{inv\}\{log\}[-7.00] = 1.0 \times 10^{-7}\ M$

c. $pH = 14 - 12.94 = 1.06$

$[H^+] = \{inv\}\{log\}[-1.06] = 8.7 \times 10^{-2}\ M$

d. $pH = 14 - 1.02 = 12.98$

$[H^+] = \{inv\}\{log\}[-12.98] = 1.0 \times 10^{-13}\ M$

52.   a. $pH = 14 - 3.91 = 10.09$

$[H^+] = \{inv\}\{log\}[-10.09] = 8.1 \times 10^{-11}\ M$

b. $pH = 14 - 12.56 = 1.44$

$[H^+] = \{inv\}\{log\}[-1.44] = 3.6 \times 10^{-2}\ M$

c. $pH = 14 - 1.15 = 12.85$

$[H^+] = \{inv\}\{log\}[-12.85] = 1.4 \times 10^{-13}\ M$

d. $pH = 14 - 8.77 = 5.23$

$[H^+] = \{inv\}\{log\}[-5.23] = 5.9 \times 10^{-6}\ M$

53.   a. $[H^+] = \{inv\}\{log\}[-8.51] = 3.1 \times 10^{-9}\ M$

$pOH = 14 - 8.51 = 5.49$

$[OH^-] = \{inv\}\{log\}[-5.49] = 3.2 \times 10^{-6}\ M$

b. $[OH^-]$ = {inv}{log}[-9.39] = 4.1 × 10^{-10} *M*

pH = 14 - 9.39 = 4.61

$[H^+]$ = {inv}{log}[-4.61] = 2.5 × 10^{-5} *M*

c. $[H^+]$ = {inv}{log}[-2.54] = 2.9 × 10^{-3} *M*

pOH = 14 - 2.54 = 11.46

$[OH^-]$ = {inv}{log}[-11.46] = 3.5 × 10^{-12} *M*

d. $[OH^-]$ = {inv}{log}[-4.82] = 1.5 × 10^{-5} *M*

pH = 14 - 4.82 = 9.18

$[H^+]$ = {inv}{log}[-9.18] = 6.6 × 10^{-10} *M*

54. a.   pOH = 14 - 5.12 = 8.88

$[H^+]$ = {inv}{log}[-5.12] = 7.6 × 10^{-6} *M*

$[OH^-]$ = {inv}{log}[-8.88] = 1.3 × 10^{-9} *M*

b.   pH = 14 - 5.12 = 8.88

$[H^+]$ = {inv}{log}[-8.88] = 1.3 × 10^{-9} *M*

$[OH^-]$ = {inv}{log}[-5.12] = 7.6 × 10^{-6} *M*

c.   pOH = 14 - 7.00 = 7.00

$[H^+]$ = $[OH^-]$ {inv}{log}[-7.00] = 1.0 × 10^{-7} *M*

d.   pH = 14 - 13.00 = 1.00

$[H^+]$ = {inv}{log}[-1.00] = 1.0 × 10^{-1} *M*

$[OH^-]$ = {inv}{log}[-13.00] = 1.0 × 10^{-13} *M*

55. Effectively *no* molecules of HCl remain in solution. HCl is a strong acid for which the equilibrium with water lies far to the right. All the HCl molecules originally dissolved in the water will ionize.

56. The solution contains water molecules, H_3O^+ ions (protons), and NO_3^- ions. Because HNO_3 is a strong acid, which is completely ionized in water, there are no HNO_3 molecules present.

57.   a.   HCl is a strong acid and completely ionized so

$[H^+] = 1.04 \times 10^{-4}$ M

$pH = -\log[1.04 \times 10^{-4}] = 3.983$

     b. HNO_3 is a strong acid and completely ionized so

$[H^+] = 0.00301$ M

$pH = -\log[0.00301] = 2.521$

     c. $HClO_4$ is a strong acid and completely ionized so

$[H^+] = 5.41 \times 10^{-4}$ M

$pH = -\log[5.41 \times 10^{-4}] = 3.267$

     d. HNO_3 is a strong acid and completely ionized so

$[H^+] = 6.42 \times 10^{-2}$ M

$pH = -\log[6.42 \times 10^{-2}] = 1.192$

58.   a.   HCl is a strong acid and completely ionized so

$[H^+] = 0.00010$ M and pH = 4.00

     b. HNO_3 is a strong acid and completely ionized so

$[H^+] = 0.0050$ M and pH = 2.30

     c. $HClO_4$ is a strong acid and completely ionized so

$[H^+] = 4.21 \times 10^{-5}$ M and pH = 4.376

     d. HNO_3 is a strong acid and completely ionized so

$[H^+] = 6.33 \times 10^{-3}$ M and pH = 2.199

59.   A buffered solution is one that resists a change in its pH even when a strong acid or base is added to it. A solution is buffered by the presence of the combination of a weak acid and its conjugate base.

60.   A buffered solution consists of a mixture of a weak acid and its conjugate base; one example of a buffered solution is a mixture of acetic acid (CH_3COOH) and sodium acetate ($NaCH_3COO$).

61.   The conjugate *base* component of the buffer mixture is capable of combining with any strong acid that might be added to the buffered solution. For the example of acetate ion ($C_2H_3O_2^-$) given in the solution to question 60, the equation is

$$HCl(aq) + C_2H_3O_2^-(aq) \rightarrow HC_2H_3O_2(aq) + Cl^-(aq)$$

62.   The weak acid component of a buffered solution is capable of reacting with added strong base. For example, using the buffered solution given as an example in Question 60, acetic acid would consume added sodium hydroxide as follows:

$$CH_3COOH(aq) + NaOH(aq) \rightarrow NaCH_3COO(aq) + H_2O(l)$$

Acetic acid *neutralizes* the added NaOH and prevents it from having much effect on the overall pH of the solution.

63.   a.   not a buffer: although HCl and Cl^- are conjugates, HCl is *not* a weak acid.

b.   a buffer: CH_3COOH and CH_3COO^- are conjugates

c.   a buffer: H_2S and HS^- are conjugates

d.   not a buffer: S^{2-} (of Na_2S) is *not* the conjugate base of H_2S

64.   added NaOH: $CH_3COOH + OH^- \rightarrow CH_3COO^- + H_2O$

added HCl: $CH_3COO^- + H_3O^+ \rightarrow CH_3COOH + H_2O$

added NaOH: $H_2S + OH^- \rightarrow HS^- + H_2O$

added HCl: $HS^- + H_3O^+ \rightarrow H_2S + H_2O$

65.   In whatever solvent is used, a Brönsted-Lowry acid will still be a proton donor. In liquid ammonia, HCl would still be an acid through the following equation

$$HCl + NH_3 \rightarrow Cl^- + NH_4^+$$

in which the proton is transferred from HCl to NH_3. Similarly, OH^- would still be a base (proton acceptor) in liquid ammonia as indicated in the equation

$$OH^- + NH_3 \rightarrow H_2O + NH_2^-$$

in which OH^- could receive a proton from ammonia.

66.   a.   NaOH is completely ionized, so $[OH^-] = 0.10$ *M*

pOH = $-\log[0.10]$ = 1.00

pH = 14 − 1.00 = 13.00

b.   KOH is completely ionized, so $[OH^-] = 2.0 \times 10^{-4}$ *M*

pOH = $-\log[2.0 \times 10^{-4}]$ = 3.70

pH = 14 − 3.70 = 10.30

c.   CsOH is completely ionized, so $[OH^-] = 6.2 \times 10^{-3}$ *M*

pOH $= -\log[6.2 \times 10^{-3}] = 2.21$

pH $= 14 - 2.21 = 11.79$

d.   NaOH is completely ionized, so $[OH^-] = 0.0001$ *M*

pOH $= -\log[0.0001] = 4.0$

pH $= 14 - 4.0 = 10.0$

67.   *a*, *c*, and *d* represent acidic solutions; *b* represents a *basic* solution because there is more hydroxide ion present than there is hydrogen ion.

68.   *a*, *b*, and *d* represent basic solutions; *c* represents an *acidic* solution because there is less hydroxide ion than hydrogen ion.

69.   In order to be able to consume added acid, a buffered solution must contain a species capable of strongly attracting protons. The conjugate base of a *weak* acid is capable of strongly attracting protons, but the conjugate base of a *strong* acid does *not* have a strong affinity for protons.

70.   *a*, *c*, and *e* represent strong acids; *b* and *d* are typical *weak* acids.

71.   No. For any aqueous solution, the concentrations of $[H^+]$ and $[OH^-]$ are related by K_w. The product of the given concentrations would not equal the value of K_w.

72.   Ordinarily in calculating the pH of strong acid solutions, the major contribution to the concentration of hydrogen ion present is from the dissolved strong acid; we ordinarily neglect the small amount of hydrogen ion present in such solutions due to the ionization of water. With 1.0×10^{-7} *M* HCl solution, however, the amount of hydrogen ion present due to the ionization of *water* is *comparable* to that present due to the addition of *acid* (HCl) and must be considered in the calculation of pH.

73.   hydroxide

74.   accepts

75.   proton

76.   base

77.   strong

78.   carboxyl (-COOH)

79.   autoionization

80. 1.0×10^{-14}

81.   decimal places

82.   higher

83.   0.20, 0.20

84.   pH

85.   conjugate base

86.   weak acid

87.   conjugate base

88.   a. H_2O and OH^- represent a conjugate acid-base pair (H_2O is the acid, having one more proton than the base, OH^-).

     b. H_2SO_4 and SO_4^{2-} are *not* a conjugate acid-base pair (they differ by *two* protons). The conjugate base of H_2SO_4 is HSO_4^-; the conjugate acid of SO_4^{2-} is also HSO_4^-.

     c. H_3PO_4 and $H_2PO_4^-$ represent a conjugate acid-base pair (H_3PO_4 is the acid, having one more proton than the base $H_2PO_4^-$).

     d. $HC_2H_3O_2$ and $C_2H_3O_2^-$ represent a conjugate acid-base pair ($HC_2H_3O_2$ is the acid, having one more proton than the base $C_2H_3O_2^-$).

89.   a. CH_3NH_2 (base), $CH_3NH_3^+$ (acid); H_2O (acid), OH^- (base)

     b. CH_3COOH (acid), CH_3COO^- (base); NH_3 (base), NH_4^+ (acid)

     c.   HF (acid), F^- (base); NH_3 (base), NH_4^+ (acid)

90.   The conjugate *acid* of the species indicated would have *one additional proton*:

     a. NH_4^+

     b. NH_3

     c. H_3O^+

     d. H_2O

91.   The conjugate *bases* of the species indicated would have *one less proton*:

     a. $H_2PO_4^-$

     b. CO_3^{2-}

    c. F^-

    d. HSO_4^-

92.   When an acid ionizes in water, a proton is released to the water as an H_3O^+ ion:

    a. $CH_3CH_2COOH + H_2O \rightleftarrows CH_3CH_2COO^- + H_3O^+$

    b. $NH_4^+ + H_2O \rightleftarrows NH_3 + H_3O^+$

    c. $H_2SO_4 + H_2O \rightarrow HSO_4^- + H_3O^+$

    d. $H_3PO_4 + H_2O \rightleftarrows H_2PO_4^- + H_3O^+$

93.   Bases that are *weak* have relatively strong conjugate acids:

    a. F^- is a relatively strong base; HF is a weak acid.

    b. Cl^- is a very weak base; HCl is a strong acid.

    c. HSO_4^- is a very weak base; H_2SO_4 is a strong acid.

    d. NO_3^- is a very weak base; HNO_3 is a strong acid.

94. $K_w = [H^+][OH^-] = 1.0 \times 10^{-14}$ at 25°C

$$[H^+] = \frac{1.0 \times 10^{-14}}{[OH^-]}$$

    a. $[H^+] = \dfrac{1.0 \times 10^{-14}}{4.22 \times 10^{-3}\ M} = 2.4 \times 10^{-12}\ M$; solution is basic

    b. $[H^+] = \dfrac{1.0 \times 10^{-14}}{1.01 \times 10^{-13}\ M} = 9.9 \times 10^{-2}\ M$; solution is acidic

    c. $[H^+] = \dfrac{1.0 \times 10^{-14}}{3.05 \times 10^{-7}\ M} = 3.3 \times 10^{-8}\ M$; solution is basic

    d. $[H^+] = \dfrac{1.0 \times 10^{-14}}{6.02 \times 10^{-6}\ M} = 1.7 \times 10^{-9}\ M$; solution is basic

95. $[OH^-] = \dfrac{1.0 \times 10^{-14}}{[H^+]}$

    a. $[OH^-] = \dfrac{1.0 \times 10^{-14}}{4.21 \times 10^{-7}\ M} = 2.4 \times 10^{-8}\ M$; solution is acidic

    b. $[OH^-] = \dfrac{1.0 \times 10^{-14}}{0.00035\ M} = 2.9 \times 10^{-11}\ M$; solution is acidic

    c. $[OH^-] = \dfrac{1.0 \times 10^{-14}}{0.00000010\ M} = 1.0 \times 10^{-7}\ M$; solution is neutral

d. $[OH^-] = \dfrac{1.0 \times 10^{-14}}{9.9 \times 10^{-6} \ M} = 1.0 \times 10^{-9} \ M$; solution is acidic

96.   a. $[OH^-] = 0.0000032 \ M$ is more basic

b. $[OH^-] = 1.54 \times 10^{-8} \ M$ is more basic

c. $[OH^-] = 4.02 \times 10^{-7} \ M$ is more basic

97. $pH = -\log[H^+]$ $pOH = -\log[OH^-]$ $pH + pOH = 14$

a. $pH = -\log[1.49 \times 10^{-3} \ M] = 2.827$; solution is acidic

b. $pOH = -\log[6.54 \times 10^{-4} \ M] = 3.184$

$pH = 14 - 3.184 = 10.816$; solution is basic

c. $pH = -\log[9.81 \times 10^{-9} \ M] = 8.008$; solution basic

d. $pOH = -\log[7.45 \times 10^{-10} \ M] = 9.128$

$pH = 14 - 9.128 = 4.872$; solution is acidic

98. $pOH = -\log[OH^-]$ $pH = 14 - pOH$

a. $pOH = -\log[1.4 \times 10^{-6} \ M] = 5.85$

$pH = 14 - 5.85 = 8.15$; solution is basic

b. $pOH = -\log[9.35 \times 10^{-9} \ M] = 8.029 = 8.03$

$pH = 14 - 8.029 = 5.971 = 5.97$; solution is acidic

c. $pOH = -\log[2.21 \times 10^{-1} \ M] = 0.656 = 0.66$

$pH = 14 - 0.656 = 13.344 = 13.34$; solution is basic

d. $pOH = -\log[7.98 \times 10^{-12} \ M] = 11.098 = 11.10$

$pH = 14 - 11.098 = 2.902 = 2.90$; solution is acidic

99. $pOH = 14 - pH$

a. $pOH = 14 - 1.02 = 12.98$; solution is acidic

b. $pOH = 14 - 13.4 = 0.6$; solution is basic

c. $pOH = 14 - 9.03 = 4.97$; solution is basic

d. $pOH = 14 - 7.20 = 6.80$; solution is basic

100. a. $[OH^-] = \dfrac{1.0 \times 10^{-14}}{5.72 \times 10^{-4} \ M} = 1.75 \times 10^{-11} \ M = 1.8 \times 10^{-11} \ M$

$pOH = -\log[1.75 \times 10^{-11} \ M] = 10.76$

$pH = 14 - 10.76 = 3.24$

b. $[H^+] = \dfrac{1.0 \times 10^{-14}}{8.91 \times 10^{-5}\ M} = 1.12 \times 10^{-10}\ M = 1.1 \times 10^{-10}\ M$

pH $= -\log[1.12 \times 10^{-10}\ M] = 9.95$

pOH $= 14 - 9.95 = 4.05$

c. $[OH^-] = \dfrac{1.0 \times 10^{-14}}{2.87 \times 10^{-12}\ M} = 3.48 \times 10^{-3}\ M = 3.5 \times 10^{-3}\ M$

pOH $= -\log[3.48 \times 10^{-3}\ M] = 2.46$

pH $= 14 - 2.46 = 11.54$

d. $[H^+] = \dfrac{1.0 \times 10^{-14}}{7.22 \times 10^{-8}\ M} = 1.39 \times 10^{-7}\ M = 1.4 \times 10^{-7}\ M$

pH $= -\log[1.39 \times 10^{-7}\ M] = 6.86$

pOH $= 14 - 6.86 = 7.14$

101. $[H^+] = \{inv\}\{log\}[-pH]$

    a. $[H^+] = \{inv\}\{log\}[-8.34] = 4.6 \times 10^{-9}\ M$

    b. $[H^+] = \{inv\}\{log\}[-5.90] = 1.3 \times 10^{-6}\ M$

    c. $[H^+] = \{inv\}\{log\}[-2.65] = 2.2 \times 10^{-3}\ M$

    d. $[H^+] = \{inv\}\{log\}[-12.6] = 3 \times 10^{-13}\ M$

102. pH $= 14 - pOH$ $[H^+] = \{inv\}\{log\}[-pH]$

    a. $[H^+] = \{inv\}\{log\}[-5.41] = 3.9 \times 10^{-6}\ M$

    b. pH $= 14 - 12.04 = 1.96$

        $[H^+] = \{inv\}\{log\}[-1.96] = 1.1 \times 10^{-2}\ M$

    c. $[H^+] = \{inv\}\{log\}[-11.91] = 1.2 \times 10^{-12}\ M$

    d. pH $= 14 - 3.89 = 10.11$

        $[H^+] = \{inv\}\{log\}[-10.11] = 7.8 \times 10^{-11}\ M$

103. a. pH $= 14 - 0.90 = 13.10$

        $[H^+] = \{inv\}\{log\}[-13.10] = 7.9 \times 10^{-14}\ M$

    b. $[H^+] = \{inv\}\{log\}[-0.90] = 0.13\ M$

    c. pH $= 14 - 10.3 = 3.7$

        $[H^+] = \{inv\}\{log\}[-3.7] = 2 \times 10^{-4}\ M$

    d. $[H^+] = \{inv\}\{log\}[-5.33] = 4.7 \times 10^{-6}\ M$

104. a. $HClO_4$ is a strong acid and completely ionized so

$[H^+]$ = 1.4×10^{-3} M and pH = 2.85

b.   HCl is a strong acid and completely ionized so

$[H^+]$ = 3.0×10^{-5} M and pH = 4.52

c. HNO_3 is a strong acid and completely ionized so

$[H^+]$ = 5.0×10^{-2} M and pH = 1.30

d.   HCl is a strong acid and completely ionized so

$[H^+]$ = 0.0010 M and pH = 3.00

105. There are many examples. For a general weak acid (HA) and its conjugate base (A^-) the general equations illustrating the consumption of added acid and base would be:

$$HA(aq) + OH^-(aq) \rightarrow A^-(aq) + H_2O$$

$$A^-(aq) + H_3O^+(aq) \rightarrow HA(aq) + H_2O$$

For example, for a buffer consisting of equimolar HF/NaF:

$$HF(aq) + OH^-(aq) \rightarrow F^-(aq) + H_2O$$

$$F^-(aq) + H_3O^+(aq) \rightarrow HF(aq) + H_2O$$

Chapter 16   Equilibrium

1.   The hydrogen-hydrogen bond of H_2 and the bromine-bromine bond of Br_2 must break. Two hydrogen-bromine bonds (one in each of the HBr molecules) must form.

2.   The nitrogen-nitrogen triple bond in N_2 and the three hydrogen-hydrogen bonds (in the three H_2 molecules) must be broken. Six nitrogen-hydrogen bonds must form (in the two ammonia molecules).

3.   The collision model pictures chemical reactions as taking place only when the reactant molecules *physically collide* with one another, with enough energy to break bonds in the reactant molecules. Not all collisions possess enough energy to break bonds in the reactant molecules. A minimum energy, the *activation energy* (E_a) is needed for a collision to result in reaction. If molecules do not possess this minimum energy when they collide, they just bounce off one another without reacting. A simple reaction is illustrated in Figure 16.2.

4.   The activation energy is the minimum energy two colliding molecules must possess in order for the collision to result in reaction. If molecules do not possess energies equal to or greater than E_a, a collision between these molecules will not result in a reaction.

5.   A catalyst is a substance which speeds up a reaction without being consumed in the reaction (the full amount of catalyst used is still present after the reaction is complete). Catalysts work by providing an alternative pathway by which a reaction can take place: this alternative pathway has a lower activation energy. See text Figures 16.3 and 16.4.

6.   Living cells contain biological catalysts called *enzymes*. Such enzymes are necessary to speed up the complicated biochemical processes that must occur in cells. Such processes would be too slow to sustain life at room temperature if such catalysts were not present.

7.   In an equilibrium system, two opposing processes are going on at the same time and at the same speed. There is no net change in a system at equilibrium with time. Every time one process occurs, the opposite process occurs at the same time elsewhere in the system. A simple equilibrium might exist for the populations of two similar size towns connected by highway. Assuming there is no great attraction in one town compared to the other, we might assume the populations of the two towns would remain constant with time as individual people drive between them, but in such a way that new people are arriving in the first town from the second town as residents of the first town leave for the second town.

8.   A state of equilibrium is attained when two opposing processes are exactly balanced. The development of a vapor pressure above a liquid in a closed container is an example of a physical equilibrium. Any chemical reaction which appears to "stop" before completion serves as an example of a chemical equilibrium.

9.   Chemical reactions are reversible if they can occur in either direction
        (as written from left to right, or the reverse of this). In principle,
        all chemical reactions are microscopically reversible. In practice, many
        (though by no means all) reactions are favored greatly in one direction
        over the other.

10.   Chemical equilibrium occurs when two *opposing* chemical reactions reach
        the *same speed* in a closed system. When a state of chemical equilibrium
        has been reached, the concentrations of reactants and products present
        in the system remain *constant* with time, and the reaction appears to
        "stop." A chemical reaction that reaches a state of equilibrium is
        indicated by using a double arrow ($\rightleftharpoons$). The points of the double arrow
        point in opposite directions, indicating that two opposite processes are
        going on.

11.   Once a system has reached equilibrium the net concentration of product
        no longer increases because molecules of product already present react
        to form the original reactants. Although there is no *net* change in the
        number of product molecules present at any one time, this is not to say
        that the *same* product molecules are always present.

12.   Although we recognize a state of chemical equilibrium by the fact that
        the concentrations of reactants and products no longer change with time,
        the lack of change results from the fact that two *opposing* processes are
        going on at the same time with the same rate (not because the reaction
        has truly "stopped"). Further reaction in the forward direction is
        canceled out by an equal extent of reaction in the reverse direction.
        The reaction is still proceeding, but the opposite reaction is also
        proceeding at the same rate.

13.   The equilibrium constant represents a ratio of the concentration of
        products present at the point of equilibrium to the concentration of
        reactants present, with the concentration of each species raised to the
        power of its coefficient in the balanced chemical equation for the
        reaction. For a general reaction

$$aA + bB \rightleftharpoons cC + dD$$

        the equilibrium constant, K, has the algebraic form

$$K = \frac{[C]^c\,[D]^d}{[A]^a\,[B]^b}$$

        where square brackets indicate the concentrations of the substances in
        moles per liter (molarity, M).

14.   The equilibrium constant is a *ratio* of the concentration of products to
        the concentration of reactants, with all concentrations measured at
        equilibrium. Depending on how much reactant a particular experiment was
        begun with, there may be different absolute amounts of reactants and
        products present at equilibrium, but the *ratio* will always be the same

for a given reaction at a given temperature. For example, the ratios (4/2) and (6/3) are different absolutely in terms of the numbers involved, but each of these ratios has the *value* of 2.

15. a. $K = \dfrac{[NO]^4 [H_2O]^6}{[NH_3]^4 [O_2]^5}$

  b. $K = \dfrac{[NO_2]^2}{[NO]^2 [O_2]}$

  c. $K = \dfrac{[CH_2O] [H_2]}{[CH_3OH]}$

16. a. $K = \dfrac{[NCl_3]^2}{[N_2] [Cl_2]^3}$

  b. $K = \dfrac{[HI]^2}{[H_2]^2 [I_2]^2}$

  c. $K = \dfrac{[N_2H_4]}{[N_2] [H_2]^2}$

17. a. $K = \dfrac{[NO_2]^2}{[N_2O_4]}$

  b. $K = \dfrac{[SiCl_4] [H_2]^2}{[SiH_4] [Cl_2]^2}$

  c. $K = \dfrac{[PCl_3]^2 [Br_2]^3}{[PBr_3]^2 [Cl_2]^3}$

18. a. $K = \dfrac{[CH_3OH]}{[CO] [H_2]^2}$

  b. $K = \dfrac{[NO]^2 [O_2]}{[NO_2]^2}$

  c. $K = \dfrac{[PBr_3]^4}{[P_4] [Br_2]^6}$

19. $CH_3OH(g) \rightleftarrows CH_2O(g) + H_2(g)$

  $K = \dfrac{[CH_2O] [H_2]}{[CH_3OH]} = \dfrac{[0.441 \ M] [0.0331 \ M]}{[0.00215 \ M]} = 6.79$

20. $N_2(g) + 3H_2(g) \rightleftarrows 2NH_3(g)$

  $K = \dfrac{[NH_3]^2}{[N_2] [H_2]^3} = \dfrac{[0.34 \ M]^2}{[4.9 \times 10^{-4} \ M] [2.1 \times 10^{-3} \ M]^3} = 2.5 \times 10^{10}$

21. $N_2(g) + O_2(g) \rightleftharpoons 2NO(g)$

$$K = \frac{[NO]^2}{[N_2][O_2]} = \frac{[4.7 \times 10^{-4}\ M]^2}{[0.041\ M][0.0078\ M]} = 6.9 \times 10^{-4}$$

22. $N_2(g) + 3Cl_2(g) \rightleftharpoons 2NCl_3(g)$

$$K = \frac{[NCl_3]^2}{[N_2][Cl_2]^3} = \frac{[0.141\ M]^2}{[0.000104\ M][0.000201\ M]^3} = 2.35 \times 10^{13}$$

23.   A *homogeneous* equilibrium system is a system in which all the substances present are in the same physical state. An example is

$$N_2(g) + O_2(g) \rightleftharpoons 2NO(g)$$

Heterogeneous equilibrium systems are those involving substances in more than one physical state (e.g., mixtures of liquids and gases, gases and solids, etc.). Examples are:

$$BaCO_3(s) \rightleftharpoons BaO(s) + CO_2(g)$$

$$NH_3(g) + HCl(g) \rightleftharpoons NH_4Cl(s)$$

24.   Equilibrium constants represent ratios of the *concentrations* of products and reactants present at the point of equilibrium. The *concentration* of a pure solid or of a pure liquid is constant and is determined by the density of the solid or liquid. For example, suppose you had a liter of water. Within that liter of water are 55.5 mol of water (the number of moles of water that is contained in one liter of water *does not vary*).

25.   a. $K = \dfrac{1}{[SO_3]}$

     b. $K = \dfrac{[H_2O]}{[NH_3]^2[CO_2]}$

     c. $K = [I_2]^2$

26.   a. $K = [H_2O(g)][CO_2(g)]$

     b. $K = [CO_2]$

     c. $K = \dfrac{1}{[\![\ _2]^3}$

27.   a. $K = [Cl_2]^3$

     b. $K = \dfrac{[H_2O]}{[CO_2]}$

c. $K = \dfrac{[UF_4][H_2O]^2}{[HF]^4}$

28.   a. $K = [Br_2]^3[N_2]$

b. $K = \dfrac{[H_2O]}{[H_2]}$

c. $K = [CO_2]$

29.   Le Châtelier's principle states that when a change is imposed on a system at equilibrium, the position of the equilibrium shifts in a direction that tends to reduce the effect of the change.

30.   When an additional amount of one of the reactants is added to an equilibrium system, the system shifts to the right and adjusts so as to use up some of the added reactant. This results in a net *increase* in the amount of product, compared to the equilibrium system before the additional reactant was added. The numerical *value* of the equilibrium constant does *not* change when a reactant is added: the concentrations of all reactants and products adjust until the correct value of K is once again achieved.

31.   When the volume of an equilibrium system involving gaseous substances is decreased suddenly, the pressure in the container increases. Reaction will occur, shifting in the direction that gives the smaller number of gas molecules, to reduce this increase in pressure.

32.   If heat is applied to an endothermic reaction (i.e., the temperature is raised), the equilibrium is shifted to the right. More product will be present at equilibrium than if the temperature had not been increased. The value of K increases.

33.   a.   shifts right (system reacts to get rid of excess O_2)

b.   shifts right (system reacts to replace water)

c.   shifts left (system reacts to replace gaseous ammonia)

34.   a.   shifts right (system reacts to get rid of excess SO_2)

b.   shifts right (system reacts to replace missing SO_3)

c.   no change (catalysts do not affect the position of equilibrium)

35.   a.   no change (water is in the *liquid* state)

b.   assuming the system is warm enough to convert the dry ice to the gaseous state, the equilibrium will shift to the left.

c.   shifts to right

d.   shifts to right

36.   a.   no effect (UO_2 is a solid)

b.   no effect (Xe is not involved in the reaction)

c.   shifts to left (if HF attacks glass, it is removed from system, causing reaction to replace the lost HF)

d.   shifts to right

e.   shifts to left (4 mol gas versus 3 mol gas)

37.   Since the reaction is endothermic, heat is effectively a reactant. Performing the reaction at a lower temperature (removing heat from the system) would shift the reaction to the left.

38.   A increase in temperature will tend to increase the yield of product. Heat is a reactant for the reaction; adding heat favors the forward reaction.

39.   Since the reaction is exothermic, heat is effectively a product of the reaction as written. Raising the temperature of the system (adding heat to the system) tends to disfavor the formation of products, and shifts the equilibrium to the left (toward reactants).

40.   For an *endo*thermic reaction, an increase in temperature will shift the position of equilibrium to the right (toward products).

41.   the production of dextrose will be favored

42.   Heat is a product of the reaction. Removing heat will tend to favor the forward reaction. The reaction is *exo*thermic and should be performed at as low a temperature as possible (consistent with the molecules still having sufficient energy to react).

43.   A large equilibrium constant means that the concentration of products is large, compared to the concentration of remaining reactants. The position of the equilibrium lies far to the right. Reactions with numerically large equilibrium constants are greatly favored as a source of product. When we calculated the theoretical yield for a reaction in earlier chapters, we tacitly assumed that the reaction had a large equilibrium constant.

44.   A small equilibrium constant means that the concentration of products is small, compared to the concentration of reactants. The position of equilibrium lies far to the left. Reactions with very small equilibrium constants are generally not very useful as a source of the products, unless Le Châtelier's principle can be applied to shift the position of equilibrium to the point where a sufficient amount of product can be isolated.

45. $$K = \frac{[N_2][Br_2]^3}{[NBr_3]^2} = \frac{[4.11 \times 10^{-2} \ M][1.06 \times 10^{-3} \ M]^3}{[2.07 \times 10^{-3} \ M]^2} = 1.14 \times 10^{-5}$$

46. $K = \dfrac{[NCl_3]^2}{[N_2][Cl_2]^3} = \dfrac{[1.9 \times 10^{-1}]^2}{[1.4 \times 10^{-3}\ M][4.3 \times 10^{-4}\ M]^3} = 3.2 \times 10^{11}$

47. $K = \dfrac{[O_3]^2}{[O_2]^3}$

$1.8 \times 10^{-7} = \dfrac{[O_3]^2}{[0.0012\ M]^3}$

$[O_3]^2 = 1.8 \times 10^{-7} \times [0.0012]^3 = 3.11 \times 10^{-16}$

$[O_3] = 1.8 \times 10^{-8}\ M$

48. $K = [CO_2] = [2.1 \times 10^{-3}\ M] = 2.1 \times 10^{-3}$

49. $K = \dfrac{[HF]^2}{[H_2][F_2]}$

$2.1 \times 10^3 = \dfrac{[HF]^2}{[0.0021\ M][0.0021\ M]}$

$[HF]^2 = 2.1 \times 10^3 \times [0.0021] \times [0.0021] = 9.26 \times 10^{-3}$

$[HF] = 9.6 \times 10^{-2}\ M$

50. $K = \dfrac{[H_2]^2[O_2]}{[H_2O]^2}$

$2.4 \times 10^{-3} = \dfrac{[1.9 \times 10^{-2}]^2[O_2]}{[1.1 \times 10^{-1}]^2}$

$[O_2] = \dfrac{(2.4 \times 10^{-3})(1.1 \times 10^{-1})^2}{(1.9 \times 10^{-2})^2} = 8.0 \times 10^{-2}\ M$

51. $K = \dfrac{[NO]^2}{[N_2][O_2]}$

$1.71 \times 10^{-3} = \dfrac{[NO]^2}{[0.0342\ M][0.0342\ M]}$

$[NO]^2 = 1.71 \times 10^{-3} \times [0.0342] \times [0.0342] = 2.00 \times 10^{-6}$

$[NO] = 1.41 \times 10^{-3}\ M$

52. $K = \dfrac{[NO_2]^2}{[N_2O_4]} = 8.1 \times 10^{-3}$

$8.1 \times 10^{-3} = \dfrac{[0.0021\ M]^2}{[N_2O_4]}$

$[N_2O_4] = 5.4 \times 10^{-4}\ M$

53.   When a crystal of ionic solute M^+X^- is placed in water, initially the crystal just dissolves producing $M^+(aq)$ ions and $X^-(aq)$ ions. As the concentration of the ions in solution increases, however, the likelihood of oppositely charged ions colliding and *reforming* the solid increases. Eventually, an equilibrium is reached in which dissolving and reforming of the solid are occurring at the same speed. Past this point in time, there is no further net increase in the concentration of the dissolved ions.

54.   solubility product, K_{sp}

55.   The equilibrium represents the balancing of the dynamic processes of dissolving and of reformation of the solid. The amount of excess solid added in preparing a solution might affect the *speed* at which the point of equilibrium is reached, but it will not affect the net amount of solute present in solution at the point of equilibrium. A given amount of solvent can only "hold" a certain amount of solute.

56.   Stirring or grinding the solute increases the speed with which the solute dissolves, but the ultimate *amount* of solute that dissolves is fixed by the equilibrium constant for the dissolving process, K_{sp}.

57.   a. $NiS(s) \rightleftharpoons Ni^{2+}(aq) + S^{2-}(aq)$

$$K_{sp} = [Ni^{2+}][S^{2-}]$$

b. $CuCO_3(s) \rightleftharpoons Cu^{2+}(aq) + CO_3^{2-}(aq)$

$$K_{sp} = [Cu^{2+}][CO_3^{2-}]$$

c. $BaCrO_4(s) \rightleftharpoons Ba^{2+}(aq) + CrO_4^{2-}(aq)$

$$K_{sp} = [Ba^{2+}][CrO_4^{2-}]$$

d. $Ag_3PO_4(s) \rightleftharpoons 3Ag^+(aq) + PO_4^{3-}(aq)$

$$K_{sp} = [Ag^+]^3[PO_4^{3-}]$$

58.   a. $PbBr_2(s) \rightleftharpoons Pb^{2+}(aq) + 2Br^-(aq)$

$$K_{sp} = [Pb^{2+}][Br^-]^2$$

b. $Ag_2S(s) \rightleftharpoons 2Ag^+(aq) + S^{2-}(aq)$

$$K_{sp} = [Ag^+]^2[S^{2-}]$$

c. $PbCO_3(s) \rightleftharpoons Pb^{2+}(aq) + CO_3^{2-}(aq)$

$$K_{sp} = [Pb^{2+}][CO_3^{2-}]$$

d. $Sr_3(PO_4)_2(s) \rightleftharpoons 3Sr^{2+}(aq) + 2PO_4^{3-}(aq)$

$K_{sp} = [Sr^{2+}]^3 [PO_4^{3-}]^2$

59. $ZnCO_3(s) \rightleftharpoons Zn^{2+}(aq) + CO_3^{2-}(aq)$

molar mass $ZnCO_3$ = 125.4 g

$$M = \frac{1.12 \times 10^{-4} \text{ g}}{1 \text{ L}} \times \frac{1 \text{ mol}}{125.4 \text{ g}} = 8.93 \times 10^{-7} \text{ } M$$

$K_{sp} = [Zn^{2+}][CO_3^{2-}] = (8.93 \times 10^{-7} \text{ } M)(8.93 \times 10^{-7} \text{ } M) = 7.98 \times 10^{-13}$

60. $ZnCO_3(s) \rightleftharpoons Zn^{2+}(aq) + CO_3^{2-}(aq)$

$K_{sp} = [Zn^{2+}][CO_3^{2-}]$

If 1.7×10^{-5} mol of $ZnCO_3$ dissolve per liter, then the concentrations of the two ions produced will each also be 1.7×10^{-5} M.

$K_{sp} = [1.7 \times 10^{-5} \text{ } M][1.7 \times 10^{-5} \text{ } M] = 2.9 \times 10^{-10}$.

61. $NiS(s) \rightleftharpoons Ni^{2+}(aq) + S^{2-}(aq)$

molar mass NiS = 90.77 g

$$3.6 \times 10^{-4} \text{ g NiS/L} \times \frac{1 \text{ mol NiS}}{90.77 \text{ g NiS}} = 3.97 \times 10^{-6} \text{ } M$$

$K_{sp} = [Ni^{2+}][S^{2-}] = (3.97 \times 10^{-6} \text{ } M)(3.97 \times 10^{-6} \text{ } M) = 1.6 \times 10^{-11}$

62. $CuCrO_4(s) \rightleftharpoons Cu^{2+}(aq) + CrO_4^{2-}(aq)$

$K_{sp} = [Cu^{2+}][CrO_4^{2-}]$

Molar mass of $CuCrO_4$ = 179.55 g

$$1.1 \times 10^{-5} \text{ g CuCrO}_4 \times \frac{1 \text{ mol}}{179.55 \text{ g}} = 6.1 \times 10^{-8} \text{ mol}$$

If 6.1×10^{-8} mol of $CuCrO_4$ dissolve per liter, then the concentrations of $Cu^{2+}(aq)$ and $CrO_4^{2-}(aq)$ are also each 6.1×10^{-8} M.

$K_{sp} = (6.1 \times 10^{-8} \text{ } M)(6.1 \times 10^{-8} \text{ } M) = 3.8 \times 10^{-15}$

63. $CaCO_3(s) \rightleftharpoons Ca^{2+}(aq) + CO_3^{2-}(aq)$

$K_{sp} = [Ca^{2+}][CO_3^{2-}] = 3.0 \times 10^{-9}$

Let x represent the number of moles of $CaCO_3(s)$ that dissolve per liter, then $[Ca^{2+}] = x$ and $[CO_3^{2-}] = x$ also from the stoichiometry of the reaction; then

$K_{sp} = [x][x] = x^2 = 3.0 \times 10^{-9}$

$x = [CaCO_3] = 5.5 \times 10^{-5} M \ (5.5 \times 10^{-3} \ g/L)$

64. $CuCrO_4(s) \rightleftarrows \Gamma\phi^{2+}(aq) + CrO_4{}^{2-}(aq)$

$K_{sp} = [Cu^{2+}][CrO_4{}^{2-}] = 3.8 \times 10^{-6}$

Let x represent the number of moles of $CuCrO_4(s)$ that dissolve per liter, then $[Cu^{2+}] = x$ and $[CrO_4{}^{2-}] = x$ also from the stoichiometry of the reaction; then

$K_{sp} = [x][x] = x^2 = 3.8 \times 10^{-6}$

$x = [CuCrO_4] = 1.9 \times 10^{-3} M$

65.   molar mass $Fe(OH)_2 = 89.87$ g

$1.5 \times 10^{-3} \ g \ Fe(OH)_2/L \times \dfrac{1 \ mol \ Fe(OH)_2}{89.87 \ g \ Fe(OH)_2} = 1.67 \times 10^{-5} \ mol \ Fe(OH)_2/L$

$Fe(OH)_2(s) \rightleftarrows = Fe^{2+}(aq) + 2OH^-(aq)$

$K_{sp} = [Fe^{2+}][OH^-]^2$

If $1.67 \times 10^{-5} M$ of $Fe(OH)_2$ dissolves then

$[Fe^{2+}] = 1.67 \times 10^{-5} M$ and

$[OH^-] = 2 \times (1.67 \times 10^{-5} M) = 3.34 \times 10^{-5} M$

$K_{sp} = (1.67 \times 10^{-5} M)(3.34 \times 10^{-5} M)^2 = 1.9 \times 10^{-14}$

66. $PbCrO_4(s) \rightleftarrows Pb^{2+}(aq) + CrO_4{}^{2-}(aq)$

$K_{sp} = [Pb^{2+}][CrO_4{}^{2-}] = 2.8 \times 10^{-13}$

Let x represent the number of moles of $PbCrO_4(s)$ that dissolve per liter. Then $[Pb^{2+}] = x$ and $[CrO_4{}^{2-}] = x$ also from the stoichiometry of the reaction; then

$K_{sp} = [x][x] = x^2 = 2.8 \times 10^{-13}$

$x = [PbCrO_4] = 5.3 \times 10^{-7} M.$

Molar mass of $PbCrO_4 = 323.2$ g

$5.3 \times 10^{-7} \ mol/L \times 323.2 \ g/mol = 1.7 \times 10^{-4} \ g/L$

67.   molar mass $MgF_2 = 62.31$ g

$8.0 \times 10^{-2} \ g \ MgF_2/L \times \dfrac{1 \ mol \ MgF_2}{62.31 \ g \ MgF_2} = 1.28 \times 10^{-3} M = 1.3 \times 10^{-3} M$

$MgF_2(s) \rightleftarrows Mg^{2+}(aq) + 2F^-(aq)$

$K_{sp} = [Mg^{2+}][F^-]^2$

If 1.28×10^{-3} M of MgF_2 dissolves, then

$[Mg^{2+}] = 1.28 \times 10^{-3}$ M and

$[F^-] = 2 \times 1.28 \times 10^{-3}$ $M = 2.56 \times 10^{-3}$ M

$K_{sp} = (1.28 \times 10^{-3} M)(2.56 \times 10^{-3} M)^2 = 8.4 \times 10^{-9}$

68. $PbCl_2(s) \rightleftarrows Pb^{2+}(aq) + 2Cl^-(aq)$

$K_{sp} = [Pb^{2+}][Cl^-]^2$

If $PbCl_2$ dissolves to the extent of 3.6×10^{-2} M, then

$[Pb^{2+}] = 3.6 \times 10^{-2}$ M and

$[Cl^-] = 2 \times (3.6 \times 10^{-2}) = 7.2 \times 10^{-2}$ M

$K_{sp} = (3.6 \times 10^{-2} M)(7.2 \times 10^{-2} M)^2 = 1.9 \times 10^{-4}$

molar mass $PbCl_2 = 278.1$ g

$3.6 \times 10^{-2} \dfrac{mol}{1\ L} \times \dfrac{278.1\ g}{1\ mol} = 10.\ g/L$

69. $Hg_2Cl_2(s) \rightleftarrows Hg_2^{2+}(aq) + 2Cl^-(aq)$

$K_{sp} = [Hg_2^{2+}][Cl^-]^2$

let x represent the number of moles of Hg_2Cl_2 that dissolve per liter; then

$[Hg_2^{2+}] = x$ and $[Cl^-] = 2x$

$K_{sp} = [x][2x]^2 = 4x^3 = 1.3 \times 10^{-18}$

$x^3 = 3.25 \times 10^{-19}$

$x = [Hg_2^{2+}] = 6.9 \times 10^{-7}$ M

70. $Fe(OH)_3(s) \rightleftarrows Fe^{3+}(aq) + 3OH^-(aq)$

$K_{sp} = [Fe^{3+}][OH^-]^3 = 4 \times 10^{-38}$

Let x represent the number of moles of $Fe(OH)_3$ that dissolve per liter; then $[Fe^{3+}] = x$.

The amount of hydroxide ion that would be produced by the dissolving of the $Fe(OH)_3$ would then be $3x$, but pure water itself contains hydroxide ion at the concentration of 1.0×10^{-7} M (see Chapter 17). The total concentration of hydroxide ion is then $[OH^-] = (3x + 1.0 \times 10^{-7})$. Since *x* must be a very small number [since $Fe(OH)_3$ is not very soluble], we can save ourselves a lot of arithmetic if we use the approximation that $(3x + 1.0 \times 10^{-7} M) = 1.0 \times 10^{-7}$

$$K_{sp} = [x][1.0 \times 10^{-7}]^3 = 4 \times 10^{-38}$$

$$x = 4 \times 10^{-17} M$$

molar mass $Fe(OH)_3$ = 106.9 g

$$\frac{4 \times 10^{-17} \text{ mol}}{1.00 \text{ L}} \times \frac{106.9 \text{ g}}{1 \text{ mol}} = 4 \times 10^{-15} \text{ g/L}$$

71. Collision between molecules is *not* the only prerequisite for a reaction. The molecules must also possess sufficient energy to react with each other, and must have the proper spatial orientation for reaction.

72. An increase in temperature increases the fraction of molecules that possess sufficient energy for a collision to result in a reaction.

73. activation

74. catalyst

75. balancing

76. constant

77. To say a reaction is *reversible* means that, to one extent or another, the reaction may occur in either direction.

78. When we say that a chemical equilibrium is *dynamic*, we are recognizing the fact that even though the reaction has appeared macroscopically to have stopped, on a microscopic basis the forward and reverse reactions are still taking place, at the same speed.

79. equals

80. heterogeneous

81. increase

82. position

83. pressure (and concentration)

84. Heat is considered a *product* of an exothermic process. Adding a product to a system in equilibrium causes the reverse reaction to occur (producing additional reactants).

85. The solubility product (K_{sp}) for a sparingly soluble salt is the equilibrium constant for the dynamic equilibrium between solution and undissolved solute in a saturated solution of the salt. Consider the sparingly soluble salt AgCl.

$$AgCl(s) \rightleftarrows Ag^+(aq) + Cl^-(aq) \qquad K_{sp} = [Ag^+(aq)][Cl^-(aq)]$$

86. An equilibrium reaction may come to many *positions* of equilibrium, but at each possible position of equilibrium, the numerical value of the equilibrium constant is fulfilled. If different amounts of reactant are taken in different experiments, the *absolute amounts* of reactant and product present at the point of equilibrium reached will differ from one experiment to another, but the *ratio* that defines the equilibrium constant will be the same.

87. alpha $\rightleftarrows$ beta

$$K = \frac{[beta]}{[alpha]}$$

At equilibrium, [alpha] = 2 × [beta]

$$K = \frac{[beta]}{2 \times [beta]} = 0.5$$

88. $PCl_5(g) \rightleftarrows PCl_3(g) + Cl_2(g)$

$$K = \frac{[PCl_3][Cl_2]}{[PCl_5]} = 4.5 \times 10^{-3}$$

The concentration of PCl_5 is to be twice the concentration of PCl_3:

$$[PCl_5] = 2 \times [PCl_3]$$

$$K = \frac{[PCl_3][Cl_2]}{2 \times [PCl_3]} = 4.5 \times 10^{-3}$$

$$K = \frac{[Cl_2]}{2} = 4.5 \times 10^{-3} \quad \text{and} \quad [Cl_2] = 9.0 \times 10^{-3} \ M$$

89. density $CaCO_3(s)$ = 2.930 g/cm^3 \qquad molar mass $CaCO_3$ = 100.1 g

$$\frac{2.930 \text{ g}}{1 \text{ cm}^3} \times \frac{1 \text{ mol}}{100.1 \text{ g}} \times \frac{1000 \text{ cm}^3}{1 \text{ L}} = 29.27 \ M \text{ for the solid}$$

density $CaO(s)$ = 3.30 g/cm^3 (lime)   molar mass CaO = 56.08 g

$$\frac{3.30 \text{ g}}{1 \text{ cm}^3} \times \frac{1 \text{ mol}}{56.08 \text{ g}} \times \frac{1000 \text{ cm}^3}{1 \text{ L}} = 58.8 \ M \text{ for the solid}$$

90. Since all of the metal carbonates indicated have the metal ion in the +2 oxidation state, we can illustrate the calculations for a general metal carbonate, MCO_3:

$$MCO_3(s) \rightleftarrows M^{2+}(aq) + CO_3^{2-}(aq) \qquad K_{sp} = [M^{2+}(aq)][CO_3^{2-}(aq)]$$

If we then let x represent the number of moles of MCO_3 that dissolve per liter, then $[M^{2+}(aq)] = x$ and $[CO_3^{2-}(aq)] = x$ also since the reaction is of 1:1 stoichiometry. Therefore,

$K_{sp} = [M^{2+}(aq)][CO_3^{2-}(aq)] = x^2$ for each salt. Solving for x gives the following results.

$$[BaCO_3] = x = 7.1 \times 10^{-5}\ M$$

$$[CdCO_3] = x = 2.3 \times 10^{-6}\ M$$

$$[CaCO_3] = x = 5.3 \times 10^{-5}\ M$$

$$[CoCO_3] = x = 3.9 \times 10^{-7}\ M$$

91. $Ca_3(PO_4)_2(s) \rightleftarrows 3Ca^{2+}(aq) + 2PO_4^{3-}(aq)$

let x represent the number of moles of $Ca_3(PO_4)_2$ that dissolve per liter; then

$[Ca^{2+}] = 3x$ and $[PO_4^{3-}] = 2x$

$K_{sp} = [Ca^{2+}]^3[PO_4^{3-}]^2 = 1.3 \times 10^{-32}$

$\qquad [3x]^3[2x]^2 = 1.3 \times 10^{-32}$

$\qquad 108x^5 = 1.3 \times 10^{-32}$

$\qquad x^5 = 1.20 \times 10^{-34}$

$\qquad x = 1.64 \times 10^{-7}\ M$

$\qquad [Ca^{2+}] = 3x = 3 \times 1.64 \times 10^{-7}\ M = 4.9 \times 10^{-7}\ M$

92.   Although a small solubility product generally implies a small solubility, comparisons of solubility based directly on K_{sp} values are only valid if the salts produce the same numbers of positive and negative ions per formula when they dissolve. For example, one can compare the solubilities of $AgCl(s)$ and $NiS(s)$ directly using K_{sp}, since each salt produces one positive and one negative ion per formula when dissolved. One could not directly compare $AgCl(s)$ with a salt such as $Ca_3(PO_4)_2$, however.

93.   A higher concentration means there are more molecules present, which results in a greater frequency of collision between molecules.

94.   At higher temperatures, the average kinetic energy of the reactant molecules is larger. At higher temperatures, the probability that a collision between molecules will be energetic enough for reaction to take place is larger. On a molecular basis, a higher temperature means a given molecule will be moving faster.

95.   When a liquid is confined in an otherwise empty closed container, the liquid begins to evaporate, producing molecules of vapor in the empty space of the container. As the amount of vapor increases, molecules in the vapor phase begin to condense and reenter the liquid state. Eventually the opposite processes of evaporation and condensation will

be going on at the same speed: beyond this point, for every molecule that leaves the liquid state and evaporates, there is a molecule of vapor which leaves the vapor state and condenses. We know the state of equilibrium has been reached when there is no further change in the pressure of the vapor.

96. a. $$K = \frac{[HBr]^2}{[H_2][Br_2]}$$

 b. $$K = \frac{[H_2S]^2}{[H_2]^2[S_2]}$$

 c. $$K = \frac{[HCN]^2}{[H_2][C_2N_2]}$$

97. a. $$K = \frac{[O_2]^3}{[O_3]^2}$$

 b. $$K = \frac{[CO_2][H_2O]^2}{[CH_4][O_2]^2}$$

 c. $$K = \frac{[C_2H_4Cl_2]}{[C_2H_4][Cl_2]}$$

98. $$K = \frac{[Br]^2}{[Br_2]} = \frac{(0.034 \; M)^2}{(0.97 \; M)} = 1.2 \times 10^{-3}$$

99. $$K = \frac{[PCl_3][Cl_2]}{[PCl_5]} = \frac{(0.325 \; M)(3.9 \times 10^{-3} \; M)}{(1.1 \times 10^{-2} \; M)} = 0.12$$

100. a. $$K = \frac{1}{[O_2]^3}$$

 b. $$K = \frac{1}{[NH_3][HCl]}$$

 c. $$K = \frac{1}{[O_2]}$$

101. a. $$K = \frac{1}{[O_2]^5}$$

 b. $$K = \frac{[H_2O]}{[CO_2]}$$

 c. $$K = [N_2O][H_2O]^2$$

102. An *exo*thermic reaction is one which liberates heat energy. Increasing the temperature (adding heat) for such a reaction is fighting against the reaction's own tendency to liberate heat. The net effect of raising the temperature will be a shift to the left to decrease the amount of

product. If it is desired to increase the amount of product in an exothermic reaction, heat must be *removed* from the system. Changing the temperature *does* change the numerical value of the equilibrium constant for a reaction.

103. $2NO(g) + O_2(g) \rightleftharpoons 2NO_2(g)$

a.   shifts to right

b.   shifts to right

c.   no effect (He is not involved in the reaction)

104.   The reaction is *exothermic* as written. An increase in temperature (addition of heat) will shift the reaction to the left (toward reactants).

105. $K = \dfrac{[CO_2][H_2]}{[CO][H_2O]} = \dfrac{(1.3\ M)(1.4\ M)}{(0.71\ M)(0.66\ M)} = 3.9$

106. $K = \dfrac{[NH_3]^2}{[N_2][H_2]^3}$

$1.3 \times 10^{-2} = \dfrac{[NH_3]^2}{(0.10\ M)(0.10\ M)^3}$

$[NH_3]^2 = 1.3 \times 10^{-2} \times (0.10) \times (0.10)^3 = 1.3 \times 10^{-6}$

$[NH_3] = 1.1 \times 10^{-3}\ M$

107. $K = \dfrac{[NO]^2[Cl_2]}{[NOCl]^2}$

$9.2 \times 10^{-6} = \dfrac{(1.5 \times 10^{-3})^2[Cl_2]}{(0.44\ M)^2}$

$[Cl_2] = \dfrac{(9.2 \times 10^{-6})(0.44)^2}{(1.5 \times 10^{-3})^2} = \dfrac{1.781 \times 10^{-6}}{2.25 \times 10^{-6}} = 0.79\ M$

108.   a. $Cu(OH)_2(s) \rightleftharpoons Cu^{2+}(aq) + 2OH^-(aq)$

$K_{sp} = [Cu^{2+}][OH^-]^2$

b. $Cr(OH)_3(s) \rightleftharpoons Cr^{3+}(aq) + 3OH^-(aq)$

$K_{sp} = [Cr^{3+}][OH^-]^3$

c. $Ba(OH)_2(s) \rightleftharpoons Ba^{2+}(aq) + 2OH^-(aq)$

$K_{sp} = [Ba^{2+}][OH^-]^2$

d. $Sn(OH)_2(s) \rightleftharpoons Sn^{2+}(aq) + 2OH^-(aq)$

$K_{sp} = [Sn^{2+}][OH^-]^2$

109.   Since the calculations for each of the silver halides would be similar, we can illustrate the calculations for a general silver halide, AgX:

$$AgX(s) \rightleftharpoons Ag^+(aq) + X^-(aq) \qquad\qquad K_{sp} = [Ag^+(aq)][X^-(aq)]$$

If we then let x represent the number of moles of AgX that dissolve per liter, then $[Ag^+(aq)] = x$ and $[X^-(aq)] = x$ also since the reaction is of 1:1 stoichiometry. Therefore,

$[Ag^+(aq)][X^-(aq)] = x^2 = K_{sp}$ for each salt.   Solving for x gives the following results.

$$[AgCl] = x = 1.3 \times 10^{-5}\ M$$

$$[AgBr] = x = 7.1 \times 10^{-7}\ M$$

$$[AgI] = x = 9.1 \times 10^{-9}\ M$$

110.   molar mass AgCl = 143.4 g

$$9.0 \times 10^{-4}\ g\ AgCl/L \times \frac{1\ mol\ AgCl}{143.4\ g\ AgCl} = 6.28 \times 10^{-6}\ mol\ AgCl/L$$

$$AgCl(s) \rightleftharpoons Ag^+(aq) + Cl^-(aq)$$

$$K_{sp} = [Ag^+][Cl^-] = (6.28 \times 10^{-6}\ M)(6.28 \times 10^{-6}\ M) = 3.9 \times 10^{-11}$$

111. $HgS(s) \rightleftharpoons Hg^{2+}(aq) + S^{2-}(aq)$

$$K_{sp} = [Hg^{2+}][S^{2-}] = 1.6 \times 10^{-54}$$

Let x represent the number of moles of HgS that dissolve per liter; then

$[Hg^{2+}] = x$ and $[S^{2-}] = x$

$$K_{sp} = [x][x] = x^2 = 1.6 \times 10^{-54}$$

$$x = 1.3 \times 10^{-27}\ M$$

molar mass HgS = 232.7 g

$$1.3 \times 10^{-27}\ M \times \frac{232.7\ g}{1\ mol} = 2.9 \times 10^{-25}\ g/L$$

112.   molar mass $Ni(OH)_2$ = 92.71 g

$$\frac{0.14\ g\ Ni(OH)_2}{1.00\ L} \times \frac{1\ mol\ Ni(OH)_2}{92.71\ g\ Ni(OH)_2} = 1.510 \times 10^{-3}\ M$$

$$Ni(OH)_2(s) \rightleftharpoons Ni^{2+}(aq) + 2OH^-(aq)$$

$$K_{sp} = [Ni^{2+}][OH^-]^2$$

If $1.510 \times 10^{-3}\ M$ of $Ni(OH)_2$ dissolves, then

$[Ni^{2+}] = 1.510 \times 10^{-3}$ *M* and

$[OH^-] = 2 \times (1.510 \times 10^{-3}$ *M*$) = 3.020 \times 10^{-3}$ *M*

$K_{sp} = (1.510 \times 10^{-3}$ *M*$)(3.020 \times 10^{-3}$ *M*$)^2 = 1.4 \times 10^{-8}$

Cumulative Review: Chapters 15 and 16

1.   Arrhenius defined acids and bases in terms of the ions that show acidic and basic properties in *aqueous solution*: an acid is a substance which produces H^+ ions in aqueous solution, and a base is a substance that produces OH^- ions in aqueous solution. This definition is too restrictive, since it only considers aqueous systems. For example, Arrhenius recognized HCl as an acid when it is dissolved in water, but what about gaseous hydrogen chloride? Or how about HCl dissolved in some other solvent? The Arrhenius theory also only allows for only one kind of base, the hydroxide ion.

   The Brönsted-Lowry model for acids and bases extends some of the concepts of the Arrhenius theory, and adapts them to more general situations, defining acids and bases in a more fundamental manner. In the Brönsted-Lowry model, an acid still represents a source of H^+ ions (specifically, a Brönsted-Lowry acid is a proton donor), but there is no restriction as to the solvent being only water. So in the Brönsted-Lowry model, if HCl transfers H^+ to another species, then HCl is an acid regardless of any other consideration. Where the Brönsted-Lowry theory really extends our idea of acid-base chemistry is in defining what represents a base: a Brönsted-Lowry base is any species that accepts a proton from an acid. According to the Brönsted-Lowry theory, the hydroxide ion in aqueous solution would still be a base, because if an acid is added to a hydroxide ion solution, the hydroxide ions would accept protons from the acid

$$HCl + OH^- \rightarrow H_2O + Cl^-$$

   The Brönsted-Lowry theory allows for other bases, however, and does not require water to be the solvent. For example, ammonia and hydrogen chloride react with each other in the gas phase

$$HCl(g) + NH_3(g) \rightarrow NH_4^+Cl^-(s)$$

   While this gas phase reaction would be difficult to explain in the Arrhenius theory, in the Brönsted-Lowry model all that has happened is that a proton has been transferred from the acid (HCl) to the base (NH_3).

2.   A conjugate acid-base pair consists of two species related to each other by the donating or accepting of a single proton, H^+. An acid has one more H^+ than its conjugate base; a base has one less H^+ than its conjugate acid.

   Brönsted-Lowry acids:

$$HCl(aq) + H_2O(l) \rightarrow Cl^-(aq) + H_3O^+(aq)$$

$$H_2SO_4(aq) + H_2O(l) \rightarrow HSO_4^-(aq) + H_3O^+(aq)$$

$$H_3PO_4(aq) + H_2O(l) \rightleftarrows H_2PO_4^-(aq) + H_3O^+(aq)$$

$$NH_4^+(aq) + H_2O(l) \rightleftarrows NH_3(aq) + H_3O^+(aq)$$

Brönsted-Lowry bases:

$$NH_3(aq) + H_2O(l) \rightleftarrows NH_4^+(aq) + OH^-(aq)$$

$$HCO_3^-(aq) + H_2O(l) \rightleftarrows H_2CO_3(aq) + OH^-(aq)$$

$$NH_2^-(aq) + H_2O(l) \rightarrow NH_3(aq) + OH^-(aq)$$

$$H_2PO_4^-(aq) + H_2O(l) \rightleftarrows H_3PO_4(aq) + OH^-(aq)$$

3.   When we say that acetic acid is a weak acid, we can take either of two points of view. Usually we say that acetic acid is a weak acid because it doesn't ionize very much when dissolved in water: we say that not very many acetic acid molecules dissociate. However, we can describe this situation from another point of view. We could say that the reason acetic acid doesn't dissociate much when we dissolve it is water is because the acetate ion (the conjugate base of acetic acid) is extremely effective at holding on to protons, and specifically is better at holding on to protons than water is in attracting them. So, acetic acid doesn't dissociate much because the acetate ion won't let the proton go!

$$HC_2H_3O_2 + H_2O \rightleftarrows C_2H_3O_2^- + H_3O^+$$

Now what would happen if we had a source of free acetate ions (for example, sodium acetate) and placed them into water? Since acetate ion is better at attracting protons than is water, the acetate ions would pull protons out of water molecules, leaving hydroxide ions. That is,

$$C_2H_3O_2^- + H_2O \rightarrow HC_2H_3O_2 + OH^-$$

Since an increase in hydroxide ion concentration would take place in the solution, the solution would be basic. Although acetic acid is a weak acid, the acetate ion is a base in aqueous solution.

4.   The strength of an acid is a direct result of the position of the acid's ionization equilibrium. We call acids whose ionization equilibrium positions lie far to the right strong acids, and we call those acids whose equilibrium positions lie only slightly to the right weak acids. For example, HCl, HNO_3, and $HClO_4$ are all strong acids, which means that they are completely ionized in aqueous solution (the position of equilibrium is very far to the right):

$$HCl(aq) + H_2O(l) \rightarrow Cl^-(aq) + H_3O^+(aq)$$

$$HNO_3(aq) + H_2O(l) \rightarrow NO_3^-(aq) + H_3O^+(aq)$$

$$HClO_4(aq) + H_2O(l) \rightarrow ClO_4^-(aq) + H_3O^+(aq)$$

Since these are very strong acids, we know that their anions (Cl^-, NO_3^-, ClO_4^-) must be very weak bases, and that solutions of the sodium salts of these anions would *not* be appreciably basic. Since these acids have a strong tendency to lose protons, there is very little tendency for the anions (bases) to gain protons.

5. When we say that water is an amphoteric substance, we are just recognizing that water will behave as a Brönsted-Lowry base if a strong acid is added to it, but will behave as a Brönsted-Lowry acid if a strong base is added to it. For example, water behaves as a base when HCl is dissolved in it

$$HCl + H_2O \rightarrow Cl^- + H_3O^+$$

However, water would behave as an acid if the strong base $NaNH_2$ were added to it

$$NH_2^- + H_2O \rightarrow NH_3 + OH^-$$

We can also demonstrate the amphoterism of water by the fact that water undergoes autoionization, in which some water molecules behave as an acid and some behave as a base

$$H_2O + H_2O \rightleftharpoons H_3O^+ + OH^-$$

Because this reaction is so important to our understanding the relative acidity and basicity of aqueous solution, the equilibrium constant for the autoionization of water is given a special symbol, K_w

$$K_w = [H_3O^+][OH^-]$$

This equilibrium constant has the value 1.0×10^{-14} at 25°C. Because of the fact that hydronium ions and hydroxide ions are produced in equal numbers when water molecules undergo autoionization, and with the value for the equilibrium constant given, we know that in pure water

$$[H_3O^+] = [OH^-] = 1.0 \times 10^{-7} \ M$$

If a solution has a higher concentration of H_3O^+ ion than OH^- ion, we say the solution is acidic. If a solution has a lower concentration of H_3O^+ ion than OH^- ion we say the solution is basic.

6. The pH of a solution is defined as the negative of the base 10 logarithm of the hydrogen ion concentration in the solution; that is

$$pH = -\log_{10}[H^+]$$

for a solution. Since in pure water, the amount of $H^+(aq)$ ion present is equal to the amount of $OH^-(aq)$ ion, we say that pure water is *neutral*. Since $[H^+] = 1.0 \times 10^{-7} \ M$ in pure water, this means that the pH of pure water is $-\log[1.0 \times 10^{-7} \ M] = 7.00$. Solutions in which the hydrogen ion concentration is greater than $1.0 \times 10^{-7} \ M$ (pH < 7.00) are *acidic*; solutions in which the hydrogen ion concentration is less than $1.0 \times 10^{-7} \ M$ (pH > 7.00) are *basic*. Since the pH scale is logarithmic, when the pH changes by one unit, this corresponds to a change in the hydrogen ion concentration by a factor of *ten*.

In some instances, it may be more convenient to speak directly about the hydroxide ion concentration present in a solution, and so an analogous logarithmic expression is defined for the hydroxide ion concentration:

$$pOH = -\log_{10}[OH^-]$$

The concentrations of hydrogen ion and hydroxide ion in water (and in aqueous solutions) are *not* independent of one another, but rather are related by the dissociation equilibrium constant for water,

$$K_w = [H^+][OH^-] = 1.0 \times 10^{-14} \text{ at } 25°C.$$

From this constant it is obvious that pH + pOH = 14.00 for water (or an aqueous solution) at 25°C.

7.   A buffered solution is one that resists a change in its pH even when a strong acid or base is added to it. Buffered solutions consist of approximately equal amounts of two components: a weak acid (or base) and its conjugate base (or acid). The weak acid component of the buffered solution is capable of reacting with added strong base. The conjugate base component of the buffered solution is able to react with added strong acid. By reacting with (and effectively neutralizing) the added strong acid or strong base, the buffer is able to maintain its pH at a relatively constant level. Consider the following three buffered solutions:

$0.10 \text{ M } HC_2H_3O_2/0.10 \text{ M } NaC_2H_3O_2$

$0.50 \text{ M } HF/0.50 \text{ M } KF$

$0.25 \text{ M } NH_4Cl/0.25 \text{ M } NH_3$

The *acidic* component of each of these buffered solutions can neutralize added OH^- ion as shown below:

$$HC_2H_3O_2 + OH^- \rightarrow C_2H_3O_2^- + H_2O$$
$$HF + OH^- \rightarrow F^- + H_2O$$
$$NH_4^+ + OH^- \rightarrow NH_3 + H_2O$$

Notice that in each case, the added hydroxide ion has been neutralized and converted to a water molecule. The *basic* component of the buffered solutions can neutralize added H^+ ion as shown below:

$$C_2H_3O_2^- + H^+ \rightarrow HC_2H_3O_2$$
$$F^- + H^+ \rightarrow HF$$
$$NH_3 + H^+ \rightarrow NH_4^+$$

Notice that in each case the added hydrogen ion is converted to some other species.

Buffered solutions are crucial to the reactions in biological systems because many of these reactions are extremely pH dependent: a change in pH of only one or two units can make some reactions impossible or extremely slow. Many biological molecule have 3-dimensional structures which are extremely dependent on the pH of their surroundings. For example, protein molecules can lose part of their necessary structure and shape if the pH of their environment changes (if a protein's structure is changed it may not work correctly). For example, if a small amount of vinegar is added to whole milk, the milk instantly curdles: the solid which forms is the protein portion of the milk, which becomes less soluble at lower pH values.

8.   Chemists envision that a reaction can only take place between molecules if the molecules physically *collide* with each other. Furthermore, when molecules collide, the molecules must collide with enough force for the reaction to be successful (there must be enough energy to break bonds in the reactants), and the colliding molecules must be positioned with the correct relative orientation for the products (or intermediates) to form. Reactions tend to be faster if higher concentrations are used for the reaction, because, if there are more molecules present per unit volume there will be more collisions between molecules in a given time period. Reactions are faster at higher temperatures because at higher temperatures the reactant molecules have a higher average kinetic energy, and the number of molecules that will collide with sufficient force to break bonds increases.

9.   A graph illustrating the activation energy barrier for a reaction is given as Figure 16.4 in the text. The activation energy for a reaction represents the minimum energy the reactant molecules must possess for a reaction to occur when the molecules collide. Although an increase in temperature does not change the activation energy for a reaction itself, at higher temperatures, the reactant molecules have a higher average kinetic energy, and a larger fraction of reaction molecules will possess enough energy for a collision to be effective: you will remember that in the kinetic-molecular theory, temperature was a direct measure of average kinetic energy. A catalyst speeds up a reaction by providing an alternate mechanism or pathway by which the reaction can occur, with such a mechanism or pathway having a lower activation energy than the original pathway.

10.   Chemists define equilibrium as the exact balancing of two exactly opposing processes. When a chemical reaction is begun by combining pure reactants, the only process possible initially is

reactants → products

However, for many reactions, as the concentration of product molecules increases, it becomes more and more likely that product molecules will collide and react with each other

products → reactants

giving back molecules of the original reactants. At some point in the process the rates of the forward and reverse reactions become equal, and the system attains chemical equilibrium. To an outside observer, the system appears to have stopped reacting. On a microscopic basis, though, both the forward and reverse processes are still going on: every time additional molecules of the product form, however, somewhere else in the system molecules of product react to give back molecules of reactant.

Once the point is reached that product molecules are reacting at the same speed at which they are forming, there is no further net change in concentration. A graph showing how the rates of the forward and reverse reactions change with time is given in the text as Figure 16.8. At the start of the reaction, the rate of the forward reaction is at its maximum, while the rate of the reverse reaction is zero. As the reaction proceeds, the rate of the forward reaction gradually decreases as the concentration of reactants decreases, whereas the rate of the reverse reaction increases as the concentration of products increases. Once the two rates have become equal, the reaction has reached a state of equilibrium.

11.   The expression for the equilibrium constant for a reaction has as its numerator the concentrations of the products (raised to the powers of their stoichiometric coefficients in the balanced chemical equation for the reaction), and as its denominator the concentrations of the reactants (also raised to the powers of their stoichiometric coefficients). In general terms, for a reaction

$$aA + bB = cC + dD$$

the equilibrium constant expression has the form

$$K = \frac{[C]^c[D]^d}{[A]^a[B]^b}$$

in which square brackets [] indicate molar concentration. For example, here are three simple reactions and the expression for their equilibrium constants:

$N_2(g) + O_2(g) \rightleftharpoons 2NO(g)$ $K = [NO]^2/[N_2][O_2]$

$2SO_2(g) + O_2(g) \rightleftharpoons 2SO_3(g)$ $K = [SO_3]^2/[SO_2]^2[O_2]$

$N_2(g) + 3H_2(g) \rightleftharpoons 2NH_3(g)$ $K = [NH_3]^2/[N_2][H_2]^3$

12.   The equilibrium constant for a reaction is a *ratio* of the concentration of products present at the point of equilibrium to the concentration of reactants still present. A *ratio* means that we have one number divided by another number (for example, the density of a substance is the ratio of a substance's mass to its volume). Since the equilibrium constant is a ratio, there are an infinite number of sets of data which can give the same ratio: for example, the ratios 8/4, 6/3, 100/50 all have the same value, 2. The actual concentrations of products and reactants will differ from one experiment to another involving a particular chemical

reaction, but the ratio of the amount of product to reactant at equilibrium should be the same for each experiment.

Consider this simple example: suppose we have a reaction for which $K = 4$, and we begin this reaction with 100 reactant molecules. At the point of equilibrium, there should be 80 molecules of product and 20 molecules of reactant remaining (80/20 = 4). Suppose we perform another experiment involving the same reaction, only this time we begin the experiment with 500 molecules of reactant. This time, at the point of equilibrium, there will be 400 molecules of product present and 100 molecules of reactant remaining (400/100 = 4). Since we began the two experiments with different numbers of of reactant molecules, it's not troubling that there are different absolute numbers of product and reactant molecules present at equilibrium: however, the ratio, K, is the same for both experiments. We say that these two experiments represent two different positions of equilibrium: an equilibrium position corresponds to a particular set of experimental equilibrium concentrations which fulfill the value of the equilibrium constant. Any experiment that is performed with a different amount of starting material will come to its own unique equilibrium position, but the equilibrium constant ratio, K, will be the same for a given reaction regardless of the starting amounts taken.

13. In a homogeneous equilibrium, all the reactants and products are in the same phase and have the same physical state (solid, liquid, or gas). For a heterogeneous equilibrium, however, one or more of the reactant or products exists in a phase or physical state different from the other substances. When we have a heterogeneous equilibrium, the concentrations of solids and pure liquids are left out of the expression for the equilibrium constant for the reaction: the concentration of a solid or pure liquid is constant.

$C(s) + O_2(g) \rightleftarrows CO_2(g)$ heterogeneous (solid, gases)

$$K = [CO_2]/[O_2]$$

$2CO(g) + O_2(g) \rightleftarrows 2CO_2(g)$ homogeneous (all gases)

$$K = [CO_2]^2/[CO]^2[O_2]$$

14. Your paraphrase of Le Châtelier's principle should go something like this: "when you make any change to a system in equilibrium, this throws the system temporarily out of equilibrium, and the system responds by reacting in whichever direction will be able to reach a new position of equilibrium". There are various changes that can be made to a system in equilibrium. Here are examples of some of them.

a. the concentration of one of the reactants is increased.

Consider the reaction: $2SO_2(g) + O_2(g) \rightleftarrows 2SO_3(g)$

Suppose the reactants have already reacted and a position of equilibrium has been reached which fulfills the value of K for the reaction. At this point there will be present particular amounts of each reactant and of the product. Suppose then 1 additional mole of O_2 is added to the system from outside. At the instant the additional O_2 is added, the system will not be in equilibrium: there will be too much O_2 present in the system to be compatible with the amounts of SO_2 and SO_3 present. The system will respond by reacting to get rid of some of the excess O_2 until the value of the ratio K is again fulfilled. If the system reacts to get rid of the excess of O_2, additional product SO_3 will form. The net result is more SO_3 produced than if the the change had not been made.

b.   the concentration of one of the products is decreased by selectively removing it from the system

Consider the reaction: $CH_3COOH + CH_3OH \rightleftarrows H_2O + CH_3COOCH_3$

This reaction is typical of many reactions involving organic chemical substances, in which two organic molecules react to form a larger molecule, with a molecule of water split out during the combination. This type of reaction on its own tends to come to equilibrium with only part of the starting materials being converted to the desired organic product (which effectively would leave the experimenter with a mixture of materials). A technique which is used by organic chemists to increase the effective yield of the desired organic product is to *separate* the two products (if the products are separated, they cannot react to give back the reactants). One method used is to add a drying agent to the mixture: such a drying agent chemically or physically absorbs the water from the system, removing it from the equilibrium. If the water is removed, the reverse reaction cannot take place, and the reaction proceeds to a greater extent in the forward direction than if the drying agent had not been added. In other situations, an experimenter may separate the products of the reaction by distillation (if the boiling points make this possible): again, if the products have been separated, then the reverse reaction will not be possible, and the forward reaction will occur to a greater extent.

c.   the reaction system is compressed to a smaller volume

Consider the example: $3H_2(g) + N_2(g) \rightleftarrows 2NH_3(g)$

For equilibria involving gases, when the volume of the reaction system is compressed suddenly, the pressure in the system increases. However, if the reacting system can relieve some of this increased pressure by reacting, it will do so. This will happen by the reaction occurring in whichever direction will give the smaller number of moles of gas (if the number of moles of gas is decreased in a particular volume, the pressure will decrease).
        For the reaction above, there are two moles of the gas on the right side of the equation, but there is a total of four moles on the left side. If this system at equilibrium were to be

suddenly compressed to a smaller volume, the reaction would proceed further to the right (in favor of more ammonia being produced).

d.   the temperature is increased for an endothermic reaction

Consider the reaction: $2NaHCO_3$ + heat $\rightleftharpoons$ Na_2CO_3 + H_2O + CO_2

Although a change in temperature actually does change the *value* of the equilibrium constant, we can simplify reactions involving temperature changes by treating heat energy as if it were a chemical substance: for this endothermic reaction, heat is one of the reactants. As we saw in the example in part (a) of this question, increasing the concentration of one of the reactants for a system at equilibrium causes the reaction to proceed further to the right, forming additional product. Similarly for the endothermic reaction given above, increasing the temperature causes the reaction to proceed further in the direction of products than if no change had been made. It is as if there were too much "heat" to be compatible with the amount of substances present. The substances react to get rid of some of the energy.

e.   the temperature is decreased for an exothermic process.

Consider the reaction: PCl_3 + Cl_2 $\rightleftharpoons$ PCl_5 + heat

As discussed in part (d) above, although changing the temperature at which a reaction is performed does change the numerical value of K, we can simplify our discussion of this reaction by treating heat energy as if it were a chemical substance. Heat is a product of this reaction. If we are going to lower the temperature of this reaction system, the only way to accomplish this is to remove energy from the system. Lowering the temperature of the system is really working with this system in its attempt to release heat energy. So lowering the temperature should favor the production of more product than if no change were made.

15.   When a slightly soluble salt is placed in water, ions begin to leave the crystals of salt and to enter the solvent to form a solution. As the concentration of ions in solution increases, eventually ions from the solution are attracted to and rejoin the crystals of undissolved salt. Eventually things get to the point that every time ions leave the crystals to enter the solution in one place in the system, somewhere else ions are leaving the solution to rejoin the solid. At the point where dissolving and "undissolving" are going on at the same rate, we arrive at a state of dynamic equilibrium. We write the equilibrium constant (the solubility product), K_{sp}, for the dissolving of a slightly soluble salt in the usual manner: since the concentration of the solid material is constant, we do not include it in the expression for K_{sp}:

$$AgCl(s) \rightleftarrows Ag^+(aq) + Cl^-(aq) \qquad K_{sp} = [Ag^+][Cl^-]$$

$$PbCl_2(s) \rightleftarrows Pb^{2+}(aq) + 2Cl^-(aq) \qquad K_{sp} = [Pb^{2+}][Cl^-]^2$$

$$BaSO_4(s) \rightleftarrows Ba^{2+}(aq) + SO_4^{2-}(aq) \qquad K_{sp} = [Ba^{2+}][SO_4^{2-}]$$

If the solubility product constant for a slightly soluble salt is known, the solubility of the salt in mol/L or g/L can be easily calculated. For example, for $BaSO_4$, $K_{sp} = 1.5 \times 10^{-9}$ at 25°C. Suppose x moles of $BaSO_4$ dissolve per liter; since the stoichiometric coefficients for the dissolving of $BaSO_4$ are all the same, this means that x moles of $Ba^{2+}(aq)$ and x moles of $SO_4^{2-}(aq)$ will be produced per liter when $BaSO_4$ dissolves.

$$K_{sp} = [Ba^{2+}][SO_4^{2-}] = [x][x] = 1.5 \times 10^{-9}$$

$$x^2 = 1.5 \times 10^{-9} \quad \text{and therefore } x = 3.9 \times 10^{-5} \ M$$

So the molar solubility of $BaSO_4$ is $3.9 \times 10^{-5} \ M$; this could be converted to the number of grams of $BaSO_4$ that dissolve per liter using the molar mass of $BaSO_4$ (233.4 g):

$$(3.9 \times 10^{-5} \ mol/L)(233.4 \ g/mol) = 9.10 \times 10^{-3} \ g/L$$

16. a. HSO_3^- f. HNO_3

   b. H_2SO_3 g. H_2SO_4

   c. HF h. HS^-

   d. CH_3COOH i. H_2S

   e. H_3O^+

17. a. $C_2H_3O_2^-$ f. SO_4^{2-}

   b. HS^- g NH_2^-

   c. S^{2-} h. HSO_4^-

   d. CO_3^{2-} i. $H_2PO_4^-$

   e. HCO_3^-

18. Bases (from Question 16)

$$SO_3^{2-} + H_2O \rightleftarrows HSO_3^- + OH^-$$

$$F^- + H_2O \rightleftarrows HF + OH^-$$

$$CH_3COO^- + H_2O \rightleftarrows CH_3COOH + OH^-$$

$H_2O + H_2O \rightleftarrows H_3O^+ + OH^-$

$NO_3^- + H_2O \rightarrow$ (no reaction)

$S^{2-} + H_2O \rightleftarrows HS^- + OH^-$

$HS^- + H_2O \rightleftarrows H_2S + OH^-$

Note: HSO_4^- and HSO_3^- are stronger acids than water and do not behave as bases in water

Acids (from Question 17)

$HC_2H_3O_2 + H_2O \rightleftarrows C_2H_3O_2^- + H_3O^+$

$H_2S + H_2O \rightleftarrows HS^- + H_3O^+$

$HS^- + H_2O \rightleftarrows S^{2-} + H_3O^+$

$H_2CO_3 + H_2O \rightleftarrows HCO_3^- + H_3O^+$

$HSO_4^- + H_2O \rightleftarrows SO_4^{2-} + H_3O^+$

$H_2SO_4 + H_2O \rightarrow HSO_4^- + H_3O^+$

$H_3PO_4 + H_2O \rightarrow H_2PO_4^- + H_3O^+$

Note: HCO_3^- and NH_3 are stronger bases than water, and do not behave as acids in water; see also above.

19.   a. $[H^+] = 4.01 \times 10^{-3}$ *M*

pH $= -\log[4.01 \times 10^{-3}] = 2.397$

b. $[OH^-] = 7.41 \times 10^{-8}$ *M*

pOH $= -\log[7.41 \times 10^{-8}] = 7.130$

c. $[H^+] = 9.61 \times 10^{-6}$ *M*

pH $= -\log[9.61 \times 10^{-6}] = 5.017$

pOH $= 14 - 5.017 = 8.98$

d. $[OH^-] = 6.62 \times 10^{-3}$ *M*

pOH $= -\log[6.62 \times 10^{-3}] = 2.179$

pH $= 14 - 2.179 = 11.82$

e.   pH = 6.325

pOH = 14 - 6.325 = 7.68

$[OH^-]$ = {inv}{log}(-7.675) = 2.1×10^{-8}

f.   pH = 9.413

$[H^+]$ = {inv}{log}(-9.413) = 3.86×10^{-10} *M*

20.   a. HNO_3 is a strong acid, so

$[H^+]$ = 0.00141 *M*

pH = -log(0.00141) = 2.851

pOH = 14 - 2.851 = 11.15

b.   NaOH is a strong base, so

$[OH^-]$ = 2.13×10^{-3} *M*

pOH = -log(2.13×10^{-3}) = 2.672

pH = 14 - 2.672 = 11.33

c.   HCl is a strong acid, so

$[H^+]$ = 0.00515 *M*

pH = -log(0.00515) = 2.288

pOH = 14 - 2.288 = 11.71

d. $Ca(OH)_2$ is a strong, but not very soluble base. Each formula unit of $Ca(OH)_2$ produces two formula units of OH^- ion.

$[OH^-]$ = $2 \times 5.65 \times 10^{-5}$ *M* = 1.13×10^{-4} *M*

pOH = -log(1.13×10^{-4}) = 3.947

pH = 14 - 3.947 = 10.05

21.   a. $K = [HBr(g)]^2 / [H_2(g)][Br_2(g)]$

b. $K = [NO_2(g)]^2 / [NO(g)]^2[O_2(g)]$

c. $K = [N_2(g)][H_2O(g)]^2 / [O_2(g)]$

d. $K = [SO_2(g)][Cl_2(g)] / [SO_2Cl_2(g)]$

e. $K = [CO_2(g)][NO(g)] / [CO(g)][NO_2(g)]$

22. $2SO_2(g) + O_2(g) \rightleftharpoons 2SO_3(g)$

$$K = \frac{[SO_3]^2}{[SO_2]^2[O_2]} = \frac{[0.42]^2}{[1.4 \times 10^{-3}]^2[4.5 \times 10^{-4}]} = 2.0 \times 10^8$$

23. a. $K_{sp} = [Fe^{3+}][OH^-]^3$ e. $K_{sp} = [Cd^{2+}][OH^-]^2$

     b. $K_{sp} = [Hg^{2+}][Cl^-]^2$ f. $K_{sp} = [Zn^{2+}][S^{2-}]$

     c. $K_{sp} = [La^{3+}][F^-]^3$ g. $K_{sp} = [Cr^{3+}][OH^-]^3$

     d. $K_{sp} = [Ba^{2+}]^3[PO_4^{3-}]^2$ h. $K_{sp} = [Co^{2+}][OH^-]^2$

Chapter 17   Oxidation-Reduction Reactions/Electrochemistry

1.   Oxidation can be defined as the loss of electrons by an atom, molecule, or ion. Oxidation may also be defined as an increase in oxidation state for an element, but since elements can only increase their oxidation states by losing electrons, the two definitions are equivalent. The following equation shows the oxidation of copper metal to copper(II) ion

$$Cu(s) \rightarrow Cu^{2+}(aq) + 2e^-$$

2.   Reduction can be defined as the gaining of electrons by an atom, molecule, or ion. Reduction may also be defined as a decrease in oxidation state for an element, but naturally such a decrease takes place by the gaining of electrons (so the two definitions are equivalent).

   $S + 2e^- \rightarrow S$ is an example of a reduction process.

   $Na \rightarrow Na^+ + e^-$ is an example of an oxidation process.

3.   Each of these reactions involves a *metallic* element in the form of the *free* element on the left side of the equation; on the other side of the equation, the metallic element is *combined* in an ionic compound. If a metallic element goes from the free metal to the ionic form, the metal is oxidized (loses electrons).

   a.   iron is oxidized, oxygen is reduced

   b.   zinc is oxidized, silver ion is reduced

   c.   potassium is oxidized, chlorine is reduced

   d.   calcium is oxidized, oxygen is reduced

4.   Each of these reactions involves a *metallic* element in the form of the *free* element on one side of the equation; on the other side of the equation, the metallic element is *combined* in an ionic compound. If a metallic element goes from the free metal to the ionic form, the metal is oxidized (loses electrons).

   a.   sodium is oxidized, nitrogen is reduced

   b.   magnesium is oxidized, chlorine is reduced

   c.   aluminum is oxidized, bromine is reduced

   d.   iron is oxidized, oxygen is reduced

5.   Each of these reactions involves a *metallic* element in the form of the *free* element on one side of the equation; on the other side of the equation, the metallic element is *combined* in an ionic compound. If a metallic element goes from the free metal to the ionic form, the metal is oxidized (loses electrons).

a.   copper is oxidized, chlorine is reduced

b.   nickel is oxidized, oxygen is reduced

c.   mercury is oxidized, sulfur is reduced

d.   potassium is oxidized, iodine is reduced

6.   Most of these reactions involve a *metallic* element in the form of the *free* element on one side of the equation; on the other side of the equation, the metallic element is *combined* in an ionic compound. If a metallic element goes from the free metal to the ionic form, the metal is oxidized (loses electrons).

a.   magnesium is oxidized, bromine is reduced

b.   sodium is oxidized, sulfur is reduced

c.   bromide ion is oxidized, chlorine is reduced

d.   potassium is oxidized, nitrogen is reduced

7.   The assignment of oxidation states is a bookkeeping method by which *charges* are assigned to the various atoms in a compound: this method allows us to keep track of electrons transferred between species in oxidation-reduction reactions.

8.   The oxidation state of a *pure element* is *zero*, regardless of whether the element occurs naturally as single atoms or as a molecule.

9.   For the very electronegative elements (such as oxygen), we assign each of these elements an oxidation state equal to its charge when the element forms an anion. Since oxygen forms O^{2-} ions, we assign oxygen an oxidation state of -2 even in compounds where no ions exist. The most common situation in which oxygen is *not* assigned the -2 oxidation state occurs with the *peroxide* ion, O_2^{2-}, in which each oxygen atom is in the -1 oxidation state.

10. Fluorine is always assigned a negative oxidation state (-1) because all other elements are less electronegative than fluorine. The other halogens are *usually* assigned an oxidation state of -1 in compounds. In interhalogen compounds such as ClF, fluorine is assigned oxidation state -1 (F is more electronegative than Cl), which means that chlorine must be assigned a $+1$ oxidation state in this instance.

11. Oxidation states represent a bookkeeping method to assign electrons in a molecule or ion. Since a neutral molecule has an overall charge of zero, the sum of the oxidation states in a neutral molecule must be zero. For example, water (H_2O) is a neutral molecule with zero overall charge. Each hydrogen in water has an oxidation state of $+1$, whereas oxygen has an oxidation state of -2: $2(+1) + (-2) = 0$

12. Oxidation states represent a bookkeeping method to assign electrons in a molecule or ion. Since an ion has a net charge, the sum of the oxidation

states of the atoms in the ion must equal the charge on the ion. For example, the hydroxide ion (OH^-) has an overall charge of -1 because hydrogen has an oxidation state of $+1$, whereas oxygen has an oxidation state of -2 in the hydroxide ion: $(-2) + (+1) = -1$

13.   The rules for assigning oxidation states are given in Section 17.2 of the text. The rule which applies for each element in the following answers is given in parentheses after the element and its oxidation state.

  a.   F, -1 (Rule 5); N, $+3$ (Rule 6)

  b.   O, -2 (Rule 3); N, $+4$ (Rule 6)

  c.   H, $+1$ (Rule 4); O, -2 (Rule 3); Cl, $+1$ (Rule 6)

  d.   S, 0 (Rule 1)

14.   The rules for assigning oxidation states are given in Section 17.2 of the text. The rule which applies for each element in the following answers is given in parentheses after the element and its oxidation state.

  a.   N, $+3$ (Rule 6); Cl, -1 (Rule 5)

  b.   S, $+6$ (Rule 6); F, -1 (Rule 5)

  c.   P, $+5$ (Rule 6); Cl, -1 (Rule 5)

  d.   Si, -4 (Rule 6); H, $+1$ (Rule 4)

15.   The rules for assigning oxidation states are given in Section 17.2 of the text. The rule which applies for each element in the following answers is given in parentheses after the element and its oxidation state.

  a.   O 0 (Rule 1)

  b.   O 0 (Rule 1)

  c.   Fe $+3$ (Rule 2); Cl -1 (Rule 2)

  d.   Fe $+2$ (Rule 2); Cl -1 (Rule 2)

16.   The rules for assigning oxidation states are given in Section 17.2 of the text. The rule which applies for each element in the following answers is given in parentheses after the element and its oxidation state.

  a.   H, $+1$ (Rule 4); Br, -1 (Rule 6 or Rule 5)

  b.   H, $+1$ (Rule 4); O, -2 (Rule 3); Br, $+1$ (Rule 6)

  c.   Br, 0 (Rule 1)

  d.   H, $+1$ (Rule 4); O, -2 (Rule 3); Br, $+7$ (Rule 6)

17.   The rules for assigning oxidation states are given in Section 17.2 of the text. The rule which applies for each element in the following answers is given in parentheses after the element and its oxidation state.

   a.   Na, +1 (Rule 2); P, +5 (Rule 6); O, -2 (Rule 3)

   b.   Na, +1 (Rule 2); H, +1 (Rule 4); P, +5 (Rule 6); O, -2 (Rule 3)

   c.   Na, +1 (Rule 2); H, +1 (Rule 4); P, +5 (Rule 6); O, -2 (Rule 3)

   d.   Na, +1 (Rule 2); P, -3 (Rule 6 or Rule 2)

18.   The rules for assigning oxidation states are given in Section 17.2 of the text. The rule which applies for each element in the following answers is given in parentheses after the element and its oxidation state.

   a.   H, +1 (Rule 4); O, -2 (Rule 3); N, +5 (Rule 6)

   b.   H, +1 (Rule 4); O, -2 (Rule 3); P, +5 (Rule 7)

   c.   H, +1 (Rule 4); O, -2 (Rule 3); S, +6 (Rule 7)

   d.   O, -1 (Rule 3)

19.   The rules for assigning oxidation states are given in Section 17.2 of the text. The rule which applies for each element in the following answers is given in parentheses after the element and its oxidation state.

   a.   Na, +1 (Rule 2); O, -2 (Rule 3); Cr, +6 (Rule 6)

   b.   Na, +1 (Rule 2); O, -2 (Rule 3); Cr, +6 (Rule 6)

   c.   Cl, -1 (Rule 2); Cr, +3 (Rule 6)

   d.   O, -2 (Rule 3); Cr, +3 (Rule 6)

20.   The rules for assigning oxidation states are given in Section 17.2 of the text. The rule which applies for each element in the following answers is given in parentheses after the element and its oxidation state.

   a.   Cu, +2 (Rules 2,6); Cl, -1 (Rules 2,5)

   b.   Cr, +3 (Rules 2,6); Cl, -1 (Rules 2,5)

   c.   H, +1 (Rule 4); O, -2 (Rule 3); Cr, +6 (Rule 7)

   d.   Cr, +3 (Rule 2,6); O, -2 (Rules 2,3)

21.   The rules for assigning oxidation states are given in Section 17.2 of the text. The rule which applies for each element in the following answers is given in parentheses after the element and its oxidation state.

a.   S +6 (Rule 7); O −2 (Rule 3)

b.   C +4 (Rule 7); O −2 (Rule 3)

c.   S +4 (Rule 7); O −2 (Rule 3)

d.   H +1 (Rule 4); C +4 (Rule 7); O −2 (Rule 3)

22.   The rules for assigning oxidation states are given in Section 17.2 of the text. The rule which applies for each element in the following answers is given in parentheses after the element and its oxidation state.

a.   H, +1 (Rule 4); C, −4 (Rule 6)

b.   Na, +1 (Rule 2); O, −2 (Rule 3); C, +4 (Rule 6)

c.   K, +1 (Rule 2); H, +1 (Rule 4); O, −2 (Rule 3); C, +4 (Rule 6)

d.   O, −2 (Rule 3); C, +2 (Rule 6)

23.   Consider the following simple oxidation reaction

$Na \rightarrow Na^+ + e^-$

Clearly the sodium atom on the left side of the equation is losing an electron in forming the sodium ion on the right side of the equation. The sodium atom on the left side of the equation is in the *zero* oxidation state because it represents a pure element. The sodium ion on the right side of the equation is in the +1 oxidation state (the same as the charge on the simple ion). Thus, by losing one electron, sodium has increased in oxidation state by one unit.

24.   Electrons are negative; when an atom gains electrons, it gains one negative charge for each electron gained. For example, in the reduction reaction $Cl + e^- \rightarrow Cl^-$, the oxidation state of chlorine decreases from 0 to −1 as the electron is gained.

25.   An oxidizing *agent* is a molecule, atom, or ion which *causes* the oxidation of some other species, while itself being reduced. A reducing *agent* is a molecule, atom, or ion which *causes* the reduction of some other species, while itself being oxidized.

26.   An oxidizing agent *causes* another species to be oxidized (to lose electrons). In order to make another species lose electrons, the oxidizing agent must be capable of gaining the electrons; an oxidizing agent is itself reduced. On the contrary, a reducing agent is itself oxidized.

27.   Oxidizing agents gain the electrons they cause some other species to lose. Reducing agents donate the electrons needed for the reduction of some other species.

28. An oxidizing agent oxidizes another species by gaining the electrons lost by the other species; therefore, an oxidizing agent itself decreases in oxidation state. A reducing agent increases its oxidation state when acting on another atom or molecule.

29. a. $2NO(g) + O_2(g) \rightarrow 2NO_2(g)$

N +2   O 0   N +4

O -2   O -2

nitrogen is oxidized; oxygen is reduced

b. $CH_4(g) + 2O_2(g) \rightarrow CO_2(g) + 2H_2O(g)$

C -4   O 0   C +4   H +1

H +1   O -2   O -2

carbon is oxidized; oxygen is reduced

c. $2Al(s) + 3Cl_2(g) \rightarrow 2AlCl_3(s)$

Al 0   Cl 0   Al +3

                    Cl -1

aluminum is oxidized; chlorine is reduced

d. $12Li(s) + P_4(s) \rightarrow 4Li_3P(s)$

Li 0   P 0   Li +1

                   P -3

lithium is oxidized; phosphorus is reduced

30. a. $Zn(s) + 2HNO_3(g) \rightarrow Zn(NO_3)_2(aq) + H_2(g)$

Zn 0   H +1   Zn +2   H 0

          N +5   N +5

          O -2   O -2

zinc is oxidized; hydrogen is reduced

b. $H_2(g) + CuSO_4(aq) \rightarrow Cu(s) + H_2SO_4(aq)$

H 0   Cu +2   Cu 0   H +1

         S +6   S +6

         O -2   O -2

hydrogen is oxidized; copper is reduced

c. $N_2(g) + 3Br_2(l) \rightarrow 2NBr_3(g)$

N 0   Br 0   N −3

                Br +1

N is more electronegative than Br

nitrogen is reduced; bromine is oxidized

d. $2KBr(aq) + Cl_2(g) \rightarrow 2KCl(aq) + Br_2(l)$

K +1   Cl 0   K +1   Br 0

Br −1   Cl −1

bromine is oxidized; chlorine is reduced

31. a. $2Cu(s) + S(s) \rightarrow Cu_2S$

Cu 0   S 0   Cu +1

                S −2

copper is oxidized; sulfur is reduced

b. $2Cu_2O(s) + O_2(g) \rightarrow 4CuO(s)$

Cu +1   O 0   Cu +2

 O −2   O −2

copper is oxidized; oxygen (of O_2) is reduced

c. $4B(s) + 3O_2(g) \rightarrow 2B_2O_3(s)$

B 0   O 0   B +3

                O −2

boron is oxidized; oxygen is reduced

d. $6Na(s) + N_2(g) \rightarrow 2Na_3N(s)$

Na 0   N 0   Na +1

                N −3

sodium is oxidized; nitrogen is reduced

32. a. $Cu(s) + 2AgNO_3(aq) \rightarrow 2Ag(s) + Cu(NO_3)_2(aq)$

Cu 0   Ag +1   Ag 0   Cu +2

          N +5   N +5

          O −2   O −2

copper is oxidized; silver is reduced

b. $N_2(g) + 3F_2(g) \rightarrow 2NF_3(g)$

N 0   F 0   F -1

N +3

nitrogen is oxidized; fluorine is reduced

c. $2Fe_2O_3(s) + 3S(s) \rightarrow 4Fe(s) + 3SO_2$

Fe +3   S 0   Fe 0   S +4

O -2   O -2

sulfur is oxidized; iron is reduced

d. $2H_2O_2(l) \rightarrow 2H_2O(l) + O_2(g)$

H +1   H +1   O 0

O -1   O -2

oxygen is both oxidized and reduced

33.   Silver is reduced [+1 in $AgBr(s)$, 0 in $Ag(s)$]; bromine is oxidized [-1 in AgBr, 0 in $Br_2(g)$].

34.   Iron is reduced [+3 in $Fe_2O_3(s)$, 0 in $Fe(l)$]; carbon is oxidized [+2 in $CO(g)$, +4 in $CO_2(g)$]. $Fe_2O_3(s)$ is the oxidizing agent; $CO(g)$ is the reducing agent.

35.   Magnesium is oxidized [0 in $Mg(s)$, +2 in $Mg(OH)_2(s)$]; hydrogen is reduced [+1 in $H_2O(l)$, 0 in $H_2(g)$].

36.   Chlorine is reduced [0 in $Cl_2(g)$, -1 in $NaCl(s)$]; bromine is oxidized [-1 in $NaBr(aq)$, 0 in $Br_2(l)$]. $Cl_2(g)$ is the oxidizing agent; $NaBr(aq)$ is the reducing agent.

37.   Oxidation-reduction reactions must be balanced with respect to *mass* (the total number of each type of atom on each side of the balanced equation must be the same) and with respect to *charge* (whatever number of electrons is lost in the oxidation process must be gained in the reduction process, with no "extra" electrons).

38.   Oxidation-reduction reactions are often more complicated than "regular" reactions; frequently the coefficients necessary to balance the number of electrons transferred come out to be large numbers. We also have to make certain that we account for the electrons being transferred.

39.   When an overall equation is split into separate partial equations representing the oxidation and the reduction processes, these partial equations are called the *half-reactions* for the reaction.

40.   Under ordinary conditions it is impossible to have "free" electrons that are not part of some atom, ion, or molecule. For this reason, the total

number of electrons lost by the species being oxidized must equal the total number of electrons gained by the species being reduced.

41.   a. $O_2(g) \rightarrow O^{2-}(s)$

Balance mass: $O_2(g) \rightarrow \mathbf{2}O^{2-}(s)$

Balance charge: $O_2(g) + \mathbf{4e^-} \rightarrow 2O^{2-}(s)$

Balanced half-reaction: $O_2(g) + 4e^- \rightarrow 2O^{2-}(g)$

b. $H^+(aq) \rightarrow H_2(g)$

Balance mass: $\mathbf{2}H^+(aq) \rightarrow H_2(g)$

Balance charge: $2H^+(aq) + \mathbf{2e^-} \rightarrow H_2(g)$

Balanced half-reaction: $2H^+(aq) + 2e^- \rightarrow H_2(g)$

c. $Hg_2^{2+}(aq) \rightarrow Hg^{2+}(aq)$

Balance mass: $Hg_2^{2+}(aq) \rightarrow \mathbf{2}Hg^{2+}(aq)$

Balance charge: $Hg_2^{2+}(aq) \rightarrow 2Hg^{2+}(aq) + \mathbf{2e^-}$

Balanced half-reaction: $Hg_2^{2+}(aq) \rightarrow 2Hg^{2+}(aq) + 2e^-$

d. $Sn^{4+}(aq) \rightarrow Sn^{2+}(aq)$

Balance charge: $Sn^{4+}(aq) + \mathbf{2e^-} \rightarrow Sn^{2+}(aq)$

Balanced half-reaction: $Sn^{4+}(aq) + 2e^- \rightarrow Sn^{2+}(aq)$

42.   a. $N_2(g) \rightarrow N^{3-}(s)$

Balance nitrogen: $N_2(g) \rightarrow \mathbf{2}N^{3-}(s)$

Balance charge: $\mathbf{6e^-} + N_2(g) \rightarrow 2N^{3-}(s)$

Balanced half reaction: $6e^- + N_2(g) \rightarrow 2N^{3-}(s)$

b. $O_2^{2-}(aq) \rightarrow O_2(g)$

Balance charge: $O_2^{2-}(aq) \rightarrow O_2(g) + \mathbf{2e^-}$

Balanced half reaction: $O_2^{2-}(aq) \rightarrow O_2(g) + 2e^-$

c. $Zn(s) \rightarrow Zn^{2+}(aq)$

Balance charge: $Zn(s) \rightarrow Zn^{2+}(aq) + \mathbf{2e^-}$

Balanced half reaction: $Zn(s) \rightarrow Zn^{2+}(aq) + 2e^-$

d. $F_2(g) \rightarrow F^-(aq)$

Balance fluorine: $F_2(g) \rightarrow \mathbf{2}F^-(aq)$

Balance charge: $2e^- + F_2(g) \rightarrow 2F^-(aq)$

Balanced half reaction: $2e^- + F_2(g) \rightarrow 2F^-(aq)$

43.   a. $NO_3^-(aq) \rightarrow NO(g)$

Balance oxygen: $NO_3^-(aq) \rightarrow NO(g) + 2H_2O(l)$

Balance hydrogen: $4H^+(aq) + NO_3^-(aq) \rightarrow NO(g) + 2H_2O(l)$

Balance charge: $4H^+(aq) + NO_3^-(aq) + 3e^- \rightarrow NO(g) + 2H_2O(l)$

Balanced half reaction: $4H^+(aq) + NO_3^-(aq) + 3e^- \rightarrow NO(g) + 2H_2O(l)$

   b. $NO_3^-(aq) \rightarrow NO_2(g)$

Balance oxygen: $NO_3^-(aq) \rightarrow NO_2(g) + H_2O(l)$

Balance hydrogen: $2H^+(aq) + NO_3^-(aq) \rightarrow NO_2(g) + H_2O(l)$

Balance charge: $2H^+(aq) + NO_3^-(aq) + 1e^- \rightarrow NO_2(g) + H_2O(l)$

Balanced half reaction: $2H^+(aq) + NO_3^-(aq) + e^- \rightarrow NO_2(g) + H_2O(l)$

   c. $H_2SO_4(l) \rightarrow SO_2(g)$

Balance oxygen: $H_2SO_4(l) \rightarrow SO_2(g) + 2H_2O(l)$

Balance hydrogen: $2H^+(aq) + H_2SO_4(l) \rightarrow SO_2(g) + 2H_2O(l)$

Balance charge: $2H^+(aq) + H_2SO_4(l) + 2e^- \rightarrow SO_2(g) + 2H_2O(l)$

Balanced half reaction: $2H^+(aq) + H_2SO_4(l) + 2e^- \rightarrow SO_2(g) + 2H_2O(l)$

   d. $H_2O_2(aq) \rightarrow H_2O(l)$

Balance oxygen: $H_2O_2(aq) \rightarrow 2H_2O(l)$

Balance hydrogen: $2H^+(aq) + H_2O_2(aq) \rightarrow 2H_2O(l)$

Balance charge: $2H^+(aq) + H_2O_2(aq) + 2e^- \rightarrow 2H_2O(l)$

Balanced half reaction: $2H^+(aq) + H_2O_2(aq) + 2e^- \rightarrow 2H_2O(l)$

44.   a. $O_2(g) \rightarrow H_2O(l)$

Balance oxygen: $O_2(g) \rightarrow 2H_2O(l)$

Balance hydrogen: $4H^+(aq) + O_2(g) \rightarrow 2H_2O(l)$

Balance charge: $4e^- + 4H^+(aq) + O_2(g) \rightarrow 2H_2O(l)$

Balanced half reaction: $4e^- + 4H^+(aq) + O_2(g) \rightarrow 2H_2O(l)$

   b. $IO_3^-(aq) \rightarrow I_2(s)$

Balance iodine: $2IO_3^-(aq) \rightarrow I_2(s)$

Balance oxygen: $2IO_3^-(aq) \rightarrow I_2(s) + 6H_2O(l)$

Balance hydrogen: $12H^+$ + $2IO_3^-(aq)$ → $I_2(s)$ + $6H_2O(l)$

Balance charge: $12H^+(aq)$ + $2IO_3^-(aq)$ + $10e^-$ → $I_2(s)$ + $6H_2O(l)$

Balanced half reaction: $12H^+(aq)$ + $2IO_3^-(aq)$ + $10e^-$ → $I_2(s)$ + $6H_2O(l)$

c. $VO^{2+}(aq)$ → $V^{3+}(aq)$

Balance oxygen: $VO^{2+}(aq)$ → $V^{3+}(aq)$ + $H_2O(l)$

Balance hydrogen: $2H^+(aq)$ + $VO^{2+}(aq)$ → $V^{3+}(aq)$ + $H_2O(l)$

Balance charge: e^- + $2H^+(aq)$ + $VO^{2+}(aq)$ → $V^{3+}(aq)$ + $H_2O(l)$

Balanced half reaction: e^- + $2H^+(aq)$ + $VO^{2+}(aq)$ → $V^{3+}(aq)$ + $H_2O(l)$

d. $BiO^+(aq)$ → $Bi(s)$

Balance oxygen: $BiO^+(aq)$ → $Bi(s)$ + $H_2O(l)$

Balance hydrogen: $2H^+(aq)$ + $BiO^+(aq)$ → $Bi(s)$ + $H_2O(l)$

Balance charge: $3e^-$ + $2H^+(aq)$ + $BiO^+(aq)$ → $Bi(s)$ + $H_2O(l)$

Balanced half reaction: $3e^-$ + $2H^+(aq)$ + $BiO^+(aq)$ → $Bi(s)$ + $H_2O(l)$

45.   For simplicity, the physical states of the substances have been omitted until the final balanced equation is given.

a. $Mg(s)$ + $Hg^{2+}(aq)$ → $Mg^{2+}(aq)$ + $Hg_2^{2+}(aq)$

Mg → Mg^{2+}

Balance charge: Mg → Mg^{2+} + $2e^-$

Balanced half-reaction: Mg → Mg^{2+} + $2e^-$

Hg^{2+} → Hg_2^{2+}

Balance mercury: $2Hg^{2+}$ → Hg_2^{2+}

Balance charge: $2Hg^{2+}$ + $2e^-$ → Hg_2^{2+}

Balanced half-reaction: $2Hg^{2+}$ + $2e^-$ → Hg_2^{2+}

Since the number of electrons is the same in both half-reactions, the half-reactions can be directly combined for the overall equation

$Mg(s)$ + $2Hg^{2+}(aq)$ → $Mg^{2+}(aq)$ + $Hg_2^{2+}(aq)$

b. $NO_3^-(aq)$ + $Br^-(aq)$ → $NO(g)$ + $Br_2(l)$

NO_3^- → NO

Balance oxygen: NO_3^- → NO + $2H_2O$

Balance hydrogen: $4H^+$ + NO_3^- → NO + $2H_2O$

Balance charge: $4H^+ + NO_3^- + \mathbf{3e^-} \rightarrow NO + \mathbf{2H_2O}$

Balanced half reaction: $4H^+ + NO_3^- + 3e^- \rightarrow NO + 2H_2O$

$Br^- \rightarrow Br_2$

Balance bromine: $\mathbf{2Br^-} \rightarrow Br_2$

Balance charge: $2Br^- \rightarrow Br_2 + \mathbf{2e^-}$

Balanced half-reaction: $2Br^- \rightarrow Br_2 + 2e^-$

Combine the half-reactions: $2 \times (4H^+ + NO_3^- + 3e^- \rightarrow NO + 2H_2O)$

$3 \times (2Br^- \rightarrow Br_2 + 2e^-)$

$8H^+(aq) + 2NO_3^-(aq) + 6Br^-(aq) \rightarrow 3Br_2(l) + 2NO(g) + 4H_2O(l)$

c. $Ni(s) + NO_3^-(aq) \rightarrow Ni^{2+}(aq) + NO_2(g)$

$Ni \rightarrow Ni^{2+}$

Balance charge: $Ni \rightarrow Ni^{2+} + \mathbf{2e^-}$

Balanced half-reaction: $Ni \rightarrow Ni^{2+} + 2e^-$

$NO_3^- \rightarrow NO_2$

Balance oxygen: $NO_3^- \rightarrow NO_2 + \mathbf{H_2O}$

Balance hydrogen: $NO_3^- + \mathbf{2H^+} \rightarrow NO_2 + H_2O$

Balance charge: $NO_3^- + 2H^+ + \mathbf{e^-} \rightarrow NO_2 + H_2O$

Balanced half-reaction: $NO_3^- + 2H^+ + e^- \rightarrow NO_2 + H_2O$

Combine the half-reactions: $2 \times (NO_3^- + 2H^+ + e^- \rightarrow NO_2 + H_2O)$

$Ni \rightarrow Ni^{2+} + 2e^-$

$2NO_3^-(aq) + 4H^+(aq) + Ni(s) \rightarrow 2NO_2(g) + 2H_2O(l) + Ni^{2+}(aq)$

d. $ClO_4^-(aq) + Cl^-(aq) \rightarrow ClO_3^-(aq) + Cl_2(g)$

$ClO_4^- \rightarrow ClO_3^-$

Balance oxygen: $ClO_4^- \rightarrow ClO_3^- + \mathbf{H_2O}$

Balance hydrogen: $\mathbf{2H^+} + ClO_4^- \rightarrow ClO_3^- + H_2O$

Balance charge: $2H^+ + ClO_4^- + \mathbf{2e^-} \rightarrow ClO_3^- + H_2O$

Balanced half reaction: $2H^+ + ClO_4^- + 2e^- \rightarrow ClO_3^- + H_2O$

$$Cl^- \rightarrow Cl_2$$

Balance chlorine: $\mathbf{2}Cl^- \rightarrow Cl_2$

Balance charge: $2Cl^- \rightarrow Cl_2 + \mathbf{2e^-}$

Balanced half-reaction: $2Cl^- \rightarrow Cl_2 + 2\ e^-$

Since the number of electrons transferred is the same in both half-reactions, the half-reactions can be combined directly to give the overall equation for the reaction:

$$2H^+(aq) + ClO_4^-(aq) + 2Cl^-(aq) \rightarrow ClO_3^-(aq) + H_2O(l) + Cl_2(g)$$

46.   For simplicity, the physical states of the substances have been omitted until the final balanced equation is given.

a. $MnO_4^-(aq) + Zn(s) \rightarrow Mn^{2+}(aq) + Zn^{2+}(aq)$

$MnO_4^- \rightarrow Mn^{2+}$

Balance oxygen: $MnO_4^- \rightarrow Mn^{2+} + \mathbf{4H_2O}$

Balance hydrogen: $\mathbf{8H^+} + MnO_4^- \rightarrow Mn^{2+} + 4H_2O$

Balance charge: $\mathbf{5e^-} + 8H^+ + MnO_4^- \rightarrow Mn^{2+} + 4H_2O$

$Zn \rightarrow Zn^{2+}$

Balance charge: $Zn \rightarrow Zn^{2+} + \mathbf{2e^-}$

Combine half reactions: $2 \times (5e^- + 8H^+ + MnO_4^- \rightarrow Mn^{2+} + 4H_2O)$

$5 \times (Zn \rightarrow Zn^{2+} + 2e^-)$

$16H^+(aq) + 2MnO_4^-(aq) + 5Zn(s) \rightarrow 2Mn^{2+}(aq) + 8H_2O(l) + 5Zn^{2+}(aq)$

b. $Sn^{4+}(aq) + H_2(g) \rightarrow Sn^{2+}(aq) + H^+(aq)$

$Sn^{4+} \rightarrow Sn^{2+}$

Balance charge: $Sn^{4+} + \mathbf{2e^-} \rightarrow Sn^{2+}$

$H_2 \rightarrow H^+$

Balance hydrogen: $H_2 \rightarrow \mathbf{2H^+}$

Balance charge: $H_2 \rightarrow 2H^+ + \mathbf{2e^-}$

$Sn^{4+}(aq) + H_2(g) \rightarrow Sn^{2+}(aq) + 2H^+(aq)$

c. $Zn(s) + NO_3^-(aq) \rightarrow Zn^{2+}(aq) + NO_2(g)$

$Zn \rightarrow Zn^{2+}$

Balance charge: $Zn \rightarrow Zn^{2+} + \mathbf{2e^-}$

$NO_3^- \rightarrow NO_2$

Balance oxygen: $NO_3^- \rightarrow NO_2 + \mathbf{H_2O}$

Balance hydrogen: $NO_3^- + \mathbf{2H^+} \rightarrow NO_2 + H_2O$

Balance charge: $NO_3^- + 2H^+ + \mathbf{e^-} \rightarrow NO_2 + H_2O$

Balanced half-reaction: $NO_3^- + 2H^+ + e^- \rightarrow NO_2 + H_2O$

Combine half reactions: $Zn \rightarrow Zn^{2+} + 2e^-$

$2 \times (NO_3^- + 2H^+ + e^- \rightarrow NO_2 + H_2O)$

$Zn(s) + 2NO_3^-(aq) + 4H^+(aq) \rightarrow Zn^{2+}(aq) + 2NO_2(g) + 2H_2O(l)$

d. $H_2S(g) + Br_2(l) \rightarrow S(s) + Br^-(aq)$

$H_2S \rightarrow S$

Balance hydrogen: $H_2S \rightarrow S + \mathbf{2H^+}$

Balance charge: $H_2S \rightarrow S + 2H^+ + \mathbf{2e^-}$

Balanced half-reaction: $H_2S \rightarrow S + 2H^+ + 2e^-$

$Br_2 \rightarrow Br^-$

Balance bromine: $Br_2 \rightarrow 2Br^-$

Balance charge: $\mathbf{2e^-} + Br_2 \rightarrow 2Br^-$

Balanced half-reaction: $2e^- + Br_2 \rightarrow 2Br^-$

$H_2S(g) + Br_2(l) \rightarrow S(s) + 2H^+(aq) + 2Br^-(aq)$

47.   For simplicity, the physical states of the substances have been omitted until the final balanced equation is given.

For the oxidation of iodide ion, I^-, in acidic solution, the half-reaction is always the *same*:

$I^- \rightarrow I_2$

Balance iodine: $\mathbf{2}I^- \rightarrow I_2$

Balance charge: $2I^- \rightarrow I_2 + \mathbf{2e^-}$

Balanced half-reaction: $2I^- \rightarrow I_2 + 2e^-$

a. $IO_3^- \rightarrow I_2$

Balance iodine: $\mathbf{2}IO_3^- \rightarrow I_2$

Balance oxygen: $2IO_3^- \rightarrow I_2 + \mathbf{6H_2O}$

Balance hydrogen: $2IO_3^- + \mathbf{12H^+} \rightarrow I_2 + 6H_2O$

Balance charge: $2IO_3^- + 12H^+ + \mathbf{10e^-} \rightarrow I_2 + 6H_2O$

Balanced half-reaction: $2IO_3^- + 12H^+ + 10e^- \rightarrow I_2 + 6H_2O$

Combine the half-reactions: $2IO_3^- + 12H^+ + 10e^- \rightarrow I_2 + 6H_2O$
$$5 \times (2I^- \rightarrow I_2 + 2e^-)$$

$2IO_3^-(aq) + 12H^+(aq) + 10I^-(aq) \rightarrow 6I_2(aq) + 6H_2O(l)$

$IO_3^-(aq) + 6H^+(aq) + 5I^-(aq) \rightarrow 3I_2(aq) + 3H_2O(l)$

b. $Cr_2O_7^{2-} \rightarrow Cr^{3+}$

Balance chromium: $Cr_2O_7^{2-} \rightarrow \mathbf{2}Cr^{3+}$

Balance oxygen: $Cr_2O_7^{2-} \rightarrow 2Cr^{3+} + \mathbf{7H_2O}$

Balance hydrogen: $Cr_2O_7^{2-} + \mathbf{14H^+} \rightarrow 2Cr^{3+} + 7H_2O$

Balance charge: $Cr_2O_7^{2-} + 14H^+ + \mathbf{6e^-} \rightarrow 2Cr^{3+} + 7H_2O$

Balanced half-reaction: $Cr_2O_7^{2-} + 14H^+ + 6e^- \rightarrow 2Cr^{3+} + 7H_2O$

Combine the half-reactions: $3 \times (2I^- \rightarrow I_2 + 2e^-)$
$$Cr_2O_7^{2-} + 14H^+ + 6e^- \rightarrow 2Cr^{3+} + 7H_2O$$

$6I^-(aq) + Cr_2O_7^{2-}(aq) + 14H^+(aq) \rightarrow 3I_2(aq) + 2Cr^{3+}(aq) + 7H_2O(l)$

c. $Cu^{2+} \rightarrow CuI$

Balance iodine: $Cu^{2+} + \mathbf{I^-} \rightarrow CuI$

Balance charge: $Cu^{2+} + I^- + \mathbf{e^-} \rightarrow CuI$

Balanced half-reaction: $Cu^{2+} + I^- + e^- \rightarrow CuI$

Combine the half-reactions: $2I^- \rightarrow I_2 + 2e^-$
$$2 \times (Cu^{2+} + I^- + e^- \rightarrow CuI)$$

$2Cu^{2+}(aq) + 4I^-(aq) \rightarrow 2CuI(s) + I_2(aq)$

48.   The half reaction for the reduction of Ce^{4+} is the *same* in each of these processes:

$$Ce^{4+} + e^- \rightarrow Ce^{3+}$$

a. $H_3AsO_3 \rightarrow H_3AsO_4$

Balance oxygen: **H_2O** $+ H_3AsO_3 \rightarrow H_3AsO_4$

Balance hydrogen: $H_2O + H_3AsO_3 \rightarrow H_3AsO_4 +$ **$2H^+$**

Balance charge: $H_2O + H_3AsO_3 \rightarrow H_3AsO_4 + 2H^+ +$ **$2e^-$**

Balanced half reaction: $H_2O + H_3AsO_3 \rightarrow H_3AsO_4 + 2H^+ + 2e^-$

Combine half reactions: $H_2O + H_3AsO_3 \rightarrow H_3AsO_4 + 2H^+ + 2e^-$
$$2 \times (Ce^{4+} + e^- \rightarrow Ce^{3+})$$

$$H_2O(l) + H_3AsO_3(aq) + 2Ce^{4+}(aq) \rightarrow H_3AsO_4(aq) + 2H^+(aq) + 2Ce^{3+}(aq)$$

b. $Fe^{2+} \rightarrow Fe^{3+}$

Balance charge: $Fe^{2+} \rightarrow Fe^{3+} +$ **e^-**

Balanced half reaction: $Fe^{2+} \rightarrow Fe^{3+} + e^-$

Combine half reactions: $Fe^{2+} \rightarrow Fe^{3+} + e^-$
$$Ce^{4+} + e^- \rightarrow Ce^{3+}$$

$$Ce^{4+}(aq) + Fe^{2+}(aq) \rightarrow Ce^{3+}(aq) + Fe^{3+}(aq)$$

c. $I^- \rightarrow I_2$

Balance iodine: **$2I^-$** $\rightarrow I_2$

Balance charge: $2I^- \rightarrow I_2 +$ **$2e^-$**

Balanced half reaction: $2I^- \rightarrow I_2 + 2e^-$

Combine half reactions: $2I^- \rightarrow I_2 + 2e^-$
$$2 \times (Ce^{4+} + e^- \rightarrow Ce^{3+})$$

$$2Ce^{4+}(aq) + 2I^-(aq) \rightarrow 2Ce^{3+}(aq) + I_2(s)$$

49. An oxidation-reduction is made useful as a galvanic cell (battery) by physically separating the oxidation half-reaction from the reduction half-reaction, and by causing the electrons to be transferred through a *wire* connecting the two. The passage of electrons through the wire represents an electrical current, which might be used to drive a motor or some other device.

50. A salt bridge typically consists of a *U*-shaped tube filled with an inert electrolyte (one involving ions that are not part of the oxidation-reduction reaction). A salt bridge is used to complete the electrical circuit in a cell. Any method which allows transfer of charge without allowing bulk mixing of the solutions may be used (another common

method is to set up one half-cell in a porous cup, which is then placed in the beaker containing the second half-cell).

51.   In a galvanic cell, electrons flow from the anode (where oxidation occurs) to the cathode (where reduction occurs).

52.   In a galvanic cell, the anode is the electrode where oxidation occurs; the cathode is the electrode where reduction occurs.

53.

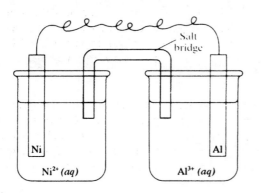

$Ni^{2+}(aq)$ ion is reduced; $Al(s)$ is oxidized.

The reaction at the anode is $Al(s) \rightarrow Al^{3+}(aq) + 3e^-$.

The reaction at the cathode is $Ni^{2+}(aq) + 2e^- \rightarrow Ni(s)$.

54.

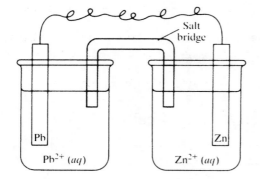

$Pb^{2+}(aq)$ ion is reduced; $Zn(s)$ is oxidized.

The reaction at the anode is $Zn(s) \rightarrow Zn^{2+}(aq) + 2e^-$.

The reaction at the cathode is $Pb^{2+}(aq) + 2e^- \rightarrow Pb(s)$

55.   The overall reaction is

$$Pb(s) + PbO_2(s) + 2H_2SO_4(aq) \rightarrow 2PbSO_4(s) + 2H_2O(l)$$

in which $Pb^0(s)$ is oxidized to Pb^{2+} and $Pb^{IV}O_2$ is reduced to Pb^{2+}. This reaction can be reversed by *electrolysis* of the mixture of water and $PbSO_4(s)$ (passing electrical energy into the mixture from the outside).

56.   Both normal and alkaline cells contain zinc as one electrode; zinc corrodes more slowly under alkaline conditions than in the highly acidic environment of a normal dry cell.

anode: $Zn(s) + 2OH^-(aq) \rightarrow ZnO(s) + H_2O(l) + 2e^-$

cathode: $2MnO_2(s) + H_2O(l) + 2e^- \rightarrow Mn_2O_3(s) + 2OH^-(aq)$

57.   Corrosion represents returning metals to the natural state (ore) and involves *oxidation* of the metal. Corrosion of a metal is undesirable because, as the metal is converted to its oxide, the bulk of the metal loses its strength, flexibility, and other metallic properties. If the metal were part of some constructed item, the item would slowly disintegrate.

58.   Aluminum is a very reactive metal when freshly isolated in the pure state. However, on standing for even a relatively short period of time, aluminum metal forms a thin coating of Al_2O_3 on its surface from reaction with atmospheric oxygen. This coating of Al_2O_3 is much less reactive than the metal and serves to protect the surface of the metal from further attack.

59.   Most steels contain additives such as chromium or nickel. These additives are able to form protective oxide coatings on the surface of the steel which tend to prevent further oxidation.

60.   In cathodic protection of steel tanks and pipes, a more reactive metal than iron is connected to the item to be protected. The active metal is then preferentially oxidized rather than the iron of the tank or pipe.

61.   Electrolysis is the process of forcing an electrical current through a cell to produce a chemical change that would otherwise not occur on its own.

62.   The main recharging reaction for the lead storage battery is

$2PbSO_4(s) + 2H_2O(l) \rightarrow Pb(s) + PbO_2(s) + 2H_2SO_4(aq)$

A major side reaction is the electrolysis of water

$2H_2O(l) \rightarrow 2H_2(g) + O_2(g)$

resulting in the production of an explosive mixture of hydrogen and oxygen, which accounts for many accidents during the recharging of such batteries.

63.   Many metals can be produced by electrolysis of aqueous solutions of their salts, or by electrolysis of molten salts (for those metals that would react with water). Aluminum combines so readily with oxygen that it cannot be prepared by either of these methods. Aluminum is most commonly prepared by the Hall process, which is the electrolysis of a molten mixture of Al_2O_3 and Na_3AlF_6.

64. Electrolysis is applied in electroplating by making the item to be plated the cathode in a cell containing a solution of ions of the desired plating metal.

65. electrons

66. loss; oxidation state

67. gain, oxidation number

68. electronegative

69. charge

70. An *oxidizing agent* is an atom, molecule, or ion which causes the oxidation of another species. During this process, the oxidizing agent itself is reduced.

71. oxidation, reduced

72. lose

73. equal

74. separate from

75. galvanic

76. oxidation

77. cathode

78. An electrolysis reaction results when an electrical current from an outside source is used to cause an otherwise nonspontaneous reaction to occur. An example is the electrolysis of water: $2H_2O(l) \rightarrow 2H_2(g) + O_2(g)$; this reaction only takes place if an electrical current of sufficient voltage is passed through the water.

79. voltage or potential

80. hydrogen; oxygen

81. zinc

82. oxidation

83. aluminum oxide

84. a. $4Fe(s) + 3O_2(g) \rightarrow 2Fe_2O_3(s)$

    iron is oxidized, oxygen is reduced

b. $2Al(s) + 3Cl_2(g) \rightarrow 2AlCl_3(s)$

aluminum is oxidized, chlorine is reduced

c. $6Mg(s) + P_4(s) \rightarrow 2Mg_3P_2(s)$

magnesium is oxidized, phosphorus is reduced

85. a.   zinc is oxidized, hydrogen (as H^+ in HCl) is reduced

b.   copper(I) is both oxidized to copper(II) and reduced to copper(0)

c.   iron (as Fe^{2+}) is oxidized to Fe^{3+}, chromium(VI) (in $Cr_2O_7^{2-}$) is reduced to Cr^{3+}

86. a.   aluminum is oxidized; hydrogen is reduced

b.   hydrogen is reduced; iodine is oxidized

c.   copper is oxidized; hydrogen is reduced

87. a. $CH_2{=}CH_2(g) + Cl_2(g) \rightarrow ClCH_2{-}CH_2Cl(l)$

C −2   0   Cl −1

H +1   C −1

                         H +1

carbon is oxidized, chlorine is reduced

Cl_2 is the oxidizing agent, $CH_2{=}CH_2$ is the reducing agent

b. $CH_2{=}CH_2(g) + Br_2(g) \rightarrow BrCH_2{-}CH_2Br(l)$

C −2   0   Br −1

H +1   C −1

                         H +1

carbon is oxidized, bromine is reduced

Br_2 is the oxidizing agent, $CH_2{=}CH_2$ is the reducing agent

c. $CH_2{=}CH_2(g) + HBr(g) \rightarrow CH_3{-}CH_2Br(l)$

C −2   H +1   C −2

H +1   Br −1   Br −1

                             H +1

The process appears not to involve electron transfer.

d. $CH_2=CH_2(g) + H_2(g) \rightarrow CH_3-CH_3$

C -2 H 0 C -3

H $+1$ H $+1$

carbon is reduced, hydrogen is oxidized

hydrogen is the reducing agent, $CH_2=CH_2$ is the oxidizing agent

88.   a. $C_3H_8(g) + 5O_2(g) \rightarrow 3CO_2(g) + 4H_2O(g)$

b. $CO(g) + 2H_2(g) \rightarrow CH_3OH(l)$

c. $SnO_2(s) + 2C(s) \rightarrow Sn(s) + 2CO(g)$

d. $C_2H_5OH(l) + 3O_2(g) \rightarrow 2CO_2(g) + 3H_2O(g)$

89.   a. $2MnO_4^-(aq) + 6H^+(aq) + 5H_2O_2(aq) \rightarrow 2Mn^{2+}(aq) + 8H_2O(l) + 5O_2(g)$

b. $6Cu^+(aq) + 6H^+(aq) + BrO_3^-(aq) \rightarrow 6Cu^{2+}(aq) + Br^-(aq) + 3H_2O(l)$

c. $2HNO_2(aq) + 2H^+(aq) + 2I^-(aq) \rightarrow 2NO(g) + I_2(aq) + 2H_2O(l)$

90.   Each of these reactions involves a *metallic* element in the form of the *free* element on one side of the equation; on the other side of the equation, the metallic element is *combined* in an ionic compound. If a metallic element goes from the free metal to the ionic form, the metal is oxidized (loses electrons).

a.   sodium is oxidized, oxygen is reduced

b.   iron is oxidized, hydrogen is reduced

c.   oxygen (O^{2-}) is oxidized, aluminum (Al^{3+}) is reduced (this reaction is the reverse of the type discussed above)

d.   magnesium is oxidized, nitrogen is reduced

91.   Each of these reactions involves a *metallic* element in the form of the *free* element on one side of the equation; on the other side of the equation, the metallic element is *combined* in an ionic compound. If a metallic element goes from the free metal to the ionic form, the metal is oxidized (loses electrons).

a.   zinc is oxidized, nitrogen is reduced

b.   cobalt is oxidized, sulfur is reduced

c.   potassium is oxidized, oxygen is reduced

d.   silver is oxidized, oxygen is reduced

92.   The rules for assigning oxidation states are given in Section 17.2 of the text. The rule which applies for each element in the following answers is given in parentheses after the element and its oxidation state.

a.   H +1 (Rule 4); N −3 (Rule 6)

b.   C +2 (Rule 6); O −2 (Rule 3)

c.   C +4 (Rule 6); O −2 (Rule 3)

d.   N +3 (Rule 6); F −1 (Rule 5)

93.   The rules for assigning oxidation states are given in Section 17.2 of the text. The rule which applies for each element in the following answers is given in parentheses after the element and its oxidation state.

a.   P +3 (Rule 6); Br −1 (Rule 5)

b.   C −(8/3) (Rule 6); H +1 (Rule 4)

c.   K +1 (Rule 2); Mn +7 (Rule 6); O −2 (Rule 3)

d.   C 0 (Rule 6); H +1 (Rule 4); O −2 (Rule 3)

94.   The rules for assigning oxidation states are given in Section 17.2 of the text. The rule which applies for each element in the following answers is given in parentheses after the element and its oxidation state.

a.   Mn +4 (Rule 6); O −2 (Rule 3)

b.   Ba +2 (Rule 2); Cr +6 (Rule 6); O −2 (Rule 3)

c.   H +1 (Rule 4); S +4 (Rule 6); O −2 (Rule 3)

d.   Ca +2 (Rule 2); P +5 (Rule 6); O −2 (Rule 3)

95.   The rules for assigning oxidation states are given in Section 17.2 of the text. The rule which applies for each element in the following answers is given in parentheses after the element and its oxidation state.

a.   Cr +3 (Rule 6); Cl −1 (Rule 2)

b.   K +1 (Rule 2); Cr +6 (Rule 6); O −2 (Rule 3)

c.   K +1 (Rule 2); Cr +6 (Rule 6); O −2 (Rule 3)

d.   Cr +2 (Rule 6); C 0 (Rule 7); H +1 (Rule 4); O −2 (Rule 3)

For chromous acetate, first the oxidation state of carbon in the acetate ion, $C_2H_3O_2^-$, is determined by Rule 7 (the sum of the oxidation numbers must equal the charge on the ion), then the oxidation state of Cr may be determined by Rule 6).

96.   The rules for assigning oxidation states are given in Section 17.2 of the text. The rule which applies for each element in the following answers is given in parentheses after the element and its oxidation state.

a.   Bi +3 (Rule 7); O –2 (Rule 3)

b.   P +5 (Rule 7); O –2 (Rule 3)

c.   N +3 (Rule 7); O –2 (Rule 3)

d.   Hg +1 (Rule 7)

97. a. $C(s) + O_2(g) \rightarrow CO_2(g)$

     C 0   O 0   C +4

                     O –2

     carbon is oxidized; oxygen is reduced

b. $2CO(g) + O_2(g) \rightarrow 2CO_2(g)$

     C +2   O 0   C +4

     O –2   O –2

     carbon (of CO) is oxidized; oxygen (of O_2) is reduced

c. $CH_4(g) + 2O_2(g) \rightarrow CO_2(g) + 2H_2O(g)$

     C –4   O 0   C +4   H +1

     H +1   O –2   O –2

     carbon (of CH_4) is oxidized; oxygen (of O_2) is reduced

d. $C_2H_2(g) + 2H_2(g) \rightarrow C_2H_6(g)$

     C –1   H 0   C –3

     H +1   H +1

     hydrogen (of H_2) is oxidized; carbon (of C_2H_2) is reduced

98. a. $2B_2O_3(s) + 6Cl_2(g) \rightarrow 4BCl_3(1) + 3O_2(g)$

     B +3   Cl 0   B +3   O 0

     O –2   Cl –1

     oxygen is oxidized; chlorine is reduced

b. $GeH_4(g) + O_2(g) \rightarrow Ge(s) + 2H_2O(g)$

     Ge –4   O 0   Ge 0   H +1

     H +1   O –2

     germanium is oxidized; oxygen is reduced

c. $C_2H_4(g)$ + $Cl_2(g)$ → $C_2H_4Cl_2(l)$

C -2 Cl 0   C -1

H $+1$ H $+1$; Cl -1

carbon is oxidized; chlorine is reduced

d. $O_2(g)$ + $2F_2(g)$ → $2OF_2(g)$

O 0   F 0   O $+2$

F -1

oxygen is oxidized; fluorine is reduced

99. a. $I^-(aq)$ → $I_2(s)$

Balance iodine: $2I^-(aq)$ → $I_2(s)$

Balance charge: $2I^-(aq)$ → $I_2(s)$ + **2e⁻**

Balanced half reaction: $2I^-(aq)$ → $I_2(s)$ + $2e^-$

b. $O_2(g)$ → $O^{2-}(s)$

Balance oxygen: $O_2(g)$ → **2O²⁻**(s)

Balance charge: $O_2(g)$ + **4e⁻** → $2O^{2-}(s)$

Balanced half reaction: $O_2(g)$ + $4e^-$ → $2O^{2-}(s)$

c. $P_4(s)$ → $P^{3-}(s)$

Balance phosphorus: $P_4(s)$ → **4P³⁻**(s)

Balance charge: $P_4(s)$ + **12e⁻** → $4P^{3-}(s)$

Balanced half reaction: $P_4(s)$ + $12e^-$ → $4P^{3-}(s)$

d. $Cl_2(g)$ → $Cl^-(aq)$

Balance chlorine: $Cl_2(g)$ → **2Cl⁻**(aq)

Balance charge: $Cl_2(g)$ + **2e⁻** → $2Cl^-(aq)$

Balanced half reaction: $Cl_2(g)$ + $2e^-$ → $2Cl^-(aq)$

100. a. $SiO_2(s)$ → $Si(s)$

Balance oxygen: $SiO_2(s)$ → $Si(s)$ + **2H₂O**(l)

Balance hydrogen: $SiO_2(s)$ + **4H⁺**(aq) → $Si(s)$ + $2H_2O(l)$

Balance charge: $SiO_2(s)$ + $4H^+(aq)$ + **4e⁻** → $Si(s)$ + $2H_2O(l)$

Balanced half reaction: $SiO_2(s)$ + $4H^+(aq)$ + $4e^-$ → $Si(s)$ + $2H_2O(l)$

b. $S(s) \rightarrow H_2S(g)$

Balance hydrogen: $S(s) + \mathbf{2H^+}(aq) \rightarrow H_2S(g)$

Balance charge: $S(s) + 2H^+(aq) + \mathbf{2e^-} \rightarrow H_2S(g)$

Balanced half reaction: $S(s) + 2H^+(aq) + 2e^- \rightarrow H_2S(g)$

c. $NO_3^-(aq) \rightarrow HNO_2(aq)$

Balance oxygen: $NO_3^-(aq) \rightarrow HNO_2(aq) + \mathbf{H_2O}(l)$

Balance hydrogen: $NO_3^-(aq) + \mathbf{3H^+}(aq) \rightarrow HNO_2(aq) + H_2O(l)$

Balance charge: $NO_3^-(aq) + 3H^+(aq) + \mathbf{2e^-} \rightarrow HNO_2(aq) + H_2O(l)$

Balanced half reaction: $NO_3^-(aq) + 3H^+(aq) + 2e^- \rightarrow HNO_2(aq) + H_2O(l)$

d. $NO_3^-(aq) \rightarrow NO(g)$

Balance oxygen: $NO_3^-(aq) \rightarrow NO(g) + \mathbf{2H_2O}(l)$

Balance hydrogen: $NO_3^-(aq) + \mathbf{4H^+}(aq) \rightarrow NO(g) + 2H_2O(l)$

Balance charge: $NO_3^-(aq) + 4H^+(aq) + \mathbf{3e^-} \rightarrow NO(g) + 2H_2O(l)$

Balanced half reaction: $NO_3^-(aq) + 4H^+(aq) + 3e^- \rightarrow NO(g) + 2H_2O(l)$

101.   For simplicity, the physical states of the substances have been omitted until the final balanced equation is given.

a. $I^-(aq) + MnO_4^-(aq) \rightarrow I_2(aq) + Mn^{2+}(aq)$

$I^- \rightarrow I_2$

Balance iodine: $\mathbf{2}I^- \rightarrow I_2$

Balance charge: $2I^- \rightarrow I_2 + \mathbf{2e^-}$

$MnO_4^- \rightarrow Mn^{2+}$

Balance oxygen: $MnO_4^- \rightarrow Mn^{2+} + \mathbf{4H_2O}$

Balance hydrogen: $\mathbf{8H^+} + MnO_4^- \rightarrow Mn^{2+} + 4H_2O$

Balance charge: $8H^+ + MnO_4^- + \mathbf{5e^-} \rightarrow Mn^{2+} + 4H_2O$

Combine the half reactions: $5 \times (2I^- \rightarrow I_2 + 2e^-)$

$2 \times (8H^+ + MnO_4^- + 5e^- \rightarrow Mn^{2+} + 4H_2O)$

$16H^+(aq) + 2MnO_4^-(aq) + 10I^-(aq) \rightarrow 2Mn^{2+}(aq) + 8H_2O(l) + 5I_2(aq)$

b. $S_2O_8^{2-} + Cr^{3+} \rightarrow SO_4^{2-} + Cr_2O_7^{2-}$

$S_2O_8^{2-} \rightarrow SO_4^{2-}$
Balance sulfur: $S_2O_8^{2-} \rightarrow$ **2**SO_4^{2-}
Balance charge: $S_2O_8^{2-} +$ **2e**$^- \rightarrow 2SO_4^{2-}$

$Cr^{3+} \rightarrow Cr_2O_7^{2-}$
Balance chromium: **2**$Cr^{3+} \rightarrow Cr_2O_7^{2-}$
Balance oxygen: **7H$_2$O** $+ 2Cr^{3+} \rightarrow Cr_2O_7^{2-}$
Balance hydrogen: $7H_2O + 2Cr^{3+} \rightarrow Cr_2O_7^{2-} +$ **14H$^+$**
Balance charge: $7H_2O + 2Cr^{3+} \rightarrow Cr_2O_7^{2-} + 14H^+ +$ **6e**$^-$

Combine the half reactions: $3 \times (S_2O_8^{2-} + 2e^- \rightarrow 2SO_4^{2-})$
$$7H_2O + 2Cr^{3+} \rightarrow Cr_2O_7^{2-} + 14H^+ + 6e^-$$

$7H_2O(l) + 2Cr^{3+}(aq) + 3S_2O_8^{2-}(aq) \rightarrow Cr_2O_7^{2-}(aq) + 14H^+(aq) + 6SO_4^{2-}(aq)$

c. $BiO_3^- + Mn^{2+} \rightarrow Bi^{3+} + MnO_4^-$

$BiO_3^- \rightarrow Bi^{3+}$
Balance oxygen: $BiO_3^- \rightarrow Bi^{3+} +$ **3H$_2$O**
Balance hydrogen: **6H$^+$** $+ BiO_3^- \rightarrow Bi^{3+} + 3H_2O$
Balance charge: $6H^+ + BiO_3^- +$ **2e**$^- \rightarrow Bi^{3+} + 3H_2O$

$Mn^{2+} \rightarrow MnO_4^-$
Balance oxygen: **4H$_2$O** $+ Mn^{2+} \rightarrow MnO_4^-$
Balance hydrogen: $4H_2O + Mn^{2+} \rightarrow MnO_4^- +$ **8H$^+$**
Balance charge: $4H_2O + Mn^{2+} \rightarrow MnO_4^- + 8H^+ +$ **5e**$^-$

Combine the half reactions: $5 \times (6H^+ + BiO_3^- + 2e^- \rightarrow Bi^{3+} + 3H_2O)$
$$2 \times (4H_2O + Mn^{2+} \rightarrow MnO_4^- + 8H^+ + 5e^-)$$

$2Mn^{2+}(aq) + 14H^+(aq) + 5BiO_3^-(aq) \rightarrow 2MnO_4^-(aq) + 5Bi^{3+}(aq) + 7H_2O(l)$

102.   For simplicity, the physical states of the substances have been omitted until the final balanced equation is given.

For the reduction of the permanganate ion, MnO_4^-, in acid solution, the half reaction is always the *same*:

$MnO_4^- \rightarrow Mn^{2+}$

Balance oxygen: $MnO_4^- \rightarrow Mn^{2+} + \mathbf{4H_2O}$

Balance hydrogen: $\mathbf{8H^+} + MnO_4^- \rightarrow Mn^{2+} + 4H_2O$

Balance charge: $8H^+ + MnO_4^- + \mathbf{5e^-} \rightarrow Mn^{2+} + 4H_2O$

a. $C_2O_4^{2-} \rightarrow CO_2$

Balance carbon: $C_2O_4^{2-} \rightarrow \mathbf{2CO_2}$

Balance charge: $C_2O_4^{2-} \rightarrow \mathbf{2CO_2 + 2e^-}$

Combine half reactions: $5 \times (C_2O_4^{2-} \rightarrow \mathbf{2}CO_2 + 2e^-)$

$2 \times (8H^+ + MnO_4^- + 5e^- \rightarrow Mn^{2+} + 4H_2O)$

$16H^+(aq) + 2MnO_4^-(aq) + 5C_2O_4^{2-}(aq) \rightarrow 2Mn^{2+}(aq) + 8H_2O(l) + 10CO_2(g)$

b. $Fe^{2+} \rightarrow Fe^{3+}$

Balance charge: $Fe^{2+} \rightarrow Fe^{3+} + \mathbf{e^-}$

Combine half reactions: $5 \times (Fe^{2+} \rightarrow Fe^{3+} + e^-)$

$8H^+ + MnO_4^- + 5e^- \rightarrow Mn^{2+} + 4H_2O$

$8H^+(aq) + MnO_4^-(aq) + 5Fe^{2+}(aq) \rightarrow Mn^{2+}(aq) + 4H_2O(l) + 5Fe^{3+}(aq)$

c. $Cl^- \rightarrow Cl_2$

Balance chlorine: $\mathbf{2}Cl^- \rightarrow Cl_2$

Balance charge: $2Cl^- \rightarrow Cl_2 + \mathbf{2e^-}$

Combine half reactions: $5 \times (2Cl^- \rightarrow Cl_2 + 2e^-)$

$2 \times (8H^+ + MnO_4^- + 5e^- \rightarrow Mn^{2+} + 4H_2O)$

$16H^+(aq) + 2MnO_4^-(aq) + 10Cl^-(aq) \rightarrow 2Mn^{2+}(aq) + 8H_2O(l) + 5Cl_2(g)$

103.

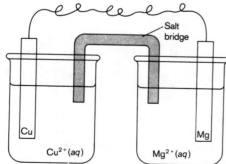

$Cu^{2+}(aq)$ ion is reduced; $Mg(s)$ is oxidized.

The reaction at the anode is $Mg(s) \rightarrow Mg^{2+}(aq) + 2e^-$.

The reaction at the cathode is $Cu^{2+}(aq) + 2e^- \rightarrow Cu(s)$.

Chapter 18   Radioactivity and Nuclear Energy

1. The nucleus of an atom has little or *no* effect on the atom's chemical properties. The chemical properties of an atom are determined by the number and arrangement of the atom's electrons (which are outside the nucleus).

2. The radius of a typical atomic nucleus is on the order of 10^{-13} cm, which is about one hundred thousand times smaller than the radius of an atom overall.

3. Nuclei are made up of two types of particles, protons and neutrons. These particles have comparable (but not exactly the same) masses. Since so much of the atom's mass is concentrated inside a very small volume, the nucleus of an atom is extremely dense.

particle	relative mass	relative charge
proton	1836	+1
neutron	1839	0

4. The atomic number (Z) of a nucleus represents the number of protons present in the nucleus. The mass number (A) of a nucleus represents the total number of protons and neutrons in the nucleus. For example, for the nuclide $^{13}_{6}C$, with six protons and seven neutrons, we have $Z = 6$ and $A = 13$.

5. Isotopes are atoms of the same element which differ in the number of neutrons present in the nuclei. Since the number of protons is the same in each such nucleus (the atoms are of the same element), isotopes have the same atomic number (Z). Since the number of neutrons present differs between the nuclei, the mass numbers of the nuclei (A) are different. Isotopes are atoms of the same element which differ in mass. For example, $^{13}_{6}C$ and $^{14}_{6}C$ both represent carbon atoms. However, $^{13}_{6}C$ has one less neutron than does $^{14}_{6}C$.

6. The atomic number (Z) is written in such formulas as a left subscript, while the mass number (A) is written as a left superscript. That is, the general symbol for a nuclide is $^{A}_{Z}X$. As an example, consider the isotope of oxygen with 8 protons and 8 neutrons: its symbol would be $^{16}_{8}O$.

7. Beta particle: charge –1, mass number 0, symbol $^{0}_{-1}e$ or $^{0}_{-1}\beta$

8. Alpha particle: charge 2+, mass number 4, symbol $^{4}_{2}He$

9. When a nucleus produces an alpha (α) particle, the atomic number of the nucleus decreases by two units.

10.   When a nucleus produces a beta (β) particle, the atomic number of the parent nucleus is *increased* by *one* unit. The beta particle has a mass number of zero, but an "atomic number" of -1.

11.   When a nucleus produces an alpha (α) particle, the mass number of the original nucleus decreases by four units. When a nucleus produces a beta (β) particle, the mass number of the original nucleus is unchanged.

12.   Gamma rays are high energy photons of electromagnetic radiation. Gamma rays are not considered to be particles. When a nucleus produces only gamma radiation, the atomic number and mass number of the nucleus do not change. Gamma rays represent the energy changes associated with transitions and rearrangement of the particles within the nucleus.

13.   A positron is a particle with the same mass as an electron, but with the opposite charge: a positron is *positively* charged. It's mass number is therefore zero, and its "atomic number" is +1. When an unstable nucleus produces a positron, the mass number of the original nucleus is unchanged, but the atomic number of the original nucleus decreases by one unit.

14.   Electron capture occurs when one of the inner orbital electrons is pulled into and becomes part of the nucleus.

15. $^{20}_{10}\text{Ne}$ $^{21}_{10}\text{Ne}$ $^{22}_{10}\text{Ne}$

       10 neutrons   11 neutrons   12 neutrons

16.   The average atomic mass listed on the Periodic Table is 20.18, which suggests that the isotope of mass number 20 predominates in naturally occurring neon. The average atomic mass given in the periodic table is a *weighted* average which includes not only the masses of the isotopes, but also their relative abundances.

17. $^{24}_{12}\text{Mg}$ (12 protons, 12 neutrons)

       $^{25}_{12}\text{Mg}$ (12 protons, 13 neutrons)

       $^{26}_{12}\text{Mg}$ (12 protons, 14 neutrons)

18.   The approximate atomic molar mass could be calculated as follows: $0.79(24) + 0.10(25) + 0.11(26) = 24.3$. This is *only* and approximation since the mass numbers, rather than the actual isotopic masses, were used. The fact that the approximate mass calculated is slightly above 24 shows that the isotope of mass number 24 predominates.

19. a. $_{-1}^{0}e$ or $_{-1}^{0}\beta$

 b. $_{2}^{4}He$ or $_{2}^{4}\alpha$

 c. $_{0}^{1}n$

 d. $_{1}^{1}H$

20. a. $_{-1}^{0}e$ or $_{-1}^{0}\beta$

 b. $_{+1}^{0}e$ or $_{+1}^{0}\beta$

 c. $_{0}^{0}\gamma$

21. a. $_{-1}^{0}e$

 b. $_{25}^{56}Mn$

 c. $_{31}^{72}Ga$

22. a. $_{83}^{192}Bi$

 b. $_{82}^{204}Pb$

 c. $_{84}^{206}Po$

23. a. $_{87}^{206}Fr$

 b. $_{-1}^{0}e$

 c. $_{0}^{1}n$

24. a. $_{-1}^{0}e$

b. $_{-1}^{0}e$

c. $_{83}^{210}Bi$

25.   a. $_{23}^{55}V \rightarrow _{-1}^{0}e + _{24}^{55}Cr$

b. $_{47}^{116}Ag \rightarrow _{-1}^{0}e + _{48}^{116}Cd$

c. $_{89}^{229}Ac \rightarrow _{-1}^{0}e + _{90}^{229}Th$

26.   a. $_{53}^{136}I \rightarrow _{54}^{136}Xe + _{-1}^{0}e$

b. $_{51}^{133}Sb \rightarrow _{52}^{133}Te + _{-1}^{0}e$

c. $_{49}^{117}In \rightarrow _{50}^{117}Sn + _{-1}^{0}e$

d. $_{20}^{47}Ca \rightarrow _{21}^{47}Sc + _{-1}^{0}e$

27.   a. $_{90}^{227}Th \rightarrow _{2}^{4}He + _{88}^{223}Ra$

b. $_{83}^{211}Bi \rightarrow _{2}^{4}He + _{81}^{207}Tl$

c. $_{96}^{244}Cm \rightarrow _{2}^{4}He + _{94}^{240}Pu$

28.   a. $_{88}^{226}Ra \rightarrow _{86}^{222}Rn + _{2}^{4}He$

b. $_{86}^{222}Rn \rightarrow _{84}^{218}Po + _{2}^{4}He$

c. $_{94}^{239}Pu \rightarrow _{92}^{235}U + _{2}^{4}He$

d. $_{4}^{8}Be \rightarrow _{2}^{4}He + _{2}^{4}He$

29.   A nuclear transformation represents the change of one element into another. Nuclear transformations are generally accomplished by

bombardment of a target nucleus with some small, energetic particle that effects the desired transformation of the target nucleus.

30. There is often considerable repulsion between the target nucleus and the particles being used for bombardment (especially if the bombarding particle is positively charged like the target nucleus). Using accelerators to greatly speed up the bombarding particles can overcome this repulsion.

31. The elements with atomic number greater than 92 are referred to as the *transuranium* elements. The transuranium elements have been prepared by bombardment reactions of other nuclei.

32. $$^{27}_{13}\text{Al} + \ ^{4}_{2}\text{He} \rightarrow \ ^{30}_{15}\text{P} + \ ^{1}_{0}\text{n}$$

33. Geiger (Geiger-Müller) counters contain a probe which contains argon gas. The argon atoms themselves have no charge, but they can be ionized by high-energy particles from a radioactive decay process. Although a sample of normal uncharged argon gas does not conduct an electrical current, argon gas that has been ionized will briefly conduct an electrical current (until the argon ions and electrons recombine). If an electric field is applied to the argon gas probe, then a brief pulse of electricity will be passed through the argon every time an ionization event occurs (every time a high-energy particle strikes the argon gas probe). The Geiger counter detects each pulse of current, and these pulses are then counted and displayed on the meter of the device. A scintillation counter uses a substance like sodium iodide, which emits light when struck by a high-energy particle from a radioactive decay. A detector senses the flashes of light from the sodium iodide, and these flashes are then counted and displayed on the meter of the device.

34. The half-life of a nucleus is the time required for one-half of the original sample of nuclei to decay. A given isotope of an element always has the same half-life, although different isotopes of the same element may have greatly different half-lives. Nuclei of different elements typically have different half-lives.

35. When we say that one nucleus is "hotter" than another, we mean that the "hot" nucleus undergoes more decay events per time period. The "hotness" of radionuclei is most commonly indicated by their *half-lives* (the amount of time required for half a sample to undergo the decay process). A nucleus with a short half-life will undergo more decay events in a given time than a nucleus with a long half-life.

36. $^{226}_{88}\text{Ra}$ is the most stable (longest half-life)

   $^{224}_{88}\text{Ra}$ is the "hottest" (shortest half-life)

37.   highest   lowest

^{24}Na $>$ ^{131}I $>$ ^{60}Co $>$ ^{3}H $>$ ^{14}C

38.   highest activity   lowest activity

^{87}Sr $>$ ^{99}Tc $>$ ^{24}Na $>$ ^{99}Mo $>$ ^{133}Xe $>$ ^{131}I $>$ ^{32}P $>$ ^{51}Cr $>$ ^{59}Fe

39.

time, days	0	2.7	5.4	8.1
mass, μg	50	25	12.5	6.25

After 8 days, slightly more than 6 μg of ^{198}Au remains.

40.   For ^{223}Ra, the half-life is 12 days. After two half-lives (24 days), 250 mg remains; after three half-lives (36 days), 125 mg remains.

For ^{224}Ra, the half-life is 3.6 days. One month would be approximately 8 half-life periods (29 days), and approximately 4 mg remains.

For ^{225}Ra, the half-life is 15 days. One month would be two half-life periods, and 250 mg remains.

41.   Kr-81 is the most stable (longest half life); Kr-73 is the "hottest" (shortest half life). Since the half-lives of Kr-73 and Kr-74 are so short, after 24 hours there would essentially be no detectable amount of these isotopes remaining. Since 24 hours is very approximately two half life periods for Kr-76, approximately one fourth of the original sample would remain. Since the half life of Kr-81 is much, much larger than the 24-hour time period under consideration, essentially all of the sample would remain.

42.   For an administered dose of 100 μg, 0.39 μg remains after 2 days. The fraction remaining is 0.39/100 = 0.0039; on a percentage basis, less than 0.4 % of the original radioisotope remains.

43.   Carbon-14 ($^{14}_{6}$C) is most commonly used in the radiodating of archaeological artifacts.

44.   Carbon-14 is produced in the upper atmosphere by the bombardment of ordinary nitrogen with neutrons from space:

$$^{14}_{7}N + ^{1}_{0}n \rightarrow ^{14}_{6}C + ^{1}_{1}H$$

45.   The quantity of $^{14}_{6}$C in the atmosphere is assumed to remain constant because a balance exists between the continued *production* of $^{14}_{6}$C from bombardment of nitrogen in the upper atmosphere by cosmic rays, and the *decay* of $^{14}_{6}$C through beta particle production.

46.   We assume that the concentration of C-14 in the atmosphere is effectively constant. A living organism is constantly replenishing C-14

either through the processes of metabolism (sugars ingested in foods contain C-14), or photosynthesis (carbon dioxide contains C-14). When a plant dies, it no longer replenishes itself with C-14 from the atmosphere, and as the C-14 undergoes radioactive decay, its amount decreases with time.

47. A *radiotracer* is a radioactive nuclide that can be introduced into an organism in food or drugs, whose pathway through the body can then be traced by monitoring of the radioactivity of the nuclide. Carbon-14 and Phosphorus-32 have been used to study the conversion of nutriets into energy by living cells.

48. These isotopes and their uses are listed in Table 18.4 Some important examples include the use of I-131 (and other iodine isotopes) in the diagnosis and treatment of thyroid disease (iodine is used in the body primarily in the thyroid gland); Fe-59 in the study of the function of red blood cells (iron is a constituent of hemoglobin which is found in the red blood cells); Sr-87 in the study of bones (Sr is a Group 2 element, and is able to take the place of Ca in bone structures).

49. The forces that hold protons and neutrons together in the nucleus are *much greater* than the forces that bind atoms together in molecules.

50. Combining two light nuclei to form a heavier, more stable nucleus is called nuclear *fusion*. Splitting a heavy nucleus into nuclei with smaller mass numbers is called nuclear *fission*.

51. The energies released by nuclear processes are on the order of 10^6 times more powerful than those associated with ordinary chemical reactions.

52. $^1_0 n + ^{235}_{92} U \rightarrow ^{142}_{56} Ba + ^{91}_{36} Kr + 3 ^1_0 n$ is one possibility.

53. The fission of $^{235}_{92}U$ is initiated by bombardment of the nucleus with neutrons from an outside source. For every nucleus of $^{235}_{92}U$ that decays, however, three neutrons are produced by the process. Once the reaction has been started with neutrons from an outside source, the neutrons generated by the reaction itself can go on to cause other nuclei of $^{235}_{92}U$ to decay, thereby producing still more neutrons, and so on. All that is needed to sustain such a chain reaction is a sufficient density of $^{235}_{92}U$, so that the emitted neutrons are not lost to the outside.

54. A critical mass of a fissionable material is the amount needed to provide a high enough internal neutron flux to sustain the chain reaction (enough neutrons are produced to cause the continuous fission of further material). A sample with less than a critical mass is still radioactive, but cannot sustain a chain reaction.

55. The *moderator* in a uranium fission reactor surrounds the fuel rods and slows down the neutrons produced by the uranium decay process so that they can be absorbed more easily by other uranium atoms. The *control*

rods are constructed of substances that absorb neutrons, and can be inserted into the reactor core to control the power level of the reactor. The *containment* of a reactor refers to the building in which the reactor core is located, which is designed to contain the radioactive core in the event of a nuclear accident. A *cooling liquid* (usually water) is circulated through the reactor to draw off the heat energy produced by the nuclear reaction, so that this heat energy can be converted to electrical energy in the power plant's turbines.

56.   An actual nuclear explosion, of the type produced by a nuclear weapon, cannot occur in a nuclear reactor because the concentration of the fissionable materials is not sufficient to form a supercritical mass. However, since many reactors are cooled by water, which can decompose into hydrogen and oxygen gases, a *chemical* explosion is possible which could scatter the radioactive material used in the reactor.

57.   If the system used to cool a reactor core fails, the reactor may reach temperatures high enough to melt the core itself. In a scenario referred to as the "China Syndrome," the molten reactor core could become hot enough so as to melt through the bottom of the reactor building and into the earth itself (eventually the molten material would reach cool ground water and resolidify, with possible release of radioactivity). If water is used to cool the reactor core, and the cooling system becomes blocked, it is possible for the heat from the reactor to cause a steam explosion (which would also release radioactivity), or to break down the coolant water into hydrogen gas (which could also explode).

58.
$$^{238}_{92}U + ^{1}_{0}n \rightarrow ^{239}_{92}U$$

$$^{239}_{92}U \rightarrow ^{239}_{93}Np + ^{0}_{-1}e$$

$$^{239}_{93}Np \rightarrow ^{239}_{94}Pu + ^{0}_{-1}e$$

59.   Nuclear *fusion* is the process of combining two light nuclei into a larger nucleus, with an energy release larger even than that provided by fission processes.

60.   In one type of fusion reactor, two $^{2}_{1}H$ atoms are fused to produce $^{4}_{2}He$. Because the hydrogen nuclei are positively charged, extremely high energies (temperatures of 40 million K) are needed to overcome the repulsion between the nuclei as they are shot into each other.

61.   Fusion produces an enormous amount of energy per gram of fused material. If it is hydrogen that is to be fused, the earth possesses an enormous supply of the needed raw materials in the oceans; the product nuclei from the fusion of hydrogen (helium isotopes) are far less dangerous than those produced by fission processes.

62.   In the theory of stellar nucleosynthesis, it is considered that the nucleus began as a cloud of neutrons which exploded (the Big Bang). After this initial explosion, neutrons were thought to have decomposed into protons and electrons

$$_0^1n \rightarrow _{.1}^1H + _{-1}^0e$$

The products of this decomposition were then thought to have combined to form large clouds of hydrogen atoms. As the hydrogen clouds became larger, gravitational forces caused these clouds to contract and heat up. Eventually the clouds of hydrogen were so dense and so hot that fusion of hydrogen nuclei into helium nuclei took place, with a great release of energy. When the tendency for the hydrogen clouds to expand from the heat of fusion was counter-balanced by the gravitational forces of the cloud, a small star had formed. In addition to the fusion of hydrogen nuclei into helium mentioned already, as the star's hydrogen supply is exhausted, the helium present in the star also begins to undergo fusion into nuclei of other elements.

63.   Although the energy transferred per event to a living creature is small, the quantity of energy is enough to break chemical bonds which may cause malfunctioning of cellular systems. In particular, many biochemical processes are chain-like in nature, and the production of a single odd ion in a cell by a radioactive event may have a cumulative effect. For example, ionization of a single bond in a sex cell may cause a drastic mutation in the creature resulting.

64.   Somatic damage is damage directly to the organism itself, causing nearly immediate sickness or death to the organism. Genetic damage is damage to the genetic machinery of the organism, which will be manifested in future generations of offspring.

65.   Alpha particles are stopped by the outermost layers of skin; beta particles penetrate only about 1 cm into the body; gamma rays are deeply penetrating.

66.   Gamma rays penetrate long distances, but seldom cause ionization of biological molecules. Alpha particles, because they are much heavier although less penetrating, are very effective at ionizing biological molecules and leave a dense trail of damage in the organism. Isotopes which release alpha particles can be ingested or breathed into the body where the damage from the alpha particles will be more acute.

67.   Nuclei of atoms that are chemically inert, or which are not ordinarily found in the body, tend to be excreted from the body quickly and do little damage. Other nuclei of atoms which form a part of the body's structure or normal metabolic processes are likely to be incorporated into the body. When a radioactive nuclide is ingested into the body, its capacity to cause damage also depends on how long it remains in the body. If the nuclide has been incorporated into the body, the danger is greatest.

68.   The exposure limits given in Table 18.5 as causing no detectable clinical effect are 0-25 rem. The total yearly exposures from natural and human-induced radioactive sources are estimated in Table 18.6 as less than 200 *milli*rem (0.2 rem), which is well within the acceptable limits.

69.   atomic number

70.   radioactive

71.   electron

72.   mass

73.   alpha

74.   neutron; proton

75.   gamma (γ)

76.   radioactive decay

77.   higher

78.   mass number

79.   particle accelerators

80.   transuranium

81.   Geiger

82.   half-life

83. $^{14}_{6}$C (carbon-14)

84.   radiotracers

85.   fusion

86.   chain

87. $^{235}_{92}$U

88.   breeder

89.   The decay series, in order from the top right of the diagram, is: alpha, beta, beta, alpha, alpha, alpha, alpha, alpha, beta, beta, alpha, beta, beta, alpha. This decay is indicated in color in the figure.

90. 4.5×10^9 dollars ($4.5 billion)

91. a.   cobalt is a component of Vitamin B-12

     b.   bones consist partly of $Ca_3(PO_4)_2$

     c.   red blood cells contain hemoglobin, an iron-protein compound

     d.   mercury is absorbed by substances in the brain (this is part of the reason mercury is so hazardous in the environment)

92. 3.5×10^{-11} J/atom; 8.9×10^{10} J/g

93. In order to sustain a nuclear chain reaction, the neutrons produced by the fission must be contained within the fissionable material, so that they can go on to cause other fissions. In order that the neutrons are contained, the fissionable material must be closely enough packed together that it is more likely for a neutron to encounter a fissionable nucleus than to be lost to the outside.

94. Despite the fact that nuclear waste has been generated for over 40 years, no permanent disposal plan has been implemented as yet. One proposal to dispose of such waste calls for the waste to be sealed in blocks of glass, which in turn are sealed in corrosion-proof metal drums, which would then be buried in deep, stable rock formations away from earthquake and other geologically active zones. In these deep storage areas, it is hoped that the waste could decay safely undisturbed until the radioactivity drops to "safe" levels.

95. $^{64}_{30}$Zn (30 protons, 34 neutrons)

     $^{66}_{30}$Zn (30 protons, 36 neutrons)

     $^{67}_{30}$Zn (30 protons, 37 neutrons)

     $^{68}_{30}$Zn (30 protons, 38 neutrons)

     $^{70}_{30}$Zn (30 protons, 40 neutrons)

96. $^{27}_{13}$Al: 13 protons, 14 neutrons

     $^{28}_{13}$Al: 13 protons, 15 neutrons

     $^{29}_{13}$Al: 13 protons, 16 neutrons

97.   a. ^4_2He

      b. ^4_2He

      c. ^1_0n

98.   a. $^0_{-1}e$

      b. $^{74}_{34}Se$

      c. $^{240}_{92}U$

99. $^{14}_7N + ^4_2He \rightarrow ^{17}_8O + ^1_1H$

100. For a decay of 10 μg to 1/1000 of this amount, we want to know when the amount of remaining ^{131}I is on the order of 0.01 μg.

time, days	0	8	16	24	32	40
mass, μg	10	5	2.5	1.25	0.625	0.313
time, days	48	56	64	72	80	
mass, μg	0.156	0.078	0.039	0.020	0.01	

Approximately 80 days are required.

101. ^{131}I is used in the diagnosis and treatment of thyroid cancer and other dysfunctions of the thyroid gland. The thyroid gland is the only place in the human body which uses and stores iodine. I-131 that is administered concentrates in the thyroid, and can be used to cause an image on a scanner or x-ray film, or in higher doses, to selectively kill cancer cells in the thyroid. ^{201}Tl concentrates in healthy muscle cells when administered, and can be used to detect and assess damage to heart muscles after a heart attack: the damaged muscles show a lower uptake of Tl-201 than normal muscles.

102. Breeder reactors are set up to convert non-fissionable ^{238}U into fissionable ^{239}Pu. The material used for fission in a breeder reactor is a combination of U-235 (which undergoes fission in a chain reaction) and the more common U-238 isotope. Excess neutrons from the U-235 fission are absorbed by the U-238 converting it to the fissionable plutonium isotope Pu-239. Although Pu-239 is fissionable, its chemical and physical properties make it very difficult and expensive to handle and process.

Chapter 19   Organic Chemistry

1. Carbon has the unusual ability of bonding strongly to itself, forming long chains or rings of carbon atoms. Since there are many different possible arrangements for a long chain of carbon atoms, there exists a great multitude of possible carbon compounds.

2. A given carbon atom can be attached to a maximum of four other atoms. Carbon atoms have four valence electrons. By making four bonds, carbon atoms exactly complete their valence octet.

3. A double bond represents the sharing of an extra pair of electrons between two bonded atoms. Two examples are

```
    H H              H H H
    | |              | | |
    C=C     and      C=C-C-H
    | |              |   |
    H H              H   H
```

4. A triple bond represents the sharing of *six* electrons (three *pairs* of electrons). The simplest example of an organic molecule containing a triple bond is acetylene, H:C:::C:H (H-C≡C-H).

5. When a carbon atom is bonded to four other atoms, the electron pairs of the carbon atom will be arranged with the tetrahedral configuration. This represents the electron pairs being as far away from each other as possible, separated by the tetrahedral angle of 109.5°.

6. Each carbon atom in ethane is bonded to *four* other atoms. According to VSEPR theory, each carbon atom has its electron pairs arranged *tetrahedrally*.

7. A saturated hydrocarbon is one in which all the carbon-carbon bonds are single bonds, with each carbon atom forming bonds to four other atoms. The saturated hydrocarbons are called alkanes.

8. An unsaturated hydrocarbon is one that contains an area of multiple bonding between some of the carbon atoms. Such a hydrocarbon is called "unsaturated" because each carbon atom of the multiple bond could bond to additional atoms (rather than to each other). Such unsaturated hydrocarbons undergo addition reactions in which atoms or groups from an outside reagent become bonded to the carbon atoms of the multiple bond, producing a saturated compound. The structural features that characterize unsaturated hydrocarbons are the carbon-carbon double bond or triple bond.

9. A "straight-chain" alkane is not really straight because the electron pairs on the carbon atoms have a *tetrahedral* orientation, separated by an angle of 109.5°. In order to give a truly straight chain, the angle between electron pairs would have to be 90° and multiples of 90°.

10. Each successive member of this family differs from the previous member by a $-CH_2-$ unit (which is sometimes called a "methylene" unit). Such a family of compounds is sometimes referred to as a *homologous series*.

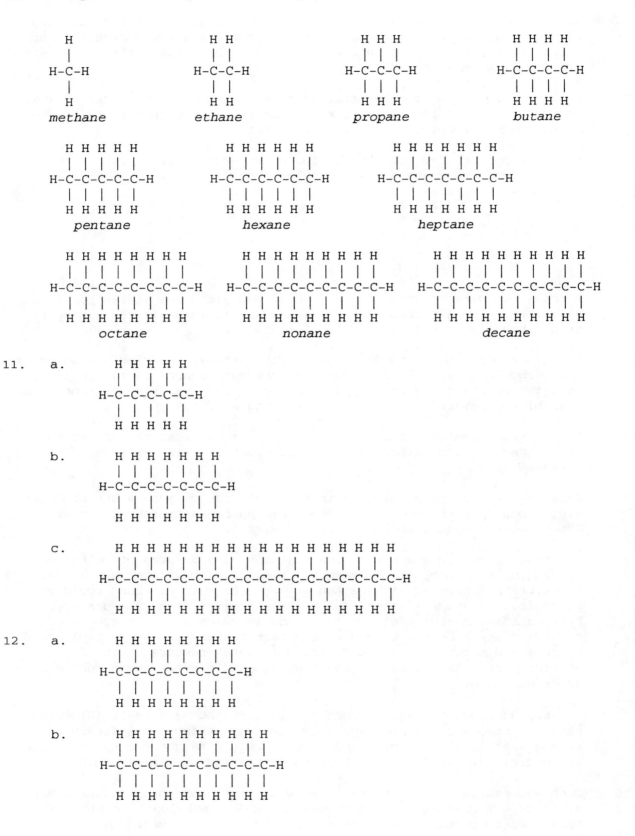

```
      H
      |
   H-C-H
      |
      H
   methane
```

```
    H H
    | |
  H-C-C-H
    | |
    H H
   ethane
```

```
   H H H
   | | |
 H-C-C-C-H
   | | |
   H H H
  propane
```

```
  H H H H
  | | | |
H-C-C-C-C-H
  | | | |
  H H H H
  butane
```

```
   H H H H H
   | | | | |
 H-C-C-C-C-C-H
   | | | | |
   H H H H H
    pentane
```

```
   H H H H H H
   | | | | | |
 H-C-C-C-C-C-C-H
   | | | | | |
   H H H H H H
     hexane
```

```
   H H H H H H H
   | | | | | | |
 H-C-C-C-C-C-C-C-H
   | | | | | | |
   H H H H H H H
      heptane
```

```
   H H H H H H H H
   | | | | | | | |
 H-C-C-C-C-C-C-C-C-H
   | | | | | | | |
   H H H H H H H H
       octane
```

```
   H H H H H H H H H
   | | | | | | | | |
 H-C-C-C-C-C-C-C-C-C-H
   | | | | | | | | |
   H H H H H H H H H
       nonane
```

```
   H H H H H H H H H H
   | | | | | | | | | |
 H-C-C-C-C-C-C-C-C-C-C-H
   | | | | | | | | | |
   H H H H H H H H H H
        decane
```

11. a.
```
      H H H H H
      | | | | |
    H-C-C-C-C-C-H
      | | | | |
      H H H H H
```

b.
```
      H H H H H H H
      | | | | | | |
    H-C-C-C-C-C-C-C-H
      | | | | | | |
      H H H H H H H
```

c.
```
      H H H H H H H H H H H H H H H H H H H
      | | | | | | | | | | | | | | | | | | |
    H-C-C-C-C-C-C-C-C-C-C-C-C-C-C-C-C-C-C-C-H
      | | | | | | | | | | | | | | | | | | |
      H H H H H H H H H H H H H H H H H H H
```

12. a.
```
      H H H H H H H H
      | | | | | | | |
    H-C-C-C-C-C-C-C-C-H
      | | | | | | | |
      H H H H H H H H
```

b.
```
      H H H H H H H H H H
      | | | | | | | | | |
    H-C-C-C-C-C-C-C-C-C-C-H
      | | | | | | | | | |
      H H H H H H H H H H
```

c.
```
    H H H H H H H H H H H H
    | | | | | | | | | | | |
H-C-C-C-C-C-C-C-C-C-C-C-C-H
    | | | | | | | | | | | |
    H H H H H H H H H H H H
```

13. a.
```
    H H H H H H H
    | | | | | | |
H-C-C-C-C-C-C-C-H
    | | | | | | |
    H H H H H H H
```

heptane $CH_3CH_2CH_2CH_2CH_2CH_2CH_3$

b.
```
    H H H H H H H H H
    | | | | | | | | |
H-C-C-C-C-C-C-C-C-C-H
    | | | | | | | | |
    H H H H H H H H H
```

nonane $CH_3CH_2CH_2CH_2CH_2CH_2CH_2CH_2CH_3$

c.
```
    H H H
    | | |
H-C-C-C-H
    | | |
    H H H
```

propane $CH_3CH_2CH_3$

d.
```
    H H H H H H H H H H
    | | | | | | | | | |
H-C-C-C-C-C-C-C-C-C-C-H
    | | | | | | | | | |
    H H H H H H H H H H
```

decane $CH_3CH_2CH_2CH_2CH_2CH_2CH_2CH_2CH_2CH_3$

14. a.
```
    H H H H
    | | | |
H-C-C-C-C-H
    | | | |
    H H H H
```

butane $CH_3CH_2CH_2CH_3$

b.
```
     H H H H H H H H
     | | | | | | | |
   H-C-C-C-C-C-C-C-H
     | | | | | | | |
     H H H H H H H H
```

octane $CH_3CH_2CH_2CH_2CH_2CH_2CH_2CH_3$

c.
```
     H H H H H
     | | | | |
   H-C-C-C-C-C-H
     | | | | |
     H H H H H
```

pentane $CH_3CH_2CH_2CH_2CH_3$

d.
```
     H H H H H H
     | | | | | |
   H-C-C-C-C-C-C-H
     | | | | | |
     H H H H H H
```

hexane $CH_3CH_2CH_2CH_2CH_2CH_3$

15.   Structural isomerism occurs when two molecules have the same atoms present, but those atoms are bonded differently. The molecules have the same formulas but different arrangements of the atoms. The alkane butane is the first alkane to have an isomer:

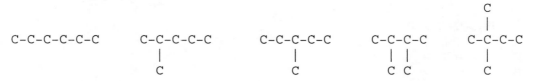

$CH_3CH_2CH_2CH_3$

butane

$$CH_3$$
$$|$$
$$CH_3CHCH_3$$

2-methylpropane

16.   branch or substituent

17.   With six carbon atoms, there are five isomers possible. Here are the carbon skeletons:

```
                                                                        C
                                                                        |
C-C-C-C-C-C     C-C-C-C-C     C-C-C-C-C     C-C-C-C     C-C-C-C
                    |             |           | |           |
                    C             C           C C           C
```

18.   With eight carbon atoms, there are a *lot* of isomers possible. Here are carbon skeletons for some of them:

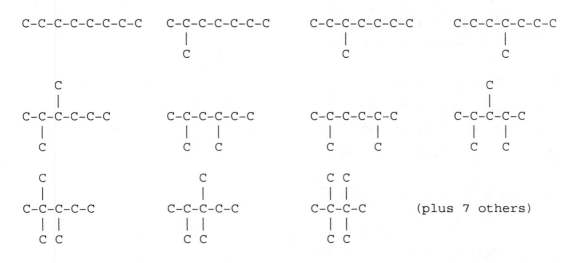

19.   *Number of carbons*   *root name*

5   pentane (*pent-*)

6   hexane (*hex-*)

7   heptane (*hept-*)

8   octane (*oct-*)

9   nonane (*non-*)

10   decane (*dec-*)

20.   The root name is derived from the number of carbon atoms in the *longest continuous chain* of carbon atoms.

21.   An alkyl group represents a hydrocarbon *branch* occurring along the principal carbon atom chain of an organic molecule. An alkyl group has one fewer hydrogen atom than the corresponding alkane with the same carbon atom skeleton.

22.   The position of a substituent is indicated by a number which corresponds to the carbon atom in the longest chain to which the substituent is attached.

23.   If multiple substituents of the same type occur in an organic molecule, the total number of such substituents is indicated by a prefix before the name of the substituent [*di-* (2), *tri-* (3), *tetra-* (4), etc.]

24.   Multiple substituents are listed in alphabetical order, disregarding any prefix.

25.   a.   3-methylheptane (look for the *longest* carbon chain)

   b.   2,3-dimethylbutane

   c.   2,3-dimethylbutane (compare to part b above)

   d.   2,3,4-trimethylheptane

26.   a.   3-ethylpentane

   b.   2,2-dimethylbutane

   c.   2,2-dimethylpropane

   d.   2,3,4-trimethylpentane

27.   a. 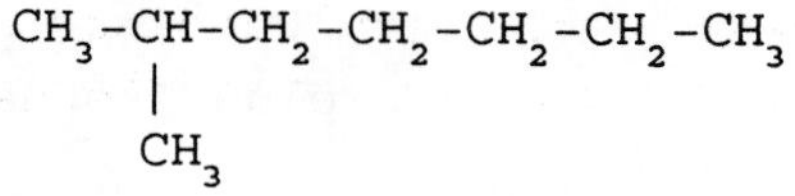 $CH_3-CH-CH_2-CH_2-CH_2-CH_2-CH_3$
                    |
                    CH_3

   b. 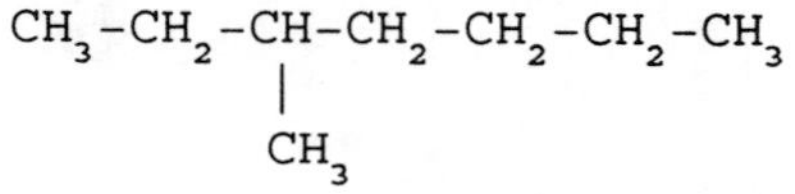 $CH_3-CH_2-CH-CH_2-CH_2-CH_2-CH_3$
                        |
                        CH_3

   c. 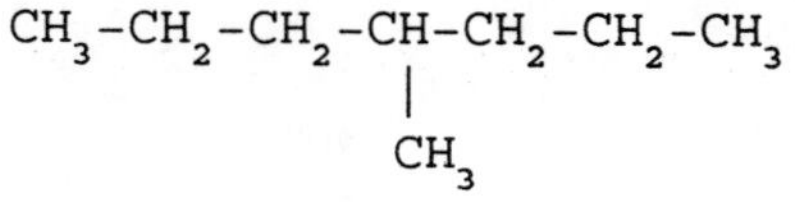 $CH_3-CH_2-CH_2-CH-CH_2-CH_2-CH_3$
                            |
                            CH_3

   d. 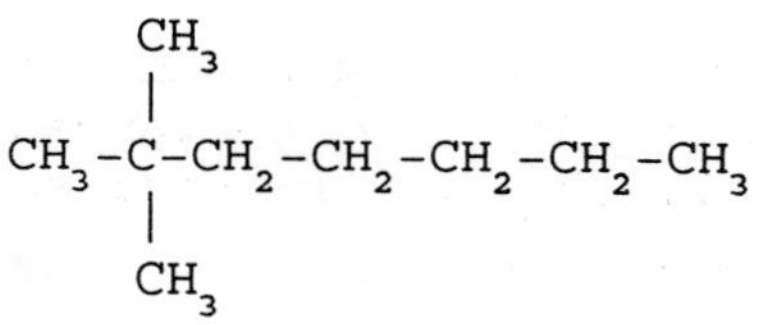 $\begin{array}{c} CH_3 \\ | \\ CH_3-C-CH_2-CH_2-CH_2-CH_2-CH_3 \\ | \\ CH_3 \end{array}$

   e. 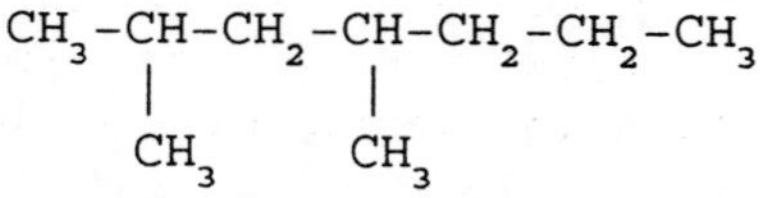 $CH_3-CH-CH_2-CH-CH_2-CH_2-CH_3$
                    | |
                    CH_3 CH_3

28.   a. 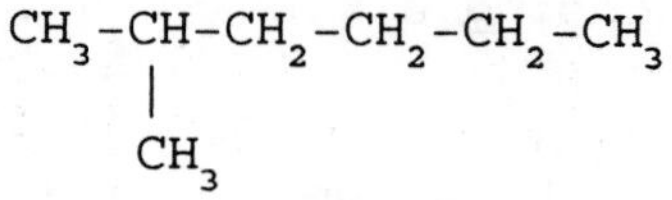 $CH_3-CH-CH_2-CH_2-CH_2-CH_3$
                    |
                    CH_3

   b. 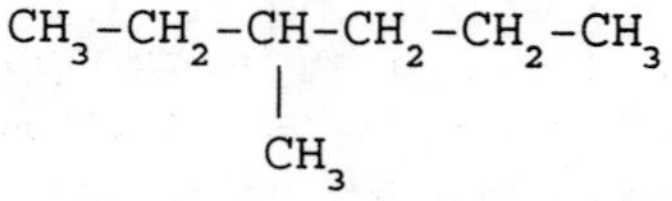 $CH_3-CH_2-CH-CH_2-CH_2-CH_3$
                        |
                        CH_3

   c. 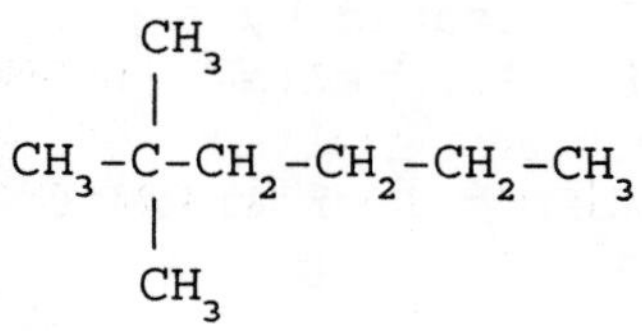 $\begin{array}{c} CH_3 \\ | \\ CH_3-C-CH_2-CH_2-CH_2-CH_3 \\ | \\ CH_3 \end{array}$

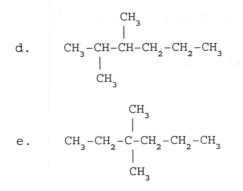

d.

e.

29.   Petroleum is a thick, dark liquid composed largely of hydrocarbons
        containing from 5 to more than 25 carbon atoms. Natural gas consists
        mostly of methane, but also may contain significant amounts of ethane,
        propane, and butane. These substances were formed over the eons from the
        decay of living organisms.

30.

Number of C atoms	*Use*
C_5-C_{12}	gasoline
C_{10}-C_{18}	kerosene, jet fuel
C_{15}-C_{25}	diesel fuel, heating oil, lubrication
C_{25}-	asphalt

31.   In the pyrolytic cracking of petroleum, the more abundant kerosene
        fraction of petroleum is heated to about 700°C, which causes the large
        molecules of the kerosene fraction to break into the smaller molecules
        characteristic of the gasoline fraction.

32.   Tetraethyl lead was added to gasolines to prevent "knocking" of high
        efficiency automobile engines. The use of tetraethyl lead is being
        phased out because of the danger to the environment of the lead in this
        substance.

33.   Alkanes are relatively unreactive because the C–C and C–H bonds that
        characterize these substances are relatively strong and difficult to
        break.

34.   Combustion represents the vigorous reaction of a hydrocarbon (or other
        substance) with oxygen. The combustion of alkanes has been made use of
        as a source of heat, light, and mechanical energy.

35.   In a substitution reaction, one or more of the hydrogen atoms of an
        alkane is *replaced* by another type of atom. Because of the unreactivity
        of alkanes, only very vigorous reactants (such as the halogens) are able
        to substitute for the hydrogen atoms of alkanes.

36.   Dehydrogenation reactions involve the removal of hydrogen atoms from
        adjacent carbon atoms in an alkane (or other substance). When two

hydrogen atoms are removed from an alkane or related compound, a double bond is created.

37.   a. $C_3H_8(g) + 5O_2(g) \rightarrow 3CO_2(g) + 4H_2O(g)$

      b. $C_5H_{12}(l) + 8O_2(g) \rightarrow 5CO_2(g) + 6H_2O(g)$

      c. $C_7H_{16}(l) + 11O_2(g) \rightarrow 7CO_2(g) + 8H_2O(g)$

38.   a. $2C_6H_{14}(l) + 19O_2(g) \rightarrow 12CO_2(g) + 14H_2O(g)$

      b. $CH_4(g) + Cl_2(g) \rightarrow CH_3Cl(l) + HCl(g)$

      c. $CHCl_3(l) + Cl_2(g) \rightarrow CCl_4(l) + HCl(g)$

39.   Alkenes are hydrocarbons which contain a carbon-carbon double bond.

      The general formula for alkenes is C_nH_{2n} where *n* is the number of carbon atoms present.

40.   An alkyne is a hydrocarbon containing a carbon-carbon triple bond. The general formula is C_nH_{2n-2}.

41.   To show that a hydrocarbon contains a double bond, the ending of the name of the corresponding alkane is changed to -*ene*. To show that a triple bond is present, the ending -*yne* is used.

42.   The location of a double or triple bond in the longest chain of an alkene or alkyne is indicated by giving the *number* of the lowest number carbon atom involved in the double or triple bond.

43.   a. $CH{\equiv}C{-}CH_3(g) + 2H_2(g) \rightarrow CH_3{-}CH_2{-}CH_3(g)$

      b. $CH_3{-}CH{=}CH{-}CH_3(l) + Br_2(l) \rightarrow CH_3{-}CH{-}CH{-}CH_3(l)$
                                                            | |
                                                            Br Br

      c. $2CH_3{-}C{\equiv}C{-}CH_3(l) + 11O_2(g) \rightarrow 8CO_2(g) + 6H_2O(g)$

44.   hydrogenation

45.   a.   2-butene

      b.   3-methyl-1-butene

      c.   1-butyne

      d.   3-chloro-1-butene

46. a.   1-butyne

     b.   3-methyl-1-butyne

     c.   3-heptyne

47. The most obvious choices would be the *normal* alkenes with seven carbon atoms:

$CH_2=CH-CH_2-CH_2-CH_2-CH_2-CH_3$ 1-heptene

$CH_3-CH=CH-CH_2-CH_2-CH_2-CH_3$ 2-heptene

$CH_3-CH_2-CH=CH-CH_2-CH_2-CH_3$ 3-heptene

Additional choices are shorter-chain alkenes with branches, such as

$CH_2=C-CH_2-CH_2-CH_2-CH_3$ $CH_3-C=CH-CH_2-CH_2-CH_3$
    | |
    CH_3 CH_3

2-methyl-1-hexene   2-methyl-2-hexene

48. Shown are carbon skeletons:

$C≡C-C-C-C-C$ $C-C≡C-C-C-C$ $C-C-C≡C-C-C$ $C≡C-C-C-C$
                                                            | |
                                                            C   C

$C-C≡C-C-C$ $C≡C-C-C-C$ $C≡C-C-C$
        | | |
        C   C   C

49. Aromatic hydrocarbons have in common the presence of the *benzene ring* (phenyl group)

50. For benzene, a *set* of equivalent Lewis structures can be drawn, differing only in the *location* of the three double bonds in the ring. Experimentally, however, benzene does not demonstrate the chemical properties expected for molecules having *any* double bonds. We say that the "extra" electrons that would go into making the second bond of the three double bonds are delocalized around the entire benzene ring: this delocalization of the electrons explains benzene's unique properties.

51. The systematic method for naming monosubstituted benzenes uses the substituent name as a *prefix* for the word benzene. Examples are

chlorobenzene

ethylbenzene

Two monosubstituted benzenes with their own special names are

toluene (methylbenzene)

phenol (hydroxybenzene)

52. When named as a substituent, the benzene ring is called the *phenyl* group. Two examples are

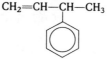

3-phenyl-1-butene

2-phenylhexane

53. For benzene rings with more than one substituent, *locator numbers* are used to indicate the position of the substituents around the ring. For this purpose, one of the carbon atoms holding a substituent is chosen to be carbon number-1, and the location of the other substituents is indicated relative to carbon number-1 (counting in the direction that leads to the smallest possible locator numbers).

54. *ortho-* refers to adjacent substituents (1,2-); *meta-* refers to two substituents with one unsubstituted carbon atom between them (1,3-); *para-* refers to two substituents with two unsubstituted carbon atoms between them (1,4-).

55. a.

b.

c.

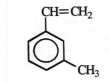

d.

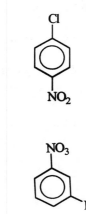

e.

56. a.   1,2-dimethylbenzene (*o*-xylene is its common name)

b.   1,2,3,4,5,6-hexachlorobenzene

c.   anthracene

d.   3,5-dichloro-1-methylbenzene (3,5-dichlorotoluene is another name)

57. a.   alchohol (primary)

b.   ketone

c.   amine

d.   aldehyde

58. a.   ether

b.   alcohol

    c.   alcohol

    d.   organic (carboxylic) acid

59.   Alcohols are characterized by the presence of the hydroxyl group, –OH. To name an alcohol, the final *-e* is dropped from the name of the parent hydrocarbon, and the ending *ol* is added. A locator number may also be necessary to indicate the location of the hydroxyl group.

60.   Primary alcohols have *one* hydrocarbon fragment (alkyl group) bonded to the carbon atom where the –OH group is attached. Secondary alcohols have *two* such alkyl groups attached, and tertiary alcohols contain *three* such alkyl groups. Examples are

ethanol (primary) CH_3-CH_2-OH

2-propanol (secondary) $CH_3-CH-CH_3$
$$\qquad\qquad\qquad\qquad\qquad\quad |$$
$$\qquad\qquad\qquad\qquad\qquad\ OH$$

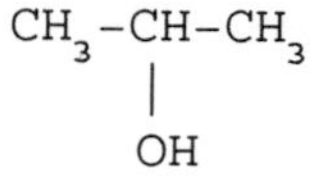

$$\qquad\qquad\qquad\qquad\qquad\quad CH_3$$
$$\qquad\qquad\qquad\qquad\qquad\quad\ |$$
2-methyl-2-propanol (tertiary) CH_3-C-CH_3
$$\qquad\qquad\qquad\qquad\qquad\quad\ |$$
$$\qquad\qquad\qquad\qquad\qquad\ OH$$

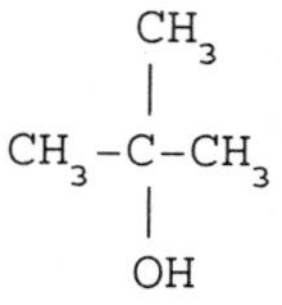

61.   a.   1-pentanol (primary)

        b.   2-methyl-2-butanol (tertiary)

        c.   3-pentanol (secondary)

        d.   1-propanol (primary)

62.   a. $CH_3-CH_2-CH_2-CH_2-CH_2-OH$ primary

        b. $CH_3-CH-CH_2-CH_2-CH_3$ secondary
$$\qquad\qquad\quad |$$
$$\qquad\qquad\ OH$$

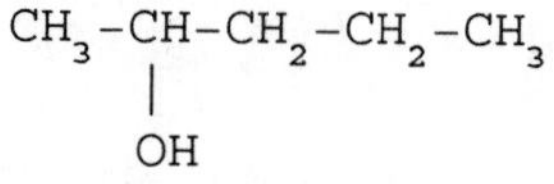

        c. $CH_3-CH_2-CH-CH_2-CH_3$ secondary
$$\qquad\qquad\qquad\quad |$$
$$\qquad\qquad\qquad\ OH$$

$$\qquad\qquad\qquad OH$$
$$\qquad\qquad\qquad |$$
        d. $CH_2-CH_2-C-CH_2-CH_3$ tertiary
$$\qquad\qquad\qquad\quad |$$
$$\qquad\qquad\qquad\ CH_3$$

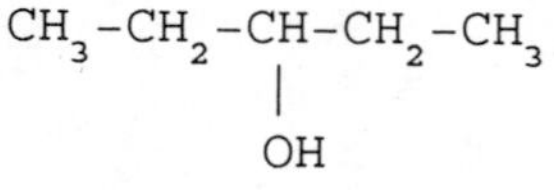

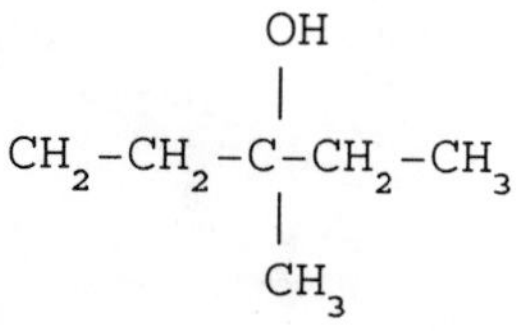

63. Methanol is sometimes called "wood" alcohol, because it formerly was obtained by the heating of wood in the absence of air (this process was called destructive distillation of wood). Currently methanol is most commonly prepared by the catalyzed hydrogenation of carbon monoxide

$$CO(g) + 2H_2(g) \rightarrow CH_3OH(g)$$

Methanol is an important industrial chemical produced in large amounts every year. It is used as a starting material for the synthesis of acetic acid (CH_3COOH) and of many other important substances. Use has also been made of methanol as a motor fuel for high-performance engines.

64. $C_6H_{12}O_6$ –yeast→ $2CH_3-CH_2-OH + 2CO_2$

The yeast necessary for the fermentation process are killed if the concentration of ethanol is over 13%. More concentrated ethanol solutions are most commonly made by distillation.

65. Although much ethanol is produced each year by means of the fermentation process, ethanol is also produced synthetically by hydration of ethene (ethylene)

$$CH_2=CH_2 + H_2O \rightarrow CH_3-CH_2OH$$

Ethanol is used in industry as a solvent and as a starting material for the synthesis of more complicated molecules. Mixtures of ethanol and gasoline are used as automobile motor fuels (gasohol).

66. methanol (CH_3OH) - starting material for synthesis of acetic acid and many plastics

ethylene glycol (CH_2OH-CH_2OH) - automobile antifreeze

isopropyl alcohol (2-propanol, $CH_3-CH(OH)-CH_3$) - rubbing alcohol

67. Aldehydes and ketones both contain the *carbonyl* functional group

68. Aldehydes and ketones both contain the carbonyl group $\diagdown$C=O.

Aldehydes and ketones differ in the *location* of the carbonyl function: aldehydes contain the carbonyl group at the end of a hydrocarbon chain (the carbon atom of the carbonyl group is bonded only to at most one other carbon atom); the carbonyl group of ketones represents one of the interior carbon atoms of a chain (the carbon atom of the carbonyl group is bonded to two other carbon atoms).

69.   The simplest aldehyde, methanal (formaldehyde), is used as a tissue
       preservative. Several important aldehydes are used as artificial
       flavorings and aromas (benzaldehyde, cinnamaldehyde, vanillin). The most
       common ketone is propanone (acetone) which is used in great quantity as
       a solvent; acetone can be a product of metabolism in persons with
       certain diseases (e.g., diabetes). Butanone (methyl ethyl ketone) is
       another ketone that is used frequently as a solvent.

70.   Aldehydes and ketones are produced by the oxidation of primary and
       secondary alcohols, respectively.

       CH_3-CH_2-OH ---oxidation--→ $CH_3-C=O$
       $\qquad\qquad\qquad\qquad\qquad\qquad\qquad |$
       $\qquad\qquad\qquad\qquad\qquad\qquad\qquad H$

       $CH_3-CH-OH$ ---oxidation--→ $CH_3-C=O$
       $\qquad\quad |$
       $\qquad\quad CH_3 \qquad\qquad\qquad\qquad\qquad CH_3$

71.   To name an aldehyde, the final -e of the parent hydrocarbon is dropped,
       and the ending -al is added. No locator number is needed to locate the
       carbonyl group in aldehydes because the carbonyl carbon is always
       assumed to be carbon number-1 of the chain. The ending -*one* is used to
       show that a molecule is a ketone. A locator number is needed to locate
       the carbonyl group in ketones with 5 or more carbons in the principal
       carbon atom chain.

72.   In addition to their systematic names (based on the hydrocarbon root,
       with the ending -*one*), ketones can also be named by naming the groups
       attached to either side of the carbonyl carbon as alkyl groups, followed
       by the word "ketone". Examples are

       $CH_3-C(=O)-CH_2CH_3$ methyl ethyl ketone (2-butanone, butanone)
       $CH_3CH_2-C(=O)-CH_2CH_3$ diethyl ketone (3-pentanone)

73.   a.   3-hexanone   (ethyl propyl ketone)

       b.   2,3-dichlorobutanal   (2,3-dichlorobutyraldehyde)

       c.   3,4-dimethylpentanal

       d.   2-methylpropanal

       e.   ethyl phenyl ketone

74.   a. $CH_3-C-\phi$ [ϕ represents the phenyl group (benzene ring)]
             $\qquad\ \|$
             $\qquad\ O$

       b. $CH_3-CH_2-CH_2-C=O$
             $\qquad\qquad\qquad\qquad |$
             $\qquad\qquad\qquad\qquad H$

c.   CH$_3$–CH$_2$–C–CH$_3$
                    ‖
                    O

d.   CH$_3$–CH$_2$–CH$_2$–C–CH$_2$–CH$_2$–CH$_3$
                            ‖
                            O

e.   CH$_3$–CH$_2$–CH$_2$–C–CH$_2$–CH$_2$–CH$_3$ (same molecule as above)
                            ‖
                            O

75.   Organic (carboxylic) acids contain the carboxyl group, –COOH

        –C=O
         |
         OH

The general formula for organic acids is usually indicated in print as RCOOH, where R represents the hydrocarbon fragment.

76.   Carboxylic acids are typically *weak* acids.

CH$_3$–CH$_2$–COOH(aq) ⇌ H$^+$$(aq)$ + CH$_3$–CH$_2$–COO$^-$$(aq)$

77.   To name an organic acid, the final -*e* of the name of the parent hydrocarbon is dropped, and the ending -*oic acid* is added. For example, the organic acid CH$_3$CH$_2$COOH contains three carbon atoms, and is considered as if it were derived from propane, with the name as propan*oic acid*.

78.   a.   CH$_2$–CH$_2$–COOH

       b.   CH$_3$–CH$_2$–C–CH$_3$
                          ‖
                          O

       c.   no reaction (tertiary alcohols are not oxidized in this manner)

79.   Esters are synthesized by the reaction of organic acids with alcohols,

        RCOOH + R´OH → RCOOR´ + H$_2$O

The general structural formula showing the linkage in esters is

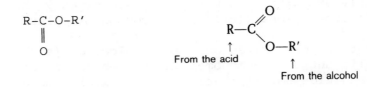

R–C–O–R´
    ‖
    O

80.   Acetylsalicylic acid is synthesized from salicylic acid (behaving as an alcohol through its -OH group) and acetic acid.

81.   a.   3-methylbutanoic acid

      b.   benzoic acid

      c.   2-hydroxypropanoic acid

      d.   3,4-dimethylhexanoic acid

82.   a.   CH$_3$-CH$_2$-CH-CH$_2$-C=O
                            | |
                           CH$_3$ OH

      b.   H-C-O-CH$_2$-CH$_3$
                ‖
                O

      c.   φ-C-O-CH$_3$ [φ represents the pheynyl group (benzene ring)]
              ‖
              O

      d.   CH$_3$-CH$_2$-CH-C=O
                        | |
                       Br OH

                      Cl   OH
                       | |
      e.   CH$_3$-CH$_2$-CH-CH-CH-C=O
                        | |
                       CH$_3$ CH$_3$

83.   Polymers are large, usually chain-like molecules, that are built up from smaller molecules. The smaller molecules may combine together and repeat in the chain of the polymer hundreds or thousands of time. The small molecules from which polymers are built up are called *monomers*.

84.   In addition polymerization, the monomer units simply add together to form the polymer, with no other products. Polyethylene and polytetrafluoroethylene (Teflon) are common examples.

85.   In condensation polymerization, small molecules (such as H$_2$O) are formed and are split out as the monomer units combine to form the polymer chain. In addition polymerization, monomer units merely "add together" to form a longer chain. The polymer Nylon-66 is an example of a condensation polymer.

86. A polyester is formed from the reaction of a dialcohol (two -OH groups) with a diacid (two -COOH groups). One -OH group of the alcohol forms an *ester linkage* with one of the -COOH groups of the acid. Since the resulting dimer still possesses an -OH and a -COOH group, the dimer can undergo further esterification reactions. Dacron is a common polyester.

87.

acrylonitrile

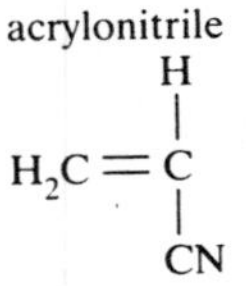

polyacrylnitrile (PAN) 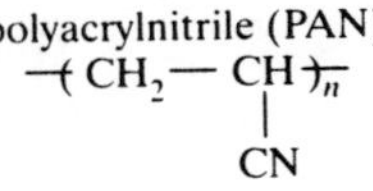   carpets, fabrics

butadiene

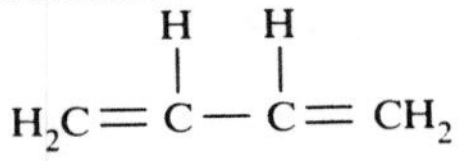

polybutadiene   tire tread, coating resin

88.

nylon   **dacron**

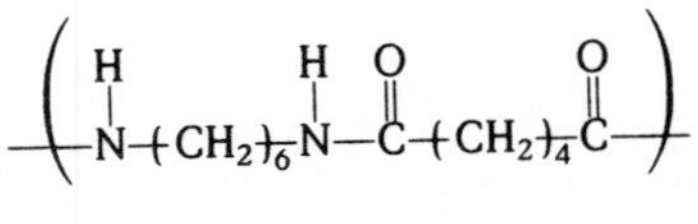

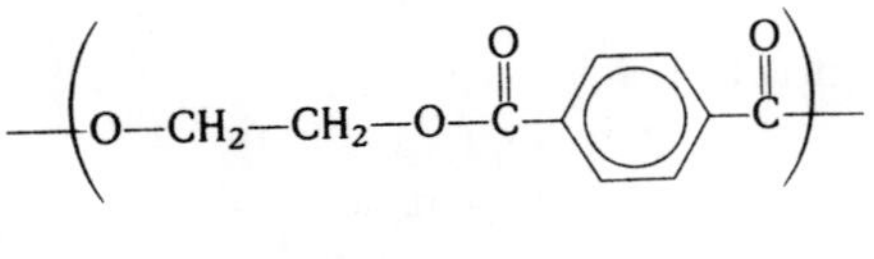

89. urea, ammonium cyanate

90. saturated

91. tetrahedral

92. straight-chain or normal

93. bonds

94. *-ane*

95. longest

96. number

97. pyrolytic cracking

98. anti-knocking

99. combustion

100. substitution

101. addition

102. hydrogenation

103. aromatic

104. functional

105. primary

106. carbon monoxide

107. fermentation

108. carbonyl

109. oxidation

110. carboxyl

111. esters, alcohol

112. addition

113. The general formula is C_nH_{2n+2}. Each succesive alkane differs from the previous or following alkane by CH_2 (sometimes called a methylene unit).

114. The carbon skeletons are

```
                                                    C
                                                    |
C-C-C-C-C         C-C-C-C              C-C-C
                       |                   |
                       C                   C
```

115. There is an extremely large number of isomers. Only a few are shown here, including the normal alkane, as well as a series of alkanes having 19 carbon atoms in the longest chain, with a single methyl group branch. Considering all the other possibilities for isomerism, the reader can perhaps understand why organic chemistry is sometimes considered a difficult subject!

```
C-C-C-C-C-C-C-C-C-C-C-C-C-C-C-C-C-C-C-C-C

C-C-C-C-C-C-C-C-C-C-C-C-C-C-C-C-C-C-C-C
    |
    C

C-C-C-C-C-C-C-C-C-C-C-C-C-C-C-C-C-C-C-C
      |
      C

C-C-C-C-C-C-C-C-C-C-C-C-C-C-C-C-C-C-C-C
        |
        C
```

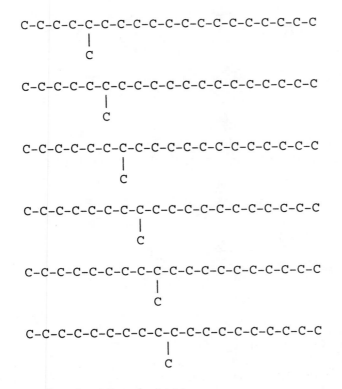

116. a.   2-chlorobutane

     b.   1,2-dibromoethane

     c.   triiodomethane (common name: iodoform)

     d.   2,3,4-trichloropentane

     e.   2,2-dichloro-4-isopropylheptane

117. Several examples of molecules containing two or more fused benzene rings are shown in Table 19.4 of the text.

118. a.
$$CH_3-CH-CH-CH_2-CH_2-CH_2-CH_3$$
with CH_3 on the second carbon and CH_3 on the third carbon

     b.
$$HO-CH_2-C--CH-CH_2-CH_2-CH_2-CH_2-CH_3$$
with CH_3 above, CH_3 and Cl below

     c.
$$CH_2=C-CH_2-CH_2-CH_2-CH_3$$
with Cl below

d. $CH_2-CH=CH-CH_2-CH_2-CH_3$
      $|$
      Cl

e. 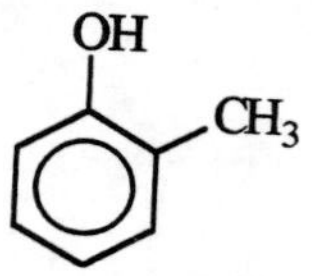
OH
      CH_3

119. a. CH_3-CH_2Cl, CH_2Cl-CH_2Cl, and various other chlorosubstituted ethanes.

b. $CH_3-CH_2-CH_2-CH_3$

c. CH_3-CH_2
                  $\backslash$
                      $CBr-CHBr-CH_3$
                  $/$
      CH_3-CH_2

120. primary $CH_3-CH_2-CH_2-CH_2-CH_2-CH_2-OH$

      secondary $CH_3-CH_2-CH_2-CH_2-CH-CH_3$
                                                $|$
                                                OH

      tertiary $CH_3-CH_2-\overset{CH_3}{\underset{OH}{C}}-CH_2-CH_3$

121. 1,2,3-trihydroxypropane (1,2,3-propanetriol)

122. $CH_2-CH-CH-CH-CH-C=O$
      $|$ $|$ $|$ $|$ $|$ $|$
      OH OH OH OH OH H

123. a. $CH_3-CH_2-CH_2-CH-\overset{H}{\underset{CH_3}{C}}=O$

b. $CH_3-CH-CH_2-COOH$
              $|$
              OH

c. $CH_3-CH-\overset{H}{\underset{NH_2}{C}}=O$

d.   CH$_3$-C-CH$_2$-C-CH$_2$-CH$_3$
        ‖   ‖
        O   O

e.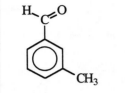

124. a.   CH$_3$-C-CH$_2$-CH$_2$-CH$_2$-CH$_2$-CH$_3$
           ‖
           O

b.   CH$_3$-CH$_2$-CH-CH$_2$-C=O
             | |
            CH$_3$ H

c.   CH$_3$-CH$_2$-CH$_2$-CH-CH$_2$-OH
                  |
                CH$_3$

           OH
           |
d.   CH$_2$-CH-CH$_2$
     | |
    OH   OH

         CH$_3$
         |
e.   CH$_3$-CH-C-CH$_2$-CH$_2$-CH$_3$
          ‖
          O

125. acetylsalicylic acid

methyl salicylate

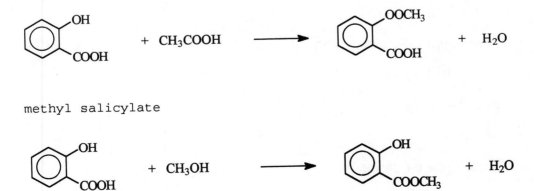

126.

$$
\begin{array}{l}
\text{HO}-\text{C}\!=\!\text{O} \\
\quad\;\; | \\
\text{CH}_3-\text{CH}-\text{N}-\!(\text{H} + \text{HO})\!-\text{C}\!=\!\text{O} \rightarrow \\
\qquad\qquad\; | \qquad\qquad\quad | \\
\qquad\qquad\; \text{H} \qquad\qquad\;\; \text{CH}_2-\text{NH}_2
\end{array}
$$

$$
\begin{array}{l}
\text{HO}-\text{C}\!=\!\text{O} \\
\quad\;\; | \\
\text{CH}_3-\text{CH}-\text{N}-\text{C}\!=\!\text{O} + \text{H}_2\text{O} \\
\qquad\qquad\; | \quad\;\; | \\
\qquad\qquad\; \text{H} \quad \text{CH}_2-\text{NH}_2
\end{array}
$$

One end has —NH$_2$, which can react with the —COOH end of another of these dipeptides.

127. a.

$$
\begin{array}{c}
\text{H H H H H H H} \\
| \;\; | \;\; | \;\; | \;\; | \;\; | \;\; | \\
\text{H}-\text{C}-\text{C}-\text{C}-\text{C}-\text{C}-\text{C}-\text{C}-\text{H} \\
| \;\; | \;\; | \;\; | \;\; | \;\; | \;\; | \\
\text{H H H H H H H}
\end{array}
$$

b.

$$
\begin{array}{c}
\text{H H H H H H H H H H H} \\
| \;\; | \;\; | \;\; | \;\; | \;\; | \;\; | \;\; | \;\; | \;\; | \;\; | \\
\text{H}-\text{C}-\text{C}-\text{C}-\text{C}-\text{C}-\text{C}-\text{C}-\text{C}-\text{C}-\text{C}-\text{C}-\text{H} \\
| \;\; | \;\; | \;\; | \;\; | \;\; | \;\; | \;\; | \;\; | \;\; | \;\; | \\
\text{H H H H H H H H H H H}
\end{array}
$$

c.

$$
\begin{array}{c}
\text{H H H H H H H H H H H H H H H H} \\
| \;\; | \;\; | \;\; | \;\; | \;\; | \;\; | \;\; | \;\; | \;\; | \;\; | \;\; | \;\; | \;\; | \;\; | \;\; | \\
\text{H}-\text{C}-\text{C}-\text{C}-\text{C}-\text{C}-\text{C}-\text{C}-\text{C}-\text{C}-\text{C}-\text{C}-\text{C}-\text{C}-\text{C}-\text{C}-\text{C}-\text{H} \\
| \;\; | \;\; | \;\; | \;\; | \;\; | \;\; | \;\; | \;\; | \;\; | \;\; | \;\; | \;\; | \;\; | \;\; | \;\; | \\
\text{H H H H H H H H H H H H H H H H}
\end{array}
$$

128. a.

$$
\begin{array}{c}
\text{H H H H H H H H} \\
| \;\; | \;\; | \;\; | \;\; | \;\; | \;\; | \;\; | \\
\text{H}-\text{C}-\text{C}-\text{C}-\text{C}-\text{C}-\text{C}-\text{C}-\text{C}-\text{H} \\
| \;\; | \;\; | \;\; | \;\; | \;\; | \;\; | \;\; | \\
\text{H H H H H H H H}
\end{array}
$$

octane CH$_3$CH$_2$CH$_2$CH$_2$CH$_2$CH$_2$CH$_2$CH$_3$

b.

$$
\begin{array}{c}
\text{H H H H H H} \\
| \;\; | \;\; | \;\; | \;\; | \;\; | \\
\text{H}-\text{C}-\text{C}-\text{C}-\text{C}-\text{C}-\text{C}-\text{H} \\
| \;\; | \;\; | \;\; | \;\; | \;\; | \\
\text{H H H H H H}
\end{array}
$$

hexane CH$_3$CH$_2$CH$_2$CH$_2$CH$_2$CH$_3$

c.

$$
\begin{array}{c}
\text{H H H H} \\
| \;\; | \;\; | \;\; | \\
\text{H}-\text{C}-\text{C}-\text{C}-\text{C}-\text{H} \\
| \;\; | \;\; | \;\; | \\
\text{H H H H}
\end{array}
$$

butane CH$_3$CH$_2$CH$_2$CH$_3$

d.

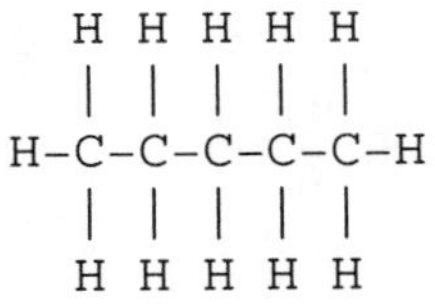

```
    H H H H H
    | | | | |
H-C-C-C-C-C-H
    | | | | |
    H H H H H
```

pentane $CH_3CH_2CH_2CH_2CH_3$

129. Some of the carbon skeletons are

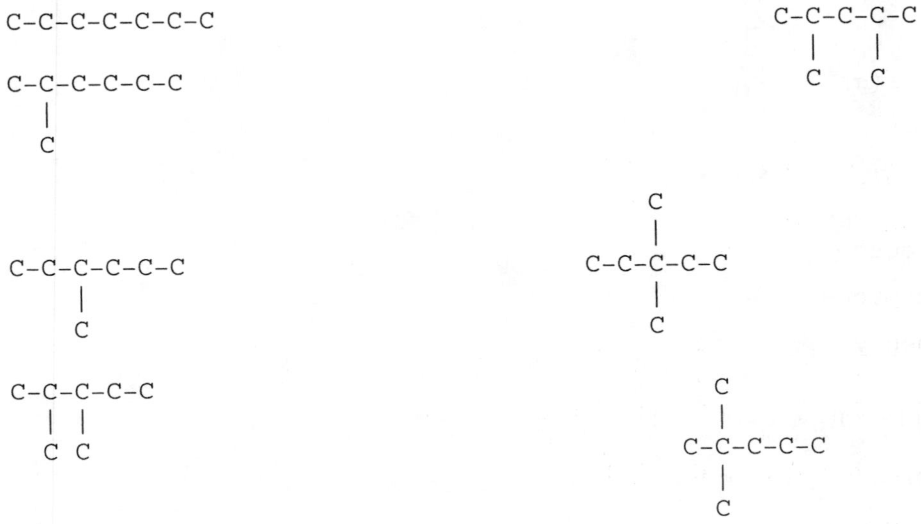

```
C-C-C-C-C-C-C
```

```
C-C-C-C-C
  |       |
  C       C
```

```
C-C-C-C-C-C
    |
    C
```

```
    C
    |
C-C-C-C-C
    |
    C
```

```
C-C-C-C-C-C
      |
      C
```

```
      C
      |
C-C-C-C-C
      |
      C
```

```
C-C-C-C-C
  | |
  C C
```

130. a.   2,3-dimethylbutane

b.   3,3-diethylpentane

c.   2,3,3-trimethylhexane

d.   2,3,4,5,6-pentamethylheptane

131. a.

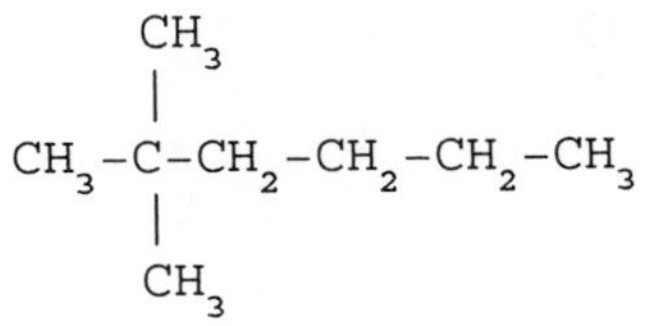

```
        CH_3
        |
CH_3-C-CH_2-CH_2-CH_2-CH_3
        |
        CH_3
```

b.

```
            CH_3
            |
CH_3-CH-CH-CH_2-CH_2-CH_3
        |
        CH_3
```

c.

```
            CH_3
            |
CH_3-CH_2-C-CH_2-CH_2-CH_3
            |
            CH_3
```

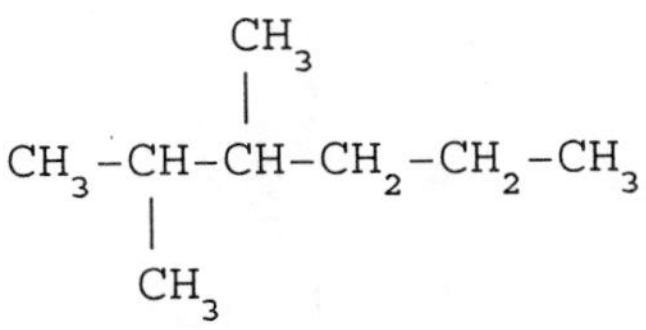

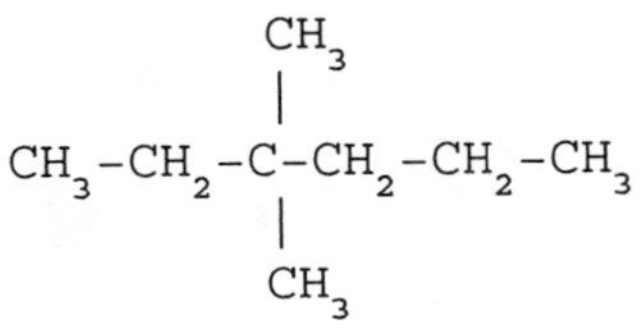

d.

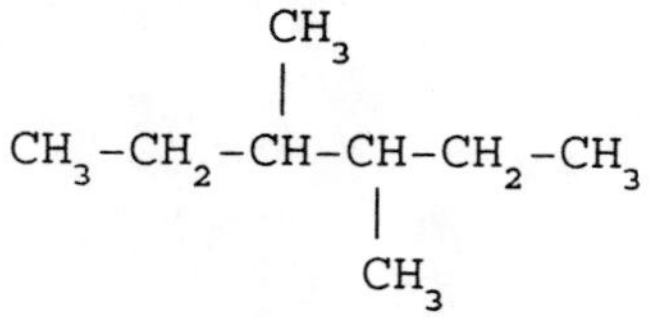

$$CH_3-CH_2-\underset{\underset{CH_3}{|}}{\overset{\overset{CH_3}{|}}{CH}}-CH-CH_2-CH_3$$

e.

$$CH_3-\overset{\overset{CH_3}{|}}{CH}-CH_2-\underset{\underset{CH_3}{|}}{CH}-CH_2-CH_3$$

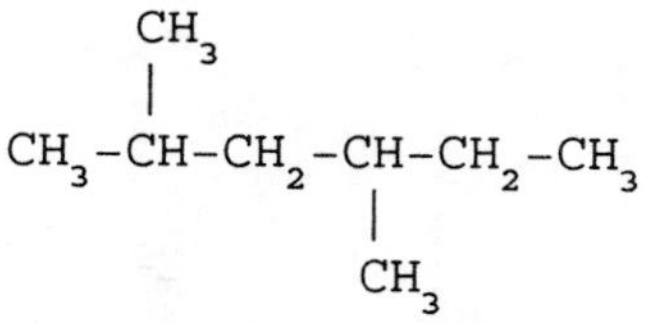

132.   a. $CH_3Cl(g)$

     b. $H_2(g)$

     c. $HCl(g)$

133.   a.   2-decene

     b.   2-heptene

     c.   2-pentyne

134. $CH\equiv C-CH_2-CH_2-CH_2-CH_2-CH_2-CH_3$ 1-octyne

     $CH_3-C\equiv C-CH_2-CH_2-CH_2-CH_2-CH_3$ 2-octyne

     $CH_3-CH_2-C\equiv C-CH_2-CH_2-CH_2-CH_3$ 3-octyne

     $CH_3-CH_2-CH_2-C\equiv C-CH_2-CH_2-CH_3$ 4-octyne

135.   a.   1,2-dimethylbenzene   (2-methyltoluene)

     b.   1,3,5-tribromobenzene

     c.   2-chloronitrobenzene

     d.   naphthalene

136.   a.   carboxylic acid

     b.   ketone

     c.   ester

     d.   alcohol (phenol)

137.   a.   2-propanol (secondary)

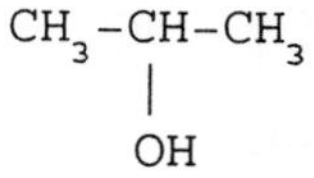

$$CH_3-\underset{\underset{OH}{|}}{CH}-CH_3$$

b.   2-methyl-2-propanol (tertiary)

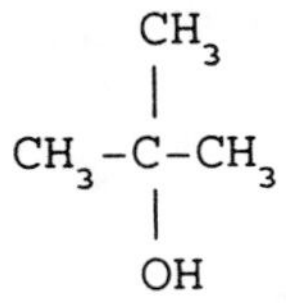

$$CH_3-\underset{\underset{OH}{|}}{\overset{\overset{CH_3}{|}}{C}}-CH_3$$

c.   4-isopropyl-2-heptanol (secondary)

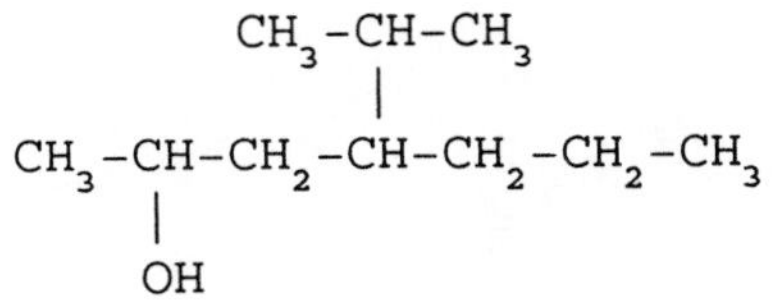

$$CH_3-\underset{\underset{OH}{|}}{CH}-CH_2-\underset{\overset{|}{CH}}{CH}-CH_2-CH_2-CH_3$$
$$\overset{CH_3-CH-CH_3}{|}$$

d.   2,3-dichloro-1-pentanol (primary)

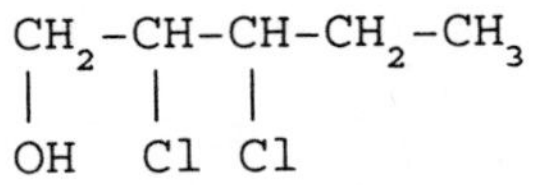

$$\underset{\underset{OH}{|}}{CH_2}-\underset{\underset{Cl}{|}}{CH}-\underset{\underset{Cl}{|}}{CH}-CH_2-CH_3$$

138. a.   3-methylpentanal

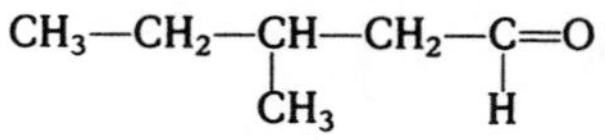

$$CH_3-CH_2-\underset{\underset{CH_3}{|}}{CH}-CH_2-\underset{\underset{H}{|}}{C}=O$$

b.   3-methyl-2-pentanone

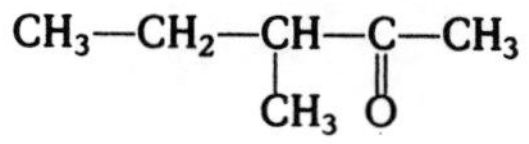

$$CH_3-CH_2-\underset{\underset{CH_3}{|}}{CH}-\underset{\overset{||}{O}}{C}-CH_3$$

c.   methyl phenyl ketone

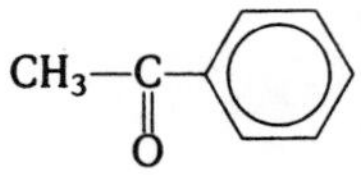

$$CH_3-\underset{\overset{||}{O}}{C}-\bigcirc$$

d.   2-hydroxybutanal

$$CH_3-CH_2-\underset{\underset{OH}{|}}{CH}-\underset{\underset{H}{|}}{C}=O$$

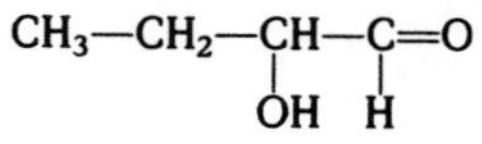

e.   propanal

$$CH_3-CH_2-\underset{\underset{H}{|}}{C}=O$$

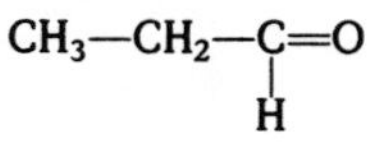

139. Carboxylic acids are synthesized from the corresponding primary alcohol by strong oxidation with a reagent such as potassium permanganate

$CH_3-CH_2-CH_2-OH$ --KMnO$_4$--> CH_3-CH_2-COOH

The synthesis of carboxylic acids from alcohols is an oxidation/reduction reaction.

140. a. $CH_3-CH-CH_2-COOH$
                    |
                   CH_3

   b.

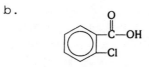

   c. $CH_3-CH_2-CH_2-CH_2-CH_2-COOH$

   d. CH_3-COOH

141. a.   polyethylene

$H_2C{=}CH_2$ $-(CH_2{-}CH_2)_n$

   b.   polyvinyl chloride

$-(CH_2{-}CH)_n$
           H
$H_2C{=}C$ Cl
           |
           Cl

   c.   Teflon

$F_2C{=}CF_2$ $-(CF_2{-}CF_2)_n$

   d.   polypropylene

           H $-(CH{-}CH_2CH{-}CH_2)_n$
$H_2C{=}C$ CH_3 CH_3
           |
           CH_3

   e.   polystyrene

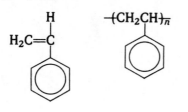

Chapter 20   Biochemistry

1.   Oxygen is the element present in the human body in the largest percentage by mass (65%). Other elements present in the body and there uses are given in Table 20.1.

2.   Proteins represent biopolymers of α-amino acids used for many purposes in the human body (structure, enzymes, antibodies, etc.). Proteins make up about 15% of the body by mass.

3.   Molar masses of proteins range from a few thousand amu to over 1 million amu. Such molar masses are consistent with proteins being large polymeric molecules.

4.   Fibrous proteins provide the structural material of many tissues in the body, and are the chief constituents of hair, cartilage, and muscles. Fibrous proteins consist of lengthwise bundles of polypeptide chains (a fiber). Globular proteins have their polypeptide chains folded into a basically spherical shape and tend to be found in the bloodstream, where they transport and store various needed substances, act as antibodies to fight infections, act as enzymes to catalyze cellular processes, participate in the body's various regulatory systems, and so on.

5.   The general structural formula for the alpha amino acids is

All alpha amino acids contain the carboxyl group (–COOH) and the amino group (–NH$_2$) attached to the α-carbon atom as indicated. In this general formula, *R* represents the remainder of the amino acid molecule (side-chain): it is this portion of the molecule that differentiates one amino acid from another.

6.   The structures of the amino acids are given in detail in Figure 20.2. Generally a side chain is nonpolar if it is mostly hydrocarbon in nature (e.g., alanine, in which the side chain is a methyl group). Side chains are polar if they contain the hydroxyl group (–OH), the sulfhydryl group (–SH), or a second amino (–NH$_2$) or carboxyl (–COOH) group.

7.   Since most proteins exist in aqueous media (water) in living creatures, the presence of hydro*phobic* (water-fearing) and hydro*philic* (water-loving) side chains on the amino acids in a protein will greatly influence how that protein's chain interacts with water. In particular, the three-dimensional structure of the protein is greatly influenced by what type of side chains are present in its constituent amino acids.

8.   Figure 20.2 shows the amino acids separated into the hydrophilic and hydrophobic subgroupings. Notice that the hydrophobic amino acids contain R groups which are basically hydrocarbon (or substituted hydrocarbon) in nature. This makes these R groups nonpolar and unlikely to interact with very polar water molecules. Notice that the hydrophilic amino acids all

contain a very polar functional group (e.g., –OH, –SH, –C=O, etc.) which enable the amino acid R groups to interact with water. For a protein in an aqueous medium, the hydrophilic R groups will orient themselves towards the aqueous medium, while the hydrophobic R groups will turn away from the aqueous medium, causing a profound effect on the protein's shape.

9.

```
     H O H H O
     | ‖ | | ‖
H–N–C–C–N–C–C–OH    gly-ala
     | |     |
     H H     CH₃
```

```
   H H O H H O
   | | ‖ | | ‖
H–N–C–C–N–C–C–OH    ala-gly
     |     |
     CH₃   H
```

These dipeptides (as is evident from their structures) are *not* identical. In abbreviating primary structures, the first named amino acid is assumed to have a free amino group, and the last named amino acid is assumed to have a free carboxyl group.

10.   There are six tripeptides possible.

cys-ala-phe   *ala-cys-phe*   *phe-ala-cys*

cys-phe-ala   *ala-phe-cys*   *phe-cys-ala*

11.   a.   *ile-ala-gly*

```
     H O H H O H H O
     | ‖ | | ‖ | | ‖
H–N–C–C–N–C–C–N–C–C–OH
     | |     |     |
     H CH    CH₃   H
       /\
    H₃C  CH₂CH₃
```

    b.   *gln-ser*

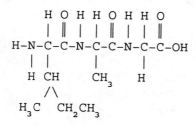

```
     H O H H O
     | ‖ | | ‖
H–N–C–C–N–C–C–OH
     | |     |
     H CH₂   CH₂–OH
       |
       CH₂
       |
    H₂N–C=O
```

c.   *ser-gln*

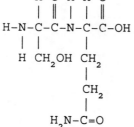

d.   *cys-asn-gly*

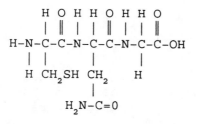

12.   phe-ala-gly

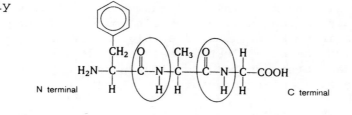

phe-gly-ala

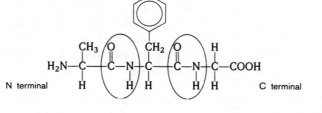

ala-phe-gly

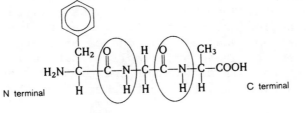

ala-gly-phe

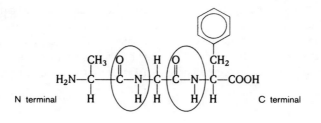

gly-phe-ala

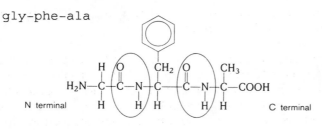

gly-ala-phe

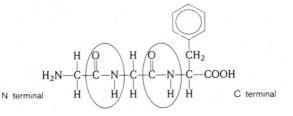

13.   The secondary structure of a protein describes, in general, the
      arrangement in space of the protein's polypeptide chain. The most common
      secondary structures are the alpha-helix and the beta-pleated sheet.

14.   Long, thin, resilient proteins, such as hair, typically contain
      elongated, elastic alpha-helical protein molecules. Other proteins, such
      as silk, which in bulk form sheets or plates, typically contain protein
      molecules having the beta pleated sheet secondary structure. Proteins
      which do not have a structural function in the body, such as hemoglobin,
      typically have a globular structure.

15.   In the pleated sheet secondary structure, a large number of similar
      polypeptide chains are arranged lengthwise next to each other to form a
      wide sheet of protein. Because the individual polypeptide chains contain
      the normal bond angles associated with the atoms involved they are not
      themselves linear, and when several chains are arranged next to each
      other to form a sheet, there are ripples ("pleats") in the overall sheet
      of protein due to this. A drawing of the pleated sheet is given in the
      text as Figure 20.6. Silk and muscle fibers have the pleated sheet
      structure

16.   The secondary structure, in general, describes the arrangement of the
      long polypeptide chain of the protein. In the alpha-helical secondary
      structure, the chain forms a coil or spiral, which gives proteins
      consisting of such structures an elasticity or resilience. Such proteins
      are found in wool, hair, and tendons.

17.   The tertiary structure of a protein represents its specific, overall
      shape when it occurs in its natural environment and is influenced by that
      environment. To distinguish between the secondary and tertiary
      structures, consider this example: a given protein has an alpha helical
      secondary structure (the protein's own amino acid chain coils in a
      helix); in the body, however, this helix itself is folded and twisted by
      interactions with the protein's environment until it forms a tight

sphere. The fact that the helical protein is folded into a tight sphere indicates the tertiary structure of the protein.

18. Cysteine, an amino acid containing the sulfhydryl (-SH) group in its side chain, is capable of forming disulfide linkages (-S-S-) with other cysteine molecules in the same polypeptide chain. If such a disulfide linkage is formed, this effectively ties together two portions of the polypeptide, producing a kink or knot in the chain, which leads in part to the protein's overall 3-dimensional shape (tertiary structure). Cysteine, and the disulfide linkages it forms, is responsible for the curling of hair (whether naturally or by a permanent wave).

19. Denaturation of a protein represents the breaking down of the protein's tertiary structure. If the environment of a protein is changed from the normal environment of the protein, the specific folding and twisting of the protein's polypeptide chain will change to accommodate the new environment. If the protein's tertiary structure is changed, the protein most likely will no longer have whatever function in the body it ordinarily possesses. Cooking of an egg (adding heat to the environment of the protein) causes the protein albumin in the white of the egg to coagulate. Adding heavy metal ions (lead or mercury, for example) can disrupt the inter-chain linkages that contribute to the protein's tertiary structure. A permanent hair wave works by deliberately changing the hair protein's structure.

20. Collagen has an alpha-helical secondary structure. Collagen's function in the body is as the raw material of which tendons are constructed. The long, springy structure of the alpha-helix is responsible for collagen's strength and elasticity.

21. Proteins that catalyze biochemical processes are called *enzymes*.

22. Antibodies are special proteins which are synthesized in the body in response to foreign substances such as bacteria or viruses. Although there are usually specific antibodies for specific invaders, the antibody interferon offers general protection against invasion by viruses.

23. Antibodies are special proteins that are synthesized in the body in response to foreign substances such as bacteria. Interferon is a protein that helps to protect cells against viral infection. The process of blood-clotting involves several proteins.

24. In a permanent wave, cross-linkages between adjacent polypeptide chains of the protein are broken chemically, and then reformed chemically in a new location. The primary cross-linkage involved is a disulfide linkage between cysteine units in the polypeptide chains. It is primarily the tertiary structure of the hair protein which is affected by a permanent wave, although if the waving lotion is left on the hair too long, the secondary structure can also be affected (making the hair very "frizzy").

25. Enzymes are typically 1 to 10 *million* times more efficient than inorganic catalysts. Enzymes are much more efficient than any inorganic catalyst.

26.   The molecule acted upon by an enzyme is referred to as the enzyme's substrate. When we say that an enzyme is specific for a particular substrate, we mean that the enzyme will catalyze the reactions of that molecule and that molecule only.

27.   The action of an enzyme on its substrate takes place at a specific portion of the polypeptide chain called the *active site*.

28.   Figure 20.11 illustrates the lock and key model clearly. The lock-and-key model for enzyme action postulates that the structures of the enzyme and its substrate are complementary, such that the active site of the enzyme and the portion of the substrate molecule to be acted upon can fit together very closely. The structures of these portions of the molecules are unique to the particular enzyme-substrate pair, and they fit together much like a particular key is necessary to work in a given lock.

29.   Simple sugars typically contain several hydroxyl (–OH) groups, as well as the carbonyl (C=O) function (making the sugar either an aldehyde or a ketone, as well as a polyalcohol).

30.   Sugars contain an aldehyde or ketone functional group (carbonyl group), as well as several (OH groups (hydroxyl group).

31.   In solution, functional groups at opposite ends of the simple sugar molecules react with each other, forming the sugar into a *ring* or *cyclic* structure (see Figure 20.12 in the text for the structure).

32.   a.   glucose

$$
\begin{array}{c}
\text{CHO} \\
| \\
\text{H}-\text{C}-\text{OH} \\
| \\
\text{HO}-\text{C}-\text{H} \\
| \\
\text{H}-\text{C}-\text{OH} \\
| \\
\text{H}-\text{C}-\text{OH} \\
| \\
\text{CH}_2\text{OH}
\end{array}
$$

b.   ribose

$$
\begin{array}{c}
\text{CHO} \\
| \\
\text{H}-\text{C}-\text{OH} \\
| \\
\text{H}-\text{C}-\text{OH} \\
| \\
\text{H}-\text{C}-\text{OH} \\
| \\
\text{CH}_2\text{OH}
\end{array}
$$

c.   ribulose

$$
\begin{array}{c}
\text{CH}_2\text{OH} \\
| \\
\text{C}=\text{O} \\
| \\
\text{H}-\text{C}-\text{OH} \\
| \\
\text{H}-\text{C}-\text{OH} \\
| \\
\text{CH}_2\text{OH}
\end{array}
$$

d.   galactose

$$CHO$$
$$H-C-OH$$
$$HO-C-H$$
$$HO-C-H$$
$$H-C-OH$$
$$CH_2OH$$

33.   A disaccharide consists of two monosaccharide units bonded together into a single molecule. Sucrose consists of a glucose molecule and a fructose molecule connected by an alpha-glycosidic linkage.

34.   A polysaccharide is a large polymeric substance, containing as its building blocks repeating simple sugar (monosaccharide) monomer units. Both starch and cellulose consist of long chains of bonded *glucose* molecules: the differences in properties between starch and cellulose are derived from the different manner in which the glucose units are attached to one another to form the polysaccharide chains.

35.   Sucrose is a disaccharide formed from glucose and fructose by elimination of a water molecule to form a C-O-C linkage between the rings (called a glycosidic linkage). The structure of sucrose is shown in Figure 20.13.

36.   ribose (aldopentose); arabinose (aldopentose); ribulose (ketopentose); glucose (aldohexose); mannose (aldohexose); galactose (aldohexose); fructose (ketohexose).

37.   Deoxyribonucleic acid (DNA) is the molecule responsible for coding and storing genetic information in the cell, and for subsequently transmitting that information. DNA is found in the nucleus of each cell. The molar mass of DNA depends on the complexity of the plant or animal species involved, but human DNA may have a molar mass as large as 2 billion grams.

38.   A nucleotide consists of three components: a five-carbon sugar, a nitrogen-containing organic base, and a phosphate group. The phosphate and nitrogen base are each bonded to respective sites on the sugar, but are not bonded to each other.

39.   Deoxyribose is the pentose sugar found in DNA molecules, whereas the sugar ribose is found in RNA molecules.

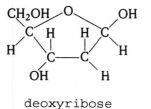

deoxyribose

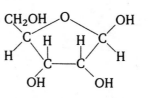

ribose

40.   Uracil (RNA only); cytosine (DNA, RNA); thymine (DNA only); adenine (DNA, RNA); guanine (DNA, RNA)

41.   In a strand of DNA, the phosphate group and the sugar molecule of adjacent nucleotides become bonded to each other. The chain-portion of the DNA molecule, therefore, consists of alternating phosphate groups and sugar molecules. The nitrogen bases are found sticking out from the side of this phosphate-sugar chain, being bonded to the sugar molecules.

42.   When the two strands of a DNA molecule are compared, it is found that a given base in one strand is always found paired with a particular base in the other strand. Because of the shapes and side atoms along the rings of the nitrogen bases, only certain pairs are able to approach and hydrogen-bond with each other in the double helix. Adenine is always found paired with thymine; cytosine is always found paired with guanine. When a DNA helix unwinds for replication during cell division, only the appropriate complementary bases are able to approach and bond to the nitrogen bases of each strand. For example, for a guanine-cytosine pair in the original DNA, when the two strands separate, only a new cytosine molecule can approach and bond to the original guanine, and only a new guanine molecule can approach and bond to the original cytosine.

43.   A given section of the DNA molecule called a *gene* contains the specific information necessary for construction of a particular protein.

44.   Messenger RNA molecules are synthesized to be complementary to a portion (gene) of the DNA molecule in the cell, and serve as the template or pattern upon which a protein will be constructed (a particular group of nitrogen bases on *m*-RNA is able to accommodate and specify a particular amino acid in a particular location in the protein). Transfer RNA molecules are much smaller than *m*-RNA, and their structure accommodates only a single specific amino acid molecule: transfer RNA molecules "find" their specific amino acid in the cellular fluids, and bring it to *m*-RNA where it is added to the protein molecule being synthesized.

45.   Rather than having some common structural feature, substances are classified as lipids based on their solubility characteristics. Lipids are water-insoluble substances that can be extracted from cells by nonpolar organic solvents such as benzene or carbon tetrachloride.

46.   A triglyceride typically consists of a glycerol backbone, to which three separate fatty acid molecules are attached by ester linkages

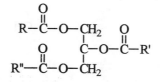

47.   Saturated: butyric acid, caproic acid, lauric acid, stearic acid
       Unsaturated: oleic acid, linoleic acid, linolenic acid
       Most unsaturated fatty acids are derived from vegetable matter (plants).

48. Saponification is the production of a *soap* by treatment of a triglyceride with a strong base such as NaOH.

triglyceride + 3NaOH → glycerol + 3Na⁺soap⁻

$$CH_2-O-\overset{\overset{O}{\|}}{C}-R$$
$$CH-O-\overset{\overset{O}{\|}}{C}-R' + 3NaOH \rightarrow$$
$$CH_2-O-\overset{\overset{O}{\|}}{C}-R''$$

$$CH_2-OH \quad RCOONa$$
$$CH-OH + R'COONa$$
$$CH_2-OH \quad R''COONa$$

49. Fatty acid salts have both a long hydrocarbon chain (that tends to be nonpolar in nature), but also are ionic (at the carboxylate end). Fatty acids are able to dissolve both in nonpolar substances (oils and grease) and also in water. In water, a large number of fatty acid molecules combine to form a spherical grouping called a *micelle*, in which the polar (ionic) ends of the fatty acids face out into the water, and the nonpolar chains of the fatty acids are positioned into the interior of the micelle. Fatty acid salts work as soaps to remove grease and oil from clothing by taking the grease or oil molecules into the interior of the micelles, allowing the grease or oil to be dispersed in the water in which the fatty acid salts are themselves dispersed.

50. Soaps have both a nonpolar nature (due to the long chain of the fatty acid) and an ionic nature (due to the charge on the carboxyl group). In water, soap anions form aggregates called micelles, in which the water-repelling hydrocarbon chains are oriented towards the interior of the aggregate, with the ionic, water-attracting carboxyl groups oriented towards the outside. Most dirt has a greasy nature. A soap micelle is able to interact with a grease molecule, pulling the grease molecule into the hydrocarbon interior of the micelle. When the clothing is rinsed, the micelle containing the grease is washed away. See Figures 20.22 and 20.23.

51. The group of lipids called *steroids* all contain the same basic cluster of four rings.

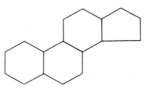

This common structure is sometimes referred to as the steroid nucleus or kernel.

Some important steroids are shown in Figure 20.25 in the text.

52.   Cholesterol is the naturally occurring steroid from which the body synthesizes other needed steroids. Since cholesterol is insoluble in water, it is thought that having too large a concentration of this substance in the bloodstream may lead to its deposition and build up on the walls of blood vessels, causing their eventual blockage.

53.   testosterone: male sex hormone that controls development of male reproductive organs and secondary sex characteristics (deep voice, muscle structure, hair patterns)
estradiol: female sex hormone that controls development of female reproductive organs and secondary sex characteristics
progesterone: female hormone secreted during pregnancy that prevents further ovulation during and immediately after the pregnancy; birth-control pills are often synthetic progesterone derivatives

54.   Phospholipids have a similar structure to triglycerides, except that one of the fatty acids attached to the glycerol backbone is replaced by a phosphate group (phospholipids are sometimes referred to as phosphodiglycerides). An important phospholipid is lecithin, which behaves very strongly as an emulsifying agent (allowing polar and nonpolar substances to mix). Lecithin is found in high concentration in egg yolks, and is being used in baking in place of whole eggs: the emulsifying properties of the egg yolk are due to the lecithin, and using lecithin itself avoids the cholesterol problem associated with whole eggs.

55.	v	56.	i
57.	t	58.	m
59.	x	60.	u
61.	q	62.	f
63.	k	64.	g
65.	y	66.	r
67.	c	68.	p
69.	n	70.	o
71.	e	72.	b
73.	s	74.	d
75.	h	76.	a
77.	deoxyribonucleic acid	78.	nucleotides
79.	ribose	80.	ester

81. complementary paired

82. thymine, guanine

83. gene

84. transfer, messenger

85. DNA

86. lipids

87. triglycerides

88. unsaturated, saturated

89. saponification

90. ionic, nonpolar

91. micelles

92. fatty (long chain)

93. cholesterol

94. progesterone

95. emulsifying

96. The primary structure of a protein refers to the specific identity and ordering of amino acids in a protein's polypeptide chain. The primary structure is sometimes referred to as the protein's amino acid *sequence*.

97. 24 (assuming no amino acid repeats)

98. tendons, bone (with mineral constituents), skin, cartilage, hair, fingernails.

99. hemoglobin

100. Proteins contain both acidic (–COOH) and basic (–NH$_2$) groups in their side chains, which can neutralize both acids and bases.

101. An enzyme is inhibited if some other molecule, other than the enzyme's correct substrate, blocks the active sites of the enzyme. If the enzyme is inhibited irreversibly, the enzyme can no longer function and is said to have been inactivated.

102. pentoses (5 carbons); hexoses (6 carbons); trioses (3 carbons)

103. Although starch and cellulose are both polymers of glucose, the glucose rings in cellulose are connected in such a manner that the enzyme which ordinarily causes digestion of polysaccharides is not able to fit the shape of the substrate, and is not able to act upon it.

104. In a strand of DNA, the phosphate group and the sugar molecule of adjacent nucleotides become bound to each other. The chain-portion of the DNA molecule, therefore, consists of alternating phosphate groups and sugar molecules. The nitrogen bases are found sticking out from the side of this phosphate-sugar chain, being bonded to the sugar molecules.

105. A wax is an ester of a fatty acid with a long chain monohydroxy alcohol. Waxes are solids that provide waterproof coatings on the fruits and leaves of plants, and on the skins and feathers of animals.

106. The primary human bile acid is cholic acid, which helps to emulsify fats in the intestinal tract. In order to be digested by enzymes for absorption into the bloodstream, large clumps of fat must be dispersed into fine droplets in the liquid of the small intestine. Cholic acid basically acts as a detergent.

In-Class Discussion Questions

Instructor's Guide

At the University of Illinois at Urbana-Champaign we have been trying to find ways to encourage "active learning" in our chemistry courses. We want students to be active participants in the learning process, not just passive sponges for information. We also want the students to recognize that learning chemistry goes beyond "getting the right answer" to algorithm-based exercises. We want them to learn to think like a chemist – to be able to solve problems because they truly understand the underlying concepts, not because they have memorized a solution to a particular type of problem.

A crucial part of active learning involves true discussion of the concepts using question that require the students to probe their understanding of the concepts. All of us know that trying to teach something to someone is one of the surest ways to expose our misunderstandings of the underlying concepts. Peer teaching is one of the best features of group discussions. However, for group work to yield real value, the questions must be carefully chosen. The "In-Class Discussion Questions" in *Introductory Chemistry* come from our own experiences with active learning at the University of Illinois. We hope you will find them useful in your own courses as well.

What are "In-Class Discussion Questions", and how do they differ from traditional questions?

"In-Class Discussion Questions" are challenging questions designed to get students to consider the underlying concepts involved in understanding chemistry. Research has shown that students can be adept at solving even relatively difficult traditional problems yet still not have a firm understanding of chemical principles. This is partly due to the fact that students generally solve traditional problems by using memorized rules, algorithms, or equations. While we as instructors mean for the traditional problems to be conceptual in nature, students often exchange thinking about the chemistry for finding a short cut to solving a specific problem. Because of this, many of the "In-Class Discussion Questions" ask the students to explain a term, equation, rule, or algorithm. In other words, we ask the students to explain what we have long been assuming they had to know to solve the traditional problems.

Why should you use "In-Class Discussion Questions"?

The "In-Class Discussion Questions" bring to light the students' initial ideas and "content misconceptions." This can be beneficial to both the instructor and the students. While these "content misconceptions" undoubtedly play a role in students' lack of understanding, there is an even more fundamental difficulty: misconceptions about what it means to really understand For example, we have found:

1) Students are passive readers of textbooks. They often view the textbook as simply a place to find their homework assignments, and perhaps to look for sample problems and solutions. Even students who take the time to read some of the text will often skip over graphs and figures, crucial aids for increasing conceptual understanding. Students generally do not see the importance of the type of understanding that graphs and figures provide, but only see the importance of example problems and bold-faced words.

2) Students are not very proficient at thinking through problems in chemistry. Most students can solve (or be taught to solve) problems once these

problems have been "set-up" for the students. Many students will even make claims such as "Once I am shown how to set up a problem I can usually solve it", and genuinely believe that this demonstrates understanding. It is not so much that they are trying to get out of thinking, but that they are defining understanding in terms of algorithms. In addition, students often define understanding in terms of rules, terms, and equations. For example, many students genuinely believe they understand the nature of gases because they have memorized "PV=nRT" or that they understand the concept of bonding because they know "elements want to be like Noble gases."

3) Students often believe that coming to a correct answer on a traditional problem demonstrates conceptual understanding. However, this is simply not a good assumption.

All three of these are related to passivity on the part of the students, whether it be a passive reading of the text or a passive acceptance of algorithms, terms, rules, and equations. This passivity is ironic in a science course in which we would like to teach our students to question, and to understand.

How do the "In-Class Discussion Questions" address these concerns?

There are several types of "In-Class Discussion Questions" provided, each with differing but related rationale:

1) Many problems explicitly ask the students to explain a term, equation, or rule. This helps the students to see that there are reasons for the terms, equations, and rules we have in chemistry instead of passively accepting that this is "just the way things are."

2) Several questions ask the students to discuss specific models. All too often students equate models with reality as opposed to understanding that models are man-made constructs to try to better understand observations.

3) Some of the problems include the use of pictorial representations of microscopic views of matter. This includes both drawing the pictures and evaluating them. These are to help the students relate the macroscopic and the microscopic worlds.

4) The multiple choice questions were developed from open-ended problems given to both university and high school students. The most popular responses were included as choices. The greatest benefit of these questions is having the students explain what they believe is wrong with the choices they do not choose. We have noticed that while students can be adept at defending a choice they believe to be correct, they find it much more difficult to find fault with the other responses. Students become more active, critical thinkers when they have to evaluate choices which are very tempting (and sometimes correct to some extent).

5) Some of the problems ask the students to determine the type of data that is needed to answer the question. These are not exercises in looking up constants, but problems which require the students to explicitly think about the approach they will use to solve the problem. The goal is to help the students develop their own strategies for solving the problems.

6) Some of the problems contradict or question what students "know to be true" (such as the pressure of a gas always being inversely related to its volume). There are a couple of reasons for this: first, to help the students understand the limits of such "knowns"; and second, to keep the students from passively accepting these "knowns."

7) Some of the problems come from listening to students' incorrect ideas over several years. As mentioned, it is a good idea to directly confront students with their misconceptions, not only to get the students to change their ideas, but to keep the students from passively accepting and holding onto these ideas.

How should the "In-Class Discussion Questions" be used?

The ideal way to use these questions is to have relatively small groups of students (6-8) working together. This serves at least a couple of purposes:

1) The students are effectively modeling how to think about problems -- many ideas surface, debates occur, students often go down "wrong paths", and they sometimes discuss important issues which are not explicitly written into the questions. This type of environment also teaches the students the benefits of actively thinking through a problem.

2) Students are required to be active participants in their own education. This is important for reasons already mentioned and one more -- we have found that many times students need to say something out loud before they can really evaluate it. For example, a student who believes he/she understands a concept (but does not) will often start out speaking quickly and confidently and then begin to trail off as he/she "listens" to what he/he is saying.

In addition:

• Group discussions do not always work well for traditional (algorithm-based) problems. A main goal of the "In-Class Discussion Questions" is to bring ideas to the surface so they can be debated (although the eventual answer is also important the emphasis is on the process of getting to the answer). The main goal of traditional problems is usually to get the correct answer (although the process is also important, the emphasis is usually on the answer). That is not to say that one type of problem is more important than the other, but that both types need to be provided to the students. Generally, group work is better for generating many ideas, and individual work is better for solving algorithm-based problems.

• The goal of the group discussions using these questions is different from tutoring. While tutoring has its place, it often turns into one student training another student, generally with the algorithms and short cuts discussed previously.

• It is helpful to have discussions during class time:

  1) You can interact with the students and question them further. This is important to keep students from using short cuts to just get a correct answer, and to question the students even when they are correct (to keep them from being passive acceptors of answers. The answers we accept from the student are as important as the questions we ask of them.

  2) You get to know the students better more quickly. This includes a better understanding of how they approach problems, their misconceptions, and group dynamics.

Chapter 1

1.   Many students memorize the terms "hypothesis", "theory" and "law" from the definitions given in the text. Asking students a question such as this allows you to get an idea of how the students are applying the definitions. For example, a theory cannot become a law, although many students will think of a law as a time tested theory.

2.   By having the students make these observations, you can get a better idea about how they differentiate between the terms "qualitative" and "quantitative." Also, the students see that they make observations everyday about their environments; that is, observations are not foreign to them, or only done in the context of a formal lab.

3.   Similar to question number 2, this allows the students to see that there are many chemical reactions that they are a part of (either directly or indirectly) everyday (for example, digesting their food). This also gives you an opportunity to see what the students think of when they hear the term "chemical reactions".

4.   A good discussion of this question will help you get a better feel for the students' ideas about what science is. How is a theory tested? What does it mean when a reporter, for example, claims a study or a poll is scientific?

5.   Instead of merely reciting steps to a scientific method, this question has students describe how they have "been scientific" outside of school. Like question number 4, it begs the question "What do we mean by scientific?" When possible it is generally good to ask questions that get at the applications of terms, because the students are going to have to define the terms at some point in the discussion. This question should also get students to realize that there is not one set method of science.

6.   This text emphasizes the role of models in scientific study. For students to have a good understanding of what science is about, it is important for them to understand what models are, why we use them, and their limitations.

7.   Similar to other In-Class Discussion Questions in this chapter, this question makes students decide what is meant by a scientific theory (they will have to do this in order to choose one to discuss). It also shows the limitations of the theories because questions will always arise. It is crucial for the students to realize that this is one aspect of science: formulating a theory, and testing it with questions.

8.   By evaluating the responses to this question you can get a better understanding of what the students mean by a scientific test. Are there controls? What about sample size? Could there be other explanations to the results? See if the students think of these types of questions before directly asking them.

9.   Students often think of science as a body of infallible knowledge and are surprised to learn that scientists can have debates over issues. Many students who have heard of the scientific method feel that it is taught as a method which always leads to only one possible conclusion. A discussion of this question will get at the initial ideas of the students regarding their views of science and can help them see that the same method can lead to different conclusions.

Chapter 2

1.   (a) 43,800 minutes; (b) 40,320 minutes; (c) These are different due to differences in conversion factors. Answer "a" could be said to be more correct because the conversion factor "4 weeks/1 month" is less exact than those in response "a." The problem is useful to show students that they can get different answers with different conversion factors.

2.   This problem is useful to show the students that they have an intuitive feel for solving these types of problems. Once you get to Chapter 9, you can make an analogy between this problem and chemical stoichiometry (which is explicitly asked for in In-Class Discussion Question 1 from Chapter 9). (a) 210 pennies; (b) 140 dimes; (c) 321 g; (d) 70 pieces; (e) 716.1 g; (f) 70 pieces (unless you had more pennies as well).

3.   Choice "c" is the best response, but it still does not explain why such an object would sink. One of the benefits of these types of questions is to let the students know that one can always achieve a deeper level of understanding. Choice "a" is a very popular answer as is choice "d." More important than stressing the answer, however, is finding what the students understand about density and if they use it as an explanatory device.

4.   It is important for the students to apply the rules of significant figures to measurements in the lab. This question is related to number 10 in this chapter.

5.   Problems such as these are good in that they require the students to decide what information is necessary and how to use this information. Students can often enter numbers into an equation correctly if we give them only the necessary numbers and the equation. However, a problem such as this requires the student to think about the problem solving approach that is needed.

6-10. Students are often confused about significant figures, and many times even those students who can correctly use them are not sure about the purpose or the application. Problems such as these require that the student understand, not merely know, the rules of significant figures, especially with the application to lab measurements (9 and 10).

11.   An actual understanding of this observation may be premature at this point. However, viscosity and density are confusing to the students and so this is a good problem to leave them with (a little frustration can motivate students, especially if they find the question intriguing or discrepant).

12.   Like significant figures, scientific notation is sometimes viewed by the students as a concept made up just to make things difficult. This usually is because the students try to memorize their way out of problems instead of thinking their way through them. It is also good to be able to relate different concepts so chemistry is not seen as consisting of many unrelated facts or ideas.

13.   This is a relatively typical problem which can be used to show the students general ideas behind unit conversion. It is also a good problem to have students estimate an answer before they do calculations.

14.   Mass and volume are often confused or used interchangeably. While both
       objects will displace the same amount of water, many students will
       think the lead will displace more water since it is "heavier". This
       problem also allows for a discussion of measuring volume by water
       displacement.

Chapter 3

1.   Students tend to like questions such as these which discuss something
       familiar to them and that can be explained with what they have learned.
       The key to this question is the differing heat capacities of the
       different substances and it is important that the students are not
       allowed to merely say "Because of.the heat capacities" but to explain
       their ideas.

2.   Of several hundred incoming UIUC students, the breakdown for responses
       was: (a) 7%, (b) 40%, (c) 12%, (d) 37%, (e) 3%

       Note that the majority of the students believed that the bubbles are
       hydrogen and oxygen gases. It seems, then, that if we merely tell the
       students that the boiling of water is a physical change, yet they
       believe that the product is hydrogen and oxygen gases, they will be more
       confused than they were initially. Also, one of the indicators of a
       chemical change (with which the students may be familiar) is that a gas
       is given off, which, from their perspective, is what occurs as water
       boils.

3.   Students may have good reasons for listing processes as chemical or
       physical changes even if they are incorrect. In many ways, their
       reasons are more telling than their answers. It might be helpful to
       perform this as a demonstration for the students or to have them
       experiment with this on their own.

4.   This question helps students to see the limitations of any
       classification system while at the same time it allows you to see how
       the students are using the system. For example, a bucketful of sand
       takes up the shape of its container, so is it a liquid?

5.   Students often assert that the boiling of water is a physical change,
       but that hydrogen and oxygen gases are a product of boiling water. In a
       problem such as this, have the students not only defend the answer they
       choose, but also critique the others.

6.   This question gets to the differences between a mixture and a compound.
       Many students believe that because the formula for water is H_2O, a 2:1
       mixture of hydrogen and oxygen gases is equivalent to water. Having the
       students draw molecular level pictures of the mixture and the compound
       should help students to relate the macroscopic to the microscopic, which
       is an important idea in chemistry.

7.   Like question number 6, this is a good time to have the students drawing
       molecular level pictures. The drawings that the students submit will go
       much further in letting us know their understanding of the concept than
       their reciting a text definition.

8,10. These questions are another way of getting at the differences between
       chemical and physical changes. As with other In-Class Discussion
       Questions, it is just as important to listen to the students'
       explanations as it is to know the students' answers. Many times a

student can be correct for the wrong reasons or incorrect with mostly correct thinking.

9. This problem allows the students to apply what is meant by the term pure from a chemist's perspective. Technically, only elements and compounds can be pure to a chemist (which could lead to an interesting discussion with the question, "But aren't atoms made up of other particles?").

Chapter 4

1. Students should realize that it is the number of protons that "define" an element. Thus, choice "d" is correct (because choices b and c are correct).

2. This question could be followed by a discussion of what average mass means. In this case, "a" is correct -- no carbon atom has a mass of 12.011.

3. Some students will believe that "a" and "c" are correct, although only "c" is correct. While this is not widespread it should be addressed if it comes up.

4. Answer "b" is correct. Some students will believe that the 2 in the formula suggests something about the mass of hydrogen or oxygen. While this is not widespread it should be addressed if it comes up.

5. There should be no difference. It does not matter how a substance is produced, it is still that substance.

6. Yes, many questions are raised from Dalton's theory. For example: What are the masses of the atoms?, Are atoms really without structure?, What forces hold atoms together in compounds?, etc.

7. We now know that some atoms of the same element have different masses. We have had to include the existence of isotopes in our models.

8. Compounds of the same element differ only in the number of atoms of the elements forming them, i.e. NO, N_2O, NO_2.

9. Over 70% of the several hundred incoming UIUC students correctly chose response "e". However, almost 25% of the students chose response "d". Again, the largest benefits of a question such as this are to have the students explain why they believe incorrect explanations, and to hear the students' ideas. For example, by choosing "d" we could believe that the students do not understand the atomic theory. On the other hand, they may simply be confusing the terms "atom" and "element". These types of insights are important for us to make.

10. The purpose of this question is to get the students to appreciate, in general, the purpose of a model, and to consider, more specifically, Thomson's model. The answers to these will vary from student to student, and what is important here is to stress that the answers are more contingent on their support than an absolute "correctness". However, most students will probably claim in "a" that electrons are the most important for the formation of compounds (especially due to Thomson's findings that the electrons so easily removed). In the case with "c" it is most important to stress that any model that explains Thomson's findings is reasonable, and that this is what developing

models is about--matching observations, not necessarily reality. This emphasis on models is extremely important in chemistry.

11.   In asking several hundred incoming UIUC students about what happens to the size of molecules, and to the mass as the ice is heated (until it is steam), about one-third of the students believed that the mass and molecular size varied. Most of these students believed that the mass of the ice was greater than that of the steam, and that the size of the "steam molecules" was greater than those of the "ice molecules." The drawings in conjunction with the explanations can reveal quite a bit about the students' ideas.

12.   This question allows students to explain their understanding of subatomic particles.

13.   The number of protons in an atom is what "defines" the element, so by changing the number of protons, the element will be transformed. This is not possible by chemical means, however. A discussion of how this transformation would differ from a chemical change would be fruitful.

14.   As stated earlier, an understanding of the importance and limitations of models is crucial in developing an understanding of science. It is worthwhile for the students to consider explicitly these different models of the atoms while understanding that each has advantages and each has flaws.

15.   This question is a rather traditional question but allows the students to apply their knowledge of the set up of the periodic table. Especially troublesome for students is part b.

16.   This question goes well with number 14. Dalton's model can be quite useful in discussing gas laws, especially because of its simplicity. But there are many phenomena it does not explain (for example, how/why atoms bond to form molecules).

17.   The periodic table shows the average mass of all of the isotopes. Therefore ^{35}Cl must be more abundant since the average mass is closer to 35 than 37. You may also wish to have the students calculate the relative abundances of these two isotopes.

Chapter 5

1-5.   Students all too often memorize rules for naming compounds without understanding that the names are systematic, and that the rules are made to be as simple as possible. For example, roman numerals and prefixes are only used when necessary (that is, if there are more than one possible compound to fit the name, like "iron oxide" for example). The more we stress the purpose of rules with students, the more they expect there to be rules, and the greater the chance they will achieve understanding.

Chapter 6

1.   As stated in the question, the given choices are actual student responses (incoming students to UIUC). Again, the most important goal of a problem such as this is to get the students talking about why they believe certain responses to be incorrect. Most students will undoubtedly know that "d" is correct, but many of them will also be

surprised that some of the other responses (especially "a" and "e" it seems) are not correct.

2.   The main purpose of this question is to have the students come to the same definition of what is meant by a formula, and what is meant by an equation (many times students will use these terms interchangeably). Also, if the students are more clear on what information is given by a formula (the elements in the compound and the ratio of different atoms in the molecule) they will be more likely to understand what is meant by a balanced equation.

3.   Molecular level pictures are a good way at gauging student understanding. Their pictures in this case should clearly distinguish the meaning of coefficients from subscripts. This also teaches the students that relating the macroscopic to the microscopic is useful in chemistry.

4-7.   Even students who can balance equations often have difficulty with these questions. These go well with #1 in that the student has to understand why we balance equations, and what the coefficients and subscripts symbolize in order to answer them. After all, a balanced equation is just letters and numbers with an arrow. Its meaning is not intuitively obvious.

8,9.   When possible it is good to have students critically examine a graph or figure from the text. This stresses the importance of becoming active readers of the text (instead of viewing it merely as the place in which to find the homework). Questions 8 and 9 also help the students to see that macroscopic definitions in chemistry can be quite limiting and that a microscopic perspective is sometimes a better way of understanding chemical processes and phenomena.

Chapter 7

1.   This problem is to get the students to consider a representation of a reaction in solution. Given the chemical equation, most all of your students can undoubtedly balance this equation, although it is not clear how many students will know what to do when you ask the students to draw a representation. The equation is:

$$Pb(NO_3)_2 \text{ (aq)} + 2KI \text{ (aq)} \rightarrow PbI_2 \text{ (s)} + 2KNO_3. \text{(aq)}$$

2.   This question is consistent with emphasizing pictorial representations of ions, molecules, and reactions in solutions, and stems from research which points to the fact that while many students are successful at balancing equations, they are not able to represent these. The main point here is to use the students' drawings to get a better idea of their thoughts.

3.   This problem requires the students to think about the application of the solubility rules. The answer to this is "a". The precipitate formed is barium sulfate, and the other product is water. Thus, the ion concentration decreases, and the bulb grows dim.

4,7,9,10.   As with questions 8 and 9 from Chapter 6, it is often important to take a microscopic perspective when considering chemical reactions. In the drawings, the students should show that the products are chemically different from the reactants, although the same atoms appear on each side. While a chemical equation serves the same purpose to a chemist, this is not always obvious (especially to first time students). The students should be asked to make an explicit link between their drawings and balanced equations.

5.   As stated previously, text definitions supplied by the students are of limited value in gauging their understanding of chemical concepts. On the other hand, their drawings of the same concepts (along with explanations of these drawings) can go a long way in helping us better understand their ideas.

6.   Students need to draw or write out a net ionic equation for this (which could be accomplished with a molecular level picture). Since no new products are formed, this does not qualify as a chemical reaction.

8.   In simplest terms the net ionic reaction would be $H^+ + OH^- \rightarrow H_2O$.

Chapter 8

1.   Although many students at this level have had a great deal of chemistry instruction, a lot of the students do not understand why we use the mole concept in chemistry. Many students cannot explain what a mole is or what it is used for. In answering this question, students will often claim the mole is "how much the compound weighs", or something like "a mole is the mass of the atoms in a compound". Students do not always appreciate that the mole is used to equate mass and number so that we can, in effect, count by weighing.

2.   An empirical formula represents the simplest whole-number ratio of the various types of atoms in a compound, while the molecular formula represents the actual formula. They can be the same, such as with water, H_2O.

3,4. These are rather traditional problems, but students have difficulty with them (especially #3 since it is worded differently from most of these types of problems). The element in #3 is Si, and the formula for #4 is N_2O_3. Make sure that the students can also explain what they are doing instead of just plugging numbers into a formula.

5.   Students find this very difficult, especially since it uses the concept of relative masses. Even students who use this concept to state that the relative masses of A and B are 30 and 40 respectively will then be confused on how AB_2 can add up to 110% (claiming 30 + 40 + 40 = 110%).

6.   A relatively traditional problem although part b is difficult for many students.

7.   This question is to get the students to start thinking about the conversion between mass and number (which will be useful for the mole concept). One way of solving this problem would be to find the mass of the chalk before and after writing one's name, and find, by subtraction, the mass of chalk it takes to write the name. Then, by knowing the mass of a "chalk molecule", one could calculate the number of "chalk molecules".

8-12. These are all problems which the students should be expected to do (and many can). However, these problems also reveal some conceptual misunderstandings of students. For example, the idea that the unit of molar mass is grams per 1 mole, and that this can be determined by dividing the mass by the number of moles that one is given (8, 12). Or that there are twice as many hydrogen atoms as there are water molecules in a sample (9). Or that the mass of one molecule should be extremely small (10). Or finally, that a molecule can have a relatively high percent by mass of an element with a subscript of one (11).

13. Another problem in which we don't want to just accept the students giving us the text definition, but in which we have them discuss the meaning or relevance of the terms.

Chapter 9

1. If you used the question from Chapter 2 and the students could successfully solve it, relate the ideas to chemical stoichiometry to let them know that they do understand some of the principles involved in solving such a problem.

2. Like number 1 above (and number 2 from Chapter 2), many students will be able to solve this, even the limiting reactant analogy. Use this opportunity to emphasize the similarities between something they know and something they may be struggling with (chemical stoichiometry).

3. Even given that the students can balance equations and perform limiting reactant calculations, many times student have difficulty drawing representations of the reactions. In fact, when incoming students at UIUC were given an open-ended question asking them to represent the equation in this question, many of them drew "tri-atomic" hydrogen (presumably because there is a coefficient of three with respect to the hydrogen). In the multiple choice version given to several hundred students, almost 25% of them choose answers with tri-atomic hydrogen, and only slightly more than half choose the correct response. Their solution should include 4 molecules of ammonia and 4 molecules of diatomic nitrogen.

4. Research on several hundred incoming UIUC students suggests that many of the students will choose "a" from the correct drawing in question #5 (almost two-thirds chose it). While it simplifies to the correct answer ("d") it suggests that perhaps students do not understand what information is being conveyed by a chemical equation. Again, the answer they give is important, but it is perhaps more important to try to understand their reasoning for their answers.

5. This type of problem is good in that it makes the students really think about what they need to know to solve a problem, as opposed to trying to figure out how to "plug and chug" the numbers to arrive at a correct answer. In this case, they need to know: the balanced equation, the molar masses of A and B, and the molar mass of the product that is formed. Have the student explain both "how" they will use the information and "why" they need the information they claim to need.

6. Because of the way this question is worded, many students believe the answer to be 20.0 grams. Have the students also determine the mass of left over reactant, but don't ask for this until they have all realized that 20.0 g is incorrect and why.

7,8. Only about half of the several hundred incoming UIUC students correctly chose "d" for question 7. Answer "d" is the best choice for number 8 (although "c" is a reasonable choice as well). About half of the students chose "d", and 20% chose "c". Again, it is important to get at the reasons for the answers, especially since students seem stuck on the Law of Conservation of Mass, although not necessarily in this case. Also, in the case of question 8, over ten percent chose "a", presumably because more of chemical A (by mass) is involved in the reaction (only about 3% chose "b"). As with many of the other questions, it is a good idea to use this question to better understand the students' ideas.

9.   Limiting reactant problems can be difficult for students, although many students at this level can solve them. Students who have difficulty with these often try to memorize an algorithm and may multiply by an incorrect ratio of coefficients. This type of question requires that the students think about which reactant is limiting and why. It is important to have the students explain their answers.

10.   Students who have difficulty with limiting reactant problems often confuse the amount of a reactant they have with the amount that is needed for a complete reaction. In this problem, the answer is "b".

11.   In this case, only about ten percent of the several hundred UIUC students given a multiple choice version of this type of question correctly choose a response in which the gases had a mass greater than that of the object being burned (since it is becoming an oxide --or oxides--of that sample). In fact, about half of the students believed the mass of the gases would weigh the same as that which was being burned (presumably due to the memorized "Law of Conversation of Mass").

12.   Results from several hundred incoming students at UIUC reveal that about half of the students believed that the mass of an iron bar decreased when it rusts, and almost 25% believed that the mass stayed the same. Less than 20% correct chose "b". Again, it is important in a question like this to allow the students to discuss their ideas, especially in deciding which choices they believe are incorrect and why.

13.   In this question, over one-third of several hundred incoming UIUC students incorrectly believed that the answer to this is "yes". More important that this, though, is to get the students to vocalize their explanations to this.

14.   In asking several hundred incoming UIUC students this question, almost 40% of the students believed that the mass of this system would decrease, presumably because the chemical has either "disappeared" or has been converted into a gas (which many believe has less mass than the solid). Most of the rest correctly believe that the system ends up with the same mass, although it again is interesting to ask them explain why (especially without using the phrase "Law of Conservation of Mass").

15.   Many students say 2.0 moles (analogous to 20.0 g from number 6 above). Some students are uncomfortable with the answer 0.50 mol, presumably because it is a fraction.

16.   This question is an application of the idea of percent yield and is better than having the students merely define percent yield.

17.   This is a complement to question number 6. After students have done a problem like number 6, make sure they can explain

Chapter 10

1. Like other In-Class Discussion Questions, this relies on students drawing pictures of their ideas. High energy waves having shorter wavelengths makes a lot more sense to students when they are looking at three waves of different wavelength. Look for a confusion between wavelength and amplitude.

2. Students have a notion that we know exactly where the electrons are and that they move in predictable orbits. We need to help them accept the idea that our models are based on probability.

3. The term orbital is unfortunate in that many students infer a circular orbit from it. However, it represents a region of probability in which one is likely to find an electron. This distinction is crucial.

4. Students have noticed this trend and are not sure why. In fact some students have just accepted this as "the way that it is," which is an attitude that should be diminished as soon as possible. Questions such as this which ask the students to explain something that they may have been merely accepting is a good thing. Even if we are not sure of the answer, it is good for the students to see that we can make educated hypotheses based on previous information. Students may equate metallic behavior with atomic size and answer accordingly, or you may have to lead them through this a bit; whatever the case, allow the students time to discuss their ideas.

5. As with other questions for this chapter, this is to get to students' ideas about ionization energy when an atom losing an electron is isoelectronic with a noble gas. What is most important here (as with the other questions) is not to just allow students to answer either "true" or "false" but to explain their ideas. In this case, energy is still required for a potassium atom to lose an electron even though many students will claim that this is what a potassium atom "wants to do," and will therefore do it spontaneously (sometimes even claiming that energy will be given off).

6. The main reason for this questions stems from the observation that many times students merely memorize trends across and down the periodic table, or, at best, use a memorized rule as an explanation (such as "there is an increase in electrons"). Thus, this question provides a discrepant situation--if a student uses the "increase in electron" rule as an explanation, this question serves to show the students that, this being a cause, it has opposite effects. It would be good here to have the students explain the trends instead of just memorizing them.

7. The Li atom is larger, but the Li 1s orbital is smaller (compared to the H atom, and H 1s orbital).

8. This is true although some students will say it is false and claim the hydrogen atom only has a 1s orbital (of course, orbitals don't really exist at all, and the depth to which you decide to discuss this is up to you). This question can be followed by a discussion of the concept of orbitals.

9. Again, have the students describe the relevance of these terms in their own words as opposed to merely citing the text definition.

10. This question requires that the students apply their knowledge of the way in which the periodic table is set up. It also goes well with number 4 above.

11. While discussing this problem, emphasize to the students that they need not memorize or use mnemonics to learn electron configurations, but only need to understand the periodic table.

12. Many students think of the first ionization energy for a noble gas to be higher than the second because of a memorized rule such as "All elements want to be like noble gases." While this statement is true to an extent, many students misuse it to mean that an atom such as He "really does not want to" lose an electron; but if it already has, then it is not so difficult to lose the next one. In this way, student will also claim that the second ionization energy for an atom such as Mg will actually be negative so that it can be like Ne.

13. Many students realize that taking a second electron from lithium will be difficult (take quite a bit of energy) because after taking away the first, the ion will have the same configuration as He. However, as mentioned above, many students will also claim that the second ionization energy for beryllium will be negative (exothermic) because the beryllium ion will "want" to lose another electron to be like He. Thus, do not allow the students to look up the numbers before answering this (although it might be a good idea to do so after a lengthy discussion) and make sure that the students do not just provide a quick answer (such as "The second IE for Li is greater") but that they explain their reasoning.

14. In this problem the students should note that there is a great change between the second and third ionization energies for both elements X and Y. This could indicate that the elements are alkaline earth metals. Because the ionization energies of Y are greater than X, element Y should be above X on the periodic table (so, for example, Y could be Mg and X could be Ca). The purpose here is to get the students of thinking about what these numbers mean and how to use the learned trends.

Chapter 11

1.   Have the students answer this question without using the textbook. The goal here is for the students to explain their reasoning rather than simply use a catch-phrase. It is important to allow the students to discuss their predictions once they have looked up the answers in the text as this could provide you with more insight into their ideas.

2.   A relatively traditional problem, but one which often brings with it quite a bit of discussion. Make sure the students explain the radii trends instead of merely listing them.

3,4. Question 3 is asking for students to explain chemical bonds in their own terms, and question 4 gets to the relevance of bonding; that is, why should bonds form at all? Instead of just knowing the "what" the students should also consider the "why?".

5,7. Students often memorize the definitions of ionic and covalent but cannot explain the difference between them. Again, asking the students "why?" instead of "what?" gets to a whole new level of understanding.

6,8.   It would be best to have the students answer this question only using a periodic table (without the textbook). Having the students understand how these properties are related will decrease the likelihood that the students merely memorize the trends.

9.   Another example of a question which does not ask the student to define something, but to explain why.

10.   Many first time students think the answer to this is yes and can "prove" it with simple examples such as water. However, a discussion of this can get students to see that our models change when atoms come together to form molecules (while a molecular orbital theory is beyond this material, you can set the stage for its later acceptance).

Chapter 12

1.   In this case, the density of a gas will not change if the sample is kept at constant volume, but will if placed in a piston and increase the temperature (in that case, the density will decrease as an increase in temperature increases the volume). Many students believe that the density of a substance cannot be changed (even after doing calculations of gas density). It would be a good idea to have the students draw pictures of these situations, as emphasized in the chapter.

2.   Of several hundred incoming UIUC students given this question, just over half correctly claimed that nothing is between the "dots". However, almost a third of the students believed that there was either air or oxygen between the air molecules. Again, this shows the need for having the students considering magnified representations of gases (as emphasized in the chapter and in these questions) because while most students can solve $PV = nRT$ type problems, almost a third of the students believe that air molecules are located in the space between air molecules.

3.   Chemistry majors at UIUC have been asked to discuss this question and initially most claim that they have done this with straws for years; however, they are hard pressed to explain it, especially when asked to explain this phenomenon by using the kinetic molecular theory. Actual student models that have been proposed include: one's finger blocks gravity; because there is less air in the straw than in the room, there is less pressure in the straw and the water is pushed up (thus, at the surface they are correct by claiming that there is less pressure, but their explanation is incorrect). It might be a good idea to have the materials available (straws and water) so that the students can observe this phenomenon; many notice that a drop (or so) of water comes out of the straw, and some are able to then make the connection that because of this increase in volume of air in the straw (with the same amount of air) the pressure decreases. However, the point is not about telling the students the right answer, but allowing the students to discuss their ideas.

4.   Many students are confused by this question and some almost believe that this is proof that Boyle's Law doesn't work (in fact, one student claimed that this is true because air is a real gas, and Boyle's Law is for ideal gases). It seems that many students use either Boyle's or Charles's laws without consideration of the conditions (in this case because more air is added, both pressure and volume can increase, as long as the tire is pliable).

5.   It might be a good idea to have the students draw a picture of this. Hopefully by this point they are seeing the advantages of pictures on their own, but you may have to remind them of it. In this problem, two moles of gas become one mole, and according to the KMT, this gas (XY) should take up half the volume of X and Y separately. Of several hundred incoming UIUC students given this question, almost half (47%) claimed that the volume would not change, and the remaining half were evenly split between the volume increasing and the volume decreasing.

6.   The most popular response of several hundred incoming UIUC students to this question is "b" (about 40%)--that hot air rises. The correct response ("d") was chosen by only 20% of the students, and some of them chose it merely because it included the term "density" and they knew this should be part of the answer. Choice "e" is also popular (23%). Again, the emphasis should be on letting the students discuss their ideas and to have them try to explain why they believe the choices they did not choose are incorrect. This is difficult because all of the responses are correct to some extent. Merely telling the students that the answer is "d" will not help the students understand the nature of gases.

7.   In asking several hundred incoming UIUC students, only about 27% correctly claimed that the situations would all look the same with a static drawing by merely changing the temperature. The most popular response (42%) when cooling the gas was that the molecules will become significantly closer together. Again, the emphasis is to have the students represent gas molecules and the KMT. In the case of evacuating the gas, most students will draw a picture with fewer gas particles evenly spread (not all pay attention to the detail of the actual number of "dots"), although some leave a lot of open space at the top of the drawing (which makes sense if they think this empty space is air anyway, as cited in question 2).

8.   In this case pressure outside the balloon is decreasing, and thus the balloon will expand in order to equalize pressures.

9.   The question is essentially having them explain the ideal gas law, so do not let them use PV=nRT to explain it. That is, have them explain why "PV=nRT" works. This is to help them understand the models which we use when dealing with gases.

10.   This question focuses the students on explaining these laws as opposed to merely plugging number into the appropriate formulas. It helps students to see that there are explanations to the equations we use. Charles's law is especially tricky for the students when they try to explain how pressure is kept constant.

11.   This question is meant to demonstrate to students that we can explain "real-world" events with our knowledge of chemistry.

   a.   Heating the can will increase the pressure of the gas inside the can. As the pressure increases, it may be enough to rupture the can. Couple this with question 14 to have the students explain why heating the can will increase the pressure.

   b.   As you draw a vacuum in your mouth, atmospheric pressure pushes the liquid up the straw.

c.   The external atmospheric pressure pushes on the can. Since there is no opposing pressure from the air in the inside, the can collapses.

d.   How hard the tennis ball is depends on the difference between the pressure of the air inside the tennis ball and atmospheric pressure. A "sea level" ball will be much "harder" at high altitude since the external pressure is lower at high altitude. A high altitude ball will be "soft" at sea level.

12.   All too often, students think of the ideal gas law, Boyle's Law, and Charles's Law as three disparate equations, and many students will memorize all three of them. It is good to point out to the students that by knowing the ideal gas law, they can derive many other equations.

13.   Students will often relate pressure to volume or pressure to amount of gas without considering the other variables. Once the students have consider this, ask them to discuss the same question if the balloon is larger or smaller than the flask.

14.   It would still work, but not as well (the hot air would not condense like the steam). Have the students explain both experiments. They can even make estimations and calculations of the percent change in volume of the cans in both cases.

15.   For Dalton's law of partial pressures to hold true, the simplifications of no interactions among gas particles and negligible particle size must hold true. Have the students explain why.

16.   Another question emphasizing a molecular perspective.

17,18. Similar to question #10 above. Make sure the students explain the significance of keeping two of the variables constant.

Chapter 13

1.   Of several hundred UIUC students given this question, about 40% correctly say "d". However, a b and c are all popular (each chosen by about 20% of the students). It is helpful to get an idea about what the students think about physical equilibrium because many times these ideas re-surface when discussing chemical equilibrium. As with other questions, it is more important to listen to how the students defend their choices and critique the others than to simply tell them the answer.

2.   Many students think of the term boiling point as meaning boiling temperature. This also gets the students thinking about how dynamic physical (and eventually, hopefully, chemical) processes are and about vapor pressure. If possible it would help for the students to see this as a demonstration.

3.   Yes, there are some substances in which only dispersion forces are present such as naphthalene, C_4H_{10}, and polyethylene that are solids at room temperature. That these substances are solids at room temperature tells us that their interparticle forces are stronger than those that are liquids at room temperature, such as water in which there are hydrogen bonds.

4.   The nature of the force stays the same. As the temperature increases
        and the phase changes, solid→liquid→gas occur, a greater fraction of
        the forces are overcome by the increased thermal (kinetic) energy of the
        particles.

5.   Vapor pressure is dependent on temperature and intermolecular forces.
        Many students will claim that a large bucket of water has a greater
        vapor pressure than a glass of water at the same temperature.

6,7,8,9.   Students have difficulty with explaining what the term vapor
             pressure means, even though it is explained in the text. Make
        sure that the students explain using their own words. Also, many
        students do not think of solids as having a vapor pressure.

10,11. Many students will think that vapor pressure decreases over time as the
        water evaporates (less water means less vapor pressure). Also, some
        will not realize that the vapor pressure of water at 100°C is 1 atm.

12.   As with the other In-Class Discussion Questions, it is most important to
        have the students explain the relationships. Too often students will
        try to memorize these (thus knowing that as intermolecular forces
        increase, so do surface tension, viscosity, melting point, and boiling
        point), but cannot explain these. Once students realize that these
        properties can be explained, they are on their way to a better
        understanding of chemistry as a logical science as opposed to disparate
        facts.

13.   The students should be able to explain this from their reading in the
        text, but make sure they explain it in their own words. This will help
        them to become more active and critical readers.

14.   Intramolecular forces will be greater if the molecule melts and boils
        before it decomposes. This question gets to students understandings of
        these terms, as opposed to just their knowledge of the text definition.

15.   This is similar to the question "Why do bonds form at all between
        atoms?" in that it gets at the "why?" instead of just the "what?".
        Asking these of students (and allowing the students to ask them of us)
        helps the students become more critical thinkers.

Chapter 14

1.   Of several hundred UI students given this question, almost 60% correctly
        stated that the concentration increased. However, the remaining 40%
        were about evenly split between claiming the concentration either
        decreased or stayed the same. This is presumably because the students
        are not visualizing what is occurring when the water in a solution
        vaporizes, and/or because they are using an incorrect definition of
        concentration.

2.   This question is to get the students thinking qualitatively (and perhaps
        semi-quantitatively) about concentration. Again, students are generally
        good problem solvers in an algorithmic sense, although they do not
        always consider the concepts in the problems. In this case, the answers
        are a) the amount of sugar in solution A is twice that in solution B; b)
        the volumes of the two solutions are equal ; c) the concentration of
        sugar in A is twice that of solution B.

3. In this case, the person with the solid should add 0.88 g of NaCl to 150.0 mL solution. The lab partner should add 6.0 mL of 2.5 M NaCl to 144 mL of water.

4. Students find problems such as this (in which students must decide which data is needed to answer a question) difficult. The molar mass of A is not needed because the students do not need to solve for the concentration, they just need to compare relative concentrations. Choices "a" and "c" will suffice, although "d" would need to be known for an actual calculation.

5. Similar to question 4, this problem requires the students to decide which data is needed. Choices "a", "b", and "d" need to be known.

6. This requires the students to understand the what the mole to mole ratio means. Often students will incorrectly use a coefficient (multiply by the coefficient instead of divide, for example). In this case, the answer is "b".

7. Students often claim that non-polar bonds are very weak, and sometimes extrapolate this to mean that solids always have polar or ionic bonds. This question should get them to see that many non-polar bonds can make for a strong interaction.

8. Another example of having the students use pictures to convey their ideas. These should be accompanied, as always, by an explanation.

9. This question has the students apply their understanding of the terms "weight percent" and "molarity". The answer is also surprising and enlightening to many students.

10. Both of these terms have to do with ratios (and the more dense the sugar water, for example, the higher its concentration). If students can see how these are related, they are more likely to understand each.

11. Questions such as these keep students from merely memorizing formulas that can often be misapplied. Anytime students use a formula, make them explain it.

Chapter 15

1. This question is an actual UIUC student question. It has also come up when students are asked to calculate the hydroxide concentration of a solution with a pH less than 7. This question is to get at the idea that chemical equilibrium is a dynamic process.

2. Many students memorize the statement "the conjugate base of a weak acid is a strong base". This is presumably because students think of acids and bases as opposites and the terms weak and strong as opposites. The students should consider the reaction of a conjugate base of a weak acid with water, and think about what the K_b value would be before jumping to a conclusion. Another example of students trying to memorize a simple statement as opposed to thinking about the situation.

3. This question should be easily answered after an active read of the text.

4.   Strength and concentration are confusing to students and often equated. For example, HCl is always a strong acid but its concentration can vary; along the same lines, ammonia is always a weak base.

5.   Make sure the students explain what pH means in their own terms. The second part of this question is false (concentration plays a factor).

6.   This question is consistent with the increased emphasis on representing reactions. With 10 molecules, you must be careful about the K for HCl, and the relatively small value of K for the weak acid (since many students will have 9 of the 10 molecules dissociate). For part D, from strongest to weakest base the answers are A^-, H_2O, and Cl^-. Make sure the students explain their answers, even if they are correct.

7.   Another "why" question. Students can memorize this number, but should also have an understanding of where it comes from.

8.   The answer (yes) is easy enough to prove, but many students think the answer is no.

9.   Students should understand that the "p" merely tells us to take the "-log" of whatever term we are considering.

10.   This question come from actual students and is good to ask if for no other reason than to surface unasked questions. This also gets the students to consider that a buffered solution will change pH and reacts just as they could predict with major species, yet the ratio of conjugate base to acid stays relatively constant.

11,12. As with question 10, this question gets the students to critically think about a buffered solution to the extent of how they work, and what makes one better than another. Asking the students to explain a question such as this should shed some light on the students ideas, and will hopefully help to make the students more critical and more active readers.

Chapter 16

1.   These questions were also asked of several hundred incoming UIUC students, and the results were quite interesting. In the case of adding chemical A to the flask, 85% of the students correctly claimed that the concentration of A would be higher once a new equilibrium was established, yet only 55% claimed that the concentration of B would be lower. In fact, 36% claimed that the concentration of B would remain unchanged, making one wonder how the reaction could proceed at all. Yet, at least half of the students claimed that the concentrations of C and D would change (most believed they would increase). Many students are confused, when directly asked, by the fact that adding only one reactant causes an increase in the amount of product; "But you are not adding any more B" they will claim. Also, many students seem to believe that the reactions are uni-directional, even though they will be able to solve the problems. Allow the students ample time to discuss their ideas.

2.   This question asks the students to graphically represent the product, and is therefore a combination of qualitative and quantitative. Again, the goal is to get the students to better understand what is occurring with chemical equilibrium.

3. It may be worthwhile to have the students perform the calculation in checking on their answer after discussion of what they believe should happen (you would have to provide them with a value for the equilibrium constant, or you could ask them what information they would need to know in order to solve this problem). When the H_2 is added should not matter, but hearing what the students say is important.

4. In terms of increasing equilibrium concentrations of D, the answer is: b, a, and c. In terms of B the answer is: c, a, and b. This question goes well with question #1 above.

5. For part a) the range should be between 1 and 2 M (closer to 2 as K decreases); for b) the range should be between 1 and 3 M (closer to 3 as K decreases); for c) the range should be between 1 and 2 M (closer to 2 as K increases); and for d) the range should be between 0 and 1 M (closer to 1 as K increases). Students have had quite a bit of difficulty with this one.

6. As stated in question 1, this question has been asked by several students (and probably wondered but unasked by many others). It therefore surfaces what these students may be too shy to ask, and then allows them the opportunity to discuss it. Having the students draw pictures here would be helpful.

7. Students have believed this to be true, indicating that they believe that all that is important is that K stays constant; that is, that they do not necessarily consider the relevant chemistry (such as in question 5). In this case, the amount of C is impossible, but it allows for the "correct" K value. Again, it is important not to just treat this question as a "trick" and quickly tell the students the answer, but to allow them ample opportunity to discuss these issues themselves.

8. Students are often confused between equilibrium condition and equilibrium constant. In this case, the answers are c and d, but many students believe that by changing the concentrations of the reactants or products, one changes the equilibrium constant.

9. Another example of relating theory and practice; it is good practice for the students to try to develop experimental verification on their own. This type of question also allows you to better assess their understandings of Ksp.

10. Students often become confused about what Ksp values actually measure and how they are related to solubilities. If a Ksp value were zero, it could mean that the solid does not dissolve into ions at all (the product of the ions is zero).

11. Many students will equate Ksp values with solubilities such that a higher Ksp necessarily means a greater solubility. While they are related, it is important for the students to understand that they are not the same thing, and why they are different (that the number of ions is important in this relationship).

12. In general, the Ksp of a solid will increase with increasing temperature. However, this is not always the case and you must decide how in-depth you wish to discuss this with your students (the fact that some solids become less soluble with an increase in temperature of the solvent).

Chapter 17

1.   This serves as a good introductory problem in that the students should
      conceptually explain the workings of a cell before doing any
      calculations. Again, this is explained in the text, but this does not
      guarantee that the students are actively reading it. Having them
      explain figures in the text is a good way of assuring that the students
      critically read the book.

2.   This question allows the student to see that the same element can have
      many different oxidation states, even without being an ion.

3.   The students can do this by finding the oxidation states of all species
      (which you may wish them to do), but the students should also understand
      how they can easily spot redox equations by noticing an element in its
      standard state.

4.   Having students write half-reactions is a helpful way to get them to
      balance redox equations, but it has the side-effect of making some
      believe that the reactions occur independently of one another. Many
      students think that the first statement is true (cannot occur
      independently of each other), presumably because of our emphasis on
      half-reactions.

5.   Students often want mnemonics (and use some with redox questions).
      While these may help the student know the "what", they do little, if
      anything for the "why." By gaining electrons, the oxidation state is
      reduced, since electrons are negatively charged. Thus "gaining" and
      "reduced" make sense in this context, and one need not rely on a
      mnemonic device.